P9-DBJ-840

Senegal

the Bradt Travel Guide

Sean Connolly

edition
1

www.bradtguides.com

Bradt Travel Guides Ltd, UK
The Globe Pequot Press Inc, USA

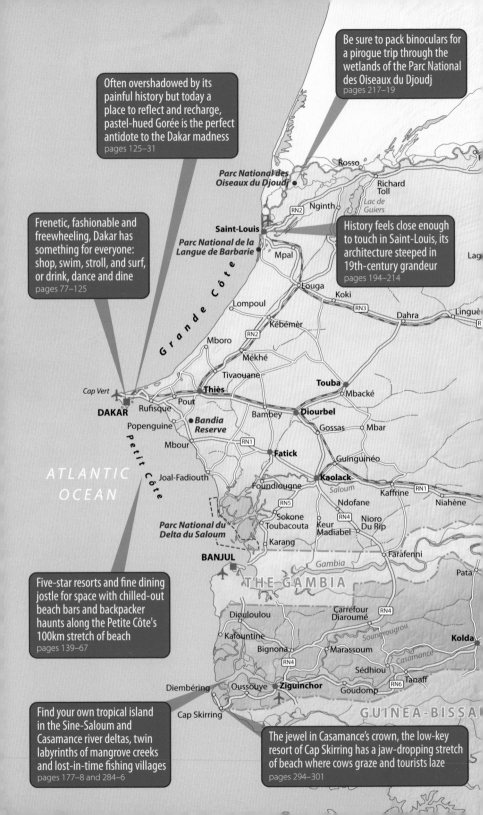

Be sure to pack binoculars for a pirogue trip through the wetlands of the Parc National des Oiseaux du Djoudj
pages 217–19

Often overshadowed by its painful history but today a place to reflect and recharge, pastel-hued Gorée is the perfect antidote to the Dakar madness
pages 125–31

Frenetic, fashionable and freewheeling, Dakar has something for everyone: shop, swim, stroll, and surf, or drink, dance and dine
pages 77–125

History feels close enough to touch in Saint-Louis, its architecture steeped in 19th-century grandeur
pages 194–214

Five-star resorts and fine dining jostle for space with chilled-out beach bars and backpacker haunts along the Petite Côte's 100km stretch of beach
pages 139–67

Find your own tropical island in the Sine-Saloum and Casamance river deltas, twin labyrinths of mangrove creeks and lost-in-time fishing villages
pages 177–8 and 284–6

The jewel in Casamance's crown, the low-key resort of Cap Skirring has a jaw-dropping stretch of beach where cows graze and tourists laze
pages 294–301

Map labels:

ATLANTIC OCEAN

Rosso
Parc National des Oiseaux du Djoudj
Richard Toll
Nginth
Lac de Guiers
RN2
Saint-Louis
Parc National de la Langue de Barbarie
Mpal
Louga
Koki
RN3
Dahra
Linguèr
Grande Côte
Lompoul
Kébémèr
Mboro
RN2
Mékhé
Tivaouane
Touba
Mbacké
Cap Vert
Thiès
Pout
Bambey
Diourbel
DAKAR
Rufisque
Popenguine
Bandia Reserve
Gossas
Mbar
Mbour
RN1
Fatick
Guinguinéo
Petit Côte
Joal-Fadiouth
Kaolack
Saloum
Kaffrine
RN1
Niahène
Foundiougne
RN5
Ndofane
RN4
Nioro Du Rip
Parc National du Delta du Saloum
Sokone
Toubacouta
Keur Madiabel
Karang
BANJUL
Gambia
Farafenni
Pata
THE GAMBIA
Diouloulou
Carrefour Diaroumé
RN4
Kolda
Kafountine
Soungrougrou
Bignona
Marassoum
Casamance
RN4
Sédhiou
Diembéring
Oussouye
Ziguinchor
Goudomp
RN6
Tanaff
Cap Skirring
GUINEA-BISSAU

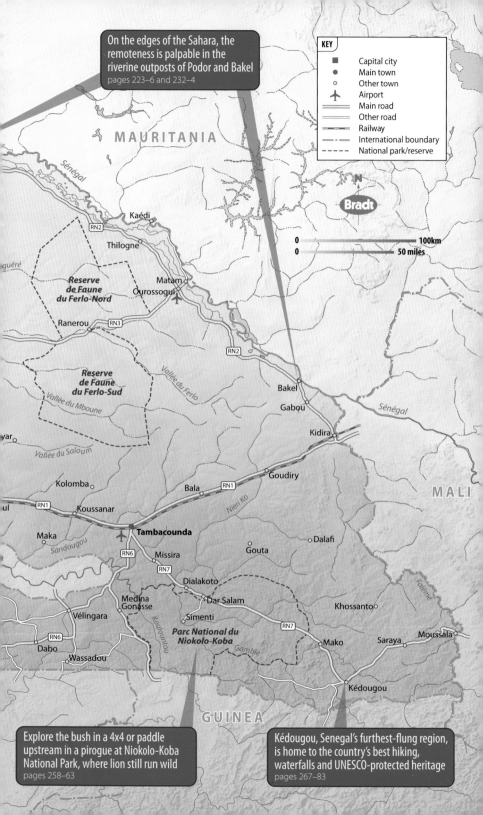

On the edges of the Sahara, the remoteness is palpable in the riverine outposts of Podor and Bakel
pages 223–6 and 232–4

KEY

■	Capital city
●	Main town
○	Other town
✈	Airport
	Main road
	Other road
	Railway
—·—·	International boundary
- - -	National park/reserve

MAURITANIA

Sénégal

Kaédi

RN2

Thilogne

Reserve de Faune du Ferlo-Nord

Matam

Ourossogui

Ranerou   RN3

Vallée du Ferlo

Vallée du Mboune

Reserve de Faune du Ferlo-Sud

Bakel

Gabou

Sénégal

Vallée du Saloum

Kidira

yar

Kolomba

Bala   RN1

Goudiry

MALI

Nieri Ko

RN1   Koussanar

Maka

Sandougou

Tambacounda

Dalafi

Missira

Gouta

RN6

RN7   Dialakoto

Medina Gonasse

Dar Salam

Khossanto

Vélingara

Simenti

Kouloumtou

Parc National du Niokolo-Koba

RN7

Mako

Saraya

Moussala

RN6

Dabo

Wassadou

Gambie

Falémé

Kédougou

GUINEA

0   100km

0   50 miles

Bradt

N

Explore the bush in a 4x4 or paddle upstream in a pirogue at Niokolo-Koba National Park, where lion still run wild
pages 258–63

Kédougou, Senegal's furthest-flung region, is home to the country's best hiking, waterfalls and UNESCO-protected heritage
pages 267–83

Senegal
Don't
miss...

Dakar's music scene
Baaba Maal is one of the many internationally renowned artists who can be seen at venues across the capital
(SB/S) page 27

Wildlife excursions
The private Réserve de Bandia offers a genuine bush atmosphere and reliable sightings of roan antelope and other game
(AVZ) pages 146–7

Journeys by pirogue

There's no better way to traverse the vast, watery knot of mangrove swamps and shell islands that make up the Sine-Saloum Delta than in a motorised canoe

(AVZ) pages 177–8

Historical architecture

Podor's colonial houses share the burnt saffron hue of the surrounding dunescape

(AVZ) pages 223–6

Miles of unspoilt beaches

Arcing their way up the coastline in a series of shallow, sheltered coves, the sands of Cap Skirring are justifiably popular as a summer getaway

(AVZ) pages 294–301

Senegal in colour

REGIE DES CHEMINS DE FER DU SENEGAL

above   The Marché du Poisson in Yoff is the ideal spot to watch the catch being hauled in, as dozens of pirogues hit the beach at the same time (S/DT) page 115

left   Trains may no longer run to Dakar's appealing train station, but its recent landmark status and plans for renovation mean that it is set to gain a new lease of life within the lifetime of this guide (DS1/DT) page 122

below   Yoff is home to one of the most conservative communities on the Cap-Vert Peninsula, including the Seydina Limamou Laye Mausoleum, which holds the tomb of the founder of the Layenne order (NP/DT) page 124

above & below left Crossed by car-free sand-and-cobblestone streets shaded with palms, quiet Île de Gorée is a massive contrast to Dakar across the water, but its bucolic atmosphere belies its tragic history as a slaving depot, as seen in the haunting Maison des Esclaves (S/DT and SC) pages 125–131

below right In season, the salt-encrusted Pepto-Bismol waters of Lac Rose are a startling sight (NW/A) pages 132–4

top The seven-spanned Pont Faidherbe is Saint-Louis' iconic sight (BP/DT) pages 209–10

above left The tiny city-island of Saint-Louis is lapped on either side by the waters of the Senegal River (A/DT) pages 194–211

above right A painted house-front in Saint-Louis: images of famous Sufis dominate all over the country, from shop displays to famous shrines (SC) page 23

below The Maison des Sœurs, a former convent, contains a striking dual staircase that was featured in the Oscar-nominated film *Coup de Torchon* (AVZ) page 211

AUTHOR

Sean Connolly first travelled to West Africa in 2008, and has been returning to study, work or backpack around the region ever since. When he's not discussing verb tenses, diplomatic recognition or the merits of camel meat, you may find him riding in the back of a grain truck, sampling questionable local delicacies or seeking out a country's funkiest records – a distinct pleasure in as music-mad a country as Senegal. Raised in Chicago and educated in New York, Sean is a full-time culture

fiend (read: Anthropology graduate) and stays on the move whenever possible, though lately you'll most often find him in Berlin.

AUTHOR'S STORY

While it would be impossible to distil the months I spent in Senegal into just one experience or pithy anecdote, perhaps nothing was so illustrative of Senegal's contrasts and charms during my time there as running out of fuel on the Vélingara–Kolda road. Seeking to wring a few cents' more profit out of his trip, our *sept-place* driver played a bit fast and loose with the amount of petrol we'd need to reach our destination, and we wound up puttering to a stop, at sunset, in an uninhabited patch of forest somewhere about 25km outside of Kolda. Amid sarcastic jeers and cries of '*Economiser!*', our driver took off on foot into the increasingly inky night with nothing but a jerrycan, and we were left at the roadside to fend for and/or entertain ourselves.

Thinking the situation a bit grim, I was resigned to my fate until the two savvy Dakarois sitting next to me pulled out their laptop and invited the car to watch a film with them. Moments later we were sharing snacks and taking pictures on the roof rack together, taking turns trying to wave down passing traffic for a lift. It was there, on the side of a dirt road illuminated by nothing but a few stars above and the glow of a pirated Kate Hudson movie, that I first noticed the easy grace with which Senegal has put on the mantle of modernity. Today, everyone has a mobile, but they'll still look up from it long enough to invite a total stranger to share their bowl of rice and, when you're stuck on the side of the road together because your clapped-out *sept-place* has called it quits, you go home with a phone full of photos and a bunch of new Facebook friends. Chalk it up to *teranga* or whatever you like, but Senegal walks the tightrope between the traditional and the modern with an effortless poise.

After a couple of hours, the Dakarois and I were the only passengers who had yet to find a lift when an ancient, hulking beast of a truck finally shuddered to a stop and offered us a ride into town; the only problem was that there was hardly room for two inside, let alone three. No matter, it was decided, we'd all go or none of us would, and we piled into the cab – air already thick with diesel and day-old sweat – and my two new friends, unprompted, sat on each others' laps for the whole of the excruciatingly slow last few miles into Kolda, just to make sure there was enough room for me. We never did see the thrifty *sept-place* driver again, but, after getting dropped off at my hotel door in Kolda, I had plenty of fantastic shots from what I thought would be a horrible night stuck out on the roads, and some new friends to share them with.

PUBLISHER'S FOREWORD   *Adrian Phillips, Managing Director*

Senegal is stable, easily accessible and offers a range of travel options (from all-inclusive resorts to more rural and 'authentic' experiences). It's been on the Bradt commissioning wish-list for a long time now, but the wait has been thoroughly worthwhile. A seasoned visitor to West Africa over many years – variously as student, worker and backpacker – Sean Connolly knows the region inside out. And having worked with Philip Briggs on updating several of our flagship titles, he is well-versed in what it takes to write an outstanding guidebook. You couldn't be in better hands.

First edition published November 2015

Bradt Travel Guides Ltd
IDC House, The Vale, Chalfont St Peter, Bucks SL9 9RZ, England
www.bradtguides.com
Print edition published in the USA by The Globe Pequot Press Inc,
PO Box 480, Guilford, Connecticut 06437-0480

Text copyright © 2015 Sean Connolly
Maps copyright © 2015 Bradt Travel Guides Ltd
Photographs copyright © 2015 Individual photographers (see below)
Project Manager: Maisie Fitzpatrick
Cover research: Pepi Bluck, Perfect Picture

The author and publisher have made every effort to ensure the accuracy of the information in this book at the time of going to press. However, they cannot accept any responsibility for any loss, injury or inconvenience resulting from the use of information contained in this guide. All rights reserved. No part of this publication may be reproduced, stored in a retrieval system, or transmitted in any form or by any means, electronic, mechanical, photocopying, recording or otherwise without the prior consent of the publisher. Requests for permission should be addressed to Bradt Travel Guides Ltd in the UK (print and digital editions), or to The Globe Pequot Press Inc in North and South America (print edition only).

ISBN: 978 1 84162 913 1 (print)
e-ISBN: 978 1 78477 124 9 (e-pub)
e-ISBN: 978 1 78477 224 6 (mobi)

British Library Cataloguing in Publication Data
A catalogue record for this book is available from the British Library

Photographs Alamy: Friedrick Stark (FS/A), Nik Wheeler (NW/A); Sean Connolly (SC); Dreamstime: Antpun (A/DT), Jeanne Coppens (JC/DT), DiversityStudio1 (DS1/DT), Djembe (D/DT), Elisabethandi (E/DT), Guillohmz (G/DT), Eduardo Huelin (EH/DT), Nael_Pictures (NP/DT), Beatrice Preve (BP/DT), Robhainer (R/DT), Susan Robinson (SR/DT), Smandy (S/DT); Marco Muscarà (MM); Shutterstock: Sergei Bachlakov (SB/S); Ariadne Van Zandbergen (AVZ)

Front cover Girl swinging from a boat in Cap Skirring (FS/A)
Back cover Grand Mosque in Touba (JC/DT)
Title page A *case d'étage* in Mlomp (AVZ); red-throated bee-eater (*Merops bulocki*) (SR/DT); *pirogue* in Dakar (AVZ)

Maps David McCutcheon FBCart.S. Some maps include data (c) OpenStreetMap contributors (under open Database License).

Colour map Relief map bases by Nick Rowland FRGS

Typeset by Ian Spick, Bradt Travel Guides and Sally Brock, Wakewing
Production managed by Jellyfish Print Solutions; printed in Turkey By Imak
Digital conversion by www.dataworks.co.in

MAJOR CONTRIBUTORS

SIMON FENTON (*www.anaccidentalafrican.com*) Today, Simon Fenton is a Senegal-based travel writer and photographer. After an early career in the morgues and pools of southern England, he lived, worked and travelled in Asia for several years, travelling independently through bush, mountain, desert and jungle, financing himself by teaching English, acting in Bollywood movies and working as a pig farmer in Vietnam.

He eventually returned to the UK to 'settle down', got married, and set up the award-winning social enterprise StreetShine before a perfect storm of events re-ignited his wanderlust. He found himself in Abéné, Senegal, where he now lives and runs his own guesthouse with his Senegalese partner, Khady, and their sons, Gulliver and Alfie.

JULIANA PELUSO (e *juliana.m.peluso@gmail.com*) As a self-proclaimed expert when it comes to finding premium shade, Juliana was able to hone her lounging talents in the sun-soaked, sandy locale of Kanel, northern Senegal, where she lived and worked during her Peace Corps service. Having consumed her fill of organ meats, she then moved on to teach English in France, which she would realistically describe as ⅔ espresso breaks, ⅓ days off due to union striking. Educated at Temple University in Philadelphia, Juliana is always on the hunt for weird cultural titbits and 'sponsored' travel opportunities.

Acknowledgements

It's hard to know where to begin thanking the vast number of people who shared their expertise, helped me on my way, sacrificed their time, opened their homes, or simply put up with an irritable writer making his way through a project that just wouldn't seem to end, but a good place to start would be with my long-suffering editor, Maisie Fitzpatrick, commissioning editor Rachel Fielding, and everyone at Bradt Guides for their patience and encouragement throughout this process, and not least Philip Briggs for his continual advocacy, advice and encouragement.

In Senegal, the list of people without whom this project would have never seen the light of day is enormous – sending a huge thank you to Simon Fenton and Khady Mané (and family), Omar Jammeh, Lamine Ndiaye, Camille Grif, Mireya Millan Gomez, Tacko Sakho, Dr Eric Ross, Pierre Thiam, Whitney Jenkins, Anthony Scavone, Tim Johnson, Lily Grabill, Clintandra Tea, Tegan Plock, Kat Caroll, Juliana Peluso, Alison Souders, Phillip Kim, Cristina May, Danny White, Margaret Davidson, Jo Diouf, Edens Duphresne, Carson Leigh, Karen Chiang, Emily Johnson, Laurie Ohlstein, Janelle Kibler, Katie Wallner, Alia Kroos, Ian-Huei Yau, Ethan Leatherbarrow, Carlisle Bell, Hadiel Mohamed, Hattie Hill, Timothy Van Vliet, Karolien Pieters, Jack Wijnker, Bert Stikema, Stephen Chandler, Jean-Pierre Gaborit, Olivier Jacquemain, Lieutenant Colonel Ousmane Kane, Malamine Ndiaye, Youba Sonko, Gérard Chenet, Francina Terblanche, Kathrine Roldsgaard Nielsen, Elisabeth Ancely, Eric Balland, Muriel Bancal, Sabine Grégoire, Didier Coullet, Pierre Dasylva, David Oades, Al Goodridge, Jenny Adams, Alison Collins and Yasmina Akkouh.

And finally for everyone who put up with me throughout the writing process, your patience is more than I ever could have asked for. To my infinitely patient girlfriend, Imke Rueben, Natalie Basedow, Anna, Tom, Hanna and Mila Alboth, Hong Rui Choo, Panagiotis Stogiannos, Efthimis Theou, Richard Djif, Agatha Ritter-Martin, Jeff Martin, Magdalena Connolly, Daniel Connolly, Janina Nirenski and all the people who I promised to spend time with and didn't because my work wasn't ready yet, I can't wait to finally catch up!

FEEDBACK REQUEST AND UPDATES WEBSITE

At Bradt Travel Guides we're aware that guidebooks start to go out of date on the day they're published – and that you, our readers, are out there in the field doing research of your own. You'll find out before us when a fine new family-run hotel opens or a favourite restaurant changes hands and goes downhill. So why not write and tell us about your experiences? Contact us on ☏ 01753 893444 or e info@bradtguides.com. We will forward emails to the author who may post updates on the Bradt website at www.bradtupdates.com/senegal. Alternatively you can add a review of the book to www.bradtguides.com or Amazon.

Contents

| | Introduction | viii |

PART ONE   **GENERAL INFORMATION**   **1**

Chapter 1   **Background Information**   **3**
Geography 3, Climate 4, Environment and conservation 4,
History 7, People 17, Language 22, Religion 22,
Education 22, Culture 24, Sport 32

Chapter 2   **Practical Information**   **33**
When to visit 33, Highlights 33, Suggested itineraries 34,
Tourist information 36, Tour operators 36, Red tape 37,
Embassies 38, Getting there and away 39, Safety 43,
Hassles 46, Women travellers 47, Gay and lesbian.
travellers 48, Travellers with disabilities 49, What to take
49, Money 51, Budgeting 52, Getting around 52,
Accommodation 56, Eating and drinking 58, Public
holidays and events 62, Shopping 63, Arts and
entertainment 64, Media and communications 64,
Photography 65, Cultural etiquette 66, Investing in
Senegal 66, Travelling positively 67

Chapter 3   **Health**   **69**
Preparations 69, Potential medical problems 71, Other
safety concerns 74

PART TWO   **THE GUIDE**   **75**

Chapter 4   **Dakar**   **77**
History 78, Getting there and away 79, Orientation 82,
Getting around 83, Tourist information 88, Where to
stay 89, Where to eat and drink 101, Nightlife and live
music 107, Arts and entertainment 109, Sport 111,
Study 112, Shopping 112, Dakar for children 118, Safety
and security 119, Other practicalities 120, What to see and
do 121, Around Dakar 125

Chapter 5   **The Petite Côte**   **139**
Toubab Dialaw 140, Popenguine 142, Circuit de Dakar
Baobabs 146, Réserve de Bandia 146, Accrobaobab 147,
La Somone and Ngaparou 147, Saly-Portudal and Saly-
Niakhniakhal 150, Mbour 158, Warang 161, Nianing 163,
Mbodiène 164, Joal-Fadiouth 164, Around Joal 166

| Chapter 6 | **Kaolack and the Sine-Saloum Delta** | **169** |

Kaolack 169, Around Kaolack 174, The Sine-Saloum Delta and National Park 177, Fimela, Djilor, Simal 178, Faoye 180, Ndangane 180, Mar Lodj 182, Palmarin and Djiffer 183, Île de Guior (Dionewar and Niodior) 186, Foundiougne 187, Sokone 188, Toubacouta 188, Missirah 191, Fathala Reserve 192, Djinack 193

| Chapter 7 | **Saint-Louis and Surrounds** | **194** |

Saint-Louis 194, Parque Nationale de la Langue de Barbarie 211, Réserve Spéciale de Faune de Guembeul 213

| Chapter 8 | **Senegal River and the North** | **215** |

Diama 215, Parc National des Oiseaux du Djoudj 217, Makhana 219, Rosso-Senegal 220, Richard Toll 221, Lac de Guiers 222, Dagana 223, Podor 223, Ndioum 226, Île à Morfil 226, Ourossogui 228, Matam 230, Bakel 232

| Chapter 9 | **Central Senegal and the Grande Côte** | **235** |

Thiès 235, Tivaouane 241, Mboro 241, Lompoul 242, Louga 243, Dahra and Linguère 245, Diourbel 246, Touba-Mbacké 248

| Chapter 10 | **Tambacounda and Niokolo-Koba National Park** | **253** |

Tambacounda 253, Niokolo-Koba National Park 258, East of Tambacounda 263

| Chapter 11 | **Kédougou and Around** | **267** |

Kédougou 267, Around Kédougou 271, West of Kédougou 274, South of Kédougou 278, East of Kédougou 283

| Chapter 12 | **Ziguinchor and Basse Casamance** | **284** |

Ziguinchor (City) 286, Cap Skirring and Kabrousse 294, Boucotte 301, Diembéring 304, Cachouane 305, Île d'Égueye 306, Île d'Ehidje 306, Oussouye and Edioungou 307, Mlomp 309, Djiromait 310, Pointe Saint-Georges 311, Enampora and Séléki 311, Elinkine 312, Carabane 313, Affiniam 314, Coubalan 315, Petit Kassa 315, Kafountine 319, Abéné 324, Niafourang and Kabadio 328, Diouloulou 331, Baïla 332, Bignona 332, Thionk-Essyl 336

| Chapter 13 | **Haute Casamance** | **337** |

Sédhiou 337, Kolda 341, Diaoube 343, Vélingara 343, Manda 345

| Appendix 1 | **Language** | **347** |

| Appendix 2 | **Further Information** | **356** |

| | Index | 359 |
| | Index of Advertisers | 366 |

LIST OF MAPS

Abéné	325	Ourossogui	229
Bakel	233	Parc National des	
Basse Casamance	285	Oiseaux de Djoudj	218
Cap Skirring and Kabrousse	295	Petite Côte	138
Cap Vert Peninsula	78	Plateau	90–1
Central Senegal and		Podor	224
the Grande Côte	236	Point E and Fann	96–7
Dakar orientation	84–5	Richard Toll	222
Gorée	127	Saint-Louis North	199
Haute Casamance	338	Saint-Louis South	201
Kafountine	320	Saint-Louis surrounds	195
Kaolack	171	Saly	152
Kédougou	268	Sédhiou	340
Kédougou region	266	Senegal 1st colour section	
Kidira	264	Sine-Saloum Delta	168
Kolda	342	Tambacounda	257
Matam	231	Tambacounda region	253
Mbour	159	Thiès	238
Ngor and Les Almadies	94	Vélingara	344
Niokolo-Koba National Park	259	Yoff	99
Northern Senegal	216	Ziguinchor	289

SEND US YOUR SNAPS!

We'd love to follow your adventures using our *Senegal* guide – why not send us your photos and stories via Twitter (@BradtGuides) and Instagram (@bradtguides) using the hashtag #senegal. Alternatively, you can upload your photos directly to the gallery on the Senegal destination page via our website (*www.bradtguides.com*).

SENEGAL ONLINE

For additional online content, articles, photos and more on Senegal, why not visit www.bradtguides.com/senegal.

Introduction

Geographically, culturally and politically, Senegal has always been an African standout, and as the closest African 'winter sun' destination to Europe, it's both endlessly fascinating and eminently accessible. With some of the best flight connections in the region, Senegal has long been a popular destination for Francophone travellers escaping the long nights and low temperatures of the northern latitudes, and the swaying palms of Dakar are much closer to home than you might think. With flight times of under six hours from Paris and less than eight from Washington DC (with non-stop connections to both), Americans and Europeans alike are only a day's journey from this superlative and surprising nation at Africa's westernmost edge.

Politically, there's hardly a more stable place anywhere on the continent: there's never been a coup d'état or a particularly authoritarian government, and the population is remarkably politically engaged – people here follow the latest palace intrigues with the zeal of a soap opera. Thus, it's little surprise that the first African to serve in the French parliament hailed from here more than 100 years ago, it was the first place on the continent where a president voluntarily handed over power, and it saw sub-Saharan Africa's first-ever change of government at the ballot box. Behind this string of achievements lies a country and a people that are both confident and diverse, who have long been at ease with themselves and their neighbours, and whose knack for welcoming visitors is hard-wired into the national DNA.

Often touted as the 'land of *teranga*', which is Wolof for hospitality, the importance of welcoming guests here is not simply a tourist-brochure buzzword, but rather a concept that informs nearly all elements of Senegalese life. Whether it's welcoming cousins in from out of town or travellers from across the globe, the red carpet is rolled out just the same, and by the time you've spent a few weeks here, it'll be harder and harder to keep track of how many bowls of the national dish, *thieboudienne,* or glasses of the ubiquitous green tea *attaya,* that you've been asked to sit down and share with a complete stranger. Given the many charms of Senegalese cuisine and the warmth with which it's offered, you might find yourself accepting more of these invitations than you'd imagine.

Apart from its island neighbours in Cape Verde, Senegal is the westernmost country in Africa, and Senegal's population and economy are both inextricably tied to the coasts, which are amply blessed with mile after mile of rich fishing waters and uninterrupted, postcard-perfect powdery beach. Tourist facilities largely mirror the settlement patterns of the country as a whole and, given that nearly 25% of all Senegalese live in the Dakar region alone, the sparsely settled interior feels both literally and figuratively miles away from the twinkling lights and ocean breezes of the coastline. The deluxe seaside hotels and resorts also quickly disappear as you head inland, and are replaced by guesthouses aimed at the local market and an admirable network of rural *campements* offering a true village experience. Regardless of where you are, however, the road network has improved dramatically in recent years, so even if you've only got a week's holiday, the further reaches of the country are more accessible than ever before.

Geographically, Senegal sits squarely in the transition zone between the endless deserts of Mauritania to the north and the impenetrable forests of Guinea to the south, occupying something of a climactic middle ground. Indeed, it's perfectly possible to trek the green Fouta Djallon foothills, catch some world-class waves, and watch a sandstorm blow in from the Sahara within a day's journey of each other, and all without ever having to cross a border. And even though the whole country is accessible within a day or two's journey, it's easy to feel as on or off the beaten track as you like. Whether your aim is to dance your feet off to Senegal's frenetic *mbalax* beat at an all-night party in Dakar, loll in a hand-woven hammock somewhere along the Petite Côte, inspect the century-old manors of Saint-Louis, or escape to an island lost deep in the rivers of Casamance, the immense diversity and warm welcome to be found in all corners of the country make Senegal a thoroughly satisfying destination for both Africa first-timers and old hands alike.

HOW TO USE THE MAPS IN THIS GUIDE

KEYS AND SYMBOLS Maps include alphabetical keys covering the locations of those places to stay, eat or drink that are featured in the book. Note that regional maps may not show all hotels and restaurants in the area: other establishments may be located in towns shown on the map.

GRIDS AND GRID REFERENCES Several maps use gridlines to allow easy location of sites. Map grid references are listed in square brackets after the name of the place or sight of interest in the text, with page number followed by grid number, eg: [91 D3].

FOLLOW BRADT

For the latest news, special offers and competitions, subscribe to the Bradt newsletter via the website www.bradtguides.com and follow Bradt on:

- www.facebook.com/BradtTravelGuides
- @BradtGuides
- @bradtguides
- www.pinterest.com/bradtguides

The Senegal Experience offer high standard, carefully selected properties. Relax in a **boutique** hotel, or choose one of our **unique** hotels, set in **peaceful**, **idyllic** locations, ideal for those wanting to experience Senegal's **wildlife** and **birdlife**.

Request your brochure:
Senegal.co.uk   0845 338 8700

Part One

GENERAL INFORMATION

Location The westernmost country in mainland Africa, 1,600km north of the Equator

Neighbouring countries Mauritania, Mali, Guinea, Guinea-Bissau, The Gambia

Land Area 196,772 km² (about 1.5 times the size of England and half the size of California)

Climate Hot and humid, cooler on the coast and considerably hotter inland. Rainy season from May to November, with dry, harmattan conditions prevailing from December to April.

Terrain Mostly expansive rolling plains that eventually give way to the Fouta Djalon foothills in the extreme southeast, where the unnamed highest point (581m) is found southwest of Kédougou. The central north consists of semi-desert Sahelian savannah, central regions are primarily given over to agriculture, and the well-watered and densely vegetated river deltas in Casamance and Sine-Saloum are the greenest areas anywhere in the country.

Status Multi-party republic

Population 13.6 million (2014 estimate)

Life expectancy 61

Capital Dakar (population 3.1 million including Pikine, Rufisque and other suburbs)

Other main towns Touba-Mbacké (880,000), Mbour (641,000), Thiès (636,000) and Kaolack (466,000)

Economy Predominantly subsistence agriculture, although this is changing as exploitation of mineral resources increases.

GDP US$2,312 per capita (PPP) (2014); 4.5% annual growth (2014)

Languages 38 languages spoken overall. French is the language of government and schooling but is only mother tongue to a small percentage of Senegalese. Wolof is the most widely spoken indigenous language and acts, along with French, as a *lingua franca* throughout the country, while Wolof, Serer, Diola, Pulaar, Soninke and Mandinka are all recognised as 'national' languages.

Religion Islam, with most following one of the four major Sufi brotherhoods present: Tijãniyyah, Mouride, Qadriyya or Layene, (94%); Christianity, primarily Catholic (5%); traditional/Animist beliefs (1%)

Currency West African CFA Franc (shared with Benin, Burkina Faso, Guinea-Bissau, Ivory Coast, Mali, Niger and Togo)

Exchange rates £1 = 898F; US$1 = 575; €1 = 656F (September 2015)

National airline Senegal Airlines

International telephone code +221

Time GMT +0

Electrical voltage 220V, 50Hz

Weights and measures Metric

Flag Three vertical bands: from hoist, green, yellow, and red, with a five-pointed green star in the centre of the yellow band.

National anthem *Pincez Tous vos Koras, Frappez les Balafons* (Pluck your koras, strike the balafons)

Public holidays Senegal officially celebrates a mix of 12 Islamic, Christian and secular public holidays (see pages 62–3).

1

Background Information

GEOGRAPHY

The westernmost country on the African continent, Senegal straddles the transitional zone between the Saharan and Sahelian expanses of Mauritania to the north and the well-watered forests and mountains of Guinea and Guinea-Bissau to the south. Outside of the Senegal River valley, the remote Sahelian stretches of the north are thinly populated by a hardy collection of Fulbe herders, while the vast majority of central Senegal falls in the Sudan-Guinea Savannah biome, and much of this land is given over to agriculture, particularly peanut cultivation in Wolof-inhabited areas. Agriculture is king in the Casamance as well, where rice cultivation dominates the landscape, surrounded by Senegal's last remaining patches of Guinea-Congo Forest. As such, between the riotously green creeks and mangrove forests of the Casamance and Sine-Saloum deltas, the mercilessly hot and hardscrabble plains of the Ferlo desert and the bracingly cool ocean breezes of the Cap Vert peninsula, the country covers nearly the whole range of biomes to be found in West Africa, all without ever having to cross a border.

And while Senegal may be thrilling in its ecological diversity, topographically speaking it wouldn't be an overstatement to say that the country is as flat as the proverbial pancake. Lying in what's known among geologists as the Senegal-Mauritanian Basin, Senegal overwhelmingly consists of wide, flat plains that offer little relief from, well, the relief. The 581m highest point (which has yet to earn itself a name, it would seem) lies in the Fouta Djallon foothills on a ridge doubling as the Guinean frontier some 45km southwest of Kédougou as the crow flies, near the tiny villages of Népen Diakha and Népen Peul. (We've never heard of a tourist visiting it, so be sure to let us know if you do!) Otherwise, at 311m, Mount Assirik, in the further reaches of Niokolo-Koba National Park, is the only real elevation of note beside, and to a much lesser extent, the Mamelles of Dakar, which top out at a less-than-vertiginous 105m.

As on much of the African continent (and in the world), the environmental pressures on Senegal today are manifold, and include deforestation, desertification, coastal erosion, and biodiversity loss. Though some efforts have been made to stem the tide (Oceanium's successful mangrove reforestation programmes in Casamance and the Sine-Saloum delta are especially worthy of note), all of these issues, among others, remain major problems that are not yet being satisfactorily addressed, particularly in the face of Senegal's rapidly growing population. Because of this, as a visitor it's especially important to support what efforts are being made, and to continue building the connection between sustainable natural environments and sustainable livelihoods for those who live in them. The community nature reserves in Popenguine, La Somone and Dindefelo are excellent examples of locally run conservation and sustainable tourism initiatives that are eminently worth supporting.

CLIMATE

Senegal essentially has two seasons, rainy and dry. The rainy season, commonly known as *hivernage*, runs from about June until September or October, but it varies greatly in length and intensity depending on where you are in the country, and the north gets only 300–350mm of rain annually as compared with the 1,000–1,500mm that fall in the south.

Starting in October, the rains taper off and (relatively) cool and dry conditions prevail for the next several months. Not coincidentally, this is the peak tourism season. The hot, dry and dusty *harmattan* winds also start to blow in from the Sahara around this time, and these prevail until temperatures once again start to climb around April and the rains follow once again in June.

ENVIRONMENT AND CONSERVATION

It bears mentioning straight away that anyone seeking a 'traditional' African safari and a big-five game-viewing experience should immediately look elsewhere. While there's no doubt that Senegal's ecological charms abound, they're also considerably more discreet than the massive herds of animals that star in so many African holiday daydreams. There's still much to explore here for naturalists casual and dedicated alike, and the extensive network of protected areas in all corners of the country allows visitors easy access to the wildly diverse range of habitats and environments present throughout the country.

Senegal's national parks and preserves are managed by the Direction des Parcs Nationaux (✎ *33 832 2309*; e *dpn@sentoo.sn*) as part of the Ministère de l'Environnement et du Développement Durable (*www.environnement.gouv.sn*), and there are now six national parks and more than half a dozen ornithological, wildlife, community-run, or other special reserves established throughout the country, in addition to dozens of protected forests and silvopastoral agroforestry reserves not developed for tourism. (This is not including the two private reserves at Bandia and Fathala, which offer the most reliable wildlife viewing in the country, though much of it is non-indigenous.) Birdlife International (*www.birdlife.org*) has designated 18 sites in Senegal as Important Bird Areas, and five areas have been recognised as Wetlands of International Importance under the Ramsar convention (*www.ramsar. org*). Additionally, three of Senegal's national parks and reserves (Niokolo-Koba, Djoudj and Sine-Saloum) have been inscribed as UNESCO World Heritage Sites.

PARKS AND RESERVES Starting in the north, the Parc National des Oiseaux du Djoudj (see pages 217–19) protects 17,000ha of inland river delta and represents the first permanent water source south of the Sahara Desert, making it enormously important for Palearctic migrants heading here from northern latitudes. It's estimated that more than three million birds from some 350 species are represented here annually. The nearby 720ha Réserve Spéciale de Faune de Guembeul (see pages 213–14) also represents an important overwintering site for migrating birds, as well as being the centre of an antelope breeding and reintroduction programme for the scimitar-horned oryx, dama gazelle and dorcas gazelle, which are extinct in the wild, critically endangered and vulnerable, respectively. The animals are eventually translocated to the harsh and little-visited semi-desert savannahs of the Ferlo Nord and Ferlo Sud reserves (see box, page 247) some 200km to the east. Just south of Saint-Louis, the Parc National de la Langue de Barbarie (see pages 211–13) is unfortunately distinguished by the fact that it stands a fair chance of disappearing entirely in the coming years.

Covering 2,000ha of sand dunes at the end of an eponymous and rapidly eroding peninsula, it's currently an important nesting site for seabirds and marine turtles alike. Further south, lying just off Dakar's glimmering corniche, the Parc National des Îles de la Madeleine (see pages 131–2) covers a diminutive, 45ha set of rocky islets, making it the smallest national park in Senegal (and by some reckonings, the world). It's home to the only population of red-billed tropicbird (*Phaethon aethereus*) on (or almost on) the African mainland, as well as *Ndoek-Daour,* the Lebou protector spirit who keeps watch over Dakar. Back on land and heading down the Petite Côte, the community-run Réserve Naturelle de Popenguine (see pages 145–6) is a fabulous spot for some hiking and a bit of low-key wildlife viewing, while its neighbour to the south, the Réserve Naturelle d'Intérêt Communautaire de la Somone (see page 150), offers a walking trail and lookout tower on the fringes of Somone's mangrove-studded lagoon. Just inland from here lies the privately owned 35ha Réserve de Bandia (see pages 146–7), where game drives through the baobabs boast all but guaranteed wildlife sightings, including giraffe, buffalo, rhino and crocodiles. Finally, just before you reach the Gambian border, the UNESCO-recognised Parc National du Delta du Saloum (see pages 177–8) is a vast and breathtaking 76,000ha expanse of mangrove swamp, where, in addition to the manatees and dolphins that call these innumerable creeks home, you'll also find the world's largest breeding colony of royal tern, home to a jaw-dropping 40,000 nests. Adjacent to the national park is the privately run 6,000ha Fathala Reserve (see pages 192–3), known for its lion walks and healthy population of the critically endangered western giant (or Derby) eland.

Casamance is home to two reserves: the 5,000ha Parc National de Basse Casamance (see box, page 310), which has unfortunately been closed to the public for many years because of the unresolved status of the Casamance conflict and fears over unexploded ordinance and rebel elements remaining within the park. It's unlikely to open again soon but, even in its inactive state, it protects Senegal's last remaining stands of Guinea-Congo forest and is home to dozens of species of primates, leopards, buffalo, and the rare dwarf crocodile. Open to the public but still thoroughly remote and little visited, the Réserve Spéciale des Oiseaux de Kalissaye (see pages 323–4) is Casamance's other gazetted preserve. Covering 16ha at the end of a sandy seafront peninsula, it's a haven for all types of terns, gulls and herons, and a nesting site for sea turtles as well.

Finally, spread over a sweeping 913,000ha on the border between Tambacounda and Kédougou regions in the far southeast, Niokolo-Koba National Park is Senegal's largest and most famous national park. Set along the meandering watercourses of the Gambia River and its tributaries, the Koulountou and the park's namesake river, the Niokolo-Koba, the park may be Senegal's flagship reserve, but wildlife numbers have been in decline for many years, and the growing importance of the Tambacounda-Kédougou artery does little to help matters. With a varied environment of gallery forests, floodplains, marshes and even a few hills, the park is a worthwhile place to see a variety of primates, antelope, hippos, wild boar and, if you're incredibly lucky, maybe a couple of the elephants believed to still occupy the further reaches of the park. There are perhaps 100 lions here as well (but no one knows for sure), and although sightings of these are also fleetingly rare, we've had reports of confirmed sightings of up to four individuals along the main Tambacounda–Kédougou road as recently as late 2014. Also in the Kédougou region is the community-run Réserve Naturelle Communautaire de Dindéfélo (see pages 271–4), where cultural tourism in the area's Bassari and Bedik villages can be combined with chimpanzee trekking, waterfall visits, and stays in the local *campements villageois*.

Offshore, there are four designated marine protected areas in Saint-Louis, Kayar, Joal and Abéné, designed to combat overfishing and preserve both local environments and livelihoods.

FLORA AND FAUNA While it's true that the animal viewing in Senegal might pale in comparison to some of its East African counterparts, the thrill of hearing the chimpanzees (*Pan troglodytes*) howl and crash through the trees in the forests of Kédougou, or catching a glimpse of a bottlenose dolphin (*Tursiops truncates*) – or even their considerably more threatened brethren, the African manatee (*Trichechus senegalensis*) – from a perch on the Dakar-Ziguinchor ferry or the observation tower at Pointe Saint-Georges will still quicken the heartbeat of all but the most jaded travellers, and there's plenty more to see on air, land, and water if you know where to look.

The Casamance and Saloum river deltas are home to the aforementioned river dolphins and manatees, and the dozens of remote beaches and sandy islets also serve as nesting grounds for numerous species of turtle, including the critically endangered hawksbill turtle (*Eretmochelys imbricata*), endangered loggerhead (*Caretta caretta*) and green turtles (*Chelonia mydas*), vulnerable leatherback sea turtle (*Dermochelys coriacea*), and olive ridley sea turtle (*Lepidochelys olivacea*). They're also fertile waters for sport fishing, and outfitters in both regions can take you out angling for barracuda, grouper, hogfish and more. Rivers, particularly the Gambia near Niokolo-Koba National Park, are also home to some considerably larger residents, including numbers of hippopotamus (*Hippopotamus amphibius*) and the Nile crocodile (*Crocodylus niloticus*). Much rarer, the dwarf crocodile (*Osteolaemus tetraspis*) is thought to live around the confines of the closed Basse Casamance National Park.

For terrestrial game viewing, the privately operated Fathala and Bandia reserves are your safest bet for reliable sightings, but if your priority is getting out into the bush and you won't be crushed if you come away without spotting an eland, Niokolo-Koba National Park is much larger and more remote than either of the above. For primates, the forests around Ségou and Salemata are particularly rewarding spots, and though chimpanzee sightings aren't a guarantee here, they're probably the most likely place in the country you'll encounter them. Other primates are considerably more common, and a number of the parks and reserves (and forests outside them) are home to patas (*Erythrocebus patas*) and vervet monkeys (*Chlorocebus pygerythrus*), and Guinea baboons (*Papio papio*), along with the western red colobus (*Procolobus badius*). Antelopes of many types are also present, with the western giant eland (*Taurotragus derbianus derbianus*) the most magnificent example. Others include the scimitar-horned oryx (*Oryx dammah*), dama gazelle (*Nanger dama*), and dorcas gazelle (*Gazella dorcas*) at Guembuel Special Reserve, and an assortment of roan antelope (*Hippotragus equinus*), waterbuck (*Kobus ellipsiprymnus*), bohor reedbuck (*Redunca redunca*), kob (*Kobus kob*), oribi (*Ourebia ourebi*), western hartebeest (*Alcelaphus buselaphus major*) and common (*Sylvicapra grimmia*) and red-flanked duikers (*Cephalophus rufilatus*), which can be found in many of the reserves across the country.

Birders have plenty to look out for here, and Avibase (*http://avibase.bsc-eoc.org*) lists 675 species on their Senegalese checklist. We've listed many of the standouts and major populations under the relevant sections of the guide, but serious birders should waste no time in getting themselves a copy of Nik Borrow and Ron Demey's 2012 *Birds of Senegal and The Gambia*, which provides a plethora of beautiful depictions and descriptions in considerably more detail than we can include here.

As for flora, vegetation throughout much of the country tends to be sparse and Sahelian, with mile after mile of acacia (*Acacia nilotica*) scrub dominating the north-central regions of the country that haven't been given over to agriculture, which are occasionally punctuated by the inimitable shape of the baobab (*Adansonia digitata*), whose gnarled branches, bulbous trunks and seeming invincibility are immediately recognisable to anyone who's spent any time in Africa. Featured on Senegal's coat of arms, these regal trees can live to be thousands of years old and dozens of metres around, and their naturally hollowed-out centres were even at one time used as a burial ground for *griots* and nobility (see page 167). Senegal's other iconic tree is undoubtedly the kapok (*Ceiba pentandra*), better known in Senegal as a *fromager*, (or even *kapokier*, or sometimes ceiba), Though they may not feature on any official crests, these elegant trees can reach over 70m in height, and are often the focal point of small villages, particularly in Casamance; they are notable for their shapely buttressed roots, which can extend several metres above ground. Extra moisture allows a wider variety of plants and trees to grow, so river-fed gallery forests interrupt the savannah near the banks of many watercourses in Senegal, but deforestation has taken its toll on many of these: along the rivers in Niokolo-Koba National Park is probably the best place to see gallery forests in Senegal today.

The coastal estuaries in Casamance and the Sine-Saloum region are home to both red (*Rhizophora mangle*) and white mangroves (*Laguncularia racemosa*), of which the red mangroves features the characteristic aerial roots that jut above the water line and provide a habitat for oysters. Baobabs also thrive in the calcium-rich soils of the river deltas' many islets, which were formed from centuries of discarded oyster and other shells, while palms grow quite successfully in the surrounding regions and along much of Senegal's coastline, but most of all in Casamance thanks to the region's considerably more tropical climate. Here you'll find African oil palms (*Elaeis guineensis*), the fruits of which are the source of the red palm oil so common in West African cuisine. When the trunk is tapped (as opposed to harvesting the fruits), the African oil palm is also one of several species used to produce palm wine.

HISTORY

For a more in-depth look at Senegal's history (and the country overall), interested readers should get themselves a copy of the authoritative Culture and Customs of Senegal *by Eric Ross, PhD (www.ericrossacademic.wordpress.com), which served as an indispensable source for the history section in this guide.*

PREHISTORY Fossil evidence of human habitation in Senegal stretches deep into the early Palaeolithic era, and it's believed that the region has been more or less continually inhabited for hundreds of thousands of years, first by hunter-gatherers and subsequently by more settled populations. The amount of archaeological work on this period of Senegalese history has been somewhat limited, but a number of Palaeolithic stone tools for cutting, scraping, and other uses have been recovered here, among which are a number of Acheulean hand-axes found on the Cap Vert peninsula (some unearthed by Théodore Monod, namesake of Dakar's Cultural Museum) and others along the Senegal and Faléme rivers in the east of the country. The Neolithic period, which began in Senegal around 5000BCE, saw an expansion and specialisation in the types and varieties of materials used to make tools. Ceramics, flint, bone and other materials used for both practical and decorative purposes have all been recovered dating from this era in Senegal.

The Neolithic era began a slow transition into the Iron Age around the 4th century BCE, and a number of settled societies began to coalesce at this time, including those that would leave behind what are perhaps Senegambia's most significant prehistoric monuments, the stone circles at Siné Ngayène and Wanar in the eastern Saloum region (as well as Wassu and Kerbatch in the Gambia). These four sites are thought to date from around the 12th century CE, just before the foundation of the Jolof Empire that would soon encompass the area, but there are literally thousands of megalithic monuments, primarily stone and earthen tumuli, spread between the Sine-Saloum Delta and Tambacounda which are believed to be have been used as elite burial sites, and many of these date back significantly further than the UNESCO-inscribed sites that represent their apotheosis.

Simultaneously, fishing communities began to take root on the coasts, and it's these populations that began the centuries-long process of creating the hundreds of seashell islands – most famously Fadiouth – that dot Senegal's river deltas. Remarkably, these are quite simply a product of centuries of use as a dumping ground for leftover shells, and even if it was at first inadvertent, the practice's continuity in the coming centuries, despite the arrival of new technologies and political systems, has guaranteed their survival. The most significant of these emerging technologies was metal smelting, and the working of iron, copper, gold, and other metals started in earnest around the region circa 300 CE, and would some centuries hence give rise, all the way across the country along the Senegal River, to the first historically recorded Senegalese state, Takrur.

THE RISE OF EMPIRES AND THE ARRIVAL OF ISLAM Set along the banks of the lower Senegal River (from roughly Dagana to Matam) on either side of today's Senegal-Mauritania border, precise details of the rise of Takrur remain obscured to history, but it's thought to have been founded before 800 CE and to have been a well-established ironworking civilisation by the time it first appeared in the historical record in Andalusian Muslim geographer Al-Bakri's 1068 *Book of Roads and Kingdoms*. An important locus on Trans-Saharan trade routes for gold, salt, grain and slaves, Takrur's development was intimately linked with its trade partners further north in the Maghreb, and in the first half of the 11th century the Takruri king War Jaabi became the first West African monarch to convert to Islam, thus marking the beginning of what would eventually become Senegal's near-total conversion (and explaining why the region today remains the country's most conservative and fully Islamised).

Today, the Fouta Toro region is something of a backwater in Senegal, but at that time Takrur sat at a highly strategic junction for both Saharan and riverine trade. The population's ethnic makeup isn't fully known, but Serer, Wolof and Toucouleur (Fulbe) traditions can all be traced to the region. The rise of Takrur was also contemporaneous with that of the much larger Ghana Empire to its east (and in its later years, the Mali Empire), but Takrur is thought to have for the most part maintained at least a nominal independence from its more powerful neighbours, and also served as a southern border to the Almoravids, whose territory extended from Takrur all the way north to Andalusia after they launched several wars of expansion in the second half of the 11th century, concurrent with the founding of their capital at Marrakech.

Further downriver from Takrur, near Lac de Guiers in the area known as Waalo, Senegal's second historical empire, and perhaps its most consequential, began to take shape over the coming centuries; historians disagree on the specifics, but the Jolof Empire's foundation is likely to have taken place between 1200 and 1350 CE, and it's to here that modern-day Wolofs trace their identity. The empire's foundation is linked to a semi-legendary prince named Ndiadiane Ndiaye. Though it began in what would be Senegal's far north, the empire quickly expanded through the agricultural lands to the south, which had been administered locally by landowning chiefs known as *lamanes*, or 'owners of the land'. Now in control of the Waalo, Kayor, Baol, Sine and Saloum regions, Jolof encompassed much of the land between the Gambia and Senegal rivers, and it overtook Takrur as Senegambia's dominant state.

Meanwhile, to the east of Jolof, both Takrur and the Ghana Empire were on the decline, culminating in a newly founded (by the celebrated Sundiata Keita) and rapidly ascendant Mali Empire absorbing what was left of the Ghana Empire in 1240. This expansionist Mandé empire would soon train its sights west towards

Senegambia; under general Tiramakhan Traore the Casamance and Gambia river basins were both conquered and incorporated into the previously landlocked empire, offering it access to the sea and plentiful lands for Mandinka settlers from the east. To the north, neighbouring Jolof and Takrur were not conquered by Mali outright, but both became vassal states of the empire.

For nearly two centuries Mali was far and away the most powerful empire in the region, and it remains famous for *mansa* Musa (Kankan) Keita's 1324 *hajj*, where he sent gold prices all along his caravan route to Mecca into a years-long slump thanks to his enormous wealth and profligate spending. Such was the Malian taste for grand gestures that Musa Keita only took the throne because the previous *mansa*, Abubakari Keita II, had abdicated in order to lead a 2,000-boat expedition into the Atlantic and was never heard from again (though a small handful of scholars argue the seafarers may have reached Brazil).

Thus, while it may have had a golden age unparalleled in the region, by the mid 15th century Mali found itself firmly on the defensive. Squeezed from the east by the breakaway Songhai Empire around Gao and no longer able to effectively exert its authority over its vassals in the west, Mali lost control of Jolof when it reasserted its authority as an independent state, and the Mandinka-settled areas around the Gambia and Casamance rivers went on to form the Kabu Empire. It was just then, in 1444, that two fleets of Portuguese caravels, led by the slaver Nuno Tristão and explorer Dinis Dias, set sail down the West African coast and reached Senegal for the very first time.

EUROPEAN CONTACT In the decades that followed, the Portuguese, from their base in the Cape Verde islands offshore, would set up a handful of settlements on the Senegalese coast (notably at Joal, Saly-Portudal and Rufisque) which were populated by Luso-African *lançados*, or metis, who operated as middlemen for trade with the interior regions for slaves, ivory, spices and gold. The arrival of the Portuguese and this newly developed economy would signal a fundamental shift in the regional balance of power, with the previously undisputed primacy of the trans-Saharan trade soon taking a back seat to commercial interests on the shores of the Atlantic. Thus, coastal regions once peripheral to the major inland centres of power in Mali and Jolof suddenly became prime real estate and many took the opportunity to flex their newfound muscles and contest their allegiances to capitals that had suddenly found themselves in the hinterland (where they largely remain to this day).

The death knell for both Takrur and Jolof would stem from a similar combination of sources, when in the 1490s Koly Tenguele Ba and a group of Fulbe from the Fouta Djalon mountains rampaged their way north through Jolof and into Takrur, overthrowing the rulers of the latter and installing their own leadership, known as the Denyanke dynasty, who would rule the newly christened Fouta Toro for more than 250 years until they were overthrown during a revolt by Fouta Toro's *torodbe* clerical class in 1776. These uprisings continued off and on throughout northern and eastern Senegal for the next 100 years, until the French solidified their hold on the upper reaches of the river in the late 1800s.

Jolof itself, albeit diminished, would at least initially survive the Fulbe invasion, but the centrifugal force of the growing Atlantic trade would pull the empire apart, as the ascendant coastal provinces of Waalo, Kayor, Baol, Sine and Saloum paid tribute to an increasingly irrelevant capital near Linguère. The situation came to a head at the 1549 battle of Danky, when Kayor, under prince Amary Ngoné Sobel Fall, rebelled against Jolof rule and successfully routed the armies of the Jolof king, known as a *bourba*. Kayor's independence led to the rapid secession of all Jolof's other provinces, leaving behind a landlocked and altogether diminished rump state in the Ferlo that would, in its reduced form, come to be known as the Jolof Kingdom. These six independent Wolof and Serer kingdoms ruled for more than 300 years and were the last indigenous political structures in Senegambia before their ultimate destruction at the hands of the 19th-century French.

As Fouta Toro and the Wolof kingdoms developed, the coastal regions were rapidly becoming a game of colonialist ping-pong between the British, Dutch, French and Portuguese. Though they were the first to be established, the Portuguese trading posts manned by *lançados* were not formally declared to be Portuguese colonies as such, and their presence was quickly contested as other European powers sought to get their hands into the increasingly lucrative pot. The Dutch set up an outpost and fort on Gorée in 1617, but the island would go on to change hands no less than half a dozen times before the century was out, and this trend largely continued through the 1700s. The area around Saint-Louis was first occupied by the French in 1638 (1659 on the island itself), and it bounced back and forth between British and French control several times before it was decisively handed over to the French in 1817 at the conclusion of the Napoleonic Wars.

Further south, the same Anglo-French game of musical islands would also repeat itself on James Island in what is now The Gambia, but the British decisively controlled the island at the turn of the 18th century. In Casamance, the quadripartite rivalry between the French, British, Portuguese and Dutch plays out in a similar fashion, only running on a slightly later timeline than territories to the north. The Portuguese had been active in Ziguinchor since 1650, but after almost two centuries of rivalry, the French set up posts up- and down-river of the city in Sédhiou and Carabane in the 1830s. From here, they harried Portuguese traffic in and out of Ziguinchor, but didn't actually take possession of the city until decades later, when it was signed over after the Berlin Conference as part of the Luso-French Convention of 1886, making it the last territorial addition to the French possessions that would become modern-day Senegal.

SLAVERY The reason for these pitched battles over coastal control was of course economic. The ports of Senegambia were geographically the closest slave-exporting ports to Europe, and though their importance to the trade was eventually surpassed by regions further south (ie: Angola), Africans had been continually abducted from Senegambia since the first days of the Portuguese presence, and it's estimated that, regardless of who was controlling the ports, between 200,000 and 500,000 individuals were taken from Senegambia and sold into slavery in the Americas between the years 1600 and 1800. Given that the region as a whole is estimated to have had just over a million residents at the time, the scale of the tragedy that befell the region can hardly be overstated.

As would be expected, the loss of so many of the population, and the slave trade's pernicious economic incentive to wage war and kidnap neighbouring peoples, had a profoundly destabilising effect on the regional states, opening them up first to a series of Islamic rebellions and revolutions in the 18th and 19th centuries that were launched against leaders seen as corrupt and parasitical, such as the successful *torodbe* revolt against the Denyanke dynasty in Fouta Toro and the subsequent 1776 establishment of an *imamate* theocracy in its stead, though even this failed to extricate itself from the omnipresent slave economy that had developed.

Secondly, the chronic instability caused by the slave trade undermined the ability of local people to mount an effective and unified resistance to the growing French presence in the region, and thus paved the way for the French to venture out from their coastal redoubts and absorb broad swathes of the Senegalese interior into the growing colony. Somewhat counter-intuitively, even the slave trade's eventual abolishment in 1848 may have contributed to the Wolof states' impending downfall, as many of their economies had become so slavery-dependent in the preceding centuries that when the trade disappeared, there was nothing left to replace it, and peanuts, which were soon to become the mainstay of the Senegalese economy, had yet to come on to the scene.

COLONIAL TAKEOVER With the 1848 abolition of slavery in the wake of the French Revolution, a total rethink of the heavily slave-dependent Senegalese economy was needed. Gum Arabic became an important crop for a time, and an illicit trade in slaves continued for some decades, but as the horrors of slavery slowly came to a close, an economic lifebuoy had just arrived in the form of the humble peanut, and it would become Senegal's dominant export for the century to come and beyond.

By the mid 19th century, most of French activity in Senegal was still confined to the coast and, to a lesser extent, along the Senegal River (the fort in Bakel dates to the 1820s); but this would change dramatically by the turn of the century, as planned rail lines, cash crop agriculture, and the expansionist governor Louis Faidherbe (whose tenure began in 1854) all conspired to violently accelerate their annexation of the country. Waalo fell to the French in the late 1850s, as forts were being built in Podor (1854) and Matam (1857). At the turn of the decade, Faidherbe ordered the invasion of the remaining Wolof and Serer kingdoms. Baol, Sine, and Saloum were all taken into a 'protectorate', while Kayor was annexed outright, though thanks to the resistance of Kayor's *damel* Lat Dior Diop, this was to prove short-lived, and the kingdom reasserted its independence in 1871. Though he was no longer governor, the expansion set in motion under Faidherbe continued apace, and construction began on the Saint-Louis–Dakar railway in 1883. Its path would cut directly through Kayor, however, and resistance was fierce. Lat Dior Diop died at the Battle of Dekhlé in 1886, the railroad was completed that same year, and the last *bourba* of Jolof, Alboury Ndiaye, fled east from his kingdom in 1890 in the face of a French assault. The final border with Great Britain in the Gambia was fixed in 1890, and thus the last of Senegal's historic kingdoms were annexed or crushed, borders with neighbouring states began to crystallise, and, with the exception of a few isolated pockets of resistance in the mangroves of Casamance, the French now controlled the entire territory that would become Senegal.

Politically, however, the territory was administered in two parts: a quartet of *communes*, and the colony. The four communes enjoyed a special status, and their French, Métis and literate African residents theoretically, though very often not in practice, enjoyed all the rights of citizens living in metropolitan France. Saint-Louis (which had been the colony's capital since its return from the British in 1817) and Gorée were both awarded commune status after the French Revolution in 1848, and in Saint-Louis the Métis population, many of whom had become quite rich acting as middlemen between French traders and Wolofs in the interior, had been nominating a mayor to advocate for their interests with the colonial government since the 1700s, so the extension of these rights, though unique in colonial Africa, was in part a confirmation of rights some had already been exercising. Rufisque would go on to gain *commune* status in 1880, finally followed by Dakar in 1887. Residents of the communes were known as *originaires* and, in addition to the other benefits, they were also exempted from mandatory service in France's colonial army. Residents of the rest of the colony, known as *sujets,* were not, and nearly 100,000 Senegalese fought for France in World War I.

With the demise of Senegal's traditional political structures, a new set of leaders emerged in the form of the four Sufi brotherhoods (see box, page 23). At first sceptical of their devout followings and rapidly expanding influence, the French attempted to stifle the brotherhoods' growth by force, none more so than the Mourides, whose founder, Ahmadou Bamba, was exiled to Gabon for seven years in 1895, which backfired spectacularly; he was hailed as a saint upon his return. Realising they had little chance against the influential brotherhoods, the French entered into negotiations with them, the result being that the French took a more laissez-faire approach to administering the rural areas where the brotherhoods held sway, just so long as the brotherhoods kept the peanuts growing, and a significant portion of the proceeds of those peanuts made their way into government coffers. It was thanks to this arrangement that some of the contours of modern Senegal began to take shape. The Mourides took charge of and expanded the peanut trade throughout the Wolof heartlands, and the railways were built up around them to keep the crops rolling to the ports, where they could be exported for processing into oil. Construction began on the Dakar–Bamako line in 1906, and by the time it was complete in 1923, Senegal's centre of gravity had decisively shifted from Saint-Louis and the north to Dakar and the peanut basin.

THE 20TH CENTURY Just as they had expanded drastically into Senegal in the latter years of the 19th century, so too had the French been busy on other parts of the continent, and in 1895 the colonies were reorganised into a new federation, Afrique Occidentale Française and, as an indicator of its growing regional importance, Dakar was named capital of the entire territory. Saint-Louis remained capital of the Senegal territory, but by the dawn of the 20th century its moment had all but passed and Dakar was beginning its skyward trajectory.

As the French consolidated their hold on the rest of Senegal, political developments in the four communes were impressively dynamic, and represent some of the first steps in Senegal's extraordinary political history. In 1909 Galandou Diouf was elected to represent Rufisque in the *Conseil Général,* the colony's advisory council which sat in Saint-Louis, making him the first African ever to do so. Barely five years later, in 1914, Blaise Diagne would become the first African to be elected to the French parliament (Chamber of Deputies), and he represented the four communes in Paris for two decades until his death in 1934. Galandou Diouf was elected to Diagne's empty seat, and served there until he fled the Nazi German invasion in 1940.

As with the rest of French West Africa, Senegal allied with the Vichy regime during World War II, and Dakar even saw fighting in September 1940 as part of Operation Menace, when Charles de Gaulle and several gunboats tried unsuccessfully to force a change of allegiance to Free France. Senegal remained under Vichy control until the successful Allied invasion of French North Africa in Operation Torch persuaded the authorities in Dakar to switch sides at the end of 1942. Tens of thousands of African troops, some in divisions known as the Tirailleurs Sénégalais, fought to liberate France from the Nazi and Vichy regimes, and it was one of these returned soldiers who, after spending two years in a German POW camp, returned to a liberated France and eventually went on to free his own country from colonial domination as well.

INDEPENDENCE This soldier, of course, was Léopold Sédar Senghor, who some years later would become the first president of an independent Senegal. The war laid bare the contradictions and inequalities inherent to the colonial system, and in November

1944, before the war had even ended, more than 1,000 repatriated POW *tirailleurs* mutinied over poor conditions, unpaid salaries, and the unequal compensation they were offered in comparison with white soldiers. The mutiny ended in a massacre, when French soldiers opened fire on their African counterparts, killing dozens and galvanizing public opinion against the colonial authorities. (The incident was commemorated in Ousmane Sembène's 1988 film *Camp de Thiaroye*.) The war ended soon after, but unrest in the colonies was only set to increase, and a massive railway strike, also seeking compensation and family benefits equal to those of the railway's white workers, brought the colony to a grinding halt over six months in 1947–8. This too was immortalised by Sembène in his 1960 novel, *God's Bits of Wood*.

The 1950s saw great changes in France's administration of its colonies, but perhaps none more significant than the 1956 *loi cadre*, which extended voting rights to all of Senegal's former *sujets*, putting them on an equal legal footing with the *originaires* of the four communes for the first time in the colony's history. Meanwhile, Senghor had been teaching in France, publishing poetry and developing the *negritude* philosophy promulgated by himself, Aimé Césaire and Léon Damas, which stressed an embrace of the intrinsic value of African life and traditions in the face of a Western-dominated intellectual tradition and political situation that sought to diminish or negate their worth. In 1948, alongside Mamadou Dia, Senghor founded a political party, the *Bloc Démocratique Sénégalais*, with which he was elected into the French National Assembly in 1951, after which he went on to become mayor of Thiès in 1956. Deeply involved in Franco-Senegalese electoral politics, Senghor himself was at first not at all an advocate of independence, but favoured maintaining continued close ties with France as part of a federal system. He, along with his new political party, the *Union Progressiste Sénégalaise* (UPS), very successfully (98%!) campaigned for a vote to remain in political union with France during the 1958 referendum in French West Africa, an option only rejected by French Guinea, which would receive an abrupt and punitive independence later the same year.

Still, the winds of change were blowing on the continent, and Guinea's example hastened the demise of the envisioned but ultimately abortive French Union. More than a dozen French territories were granted independence in 1960 alone, and Senegal was no exception. Independence was originally planned as part of a union with French Sudan (today's Mali) to form the Mali Federation, with its capital at Dakar. The federation was granted independence on 4 April 1960 but collapsed within months, leaving Senghor's Senegal and Modibo Keita's Mali as two separate countries from 20 August 1960.

Commonly touted as a beacon of democracy on the continent, Senegal is indeed a rare breed in Africa – there's been nary a coup since independence, and the changes of administration here have always been peaceful. Still, while it might stand out as compared with some of its neighbours, Senegal has also been through some rocky patches in its post-independence history. Shortly after independence in 1962, its first prime minister, the socialist Mamadou Dia, was charged with plotting a coup; he spent the next 12 years in a Kédougou jail cell. A new constitution was approved by popular vote in 1963, which did away with the post of prime minister entirely. Political rivals to Senghor's UPS also began feeling the squeeze – political parties had to be approved by the state, and the state quite simply didn't approve any. In the first three presidential elections, Senghor was re-elected unopposed, and UPS became the only legal party until 1974, when Abdoulaye Wade (more on him in a minute) and his Parti Démocratique Sénégalais (PDS) were recognised by the government.

This narrowing of political space combined with a crippling drought and slump in market prices for Senegal's peanut crop led to a series of general strikes in the late 1960s which would prompt Senghor to reverse course and liberalise what had effectively become a one-party state. He reinstated the post of prime minister in 1970, appointing the former Minister for Planning, Abdou Diouf, to the position.

As would befit someone known as the poet-president, Senghor was an aggressive promoter of the arts, and during his tenure Senegal became a cultural hub for the entire continent – music, dance, art, theatre and museums were all funded by the state, Senegal became host to numerous international events, and the world-renowned quantity and quality of Senegal's cultural output remains one of the most significant legacies of his presidency. The other would reveal itself in 1980, when he became the first African president to voluntarily hand over power. (Continuing the trend, several years later he was elected as one of the 40 *immortels* of the Académie Française, becoming the first African to join the body.)

After Senghor's resignation, Abdou Diouf became the second president of Senegal, and held the office through three elections and nearly 20 years, until he was defeated when running for a fourth term in the year 2000. He continued the trend of liberalisation begun under Senghor, and a number of political parties became active under Diouf's tenure, though their activities could often be curtailed. His time in office was punctuated by more crises than perhaps any other time in Senegal's post-independence history, and they kicked off less than a year after he took office. He sent Senegalese troops into the Gambia to put down a coup against president Dawda Jawara's administration; this led to the formation of the Confederation of Senegambia, which was little more than a loose association between the two states that didn't even see the end of the decade before dissolving. A year later in 1982, the Casamance crisis started with protests in Ziguinchor (see below), and before his first decade in office came to a close, a several-year border war kicked off with Mauritania that saw hundreds die and tens of thousands – those perceived as 'belonging' to the other country – made refugees over a grazing dispute along the river. Simultaneous to all this, Senegal was also struggling beneath a series of IMF and World Bank structural adjustment programmes that saw standards of living fall throughout the country.

Except in Casamance, the 1990s proved to be considerably calmer, and Diouf won his third election in 1993 against Abdoulaye Wade, who was running for president for the fourth time. Not to be criticised for lack of persistence, Mr Wade succeeded at the fifth attempt, defeating Abdou Diouf in a run-off election in the year 2000; in another first for Senegal, the victory of Wade and his PDS party represented the first change of government at the ballot box anywhere in sub-Saharan Africa since independence.

CASAMANCE CONFLICT Today one of Africa's longest-running civil conflicts, the separatist conflict in Casamance has gone through numerous iterations in its three-decade history, with peace agreements made and broken, but today it happily seems closer to ending than at perhaps any other time. Originally launched as a movement for the rights of Casamançais (primarily Diola), who felt marginalised by the central government in Dakar, today both popular and foreign support for the rebellion has waned, and the remaining rebels appear as increasingly isolated voices in the wilderness. The proverbial tables have turned many times in the Casamance before, but signs today are decidedly hopeful.

The conflict's active phase started in 1982, when the Mouvement des Forces Démocratiques de Casamance (MFDC) launched a series of protests in Ziguinchor over perceived governmental neglect and lack of investment in the region, the appointment of outsiders (primarily Wolofs) as civil servants there, and controversial land reforms that clashed with traditional Diola systems of land tenure. The protests, after a heavy-handed government crackdown, rapidly evolved into a fully fledged rebellion against the central government in Da' papered-over geographical, ethnic, religious and political differ. Casamance and the rest of Senegal were forcibly thrust out into the open.

Since its inception, the main player in the conflict has been the MFDC, whic was founded in 1947 by Emile Badiane (who would go on to become the mayor of Bignona), Ibou Diallo and Victor Diatta. The original MFDC, it's worth noting, actually had no separatist aspirations, but was simply created to better represent Casamançais interests in Dakar, where issues pertaining to the Casamance have a long history of being brushed aside. Indeed, the original MFDC would become a constituent part of the Léopold Sédar Senghor-led Bloc Démocratique Sénégalais (BDS) in 1954, which itself would go on to become the ruling Parti Socialiste du Sénégal (PS) at independence in 1960. Apocryphal claims of a promise made by President Senghor that an independence referendum would be arranged for Casamance after 20 years of Senegalese independence from France remain unsubstantiated, but would go on to inform the grievances brought to the table by a resurrected MFDC in 1982.

After the protests in Ziguinchor were put down and many of their leaders arrested, *akita* (meaning *warrior* in Diola) groups began to form and many took to the forests in 1983, among them some defectors from the Senegalese army. These would comprise the nucleus of the new MFDC, and their small-scale actions would grow in scale and intensity towards the end of the decade; as an expansion of their usual banditry and troublemaking on the roadways, attacks on the airport and other targets inside Ziguinchor were launched in the early 1990s.

Long led by a rotating cast of characters who have for the most part been killed or died of natural causes (it has been a long war, after all), the rebel MFDC was originally founded and led by Catholic priest Father Augustine Diamacoune Senghor (no relation to the president), but it began to splinter between hard-line factions and those more open to compromise with the government after the 1991 Bissau Accord, which would become the first of half a dozen or more failed peace processes. It was not long after this that Salif Sadio began to make his name as a leader in the organisation, and today the MFDC has largely splintered into three competing factions led by Salif Sadio, César Atoute Badiatte and Ousmane Niantang Diatta; Father Augustine Diamacoune Senghor died in Paris in 2007.

The crisis reached its nadir in the 1990s under President Abdou Diouf, and accusations of support for the MFDC from neighbouring countries (particularly The Gambia, whose president since 1994, Yahya Jammeh, is a Diola himself) periodically soured relations between Senegal and its neighbours as military alliances (and refugee populations forced into Gambia and Guinea-Bissau) ebbed and flowed. Hopes were high for a resolution after the 2000 election of Abdoulaye Wade, but the conflict managed to trundle on, and the same hopes were raised once again at Macky Sall's 2012 election, when he extended an offer of dialogue to the three remaining MFDC leaders.

The offer seems to have been well received, as Salif Sadio, widely considered the most hard-line leader of the bunch, declared a unilateral ceasefire in April 2014. Negotiations for a final resolution to the conflict are ongoing under the auspices of the Community of Sant'Egidio in Rome, who are best known for having mediated the peace agreement in Mozambique's 16-year civil war. Some 5,000 people have lost their lives in the conflict and countless more have fallen victim to landmines and other violence, but hopes are high that after nearly 35 years, peace is finally returning to the Casamance.

SENEGAL TODAY After more than 25 years in opposition, Abdoulaye Wade, the longtime head of the PDS and holder of a PhD in Law and Economics from the Sorbonne, was finally sworn in as president on 1 April 2000. He pursued a liberal economic agenda, encouraging foreign direct investment in the country and spearheading a number of large-scale initiatives, including several mining projects, the Blaise Diagne International Airport outside Dakar (which may actually be open by the time you read this), and the perpetually controversial African Renaissance Monument, which has been dividing opinions across Dakar since its unveiling there in 2010. Wade was also widely fêted for negotiating a 2004 peace agreement with the MFDC in Casamance, but by 2006 several factions of the splintered movement had returned to arms.

Today, however, Wade is better remembered for the way he left office than for what he did in it. Less than a year after entering office, Wade called a successful referendum on a new constitution that devolved power to the regions and limited the president to two five-year terms, shortened from their previous seven. He would go on to perform an almost complete about-face on these limitations, controversially contesting the 2012 election against Macky Sall on the basis that his first term began before the new constitution went into effect, as well as restoring the seven-year mandate for his hypothetical third term. The constitutional court agreed, but the moves angered many Senegalese and prompted months of running street battles with a youth-led grassroots protest movement called *Y'en a Marre* (French for 'fed up'), which sprang up to firstly dissuade Wade from contesting the election, and when that didn't work, to ultimately vote him out of office. Given that Wade rode into office on a wave of youth support, their wholesale abandonment of him in favour of Macky Sall 12 years later was considered a serious indictment of his time in office.

Sall himself served as both prime minister under Wade and president of the National Assembly during his administration, until a falling out with Abdoulaye and Karim Wade led him to defect from the PDS in 2008 and form his own party, Alliance Pour la République (APR). Running on the APR ticket and riding his own wave of popular discontent into office, his alliance won the parliamentary elections and he forced Wade into a presidential runoff, neatly winning the second round with 65% of the vote and diffusing a potential descent deeper into crisis should Wade have been re-elected. Since he's entered office, he's been praised for scaling back some of the excesses of the Wade presidency, including returning once again to the two five-year term limits promulgated in the 2001 constitution, and an ongoing re-evaluation of the enormous urban renewal projects launched in Dakar that would have seen the demolition of a number of historic buildings, including the 1912 train station, as part of the *Parc culturel de Dakar* project. Halfway through his first term, Sall remains reasonably well liked, but June 2014 saw APR trounced in local elections, which led to the sacking of prime minister Aminata Toure and a wide-open race for the next presidential and parliamentary elections, scheduled for 2017.

Senegal is without question a nation of political junkies, and the latest controversy on lips and newspapers everywhere at the time of writing was the son of the former president, Karim Wade, who was a powerful minister (so powerful he earned the nickname 'Minister of Heaven and Earth') in his father's government, and widely thought to have been being groomed as his successor. In March 2015 he was accused of embezzling more than US$1.4 billion and jailed for six years on corruption charges. Macky Sall is widely expected to contest the next presidential elections, but it's unclear what the SDP will do, as they nominated Karim Wade as their candidate just two days before his prison sentence was handed down. The latest political news inevitably whips around Dakar like a harmattan sandstorm, so just be alert and you'll no doubt get an earful of the kind of conflicts and controversies that keep the voters in Africa's oldest democracy heading back to the polls year after year.

PEOPLE

WOLOF The Wolof are culturally, politically and linguistically Senegal's dominant ethnic group, and they represent a large segment of the population, with some 43% of Senegalese claiming Wolof heritage. Overwhelmingly Muslim, Wolofs live primarily in the north-central regions of the country, in areas generally following the contours of what was once the Wolof-dominated Jolof Empire (1200–1549) and subsequently the independent kingdoms of Jolof, Kayor, Waalo and Baol (1549–late 19th century). Arrayed along and inland from the Grande Côte, the kingdoms became important intermediaries for European trade, and Wolofs were the dominant African population in Senegal's colonial cities, paving the way for them to become a dominant force in trade and eventually politics in both pre- and post-colonial Senegal. The Wolof heartland is also largely concurrent with the area known as the peanut basin, where the aforementioned nut has been the main cash crop since the 1840s. The peanut industry would later come to be dominated by the Mouride brotherhood, whose adherents are largely Wolof as well. Today, major Wolof population centres include Dakar, Saint-Louis and Touba, though Wolofs live throughout the country, leading to tensions with smaller groups over the *Wolofisation* of the country, as thanks to the popular and political dominance of the Wolof, their customs, culture, and language have been adopted to a greater or lesser degree throughout the country and for outsiders have become emblematic of Senegal as a whole.

FULBE (PEUL) Senegal's second-largest group is the Fulbe, who form part of an enormous ethno-linguistic group numbering more than 40 million people living in nearly two dozen countries stretching from Senegal and Cape Verde in the west to Sudan, the DRC and the western fringes of Ethiopia in the east. Known in Senegal as Peul, and depending on where you are, by a host of other names including Fulani and Fula, they make up 24% of Senegal's population and speak Pulaar, which is also variously and confusingly known as Fulfulde, Fula and Fulani, again depending on where you are. Within this percentage is a Senegalese Fulbe subgroup known as the Toucouleur or Halpulaaren, who are culturally and ethnically similar to the Fulbe; but rather than living as nomadic pastoralists as Fulbe traditionally do, they are settled farmers and fishers in the Senegal River valley, and as such consider themselves a distinct but closely related group. With the 1030AD conversion of the king of Takrur, War Jaabi, the ancestors of the Fulbe and Toucouleur (the name Toucouleur itself is a French corruption of Takrur) living in the Senegal River valley were the first group anywhere in Senegambia to adopt Islam, and even today the region remains arguably the most devout in the country, save perhaps the Mouride holy city of Touba.

SERER Despite representing only 15% of Senegal's population, Serers punch far above their weight when it comes to Senegalese culture and politics, with first president Léopold Sédar Senghor, global music superstar Youssou N'Dour, and legendary author and filmmaker Ousmane Sembène all claiming Serer roots. Their ancestral lands are primarily concentrated in the post-Jolof Empire kingdoms of Sine, Saloum and parts of Baol, which roughly correspond with the Petite Côte south of Dakar, continuing southeast towards the Sine-Saloum Delta and Kaolack. Long resistant to Islamisation from the surrounding Wolofs, Fulbes and Mandinkas, the Serer were among the last Senegalese groups to adopt Islam, and though Serers today are largely Muslim, much like the Diola in Casamance, Christianity and traditional Animist beliefs have a considerably stronger presence among the Serer than in most parts of the country.

WOLOF PROVERBS

Excerpt from Sir Richard Burton's *Wit and Wisdom from West Africa* (1865)

During his many 19th-century forays in Africa, British explorer Sir Richard Burton collected popular proverbs and idioms in many languages, including several hundred in Wolof, which were published in 1865. Some are humorous, some serious, and all touch on ideas and expectations in society, relations, and behaviour; even though they're firmly rooted in local culture, some will seem very familiar indeed, while others enjoy a universality that comes across in any language.

Burton's introduction to the work, despite being written exactly 150 years ago, still holds largely true today:

> In Wolof the proverbs are numerous and expressive: the people are exceedingly fond of them, and a European with any knowledge of these wise sayings, can travel amongst them not only in safety, but with all respect.

Try a few of the following out on your Wolof friends, and you're sure to get a knowing nod, a good laugh, and – as Burton said so many years ago – for taking the time to learn their culture, a great deal of respect.

Jamoul aya na, tey ladhieteoul a ko raw.
Not to know is bad, not to wish to know is worse.

La diarake ama di youja sou ko niw amone diala.
What the convalescent refuses, would give pleasure to the dead.

Daw dou maee y taliba
Running about gives no scholars. (NB – our 'Rolling stone gathers no moss.')

Beugueti ma laje, bel sama bope defa bosse.
I want no boiled meat if my head must be the trivet (which supports the pot).

Faka na la, mo guenne jamou ma la
'I have forgotten thy name,' is better than 'I know thee not.'

Boigne a di sakete ou guemigne.
Teeth serve as a fence to the mouth.

Mpithie sou bagney daije, souje la niala.
If the bird drinks not at the stream, it knows its own watering place.

Garap gou nga romba mou sanni la y mbourou sou thia euluek so, nga romba fa.
If the tree under which you pass throws bread to you, you will pass it again tomorrow.

Mpethie ou sagor lou nga thia gawantou kone yoboul goube.
If you go to the sparrows' ball, take ears of corn for them.

Sou sipou ngabo guennetey pate.
If he who buys milk is proud, he who sells it should be prouder.

DIOLA Given their outsized rôle in Senegal's modern history, you could be forgiven for thinking that the Diola make up a significant chunk of the Senegalese population, but they actually clock in at a decidedly understated 4%. Long resistant to outside incursions by Africans and Europeans alike, fierce refusal to cede power to either

Yebou thia nangou thia, kou la thia yoni nga gaw thia demma.
We go quickly where we are sent when we take interest in the journey.

Demmal mo guenne do demma.
'Go!' is better than 'Don't go!'

Jalele bagna na lo mou tamma.
The child hates him who gives it all it wants.

Sou mbajaney done nana yore, kaine dou ko solla.
If the hat drank the brain, nobody would wear it.

Kou vorra kou la doul vorra, Yalla vorra la.
He who betrays one that betrays him not, Allah shall betray him.

Ella waja bou ntoute, tey deguelou bou barey.
One must talk little, and listen much.

Y waje you baje, dou mae lou gno laika.
The best words give no food.

Dou gnou laikelo nitte sou sourey.
One should not press a full man to eat.

Kou beugua jalisse ligueya.
He who loves money must labour.

Koudi di binda nopalikou.
He who writes, rests himself.

Daigue dou bour, wandey kou ko beugua joussa soumi sa y dalle.
The rivulet is not a king, yet he who would cross it removes his shoes.

Dono gueramoul kaine gaw dee a ko maee.
The heir thanks nobody but the sudden death.

Kou beugua laime, gnomel yambe.
If you like honey, fear not the bees.

Kou yakey lojo bai koudou dou ko niarel a.
He who puts aside his spoon to draw from the pot with his hand, does not do so twice.

Mbajaney mo natta thy sa bope they diekou thia bou ko natta thy sa bope ou naweley.
If the hat which you try on fits not your head, do not make your neighbour try it.

Mere mandingne, doja bou gaw a ko guenne.
It is better to walk than to grow angry with the road.

Lou nga telle telle dioka, yonne dhitou la.
He who rises early finds the way short.

their Mandinka neighbours or the French colonialists meant that the farming and fishing communities of their Basse Casamance homeland were the last place in Senegal to fall under colonial dominion. Indeed, it was barely 60 years before the largely Diola-based Mouvement des Forces Démocratiques de Casamance

(MFDC) kicked off their separatist rebellion here in 1982 against the independent Senegalese state and the notion of outside – in this case Wolof – rule. While the rebellion may have fizzled eventually and today seems to have all but burned out, the Diola spirit of resistance is alive and well. Muslims, Christians and Animists are all well represented among the Diola today, and Ziguinchor's laissez-faire vibe is testament to the live-and-let-live philosophy that reigns in the region.

MANDINKA (MALINKÉ) Tracing their history to the Mandé peoples of the Mali Empire who spread across West Africa along with the expanding empire starting around the year 1300, there are dozens of groups throughout the region whose origins can be traced to these migrations, including the Mandinka, Bambara, Soninké, Djallonké and others, but in Senegal the Mandinkas (also known as Malinké) represent the largest Mandé group, even though they only comprise 3% of Senegalese, in sharp contrast to The Gambia, where Mandinkas make up 42% of the population. Thus it's no surprise that most Mandinkas in Senegal are found near the Gambian borders, primarily along the road to Tambacounda in the north and stretching south towards the cities of Kolda and Sédhiou in Haute Casamance. Like their Wolof and Fulbe neighbours, Islam is a core component of Mandinka identity, and both the *griot* traditions found across West Africa and the prevalence of the kora have origins with the Mandé and their presence throughout the region.

SONINKÉ (SARAKOLE) Along with the Fulbe (Peul), the Soninké (also known as Sarakole) were among the first groups in Senegal to adopt Islam in 1076, and while today they represent only a sliver of the Senegalese population, their roots in the region go all the way back to the first millennium as rulers of the Ghana Empire (from which the modern state gets its name). The heartland of the empire was situated in what is now western Mali and southeastern Mauritania, but it stretched west towards the upper reaches of the Senegal River near Bakel and Matam, which is where the bulk of Senegal's Soninké population are found today.

EUROPEAN AND LEBANESE Making up a small but visible subset of the population (somewhere around 1%) are Europeans and Lebanese, many of whom trace their ancestry here back for generations. As Senegal's transition to independence was considerably smoother than that of many countries in the region, it didn't witness an exodus of European settlers on the same scale as many of its neighbours did, and today's European presence consists of both new immigrants and families who have been in Senegal for generations. Though there are thousands more from a variety of other countries, the largest European contingent in Senegal is naturally the French; today there are more than 20,000 French citizens resident in Senegal, who typically work either with multinationals active in the country, or in other professional sectors involving trade, tourism and business.

With a presence in the country dating back to the late 1800s, the Lebanese also have long roots in Senegal and today number between 15,000 and 30,000, most of whom are the second or third generation to be born in Senegal. As is true across West Africa, many are active as traders and in the professional spheres, and a significant portion of businesses in the country are Lebanese-owned. Somewhat unusually for West Africa, the Lebanese community is also involved in politics, and the Louga-born environmentalist Haïdar El Ali currently serves as Minister of Fisheries and Maritime Affairs under Macky Sall. Geographically speaking, both communities are are heavily concentrated in Dakar, with smaller pockets in other urban centres throughout the country.

OTHER All told, groups that don't fit into one of the above categories make up just under 10% of the Senegalese population; this catch-all category includes various different groups, including indigenous ethnic minorities as well as groups found along Senegal's peripheries who are a part of larger populations in neighbouring countries but wound up on the other side of a colonial border from their compatriots. Numbering no more than a few tens of thousands, Senegal's best-known ethnic minority is probably the **Bassari** people, who live in an isolated corner of the Kédougou region (and across the border in Guinea) and are renowned for their theatrical coming-of-age ceremonies. They, along with their neighbours the **Bedik**, speak their own languages and are primarily Animists and Christians. They live a traditional farming lifestyle in isolated villages along the Fouta Djalon foothills, separate from the Muslim Peul (Fulbe) herders predominant in the valleys nearby. The 'cultural landscapes' formed by the three groups in Kédougou have been a UNESCO World Heritage Site since 2012.

Thanks to an accident of geography and history, Senegal's other most famous minority would have to be the **Lébou** people, whose traditional lands sit smack on the end of the Cap Vert peninsula where Dakar stands today. The peninsula's original inhabitants, many were displaced as the city grew, but many others managed to hold on to their lands, and today large parts of greater Dakar, particularly Yoff, Ngor and Ouakam, are dominated by Lébou. Wolof-speaking and primarily fisherfolk, the Lébou are noted for their adherence to the heterodox Layène Sufi brotherhood based in Yoff, which incorporates pre-Islamic traditions along with elements of Christian worship and the veneration of their founding father, Seydina Limamou Laye, as the *madhi* or Islamic messiah set to return as a precursor to the Apocalypse.

Though their coherence as a group has somewhat diminished in the modern era, the *métis* have also been a considerable economic and political force in Senegal. Liaisons between local Wolof women and French colonialists in 18th- and 19th-century Gorée and Saint-Louis gave birth to a new culture, the métis, who rapidly grew in number and formed their own society outside of the pre-existing colonial categories. Fluent in French and Wolof, but adopting the manners and customs of the French bourgeoisie, many became traders and middlemen between the Europeans on the coast and Africans in the interior. The women, known as *signares*, were especially notable for their emancipated and entrepreneurial rôle, and métis men and women were actively involved in both pre- and post-independence politics. Today, there are still a number of métis households to be found in Gorée and Saint-Louis, and their history is on spectacular display in Saint-Louis every Christmas during the *fanal*, when the island's métis families parade across the city in their Sunday best under a procession of enormous sparkling lanterns.

As for the groups from surrounding countries with a presence in Senegal, from the north there are many **Moors** dressed in their signature blue to be found along the borders with Mauritania and in most major centres around the country, where they are heavily involved in trade. A number of **Bambaras**, a Mandé group related to Mandinkas and Soninkés, who are dominant in neighbouring Mali, live further east along the upper reaches of the river towards Bakel and the Malian border region, while further south along the Guinean border another Mandé group known as **Djallonkés** make their homes in the Fouta Djalon foothills. In Casamance, many **Balanta** and **Manjacks** live along the Guinea-Bissau border and share a staunchly egalitarian history of resistance with their Diola neighbours.

Additionally, Dakar has long been a magnet for migrants from all around West Africa, and is notably home to tens of thousands of Caboverdians, along with immigrants from Ivory Coast, Guinea and Mali, as well as small but growing populations of Chinese and Vietnamese immigrants.

LANGUAGE

The linguists at Ethnologue (*www.ethnologue.com*) list 38 individual languages as being spoken in Senegal, and mother tongues, as you might expect, tend to fall on ethnic lines. Thus, given that Wolofs represent the largest ethnic group in the country and their traditional homelands are at the political, geographical and demographic centres of the country, it's only logical that Wolof has emerged as Senegal's lingua franca. Pulaar is widely spoken in the north of the country along the Senegal River, and also in parts of the south near Kédougou and Kolda. There are a few Soninke speakers out towards Bakel, and Mandinka is prevalent around the Gambia, particularly along the route from Kaolack to Tambacounda, and south into Haute Casamance as well. Serer is largely confined to the Sine-Saloum delta region, and the numerous dialects of Diola to the riverine lands of Basse Casamance. French is taught in schools and used as a secondary lingua franca to Wolof. If you'd like to do some brushing up before you go, free resources on all the major languages spoken in Senegal are available at www.livelingua.com/peace-corps-language-courses.php.

See also *Appendix 1, Language* for a list of useful words and phrases in French, Wolof, Pulaar and Diola.

RELIGION

With 94% of the population counting themselves as Muslims, Islam is far and away the dominant religion in Senegal, though the Senegalese state is officially secular and all citizens enjoy freedom of worship. Nearly all of Senegal's Muslims follow the Sunni tradition, and most also belong to one of four Sufi brotherhoods (see box, page 23). Islam arrived in the region in the 11th century, and was quickly adopted by certain groups while actively resisted by others. Catholicism first arrived with the Portuguese in the 1400s, and gained a larger share of adherents among groups that had not already converted to Islam. Thus ethnicity often informs religion in Senegal, and the Toucouleur (Fulbe), Wolof, Mandinka and Soninke populations of the country are overwhelmingly Islamic, while the Serer and Diola have significantly larger Catholic and Animist minorities. The same goes for smaller ethnic groups like the Bassari and Bedik, who have fiercely maintained both a social and a sacred separation from their Fulbe neighbours for centuries.

EDUCATION

Public education in Senegal is secular and based on the French system, and administered by the Ministère de l'Éducation National (*www.education.gouv. sn*). Schooling is officially compulsory and free of charge until the age of 16 but, despite this, educational attainment remains low, particularly in rural areas, where schools are ill-funded and overcrowded, and the cost of uniforms, books, and other materials remains a barrier towards full school enrolment. The literacy rate is an estimated 58%, including 70% of men and 47% of women (2015 estimates), and primary school graduation rates hovered around 60% in 2010, the most recent year for which figures are available.

Cultural factors play a rôle in depressed educational outcomes as well, as many parents prefer to send their children to Islamic schools known as *daaras* than to the 'French' public schools, which are sometimes viewed as foreign and out of tune with prevailing cultural norms. The *daaras* are recognised by the Senegalese state, but there is little to no surveillance or established standards as their curriculums

Sufism is a mystical practice within Islam. By reciting religious poetry, litanies and special prayers, Sufis attain a closer, more intimate and experiential knowledge of God than can be had through the usual prescribed devotional practices (five daily prayers, Ramadan fasting, alms-giving, etc.). As such, Sufism resembles other mystical practices such as Zen in Buddhism, yoga in Hinduism and Kabbalah in Judaism. In order to practice Sufism, aspirants (*taalibe* in Wolof) on the 'path' to God find a spiritual master (a sheikh) who will guide them. Over many centuries, these networks of sheikhs and disciples have developed into institutions called Sufi orders or brotherhoods.

In Senegal, the Sufi orders are mass institutions. The two largest ones, the Tijaniya and the Murids, have several million adherents each. The two others are the Khadrs (Qadiriya) and the Layennes (mostly in the Cape Vert region). These orders were established in the late 19th century by a generation of charismatic sheikhs. Each has developed a more or less hierarchical organisational structure, with a caliph or caliph-general at the head, various levels of middle-management sheikhs, and rank-and-file *taalibe* disciples. The orders are open to all, men and women, adults and children. Family members often belong to a single order and children are socialised into them as they grow up. The Sufi orders are active in neighbourhoods, schools and work places through local associations, called *dahiras*, which organise recitations and cultural events.

While they are fundamentally religious institutions, the Sufi orders are active in all areas of Senegalese society (cultural organisations, neighbourhood associations, private religious education, healthcare and medicine) and the economy (the transportation sector, the construction industry, retail and services). Due to migration of Senegalese to western Europe, North America, the Gulf and elsewhere across Africa over past decades, Senegal's Sufi orders are now also transnational institutions with members and activities in many countries.

Senegal's Sufi orders and sheikhs permeate many areas of life. Images of famous Sufis dominate commercial art in shops and small businesses, their portraits feature in the living rooms of most Muslim homes, and they are lauded in pop songs. Sufi shrines dot the landscape and can be found in many cities. Several of Senegal's Sufi shrines have given rise to entire cities of their own, such as Touba, Darou Mousty and Madina Gounass, where the Sufi orders govern local affairs independently of the state. Sufi commemorations and pilgrimages, variously called *màggals*, *gàmmus* or *siyaares*, are the country's most important social events.

are run by holy men known as *marabouts* (*serignés* in Wolof and *thiernos* in Pulaar), and coursework typically revolves around memorisation of the Koran (in Arabic) and the tenets of Islam. Children studying at these schools are known as *talibés*, and, depending on the *daara*, begging for alms may be a central component of their education (see box, pages 196–7). Alternatively, many students will attend a public school during the week and religious education classes in their off-hours (ie: Sunday school). Private Catholic schools are also available in all of the major cities; these are closer to the standard of instruction in the public schools, with instruction in French and a standard curriculum in addition to their religious studies. After primary school, students who are able to continue their education go on to *collège* (middle school), *lycée* (high school), and, at the conclusion of *lycée*, students who wish to continue to university must sit the *baccalauréat* school-leaving exam. At tertiary level, the doyen of Senegal's institutions of higher learning is Université Cheikh Anta Diop de Dakar (*www.ucad.sn*), which was founded in 1957 and renamed in 1987 after the famed Senegalese academic Cheikh Anta Diop. It's well regarded regionally and host to many student exchange and study abroad programmes. It's also far and away the largest school in the country, with over 60,000 students in attendance. There are several other public universities throughout the country, including Université Gaston Berger in Saint Louis (*www.ugb.sn*), Université Assane Seck de Ziguinchor (*www.univ-zig.sn*), Université de Thiès (*www.univ-thies.sn*) and Université Alioune Diop de Bambey (*www.bambey.univ.sn*). Recent decades have also seen the establishment of several private universities, primarily in and around Dakar.

CULTURE

For an inside perspective on the music, faith, and politics of modern Senegal, the work of American documentarian Elizabeth Chai Vasarhelyi is an excellent introduction, including *Youssou N'Dour: I Bring What I Love* (2008), *Touba* (2013), and *Incorruptible* (2015).

LITERATURE Given that the country's first president, **Léopold Sédar Senghor**, was a poet himself, it's no wonder that Senegal boasts a rich literary tradition, and the first few decades after independence proved to be a particularly fertile time for the new-born country's novelists. Composing his works primarily in free verse, Senghor began writing in the 1930s, and published his first collection, *Shadow Songs* (*Chants d'Ombre*), in 1945, after his release from a German POW camp in 1942. He continued to write and publish poetry during his tenure as president of Senegal, and was awarded the *Prix mondial Cino Del Duca* in 1978. Today his complete œuvre can be found in *The Collected Poetry,* published most recently in 1998.

As befitting an auteur, Senegal's cinema master **Ousmane Sembène** is also perhaps the most prolific and certainly the most celebrated author in the country. With more than half a dozen books translated into English, he's also among the most accessible to a non-Francophone audience. His 1960 novel *God's Bits of Wood* (*Les bouts de bois de Dieu*) dramatising an anti-colonial train strike on the Dakar–Niger line is often considered his finest, with the cautionary tale of 1974's *Xala* not far behind. Other English translations available include his first novel *Black Docker* (*Le Docker noir*), *The Last of the Empire* (*Le dernier de l'Empire*), a collection of short stories called *Tribal Scars* (*Voltaïque*), and two sets of two novellas: *The Money-Order & White Genesis* (*Le Mandat & Vehi-Ciosane*), and *Niiwam & Taaw.*

Unfortunately, most of Senegal's other celebrated authors have at most one, sometimes two of their works translated into English – some winners of the prestigious Grand Prix Littéraire d'Afrique Noire (which Senegalese authors have claimed nine times since 1961) have still never been published in translation. Thus, the list of titles available is short but sweet.

Birago Diop won the aforementioned prize for his *Tales and Commentaries* (*Contes et Lavanes*) in 1963, but the only book of his to be translated into English is 1947's *Tales of Amadou Koumba* (*Les contes d'Amadou Koumba*), a collection of stories, fables and parables recited to Diop by the *griot* Amadou Koumba. Fellow prize-winner **Cheikh Hamidou Kane**'s *Ambiguous Adventure* (*L'Aventure ambiguë*) has become one of the most recognised works of Senegalese literature and a staple

THIAROYE BY LÉOPOLD SÉDAR SENGHOR *(from* The Collected Poetry)

Written in response to the massacre at Thiaroye (see pages 12–13), this was first published in Léopold Sédar Senghor's second collection of poetry, *Hosties Noires* (Black Hosts) in 1948, during the time he was living in France and several years after he had been freed from a German POW camp in 1942.

Black prisoners, I should say French prisoners, is it true
That France is no longer France?
Is it true that the enemy has stolen her face?
Is it true that bankers' hate has bought her arms of steel?
Wasn't it your blood that cleansed the nation
Now forgetting its former mission?
Tell me, hasn't your blood mixed with her martyr's purified blood?
Will you have the same grand funeral as the Virgin of Hope?

Blood, blood, O my black brothers' blood,
You stain my innocent bedsheets
You are the sweat bathing my anguish, you are the suffering
That makes my voice hoarse
Woi! Hear my blind voice, deaf-mute spirits of the night.
A bloody rain of red locusts! And my heart cries out for blue skies,
And for mercy.

No, you have not died in vain, O Dead! Your blood
Is not tepid water. It generously feeds our hope,
Which will bloom at twilight.
It is our thirst, our hunger for honor,
Our absolute authority.
No, you have not died in vain.
You are the witnesses of immortal Africa
You are the witnesses of the new world to come.

Sleep now, O Dead! Let my voice rock you to sleep,
My voice of rage cradling hope.

Paris, December 1944

of African literature courses since its publication shortly after independence, but it remains his only work available in translation.

The women of Senegal are impressively well represented in the nation's literary canon, and **Mariama Bâ**'s seminal 1979 novel *So Long A Letter (Une si longue lettre)* takes a gimlet-eyed look at polygamy from the perspective of a wife who's recently found out that her husband plans to take a second spouse. Bâ died before her second novel could be published, but she posthumously won the Grand Prix Littéraire d'Afrique Noire for 1982's *Scarlet Song (Le Chant écarlate)* nonetheless. Around the same time, **Aminata Sow Fall** would publish *The Beggars' Strike (La Grève des bàttu)* and win the same award for it in 1980. Published in 1984, the most controversial book of the era dealt in such untouchable topics that the author used a pseudonym – Ken Bugul, Wolof for the 'person no one wants'. Telling the semi-autobiographical tale of a young Senegalese woman who, after going to Belgium to study, found herself involved in drugs and prostitution and faces grave uncertainty on her return to Senegal, 1984's *Le Baobab Fou* was finally translated into English as *The Abandoned Baobab* in 1991.

Approaching the turn of the century, **Boubacar Boris Diop**'s 2000 novel on the Rwandan genocide, *Murambi, The Book of Bones* (*Murambi, Le livre des ossements*) was published to great admiration and remains his best-known work, though *The Knight and His Shadow* (*Le Cavalier et son ombre*) was just released in English translation at the start of 2015, despite originally being written back in 1997. A few years later, in the mid-2000s, a new Senegalese voice emerged in **Fatou Diome**, and it's a voice that represents the younger and increasingly transnational generation of Senegalese coming of age in today's globalised world. Her début novel, *The Belly of the Atlantic* (*Le Ventre de l'Atlantique*), was published in 2005 and quickly established the Senegal-born and Strasbourg-based Diome as very possibly Senegal's foremost contemporary author. France is also home to another modern literary star of Senegalese extraction in **Marie NDiaye**, though unlike Diome, she was born and raised in France and her links to West Africa are less pronounced. Thus, her books deal more in the French and immigrant experiences than they do in the Senegalese, but regardless of this, her three books translated into English so far – 2004's *All My Friends* (*Tous mes amis*), her 2005 memoir *Self-Portrait in Green* (*Autoportrait en vert*) and 2009's *Three Strong Women* (*Trois femmes puissantes*) have all received rave reviews and are well worth the read.

MUSIC Unlike growing swathes of Africa that seem to be more interested in the latest Rihanna single than what their home-grown artists are producing, Senegal posseses an easy self-assurance in the superiority of its own culture and music, and given the embarrassment of riches on offer to any music fan, they're entirely justified in the sentiment. Make no mistake, plenty of western sounds are still to be found, but nothing fires up the crowds here like a good *mbalax* beat, and with one of the most dynamic hip-hop scenes anywhere on the continent, the western influences that do arrive are refreshingly reworked and reinterpreted for a local context.

Thus, in the land where local beats are king, the off-kilter, frenetic, stuttering drums of *mbalax* hold court on dancefloors across the land. And though the rhythms have sacred origins in the Serer *njuup* initiation ceremonies, today they're the thrumming backbeat to any party worthy of the name, and inspiration for some decidedly secular dance moves as well. The genre first coalesced into its modern form with Le Sahel's 1975 track *Bamba*, and in the ensuing decades *mbalax* swept the nation, becoming nearly as ubiquitous as it is infectious. Thus, while Le Sahel may be recognised as the genre's progenitors, the real heroes of *mbalax* were soon to be revealed, and would eventually take Senegal's newest sound to the world, starting with the soon-to-be-legendary Youssou N'Dour.

With a voice that can stop you dead in your tracks, Senegal's most famous son **Youssou N'Dour** broke on to the international scene in the late 1980s, but he had been singing with Star Band de Dakar since the early 70s, when he was just a teenager, and with his own band, Étoile de Dakar, since 1979. From then on, he's been fêted around the world for his boundary-pushing albums that explore, redefine, and cement Senegal's musical ties to Egypt, Jamaica, Cuba, Europe and beyond. Along with Youssou and Étoile de Dakar, **Thione Seck** and his band Raam Daan and **Omar Pene** with his band Super Diamono, while both lesser-known internationally, are also revered in Senegal among the founding fathers of *mbalax*, and when you're on the hunt for tunes in Dakar, all the classics from the 70s and 80s are usually simply referred to as 'retro'. N'Dour, Seck and Pene all continue to record excellent music, and so do several successful alumni from their bands, such as ex-Super Diamono star

Ismael Lô, but for a taste of the newer generation of *mbalax* stars, you won't go wrong with Alioune Mbaye Nder, Fallou Dieng, Pape Diouf, or the late Ndongo Lo.

As with much of west and central Africa, Cuban music was hugely popular in mid-20th-century Senegal, and many of the musicians that would go on to redefine Senegalese popular music in the *mbalax* era got their start playing *son*, salsas and Cuban hits in nightclubs around Dakar. This African re-interpretation of what was Afro-Cuban music to begin with arguably reached its pinnacle with the Star Band de Dakar and Orchestra Baobab, who, in their 1970s primes, were arguably Senegal's most famous bands, with the latter serving as a launchpad for Thione Seck's decades-long career. **Mar Seck** was another Senegalese salsa talent, and while he sang with the Star Band de Dakar and Star Number One de Dakar, his name won't ring bells for too many in Senegal or elsewhere, despite his rôle in laying the foundations for *salsa mbalax*, which would go on to become a genre in its own right, popularised in Senegal by Super Cayor and around the world with the revival of Orchestra Baobab in the early 2000s.

While Senegal has always been incredibly fertile ground for the birth and reinvention of new genres, there are just as many artists here who defy easy categorisation. Foremost among them is perhaps the hometown hero guitarist from Podor, **Baaba Maal**, who has been releasing music that shares as much in common with Youssou N'Dour's *mbalax*-pop fusion as it does Ali Farka Touré's moody desert blues since the 1980s, and who has, much like Youssou, fearlessly explored the linkages between the music of West Africa and its descendants worldwide, like hip-hop, reggae, and even dance. Another Senegalese luminary that fiercely resists labels of any kind is **Cheikh Lô**, who, over the course of several albums since the 90s, has been producing a wildly diverse brand of multi-instrumentalist pop with influences that include everything from *Baye Fall* devotional prayers to Brazilian samba. Making slightly less eclectic but still quite fine guitar-driven African pop, both **Daby Balde** and **Nuru Kane** are also names worth investigating, and for fans of the desert blues à la Ali Farka Touré, **Lewlewal de Podor**'s 2011 début, *Yiilo Jaam*, is not to be missed.

Much like its neighbour Mali, Senegal is also renowned for its hereditary *griot* praise-singers and storytellers, a centuries-old tradition that typically goes hand in hand with the indigenous West African harp known as the kora, and the country has produced numerous masters of the beloved and otherworldly-sounding instrument, most famously perhaps being Ziguinchor native **Seckou Keita**, whose delightfully tranquil 2015 album *22 Strings* is as fine an introduction as any to the genre. Other names worth investigating in Senegal's kora canon include **Kaouding Cissokho, Diabel Cissokho** and Baaba Maal's lifelong friend and collaborator **Mansour Seck**, who is actually a guitar player but whose albums often feature phenomenal kora duets.

While Senegal no doubt reveres its musical traditions, its hip-hop scene is as forward-looking and fearless as you'll find anywhere on the continent, and its musicians draw heavily from indigenous instrumentation and the *griot* tradition to inform their rôle as not only players, but social commentators as well. American hip-hop started arriving on Senegalese shores in the late 80s and it took hardly any time at all for a dynamic local scene to take root, which has continued to mushroom in the years since. With rhymes in both Wolof and French, **Positive Black Soul**'s hard-hitting 1992 début cassette *Boul Falé* (reissued in part on their 1995 major label début *Salaam*) marks the start of an unprecedented creative period which would see the formation of groups like **Pee Froiss** and **Daara J**, all of which later had their music released internationally. The fiercely political nature of Senegalese hip-hop would remain undiluted into the next century, with artists like **Sister Fa** putting themselves at the forefront of controversial causes like ending FGM and taking a stand on the country's disputed 2012 political transition. Dakar rapper **RedBlack** led the charge

1

with his anthemic 2012 track *Na Dem*, which translates as 'Go Away' in English, and became a powerful rallying cry against former president Abdoulaye Wade's controversial bid for a third term in office. Senegal is also the birthplace of a number of famous rappers who launched their careers elsewhere after leaving Senegal as children, most notably Akon (USA) and MC Solaar (France).

Historically speaking, Senegal is of some note as the spiritual home of the banjo, whose origins can be traced convincingly to the *akonting*, a three-string lute played by the Diola of Casamance. Indeed, the traditional instruments of Senegal play such an important part in the nation's cultural identity that the national anthem *Pincez Tous vos Koras, Frappez les Balafons* exhorts its listeners to 'strum your koras' and 'strike the balafons ' (the balafon being a traditional xylophone played in the region – check out Malang Mané's *Balanta Balo: Talking Wood of Casamance* to hear it in action). Ceremonial music is still widely performed, and the *griot* vocalists are usually accompanied by a band playing a combination of *xalam* (a stringed instrument related to the *akonting*), Serer *sabar* drums, and the *tama* talking drum, with the drums commonly featured on *mbalax* recordings as well. With only a few recordings in this style ever seeing international release, the late Serer *griotte* **Yandé Codou Sène** is very likely the most famous practitioner of the genre, as she was once the official state *griotte* to president Léopold Sédar Senghor and went on to record with Youssou N'Dour in the mid 1990s.

Finally, if you noticed that *griotte* Madame Sène was the first female voice to gain a mention in the apparently masculine confines of Senegal's musical pantheon, rest assured that while *mbalax* may indeed be male-dominated, plenty of enormously talented songstresses have crashed the party, starting with **Kiné Lam** and her 1989 début *Cheickh Anta Mbacke*; she was the first Senegalese woman to see her music released internationally. This was followed by a bevy of tapes sold hand-to-hand in Dakar's dusty market stalls, including the highly-regarded *Galass*, and eventually another international release in the form of 1996's *Praise*. Also with a handful of tapes recorded in the 90s and well admired in Senegal for her swaggering, wailed delivery, **Daro Mbaye** hasn't enjoyed the international acclaim of Kiné Lam, but her recordings are no less compelling. Another diva years late in getting her worldwide dues is the late **Aby Ngana Diop**, a *griotte* who specialised in the traditional Wolof *taasu* style of poetry, only set to a synthesiser-mad *mbalax* fusion that doesn't so much pull the listener along as give them an unexpected shove from behind. Her 1994 début (and only album) *Liital* just got the full reissue treatment in 2014 and its off-the-wall cadences and clamorous, belted-out vocals are not for the faint of heart. If your tastes skew more towards the soothing, **Viviane N'Dour** (ex-wife of Youssou's brother) is considerably glossier, with a polished, clean sound that comfortably dips into *mbalax*, R&B and pop as and when it suits her, including two fabulously unexpected covers of Aaliyah's *Are You That Somebody*. The list of leading ladies goes on and on, and Fatou Laobé, Ndeye Mbaye and Fatou Guewel are all worth lending an ear.

All of the artists mentioned above are available on YouTube, Spotify, and other major streaming services, and there have been some excellent quality reissues, new recordings, and long-neglected discoveries that have come out in the past several years on blogs like Likembe (*www.likembe.blogspot.com*), and from labels like Teranga Beat (*www.terangabeat.com*), Sahel Sounds (*www.sahelsounds.com*) and Awesome Tapes from Africa (*www.awesometapes.com*).

DANCE Perhaps the most important form of dance in Senegal today is *sabar*. With its origins in the Serer traditions that also gave birth to *mbalax*, *sabar* refers to not only the dance, but the style of music accompanying it, the drums it's played on, and the events where the drumming and dancing take place. Played with one hand and one stick, the taut goatskins crackle in a flurry of syncopation, spurring the meticulously-coiffed female dancers on to a showstopping routine of extraordinarily wild leaps and unabashedly sensual manoeuvres. It's from here in the traditional *sabar* that *mbalax* gets its high-flying leaps. (Men will also sometimes dance *sabar*, but it's considerably less common.) These risqué moves have put the tradition at odds with some of the country's more conservative elements, and *sabar* was even banned at one point.

The *sabar* parties are massively loud spectacles that can be heard from blocks around and carry on until the wee hours, so the best way to check one out for yourself is simply to keep your ears open and follow the drums. Given the conservative distaste for its sexual overtones, you're most likely to catch a true *sabar* event in either the major coastal cities or the Serer heartlands of the Sine-Saloum Delta. If you don't manage to track down a party yourself, the octogenarian Doudou N'Diaye Rose, who died in August 2015, was the unquestioned monarch of *sabar* drumming, and he sired a prodigious brood of children, most of whom now also play in his *sabar* orchestra, the Drummers of West Africa. His 1992 album *Djabote* was recorded in the open air on Gorée Island with an ensemble of more than 50 drummers and 80 singers, and it's the booming, thrumming, unbelievably precise work of a master and his musicians. Whether or not you manage to catch a *sabar* for yourself, it's an enormously compelling document of the tradition.

A touch more rarefied than your average *sabar* and also eminently worth investigating is the *Ballet National du Sénégal*. Known as *La Linguère* (which means 'princess' in Wolof), this enormously talented troupe has been performing original works since their foundation in 1960, and like so many of Senegal's cultural troupes they had the enthusiastic support of president Léopold Sédar Senghor. In their more than five decades, they've toured everywhere from Chicago to Shanghai, but when they're not on the road you can see them at the Théâtre National Daniel Sorano in Dakar.

FILM Long regarded as among the leading lights of African cinema, Senegal's star has steadily fallen since the1980s, but its production in the decades following independence remains highly regarded and almost without rival on the African continent, in part thanks to president Léopold Sédar Senghor, under whose tenure the determined promotion and funding of culture and the arts turned Senegal into *the* artistic hub for West Africa and beyond.

Despite being shot in Paris, Beninese-Senegalese director **Paulin Soumanou Vieyra**'s 1955 *Afrique-sur-Seine* takes on the topic of Africans abroad and is commonly regarded as the first sub-Saharan African film, and Vieyra would go on to produce another 30 films, most of them documentaries, over the course of several decades. Senegal's brightest star was shortly to appear, however, and director **Ousmane Sembène**'s 1963 *Borom Sarret*, which was shot on the streets of Dakar and tells the tale of a down-on-his-luck *charette* driver, is also often considered for the title of first black African film.

Sembène himself is considered, with great justification, as the father of not only Senegalese but African cinema as a whole, and he went on to shape the direction of the field over a revolutionary cinematic and literary career spanning more than four decades. His award-winning 1966 *La Noire de...* became the first feature-length African film, as previous productions had all been shorts, and his fiercely political vision and uncompromising social analysis inform all of his productions. He went on to write and direct nearly a dozen feature films (most of which have now been reissued on DVD), including *Mandabi* (1968), *Emitaï* (1971), *Xala* (1975), *Ceddo* (1977), *Camp de Thiaroye* (1988), *Guelwaar* (1992), *Faat Kiné* (2001) and his final piece, *Moolaadé*, a polemic against female genital mutilation, which took home the Prix un certain regard at the 2004 Cannes Film Festival. He passed away in 2007 and has since been chronicled in a 2010 biography by Samba Gadjigo, *Ousmane Sembène: The Making of a Militant Artist*; also he was the subject of the 2015 Cannes- and Sundance-nominated documentary *Sembène!*, co-directed by Samba Gadjigo and Jason Silverman.

Despite producing the biggest cinematic star the continent has ever known, the Senegalese film industry has hardly been a one-man show. One of Sembène's contemporaries, **Djibril Diop Mambety**, made several award-winning avant-garde films, including the prescient tale of two would-be migrants to Paris, *Touki Bouki* (1973), the jarring *Badou Boy* (1970), 1992's *Hyènes* (Hyenas), and *La Petite Vendeuse de Soleil (The Little Girl Who Sold The Sun)*, which premiered posthumously in 1999.

In 1976, ten years after Semebene's *La Noire De…*, **Safi Faye's** *Kaddu Beykat* became the first Sub-Saharan African film to be directed by a woman. She produced several other films in the intervening decades, but is perhaps best known for her 1996 exploration of arranged marriages and their consequences, *Mossane*.

More recently, **Moussa Touré** represents a passing of the baton to the next generation of Senegalese directors, and got his start with 1991's *Toubab Bi*. Since then, he's been lauded for several features, including 1998's sarcastically named *TGV*, which takes place on a bus ride from Dakar to Conakry (the rest of this book will give you an idea of how uncomfortable a ride that would be), and his moving personal exploration of the perils of migration in 2012's *La Pirogue*, which took third prize at the *Festival panafricain du cinéma et de la télévision de Ouagadougou* (FESPACO). **Moussa Sene Absa** is another director who also got his start in the early 90s, and he remains best known for his 2002 drama *Madame Brouette*.

And while it is indeed true that the Senegalese film industry is little but a shadow of its former self, there are several young directors who, despite the industry's challenges, are producing works both significant and moving. Many of them have familial links to France. The French-born **Dyana Gaye's** 2013 *Des Étoiles (Under the Starry Sky)* sets out to explore the interconnectedness and separation inherent in the migrant experience, and was filmed in Senegal, Italy and New York. Also French-born, **Alain Gomis** had his directorial début with 2001's *L'afrance*, but it's his sparkling 2013 film *Tey (Today)*, starring spoken-word superstar Saul Williams, that has catapulted him into the rankings of Senegal's top directors working today.

ART AND HANDICRAFTS As in other cultural pursuits, Senegal's visual art scene is a leading light on the continent, and one only need look at the sheer number of galleries in Dakar and Saint-Louis for proof. In both traditional and modern arts, Senegalese painters, sculptors, carvers, potters, weavers, fashion designers, photographers and others are widely recognised in their respective disciplines, and it's a rare display of art from the continent that doesn't include a Senegalese contribution. Part of this robust artistic presence can again be traced back to president Léopold Sédar Senghor and his relentless promotion of cultural endeavours during his tenure, but of course the traditions themselves date back considerably further.

Perhaps the most widely recognised Senegalese artist working today is the former physiotherapist and sculptor **Ousmane Sow** (*www.ousmanesow.com*), who's known worldwide for his evocative, larger than life sculptures – some in bronze, others using organic materials like straw, mud and jute – detailing human forms with startling precision and emotion, and taking on subjects ranging from the battle of Little Big Horn to Senegalese wrestlers and the Zulus of South Africa. He also curates the Galerie Le Manège in Dakar (see page 115). Other Senegal-based sculptors worth checking out include Guibril Andre Diop, Abdoulaye Armin Kane (*www.facebook.*

com/abdoulaye.armin.kane), Henri Sagna (*www.facebook.com/henri.sagna*) and the late Moustapha Dimé. Also, while he hasn't been exhibited internationally, Djibril Sagna has a workshop on Gorée where he fashions delightfully original works from old metal, driftwood and found objects that are by turns abstract and oddly lifelike. As for painting, there are dozens of galleries in Dakar and Saint-Louis where you can see works from some of the region's most heralded artists, but the *first* art you'll see in Senegal will almost certainly be the innumerable murals of Mouride brotherhood founder **Sheikh Ahmadou Bamba** (1853–1927) painted on shops, cars, walls, and seemingly any other available space across the country. With his face half-obscured in a white shawl, this beloved and endlessly reproduced visage is based on the only extant photo of Ahmadou Bamba and has become an icon for Mourides everywhere. Bamba's first disciple and founder of the *Baye Fall* movement, Sheikh Ibrahima Fall (1855–1930), also known as Lamp Fall, as he is considered the 'light' of Mouridism, also has only one known photograph; this too is a recurring image throughout the country, where he is seen giving a serene half-smile in his trademark dark robes. The two figures are often pictured together, sometimes alongside the 87m central minaret at Touba's grand mosque – also referred to as Lamp Fall – which is another key component of Mouride iconography seen nationwide.

As mentioned, works of a more secular variety can be seen in galleries across Dakar and Saint-Louis, and painters (many of whom also work in sculpture, design and more) worth checking out include Amadou Kane Sy (*www.kan-si.com*), Zulu Mbaye (*http://zulumbaye.skynetblogs.be*), Kiné Aw (*www.kineaw.com*), Fodé Camara, and the Los Angeles-based Aly Kourouma (*www.facebook.com/aly.t.kourouma*). Photographers are also well represented in Senegal, and the doyen here is **Oumar Ly** (*www.oumarly.com*), who has been photographing the people of Podor at his Thiofy Studio since 1963. His body of work chronicles the changing faces and styles throughout the decades, and has been shown in Dakar, France and the UK. More recently, the Dakar-based **Omar Victor Diop** (*www.omarviktor.com*) has been widely fêted across the continent and beyond for his boldly imaginative and fashion-forward photography.

Another iconic Senegalese art form, *sous-verre* painting – literally 'under glass' in French, but typically called 'reverse-glass' in English – involves painting on the back of a sheet of glass, and it reached Senegal from the Maghreb sometime in the late 19th century. It was once practised in Europe as well, but by this time the invention of chromolithography – colour printing, essentially – had all but spelled its demise there. It rose to popularity in Senegal due to a combination of political and economic factors. Imported by merchants from the Levant, inexpensive prints of Muslim saints had become wildly popular in Senegal – popular enough that the colonial government, finding them potentially subversive, banned their distribution in 1911. Thus, a market was born for replicas of the now-unavailable prints, and *sous-verre* painting was budget-friendly and fit the bill nicely. As such, the early works of Senegalese *sous-verre* were largely portraits of venerated saints (Ahmadou Bamba and Ibrahima Fall most certainly among them), calligraphy, and scenes from the Koran; it was some years later before the medium would pass into the secular domain. Today, however, *sous-verre* paintings are available in dozens of galleries and just about every tourist market in the country, picturing, along with the original sacred themes, anything and everything from Dakar's colourful *car rapides* to schoolchildren, nature, doctor's visits, independence heroes, transport, animals, farming myths, proverbs and all manner of quotidian scenes, all done in an irresistibly bold and colourful style, with rich, bright hues and vivid detail shining through the glass. A few revered artists include Mor Gueye, Alexis Ngom and the late masters Mbida and Gora Mbengue. *Senegal Behind Glass* by Anne-Marie Bouttiaux-Ndiaye is the definitive work on the topic, and richly illustrated with 150 different *sous-verre* pieces.

Finally, Senegal is home to a number of talented artisans working in **textile design**, the most dramatic example of which is the *Manufactures Sénégalaises des Arts Décoratifs* in Thiès. A centre totally unique in West Africa and probably beyond, since 1966 (set up by Senghor – who else?) this collective of artisans has been producing stunningly elaborate woven textiles based on Senegalese motifs and paintings, and they're sold for princely sums the world over – their largest production took two artisans three years to complete and today hangs at the UN in New York. Batik is another popular medium here and, while much of what you'll see hawked at the tourist markets is rather derivative, some excellent pieces are to be found if you look hard enough. Mamadou Cherif Diallo at Afrika Batik in Ziguinchor is a celebrated designer, and he's more than happy to show you the batik-making ropes as well.

And as for the wearable kind of textiles, the Senegalese are snappy dressers, and perhaps none more so than the Podorois doyenne of design, **Oumou Sy** (*www.oumousy. org*), whose collections have been paraded on Parisian catwalks since 1982. She's also the founder of the annual Dakar Fashion Week (*www.dakarfashionweek.com*), where you can see the younger generation of fashion designers like **Cole Ardo Sow** (*www.facebook. com/coleardo.sow*), **Selly Rabe Kane** (*www.sellyrabykane.com*), **Rama Diaw** (*www. ramadiawfashion.com*) and dozens of others bring out their latest in *haute couture*.

SPORT

With roots in Serer, Diola, and Lebou religious ceremonies, **traditional wrestling**, or *la lutte* as it's known, is Senegal's national sport and widely beloved, particularly among the youth. With the wild theatrics and outlandish characters of pro wrestling, but minus the made-for-TV fakery of its North American counterpart, *la lutte's* combat style remains fiercely traditional and a typical match doesn't last more than a few minutes. To start with, the two competitors, typically dressed in nothing but loincloths and a normal person's weight in *gris-gris*, are daubed with protective powders, lotions and other trade secrets, all designed to confer strength and protection in the ring. More modern fights allow the competitors to strike one another with their hands, but in its most traditional form you've got to pin or throw your opponent by grappling and throwing alone; in either form, if *any* part of your body except your hands or feet touches the ground, you're out.

The biggest stars are known around the country and found stamped on to t-shirts, painted on to shop walls and flexing their super-sized muscles for all manner of product endorsements. The biggest matches unsurprisingly take place in Dakar, usually between November and July at Stade Demba Diop, and posters are glued up all over town promoting the next clash. You'll get super bonus points chatting with kids if you know some of the stars – Ballou Gaye II, Tapha Tine, Modou Lô and Eumeu Sène are all names to look out for. For a truer-to-its-roots display of *la lutte* minus the celebrity sponsorships, there's no better place than the *xulam* festival in Oussouye, held annually in September.

As with anywhere in Africa, a wide swathe of the Senegalese population is also certifiably **football**-mad, and all but the smallest of villages (and even some of those) will have a well-worn football pitch getting daily use by a troupe of youngsters with a raggedy, patched-up ball. In coastal areas, matches take place directly on the sand; from these humble beginnings hundreds of Senegalese have gone on to play professionally abroad, with over 30 having played in the Premier League alone, and dozens more in France, the European leagues and beyond. In Senegal itself, the Senegalese Premiere League consists of 14 teams from around the country.

2

Practical Information

WHEN TO VISIT

While it's perfectly possible to visit Senegal at any time of year, tourism here is highly seasonal and you'll get a very different experience depending on when you show up. November to March is the core tourist season, peaking over the holidays, when you should absolutely make reservations in advance and expect to pay a premium on all accommodation (though if you're interested in spending the holidays in Senegal, many of the larger hotels offer packages). The weather is relatively cool and dry, and you'll be glad to have your sweater – the average low temperature in Dakar is under 20°C for most of the season, with highs closer to 27°C. It's also *the* time for birders, as all the European migrants are in town.

Expect hotter temperatures from April to June, but the rain is still some months away and a number of Senegal's coolest cultural festivals take place in these months, like the Saint-Louis Jazz Fest, Dak'art Biennial, and the annual Bassari initiations. Note that Ramadan will take place over May/June for the lifetime of this edition, so some of the festival schedules may shift to avoid the effects of the holy month.

In June the rains start to hit, and they stick around until September or October, depending on where you are. (They start earlier and finish later in the south.) This is when many places (including hotels, national parks and restaurants) start to close up shop for the season and, while this means your plans might be interrupted by closures, you'll be one of the few tourists in town – hello, empty beaches and negotiable prices. Another payback for the sometimes oppressive humidity is the riot of greenery that erupts all over the country, turning parched earth lush, filling rivers and sending waterfalls crashing over their precipices nearly overnight. Transport in the wet season isn't the problem that it used to be as nearly all of Senegal's trunk roads are now surfaced, but it's still possible to run into issues off the beaten track.

October and November see the rain tapering off and the tourists slowly returning, with most seasonally closed businesses reopening around the start of November. The heat of the rainy season is still around, but the humidity is less and the vegetated landscape is still a pleasure.

HIGHLIGHTS

URBAN EXPERIENCES

Saint-Louis The best place in Senegal for an evening stroll, when the ghosts of history come out to play in this most evocative of Senegalese towns. See pages 194–211.

Dakar The unquestioned beating heart of Senegal, there's almost nothing you can't do in Dakar. Dance all night, surf all day, eat like a foodie and soak up some culture at one of the city's many festivals. See pages 77–125.

Gorée Thirty minutes and a world away from Dakar, leave the traffic on the mainland and soak up the rhythms of life on this enchanting and tragic island. See pages 125–31.

Fadiouth Surely one of the only towns in the world built on a foundation of nothing but discarded seashells, marvelling at the island's unlikely existence and feeling the shells crunch underfoot on a walk through one of Fadiouth's mazelike alleyways is an experience you won't soon repeat. See pages 164–6.

Podor Hugging tight to both the past and the northernmost curves of the Senegal River, Podor feels every bit the frontier outpost, an otherworldly holdout staunchly resisting the advance of the Sahara beyond, and seemingly also the passage of time. See pages 223–6.

Ziguinchor This steamy river town is the stuff of film sets, and there's no more iconic Casamance experience than pushing out on to the water in a pirogue and watching the crumbling colonial city disappear out of view as you head into the mangroves beyond. See pages 286–94.

NATURAL WONDERS

Désert de Lompoul Escape to the wildlands of the Sahara in this unexpected 20km² patch of towering sand dunes, and indulge your nomad fantasies with an overnight here in a traditional Mauritanian tent. See pages 242–3.

Cascade de Dindefelo Hike through the nearby forests until you're stopped by a sheer rock face – it's here that you'll find the 115m Dindefelo waterfall, and a tranquil pool at its base offering cool waters and the best swimming for miles around. See page 279.

Sine-Saloum Delta Cross the vast, watery knot of mangrove swamp, shell islands and timeless fishing villages in a motorised pirogue, where you can grill your freshly caught fish right on board and stop off on a deserted island for a post-dinner dip. See pages 177–8.

Cap Skirring's beaches The kilometres of powdery white sand here are the stuff of postcards and daydreams, and the herds of long-horned cattle that occasionally meander across the *plage* are a picture-perfect reminder that you're still in West Africa. See pages 294–301.

Parc National des Oiseaux du Djoudj Your jaw might look much like the birds' after spotting the mind-boggling 15,000 great white pelicans crammed on to a tiny island here, and there's still another 16,000ha of wetlands here to explore. See pages 217–19.

Lac Rose Though its colour ebbs and flows with the season, when it's putting on its rose-tinted show, the lake's salt-encrusted Pepto-Bismol waters and their dunescape surrounds are an unlikely scene pulled straight out of an acid trip. See pages 132–4.

SUGGESTED ITINERARIES

THE GRAND TOUR
One month For completists, this trip around Senegal's perimeter will introduce you to all of Senegal's many faces, from the arid sands and lonely towns of the

riverine north to the forests of Niokolo-Koba, swamps of Casamance and the beaches of the Petite Côte.

Start with a few nights in Dakar, where you can get your bearings and sink your teeth into the city that makes Senegal tick. Try your hand at some surfing in Yoff (page 111), buy dinner and a new dress in one of the city's many markets (pages 113–15), and spend a still night on Gorée Island (pages 125–31), where the spectres of the past still cast a long shadow.

From here, make your way towards Saint-Louis on the inland route via Touba, and spend the afternoon on a tour of the Mourides' grand mosque (page 250). Continuing on to Saint-Louis, feel the oceanic vibe of Senegal's prettiest city and take some side trips to the Langue de Barbarie (pages 211–13) and the Parc National des Oiseaux du Djoudj bird sanctuary (pages 217–19) before continuing up the river road to Podor (pages 223–6), where, in the heat of the afternoon on the historic quayside, any sense of time disappears entirely. Further down the river road you can make pit stops and explore the historical trading centres of Matam (pages 230–1) and Bakel (pages 232–4), where you'll find one of Senegal's oldest standing forts.

Rounding the bend at Kidira (pages 264–5), Tambacounda (pages 253–63) is the next stop, as it's the jumping-off point for Kédougou (pages 267–71) and the fantastic hiking in the Bassari and Bédik lands beyond (pages 271–4). It would be easy to spend several days here, so when you're ready to move on, stop at Niokolo-Koba National Park (pages 258–63) for a bit of safari on your way back to Tamba.

Heading south into Casamance, the swaying palms of Ziguinchor (pages 286–94) and five-star resorts of Cap Skirring (pages 294–301) await. If you've made it this far, splurge – you've more than earned it. From Zig or Cap, it's possible to spend weeks exploring the dozens of villages scattered throughout the Casamance River delta, and be sure to swing through the funky beachside villages of Kafountine (pages 319–24) and Abéné (pages 324–8) on your way up to the Gambian border.

Heading through The Gambia and back north into Senegal, your first stop should be another round of mangrove magic in Toubacouta (pages 188–91), where an evening swim surrounded by bioluminescent plankton is sure to be a highlight of your trip. Finally, before you roll back into the big city and finish your grand tour at the airport in Dakar, make one last stop at Senegal's original beach resort, the inimitable Saly (pages 150–8), for a night or two of frosty umbrella drinks, rowdy dance clubs and oceanfront pampering.

COASTAL EXPLORER
Two weeks Once a periphery of great inland empires, with the rise of the Atlantic trade Senegal's coastline suddenly became all-important, and in this respect little has changed from then until now. Senegal remains a coastal country, and many visitors never stray more than a few dozen kilometres from the water in their whole stay here. There's plenty to see inland as well, but a coastal foray remains one of the most rewarding ways to see Senegal.

Starting in Dakar (pages 77–126), soak up some culture at one of the city's many museums and galleries (pages 115–18) before heading out to polish up your tan on the beaches of Toubab Dialaw (pages 140–2). Here you can join in a game of seaside footy with the local kids and try your hand at some djembe drumming at the eclectic Sobo Badè (page 141) before leapfrogging your way down the coast to sleepy Popenguine (pages 142–6) and its nature reserve for some rambling, La Somone for some beginner's surfing at Secret Bay (page 150) and an eco-trail through the lagoon, and finally hedonistic Saly, where you can join the nightly bacchanal and feast, drink and dance until you can't anymore.

From here head down to the Sine-Saloum Delta (pages 169–93) and recuperate at one of the fabulous selection of lodges around Fimela (pages 178–80) or on the car-free island of Mar Lodj (pages 182–3). Take a fabulously scenic boat trip though the winding creeks of the delta to Palmarin (pages 183–6), Foundiougne (pages 187–8) or Toubacouta (pages 188–9), and start heading back up to Dakar. Spend your last night in peace on quiet Gorée (pages 125–31), and have a quick swim here before getting the boat and making your way to the airport.

THE ESSENTIALS
One week If you've only got time to scratch the surface in Senegal, start off with hitting the sights in Dakar (pages 77–126) – a day is plenty of time to check out Marché Kermel (page 113), see what you think of the controversial Monument de la Renaissance Africaine (page 123), and have a fabulous seafood dinner at Africa's westernmost edge, the Pointe des Almadies (page 125). Spend your next day at the museums of Gorée Island (pages 125–31), and then head straight up to Saint-Louis (pages 194–211), where the buildings practically shout with history and there's fabulous swimming just outside of town on the Hydrobase (page 204). Avid birders should aim for the sand dunes at Langue de Barbarie National Park (pages 211–13) just south of the city, or the Parc National des Oiseaux du Djoudj (pages 217–19) if your schedule stretches just a tiny bit further.

Heading back down the coast, depending on your timeframe you could spend a last night under the stars in the sand dunes of Lompoul (pages 242–3), or continue south through Thiès (pages 235–40) to see the beachside Bohemia at Toubab Dialaw (pages 140–2). From here, it's only 50km to get back to Dakar and catch your flight.

TOURIST INFORMATION
Tourism in Senegal is administered under the auspices of the **Ministère du Tourisme et des Transports Aériens** (*VDN, Liberté VI Extension, lots n°7/8;* ✆ *33 869 2690*; e *ministeretourisme@gouv.sn*; *www.tourisme-senegal.sn*) in Dakar; though given that national park entry and other practicalities are all handled at the individual sites, for the casual visitor there's usually not a compelling need to contact them, though there's some moderately useful information on their website.

TOUR OPERATORS
Many of the operators offering tours to Senegal are France-based, but the following US and UK firms would be a better starting point for Anglophones. Most run scheduled trips as well as tailor-made tours.

IN THE UK
Intrepid Travel ✆ (+44) 808 274 5111; e enquiries.uk@intrepidtravel.com; www. intrepidtravel.com. Specialises in locally led adventure tours.
Overlanding West Africa ✆ (+44) 172 886 2247; e info@overlandingwestafrica.com; www. overlandingwestafrica.com. Independent operator with overland trips from Dakar to destinations across north & west Africa.

AU SÉNÉGAL
An excellent source of further information on all things Senegal is www.au-senegal. com, which covers real estate, restaurants, religion and everything in between, all in fantastic detail. Unfortunately it's all in French, but with some patience and Google Translate, there's great information to be had. They also keep an up-to-date cultural calendar under the name *Le 221*.

Responsible Travel ✆(+44) 127 382 3700; e rosy@responsibletravel.com; www. responsibletravel.com. Offers river cruises, wildlife & cultural holidays with a focus on small groups.

The Senegal Experience (See ad, page x) ✆(+44) 845 338 8700; e holidays@senegal.co.uk; www.senegal.co.uk. Senegalese branch of The Gambia Experience, which has been active in the region for nearly 3 decades & offers a wide variety of customisable holidays.

IN THE USA

Absolute Travel ✆(+1) 212 627 1950; e info@ absolutetravel.com; www.absolutetravel.com. Offers a number of luxury itineraries in Senegal & the region.

Kensington Tours ✆+1 888 903 2001; e info@ kensingtontours.com; www.kensingtontours.com. Specialises in personalised luxury excursions.

IN SENEGAL

All of the following agencies are based in Dakar unless otherwise noted, & can arrange both daytrips in Dakar & excursions further afield. All have English-speaking guides on their staff.

Africa Travel Group ✆33 869 7900; e info@ africatravel-group.com; www.africatravel-group.

com. A good option for birding tours as well as beach & cultural itineraries, along with car hire & air tickets.

Andaando m 77 793 94 32; e dieng.massaer@ yahoo.fr; www.andaando.com. A locally run agency with trips throughout the country.

Boubatour (Casamance Découverte) ✆33 860 4244; m 76 668 6363; e bouba@boubatour. com; www.boubatour.com. This locally run outfit specialises in community tourism & would be a good choice for Hispanophones as well.

Nouvelle Frontière ✆33 859 4446/7; e contact@nfsenegal.com; www.nfsenegal.com. Active in Senegal for more than 25 years, can set up car hire, guided excursions, charter flight tickets & more.

Origin Africa (See ad, page 76) ✆33 860 1578; e info@origin-africa.sn; www.origin-africa.sn. With locations in Dakar & Saly, they arrange car hire & circuits all over Senegal, including to their 2 associated camps at Lac Rose & the Lompoul Desert.

Sahel Découverte ✆33 961 56 89; e jeanjacques@saheldecouverte.com; www. saheldecouverte.com. From their office in Saint-Louis they can arrange excursions to any part of Senegal, as well as passage on their boat, the *Bou el Mogdad*.

RED TAPE

From July 2013 to April 2015, **biometric visas** were required of all nationalities except ECOWAS (CEDEAO) citizens and applications had to be made online prior to arrival in Senegal. **As of 1 May 2015, this requirement has been scrapped entirely.** Today, visas are issued on arrival at Dakar airport and all official land borders free of charge for stays of up to three months to holders of more than 100 different passports, including all EU/EEA states (except Cyprus), USA, Canada, Australia, New Zealand and South Africa. This gloriously simple policy is intended to encourage tourism after the combination of visa confusion and the Ebola crisis saw a sharp decline in tourist numbers for 2014. It could conceivably change again, so we've included some information about the former application procedure (see box, page 38) in case it's reintroduced in the future (though signs indicate it won't be). Under the new procedure, visitors must still have six months' remaining validity on their passports, and may need to provide **proof of yellow fever vaccination** if arriving from a country where it's endemic.

Longer-stay visas of six months or one year are also issued for €120 and €150 respectively, but require proof of approved employment, training or study in Senegal. Visa extensions are also possible once in Senegal, but you will have to satisfy some of the same conditions. Inquiries should be directed to the Territorial Surveillance Directorate (Direction de la Surveillance du Territoire, DST) in Dakar, located at 'Cité police' on Avenue Malick Sy and Corniche Ouest.

THE FORMER E-VISA PROCEDURE (2013–15)

While the e-visa has not been required since 1 May 2015, the following information is included for reference in case of another change in visa policy and a return to the e-visa requirement.

Visas are issued for stays up to three months, either single or multiple entry, and cost €50 regardless of duration/entries.

To start the process, go to www.visasenegal.sn, where you will fill out the application, upload a number of required supporting documents (passport scan, round-trip air ticket, hotel reservation) and pay with Visa, MasterCard or Maestro. Upon completing the process online, you will be given a **'Registration Receipt'** (*Reçu d'Inscription*). This document is not valid for travel (and says as much) and is only the first of two documents you'll need in order to collect your visa.

The second is your **'Approved Pre-enrolment'** (*Pré-enrôlement approuvé*), which will typically be emailed to you within two to three business days of completing the online application. Once you have the Approved Pre-enrolment form, you can take it, along with your passport, to any of the Senegalese embassies listed on page 39, where they will fingerprint you, take your photo and place the actual visa in your passport.

Alternatively, the Approved Pre-enrolment form can also be used in lieu of a visa to board your flight, and they will take your biometric data and issue the visa upon your landing in Dakar, Cap Skirring or Saint-Louis. The same was true of travellers arriving by land at Senegal's major border crossings.

The **supporting documents** required for the online application seem to be reasonably flexible. Proof of hotel booking is only required for several days and not for the length of your stay, and overland travellers are free to enter and exit by land, with a departing air ticket from a neighbouring country usually regarded as sufficient. Travellers not planning to fly at all should consider booking and submitting a fully refundable ticket to satisfy this condition.

Alternatively, it's typically easier to pop over to a neighbouring country and renew your stay for another three months.

If you plan on driving, be sure to organise an **international driver's licence** from the country where your original licence is issued. These are typically issued by motoring organisations like the AA (*www.theaa.com*) in the UK or AAA (*www. aaa.com*) in the USA.

EMBASSIES

SENEGALESE EMBASSIES AND CONSULATES ABROAD Senegal maintains an embassy, high commission or consulate in several countries. These include the UK (*www.senegal.embassyhomepage.com*), the US (*www.ambasenegal-us.org*), The Gambia (*59 Kairaba Ave, Fajara;* ☏ *(+220) 4 373 752*) and France (*www.consulsen-paris.fr*), as well as Belgium, Brazil, Cameroon, Canada, Cape Verde, China, Ethiopia, Germany, Ghana, Guinea, Guinea-Bissau, India, Italy, Mali, Mauritania, the Russian Federation, South Africa and Spain.

FOREIGN REPRESENTATION IN SENEGAL Foreign embassies and consulates in Dakar are given below.

Ⓔ Belgium [91 E7] Av des Jambaars, Dakar; ☎ 33 889 4390; e dakar@diplobel.fed.be; www.diplomatie.belgium.be/senegal

Ⓔ Brazil Immeuble Fahd, Blvd Djily Mbaye (@ Rue Macodou Ndiaye); ☎ 33 823 1492; m 77 590 2124

Ⓔ Canada [90 D6] Rue Galliéni (@ Rue Amadou Cissé Dia), Dakar; ☎ 33 889 4700; e dakar@international.gc.ca; www.canadainternational.gc.ca/senegal

Ⓔ Cape Verde [91 G2] Immeuble Fahd, Blvd Djily Mbaye (@ Rue Macodou Ndiaye); ☎ 33 821 1873/3936; e ambcvsen@sentoo.sn

Ⓔ China [96 B5] Rue 18 Ext, Fann Residence, Dakar; ☎ 33 869 7701; e chinaemb_sn@mfa.gov.cn; www.sn.china-embassy.org

Ⓔ France [91 H3] 1 Rue El Hadji Amadou Assane Ndoye, Dakar; ☎ 33 839 5262; e cad.dakar-fslt@diplomatie.gouv.fr; www.ambafrance-sn.org. (Also consulates in most other major cities.)

Ⓔ The Gambia [91 E3] 11 Rue de Thiong, Plateau, Dakar; ☎ 33 821 7230/4476; e gambia.high.commission@gmail.com

Ⓔ Germany [90 D6] 20 Av Pasteur, Dakar; ☎ 33 889 4884; www.dakar.diplo.de

Ⓔ Guinea [97 E3] Rue de Diourbel, Point E, Dakar; ☎ 33 824 8606

Ⓔ Guinea-Bissau [97 F3] Rue 6, Point E, Dakar; ☎ 33 850 2574

Ⓔ India 5 Av Carde, Dakar; ☎ 33 849 5875; e cons.dakar@mea.gov.in; www.embassyofindiadakar.org

Ⓔ Italy [90 B5] Rue Alpha Hachamiyou Tall, Dakar; ☎ 33 889 2636; e ambasciata.dakar@esteri.it; www.ambdakar.esteri.it

Ⓔ Mali [96 B7] 23 Corniche Ouest, Fann Residence, Dakar; ☎ 33 824 6250/2; e ambamali@sentoo.sn

Ⓔ Mauritania [85 F5] Place Douala Colobane, Dakar; ☎ 33 889 5080

Ⓔ Netherlands [90 D5] 37 Rue Jacques Bugnicourt, Dakar; ☎ 33 849 0360; e dak-ca@minbuza.nl; senegal.nlembassy.org

Ⓔ Russian Federation [90 B4] 63 Blvd de la République, Dakar; ☎ 33 821 5960; e consulat.russie@gmail.com; www.senegal.mid.ru

Ⓔ South Africa [96 C2] Lotissement École de Police, Mermoz Sud, Dakar; ☎ 33 865 1959/864 2359; e ambafsud@orange.sn

Ⓔ Spain [90 D6] 30 Av Nelson Mandela, Dakar; ☎ 33 849 2999; e cog.dakar@maec.es; www.exteriores.gob.es/embajadas/dakar

Ⓔ Switzerland [90 B5] Rue René N'Diaye (@ Rue Seydou Nourou Tall); ☎ 33 823 05 90; e dak.vertretung@eda.admin.ch; www.eda.admin.ch/Dakar

Ⓔ UK [91 E7] 20 Rue du Dr Guillet, Dakar; ☎ 33 823 7392; e dakar.consularenquiries@fco.gov.uk; www.gov.uk/government/world/senegal

Ⓔ USA [94 A3] Rte des Almadies, Dakar; ☎ 33 879 4000; e dakaracs@state.gov; www.dakar.usembassy.gov

GETTING THERE AND AWAY

BY AIR Stepping into the breach left by the collapse of Air Senegal International in 2009, **Senegal Airlines** (*www.senegalairlines.aero*) has developed an extensive West African network since it started flying in 2011, but as of spring 2015, the company was reported to be bankrupt and in the midst of negotiations over possible nationalisation and restructuring of the airline once again. As this book went to print, routes were either irregularly served or cut entirely, but the government came out strongly in support of saving the airline, so if they're flying by the time you read this, they will probably serve some combination of the following from their hub in Dakar: Banjul (The Gambia), Cotonou (Benin), Ouagadougou (Burkina Faso), Douala (Cameroon), Praia (Cape Verde), Abidjan (Côte d'Ivoire), Libreville (Gabon), Conakry (Guinea), Bissau (Guinea-Bissau), Bamako (Mali), Niamey (Niger) and Nouakchott (Mauritania).

Regional carriers including **Gambia Bird** (*www.gambiabird.com*), **Arik Air** (*www.arikair.com*) and **ASKY** (*www.flyasky.com*) cover routes to Dakar from Banjul (The Gambia), Freetown (Sierra Leone), Monrovia (Liberia), Lagos (Nigeria), Accra (Ghana) and Lomé (Togo). To Praia (Cape Verde), **TACV** (*www.flytacv.com*) is your best bet.

Further afield on the continent, **Royal Air Maroc** (*www.royalairmaroc.com*) connects Dakar to Casablanca, **Air Algerie** (*www.airalgerie.dz*) to Algiers, **Tunisair** (*www.tunisair.com*) to Tunis, **Ethiopian Airlines** (*www.flyethiopian.com*) to Addis Ababa, **South African Airways** (*www.flysaa.com*) to Johannesburg and **Kenya Airways** (*www.kenya-airways.com*) to Nairobi.

From Europe, Senegal is perhaps West Africa's most easily accessible destination, and there's even a low-cost service from Barcelona with **Vueling** (*www.vueling.com*). **Iberia** (*www.iberia.com*) and **Binter Canarias** (*www.bintercanarias.com*) connect Dakar with Madrid and the Canary Islands, **Air France** (*www.airfrance.com*) and **Corsair** (*www.corsair.fr*) run flights to both of Paris's airports, **TAP Portugal** (*www.flytap.com*) will take you to Lisbon, **Meridiana** (*www.meridiana.it*) to Milan, **Turkish Airlines** (*www.turkishairlines.com*) to Istanbul, and **Brussels Airlines** (*www.brusselsairlines.com*) delivers directly to – you guessed it – Brussels.

Even given the variety of options from Europe, there's a conspicuous lack of connections to Dakar from the British Isles, and travellers originating here would be well advised to have a look at flights to Banjul in The Gambia as well, which, though not nearly as well-connected as Dakar on the whole, enjoys considerably stronger transportation links to the former British Metropole given its status as an ex-colony. **Gambia Bird** and **Thomas Cook** (*www.thomascookairlines.com*) both connect to London, with the latter also running weekly non-stop flights to Birmingham and Manchester in season.

Your best bet from North America is with either **Delta** (*www.delta.com*) or **South African Airways** (*www.flysaa.com*), both of which run non-stop flights to Washington, DC. Delta also flies directly from New York City.

Travellers coming from Australasia will likely want to aim for Dubai or Johannesburg, from where there are direct connections to Dakar with **Emirates** (*www.emirates.com*) and **South African Airways**, respectively.

Léopold Sédar Senghor International Airport in Yoff is Senegal's only international airport and the only airport serving Dakar at the time of writing, but that's likely to change during the lifespan of this edition with the opening of the long-delayed (since 2011!) **Blaise Diagne International Airport** (*www.aibd.sn*), 50km from Dakar near the village of Ndiass. The gloriously swift (and admirably on-time) **Dakar toll road** project was only complete as far as the village of Diamniadio in late 2014, but is ultimately slated to reach its terminus at the new airport within the lifespan of this edition.

OVERLAND Five countries border Senegal: Mauritania to the north, Mali to the east, Guinea to the southwest, Guinea-Bissau to the southeast, and The Gambia smack dab in the centre. (Senegal is also the closest point on the African mainland to the islands of Cape Verde, just under 600km to the west.)

Changing money is a non-issue between Senegal, Guinea-Bissau and Mali, as they're all part of the CFA Franc zone, but if you're travelling to and from Senegal's other neighbours, you'll need to get your hands on some Gambian Dalasi, Mauritanian Ouguiya, Guinean Francs, or Cape Verdean escudo. There are typically few, if any, 'official' exchange facilities to be found at the borders, so educate yourself about the going rates ahead of time (www.xe.com is a good place to do this), and be on the lookout for con artists. This is especially true at Karang and Rosso, both of which have well-earned reputations in the hassle department. Shops near the border will often be willing to change money, and are a safer alternative to the throngs of over-eager and quick-handed moneychangers that you'll find on the street.

While there are a handful of *cars mourides* (often also signed as Al-Azhar, these buses are owned and operated by the Mouride brotherhood) and other buses to neighbouring countries originating in Dakar and elsewhere (usually Tambacounda, depending on where you're going), getting to any of Senegal's neighbours usually involves making the journey in stages. In Dakar, the infamous Gare Routière Pompiers was shut down and slated for commercial redevelopment in late 2014. Thus, nearly all intercity *sept-place* and bus traffic now originates at the shiny new **Gare Routière des Baux Maraîchers** (✆ *30 228 4644;* m *70 842 9449;* e *sentransco@ gmail.com; www.sentransco.com*) in Pikine, and this will probably be your first port of call for travel in any direction.

Crossings to Mauritania For Mauritania (after getting your visa in Dakar), you'll first have to aim for the thoroughly unbecoming town of Rosso-Senegal (see page 220), to which there are regular *sept-places* from Dakar, charging 7,500F and taking about seven hours. The border here closes at 19.00 (and from 13.00 to 15.00 for a leisurely lunch), so get a reasonably early start. Better yet, sleep in Saint-Louis, from where Rosso is only 100km away on a good surfaced road. The Mauritanian government-owned ferry chugs back and forth throughout the day, and a host of pirogues make the crossing as well if you don't feel like waiting. Crossing with a vehicle costs 5,000 Ouguiya and pedestrians are free, but travellers with their own vehicles should absolutely head for the much-preferable barrage crossing at Diama, only 30km from Saint-Louis on a new surfaced road, and mercifully free of the tout/fixer/new friend swarm that tends to plague Rosso.

Further east, there are a handful of other river crossings to Mauritania, all of which see precious little in the way of tourist or other traffic. There are no ferries as such out here, only pirogues of varying size punting goods back and forth across the river, so these should be considered pedestrian-only routes. The simplest crossing is probably at Bakel, where there's an immigration post on the river beach, a good deal (relatively speaking) of cross-border trade, and a connection to surfaced roads in Gouraye on the other side. Podor also connects to a good road across the river at Lexeiba II in Mauritania, while the Matam-Toufunde Civé crossing is well and truly in the middle of nowhere (which is saying something in Mauritania). Be prepared for long waits for onward transport at any of these.

Other crossings that could theoretically be possible include at Diemet Tienel (Senegal)/Boghé (Mauritania) and Silla (Senegal)/Kaédi (Mauritania); both are remote villages on the Senegalese side facing larger towns across the river in Mauritania, so expect Mauritanian, but not Senegalese border controls and inquire as to where you ought to do Senegalese formalities if you intend to try either of these routes. All that being said, much of eastern Mauritania has been off limits to tourists for the past several years due to banditry and terrorism-related threats, so be sure to get up-to-date information on the security situation before crossing over.

Crossings to Mali There are two crossings to Mali: both are straightforward, on surfaced roads, and with new bridges across the Falémé River. At the time of writing, Malian visas were even available at the border, for most passports. Kidira is the primary crossing, and easily approached from Tambacounda or Bakel; there are even *sept-places* that will deposit you here after 11 jarring hours from Dakar, while it's a considerably more manageable three hours from Tambacounda, or just over one hour from Bakel. Transport through to Bamako or Kayes can be arranged in Tambacounda, or picked up in Diboli (Mali) once you cross the river. Alternatively, the new road via Kedougou and Kéniéba (Mali) is hugely preferable in terms of scenery, and even knocks 200km off the journey, though if you're on public transport it may well turn out to involve more vehicle changes despite the shorter distance. Note that this road was only completed in 2012 and is still missing or incorrectly marked on most maps! The official border crossing is along the new surfaced road at Moussala (❂ 12.932, -11.381), not at Sainsoutou or Satadougou, despite these villages often being marked as such.

Crossings to Guinea There are three crossings to Guinea. The most direct route heads south from Tambacounda, tracing the western fringe of Niokolo-Koba National Park via Medina Gounasse and Kalifourou, until it reaches Koundara and eventually Labé on the Guinean side. It's mostly tarred, with the notable (read: painful) exception of about 150km in Guinea, which is still being worked on. If you're coming from the north, Tambacounda is your best bet for transport, while from Casamance you could aim for the village of Diaoubé, 90km east of Kolda on the RN6, from where there's transport associated with the enormous weekly *loumo* (market) on Wednesdays. Guinea-bound transport will also stop (and sometimes originate) in Manda, 55km south of Tambacounda at The Gambia's eastern extremity and home to the RN5/RN6 junction and a customs post.

Both other routes into Guinea are via Kédougou, and there is regular transport from here to Mali-ville (via Ségou) and Labé, though it would be wise to ask about onward transport when you first get into town, as there's typically not a vehicle every day. Most transport crosses into Guinea via Ségou, but if you find yourself in Fongolimbi it's possible to cross the border here as well, though your onward transport options will be considerably more limited. Fongolimbi holds its *loumo* on Thursdays; be there for it and you'll probably find a lift with traders returning to Guinea. Note that either of these two routes into Guinea makes for decidedly rougher sledding than the Koundara route; pack some snacks, your sense of humour and all your reserves of patience. Each bump, creak and lurch over these remote earth roads might leave you questioning your decision-making skills (and by extension, your sanity) if not for the considerable payback of the Fouta Djallon's unspoilt magnificence.

Crossings to Guinea-Bissau To Guinea-Bissau, nearly all traffic goes via the Mpack/São Domingos crossing, 18km south of Ziguinchor. There's also an informal crossing south of Kabrousse at Boudédiét (see box, pages 302–3). Heading east, there are a number of routes often used by traders but rarely by tourists, including a crossing south of Sédhiou near Tanaf (Senegal) / Farim (Guinea-Bissau) and a few south of Kolda at Sare Ndiaye (to Farim), Salikénié (to Bafatá) and Coumbacara (to Bafatá), but we don't have any current reports as to their condition. From Diaoube, you can connect to Gabú via the border at Pirada.

Crossings to The Gambia Finally, there's The Gambia, Senegal's conjoined twin, with whom it shares a circuitous 740km of frontier and a fair few border crossings. (Though thanks to its diminutive stature, despite surrounding The Gambia on nearly all sides, Senegal's border with Mauritania still clocks in at 75km longer.) Though it's only 48km at its widest point, allow several hours to transit The Gambia, as the only way to cross the eponymous river is by ferry (at either Banjul, the Trans-Gambia Highway, Janjanbureh, Basse Santa Su, or Fatoto), and waits can be long. The optimistically named Trans-Gambia Highway is something of a potholed, bureaucracy-laden slog of a trip, but the road also known as the RN4 from Kaolack to Ziguinchor still represents the easiest land crossing from northern Senegal to Casamance, not least because this is the only point at which you can transit The Gambia without having to buy a visa. You'll still have to pay the Gambian authorities a small fee (1,000F) at both borders (Soma and Farafenni), but

A NOTE ABOUT THE GAMBIA

Officially speaking, Gambia is always referred to as *The* Gambia, as the definite article is an official part of the country's name, ie: Republic of The Gambia, not Republic of Gambia. (Supposedly one of only two countries in the world with such a requirement!) In colloquial speech and in the writing of this book, it's often omitted to avoid cumbersome and unnatural phrasing.

this is much less than the 1,000 Gambian Dalasi (or 20,000F – a much better deal in Dalasi) charged for a 7-day visa (even if you're just transiting) at other entry points.

The other primary route between northern Senegal and Casamance starts at Karang (Senegal) and Amdallai (The Gambia), where you'll probably be accosted by a crooked band of female moneychangers, whom you'd do best to ignore. This journey involves a trip on the Barra-Banjul ferry and crosses back into Senegal heading south at a few possible locations, namely Seleti (Senegal)/Giboroh (The Gambia), Kartong (The Gambia), or Darsilami (The Gambia). Kartong and Darsilami are both host to Gambian, but not Senegalese, immigration controls, so if you enter Senegal at either of these points, you'll have to make a trip to Seleti for the stamp anyway.

Heading east, aside from a remote crossing north of Kolda near Pata (Senegal) and Brikama Ba (The Gambia), there are few other options to cross the border until you reach Vélingara, from where you can connect to Basse Santa Su, some 25km away. For completists, you can enter or depart The Gambia's easternmost tip at Nyamanari, opposite Manda on the RN6 in Senegal. For full details on these routes, see the box *Getting through The Gambia*, pages 334–5.

BY BOAT Aside from the MV *Aline Sitoe Diatta* and its new sister vessels, the *Diambogne* and *Anguène* (see page 288), which collectively ply the waters between Dakar and Ziguinchor four times weekly, or the tourist-class *Bou el Mogdad* (see page 198) from Saint-Louis to Podor, there are no scheduled international or domestic passenger ships serving Senegal. If you're heading to or from Cape Verde, however, bespoke sailing trips can be arranged at the Dakar Sailing Club (see below) with **Chaka Croisières** (m 77 562 9253; e *stantruffaut@gmail.com; www. chakaboat.com*), with trips to Praia starting at around €330 per person.

Indeed, Dakar is a reasonably popular port of call for yachts and other pleasure boats headed north or south along the African coast or west to Cape Verde, and the noticeboard at the **Dakar Sailing Club** (*Cercle de la Voile de Dakar*, CVD) (📞 33 832 0720/4619; e *cvdkr@orange.sn; www.cvdakar.e-monsite.com*) on Hann beach is the best place to check out what boats are in town and what their crew needs might be if you want to try to hitch a lift. This approach obviously requires a great deal of flexibility, and more than likely a bit of French as well. If you're hell-bent on boat travel, it may also be possible to pick up boats to Bissau, Banjul or beyond from the pirogue launch in Ziguinchor.

SAFETY

THEFT Aside from some of Dakar's seedier districts (see page 119) and certain areas of the city by night (looking at you, Corniche!), with some common-sense precautions, the risk of being separated from your valuables, either by guile or by force, remains low in Dakar, lower still in the provincial capitals, and fleeting in smaller towns and villages throughout the country.

The usual rules all apply here: bus stations and crowded markets are a pickpocket's best friend; keep your eyes open and valuables securely stashed. Money belts are a good idea, and so is keeping cash for daily transactions in a separate location so that you don't have to dip into the money belt in public. A reserve of cash hidden in an unlikely part of your luggage (and checked on regularly) can also be a saviour if something were to happen to your money belt. If a hotel seems reasonably secure, I typically prefer to leave valuables in a locked room (better yet, a safe if they have one) than to carry them around town with me, though this is a judgement call and you should always use your discretion.

OTHER HAZARDS
Transport Road accidents present the greatest danger to travellers in Senegal, and more broadly in Africa as a whole. The continent unfortunately boasts the highest rate of road deaths in the world, and while Senegal, at 19.5 road-related deaths per 100,000 people, sits well below the continental average of 24.1 per 100,000, it's still well above the US average of 11.4 and more than five times the UK's rate of 3.7. Your power to reduce these risks is somewhat limited, but some basic precautions can go a long way. Travel by day when possible, and don't get into a vehicle if the driver seems to have been drinking (though thanks to Islamic prohibitions regarding alcohol, this is not usually much of a problem in Senegal). *Sept-places* are generally regarded as somewhat safer than their larger *car Mouride* coach-bus brethren, as these are inevitably piled comically high with goods and luggage on the roof, creating a top-heavy vehicle and a very unfunny propensity for rollover accidents.

Helmet and seatbelt laws, though widely ignored, do exist, and you'll occasionally be offered a helmet on a moto-taxi or asked to wear your belt if you're in the front seat of a *sept-place*, though this is mostly when passing through checkpoints to placate the police.

Casamance rebellion Since the rebellion began in 1982 (see pages 14–15) there have been close to a dozen ceasefires of varying durability declared and broken between the Senegalese government and various factions of the Movement of the Democratic Forces of the Casamance (MFDC). Today, however, with Macky Sall's election in 2012 and MFDC leader Salif Sadio's public declaration of a ceasefire in April 2014, chances look higher than ever that this smouldering 30-plus-year conflict is finally burning out.

While open conflict has ended in Casamance, there remains an elevated risk of road banditry when compared with the rest of the country and, to this end, there are regular military checkpoints set up on all main roads throughout Casamance, which are typically quite low-hassle assuming your papers are in order. These checkpoints also serve as roadblocks on both the RN4 (Trans-Gambia Highway) and RN5 (Seleti to Bignona), which are closed to all traffic nightly from 18.00 to 06.00, so travel early in the day to reduce the risk of getting stuck. It's worth noting that the FCO unfortunately still carries a warning advising against all road travel in Casamance to the west of Kolda, with the exception of the roads from Ziguinchor to Cap Skirring and Ziguinchor to the Guinea-Bissau border, though this seems ripe for a change as the latest ceasefire continues to hold.

Landmines Demining efforts began in 2007 and are scheduled to be complete by 2016, though clearance efforts are currently stalled and it's likely that this deadline will be missed. The delays stem from disagreement between the Senegalese military and MFDC rebels as to the order in which certain mined areas are to be cleared,

THE SENEGALESE BUSH TAXI

Simon Fenton (www.thelittlebaobab.com), author of Squirting Milk at Chameleons (Eye Books, 2015; www.eye-books.com)

I am at the garage waiting for a bush taxi. This is the real Africa. It's steaming hot and mosquitos buzz around my ankles. I'm besieged by money changers, phone credit sellers, drink sellers, cashew nut sellers, everything else sellers, people trying to carry my bag, taxis reversing erratically into me, everyone screaming that their car or bus is faster, more comfortable or will leave sooner.

There are market stalls selling just about everything – as long as it's cheap and Chinese. Women sell *bissap*, a ribena-like drink made from hibiscus, in little plastic bags. Mangos are sold from large enamel bowls carried in on their heads. A more modern phenomenon is men selling mobile phone top-up cards – the future is very much Orange in West Africa. Small stalls of dubious hygiene make omelettes and slap them in a roll with brown, lumpy, unrefrigerated mayonnaise stored in buckets.

Then there are the urchins. Little ragged boys, often barefoot, faces covered in dust and snot. Sometimes wearing a Barack Obama 'Time for change' or a UNICEF t-shirt. Groups of them, carrying old tomato purée tins, walk around chanting for spare change. Tragically, they are often victims of trafficking, controlled by gangs or unscrupulous marabouts (see box, pages 196–7).

The *Baye Fall* (see page 47), with their large turbans, masses of beads and long robes, collect for charity – the Senegalese equivalent of Hari Krishnas. Goats wander around hoovering up the discarded mango skins and other rubbish. There's a motley collection of bush taxis, buses, trucks and abandoned vehicles which are in a really bad way. On top of all of this are the mad men, the hucksters, the Liberian refugees looking for an English speaker, the baggage handlers and the mass of people all seemingly moving all of their worldly possessions.

Eventually the bush taxi is ready and we all jump in, or crawl if in the back. I look around and tick off my mental 'bush taxi check list': cracked windscreen; wires ripped out; door doesn't close properly; years of dust and crud; ripped out upholstery; live chickens on the floor; loud, to the point of distortion, religious chanting on the stereo; window winder handles missing (the great African mystery – where do they go?); exhaust hanging on by a bit of wire. All present and correct.

Imagine sitting in a sauna, fully clothed in an uncomfortable squashed position with someone throwing dust over you. It's like that. Recently I was in the passenger seat next to the driver, affording me reasonable leg room. The passenger door swung open every ten minutes or so. The driver said he normally fixed it closed with a bit of wire, but that had been jolted off by the pot holes.

This time, I was in for a shock. The car was clean and relatively new. Sure, the windscreen was cracked but it was only slight. I went to wind the window down and sure enough the handle was missing. Then the driver, tapped me on the shoulder and with a smile, pressed a button. Electric windows! Maybe things are changing?

as seemingly neither side wants to be the first to relinquish mined areas under their control that could provide a tactical advantage were open conflict to resume. MFDC forces abducted an 11-member demining crew in May 2013 in connection with this dispute and, though the crew was released unharmed two months later, mine clearance has since ground to a halt.

The amount of remaining mined territory is quite small, however: surveys conducted in December 2013 suggest that as little as 1.3km² is either confirmed or suspected to be contaminated, and all of it lies within Sédhiou and Ziguinchor regions. And though there continue to be a small handful of mine-related injuries and deaths annually in Casamance, the remaining mined areas are typically either surrounding military bases or in remote villages (that are sometimes even abandoned because of the mines), and so long as you stick to well-used paths and heed local advice while in Casamance, the risk is minimal. The only impact land mines are likely to have on travellers is the ongoing inaccessibility of Basse Casamance National Park, which remains closed due to the potential presence of mines.

HASSLES

OVERCHARGING AND BARGAINING Hotels, restaurants and supermarkets all operate using fixed prices, and it's required that hotels have their rates visibly marked at the front desk. Challenging the price at a supermarket or restaurant would be highly unusual and rather impolite unless it was clear that some sort of shenanigans were afoot. Hotels are something of a different story, and given the seasonal nature of tourism in Senegal, it's often possible to negotiate a discount on the posted rate if you happen to be travelling during low season. For reasons that should be obvious, you're considerably less likely to have such luck during peak season.

In markets and on the street, however, bargaining is very much the order of the day, and prices are typically given with every expectation that you'll bargain them down at least a bit, particularly when you're dealing with handicrafts and souvenirs. It's pretty much impossible to estimate what percentage of the asking price you ought to expect to pay, but if you approach the negotiations with a smile, take the time to greet and chat with the vendor, and don't take the inflated price as a personal slight – it's simply how these transactions are done – you'll more than likely both come away satisfied. And if you just can't see eye to eye on an amount, don't be afraid to walk away – an artificially inflated price will come tumbling down before you know it, and if it doesn't, it's usually because you were quoted a fair price to begin with. Fruit and vegetable markets operate on much the same rules; only since you've typically got a gaggle of sellers with the same products, it's easy to feel out a price by visiting a few stalls and inquiring, which is a good way to find out who's got the juiciest produce anyway!

All this being said, try not to forget that travel, even bare-bones, backpacking, shoestring budget travel, is still both a luxury and a choice, and it's one that is not afforded to most Senegalese. Next time you look up and find yourself in a heated dispute over bananas, remember that the amount of money you're arguing over is of considerably greater significance to the seller than to you, and it's a bit ridiculous to expend so much breath and energy on little more than what you might lose in the couch cushions on a given day at home.

BEGGING In addition to the aged and handicapped seen begging on streets across Africa, Senegal is home to two other types of people who you're almost sure to be approached by during your time here. The first are *talibés* (see box, pages 196–7), who are children as young as four sent away from their families to study under a *marabout* (religious teacher) at Koranic schools where they are expected to beg by day and study Koran recitation by night. The tradition is age-old, but it's an exceedingly thorny issue in Senegalese society today, with opinions sharply divided throughout the country. Even so, it remains common practice, and the sight of bands of unaccompanied child beggars is inevitably jarring. Giving is of course at your personal discretion, and there are a number of Saint-Louis-based organisations (see box, pages 196–7) working with talibé if you should feel the urge to get involved.

The second group you're likely to encounter are **Baye Fall**, devotees of Cheikh Ibrahima 'Lamp' Fall, who was himself an early disciple of Ahmadou Bamba, founder of the Mouride brotherhood. The *Baye Fall* eschew material possessions and practise a mystical, heterodox form of Islam in which devotion is expressed through manual labour and hours-long, trance-inducing chants, along with collecting alms for their *marabout* (not unlike the *talibé*). This latter part is where you come in, but with long, wild dreadlocks, multi-coloured robes, a stack of chunky wooden prayer beads and gris-gris around their necks, and a calabash full of coins in hand, they're almost as easy to spot as a *toubab*, so it's easy to steer clear if you don't feel up to making a donation.

BRIBERY AND BUREAUCRACY While Africa as a whole carries an unenviable reputation for corruption, the varying approaches to bribery from country to country indicate just how wrongheaded these sweeping generalisations of the continent really are. It would be wrong to paint Senegal as home to nothing but upstanding, principled civil servants, but the problem of bribery here is relatively mild when compared with certain regional and continental neighbours. The military and gendarmerie staffing roadside checkpoints are more professional than what one might expect coming from other parts of Africa, and so long as your papers are in order it's unlikely you'll be asked for any illicit payments or 'cold drinks'.

When dealing with Senegalese bureaucracy, it's best to quickly disabuse yourself of stereotypical images of the pernickety and inefficient African bureaucrat, and to approach your interactions with Senegalese officialdom without paranoia. An irritable and impatient attitude will firstly get you exactly nowhere, and secondly, only serve to further reinforce the stereotype of the arrogant western tourist who looks down upon the locals, despite taking advantage of the charms of their country. A modicum of respect will go a long way towards both accomplishing your goal and engendering positive attitudes between future visitors and their hosts.

WOMEN TRAVELLERS *Juliana Peluso*

Whether they want them or not, women traveling alone in Senegal will certainly not find themselves lacking for new friendship opportunities. Foreigners are the centre of attention wherever they go, and lone women only more so; it is considered unusual for a woman to travel without the company of her husband, so when the assumption of singlehood is combined with stereotypes about the relative sexual liberation of Western women, unwanted advances can at times be overwhelming. While the attention is rarely dangerous or threatening in nature, it's wise to have a plan to brush off solicitation of the romantic variety simply in order to streamline what will be a frequent shut-down process. Whether speaking with women or men, it is inadvisable to admit to being unmarried, and some female travellers will go so far as to wear a fake wedding ring in order to bolster their claims to being 'taken', which are usually respected (though not without requisite, good-natured teasing as to the superiority of Senegalese men over their Western counterparts). Even the most patient women will find it tempting to give in to their frustration at times, but this usually only ends with relentless taunting and bad blood; it's better to respond icily to particularly aggressive suitors, which should eventually garner disinterest.

TRANSPORTATION Women travelling long distances, especially in *sept-places*, would do well to choose a car with other female travellers whenever possible; bathroom breaks are begrudgingly allotted by the driver, who may not be feeling particularly generous on a given day, and having backup when vying for a petrol station or locale with enough tree cover to provide for dignity will help your case. Following other common-sense rules of thumb, such as avoiding travelling after dark whenever possible and only taking 'official' means of transport (as official as purchasing a ticket from a garage can be, that is), should go a long way in terms of self-preservation.

DRESS Expectations of modesty in dress vary dramatically by region, and women are advised to err on the side of the discreet in order to avoid even further harassment. The Northern (Fouta) region and central Senegal, known for particularly conservative Islamic practices, are by far the strictest when it comes to limiting exposed skin; while outfits are as tight as anywhere else, shoulders and calves are rarely exposed in public. In contrast, the skimpiness exhibited in Dakar's vibrant nightlife scene rivals that of any Western city, and daytime apparel can reasonably accommodate shorts, mid-thigh-length skirts, and tank tops. The best practice is usually to observe the clothing of local women your age in order to discern what's acceptable in the city, town, or village in question. Women travelling to or through Touba (coincidentally and ironically, the word for 'pants' in Pulaar) should be sure to pack a skirt in case circumstances necessitate leaving the car; this hyper-conservative holy city forbids women from donning trousers.

GAY AND LESBIAN TRAVELLERS

As in many African countries, same-sex sexual activity is illegal in Senegal, and punishable by between one and five years imprisonment and a 100,000 to 1,500,000F fine. The rhetoric here isn't nearly as heated as in other countries, and President Macky Sall had this to say in a 2013 press conference with Barack Obama: 'Senegal... is a very tolerant country which does not discriminate in terms of inalienable rights of the human being. We don't tell anybody that he will not be recruited because he is gay or he will not access a job because his sexual orientation is different. But we are still not ready to decriminalise homosexuality... we have respect for the rights of homosexuals – but for the time being, we are still not ready to change the law.' While it could be argued that such platitudinal rhetoric makes little difference in reality, it still stands in sharp contrast to Gambian president Yahya Jammeh's vitriolic pronouncements promising to slit the throats of gays in his country.

Thus gay travellers in Senegal should exercise a high degree of caution. People who are gay, or thought to be gay, often find themselves ostracised by their families and communities; this is often accompanied by physical violence, or threats of it. The gay scene here is almost totally underground, and any gay parties or congregations are clandestine and take place in private homes. Public displays of affection are unacceptable between heterosexual couples here, but any same-sex display will open you up to the possibility of prosecution or worse and, though the law is sporadically applied, in recent years there have been several successful prosecutions resulting in jail time for those accused of participating in same-sex sexual behaviour.

On a practical note, and particularly at the downmarket end of the spectrum, hotelkeepers will often refuse to rent a room with one double bed to two men or two women (regardless of whether you're doing it to save a buck or as a couple). In this case you would be expected to take a room with twin beds, or barring that, two separate rooms.

TRAVELLERS WITH DISABILITIES

Given that some of Senegal's major attractions are beaches and colonial architecture, there's no shortage of obstacles here for people with limited mobility. Streets are potholed and sidewalks rare, lifts are few and far between, and there are quite simply few concessions made here for the disabled. Still, with some determination, flexibility and organisation, a rewarding visit could still be possible, but it will require a good deal of patience and a willingness to improvise.

WHAT TO TAKE

Famed Scottish explorer Mungo Park's 1795 packing list for his first journey up the Gambia River to locate the source of the Niger included:

> ...provisions for two days; a small assortment of beads, amber and tobacco, for the purchase of a fresh supply, as I proceeded; a few changes of linen, and other necessary apparel, an umbrella, a pocket sextant, a magnetic compass and a thermometer; together with two fowling-pieces, two pairs of pistols, and some other small articles.

And while it would very much be best to leave the pistols at home (you could probably do without the sextant as well), Park's *modus operandi* of travelling light (horses and servants notwithstanding) will serve you just as well 220 years later.

Generally speaking, Senegal is quite well stocked with all of the little necessities a traveller might require, but this varies greatly depending on where in the country you are. As a rule, Dakar is home to just about anything your traveller's heart could desire, from T-shirts to tampons. Most of the brands are French but, unless your needs are quite specific, any clothing, toiletries, food, batteries, or other basic goods you might need will be readily available in Dakar and provincial capitals, though to a notably lesser extent in the latter. A major exception to this is camping/trekking equipment, which is not easy to find anywhere in the country. Pharmacies are also typically well stocked (again, particularly in Dakar), but you should plan to bring a supply of any personal medications needed for the duration of your trip. It's also advisable to carry sunscreen, as you'll have a hard time finding it outside of major tourist centres, where it's sold at a significant mark-up. Electricity is 220v at 50Hz, and plugs are European style, with two round pins.

CARRYING YOUR LUGGAGE If you're planning on hiring a vehicle, taking a guided tour, or otherwise not lugging your bags for considerable distances, you shouldn't have any problem with an average suitcase, though take care that it's a durable one so it's ready for rough roads and over-eager baggage handlers. A bag that can be padlocked can always still be slashed or otherwise broken into, but it will go a considerable way towards deterring opportunistic theft, which is far and away the most common form of thievery you're likely to encounter.

If you'll be getting around on public transport, a backpack is greatly preferable, as weaving your way through a muddy *gare routière* with a rolling suitcase is nobody's idea of a good time. As with the suitcase, the ability to lock your bag is ideal, but keeping valuables (camera, mp3 player, etc) in a daypack that stays with you when your larger bag is stowed is also a workable solution. Plus, the daypack will come in handy for any day trips or hikes you intend to go on.

CLOTHES Before you even start packing, know that it's a breeze to replace lost or worn-out clothing in markets anywhere in Senegal. If you're backpacking, the added value of additional clothing can very rapidly be eclipsed by the added hassle of dragging a considerably heavier bag around. At the minimum, you should have one, probably two pairs of trousers/skirts, three shirts, a light pullover, a medium-thickness sweater or jacket, a waterproof jacket if you plan on travelling during the rainy season, and no less than five days' worth of socks and underwear. On your feet you'll want one decent pair of walking shoes (given Senegal's overwhelmingly flat terrain, serious hiking boots are overkill) and one pair of flip-flops (available everywhere).

Jeans and their suitability for African travel are a topic of some debate. On the negative side, they are bulky, hot, and take forever to dry. On the upside, they're durable, take a good long time before looking dirty (of particular value if you're getting around on public transport), and are good to have in a place like Dakar, where your safari-ready khaki zip-offs can look decidedly out of place. Light cotton trousers or skirts have a significant advantage over jeans in shorter drying times and less space in your pack, but their dirt-hiding abilities are considerably less impressive.

Having a pullover/jacket on hand will be a lifesaver in Dakar, where the average low temperature doesn't crack 20° for five months of the year; you'll find similar oceanic chills on much of the coast from December to April. Shirts with a buttoning front pocket can be handy for cash as they're nigh impossible for a pickpocket to get to without attracting your attention. This might seem to go without saying, but socks and underwear are perhaps the most crucial item in your wardrobe. They're small and light, so bring lots, and bring only ones made from cotton or other natural fabrics. Re-wearing socks and undies can encourage athlete's foot with the former, or prickly heat with the latter (and in a neighbourhood where you'd typically be loath to have anything prickly). You can of course buy more of these in Senegal if you run short, but you'll have to shop around carefully to avoid polyester and other synthetic materials.

It's also important to bear in mind that Senegal is overwhelmingly Islamic and, while it's quite laid-back as these things go, it's worth taking note of a few considerations when planning your outfits. Women shouldn't wear skirts or shorts above the knee, and shirts that cover your shoulders would be a good idea as well. For men, knee-length shorts are acceptable but tend to be looked upon as an outfit for schoolboys, not grown men. As a rule, the most conservative areas of the country are in the north, particularly in the towns and villages along the Senegal River and in central cities like Touba and Diourbel. Attitudes are considerably more relaxed in Casamance, and western dress predominates in Dakar, though it varies greatly by the district that you happen to be in. (Attitudes in Yoff, for instance, are much more in line with their country cousins in the north than with Plateau or Almadies, neighbourhoods only a few miles away.)

OTHER USEFUL ITEMS Whether or not you plan to camp, if you're going the budget route it can be nice to have a sleeping bag in case you wind up staying in a room with not-exactly-clean bedding, which, on the lowest end of the price spectrum, is indeed possible. A mosquito net is also useful to have as places of a certain calibre will often lack these as well. Alternatively, it can also be good to have either of these if you wind up staying with a local family, which is also quite possible.

As mentioned previously, if your luggage is capable of locking it would be worthwhile to take advantage of this and bring a padlock to deter opportunistic thieves.

Aside from the obvious toiletries of soap, shampoo, toothbrush and toothpaste that you'll clearly want to have, your own stash of loo paper should be added to that list. Most Senegalese clean themselves after using the toilet using a sort of low-tech bidet system involving a scoop or kettle full of water and, while this works just fine once you're used to it, most travellers will be very happy to have something a bit more familiar in the form of a roll of two-ply at the ready in their backpacks. It's available for purchase in any shop, but only kept stocked in the toilet at the fanciest of places. Men might want a razor unless it's Movember or they're working on their hipster beard, while women will definitely want to have at least a period's worth of tampons or pads available in case Aunt Flo comes calling while far from a major city.

For the bespectacled, make sure to have either your prescription (so that you can get a new pair made up) or a spare pair of glasses along with you. Contact lens fluid is available at some shops in Dakar, but don't count on finding it anywhere else in the country, and be aware that the dust and intense sunlight can be irritating for contact wearers. For other various aches, pains, sprains, rashes, itches, cramps, grumbles and possibly even hangovers, be sure to have a basic medical kit (see page 70 for the contents of said kit).

Other bits and bobs you might like to have along include a pocketknife, torch (flashlight), pack of cards or other games, and maybe a washbasin plug for doing some sink laundry. This one is something of a no-brainer today, but having an unlocked mobile phone is useful both for making calls and as an alarm clock for the inevitable early morning bus trips.

MONEY

In Senegal and seven other West African states, the unit of currency is the **West African CFA Franc** (CFA), pronounced *say-fah* and not to be confused with the Central African CFA Franc. Notes come in 10,000CFA, 5,000CFA, 2,000CFA, 1,000CFA and 500CFA denominations, while coins are issued for 500CFA, 200CFA, 100CFA, 50CFA, 25CFA, 10CFA, 5CFA and 1CFA. You're not likely to encounter any of the coins under 25CFA except occasionally as exact change at supermarkets. The CFA Franc is pegged to the euro at 655CFA to €1, while the exchange rate as of July 2015 was around 592CFA to the US Dollar and 923CFA to the British pound.

Because of the fixed exchange rate and strong business ties to France and the Eurozone, the euro is absolutely the foreign currency to have in Senegal. You will be able to exchange pounds and dollars if need be, but at comparatively unfavourable rates. Local currency is best for most transactions, but euros are widely accepted, particularly at upmarket hotels and other high-end services. All prices are correct as of mid 2015, but will of course, as anywhere, be subject to inflationary whims during the lifespan of this book.

ORGANISING YOUR FINANCES In short: bring euros and Visa or MasterCard. Travellers' cheques are irrelevant in Senegal. The ATM network is surprisingly good, and all major centres in Senegal have at least one bank branch with an ATM accepting international cards. Both Visa and MasterCard/Maestro are accepted at BICIS, CBAO, Ecobank and SGBS ATMs. Upmarket hotels in Dakar and other major centres can usually handle credit card payments, but if you plan to pay this way it would be best to double-check ahead of time which cards they accept.

Besides the euro, the US dollar and British pound are the most widely accepted foreign currencies, although they are a distant second place indeed. You'll probably have a bit of a challenge finding someone to change dollars or pounds on the street (at an acceptable rate anyway), though most banks and private forex bureaux will do so. Banking hours are roughly 08.00–17.00 Monday–Friday (possibly with a break for lunch) and 09.00–noon Saturday. If you find yourself in a pinch, Western Union branches are found everywhere and can arrange international wire transfers, though sizeable fees make this far from the preferred method.

BUDGETING

This may go without saying, but a trip's budget is entirely dependent on where you go, how you get there, and what you do once you've arrived. Naturally, hiring a 4x4 and staying in luxury accommodation will hit your wallet considerably harder than getting around with a *sept-place* and sleeping bag. Thus, it's something of a challenge to give budget specifics in a general guide for the varying types of travellers who frequent Senegal.

If you're travelling on the middle to upper end of the spectrum, however, it's likely that much of your trip – accommodation, transport, activities, etc – will be pre-booked through an agency, and you'll be able to get a good sense for the costs you're dealing with before you touch down in Dakar. Be sure to check what is and isn't included in your package (which meals, drinks, etc) so as to avoid any nasty surprises when the bill is due.

Budget travellers will find Senegal to be decidedly middle-of-the-road when it comes to costs, although compared to the rest of West Africa – a region where you'll often find yourself paying lots for very little – value for money here is actually pretty good. One way to cut costs immediately is to travel in a pair or small group; dorm accommodation is fleetingly rare, and many hotels in Senegal charge by room and not occupancy, so a double room will often be the same price whether you're alone or with a companion. In most towns you'll be lucky to get a basic room for under €12, and AC usually won't enter the equation until you reach at least the €23 mark. Village campements are cheaper, with basic accommodation starting around €6, while finding a place to stay in Dakar for under €16 can be a real challenge.

As for the gustatory basics, at a local joint a bottled soft drink will run you about 200F, while a large beer goes for 800F, but don't be surprised to see these prices treble or even quadruple (or worse!) in a tourist-oriented restaurant or upmarket hotel. A street snack or sandwich can be had on roadsides throughout the country for under 500F, and a *Café Touba* to wash it down goes for under 100F. A simple sit-down meal, *plat du jour*, or *chawarma* at a cheap and cheerful local place will be in the 1,500–3,000F range, while plates at more upmarket or tourist-oriented restaurants start around 4,000F.

Public transport is thankfully easy enough on the pocket, with *sept-place* trips averaging 2,000–2,500F per 100km, and buses are even cheaper. Thus, scrimpers and savers should plan on spending about €25 daily (slightly less for couples), while €60–80 per day is a more likely range if you require a few more creature comforts like air-conditioned hotels and restaurant meals. These estimates don't factor in one-off excursions like boat trips, national park fees, etc.

GETTING AROUND

BY AIR There are airports in most major centres, but only a handful of them have scheduled flights as of mid 2015. **Senegal Airlines** (\ *33 865 8883 (Dakar)/33 991*

1111 (Zig); m *800 800 888 (toll-free);* e *relations.clients@senegalairlines.aero; www. senegalairlines.aero)* flies from Dakar to Ziguinchor and Cap Skirring, while **Groupe Transair** (\ *33 865 2565 (Dakar)/991 6774 (Zig);* e *sales@groupetransair.sn; www. groupetransair.sn or www.facebook.com/groupetransair)* also serves Ziguinchor and Cap Skirring, and recently began flights to Kolda, Matam and Tambacounda. If you've got the cash, **Arc en Ciel Aviation** (\ *33 820 24 67;* e *arcenciel@arc.sn; www. arcenciel-aviation.com)* does domestic and international air charters from Dakar.

SELF-DRIVE The best places to arrange **car hire** for either saloon cars or 4x4s are in Dakar, the Petite Côte and Saint-Louis. See the respective chapters for contact details of local agencies. Rates vary, but 4x4 hire can range from €95 to €160 per day depending on the vehicle, while a saloon car will be somewhat cheaper. You may or may not be asked for it, but an international driver's licence (see page 38) is technically required. Depending on the firm, it's also common practice for a driver to be included with the car hire, which adds somewhat to the cost but may represent savings on insurance fees. If fuel isn't included in the price, remember that you're looking at an average cost of over €1.20/litre.

Driving is on the right in Senegal. Be sure to check out your rental car thoroughly before heading off, including for two safety triangles, a fire extinguisher (check the bottom to ensure it's not expired) and a first aid kit. Police may ask you for any of these at checkpoints and being able to produce them eliminates an easy pretext for bribe seeking, though it should be stated that most road checkpoints are reasonably low-hassle, assuming that your papers are in order.

It's possible to cross The Gambia with a hired car, but this raises a number of issues vis-à-vis insurance, import permits and other paperwork. If you plan to cross from northern Senegal to Casamance via The Gambia, be sure to ask the car hire firm for specifics on what paperwork you might need, as well as if it would be allowed under your rental agreement in the first place. Many self-drivers cross Senegal via Tambacounda to avoid these hassles altogether.

Most **main roads** in Senegal are surfaced and in reasonable condition, with a few notable exceptions. The **RN1** begins as a traffic-choked nightmare running parallel to the (reliably empty) new toll road leaving Dakar, and continues as a simple tarmac road all the way to Kidira on the Mali border. It's surfaced the whole way, but some stretches, notably from Fatick to Kaolack, are terribly potholed. The **RN2** picks up at the village of Diamniadio outside Dakar, heads north to Saint-Louis, then follows the northern border eastwards all the way down to Kidira, where it meets the RN1 again. It's in fair to excellent shape until Ndioum, from where you're back in pothole country all the way to Kidira. The **RN3** begins in Thiès and connects to Touba, Linguère, and eventually Ourossogui. It's in good shape to Touba, rougher to Linguère, and fantastic for the last stretch to Ourossogui. The **RN4**, otherwise known as the Trans-Gambia Highway, picks up at Kaolack and is fair to good tarmac all the way through The Gambia to Ziguinchor, with the notable exception of a deplorable 25km from Nioro du Rip to the Gambian border. The **RN5** also originates in Kaolack, but starts its journey towards Toubacouta and The Gambia in rather rough shape. It's good, newish tarmac from The Gambia's southern border to the terminus at Bignona, though. The **RN6** is beautiful new tarmac from Tambacounda to Manda, terrible potholes to Vélingara, and a mixed bag of roadworks until you reach Kolda. Westwards from Kolda, the RN6 is in such deplorable shape that nearly all traffic to Ziguinchor goes via Bounkilling and Bignona (though comprehensive road works on this stretch began in 2014). Finally, the **RN7** is in good shape, some of it brand new, from Tambacounda to Kédougou.

Some maps show the RN7 continuing north from Tambacounda to Ourossogui, but this doesn't exist in any meaningful sense and all traffic between the two cities goes via Kidira. Besides the aforementioned potholes, drivers are faced with an array of **hazards** on Senegalese roads that you should be aware of before setting out. Fortunately, given Senegal's distinct lack of winding mountain roads, blind overtaking isn't the issue here that it is in some places, but you'll still probably be overtaken by speed demons, particularly on some of the newly tarmacked routes. No matter where you are, there's likely to be a cadre of cyclists, children, livestock, and any number of other people and things that seem prone to dart into the street without any semblance of notice. There's little else to say about minimising this risk than simply to take caution and slow down. If you forget this advice, there's no shortage of speed bumps to assist you in heeding it, so be on the lookout for these as well.

As in most African countries, driving at night is not recommended. Almost none of the roads are illuminated, not all of your fellow drivers will have working headlights (others will happily show you nothing but their high beams), and the same cast of people and animals is still on the roadside, only considerably more difficult to see when they enter the roadway.

CYCLING Since Senegal is generally flat, it can make a good destination for cyclists. Distances between sights along the coast are quite approachable, but interior cities and points of interest are more spread out. Both Casamance and Kédougou would make excellent destinations for bicyclists thanks to their attractive scenery, frequent villages with accommodation, and relatively compact geography. If you get tired of pedalling, it's common practice to throw your bike on top of a *sept place* (for a fee, of course). The only bikes available locally are cumbersome Chinese workhorses so you'll want to bring a nimbler steed of your own, along with a repair kit and whatever spare parts you might need.

HITCHHIKING This is doable on main routes and some auxiliary ones, depending on how long you're willing to wait. Expect to pay for rides offered by Senegalese.

PUBLIC TRANSPORT
Road Firstly, transport with 'Touba' painted on the front is *not* heading in that direction – destinations are nearly always unmarked on Senegalese transport, but drivers will rarely miss an opportunity to spruce up their vehicles with some Mouride-inspired iconography, pithy Wolof slogans, or dangling baby shoes (see box, *Cow Tails and Left Shoes*, page 57).

The *sept place* (seven place) is the bedrock of all road transportation in Senegal, and generally takes the form of a battered Peugeot 505 wagon with three rows of seats: room for two in front, three in the middle, and three in back. The seats are sold on a first-come, first-served basis, and those in the very rear are the least comfortable by far. Take solace, though, that in neighbouring Guinea the selfsame cars function as a *neuf place* (nine place), so these are downright comfortable by comparison. Ticket prices are set by the transport union, and as such are very rarely inflated or otherwise tampered with. You should receive a ticket with the price (usually illegibly) scrawled on it, and all passengers will pay the same amount. If in doubt, don't be afraid to ask a fellow passenger. Since the ticket prices are fixed, baggage fees are usually levied, and this is where conductors will try and squeeze you for some extra money. It's something of a free-for-all in terms of what you're expected to pay, though unsurprisingly, the larger the bag and the longer the ride, the higher the price. As a rough indicator, a journey of six hours or less with a medium travel backpack will run you about 500F if you're firm on the price, but for trips longer than this, heartfelt pleas are sure to be made about the length of the journey or state of the roads, and you can expect to pay about 1000F.

Besides the *sept place*, other intercity transport options include the ***ndiaga ndiaye***, which are hulking old Mercedes 508D trucks with '*Alhamdoulilah*' painted on the front, and somewhere between 30 and 40 people squeezed into the back. They're cheaper than *sept places*, but take considerably longer because passengers (and all their baggage) are constantly mounting and alighting. **Buses** (many operated by the Mouride brotherhood and known as *cars mourides*) also cover intercity transport, and these range from reasonably comfortable private services to clapped-out and overloaded jalopies. On both *ndiaga ndiayes* and buses your baggage will typically ride for free, though a small fee isn't unheard of.

Each town in Senegal has a central *gare routière* where you can pick up buses, *sept places*, and *ndiaga ndiayes* to destinations near and far. There are a small number of private bus companies that run regular cross-country services on fixed timetables,

TRAVELLING DURING RAMADAN

Though the Muslim holy month of Ramadan won't fall during the main tourist season for the lifespan of this edition (see dates on pages 62–3), if you do find yourself here during the holy month, be prepared to make a few adjustments. For the duration of the 30-day holiday, healthy adult Muslims are forbidden from eating, drinking, smoking and any sexual activity during daylight hours. Exemptions exist for the sick and the travelling, and while no one will expect you to fast, quoting the exemption for travellers is a good answer if someone asks, and your knowledge of Islam will earn you a few *halal* brownie points to boot.

For the (non-fasting) traveller, Ramadan can often mean that otherwise-simple activities like getting a bite to eat can wind up being a bit more complicated. Unless you fancy waking up before sunrise for *suhoor,* the pre-dawn meal taken to gird fasters' stomachs for the long day ahead, it can occasionally be tricky to get meals on a normal schedule during the day. Many restaurants change their hours to reflect the diminished clientele, and lots of street food sellers will also simply pack up shop during the day. Still, with a bit of poking around you'll be able to find something, but also be prepared to wait while it's prepared, since most places won't be keeping ready food on hand during daylight hours.

Also be ready for frayed tempers and lackadaisical service as the afternoon wears on – hangry reaches epidemic proportions in the hours just before sundown, and quite understandably so; the fast is an impressive feat of endurance by any measure. On the plus side, the country comes to life at sundown for the *iftar* meal – the fast is usually broken with a few dates wherever you are when the clock strikes, followed by enormous family feasts which more often than not stretch late into the night. If you're hiring a driver or a guide, it's imperative you allow time in your schedule for them to break their fast, and it's a good opportunity to share a meal. And while socialising goes on into the wee hours and many businesses stay open late, most live music venues scale back their schedules for the month, so it's not a great time to visit if you're here for the concerts.

and these arrive and depart from their own offices rather than the *gare routière*. Details for these companies are included in the relevant chapters.

Boat Plying the waters between northern Senegal and Casamance, the MV *Aline Sitoe Diatta, Diambogne* and *Anguène* (see box, pages 292–3) ferry a plethora of people, cars, and goods between Dakar and Ziguinchor (via Karabane) four times weekly. Up north, the fabulously restored *Bou el Mogdad* (see page 198) runs six-night luxury river cruises between Saint-Louis and Podor. Aside from these two vessels, any other aquatic excursions you're likely to take will be in a motorised pirogue or fishing boat. This is the best way to get around in the Sine-Saloum Delta; boat connections through the labyrinthine mangrove swamps between centres like Toubacouta, Palmarin, Mar Lodj and others are all easily arranged.

Rail Senegalese railways have unfortunately suffered a seemingly unrelenting decline in recent decades, and as of 2014 the railway system is a shadow of its former self. The only functioning passenger service is a once-daily back-and-forth between Dakar and Thies, but there's really no compelling reason to take it unless you're a serious train buff. The legendary Dakar–Bamako route has been out of commission since 2011 and won't be back anytime soon.

Taxi In Senegal taxis are mostly all yellow and black, but otherwise run the gamut from unidentifiable old heaps to pert new Chinese-built Cherys or Iranian Samands assembled locally in Thiès. They charge fixed rates in smaller cities like Ziguinchor, Tambacounda, or Kaolack, but you should bargain hard in Dakar.

The band of cab-driving women known as 'Taxi Sisters' (✆ 33 849 5949) were the subject of Swedish-Burkinabe director Theresa Traore Dahlberg's 2011 film *Taxi Sister*, and are noteworthy as a safe means of transport for female travellers in Dakar (not to mention their feminist credentials), but unfortunately there are vanishingly few of them on the roads, so if you'd like to try and arrange with them it's imperative to call ahead.

Moto-taxis Often known (perhaps in part due to their Asian provenance) as *jakartas,* these small motorcycles are increasingly widely available, and it's not hard to flag down one for lifts around town or possibly longer hires. They're present in most cities, but really dominate the roads in Kaolack, Tambacounda and Kédougou. Rates are cheaper than a taxi by one-half or one-third.

Calèches and charettes If hooved transport is more your bag, a *calèche* or *charette* will appease the wheel-weary. *Calèches* are brightly painted horse- and/or donkey-drawn carts with seating for three or four on the back that clip-clop their way around most of Senegal's villages and towns, ferrying people about at a none-too-hurried pace and with a bit of old-school flair to boot. *Charettes* operate on much the same principle, but are better suited to hauling goods than people as they're entirely bereft of seating, or any other features really, short of a flat surface to stack things on. Both can be hailed on any roadside, but surprisingly they don't boast much of a price advantage over a taxi. They do have a fair bit more charm than a bashed-up Peugeot, though!

ACCOMMODATION

Accommodation in Senegal runs the gamut from five-star luxury lodging to thoroughly déclassé dives, and the prices reflect this. The highest-standard

If you're getting around the country on public transport, you'll very quickly notice that there's no such thing as a plain vehicle on the streets of Senegal. No matter the age or condition, cars and trucks are decorated with a panoply of saints, slogans, tassels, tails and stickers to reflect the driver's credo, provide good luck or even beseech divine intervention in the case of an accident (there's clearly a calculation made between the percentage of windscreen blocked by holy images versus the percentage of protection provided by their presence).

While the whole car gets the decorative treatment, it's the back bumper that represents one of the preferred canvases for Senegal's modish motorists, and the space almost never goes to waste. Firstly, the bumper itself is typically daubed with at least one pithy Wolof or Arabic saying, including favourites like *jamm rekk* (peace only), *door waar* (hard worker) or the perennially popular *alhamdoulillahi* (thanks be to God), but dangling below these words of wisdom, just high enough to keep from dragging on the road, you might find anything from a colourfully painted strip of rubber to a cow's tail or even a (singular) baby shoe.

Perhaps the most inscrutable elements of the whole scheme, the secret of these automotive amulets eluded me for nearly my entire stay in Senegal, until I finally asked Lamine, a Senegalese friend who I thought might be in the know, what the donkey tails were actually for. Whether he was more shocked that I couldn't tell the difference between a cow's and a donkey's tail, or that I would even suggest something as ridiculous as hanging a donkey tail from one's car, I'm still not sure, but it turns out they're nothing more than a simple good luck charm – something like the vehicular version of a lucky rabbit's foot. The baby shoes are also for good luck, but, perhaps sensing my ignorance, Lamine pre-empted my question and quickly informed me that these too had a set of rules, and that all the shoes you see dangling are for the left foot and the left foot only. I stifled my question about where in Senegal the enormous pile of right-footed baby shoes was, but my quick assumption that the third element of the back bumper trio of talismans, the colourful rubber strips, must also be for good luck was quickly shot down – those, apparently, are just there to look pretty.

accommodation is found in Dakar and the Petite Côte, but international-standard hotels also exist in tourist centres like Saint-Louis, Cap Skirring and Toubacouta. Elsewhere, most cities have well-tended mid-range accommodation geared towards travelling business people as well as tourists. A notch down from these mid-range places you start to lose perks like swimming pools and the like, but these local guesthouses will usually be the first port of call for budget travellers.

Lodging in Senegal goes by a variety of names besides *hôtel*: *campement*, *auberge*, *résidence* and occasionally *gîte*. They're all more or less interchangeable, though *campements* usually (though not always) lean towards the modest end of the spectrum, while a *hôtel* or *résidence* would tend to be higher-end.

All accommodation, regardless of standard, charges a government-mandated 1,000F tourist tax per guest per night. This is often, but not always, itemised separately on your bill.

See the inside front cover for an at-a-glance breakdown of accommodation categories and prices.

EXCLUSIVE/LUXURY Representing the highest-end accommodation available in the country, this category includes international-standard four- and five-star luxury hotels as well as select smaller lodges noted for their exclusivity and character. Expect rates between €200 and €300 for a double.

UPMARKET In the €100–200 range, this category includes smart business hotels and beachy tourist resorts that cater to international visitors, all of which will be stylish and soigné, but lacking some of the *je ne sais quoi* of their more exclusive brethren.

MODERATE Perhaps best described as comfortable but not luxurious, this category operates as something of a catch-all for decent, cleanly kept accommodation, sometimes oriented towards international tourists, other times towards African business travellers and conference-goers, which will typically have A/C, an on-site restaurant, in-room TV, hot water, and often a swimming pool. Again, this could mean stalwart Dakarois business hotels or modest Saint-Louisienne resorts on the *hydrobase*, but all will be in the neighbourhood of €50–100.

BUDGET Anywhere in the country, €20–50 can get you a well-kept room that would fall short of any Michelin inspection, but can still make for a comfortable stay. Expect reasonable rooms with private ablutions (possibly with hot water – more likely as you approach the top of the range), some sort of meals available, Wi-Fi and probably A/C. If you're squeamish about sharing toilets or haven't mastered the bucket shower yet, this category still guarantees you a few creature comforts.

SHOESTRING Depending on where you are in the country, the €10–20 you're likely to spend in this range can carry you reasonably far, or not at all. It's the bottom of the pricing barrel, but there are still plenty of very pleasant village *campements* where you'll get an enjoyable rural experience, often in a traditional setting like the *cases à impluvium* of Casamance (see box, page 331), but be prepared for bucket showers, sporadic (if any) electricity and certainly no A/C. In the cities, your money doesn't go quite as far, and you're likely to encounter some less-than-pleasant accommodation in this range, though there are proper and clean rooms to be found, typically (but not always) with common showers and toilets.

CAMPING There's not a whole lot in the way of formal camping infrastructure in Senegal (the overlander mecca Zebrabar near Saint-Louis is a notable exception), but a number of hotels will let you pitch a tent on their grounds for a fee. A tent would also be good to have for a cyclist or anyone else planning to overnight in untouristed rural areas, but be sure to always ask a village official for permission before camping.

EATING AND DRINKING

Held together by the common thread of the Atlantic Ocean and a near-universal love of fish and rice, Senegalese cuisine is a rich and diverse mélange of offerings informed by the country's drastically varied geography and long, cosmopolitan history. From the locally grown rice and palm oils of the tropical south to the soured milk and traditional millet couscous much loved by pastoralist communities on the northern plains, no matter what the dish, cooking here is approached with a French-inspired flair and a reverence that will be appreciated by any traveller who's put up with one too many slapped-together meals and plates of soggy chips.

Hotels usually do **breakfast** in the French style, with an assortment of pastries, breads, butter, jam, coffee, tea and fruit, though depending on where you're staying, the spread can range from the miserly to the lavish. Out on the streets though, breakfast sandwiches are king. They're served up on either a rather uninspired machine-baked baguette or the also-baguette-shaped, slightly denser and generally more interesting handmade *tapalapa*; just scan the roadsides for a woman sitting behind a pile of stainless steel bowls arranged around her like a drum set. Inside these lurks a variety of savoury sauces, including green peas (*petit pois*), black-eyed peas (*niebe*), onion sauce (*sos soublet*), spaghetti (yes, for a spaghetti sandwich), and some hot sauce (*sos kaani*) on the side. They'll often have some coals or a gas cooker on which to fry up omelettes as well, and the whole affair comes wrapped in an old Arabic newspaper and won't run you more than a couple hundred CFA, tops.

Cooking for lunch starts not too long after breakfast is finished: all over the country, witch-sized cauldrons start to bubble and simmer in preparation for the midday meal, of which there's no plate more popular than the undisputed national dish, *thieboudienne*, or just *thieb* to its friends, potentially spelled in about 100 different ways (*Ceebu Jën* in Wolof). However you spell it, it literally means rice (*ceeb*) and fish (*jën*), and starts with a base of rice cooked in a tomato sauce (akin to Ghana's jollof rice) served with stewed cabbage, carrots, cassava, squash, okra, tomato, *jaxatu* (bitter tomato), tamarind sauce, fish stuffed with *rof*, a parsley-garlic-onion-pepper paste and finally a sprinkling of savoury burnt rice from the bottom of the pan known as *khogn*. Like most Senegalese meals, it's served communally in a big metal bowl, and there will be a couple of whole habanero peppers on top as well – add spice by giving them a good squeeze on to your section of the bowl. Though you won't see them quite as often, *thieboudienne* also has a few cousins that operate along similar lines, namely *thiebou yapp*, which comes with lamb or goat, and *thiebou ginaar*, which is served with chicken.

While *thieb* is indeed Senegal's culinary golden child and a staple in households and on restaurant menus alike, it's far from the only game in town, and you could easily try a *plat du jour* all week and not replicate a meal, though rice and sauce is a fairly consistent formula throughout. Playing Luigi to *thieboudienne*'s Mario, **yassa** is a similarly beloved dish around the country, though it originates in Casamance. Usually served with grilled chicken or fish, *yassa* is the exquisite caramelised onion and lemon sauce that gives the dish its signature zing. Another staple, the peanut-sauce based **mafé**, traces its origins to present-day Mali, and is a popular dish well beyond Senegal's borders (Ghanaian *nkatenkwan*, or groundnut soup is similar). Richly spiced and creamy, it's typically served over rice (surprise!) with beef or lamb/goat. Down in Casamance, **caldou**, which, according to Chef Pierre Thiam, a Casamançais himself, takes its name and inspiration from *caldo*, the Portuguese word for broth, is another fish and rice dish that you'll see quite often, but its light onion-lemon-pepper sauce is a world away from *thieboudienne*. As in much of Africa, *haako*, or stewed leafy greens (from potatoes, cassava, bissap and sometimes the nutrient-rich moringa) are universally popular and commonly served along with any of the dishes mentioned above.

Even though rice is most definitely king in Senegal, several other starches join it at the royal court, including a millet couscous called **lacciri**, especially common in the north of the country and often eaten with sour milk (*lait caillé*) as part of a sweet dish called *lakh* or *ngalakh*. It's thought that all couscous was millet-based until a gradual transition took place in North Africa in the 20th century, and you will see the seminola variety around in Senegal but primarily as a Moroccan import. Another grain whose fortunes have risen and fallen with the times is **fonio**, a millet relative with tiny seeds that's long been out of fashion in Senegal as people opted for rice when they could afford it, but is steadily shaking off its paupers' reputation and is even gaining some traction as the next potential 'superfood' in the West (see box, pages 280–1).

Mealtimes in Senegal tend to follow the French custom, with lunch from 11.30 to 14.30 and dinner starting from about 19.30. Thus, if you get caught out looking for a bite between these times, it can sometimes be tricky to find a sit-down meal. Fear not, though, as your snacking needs will be well met, and with a bit of international flair, no less. Thanks to the big Lebanese presence, **shawarmas** are widely available from 'fast food' joints in all the major cities, along with another Lebanese borrowing, the *fataya*, which is basically a fried dough pie (much like an empanada or samosa) that can be stuffed with anything, including mince, veggies, fish paste, and even French fries (though not all at the same time, thankfully). These same places will usually also dish up a range of burgers, which inevitably come with either an egg or French fries *on* the burger itself. Cheaper still are the *accara* fritters made from a black-eyed pea batter you'll see women dolloping into hot pans of oil on the street.

Fatayas aren't the only Senegalese street food to have their origins in a French colonial adventure, though, and the recipe for *nems*, which are essentially little eggrolls much like Chinese/Filipino *lumpia*, first came to Senegal with conscript Senegalese soldiers returning from the Indochina war. Finally, there's **dibiterie**, which is essentially a streetside barbeque, often run by Hausa immigrants from Nigeria or Niger. With a variety of meats grilled up over a wood fire and wrapped in ersatz butcher paper – usually a repurposed cement bag – *dibi* is about as no-frills as it gets, and the theatrics of the grillmaster chopping up your meal with a hatchet or a machete are worth the price of admission alone. Served with some grilled onions, mustard, salt, a few dashes of Maggi sauce and no silverware anywhere in sight, any number of corporate slogans about finger licking could have been written about *dibi*, and indeed it has inspired a song – Ismael Lô's 1994 barbeque anthem, *Dibi Dibi Rek.*

For **dessert**, some favourites include *thiakry,* which is made from sweetened *lacciri* (millet couscous) with milk or yogurt and and spiced with cinnamon and vanilla, and from Casamance there's *sombi,* a rice pudding made with coconut milk and lime, often served with slices of fresh mango. Lots of boutiques carry pre-packaged *thiakry* and sweetened *kossam* (*lait caillé,* sour milk), usually sold chilled or frozen in plastic sachets. Fresh fruit is perhaps the most common dessert, especially if you're out in the villages, where you can just pick something good off of a tree. If you're in Dakar, there are enough patisseries and gelaterias to keep even the sweetest of teeth happy. Also, while hardly considered a dessert, a social chew on some kola nuts (the original source for cola flavour) can happen at any time of day. The nuts are highly prized in Senegal for their energetic and aphrodisiac properties, and no wedding or baby-naming ceremony would be complete without the symbolic giving of these bitter, caffeinated fruits.

DRINK What to wash all this down with? If it's the afternoon, the only answer is *attaya,* the gunpowder green tea sipped scaldingly hot and eye-wateringly sweet from the daintiest of little glasses while seated under shade trees and around coal burners in a carefully choreographed ceremony that's replicated innumerable times in compounds across the country each and every afternoon. It shares a lot in common with the tea ceremonies further north in the Maghreb, but pure green tea is used here, without the addition of mint common north of the Sahara (see box, page 68 for more on *attaya*). Otherwise, in the morning you might be offered a glass of *douté,* or Kinkeliba tea, made from the boiled leaves of the *Combretum micranthum* bush, a plant held in particularly high esteem by the Mourides, as Ahmadou Bamba was known to espouse its curative properties. Today it's drunk both as an all-around health tonic and as treatment for everything from liver ailments to diabetes to migraines. Bamba was a proponent of at least one other hot beverage in his time, and today the ubiquitous and pungent *café touba*, which traces its origins to Bamba's 1902 exile in Gabon, is vying with *attaya* as the closest thing Senegal has to a national beverage. Its intensely distinctive flavour comes from the ground grains of selim that are added to the coffee before it's brewed. Much like its cousin *attaya*, *café touba* is sipped from small cups with plenty of sugar, but *café touba* lacks the rigmarole of *attaya* preparation and can be bought by the cup from hawkers on the street, where it's infinitely preferable to their Nescafé cart competitors.

For a cold and possibly spirituous drink, you could be forgiven for thinking that **alcohol** would be in short supply given that the country is upwards of 90% Islamic, but you'd also be seriously wide of the mark. Nearly all hotels and restaurants of a certain calibre serve alcohol, and drinking dens abound in the major cities and down south – you'll have no trouble getting anything from caipirinhas to champagne in Dakar. Up in the more conservative north, towns will tend to have no more than one or two dodgy drinking holes, which are usually run by one of the Christian families in town. The local brewer, *Société des brasseries de l'Ouest africain* (SOBOA), does versions of all the usual hard liquors, but most of them will put you on the highway to hangover town pretty quickly. Less likely to leave you with a crippling hangover are the products of Liqueur de Warang (see pages 162–3), where you can sample artisanal liqueurs made using local fruits like cashew apple, *corossol* (soursop), mango and *madd*. Thankfully, the local beers are much nicer on both the palate and the head, and you'll usually have a choice of four SOBOA-brewed lagers: Senegal's own *Gazelle*, along with *Flag*, *33 Export* ('*trente-trois*') and *Castel*.

In the wetter regions of the country like Casamance and Kedougou, home-brewed alcohol is popular, and **palm wine** (*bunuk* in Diola) is widely drunk across the south. The oddly milky grog is an afternoon favourite as it continues to ferment from the moment it's tapped, thus typically becoming quite bitter by the time evening rolls around. In cashew-growing regions (Casamance, mostly), you'll also find *cadjou*, a wine of sorts made from the fermented juice of cashew apples. If you like your martini dry, try *cadjou* – it takes all the astringency of the cashew apple and concentrates it into a strangely enjoyable tipple that seems to suck the moisture right out of your mouth. The Balanta people who live in the border region with Guinea-Bissau are known for brewing it, and it's sold at the same places you'll find palm wine. The cashew apples are also commonly distilled into a firewater called *kana*, but it can hardly be recommended.

Teetotallers (or simply those promising they'll never drink again) are in fine company here though, and there's a delightfully tropical selection of **juices** to be had around the country. The intensely beetroot-coloured *bissap* is made from the hibiscus flower (like the Mexican *jamaica*), and is probably the most popular juice available, followed by the creamy off-white *bouyé*, made from the fruits of the baobab tree. More conventional tropical juices like tamarind, mango and papaya are also around, along with *gingembre*, a spicy-sweet ginger-based drink, and some more exotic options, like the intensely orange *madd* (*Saba senegalensis*) or bright-green *ditakh* (*Detarium senegalense*). Depending on where you buy them, juices are sometimes mixed with water, so if you're concerned about the hygienic conditions but still want to sample the flavours, the Dakar-based Zena Exotic Fruits (*www.zenaexoticfruits.com*) produces and bottles all of the above to European standards.

EATING OUT Dakar offers a fantastic assortment of cuisines, from across the globe or across the continent. Italy, India, Argentina, Ethiopia, China, Korea, Morocco and Lebanon are all well-represented. Your second-best place for food is Saint-Louis, with an also-fashionable, albeit much smaller, restaurant scene. The Senegalese, like the French, take their food quite seriously, and standards of cuisine at smarter restaurants (where a meal will typically run you 3,500–8,000F) are reliably refined. Local canteens will dish up satisfying simpler meals for 1,500–3,000F.

No matter where you go, local restaurants will be dishing up plates of Senegalese standards like *thieboudienne*, *thiébou yapp*, *mafé*, or *yassa poulet/ poisson*, and for quicker eats, Middle Eastern kebabs, *chawarma* and *fattayah*s are relished by locals and visitors alike. *Dibiterie* remains a late-night favourite, and French-inspired staples like *steak-frites* and brochettes are everywhere too, but they're typically found at places a few notches classier than the aforementioned *dibi*. Note that **plat du jour** indicates the daily special, while *le menu* or *menu du jour* will be a fixed-course meal, usually consisting of a starter, main course and dessert. Depending on where you are, looking for food outside of standard mealtimes can result in a seemingly interminable wait. Breakfast is usually taken from early- to mid-morning, lunch between noon and 15.00 at the very latest, and a late dinner from 20.00 to 23.00.

COOKING FOR YOURSELF If you tire of the restaurant scene, Senegal offers reasonably good opportunities for self-caterers. Supermarkets in Dakar stock almost anything that you'd find at a similar store in Europe or North America, albeit at a premium. In the rest of the country, any major centre will have a shop stocking basics like pasta, rice, biscuits, frozen meats, tea, instant coffee and a variety of snacks, but you'll have more trouble getting dairy, cheese, yogurt and the like.

Fruit and veg options sold in the market are eminently affordable, but vary depending on the season and the town; avocados rarely seem to make it north of Casamance or Kédougou, for instance. Taking seasonal variation into account, there's still usually a regular enough supply of basics like tomatoes, potatoes, carrots, cabbage, onions, bananas and peppers to be found, with welcome additions like coconuts, pineapples and mangoes making an appearance in season.

DRINKS The usual varieties of soft drinks (Coke, Fanta and local brand La Gazelle) are cheaply available almost everywhere. Tap water is generally regarded as unsafe to drink, so most travellers understandably opt for bottled water. The *sachet* bags of water sold everywhere are purified and safe to drink, and at 50F for 500ml, way cheaper than their bottled cousins, also available everywhere and often referred to by the most common brand name, Kirène. Commercially bottled juices are also widely available, often under the brand name Pressea. Locally made fruit juices are delicious (if a bit sugary), and usually sold in reused bottles or frozen into baggie-sized ice pops; either may contain water, so be aware or ask.

Alcohol is widely available but, given that most Senegalese are observant Muslims, drinking isn't a core element of Senegalese social life. Beer is brewed and bottled locally, while wines are imported from either Europe or South Africa, with a good selection available at larger supermarkets.

PUBLIC HOLIDAYS AND EVENTS

Senegal officially celebrates a combination of Islamic, Christian and secular holidays, and government offices and most businesses will be closed on these days.

Senegal also is host to more than its fair share of annual festivals, which are listed in their relevant chapters.

FIXED HOLIDAYS

1 January	New Year's Day
4 April	Independence Day
1 May	Labour Day
15 August	Assumption Day
25 December	Christmas Day

ROTATING HOLIDAYS Note that Islamic holidays are based on the lunar *Hijri* calendar, and the dates below marked with a * are predictions. Islamic holidays usually shift by about 11 days annually when compared with the Gregorian calendar, but this can move around by a day or two depending on when the moon officially kicking off the holiday is sighted.

	2015	2016	2017	2018
Maouloud (Mawlid)*	2 Jan	11 Dec	30 Nov	19 Nov
Easter Monday (Pâques)	6 Apr	28 Mar	17 Apr	2 Apr
Ascension	14 May	5 May	25 May	10 May
Pentecost/Whit Monday	25 May	16 May	5 Jun	21 May
Korité (Eid al-Fitr)*	17 Jul	6 Jul	25 Jun	15 Jun
Tabaski (Eid al-Adha)*	23 Sep	11 Sep	1 Sep	21 Aug
Tamkharit (Ashura)*	23 Oct	11 Oct	30 Sep	20 Sep
Grand Magal*	1 Dec	19 Nov	8 Nov	29 Oct

Celebrated for decades, but only declared a public holiday in 2013, the Grand Magal is when over a million Mouride pilgrims from Senegal and beyond descend on Touba to commemorate the anniversary of Ahmadou Bamba's exile to Gabon. It's an enormous movement of people and, holiday or not, almost 10% of the country makes their way to Touba for it.

Other large religious pilgrimages in Senegal include the commemoration of Pentecost (descent of the Holy Spirit on to the apostles) in Popenguine, and the *Gamou* in Tivouane marking Maouloud (the birth of the Prophet Muhammad).

SHOPPING

Late *mbalax* star Ndongo Lo had a smash hit in the 2000's with *Marchands ambulants* (roving merchants), and even beyond its infectious beat, it's easy to see why. Countless Senegalese earn their living as petty traders, hawking just about anything you could imagine on the streets or in the markets, and commerce, great or small, is something of a national sport.

Dakar is by far your best option for shopping, but most basic goods (toiletries, medicines, batteries, etc) can be purchased at smaller supermarkets or pharmacies in towns throughout the country. Pharmacies stay open all night for emergencies in a rotational system. If you show up at one that's closed, look for a posted notice marked *pharmacie de garde*, which will indicate the nearest all-night drugstore.

As art and handicrafts go, Senegal is home to many talented artisans working in a huge variety of mediums, whom we've tried to highlight when their workshops or galleries merit special mention. An excellent first stop is Dakar's Village des Arts (see page 118), where you'll find some of the country's most talented visual artists working in painting, carving, sculpture, ceramics, metalwork, *sous-verre* (see pages 31–2), batik and even photographic and video art. Masks, jewellery, leatherwork, beading and woven goods are also produced throughout Senegal. Senegal's musical tradition is well represented with markets full of tapes and CDs, though trading mp3s is becoming more and more in vogue by the day. If you're interested in purchasing a musical instrument, The Kora Workshop in Kafountine (see page 323) would be a good place to start. And of course there will never be a shortage of ostentatious wax print fabrics to buy, nor one of stylish dressmakers and tailors to get you measured up and decked out in the latest styles. They're also immensely talented at copying existing garments, so you can always get your favourite shirt re-made in an African print!

ARTS AND ENTERTAINMENT

There's perhaps no finer destination in West Africa for purveyors of the arts than Senegal, and the music scene has produced luminaries recognised the world over. To a certain extent, this cornucopia of cultural expression can be traced back to the first president, Léopold Sédar Senghor, whose aggressive promotion of the arts led to the creation of dozens of dance troupes, artist's workshops, theatres and concert venues around the country (all listed in the relevant chapters). Today that funding has for the most part long since dried up, but the passion for the creative arts among the Senegalese remains wholly undiminished.

As with most things in Senegal, the action is mostly on the coast and, while most major cities will have a club or two and perhaps a gallery, Dakar (and to a lesser extent Saint-Louis) is really the place to be to take in all the music and arts Senegal has on offer. There are a number of excellent museums as well, but the privately owned galleries often feature an equally impressive selection of paintings, carvings and more. You could easily spend several days touring the galleries of Dakar and going out for a live show every single night, though when you'd sleep is another question entirely. As a general rule of thumb, concerts here start in the late evening (towards 23.00) and go on late into the night, and the streets around Dakar's nightclubs are inevitably packed with punters squinting in the sunlight when the band finally finish their umpteenth encore and take their final bow.

MEDIA AND COMMUNICATIONS

NEWSPAPERS AND MAGAZINES Senegal is known for its boisterous and critical press, and was ranked 62nd out of 180 countries in Reporters Without Borders' 2014 Press Freedom Index, placing it in the top ten African countries overall and above a number of EU states including Greece, Hungary, Croatia and Bulgaria. (The Gambia, by comparison, comes in at an unenviable 155th place, squarely in the bottom ten African countries.) A healthy complement of private dailies are published, including *Le Soleil*, *Le Quotidien*, *Sud Quotidien*, *L'Observateur* and *Wal Fadjri L'Aurore*, but they'll only be of interest if you read some French. Senegalese weeklies include *Nouvel Horizon*, *Le Témoin* and the appropriately named *Week-End Magazine*, while *Thiof*, *Icône* and *Lissa* are glossy fashion mags published every month. Unfortunately for Anglophones, these too are published exclusively in French. A slim assortment of international and English-language papers are sometimes available at upmarket hotels in Dakar, while most locations of Supermarché Casino and the Librairie aux 4 Vents in Sea Plaza Mall (\ *33 825 5514; www.librairie4vents.com*) also stock a handful of English-language magazines.

INTERNET AND EMAIL Wi-Fi is well on its way towards becoming ubiquitous in Senegal, at least in the cities. All but the cheapest of hotels now offer it, though whether or not it's working at a given time is not exactly guaranteed. It's a similar story with restaurants, and many tourist-oriented places have free Wi-Fi for customers. Internet cafés (*télécentres*) are widely available in larger towns, though less than they were a few years ago with the growing proliferation of Wi-Fi and mobile internet.

TELEPHONE The country code is 221. Mobile service is excellent throughout Senegal, and there are three providers to choose from. The French multinational Orange is the most popular (numbers starting with 77), followed by Tigo (numbers starting with 76) and Expresso (numbers starting with 70). Fixed lines are also very reliable by African standards, and use prefixes 33 or 30.

Provisioning your Smartphone with mobile data is another good way to stay connected, and 3G service is available throughout the country. Note that data provisioning is not simply topping up with call credit, but another step to be taken afterwards. Simple call credit (known as *ceddo*), purchased on scratch cards or sent from phone to phone, can also be used for data if you don't subsequently purchase a data bundle with this credit, but at considerably higher rates. Using Orange, dial #1234# to see what types of data bundles (eg: 2,000F for 500 megabytes/seven days; 5,000F for 1 gigabyte/30 days, etc) are available. If it all seems a bit complicated, any of the three providers will set this up for you at one of their bureaux.

The proliferation of mobile phones in Senegal means that many establishments don't bother with fixed-line phones anymore. Unfortunately, mobile numbers tend to be considerably more fluid than their fixed counterparts due to lost handsets, changing service providers, or even simply the receptionist moving on to another job and carrying his or her number with them when they leave. Because of this we've included both fixed and mobile numbers when available, and readers are invited to alert us to any changes they find by emailing e info@bradtguides.com or tweeting us using @BradtGuides. Any updates will be posted at www.bradtupdates.com/senegal.

POST The Senegalese Postal Service, *La Poste* (*www.laposte.sn*), is reasonably reliable and has hundreds of agencies around the country, though valuables would be better off with a courier service like DHL. Postcards cost 500/550F to Europe/ North America and take a few weeks.

RADIO AND TELEVISION Many hotels subscribe to the French Canal+/Canalsat satellite bouquet, which, not surprisingly, offers nearly all programming in French, though you'll occasionally be able to get BBC, CNN, or France24 in English. The national broadcaster, *Radiodiffusion Television Senegalaise* (RTS), operates TV and radio services throughout the country, along with a handful of private TV broadcasters such as RDV, 2S TV and TFM. Radio Nostalgie, Sud FM and Dunyaa FM are just a few of the dozens of private radio stations in Dakar and elsewhere. Depending on the station and show, broadcasts may be in French, Wolof, Pulaar (Fula), Diola, Mandinka, Serer or even Arabic. There's precious little English found on the dial, but BBC World Service is available on 105.6FM in Dakar.

PHOTOGRAPHY

Generally speaking, Senegal is a welcoming destination for photographers, but it pays to bear in mind at least a couple of tips. Attitudes towards photography are for the most part quite open, particularly in a place like Dakar but, regardless of where in the country you are, you should always ask your subjects' permission. This is especially true in the north and central regions of the country, where local attitudes are considerably more conservative.

The weather can also conspire to make a photographer's life difficult in Senegal, depending on the time of year you visit. Unfortunately, the main tourist season and the *harmattan* season, from November to March, broadly overlap. This means that the *harmattan* tradewinds that blow copious amounts of Saharan dust over the entirety of West Africa from November to March can sometimes conspire to leave the skies in your photos a dull, soupy grey rather than a bright, sparkling blue. Conditions vary, however, and there's still plenty of opportunity to put together some worthwhile shots. With this much dust in the air it does pay to keep your equipment in a sealed bag, though.

CULTURAL ETIQUETTE

The Senegalese have a well-deserved reputation for tolerance and, while this is often invoked as witness to the extraordinarily harmonious relations between religious faiths in Senegal, it could equally be applied to their attitudes towards foreigners. Known as the 'land of *teranga*', which means 'hospitality' in Wolof, welcoming guests is considered a sacred duty here, and don't be surprised when you're invited to more meals with total strangers than you could possibly eat in a day. It's not impolite to accept, should you think you'll genuinely spend a bit of time with that person, but it's equally acceptable to politely decline, should you rather continue on your way.

Thus the Senegalese are quite a forgiving bunch, and don't typically take offence at the foibles and mildly inappropriate behaviour Westerners may unknowingly commit. That being said, ultimately it is a conservative, religious society, so bear in mind that behaviour that would go completely unnoticed in Europe or North America may often be inappropriate in Senegal. Visible drunkenness and public displays of affection (for opposite- and certainly same-sex couples) are definitely unwelcome, and if the conversation should turn to religion you may find it easier to categorise yourself as Christian rather than Atheist or Agnostic, whatever your beliefs may be.

Greetings are hugely important, and just launching into conversation or asking someone questions without first taking the time to ask about their wellbeing (and usually the wellbeing of their mother, father, sister, brother, cousin, aunt, uncle and neighbour as well) is considered rude. This rule applies everywhere, including in shops, restaurants and on the street, and will usually take the form of a quick succession of inquiries and assurances that the people in question are fine (see box, *Wolof Courtesies*, page 67).

While it's rather uncommon, it's possible you'll meet someone who chooses not to shake hands with members of the opposite sex; a hand on your heart and nod of the head does the job nicely in these situations.

Issues of ethnicity are not particularly fraught in Senegal (that famed tolerance again), and it's usually OK to inquire about someone's language and background. Serers and Toucouleurs are even bound by a generations-old *cousinage* or 'joking relationship', obliging them to consider each other as extended family and to good-naturedly tease one another when they meet.

INVESTING IN SENEGAL

Senegal's official investment promotion agency, known by the rather cryptic acronym APIX (Promotion des Investissements et Grands Travaux) (*52–54 Rue*

Tim Johnson

In the Senegalese cultural context, greetings and courtesies are the best way to show someone respect, and the better you learn them, the easier time you will have here. Below are a few of the most commonly used Wolof greetings, which will invariably be warmly appreciated if you give them a try too.

Peace be upon on you	*Asalaa Maalekum*
Peace with you also	*Maalekum Salaam*
Spend the day in peace	*Nu yendu ak jamm ak salam*
How are you	*Nanga def?*
I'm fine, thank you	*Maangi fi rekk, jërëjëf*
How (where) is your family?	*Ana waa kër gui*
They are here (fine)	*Nungiy fii*

Mohamed V, Dakar; ☎ 33 849 05 55; e infos@apix.sn; *www.investinsenegal.com*) bills itself as a one-stop shop for assistance in acquiring the requisite permits and other steps involved in registering a business in Senegal.

TRAVELLING POSITIVELY

Whether or not your aim in travelling is to participate in charitable work or not, your presence in Senegal is already a net benefit for the economy and, with some intentionality behind how you spend your money, your visit can be of value to people here long after you leave. As much as possible, try to direct your spending to locally owned businesses – this could mean anything from hotels and restaurants to guides and transport. When you give your guide a fair tip, hire someone to take you on an excursion or eat at a local restaurant, you're providing much-needed employment and income; if people can make a living from legitimate employment in tourism, it encourages the further development of the sector and mitigates against some of the negatives that often engenders it, thus encouraging positive attitudes towards tourism overall. (Though attitudes to tourism in Senegal tend to be quite welcoming as it is.)

If you'd like to get involved further, or perhaps even dedicate some of your time in Senegal as a volunteer, there are a number of ways to do this. There are several locally-run NGOs working in various capacities around Senegal that accept the assistance of short-term international volunteers. These include **Maison de la Gare** (*www.mdgsl. com*) in Saint-Louis and **Empire des Enfants** (*www.empiredesenfants.com*) in Dakar, both of which offer opportunities for travellers to volunteer their time on a short- or long-term basis with *talibé* (see box, pages 196–7) children in those cities. In the realms of sport and education, **SenExperience+** (*www.senexperienceplus.com*) offers a number of programmes in Casamance, the Petite Côte and Dakar.

For dedicated volunteering trips and medium- to long-term positions, Senegal is among the most popular destinations in West Africa, and a number of different outfits offer positions ranging from two weeks to two years. Organisations work in everything from education to agriculture, and **Global Leadership Adventures** (*www.experiencegla. com*), **Projects Abroad** (*www.projects-abroad.org*), **International Voluntary Service** (*www.ivsgb.org*) and **Service Volontaire International** (*www.servicevolontaire.org*) all

ON ATTAYA

From Squirting Milk at Chameleons *(Eye Books, 2015; www.eye-books.com) by Simon Fenton*

One tradition that does perhaps link the English and the Senegalese is their love of tea, although I'm not fond of either its British or African incarnation. The local tea is taken as incredibly strong shots, like a tea version of an espresso. Often I'll bump into a friend sitting by the roadside taking part in the tradition that happens all over the Sahel. Boys and men will be hunched around a small, chipped enamel teapot, which is perched on a couple of lumps of charcoal.

Attaya, the local tea, is more than a drink. The process of making and drinking takes an hour or three and is time for chat, gossip and discussing the football. Everybody tells me that it is the drink of Africa, although the tea itself is Chinese and the process imported by Arabs from the North.

Green tea is added to a small enamel pot with some water and an equal amount of sugar. Once boiling, a shot glass is filled from the pot from a height of at least a foot, often two feet. I've only ever see one person miss. That was me. The tea is poured back and forth between the glass and the pot many times before being returned to the fire for a while, then the shot glass refilled, again from a great height. The last time I watched I counted 30 pours, which can take an hour or more. The tea is dark green and frothy. You can almost see the tannin.

The pot is refilled with water and another glass of sugar, using the same tea leaves, and the entire process is repeated. Then it is repeated again for the third and final serving, by which time the tea leaves are spent.

The first cup is strong and bitter. This is for death. The second cup is sweeter but still strong. This is for life. The third and final cup is very sweet and the one my palate can stand. This one's for love.

offer medium- to long-term volunteer positions in Senegal. If you have an interest in farming, **Development In Gardening** (*www.reaplifedig.org*) is active here as well.

For longer assignments, **Tostan** (*www.tostan.org*) hires volunteers for a one-year commitment; and with over 250 volunteers, Senegal is also home to one of the largest **Peace Corps** (*www.peacecorps.gov*) programmes in the world, though their two-year volunteer positions are only open to American citizens.

Finally, the ripple effect of your trip doesn't just continue in Senegal after you've left, but back in your home country as well. Even if you've just been in Senegal for a week, you can do great good by simply talking openly and honestly with friends at home about your trip. Misconceptions and stereotypes about Africa abound, and you can help challenge these! Sharing stories about the beauty you encountered and the welcome you received – and even the problems you had – is one of the most powerful ways of changing the dominant narrative that so often misrepresents the reality of life in Africa. You don't have to paint a perfect picture, only an honest one, and your friends may be the next ones booking a trip.

SENEGAL ONLINE

For additional online content, articles, photos and more on Senegal, why not visit www.bradtguides.com/senegal.

3

Health

with Dr Felicity Nicholson

Before the inevitable terror inspired by reading the health section sets in, it should be made quite clear that healthcare options in Senegal are among, if not the best in West Africa. There are certain health issues inherent to tropical climates, but with reasonable precautions – i.e. malaria prophylaxis – your chances of a serious incident are minute. The cast of African bogeymen so often trotted out by jittery family and friends to dissuade you from your trip (or at least question your logic) are on the whole irrelevant in Senegal, if not entirely fictitious. The one imported case of Ebola was effectively dealt with in 2014, the military are admirably professional, and if you manage to see a predator in Niokolo-Koba National park, consider yourself very lucky. As in much of Africa, road travel presents the greatest risk to life and limb you're likely to face. Medical care in regional capitals is adequate, but for anything serious Dakar is very much the place to be. As with everything in Senegal, French is the operating language, but given the education required of doctors, it's not unusual to find one who has studied some English as well. Doctor's visits, lab fees, and malaria tests are all cheap – don't hesitate to get checked out on the basis of cost. The US Embassy in Dakar maintains an updated list of recommended doctors, their specialisations, and the languages they speak at http://dakar.usembassy.gov/service/living-in-senegal-and-guinea-bissau/medical-care-in-senegal.html.

PREPARATIONS

Sensible preparation will go a long way to ensuring your trip goes smoothly. Particularly for first-time visitors to Africa, this includes a visit to a travel clinic to discuss matters such as vaccinations and malaria prevention. The Bradt website now carries an African health section (*http://www.bradtguides.com/articles/africa-health-updates/*) to help travellers prepare for their African trip, elaborating on the information below, but the following points are worth emphasising:

- Don't travel without comprehensive medical travel insurance that will fly you home in an emergency.
- Make sure all your immunisations are up to date. A yellow-fever vaccination is advised and you may need to show proof of immunisation upon entry if you are entering Senegal from another yellow-fever-endemic area. A valid yellow-fever vaccination certificate (within the preceding ten years) will then be required on entry. If the vaccine is not suitable for you then you would be wise not to travel, as West Africa has the highest prevalence of yellow fever and there is around a 50% mortality rate. It's also unwise to travel in the tropics without being up-to-date on tetanus, polio and diphtheria (now given as an all-in-one vaccine, Revaxis), hepatitis A and typhoid. Immunisation

against rabies, meningitis, hepatitis B and possibly tuberculosis (TB) may also be recommended.

- The biggest health threat is malaria. There is no vaccine against this mosquito-borne disease, but a variety of preventative drugs is available, including mefloquine, atovaquone/proguanil (Malarone) and the antibiotic doxycycline. Malarone and doxycycline need be started only two days before entering Senegal, but mefloquine should be started two to three weeks before. Doxycycline and mefloquine need to be taken for four weeks after the trip and Malarone for seven days. It is as important to complete the course as it is to take it before and during the trip. The most suitable choice of drug varies depending on the individual and the country they are visiting, so visit your GP or a specialist travel clinic for medical advice. If you will be spending a long time in Africa, and expect to visit remote areas, be aware that no preventative drug is 100% effective, so carry a cure too. It is also worth noting that no homeopathic prophylactic for malaria exists, nor can any traveller acquire effective resistance to malaria. Those who don't make use of preventative drugs risk their life in a manner that is both foolish and unnecessary.
- Though advised for everyone, a pre-exposure course of rabies vaccination, involving three doses taken over a minimum of 21 days, is particularly important if you intend to have contact with animals, or are likely to be 24 hours away from medical help. If you have not had this then exercise serious caution around stray animals, as you'll need to head for Dakar immediately and possibly evacuate for the necessary treatment.
- Anybody travelling away from major centres should carry a personal first-aid kit. Contents might include a good drying antiseptic (eg: iodine or potassium permanganate), Band-Aids, sun cream, insect repellent, aspirin or paracetamol, antifungal cream (eg: Canesten), ciprofloxacin or norfloxacin (for severe diarrhoea), antibiotic eye drops, tweezers, condoms or femidoms, a digital thermometer and a needle-and-syringe kit with accompanying letter from a healthcare professional.
- Bring any drugs or devices relating to known medical conditions with you. That applies both to those who are on medication prior to departure, and those who are, for instance, allergic to bee stings or are prone to attacks of asthma. Always check with the country website to identify any restricted medications. Carry a copy of your prescription and a letter from your GP explaining why you need the medication.
- Prolonged immobility on long-haul flights can result in deep vein thrombosis (DVT), which can be dangerous if the clot travels to the lungs to cause pulmonary embolus. The risk increases with age, and is higher in obese or pregnant travellers, heavy smokers, those taller than 6ft/1.8m or shorter than 5ft/1.5m, and anybody with a history of clots, recent major operation or varicose veins surgery, cancer, a stroke or heart disease. If any of these criteria apply, consult a doctor before you travel.

TRAVEL CLINICS AND HEALTH INFORMATION A full list of current travel clinic websites worldwide is available on www.istm.org. For other journey preparation information, consult www.nathnac.org/ds/map_world.aspx (UK) or http://wwwnc.cdc.gov/travel/ (US). Information about various medications may be found on www.netdoctor.co.uk/travel. All advice found online should be used in conjunction with expert advice received prior to or during travel.

POTENTIAL MEDICAL PROBLEMS

MALARIA This potentially fatal disease is widespread in low-lying tropical parts of Africa, a category that includes all of Senegal, and while the risk of transmission is highest in the rainy season, it is present throughout the year. Since no malaria prophylactic is 100% effective, one should take all reasonable precautions against being bitten by the nocturnal Anopheles mosquitoes that transmit the disease (see box, page 73). Malaria usually manifests within two weeks of transmission, but it can be as little as seven days and anything up to a year. Any fever occurring after seven days should be considered as malaria until proven otherwise. Symptoms typically include a rapid rise in temperature (over 38°C), and any combination of a headache, flu-like aches and pains, a general sense of disorientation, and possibly even nausea and diarrhoea. The earlier malaria is detected, the better it usually responds to treatment. So if you display possible symptoms, get to a doctor or clinic immediately (in the UK, go to accident and emergency and say that you have been to Africa). A simple test, available at even the most rural clinic in Africa, is usually adequate to determine whether you have malaria. You need three negative tests to be sure it is not the disease. And while experts differ on the question of self-diagnosis and self-treatment, the reality is that if you think you have malaria and are not within easy reach of a doctor, it would be wisest to start treatment.

TRAVELLERS' DIARRHOEA Many visitors to unfamiliar destinations suffer a dose of travellers' diarrhoea, usually as result of imbibing contaminated food or water. Rule one in avoiding diarrhoea and other sanitation-related diseases is to wash your hands regularly, particularly before snacks and meals. As for what food you can safely eat, a useful maxim is: PEEL IT, BOIL IT, COOK IT OR FORGET IT. This means that fruit you have washed and peeled yourself should be safe, as should hot cooked foods. However, raw foods, cold cooked foods, salads, fruit salads prepared by others, ice cream and ice are all risky. It is rarer to get sick from drinking contaminated water but it happens, so stick to bottled water, which is widely available. If you suffer a bout of diarrhoea, it is dehydration that makes you feel awful, so drink lots of water and other clear fluids. These can be infused with sachets of oral rehydration salts, though any dilute mixture of sugar and salt in water will do you good, for instance a bottled soda with a pinch of salt. If diarrhoea persists beyond a couple of days, it may be a symptom of a more serious sanitation-related illness (typhoid, cholera, hepatitis, dysentery, worms, etc), so get to a doctor. If the diarrhoea is greasy and bulky, and is accompanied by sulphurous (eggy) burps, one likely cause is giardia, which is best treated with tinidazole (four x 500mg in one dose, repeated seven days later if symptoms persist).

BILHARZIA Also known as schistosomiasis, bilharzia is an unpleasant parasitic disease transmitted by freshwater snails most often associated with reedy shores where there is lots of water weed. It cannot be caught in hotel swimming pools or the ocean, but should be assumed to be present in any freshwater river pond, lake or similar habitat, even those advertised as 'bilharzia free'. The most risky shores will be within 200m of villages or other places where infected people use water, wash clothes, etc. Ideally, however, you should avoid swimming in any fresh water other than an artificial pool. If you do swim, you'll reduce the risk by applying DEET insect repellent first, staying in the water for under ten minutes, and drying off vigorously with a towel. Bilharzia is often asymptomatic in its early stages, but some people experience an intense immune reaction, including fever, cough, abdominal pain and an itching rash, around four to six weeks after infection. Later symptoms vary but often include a general feeling of tiredness and lethargy. Bilharzia is difficult to diagnose, but it can be tested for at specialist travel clinics, ideally at least six weeks after likely exposure. Fortunately, it is easy to treat at present with a one-day course of praziquantel. Dosage depends on your weight, and it's available and inexpensive at most pharmacies in Senegal (but *not* in the UK due to regulatory restrictions). Given that bilharzia is often asymptomatic, it could be wise to buy a course of praziquantel to take upon your return if you think you may have been exposed.

MENINGITIS This nasty disease can kill within hours of the appearance of initial symptoms, typically a combination of a blinding headache (light sensitivity), blotchy rash and high fever. Outbreaks tend to be localised and are usually reported in newspapers. Fortunately, immunisation with meningitis ACWY vaccine (eg: Menveo, Nimenrix) protects against the most serious bacterial form of meningitis. Nevertheless, other less serious forms exist which are usually viral, but any severe headache and fever – possibly also symptomatic of typhoid or malaria – should be sufficient cause to visit a doctor immediately.

RABIES This deadly disease can be carried by any mammal and is usually transmitted to humans via a bite or a scratch that breaks the skin. In particular, beware of village dogs and monkeys habituated to people, but assume that any mammal that bites or scratches you (or even licks an open wound) might be rabid even if it looks healthy. First, scrub the wound with soap under a running tap for a good 10–15 minutes, or while pouring water from a jug, then pour on a strong iodine or alcohol solution, which will guard against infections and might reduce the risk of the rabies virus entering the body. Whether or not you underwent pre-exposure vaccination, it is vital to obtain post-exposure prophylaxis as soon as possible after the incident. You should head immediately for the Institut Pasteur in Dakar (see page 120); they will advise you if they can provide the full post-exposure treatment (whether or not you've had a pre-exposure course of the vaccine) or if you'll have to evacuate straight away. Death from rabies is probably one of the worst ways to go, and once you show symptoms it is too late to do anything – the mortality rate is 100%.

TETANUS Tetanus is caught through deep dirty wounds, including animal bites, so ensure that such wounds are thoroughly cleaned. Immunisation protects for ten years, provided that you don't have an overwhelming number of tetanus bacteria on board. If you haven't had a tetanus shot in ten years, or you are unsure, get a booster immediately.

HIV/AIDS Rates of HIV/AIDS infection are high in most parts of Africa, and other sexually transmitted diseases are rife. Condoms (or femidoms) greatly reduce the risk of transmission.

TICK BITES Ticks in Africa are not the rampant disease transmitters that they are in the Americas, but they may spread tick-bite fever along with a few dangerous rarities. They should ideally be removed complete as soon as possible to reduce the chance of infection. The best way to do this is to grasp the tick with your finger nails as close to your body as possible, and pull it away steadily and firmly at right angles to your skin (do not jerk or twist it). If possible douse the wound with alcohol (any spirit will do) or iodine. If you are travelling with small children, remember to check their heads, and particularly behind the ears, for ticks. Spreading redness around the bite and/or fever and/or aching joints after a tick bite imply that you have an infection that requires antibiotic treatment, so seek advice.

SKIN INFECTIONS Any mosquito bite or small nick is an opportunity for a skin infection in warm humid climates, so clean and cover the slightest wound in a good drying antiseptic such as dilute iodine, potassium permanganate or crystal (or gentian) violet. Prickly heat, most likely to be contracted at the humid coast, is a fine pimply rash that can be alleviated by cool showers, dabbing (not rubbing) dry and talc, and sleeping naked under a fan or in an air-conditioned room. Fungal infections also get a hold easily in hot moist climates, so wear 100%-cotton socks and underwear and shower frequently.

EYE PROBLEMS Bacterial conjunctivitis (pink eye) is a common infection in Africa, particularly for contact-lens wearers. Symptoms are sore, gritty eyelids that often stick closed in the morning. They will need treatment with antibiotic drops or ointment. Lesser eye irritation should settle with bathing in salt water and keeping the eyes shaded. If an insect flies into your eye, extract it with great care, ensuring you do not crush or damage it, otherwise you may get a nastily inflamed eye from toxins secreted by the creature.

SUNSTROKE AND DEHYDRATION Overexposure to the sun can lead to short-term sunburn or sunstroke, and increases the long-term risk of skin cancer. Wear a T-shirt and waterproof sunscreen when swimming. On safari or walking in the direct sun, cover up with long, loose clothes, wear a hat and use sunscreen. The glare and the dust can be hard on the eyes, so bring UV-protecting sunglasses. A less direct effect of the tropical heat is dehydration, so drink more fluids than you would at home.

AVOIDING MOSQUITO AND INSECT BITES

The Anopheles mosquitoes that spread malaria are active at dusk and after dark. Most bites can thus be avoided by covering up at night. This means donning a long-sleeved shirt, trousers and socks from around 30 minutes before dusk until you retire to bed, and applying a DEET-based insect repellent to any exposed flesh. It is best to sleep under a net, or in an air-conditioned room, though burning a mosquito coil and/or sleeping under a fan will also reduce (though not entirely eliminate) bites. Travel clinics usually sell a good range of nets and repellents, as well as Permethrin treatment kits, which will render even the tattiest net a lot more protective, and helps prevent mosquitoes from biting through a net when you roll against it. These measures will also do much to reduce exposure to other nocturnal biters. Bear in mind, too, that most flying insects are attracted to light: leaving a lamp standing near a tent opening or a light on in a poorly screened hotel room will greatly increase the insect presence in your sleeping quarters. It is also advisable to think about avoiding bites when walking in the countryside by day, especially in wetland habitats, which often teem with diurnal mosquitoes. Wear a long loose shirt and trousers, preferably 100% cotton, as well as proper walking or hiking shoes with heavy socks (the ankle is particularly vulnerable to bites), and apply a DEET-based insect repellent to any exposed skin.

OTHER INSECT-BORNE DISEASES Although malaria is the insect-borne disease that attracts the most attention in Africa, and rightly so, there are others, most too uncommon to be a significant concern to short-stay travellers. These include dengue fever and other arboviruses (spread by day-biting mosquitoes), sleeping sickness (tsetse flies) and river blindness (blackflies). Bearing this in mind, however, it is clearly sensible, and makes for a more pleasant trip, to avoid insect bites as far as possible (see box, page 73). Two nasty (though ultimately relatively harmless) flesh-eating insects associated with tropical Africa are tumbu or putsi flies, which lay eggs, often on drying laundry, that hatch and bury themselves under the skin when they come into contact with humans, and jiggers, which latch on to bare feet and set up home, usually at the side of a toenail, where they cause a painful boil-like swelling. Drying laundry indoors and wearing shoes are the best way to deter this pair of flesh-eaters. Symptoms and treatment of all these afflictions are described in greater detail on Bradt's website (*http://www.bradtguides.com/articles/africa-health-updates/*).

OTHER SAFETY CONCERNS

WILD ANIMALS Don't confuse habituation with domestication. Most wildlife in Africa is genuinely wild, and widespread species such as hippo or hyena might attack a person given the right set of circumstances. Such attacks are rare, however, and they almost always stem from a combination of poor judgement and poorer luck. A few rules of thumb: never approach potentially dangerous wildlife on foot except in the company of a trustworthy guide; never swim in lakes or rivers without first seeking local advice about the presence of crocodiles or hippos; never get between a hippo and water; and never leave food (particularly meat or fruit) in the tent where you'll sleep.

SNAKE AND OTHER BITES Snakes are very secretive and bites are a genuine rarity, but certain spiders and scorpions can also deliver nasty bites. In all cases, the risk is minimised by wearing closed shoes and trousers when walking in the bush, and watching where you put your hands and feet, especially in rocky areas or when gathering firewood. Only a small fraction of snakebites deliver enough venom to be life-threatening, but it is important to keep the victim calm and inactive, and to seek urgent medical attention.

CAR ACCIDENTS Dangerous driving is probably the biggest threat to life and limb in most parts of Africa. On a self-drive visit, drive defensively, being especially wary of stray livestock, gaping pot-holes and imbecilic or bullying overtaking manoeuvres. Many vehicles lack headlights and most local drivers are reluctant headlight-users, so avoid driving at night and pull over in heavy storms. On a chauffeured tour, don't be afraid to tell the driver to slow or calm down if you think he is too fast or reckless.

SEND US YOUR SNAPS!

We'd love to follow your adventures using our *Senegal* guide – why not send us your photos and stories via Twitter (@BradtGuides) and Instagram (@bradtguides) using the hashtag #senegal. Alternatively, you can upload your photos directly to the gallery on the Senegal destination page via our website (*www.bradtguides.com*).

Part Two

THE GUIDE

CAMP du DÉSERT

Nomad desert camp | Lompoul

Local : (+221) 77 705 56 95 - Agency : (+221) 33 860 92 93
cdd@espritdafrique.com - www.campdudesert.com

Esprit d'Afrique

GÎTE du LAC

Camp of charm | Lac Rose

Local : (+221) 77 452 83 44 - Agency : (+221) 33 860 92 93
gdl@espritdafrique.com - www.gitedulac.com

Esprit d'Afrique

4

Dakar

Pop: 1,081,222 (city); 2,956,023 (region)

A blast of humidity, a statue on a hill, and something sweet in the air. Arriving by air in Dakar is a thrill for the senses that begins the moment the cabin doors open. Just over a kilometre from the ocean, even the airport swims in ocean humidity, swaddling your aeroplane-desiccated body in its warm, pillowy grasp from your first step on to the tarmac. The enormous statue sits somewhere over your left shoulder and an ever-so-faint smell catches you by the nose. Perhaps it's what acclaimed Polish journalist Ryszard Kapuściński called 'the scent of the tropics', the 'almonds, cloves, dates and cocoa', the 'vanilla and laurel leaves, oranges and bananas, cardamom and saffron' that decorate the air and fight for supremacy with the ever-present fish odours, exhaust fumes and drainpipes of a major coastal city. Or perhaps it's just *thiouraye,* the gummy, herbal Senegalese incense burned over hot coals in every home, known equally for its ability to freshen a room after mealtimes as for its supposed seductive qualities.

And Dakar is a master of seduction indeed. A superlative African city in every sense, the dining here is as sophisticated as you'll get anywhere on the continent and the cultural calendar puts that of larger cities to shame. Drummers pound, singers wail, dancers flail and artists of all stripes brush, hammer, scrape and sew some of the most innovative works in West Africa, cheek-by-jowl with legions of hawkers, beggars and hustlers, and all of these dreamers and schemers crammed on to a tiny, windswept peninsula jutting deep into the Atlantic at the very edge of the continent. It's impossible to be more than 3km from the water at any given time, and the temperate ocean drafts will have you calling to thank your mother for making you pack a sweater.

The skyline teems with rusting satellite dishes, whirling construction cranes, improbably bent antennae, flamboyant laundry, towering minarets and thousands of seagulls keeping watch over it all. Surfers colonise the peninsula's periphery, catching waves in the traditional Lebou villages of Ngor and Yoff, while sellers dominate the interior, haggling over sticky cups of *attayah* in frenetic market passageways from Medina to HLM. And Plateau, the district where all Dakar's citizens come to rub shoulders, is a dizzying mix of high fashion and urban frenzy, where business suits and *boubous* jostle for space on the paving stones that more often resemble a geological fault than a reasonable place to walk. The cast of characters here is worthy of any epic; street traders bent double under their wares hawk bracelets and bangles to women in precise coiffures and vertiginous heels; businessmen in skinny neckties and horn-rimmed glasses stare aimlessly into their Smartphones over dripping bites of *chawarma*; and Lebanese and French expats cruise past in anonymity behind the mirror tints on their 4x4s.

All roads in Senegal do in fact lead to Dakar, and they could've hardly picked a better destination.

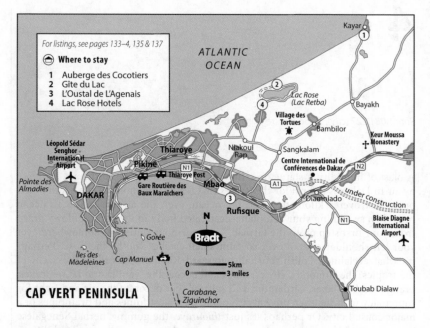

For listings, see pages 133–4, 135 & 137

Where to stay

1 Auberge des Cocotiers
2 Gîte du Lac
3 L'Oustal de L'Agenais
4 Lac Rose Hotels

ATLANTIC OCEAN

Kayar ①

Lac Rose (Lac Retba) ②
Bayakh
Village des Tortues ④
Bambilor

Léopold Sédar Senghor International Airport
Keur Moussa Monastery
Thiaroye
Niakoul Rap
Sangkalam

Pikine
N1
Thiaroye Post
Centre International de Conférences de Dakar
N2

Pointe des Almadies
DAKAR
Gare Routière des Baux Maraîchers
Mbao
A1
under construction

Diamniadio

③
Rufisque

N
Blaise Diagne International Airport

Bradt

Gorée

Îles des Madeleines
Cap Manuel

0 ——— 5km
0 ——— 3 miles

Toubab Dialaw

CAP VERT PENINSULA

Carabane, Ziguinchor

HISTORY

Prior to European contact, the Cap Vert peninsula was home to a number of Lebou fishing and farming settlements under the domination of the Cayor kingdom, which was itself a vassal of the Djolof Empire. Eventually Cayor wrested its independence from Djolof in the 15th century and, not to be outdone, the independence-minded villages of the peninsula eventually banded together under the leadership of Dial Diop and launched a 20-year rebellion against Cayor authority. The Cayor *damel* (king) eventually relented, and the tiny Lebou Republic of Cap Vert was born in 1812. It functioned as an independent hagiarchy ruled by a collection of marabouts, and kept Europeans off the peninsula until 1857.

Despite the fact that they had been fighting one another over Gorée Island just a few kilometres away for several hundred years, there was never a European settlement on the Cap Vert peninsula until the French built a fort near what is now the Place de l'Indépendance at a village called Ndakaru, eventually to become Dakar. French–Lebou relations here were relatively peaceful, particularly compared to the expansionist violence and open warfare going on inland, and, as the French presence on the peninsula grew and Dakar began to take shape, most of the Lebou villages simply remained where they were. Ngor, Yoff and Ouakam are all historical Lebou towns that were eventually surrounded by the encroaching city, making, by a pure accident of geography, one of pre-colonial Senegal's least-powerful groups into the holders of some of the most coveted real estate in the land.

With an estimated 300 residents in 1865, Dakar's significance began to be realised when it was chosen, largely because of its potential as a port, as the terminus of the Saint-Louis–Dakar railway, completed in 1886, nearly 30 years after the first French presence. A year later in 1887, Dakar was the final of the four *communes* to be recognised by the French government. All commune residents (at least nominally) enjoyed all the rights of full French citizenship, and were exempted from the forced labour and military conscription levied on the *sujets* living inland. With its recognition as a commune and the new railroad, Dakar quickly became Senegal's most important export hub for peanuts grown in the hinterlands, yet remained politically subservient to the then-capital in Saint-Louis. The French calculus changed significantly when plans for the new east–west railway were drawn up, with Dakar as the railhead for a connection all the way to Bamako, and the capital of French West Africa was relocated to Dakar in 1902, in anticipation of the railroad's completion. The last railroad spike was driven 20 years later in 1923, and by then Dakar's population had grown to 37,000.

The Medina district just north of Plateau traces its history to 1914, when panic over a cholera epidemic in the city led to mass evictions of African residents in Plateau. Their belongings were torched and they were forcibly resettled in Medina, creating Dakar's first official *quartier Africain*. In the wake of World War II, as the population continued to rise, leafier districts sprang up north of Medina, around Point E, Fann and the university. Dakar remained the capital and the most important hub of French West Africa until independence, when the breakup of the colony into eight independent countries created seven alternate power centres to compete with – most notably Abidjan in Côte d'Ivoire.

Post-independence, Dakar's importance within Senegal has only grown, as increasing numbers of upcountry Senegalese head to the big city in search of employment and opportunity. Settling in the suburbs halfway up the peninsula, these new migrant towns continue to creep their way further and further up the peninsula: a belt of shantytown suburbia absorbing anything in its path, including the once-distinct town and former *commune* of Rufisque.

By 1988, the region was home to 1,500,000 residents; 25 years later in 2013 that figure had doubled to three million, with a full 50% of Senegal's urban population and 23% of Senegalese overall living in the region, which is by far Senegal's smallest. More so than ever before, all roads in Senegal truly do lead to Dakar and, thanks to aggressive investment in Dakar's infrastructure under the last administration, those are some very fine roads indeed.

GETTING THERE AND AWAY

BY AIR See pages 39–40 for details of flights to and from Dakar, currently Senegal's only airport with international connections. As of mid 2015, all flights to Dakar were still arriving at Léopold Sédar Senghor (LSS) International Airport [94 G3] in Yoff, some 16km north of the city centre, but this will almost certainly change during the lifespan of this edition with the long-delayed opening of the new Blaise Diagne International Airport 60km away in Diass. It's not yet clear if the old airport in Yoff will be redeveloped entirely or continue to service regional flights, so be sure to double check which airport you'll be arriving at or departing from.

There's a reasonably extensive domestic network of airports in Senegal, but only a handful of them, namely Ziguinchor, Cap Skirring, Kolda Matam and Tambacounda, have scheduled passenger services, with either Senegal Airlines or Groupe Transair.

Facilities on arrival at LSS Airport are somewhat limited and, while there's no bureau de change in the airport itself, there are a few private ones in the little shops and offices outside facing the terminal. There are, however, ATMs for both Ecobank and CBAO within the building. If you need a place to hang out for a while, the first-floor restaurant-bar is open 24/7 and offers free Wi-Fi.

There is inevitably a band of hustlers in front of the airport who will try to carry your luggage, sell you an overpriced SIM card, change money or offer you some other service that you don't want or need. If you arrive and the bureaux de change are closed, you'd be much better off using one of the airport's ATMs (*guichet automatique bancaire*, occasionally GAB) than trying to change money with the people out front. Be firm in your refusals, and negotiate with the black and yellow taxi drivers directly.

Taxis have no meters, so arriving passengers can expect to be quoted wildly inflated rates, but remember that even a ride across the whole city from Plateau to *gare routière* Baux Maraîchers is only 3,500F, so you should aim to pay no more than this no matter where you're going and even less if you're headed to Ngor, Les Almadies or Yoff. (Though a small bump in prices at the airport is almost unavoidable.) To avoid the negotiations, most hotels can arrange airport pickup, or you can book a metered taxi with Les Italiens de Dakar (see page 87). See page 87 for a rough idea of standard taxi rates around Dakar, and keep in mind that all prices will go up slightly at night. If you'd rather save the cash and have some time to spare, Dakar Dem Dikk bus 8 (see box, page 86) connects LSS airport and Plateau. Note well that all of the above info is for LSS airport in Yoff, which is about 15km and, traffic depending, about 30 minutes or so from Plateau. Transport options to Dakar will change considerably with the opening of the new airport some 60km distant, so check our updates website (*www.bradtupdates.com/senegal*) for the latest.

Airlines All the airlines listed below have offices in Plateau, and several (as marked) have representation at Léopold Sédar Senghor International Airport as well. It's reasonable to assume that the Plateau offices will remain unchanged after the move to Blaise Diagne International Airport, but it's unclear exactly which airport ticket offices will migrate.

✈ **Arc en Ciel** 19 Rue Mohamed V; ☏ 33 820 2467; e arcenciel@arc.sn; www.arcenciel-aviation.com. Offers air charters around Senegal & West Africa.

✈ **Air Algerie** Place de l'Indépendance; ☏ 33 823 8081; e airalgeriedkr@orange.sn; www.airalgerie.dz

✈ **Air Burkina** [91 F2] Imm Le Goéland, Blvd Djily Mbaye; ☏ 33 822 2225/6; e Dakar@airburkina.bf; www.air-burkina.com

✈ **Air Côte d'Ivoire** [91 F2] 64 Rue Wagane Diouf; ☏ 33 889 90 70; e aircotedivoiredkr@aircotedivoire.com; www.aircotedivoire.com

✈ **Air Europa** 20 Rue Amadou Assane Ndoye; ☏ 33 821 6831; e resa.senegal@air-europa.com; www.aireuropa.com

✈ **Air France** [91 E3] 47 Av Hassan II; ☏ 33 839 7777; e mail.cto.dkr@airfrance.fr; www.airfrance.fr. Also has an office at LSS airport.

✈ **Arik Air** Imm Amsa Assurance, Rue Amadou Assane Ndoye; ☏ 33 821 7497; e customerrelationsdesk@arikair.com; www.arikair.com. Also has an office at LSS airport.

✈ **ASKY** [91 F3] Imm Dental, Rue Bérenger Féraud; ☏ 33 889 8485; e dkrkpcto@flyasky.com; www.flyasky.com

✈ **Brussels Airlines** [91 E3] Imm La Rotonde, Rue Amadou Assane Ndoye & Dr Thèse; ☏ 33 823 0460; e salessenegal@brusselsairlines.com; www.brusselsairlines.com.

✈ **Ceiba Intercontinental** 53 Rue Mousse Diop & Felix Faure; ☏ 33 821 8382; e agencia.ceibadkr@fly-ceiba.com; www.fly-ceiba.com or www.facebook.com/Official.ceiba.intercontinental

✈ **Corsair** 68 Rue Wagane Diouf & Rue Amadou Assane Ndoye; ☏ 33 889 6767; e sales@corsairfly.com; www.corsair.fr

✈ **Emirates** [91 E3] Imm La Rotonde, Rue Amadou Assane Ndoye & Dr Thèse; ☏ 33 849 5900/1018; e dakarsales@emirates.com; www.emirates.com

✈ **Ethiopian Airlines** [91 E3] Imm La Rotonde, Rue Amadou Assane Ndoye & Dr Thèse; ☏ 33 823 5552/4; e DKRCTO@ethiopianairlines.com; www.ethiopianairlines.com. Also has an office at LSS airport.

✈ **Gambia Bird** [91 F2] Imm Goéland, Blvd Djily Mbaye; ☏ 33 889 4319; e travelshop.dkr.sp@gambiabird.com; www.gambiabird.com. Also has an office at LSS airport.

✈ **Groupe Transair** [94 D2] Rte de Ngor; ☏ 33 865 2565/991 6774; e sales@groupetransair.sn;

www.groupetransair.sn or www.facebook.com/ groupetransair. Also has an office at LSS airport.

✈ **Iberia** 2 Place de l'Indépendance; ☎ 33 889 0050; e dkrfs@iberia.es; www.iberia.com

✈ **Kenya Airways** [91 E4] Imm Tamaro, 42 Rue Mohamed V; ☎ 33 823 0070; e dakar.group@ kenya-airways.com; www.kenya-airways.com

✈ **Mauritania Airlines** [91 E3] Imm La Rotonde, Rue Amadou Assane Ndoye & Dr Thèse; ☎ 33 842 4848; e dkr@mai.mr; www.mauritaniaairlines.mr

✈ **Royal Air Maroc** [91 F3] Place de l'Indépendance; ☎ 33 849 4747/9; e secretariatdakar@royalairmaroc. com; www.royalairmaroc.com

✈ **Senegal Airlines** [91 E3] Imm La Rotonde, Rue Amadou Assane Ndoye & Dr Thèse; ☎ 33 865 8881/3; m 800 800 888 (toll-free); e relations. clients@ senegalairlines.aero; www.senegalairlines. aero. Also has an office at LSS airport.

✈ **South African Airways** Imm Pinet-Laprade, 15 Blvd Djily Mbaye; ☎ 33 889 0089/869 5018; e fatoudiagne@flysaa.com; www.flysaa.com. Also has an office at LSS airport.

✈ **TACV Cabo Verde Airlines** [91 E3] 103 Rue Mousse Diop; ☎ 33 821 3968; e dakar@tacv.aero; www.flytacv.com

✈ **TAP Portugal** [91 E6] Imm Yoro Basse, 14 Ave Mandela; ☎ 33 849 4737; e cto.dkr@tap.pt; www. tapportugal.com

✈ **Tunisair** 24 Av Léopold Sédar Senghor; ☎ 33 823 1435/1723; e manager.senegal@tunisair.com. tn; www.tunisair.com

✈ **Turkish Airlines** [91 E3] Imm La Rotonde, Rue Amadou Assane Ndoye & Dr Thèse; ☎ 33 823 4444; e Dakar-sales@thy.com; www.turkishairlines.com

BY BUS AND *SEPT-PLACE* At the end of 2014, the infamous *gare routière* Pompiers was shut down and slated for redevelopment, so now all intercity transport to and from Dakar terminates at the new *gare routière* **Baux Maraîchers** [84 G3] (☎ *30 118 46 44*; m *70 842 94 49*) in Pikine. It's intentionally further from the city to alleviate traffic congestion in the centre and, while this might be annoying for travellers, the impeccable organisation here as compared with the chaos at Pompiers goes a long way towards making up for it. You can get a *sept-place* from here to any major point in the country, and it'll cost you 5,000F to Saint-Louis, 9,500F to Tambacounda, and 9,500F to Ziguinchor via the Trans-Gambia Highway.

A taxi into the city (Plateau, specifically) will run you about 3,500F, but several Dakar Dem Dikk and AFTU/Tata bus lines also serve Baux Maraîchers for a fraction of the cost. DDD lines 12, 15, and 16 all go to the Palais de Justice terminus just south of Plateau from here. Number 12 stops at Point E/University Cheikh Anta Diop and Marché Sandaga *en route*, number 15 stops at the Place de l'Indépendance, and number 16 at Marché Sandaga. Other DDD lines servicing Baux Maraîchers from around Dakar include 2, 11 214, and 231. Tata (AFTU) lines 40 and 41 both go to Terminus Petersen in Plateau, number 67 winds its way to Ouakam, and 49, 52, 54 and 65 all serve various points around the city from here.

The *petit train de banlieue* also calls here, but this would be of use only if you timed your arrival to meet the train's daily trip into Dakar, probably around 08.30.

BY CAR All Senegal's roads, both physically and metaphorically, lead to Dakar. And given Dakar's location at the far end of a peninsular bottleneck, those roads, calm in the countryside, very quickly become shuffling lines of snarled, smoke-belching traffic the closer you get to the city. This situation has been enormously improved by the recently-opened *autoroute à péage* (toll highway) that today links central Dakar with the village of Diamniadio (and eventually all 60km to the new airport), bypassing the chronically congested and not altogether charming suburbs of Pikine, Thiaroye and Rufisque. Unless you're in the market for some tissues, stickers, doo-dads, flags, fans or other tat sold by the ambulant hawkers wending their way though the paralysis, it's *absolutely* worth the few thousand CFA you'll pay for the toll road, as it can – without exaggeration – cut your time getting in and out of the city by a factor of ten.

BY TRAIN Train enthusiasts rejoice! There is still one passenger train service operating in Senegal, and it's a daily run between Dakar and Thiès, affectionately known as the *petit train bleu* (little blue train) or the *petit train de banlieue* (little suburban train). It leaves Thiès every morning at 06.55 and arrives in Dakar about two hours later, after which it turns around and heads back to Thiès at 17.15, passing through Colobane, Hann, Baux Maraîchers (Pikine), Thiaroye, Rufisque, Bargny, Sébikotane and Pout on the way. There's a first-class car with AC and soft seats for 1,250F, or second-class and benches for 500F.

BY BOAT The MVs *Aline Sitoe Diatta*, *Diambogne* and *Anguène* are operated by COSAMA (◦33 821 2900/3434; e cosama@orange.sn; www.cosamasn.com), and one of them departs the *gare maritime* [91 F1] in Dakar for Carabane and Ziguinchor every Tuesday, Thursday, Friday, and Sunday at 20.00 (see box, *Casamance by Boat*, pages 292–3, for details) Tickets often sell out, and though the addition of two new boats has alleviated this somewhat, it's wise to make the ticket office (at the *gare maritime*) your first stop when you get into town if you plan on continuing to Casamance from Dakar by boat. If your schedule is tight and you're determined to go by boat, it's sometimes possible to coordinate with a local travel agent to get your ticket in advance, although many agencies are loath to do this after clients demanded compensation for poor service or late arrivals, which the agency obviously has nothing to do with.

Dakar is also a reasonably popular port of call for yachts and other pleasure boats headed north or south along the African coast or west to Cape Verde, and La Cambuse, the resto-bar at the **Dakar Sailing Club** [84 G4] (*Cercle de la Voile de Dakar*) (CVD) (◦ 33 832 0720/4619; e cvdkr@orange.sn; www.cvdakar.e-monsite. com) on Hann beach, is the best place to check out what boats are in town and what their crew needs might be. This approach obviously requires a great deal of flexibility, and more than likely a bit of French as well.

Also based at the CVD is **Chaka Croisières** (m 77 562 9253; e stantruffaut@ gmail.com; www.chakaboat.com), who offer all kinds of customisable sailing excursions (detailed on their website) for two to eight passengers, starting around €75 per person per day. From Dakar they run short trips to the Petite Côte, and longer excursions in the Sine-Saloum Delta or inland up the Casamance and Gambia rivers. It's possible to continue on to the Bijagos Archipelago in Guinea-Bissau with them, or even to make the three-day crossing to Cape Verde for around €330 per person (which is barely more than a Dakar–Praia air ticket).

ORIENTATION

Today the urban agglomeration of Dakar covers nearly the entirety of the Cap Vert peninsula, with new and growing suburbs creeping ever further inland up the peninsula around Hann Bay towards Rufisque.

The city centre is more or less analogous with the Plateau neighbourhood at the southeast corner of the peninsula just north of Cap Manuel, with neighbourhoods and suburbs of varying characters spreading north from here. On the east side of the peninsula, the RN1 autoroute heads north from Plateau parallel to the eastern shore, passing through the largely industrial district of Hann-Bel Air on the way to the Patte d'Oie roundabout and Pikine, where the new intercity bus station (*gare routière de Baux Maraîchers*) is located.

A number of thoroughfares head up the centre of the peninsula, though they tend to be choked with traffic, so if you're transiting from Plateau to somewhere at the peninsula's north end (ie: Yoff), it's often faster to take the Route de la Corniche

Ouest. Avenue Blaise Diagne leads from Plateau through the close-packed Medina neighbourhood to University Cheikh Anta Diop and the rather leafy Point E district, continuing on as Avenue Cheikh Anta Diop until reaching the dual carriageway Voie de Dégagement Nord, which skirts the east side of the airport and connects to the northern peninsula's main east-west thoroughfare, Route de l'Aéroport. It's also possible to meander your way north through Medina, Grand Dakar, SICAP Liberté and Grand Yoff along boulevards Général de Gaulle and Dial Diop, eventually reaching either the VDN or Route de Niayes, but be ready to sit in traffic.

As the name might imply, the Route de la Corniche Ouest follows the west coast of the peninsula, passing through Fann, Fann Hock, Ouakam and Mermoz, and skirting the west side of the airport on its way up to Ngor and the Route des Almadies. The trip up here passes Dakar's five-star hotels, shopping malls, the African Renaissance Monument and some of Dakar's smartest real estate, and is the fastest way between Ngor and Plateau, two of Dakar's most-visited neighbourhoods. Thus, it's likely to be one of the most common routes used by a visitor.

Just north of the main strip of bars and clubs in Les Almadies, the Ngor roundabout is the starting point for the Route de Ngor and subsequently the Route de l'Aéroport, which generally run east from here across the north end of the peninsula through Ngor, Yoff and Parcelles Assainies – stopping at the airport, naturally – and eventually connecting to the toll road out of Dakar (or the RN1 autoroute back south to Plateau) at the Patte d'Oie roundabout.

GETTING AROUND

BUS There are no fewer than four different overlapping bus services honking and steaming their respective ways about Dakar; some are more readily comprehensible than others, but it's worth knowing what they all do if you're going to take a stab at getting around with any of them.

Before you even start to tackle the buses, know that some adept programmers recently set out to bring order to the chaos with a Dakarois public transport route planner. It's still a work in progress, but **Talibi** (*www.talibi.net*), available both online and as a Smartphone app, is a fantastic tool for anyone trying to get around Dakar. **SIG Senegal** (*www.sig-senegal.com/transport*), on the other hand, doesn't offer a route planner, but allows you to view full route maps, a feature that is so far missing from Talibi. Finally, another excellent resource is **Direction: Dakar** (*www.directiondakar.wordpress.com*), a heroic new blog by public transport expert Patricia Stichnoth. With detailed maps and route descriptions, she bravely tackles the more byzantine aspects of Dakarois public transportation and has assembled a fantastic resource for anyone planning to spend more than a few days in town without blowing their budget on taxi rides.

First, most official, and easiest to navigate among Dakar's bus options is **Dakar Dem Dikk** (↘ 33 865 1555; *www.demdikk.com*), which means 'Dakar coming and going' in Wolof and is usually abbreviated as DDD. These are the modern blue city buses with red LED signs indicating their route number and destination on the front. The stops are (usually) marked in blue with 'bus DDD' and you buy your tickets on board from the conductor sitting near the rear doors. There are a few zones, so tell him your destination and he'll charge you accordingly, but no fare will be over a few hundred CFA. Hang on to your ticket in case a controller hops aboard.

Next up are the semi-private **AFTU** (*Association de Financement des Transports Urbains*) buses, more often known simply as **Tata**, after the Indian maker of their rolling stock. Prices are similar to DDD, and these also follow a fixed route and you pay the conductor on board. Buses are white, and their route number and terminus

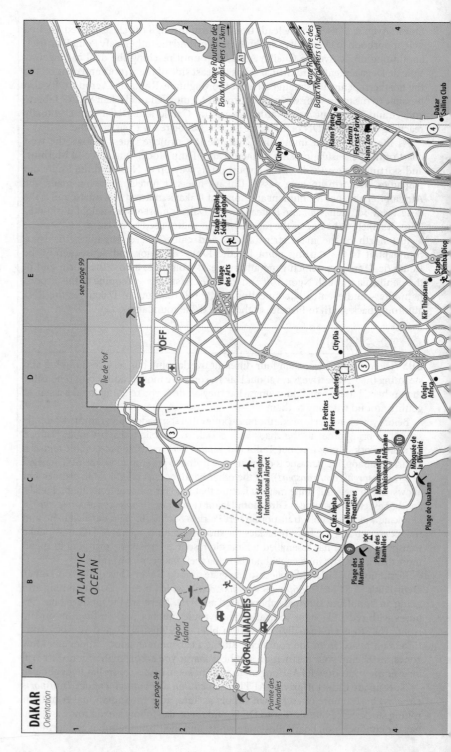

DAKAR
Orientation

ATLANTIC
OCEAN

see page 94

see page 99

Ngor Island

Pointe des
Almadies

NGOR ALMADIES

Ile de Yof

YOFF

Léopold Sédar Senghor
International Airport

Plage des
Mamelles

Phare des
Mamelles

Plage de Ouakam

Mosquée de
la Divinité

Monument de la
Renaissance Africaine

Chez Alpha

Nouvelle
Frontières

Les Petites
Pierres

Cemetery

CityPin

CityPin

Origin
Africa

Kër ThioSane

Stade
Demba Diop

Village
des Arts

Stade Léopold
Sédar Senghor

Gare Routière des
Baux Maraîchers (1.5km)

Gare Routière des
Baux Maraîchers (1.5km)

Hann Poney
Club

Hann
Forest Park

Hann Zoo

Dakar
Sailing Club

A1

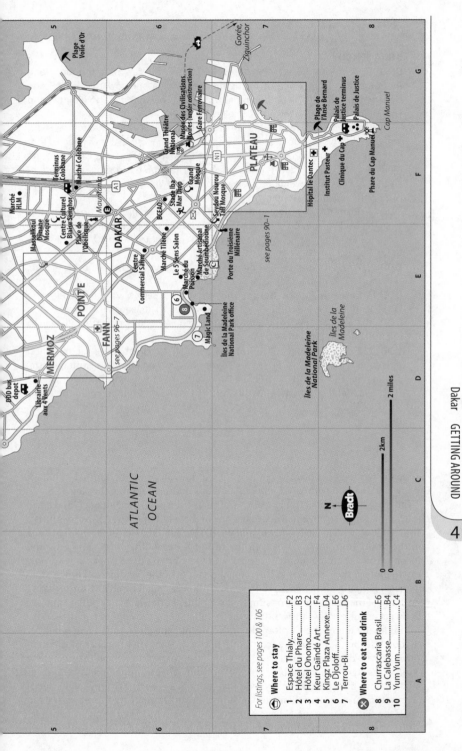

For listings, see pages 100 & 106

Where to stay

1 Espace Thialy..............F2
2 Hôtel du Phare.............B3
3 Hôtel Onomo...............C2
4 Keur Gaïndé Art..........F4
5 Kingz Plaza Annexe.....D4
6 Le Djoloff.................E6
7 Terrou-Bi.................D6

Where to eat and drink

8   Churrascaria Brasil......E6
9   La Calebasse..............B4
10 Yum Yum.................C4

2km

2 miles

ATLANTIC OCEAN

Plage Voile d'Or

Plage de l'Anse Bernard

Marché Colobane

Terminus Colobane

Marché HLM

Massalikoul Djinane Mosque

Centre Culturel Blaise Senghor

Place de l'Obélisque

DAKAR

POINT E

MERMOZ

FANN

PDD bus depot

Librairie aux 4 Vents

Mauritania

BCEAO

Stade Iba Mar Diop

Grand Mosque

Seydou Nourou Tall Mosque

Grand Théâtre National

Musée des Civilisations

Foires (under construction)

Gare Ferroviaire

PLATEAU

Hôpital le Dantec

Institut Pasteur

Clinique du Cap

Palais de Justice terminus

Palais de Justice

Phare du Cap Manuel

Cap Manuel

Marché Tilène

Le 5 Sens Salon

Marché du Poisson

Marché Artisanal de Soumbédioune

Centre Commercial Sahm

Porte du Troisième Millénaire

Magic Land

Îles de la Madeleine National Park office

Îles de la Madeleine National Park

Îles de la Madeleine

see pages 96–7

see pages 90–1

Gorée, Ziguinchor

Bradt

N

Dakar GETTING AROUND

4

85

DAKAR DEM DIKK

DDD 1: Terminus Leclerc–Parcelles Assainies You can pick this up along Av Pompidou, from where it heads though Medina and towards the Voie de Dégagement Nord (VDN), stopping at University Cheikh Anta Diop (Point E) and continuing up the VDN towards Parcelles Assainies.

DDD 8: Palais de Justice–LSS Aéroport Among the most useful lines for travellers, you can pick this one up in Plateau near the cathedral or Marché Sandaga. From here it heads north on avenues Blaise Diagne and Cheikh Anta Diop through Medina and Point E, then turning on Avenue Bourguiba towards the stadium and Village des Arts, winding its way through Yoff village north of the Route de l'Aéroport, and finally stopping at the airport terminal.

DDD 11: Terminus Lat Dior–Keur Massar For a bargain trip to Lac Rose, take this from the Lat Dior garage or Patte d'Oie roundabout to either Thiaroye Poste or its terminus at Keur Massar, from where you can connect to the AFTU/Tata 73 direct to Lac Rose.

DDD 12: Palais de Justice–Guédiawaye This line serves the new Baux Maraîchers *gare routière* via Marché Sandaga and Point E.

DDD 15: Palais de Justice–Bargny This also stops at Baux Maraîchers via Place de l'Indépendance before continuing along Hann Bay to Rufisque and beyond.

DDD 16: Palais de Justice–Malika This is another possible route from Plateau to Baux Maraîchers passing near Marché Sandaga *en route*.

DDD 232: LSS Aéroport–Baux Maraîchers An excellent route for transiting passengers, it follows the Route de l'Aéroport, VDN and Route du Front de Terre, passing the entrance to Hann Forest Park on the way to the *gare routière*.

DDD 233: Palais de Justice–Baux Maraîchers A direct run between the Palais south of Plateau and the new *gare routière*, with a stop at the HLM Marché on the way.

is usually written on a placard in the front window. Stops are signposted in blue & yellow and marked with '*arrêt minibus*' and bus numbers serving the stop.

Entering the less-penetrable realms of Dakar transport, the **Ndiaga Ndiaye** will be a familiar sight to anyone who's taken one of these hulking white Mercedes beasts (nearly all of which have *alhamdoulilah*, Arabic for 'Thanks be to god' painted on the front) from town to town in the rest of Senegal. They're equally slow and uncomfortable as their country cousins, and there are no fixed stops, so your only way to discern their route is to listen for the shouts of the conductor (known as an *apprenti*) hanging off the back. With a bit of practice, you'll be able to start picking out some of the destinations, or simply shout yours back when they pull up and see if you get an affirmative answer. Payment is collected by the *apprenti* on demand.

And finally there's the **Car Rapide**, which despite the promising name is neither car nor fast, but a Senegalese icon nonetheless, gracing any number of different souvenirs you're likely to find. Labelled with '*transport en comun*' on the side, these workhorses start out with a blue & yellow colour scheme, but by the time Dakar's painters have had their way, they look like more like they've driven straight out of a cartoon or an acid trip than from around a dusty Dakar corner. They operate in much the same way as the Ndiaga Ndiayes above, with no fixed stops and an able-bodied *apprenti* shouting himself hoarse on the back bumper.

AFTU-TATA

AFTU 3: Yoff–Terminus Petersen This heads from Yoff village to Plateau and Marché Sandaga via Ngor and Ouakam, passing Route des Almadies on the way.

AFTU 4: Yoff–Terminus Petersen Sharing its Yoff terminus with AFTU 3, this heads to Plateau and Marché Sandaga on the Route de l'Aéroport & VDN/Ave Cheikh Anta Diop through Point E.

AFTU 40: Terminus Petersen–Mbao From Petersen at the north end of Plateau, this takes the Autoroute Seydina Limamou Laye up towards the Hann Forest Park and onwards to Baux Maraîchers and Mbao.

AFTU 41: Terminus Petersen–Terminus Daroukhane Following a similar route as AFTU 40, this line also serves Baux Maraîchers before continuing on to its terminus in Guédiawaye.

AFTU 49: Ngor–Gadaye This goes from Ngor village to Baux Maraîchers (and beyond) via the Almadies roundabout, Ouakam and the African Renaissance Monument (Mamelles).

AFTU 51: Baux Maraîchers–Jaxaay If you want to get to Lac Rose and you're starting or connecting at Baux Maraîchers, take this. Keur Massar is the penultimate stop.

AFTU 56: Terminus Peterson–Keur Massar Another route to Lac Rose from Plateau.

AFTU 61: Mamelles–Keur Massar Runs from the African Renaissance Monument/ Mamelles all the way (via Ngor and Yoff) to Keur Massar, where you can catch the Tata/AFTU 73 direct to Lac Rose.

AFTU 71: Terminus Clodel (Université Cheikh Anta Diop)–Keur Massar This is another potential route to Lac Rose, starting at Terminus Clodel (outside the University's small *jardin botanique*), which can also be picked up at the rond-point UCAD in Point E.

AFTU 73: Thiaroye Poste–Lac Rose No matter where you're coming from, you'll have to transfer on to this to get to Lac Rose, most likely at either Thiaroye Poste or Keur Massar.

TAXI A never-ending fleet of black and yellow taxis prowl Dakar day and night, and it's more than likely you'll be sick of fending off over-eager drivers before you ever find yourself waiting for a lift. Burkinabe star Amadou Balaké's 1978 hit *Taximen (n'est pas gentil)* ('Taxi drivers aren't nice') hasn't been forgotten here, and you should be prepared to bargain hard or walk away. Generally speaking, a ride from Plateau up to Ngor or Yoff is about 2,500F, between Ngor and Yoff is 1,500F, and you could probably also get away with about 1,500F between Plateau and Point E. From Plateau out to Baux Maraîchers in Pikine will be 3,500F, and all prices go up at night.

If you've had enough of bargaining over space in a claptrap cab, **Les Italiens de Dakar** (\ *33 869 1212;* e *booking@dakartaxi.com; www.dakartaxi.com*) offers a 24/7 radio taxi service with air-conditioned cars and an English-speaking reservations line. Their fares are calculated by time; it's 5,000F for a ride up to 15 minutes, and 13,000F for up to an hour. This would be a good option if you're trying to arrange airport pickup, and they'll also do fixed-price trips to Lac Rose and elsewhere.

Unfortunately the female-driven **'Taxi Sisters'** (\ *33 849 5949*) project initiated under the Wade administration was small to begin with and has today all but vanished (see page 56). You can try to get in touch with the handful of ladies still on the road at the above number, or they also occasionally haunt the Novotel in Plateau.

CAR Driving in Dakar isn't exactly a walk in the park, but you're still leagues away from the madness of Lagos or Cairo, and the new motorways in town go a long, long way towards alleviating the seemingly intractable bumper-to-bumper snarls you'd be left to contend with otherwise. (The snarls are still around, mind you, but there are fewer of them.)

Car hire All of the international car hire firms listed below also have offices at Léopold Sédar Senghor International Airport.

🚗 **Avis (CFAO Equipement)** Km 2.5 Blvd du Centenaire de la Commune; ☎ 33 849 77 57; e avissenegal@cfao.com; www.avis.com

🚗 **Budget** Av Lamine Gueye & Av Faidherbe; ☎ 33 822 2513/820 2941; www.budget.com.

🚗 **Europcar** Dakar VDN & Pyrotechnique Lot; ☎ 33 869 3066/864 9509; www.europcar.com

🚗 **Hertz** [90 D4] Rue Joseph Gomis & Amadou Assane Ndoye; ☎ 33 889 81 81/820 1174; e hertz@orange.sn; www.hertz.sn

🚗 **Senecartours** [90 D4] 17 Rte de Ngor; ☎ 33 859 7777; e senecartours@senecartours.sn; www.senecartours.sn

TOURIST INFORMATION

MAPS AND GUIDES The ministry of tourism, in conjunction with Au Senegal (*www.au-senegal.com*), releases an annual ***Répertoire Touristique et Culturel*** in English and French that can be found at bookshops in Dakar and some upmarket hotels.

The **Dakar Women's Group** (*www.dakarwomensgroup.org*) puts together an English-language guide called, appropriately enough, *The Dakar Guidebook*. It's primarily aimed at English-speaking expat residents, but has a wealth of information on Dakar that would be useful for travellers too. It includes a detailed city map, proceeds go to charity, and it's available at Librairie aux 4 Vents and Chez Alpha Books.

Editions Laure Kane (*www.editionslaurekane.com*) publishes a thorough 1:16,000 map of Dakar and its suburbs, as well as a road map to Senegal, both of which are available at bookshops like Librairie aux 4 Vents and the occasional upmarket hotel or supermarket. Also be on the lookout for the well-updated and free *Le Dakar Pocket* (*www.dakarpocket.com*) map of Plateau and the centre city, available in upmarket hotels and anywhere else you find tourist flyers and the like.

TOUR OPERATORS There's no central tourist information bureau in Dakar and, while all of the operators below are knowledgeable and able to provide any relevant info, they are of course in the business of selling tours. That being said, all of the following can arrange day trips in and around Dakar (ie: to Lac Rose), as well as customisable excursions to all corners of the country.

Africa Connection Tours 52 Rue Félix Faure; ☎ 33 849 5200; e act@orange.sn; www.actours-senegal.com

Africa Travel Group [94 D4] Rte du Méridien & Rte de Ngor; ☎ 33 869 7900; info@africatravel-group.com; www.africatravel-group.com

Andaando Sicap Mbao No 199; m 77 793 94 32; e dieng.massaer@yahoo.fr; www.andaando.com

Boubatour Oukam Boulga Imm. SDE, Fann; ☎ 33 860 4244; m 76 668 6363; e bouba@boubatour.com; www.boubatour.com

Nouvelles Frontières [84 C4] Rte des Almadies lot no.1, Mamelles Aviation; ☎ 33 859 4446/7; e contact@nfsenegal.com; www.nfsenegal.com

Origin Africa [84 D4] Ancienne Piste Mermoz, Immeuble Birama; ☎ 33 860 6050; e info@origin-africa.sn; www.origin-africa.sn

Senegal Tours [91 F3] 5 Place de l'Indépendance; ☎ 33 859 5434; e Senegal-tours@senegal-tours.sn; www.senegal-tours.sn

Tropic Tour Senegal 180 Blvd Général de Gaulle; ☎ 33 821 8957/68; e tropictour@orange.sn; www.tropictour.sn

The luxury centre of gravity in Dakar leans heavily towards the Almadies neighbourhood and the west Corniche, and it's here you'll find much of the city's top-end accommodation. As a rule, clientele at any of the options in the **luxury** category (**$$$$$**) slants heavily towards those here on business, but with ample swimming pools, spa facilities and beach access they would be equally suited to well-heeled travellers seeking the highest level of comfort.

All accommodation in the **upmarket** (**$$$$**) range will be en-suite with Wi-Fi and air conditioning. Much of it is aimed at business travellers, so some hotels will have a swimming pool, some won't; all will accept credit cards as payment. Many of Dakar's nicest boutique hotels fall into this range, along with several international chains.

Many of the hotels in the **moderate** (**$$$**) category continue to be business-oriented, but there is a greater focus on the tourist market at this price. These hotels generally have air conditioning, Wi-Fi and en-suite facilities, and most (though not necessarily all) will accept credit cards.

Some of the best-value, **budget** accommodation (**$$**) in Dakar is at the north end of the Cap Vert peninsula in Yoff and Ngor, and the handful of surf camps up here represent some of the best choices for backpackers in Dakar, whether or not you've any intention of hitting the waves.

There are a handful of places offering **shoestring** (**$**) accommodation in dorms, including Ker Jahkarlo and Via Via (see pages 99–100). Some will accept credit cards; many will not, although euros are generally accepted.

PLATEAU
Map, pages 90–1.

♙ **La Villa Racine** (20 rooms) 37 Rue Jules Ferry; ☏33 889 4141; e lavillaracine@orange.sn; www.lavillaracine.com. Behind a carved wooden door, the smell of *thiouraye* (Senegalese incense) wafts out of the Moroccan-style courtyard at this newly remodelled hotel in the heart of Plateau. Rooms climb several stories above the courtyard on rather vertiginous outdoor corridors surrounded by latticework. Inside, the rooms come with TV, minibar & safe, & while the ostentatious style will be a bit overwrought for some (think high-backed chairs, spindle-legged tables & gilded trimmings), there's no denying the quality. The rooftop bar-restaurant does meat & fish dishes starting around 6,000F, and a luxury goods boutique sells perfumes & designer silk neckties downstairs. **$$$$**

♙ **Novotel** (241 rooms) Av Abdoulaye Fadiga; ☏33 849 6161; e dakar.reservation@accor.com; www.novotel.com. Upmarket neighbour to the Ibis in the same complex, the carpeted rooms here are up-to-date with modern glass-door showers, hair driers, safe, flatscreen TVs & writing desk. It's businesslike overall, but the large outdoor pool (hard to find in Plateau!) & lounge area is manicured with palms & baobabs & just fine for catching some sun after the conference ends. It's right on the eastern corniche, so sea-facing rooms have views over Gorée. **$$$$**

♙ **Rysara Hotel** 8 Av des Jambaars; ☏33 822 6060; e info@rysarahotel.sn; www.rysarahotel. sn. In a quiet neighbourhood just south of Place Soweto & opposite the British Embassy, this is a smart new addition to the hotel options in Plateau. Done up in blacks, whites & greys with brushed aluminium & chrome accents, rooms here tick all the boxes for modern business accommodation. There's a restaurant on-site, but no pool or spa facilities. **$$$$**

♙ **Ibis** (106 rooms) Av Abdoulaye Fadiga; ☏33 829 5959/849 4994; e dakar.reservation@ accor.com; www.ibis.com. Even though they're in the same compound, rooms here are half the price as at the neighbouring Novotel, & offer the type of comfortable if unremarkable business accommodation you might expect at any Ibis hotel worldwide. The considerable perk of staying here is that the Ibis shares pool & leisure facilities with its swankier neighbour, making for a noticeable upgrade from the amenities you'd usually get in this price range. **$$$**

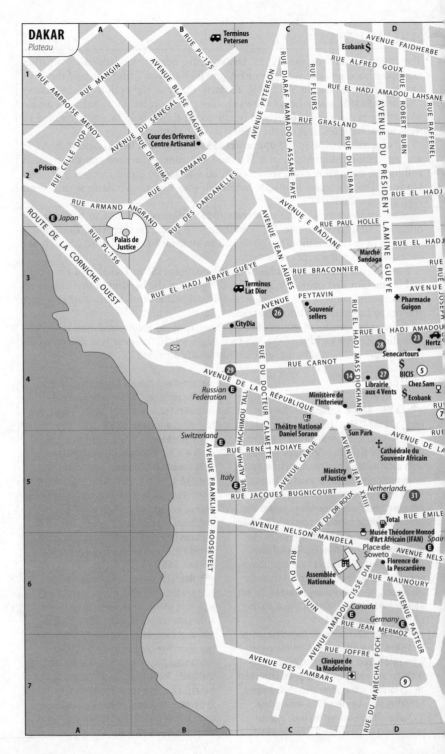

DAKAR
Plateau

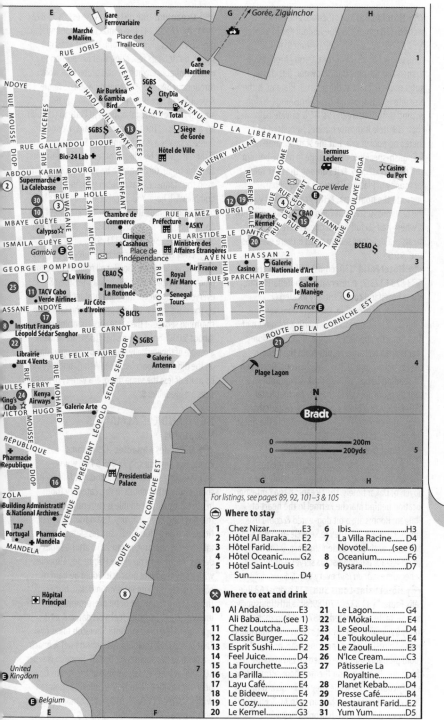

Gorée, Ziguinchor

Gare Ferroviaire
Marché Malien
Place des Tirailleurs
RUE JORIS
BVD EL HADJ DJILY MBAYE
AVENUE BALLAY
Gare Maritime
NDOYE
SGBS $
Air Burkina & Gambia Bird
CityDia
Total
AVENUE DE LA LIBÉRATION
RUE MOUSSE DIOP
RUE VINCENES
SGBS $ ☿ 13
ALLÉES DELMAS
♫ Siège de Gorée
RUE GALLANDOU DIOUF
Hôtel de Ville
RUE MALENFANT
RUE HENRY MALAN
Terminus Leclerc
Bio-24 Lab ✚
RUE P HOLLE
RUE SAINT MICHEL
RUE DAGOME
RUE CEDE
☆ **Casino du Port**
ABDOU KARIM BOURGI
Supermarché La Calebasse
② 30
10 ③
Calypso☆
RUE WAGANE DIOUF
RUE RAMEZ BOURGI
RUE RENE CAILLE
RUE DESCEMENT
Cape Verde ✉ ☰
🄱 CBAO
RUE PARENT
AVENUE ABDOULAYE FADIGA
Chambre de Commerce
12 19
④
15
RUE THANN
MBAYE GUÈYE
Préfecture
ASKY
Marché Kermel
ISMAILA GUÈYE
Clinique Casahous ✚
RUE ARISTIDE LE DANTEC
Ministère des Affaires Étrangères
20
BCEAO $
Gambia 🄴
Place de l'Indépendance
AVENUE HASSAN 2
GEORGE POMPIDOU
① ♫ **Le Viking**
CBAO $
Air France
Casino
Galerie Nationale d'Art
25
11 **TACV Cabo Verde Airlines**
Immeuble La Rotonde
Royal Air Maroc
RUE HUART
RUE PARCHAPE
Galerie le Manège
⑥
ASSANE NDOYE
Air Côte d'Ivoire
$ BICIS
Senegal Tours
RUE SALVA
France 🄴
⑧ **Institut Français Léopold Sédar Senghor**
17
RUE CARNOT
ROUTE DE LA CORNICHE EST
22
$ SGBS
Librairie aux 4 Vents
RUE FELIX FAURE
Galerie Antenna
21
ULES FERRY
King's Club ☆ 24 **Kenya Airways**
VICTOR HUGO
Galerie Arte
Plage Lagon
RÉPUBLIQUE
AVENUE DU PRÉSIDENT LÉOPOLD SÉDAR SENGHOR
RUE MOHAMED V
N
✚ **Pharmacie Republique**
Bradt
16
ZOLA
Building Administratif & National Archives
✚ **Presidential Palace**
0 ——— 200m
0 ——— 200yds
TAP Portugal
Pharmacie Mandela ✚
MANDELA
RUE DIOP
ROUTE DE LA CORNICHE EST
✚ **Hôpital Principal**
⑧
United 🄴 Kingdom
Belgium 🄴

E   F   G   H

Dakar **WHERE TO STAY**

4

For listings, see pages 89, 92, 101–3 & 105

🍴 **Where to stay**

1	Chez Nizar.................E3	6	Ibis.........................H3
2	Hôtel Al Baraka.......E2	7	La Villa Racine.......D4
3	Hôtel Farid..............E2		Novotel...........(see 6)
4	Hôtel Oceanic.........G2	8	Oceanium...............F6
5	Hôtel Saint-Louis	9	Rysara..................D7
	Sun........................D4		

✖ **Where to eat and drink**

10	Al Andaloss.............E3	21	Le Lagon............... G4
	Ali Baba...........(see 1)	22	Le Mokai............... E4
11	Chez Loutcha..........E3	23	Le Seoul................D4
12	Classic Burger.......G2	24	Le Toukouleur........ E4
13	Esprit Sushi............F2	25	Le Zaouli................ E3
14	Feel Juice...............D4	26	N'Ice Cream...........C3
15	La Fourchette........G3	27	Pâtisserie La
16	La Parilla.................E5		Royaltine.............D4
17	Layu Café................E4	28	Planet Kebab........D4
18	Le Bideew...............E4	29	Presse Café............B4
19	Le Cozy..................G2	30	Restaurant Farid....E2
20	Le Kermel...............G3	31	Yum Yum...............D5

Hôtel Al Baraka (See ad, 2nd colour section) (30 rooms) 35 Rue Abdoul Karim Bourgi; 33 822 5532; e reservation@hotelbaraka. com; www.hotelbaraka.com. Gently brought up to speed by the new Danish owner, this classic hotel spans 6 floors at the heart of Plateau, & the en-suite rooms sport all-new furnishings, fridge, writing desk, flatscreen TVs, AC & private balconies. Their clientele is mostly business-oriented so there's no pool or spa, but the staff are amenable & English-speaking. Prices come in at the bottom end of this category, & it's among the best value for money in Plateau. There's a tranquil bar opposite the front desk, & they're affiliated with the fabulous Restaurant Farid 2 blocks away, which is where half- & full-board guests here take their meals – a delicious selling point if there ever was one. **$$$**

Hôtel Farid (30 rooms) 51 Rue Vincens; 33 823 6123/7; e reservation@hotelfarid.com; www.hotelfarid.com. Centrally located & thoroughly dependable, the Farid does very comfortable accommodation with a minimum of fuss. Smartly appointed single, double & triple rooms are a welcome respite from the frenetic streets below, and all have AC, balcony, flatscreen TV, reading lamps, writing desk & wardrobe. It's slightly more upmarket than its partner hotel, Al Baraka, a few blocks away. Their restaurant across the street serves what is probably the finest Lebanese food in town. **$$$**

Hôtel Océanic 9 Rue de Thann; 33 822 2044; e hotel-oceanic@orange.sn; www.hoteloceanicsenegal.com. Probably the doyen of Dakar hotels, the Oceanic has a fantastic location behind Marché Kermel in the heart of Plateau. Rooms are a bit dog-eared & could use another update, but they're kept clean, have AC & balconies with old wooden shutters, & the easy-going terrace bar downstairs serves a different Senegalese *plat du jour* every day. **$$**

Hôtel Saint-Louis Sun (11 rooms) 68 Rue Félix Faure; 33 822 2570/8968; e htlstlouisun@ orange.sn. In a pastel red 1887 building that's lived many lives since that time, it's been plugging along as the Saint-Louis Sun for some years now and could probably safely be called an old standby at this point. Rooms are on the first floor surrounding a leafy courtyard & while they make no attempt to be stylish, they're spick & span with AC & en-suite ablutions, & some have balconies. **$$**

Oceanium Rte de la Corniche est; 33 822 2441; m 77 939 1414; e contact@oceaniumdakar. org; www.oceaniumdakar.org. It's not exactly a secret, but it bears repeating that in addition to their admirable environmental protection work throughout Senegal, Oceanium has basic single & double fan rooms that are scrupulously tidy & among the best budget options in Plateau (though it's a short list). The terrace restaurant overlooks Gorée & serves a rotating menu of Senegalese dishes. If diving, boating or other nautical pursuits are your thing, this ought to be your first stop, but even the staunchest landlubber will find little to quibble with here. You can also arrange visits here to their accommodation in Sine-Saloum (Keur Bamboung, see page 190) and Casamance (Pointe Saint-Georges, see page 311). **$$**

Chez Nizar Av Pompidou, Plateau; 77 319 1224. Long the destination for all manner of penny-pinching backpackers, hard-up businessmen & everyone in between, this Plateau standby next to & up the stairs from Ali Baba's provides the same non-charming service at the same very charming prices (about 5,000F pp) it always has. There are actually a couple of theoretically separate places operating on the different floors (eg: Chez Vieira), but they all do more or less the same thing, & a variety of room sizes are available. **$**

NGOR AND LES ALMADIES
Map, page 94.

Hôtel des Almadies (291 rooms) Pointe des Almadies; 33 869 5454; www. hoteldesalmadies.com. While today it falls well short of the other hotels in this category (both in price & quality: a double is currently 90,000F), this has long been a luxury destination in Dakar (it used to be a Club Med), and it's slated for a takeover by Sheraton in Jan 2016 after a series of delays. At the very tip of the Pointe des Almadies with its own private beach, it would be hard to have a more thrilling location in Dakar, but as things stand today the hotel overpromises & underdelivers. Facilities feel a bit dated & as if operations are coasting until Sheraton takes over. That being said, their big swimming pool & beach are open to non-guests for 5,000F (a much steeper 10,000F at weekends), & some of the rooms have been remodelled already & are nicely appointed with flatscreen TV, safe, fridge, big canopy mozzie nets & new soft furnishings. **$$$$$**

King Fahd Palace Hotel (374 rooms) Pointe des Almadies; 33 869 6969; e reservation. dakar@kingfahdpalacehotels.com; www. kingfahdpalacehotels.com. Occupying one of Dakar's most prestigious addresses since 1991, everything here is top-notch except, bafflingly, the rooms. It's all close-cropped grass, swaying palms, genteel service & marble décor until the shock of aluminium panel ceilings & motorway motel furnishings in the rooms. Ocean-facing rooms have incontestably stellar views, but it's hard to escape the notion that they've somehow cheaped out where it counts. A deluxe room at the Radisson is cheaper than a standard here, & considerably nicer. The other facilities here are suitably luxurious, with 9 holes of golf, 4 tennis courts, a big pool, ocean-side restaurant, travel agent, cigar shop, spa & beautician all available on-site. Some remodelling was going on when we visited, so perhaps those rooms will get the sprucing up they need. $$$$$

Hôtel Fleur de Lys (32 rooms) Rte des Almadies; 33 869 8687; e contact@ hotelfleurdelysdakar.com; www. hotelfleurdelysdakar.com. The 6th-floor rooftop pool & bar is hands down the best thing about this place, & non-guests are allowed to swim for 5,000F. The rooms are carpeted & on the stodgier side, but they've got writing desks, minibars, safes & all the other trimmings a business traveller might need. Staff are attentive, the restaurant has views, & there's a piano bar, of all things. An overall decent option, but overpriced for what you get. $$$$

La Résidence (12 rooms) Almadies; 33 820 8838; e info@laresidencedakar.com; www. laresidencedakar.com. On a quiet street directly between Route des Almadies and the various beach restaurants & surf shacks on the Corniche des Almadies, this tranquil owner-managed guesthouse sports immaculate poolside gardens & bright, uncluttered rooms with canopy beds & flatscreen TVs. Meals are served on the garden terrace starting at 6,500F, & serviced apartments with kitchenette are also available. $$$$

Chez Carla (La Maison d'Italie) (5 rooms) Île de Ngor; 33 821 34 35; m 77 572 4306; e reservation@chezcarlahotel.com; www. chezcarlahotel.com. Known for its excellent Italian restaurant, this charming house smack on Ngor island's waterfront also has a handful of colour-coded en-suite rooms with AC, balconies & canopy

beds, & an outcrop covered in *chaise l* which to do some serious sun-soakin you're here to snack or to sleep, they'l whisk you across from Ngor in their boat free of charge if you call them a few minutes in advance. $$$

Fana Hotel (36 rooms) Rte des Almadies; 33 820 0606/8630; m 77 633 0092; e fanahotel@orange.sn. A block off the main road, from the exterior this looks like an unprepossessing business hotel, but inside it's surprisingly lively. The décor is eclectic & there are potted plants just about everywhere you look. There's a restaurant & leafy outdoor terrace, swimming pool, & a boutique on site selling a surprisingly compelling selection of art & souvenirs. All rooms are en suite & comfortable with AC & TV, but the split-level ones will leave taller guests ducking. $$$

Hôtel Le Virage (54 rooms) Rte de Ngor; 33 820 7169; m 77 632 3263; e leviragehotel@ gmail.com; www.hotellevirage.com. Despite sitting directly atop the Plage du Virage, this new place is considerably more boardroom than boardwalk. Rooms are spacious & handsomely appointed, with AC, fridge, phone, coffee/tea facilities, full-length mirrors & private balconies. There is a big pool, as well as an on-site beautician if you need some attention before strutting your stuff. The beach-facing rooms will bump you up into the next price category. $$$

Hôtel Madrague (31 rooms) Plage de Ngor; 33 820 0223; e hotel.sbs@anfa-group. com; www.hotel-madrague.com. Much more conventionally resort-like than any of the other options on Ngor beach, the blue-&-white rooms here are spotless, with terracotta floors, flatscreen TV, AC, fridge & writing desk, & domed ceilings that make them feel a bit more spacious. Ocean-facing rooms have balconies as well. There's a swimming pool & seafood restaurant with meals starting around 6,000F. $$$

La Demeure (7 rooms) Almadies; 33 820 7679; m 77 724 9122/218 2484; e lademeureguesthouse@gmail.com; www. lademeure-guesthouse.com. In a whitewashed 3-storey building set in a prim garden just behind the Almadies roundabout, this airy family-run guesthouse is a warmly recommended option, with a small swimming pool, rooftop terrace & tranquil lounge. Rooms are tiled & en suite with big mozzie nets, safe, TV & African masks &

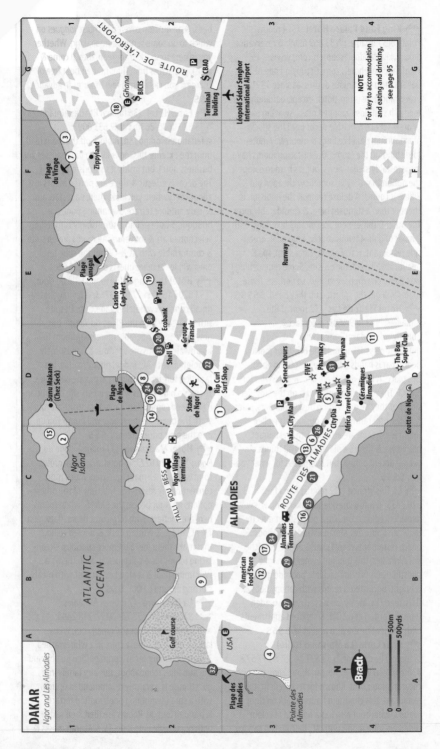

DAKAR
Ngor and Les Almadies

ATLANTIC OCEAN

Pointe des Almadies

Plage des Almadies

Golf course

USA

Ngor Island

Sunu Makane (Chez Seck)

Plage de Ngor

Plage Sunugal

Casino du Cap-Vert

Plage du Virage

Zippyland

Ghana

BICIS

ROUTE DE L'AÉROPORT

CBAO

Terminal building

Léopold Sédar Senghor International Airport

Runway

Ecobank

Total

Shell

Groupe Transair

Stade de Ngor

Rip Curl Surf Shop

Senecartours

Dakar City Mall

Duplex

FIVE

Pharmacy

Nirvana

Le Patio

Citybia

ALMADIES

Africa Travel Group

Céramiques Almadies

The Box Super'Club

ROUTE DES ALMADIES

ALMADIES

Ngor Village terminus

TALLI BOU BESS

Almadies Terminus

American Food Store

Grotte de Ngor

NOTE
For key to accommodation
and eating and drinking,
see page 95

N

Bradt

0   500m
0   500yds

NGOR AND LES ALMADIES
For listings, see pages 92–3, 95, 98 & 104–5

Where to stay

1 Auberge Maam Samba.....D2
2 Chez Carla
   (La Maison d'Italie)..........C1
3 Hôtel Cap Ouest.................F1
4 Hôtel des Almadies...........A3
5 Hôtel Fana............................D4
6 Hôtel Fleur du Lys..............C3
7 Hôtel le Virage...................F1

8 Hôtel Madrague.......D2
9 King Fahd Palace.....B2
10 La Brazzerade..........D2
11 La Demeure...............D4
12 La Résidence............B3
13 Le Lodge des
   Almadies................C3
14 Maison Abaka..........D2

15 N'gor Island Surf Camp.....C1
16 Oumar Surf Camp
   (Surfers' Paradise)............C3
17 Résidence Madamel..........B3
18 Sargal....................................G1
19 Sunugal Village...................E2

Where to eat and drink

20 Ali Baba................................D2
21 Alkimia.................................C3
22 Annapurna...........................D2
23 Bayékou.................................D2
   Charly's.........................(see 19)
24 La Cabane du Pêcheur......D2

25 La Cabane du Surfeur
   (Chez Abdou)............C3
26 Layu Café......................C3
   Le Lodge des
   Almadies............(see 13)
27 Le Ngor..........................B3
28 Le Ryad..........................C3

29 Noflaye Beach...................B3
30 Patisserie Graine d'Or..... E2
31 Planet Kebab....................D4
32 Restaurant La Marée
   (Chez Adji)...................A2
33 São Brasil...........................D2
34 Sweet Coffee.....................B3

paintings on the walls. B/fast is available daily but other meals are on request, or, uniquely, you can cook dinner for yourself in their guest kitchen. **$$$**

Le Lodge des Almadies (38 rooms) Rte des Almadies; 33 869 0345; e hotel@lodgedesalmadies.com; www.lodgedesalmadies.com. Given that both the name & the exterior of this place are on the unmemorable side, you could be forgiven for driving right past without noticing it at all. Known mostly for its impeccable French restaurant, the rooms here are mostly tasteful but still a few notches below haute cuisine. Set in 2 buildings a stone's throw apart, they all have AC, TV, safe & writing desk, & some have terraces, but other than that are something of a gamble depending on which one you get, so ask to see a few. There's a small swimming pool in the main building. **$$$**

Maison Abaka (10 rooms) Plage de Ngor; 33 820 6486; e isabelle@maison-abaka.com; www.maison-abaka.com. Lovingly designed & tended, each of the 10 rooms here is uniquely appointed with its own colour scheme & amenities, but all come standard with AC, TV, nets & some very comfortable overstuffed pillows. There's a swimming pool & beach bar, & the restaurant on site does a variety of meals as thoughtful as the accommodation. Nautilus Diving is based here, & a variety of diving, fishing, surfing & other excursions can be arranged. Recommended. **$$$**

N'gor Island Surf Camp Île de Ngor; 77 336 9150; e surfcamp@gosurf.dk; www.gosurf.dk. This breezy, bougainvillea-draped compound

on Ngor Island feels about 5,000 miles from Dakar, despite being not quite a kilometre offshore, & whether you want your feet down on a board or up in a hammock, this is every bit the *Endless Summer* type of place you can make just that happen. (Not least because parts of the surf-culture classic were filmed just offshore at the famous Ngor Right wave.) The whitewashed rooms here sport mosaic floors, cool stone walls, smart bits of artwork & the usual fans & nets, while solar heaters warm up the showers. The activities list goes on and on, with surfing, fishing, massage, yoga, drumming & dancing to keep you occupied as a start. Everybody is hosted on a HB basis; dorms go for €32, while en-suite sgl/dbl rooms are about two & three times that, respectively. **$$$**

Résidence Madamel (14 rooms) Almadies; 33 869 5964; e contact@dalalhotels.com; www.residencemadamel.com. With ceilings high enough that Gulliver would approve, the whitewashed compound here has cool, newly furnished rooms with the usual mod cons & in the reflection of the pool, the balconies around the courtyard take on the sheen of Miami Beach. The Éscale Détente spa has its hammam here & does everything from mani-pedis to reflexology. Good value for money. **$$$**

Sargal Hotel Rte de l'Aéroport; 33 869 7596; e infos@sargalhotel.com; www.sargalhotel.com. Mostly of note for its location barely 500m from the airport, the tiled rooms here aren't anything to write home about, but they're clean, air-conditioned & perfectly comfortable for a night's kip after a late flight or before an early

Dakar **WHERE TO STAY**

4

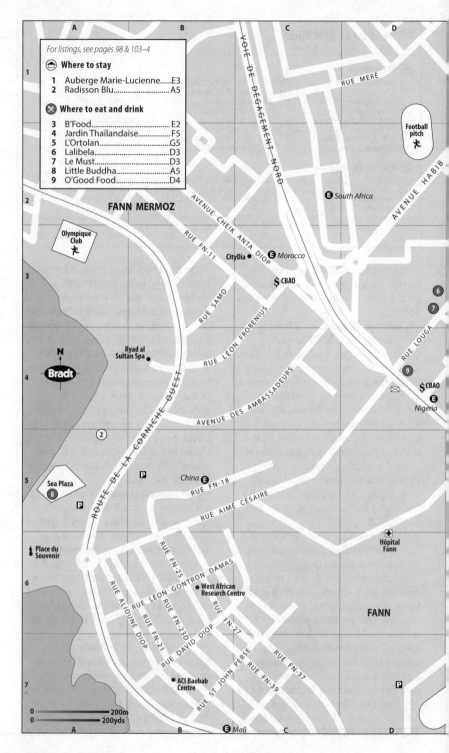

For listings, see pages 98 & 103–4

Where to stay

1 Auberge Marie-Lucienne......E3
2 Radisson Blu...........................A5

Where to eat and drink

3 B'Food.....................................E2
4 Jardin Thaïlandaise..............F5
5 L'Ortolan...............................G5
6 Lalibela.................................D3
7 Le Must.................................D3
8 Little Buddha........................A5
9 O'Good Food.........................D4

FANN MERMOZ

Olympique
Club

Ryad al
Sultan Spa

N

Bradt

Sea Plaza

8

Place du
Souvenir

VOIE DE DÉGAGEMENT NORD

RUE MÉRÉ

Football
pitch

AVENUE HABIB

South Africa

AVENUE CHEIK ANTA DIOP

RUE FN-11

CityDia

Morocco

$ CBAO

RUE SAMO

RUE LÉON FROBENIUS

RUE LOUGA

6

7

9

$ CBAO

Nigeria

AVENUE DES AMBASSADEURS

ROUTE DE LA CORNICHE OUEST

P

China

RUE FN-18

RUE AIMÉ CÉSAIRE

Hôpital
Fann

P

RUE LÉON GONTRON DAMAS

RUE FN-25

West African
Research Centre

RUE FN-27

RUE FN-23D

FANN

RUE ALIOUNE DIOP

RUE FN-21

RUE DAVID DIOP

RUE ST JOHN PERSE

RUE FN-39

RUE FN-37

P

ACI Baobab
Centre

0   200m
0   200yds

Mali

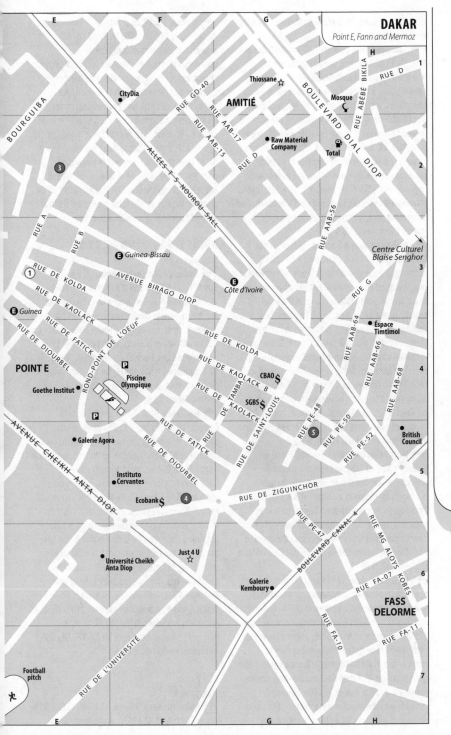

Thiossane ☆

AMITIÉ

Mosque ☪

CityDia

Raw Material Company

Total

BOULEVARD DIAL DIOP

RUE ABÉBÉ BIKILA

RUE D

RUE GD-40

RUE AAB-17

RUE AAB-15

RUE D

RUE AAB-56

RUE AAB-64

RUE AAB-66

RUE AAB-68

ALLÉES T S NOUROU SALL

BOURGUIBA

③

①

❸ *Guinea-Bissau*

❸ *Côte d'Ivoire*

AVENUE BIRAGO DIOP

RUE DE KOLDA

RUE A

RUE B

RUE DE KOLDA

RUE DE KAOLACK

RUE DE FATICK

❸ *Guinea*

RUE DE DIOURBEL

Centre Culturel Blaise Senghor

RUE G

Éspace Timtimol

POINT E

Goethe Institut ●

RUE DE L'OEUF

ROND-POINT DE L'OEUF

Ⓟ

Piscine Olympique

Ⓟ

CBAO $

RUE DE KAOLACK B

SGBS $

RUE DE TAMBA

RUE DE KAOLACK

RUE DE SAINT-LOUIS

RUE PE-48

RUE PE-50

RUE PE-52

British Council

⑤

RUE DE FATICK

● *Galerie Agora*

RUE DE DIOURBEL

AVENUE CHEIKH ANTA DIOP

Instituto ● Cervantes

Ecobank $ ④

RUE DE ZIGUINCHOR

Université Cheikh Anta Diop

Just 4 U ☆

RUE PE-47

BOULEVARD CANAL 4

RUE MG ALOYS KOBES

Galerie Kemboury ●

FASS DELORME

RUE FA-07

RUE FA-10

RUE FA-11

Football pitch

RUE DE L'UNIVERSITÉ

🚶

departure. It won't be quite so convenient once the new airport opens. **$$$**

🏠 **Sunugal Village Hotel** (21 rooms) Rte de Ngor; ☎ 33 820 0331; e sunugal@orange.sn; www.hotelsunugal.com. This long-serving favourite has 3 types of carefully maintained bungalows set in a most welcome patch of green just off the main route in Ngor. Rooms are done up in wood & mosaics; all are en-suite with AC, some have AC & TV, & the nicest add a fridge to the mix as well. The AC-only rooms dip into the budget price category & are good value. The perennially popular Charly Bar & Restaurant is attached (mains starting around 6,000F), along with a bean-shaped swimming pool, & there's a private beach for guests 150m away. **$$$**

🏠 **Auberge Maam Samba** (6 rooms) Rte Ngor Village; ☎ 33 868 1336; m 77 191 5012; e contact@aubergedakar.org; www.aubergedakar.org. Managed as a sustainable tourism endeavour in partnership with Ndem village in Diourbel region, all the décor, bedding & furniture here is made by Ndem's weavers & artisans to fair-trade standards. It's a warm & artistic space, & the simple rooms all have AC, en-suite bath & mosquito nets. The gorgeous hand-woven & naturally dyed tapestries & clothes are on sale in their boutique, along with a selection of jewellery, metalwork, carvings & baskets. Senegalese meals are available on request, but there's no alcohol served. Prices are at the upper end of this range. **$$**

🏠 **Hôtel Cap Ouest** (17 rooms) Plage du Virage; ☎ 33 820 2469; e capouest@arc.sn; www.hotel-capouest.com. The furniture here is a higgledy-piggledy assortment & it's far from stylish, but you'd have a hard time taking issue with the beachside location. There's a bar downstairs where they do *dibiterie* in the evening. Both fan & AC rooms are available, but it's middling value overall. **$$**

🏠 **La Brazzerade** (41 rooms) Plage de Ngor; ☎ 33 820 0364/9449; e labrazzerade@orange.sn; www.brazzerade.com. A bunch of old-school rooms with wood highlights & not a whole lot in the way of style are arranged in an oddly angular courtyard to the side of the restaurant here, but they're comfortable, right on the beach & good value. There are only a couple of them, but the fan-only double rooms are a stellar deal at 15,000F. Balcony & sea-facing rooms hover around the top of this price range, but still make for a pleasant choice. **$$**

🏠 **Oumar Surf Camp** Rte de la Corniche des Almadies; ☎ 33 868 1405; m 77 637 6109; e seyeoumar@hotmail.com; www.senegalsurfcamp.com. Another laid-back surfer's choice, except this time looking south over the Corniche des Almadies., this feel-good spot is run by Senegal's first ever professional surfer, Oumar Seye. Reception is at the Surfer's Paradise restaurant, which is under the same management & would be a great spot to hang out even if they didn't have their own salt-water swimming pool. As it stands it's one of several chilled out addresses along the Corniche des Almadies, & the unassuming but comfortable rooms are set in a separate house a short walk away. **$$**

POINT E, FANN AND MERMOZ
Map, pages 96–7.

🏠 **Auberge Marie-Lucienne** (25 rooms) Rue A, Point E; ☎ 33 869 0090; e auberge@orange.sn. The rooms here certainly won't change your life, but they're at the bottom end of this price category, clean enough, & if you're after a place in restaurant-heavy but accommodation-light Point E, it's a good bet. They all come with AC, fridge & TV, & rooms with balcony go for the same price as those without, so no harm in asking if they've got one available. **$$$**

🏠 **Radisson Blu** (180 rooms) Rte de la Corniche Ouest, Fann; ☎ 33 869 3333; e info.dakar@radissonblu.com; www.radissonblu.com. Opened in 2010 and competing with its neighbour Terrou-Bi for Dakar's most opulent address, Radisson's first foray into Senegal is every bit as shiny, modern & beautifully located as you would expect. Rooms are sleek & minimalist, starting at 28m² with floor-to-ceiling windows & Juliet balconies, flatscreen TV, coffee maker (espresso machine in the business rooms), rainfall showers, minibar & sea views for about €25 more than garden rooms. The 3 restaurants, infinity pool & attached bar, wellness spa, hammam, fitness centre & souvenir boutique round out the offerings, & it's right next door to the Sea Plaza mall. Non-guests can use the pool for 8,000F/10,000F weekdays/weekends. **$$$$$**

YOFF
Map, page 99.

🏠 **Auberge Keur Diame** (10 rooms) Cité Djily Mbaye, Yoff; ☎ 33 820 9676; www.keurdiame-

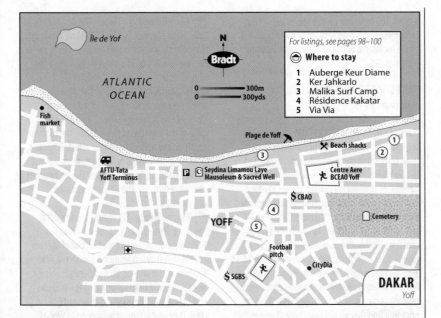

Map labels:

Île de Yof

ATLANTIC OCEAN

N

Bradt

For listings, see pages 98–100

⌂ **Where to stay**
1 Auberge Keur Diame
2 Ker Jahkarlo
3 Malika Surf Camp
4 Résidence Kakatar
5 Via Via

Fish market

0 — 300m
0 — 300yds

Plage de Yoff

Beach shacks

AFTU-Tata Yoff Terminus

Seydina Limamou Laye Mausoleum & Sacred Well

Centre Aere BCEAO Yoff

$ CBAO

YOFF

Cemetery

Football pitch

$ SGBS

CityDia

DAKAR
Yoff

---

senegal.com. Though it's not the choice if you're looking to be in the middle of the action, this peaceful family guesthouse near Yoff beach offers home-cooked meals & simple tiled rooms with fans & nets set on 2 floors around a central courtyard. Furnishings are simple & locally made (or patio chairs), & the common areas are tranquil & filled with books. **$$**

⌂ **Ker Jahkarlo** (5 rooms) Cité Djily Mbaye, Yoff; ☎77 609 5203; e jahkarlo@gmail.com; www.jahkarlo.org. This musical homestead in Yoff is family home to Fabio, the Italian percussionist owner & head of their associated community NGO. A short walk from Yoff beach, rooms here are simple & clean with fans, nets & some low-key wax prints & African décor scattered about. There are double & triple rooms, some en-suite, some not, & this is one of the very few places in Dakar to offer dorm beds (for about €11 per person). There's a rooftop terrace, meals on request, & all kinds of drum, dance & cultural activities can be arranged. **$$**

⌂ **Malika Surf Camp** Plage de Yoff; m 77 113 2791/299 1297; e info@malikasurfcamp. com; www.malikasurfcamp.com. Simple, bright, & steps from the water, it's hard not to like this surfer's hangout set amid the various beach shack restaurants in Yoff. As with the other surf camps in town, breakers are their bread & butter & lessons

are naturally available, but it's an agreeable place to stay even if you've no intention of catching anything more than some zzz. Rooms have either en-suite or shared ablutions, all have fans & nets, & all are brightly decorated with wax print designs. Accommodation is on a HB basis, but they've got a fridge for guests & have been known to throw a celebratory BBQ or two as well. **$$**

⌂ **Résidence Kakatar** (9 rooms) Yoff; ☎33 820 5308; m 77 402 8746; e contact@ kakatar.com; www.hotel-kakatar-dakar.com. A superb option for larger groups & self-caterers, this place offers 1/2-bedroom & studio flats with kitchen that sleep up to 6. Rooms are en suite & simply decorated with wood furniture & bamboo trimmings. It's a few hundred metres from Yoff beach, & there are views from the breezy roof terrace. **$$**

⌂ **Via Via** Route des Cimetières, Yoff; ☎33 820 5475; e viavia@orange.sn; www.viaviacafe.com. Part of the Belgian Via Via chain of hostels & cafes, this is one of a very few places that could be called a backpacker's hub in Dakar. A few minutes' walk from Yoff beach, they've got both en-suite & rooms with shared ablutions, & it's hard to be easier on your pocket in this town than their €13 dorm beds. Done up in vibrant greens, yellows & reds, the rooms come with fans & nets & have been the happy recipients of some late-2014 remodelling as well. The resto-bar on site serves a short but tasty menu & it's a good place to meet people if you're looking to link up & share costs on some activities. **$$**

ELSEWHERE IN DAKAR
Map, pages 84–5.

⌂ **Terrou-Bi** (118 rooms) Rte de la Corniche Ouest, Fann Hock; ☏33 839 9039; e terroubi@ terroubi.com; www.terroubi.com. This does-it-all compound on the west corniche opened in 2009 & has its own private beach, casino, a handful of restaurants & bars, fitness centre, swimming pool, boutique & elegantly equipped rooms starting at 30m². All have flatscreen TV, safe, coffee/tea facilities, king-size bed & rainfall showers. Non-guests can use the pool & beach facilities for 6,000F (8,000 at weekends). **$$$$$**

⌂ **Hôtel Onomo** Rte de l'Aéroport; ☏33 869 0610; e onomo.dakar@onomohotel.com; www. onomohotel.com. In an incongruous red-brown brick building that would look more at home in Johannesburg or Harare, this new place is shockingly hip for a business hotel that exists largely for people in transit to the airport. The exposed brick is offset by stark black & white décor in the reception hall, which is also home to the Le Ramatou restaurant (meat & fish mains 7,000F) & rotating exhibits of vogue artists & photographers from Senegal & around the continent. Rooms aren't enormous, but they've got the clean lines & angular shapes you'd associate with Scandinavia, & all come with reading lamps, flatscreen TV, safe & little terraces overlooking the courtyard. Transfers to & from the airport are included in the room price, which is already at the very bottom of this category. No swimming pool, but still excellent value. **$$$$**

⌂ **Le Djoloff** 7 Rue Nani, Fann Hock; ☏33 889 3630; e hoteldjoloff@gmail.com; www. hoteldjoloff.com. Named after one of Senegal's historic kingdoms & built using local materials & craftsmen in a charming Saint-Louisien style, the rooms here are decorated in earth tones & local artwork, with arched doorways, wrought-iron balconies & carved wooden accents throughout. The boutique has a fine selection of jewellery & *sous-verre* paintings, while the restaurant comes effusively recommended for both its rotating menu of tapas & its fantastic rooftop terrace overlooking the ocean. **$$$$**

⌂ **Keur Gaïndé Art Hotel** Rte de Cercle de la Voile, Hann Marinas; ☏33 832 2611; e yassinag@ orange.sn; www.yassineartsgallery.com. If you've ever wanted to stay in a hotel shaped like a lion with a balcony in its mouth, well, let's just say you've come to the right place. The tiled en-suite rooms here are serviceable & kitted out with African décor & mosquito nets, though lacking some of the panache of the exterior. The focus is mostly on the gallery next door, which is home to rotating exhibitions of Senegalese statuary, textiles, painting & more. There's also a nightclub, where, presumably, the lion does not sleep tonight. **$$$**

⌂ **Espace Thialy** (21 rooms) Cité Impôts et Domaines, Patte d'Oie; ☏33 855 0260; e espace. thialy@orange.sn; www.cauris.sn. Out of the way but well-loved by its clientele & connected to an NGO with active projects around Senegal, this is a cheap & cheerful destination offering fan rooms with shared ablutions starting at around €14 for a bed. They host groups of volunteers as well as individual travellers & can arrange a variety of excursions, with an eye towards ethical & solidarity tourism initiatives. With meals taken communally at a long table in the overflowing gardens, it's a warm & homely place to pitch up. There's a map on their website detailing exactly how to find them. **$$**

⌂ **Hôtel du Phare** (10 rooms) 36 Cité des Magistrats, Les Mamelles; ☏33 860 3000; e info@ hotelduphare-dakar.com; www.hotelduphare-dakar.com. Bright & casual, this welcoming place is in a quiet neighbourhood around the corner from the African Renaissance Monument & about 2km from the Route des Almadies. Rooms are simple, colourful & clean, & range from basic with fan & shared ablutions to en-suite with AC & flatscreen TV. There's a breezy roof terrace, occasional live music (which could be noisy depending on your room), & the restaurant does a rotating French-Senegalese daily menu. **$$**

⌂ **Kingz Plaza Annexe** Sacré-Cœur 3, Villa 10504; ☏33 860 4019; e info@kingzplaza.com; www.kingzplaza.com. Not quite Dakar's cheapest accommodation but a contender for it, this place has the air of a low-end business hotel that got wind of Dakar's dearth of dormitories, so they stuck a bunch of beds into one room. It's not particularly loveable or conveniently located, but the dorms go for about €10 a head.(the same price as some considerably more pleasant options elsewhere). **$**

This section was put together with the assistance of Kari Masson, long-time Dakar resident and curator of the excellent *Dakar Eats* blog (*www.dakareats.com*).

There are dozens more worthwhile restaurants that can't be fitted in here and Dakar's food scene moves fast, so it would be eminently worth giving the site a peruse to see what's opened up since this book went to print.

If you're loath to leave your room and don't fancy eating the hotel fare, www. hellofood.sn lets you order delivery online from over 60 Dakar restaurants, including many of those mentioned here. Most nicer (and even some not-so-nice) restaurants offer free Wi-Fi.

PLATEAU
Map, pages 90–1.

✗ **Al Andaloss** 24 Rue Sandiniéry; ☎ 33 889 5099/823 1423; m 77 639 1039; ⊕ 11.00–midnight daily. This is a good place to know if you're in the mood for a quick spot of Lebanese that's less fancy than Farid but more authentic than Ali Baba. They do dine-in, take-away & delivery, & all the hummus, falafel, dolma, kefta & labneh you could ask for, along with a long menu of wraps, burgers, sandwiches & even Moroccan tajines. Finish things off with some baklava & café au lait, or a round at one of their 10 billiard tables.

✗ **Ali Baba** 23 Av Pompidou; ☎ 33 822 5297/823 5589; ⊕ 09.00–02.00 daily. A Dakar landmark since 1986, Ali Baba is almost as useful for taxi navigation as it is for the food. They do pizzas, burgers & some Lebanese fare like hummus & falafel, but the *chawarma* is their (pita) bread & butter. The long green tables are somehow never empty, despite the fact you'll have barely sat down by the time your food arrives. Their new second place in Ngor makes the original location look like a greasy cave, which isn't all that inaccurate.

✗ **Chez Loutcha** 101 Rue Moussa Diop; ☎ 33 821 0302; ⊕ noon–15.00 & 19.00–22.00. The tables here have been groaning under heaped plates of Senegalese & Cape Verdean favourites for decades, & it's the lunchtime go-to for legions of hungry Dakarois. The *plat du jour* rotates daily & covers the usual suspects like *thieboudienne*, *mafé* & *yassa*, but go for the *cachupa* (Cape Verdean hominy stew with meat & beans) if you're in the mood for something different.

✗ **Classic Burger** 10 Rue Ramez Bourgi; ☎ 33 822 0010/20; www.facebook.com/classic. burger.90; ⊕ 11.30–15.30 & 18.00–23.30 Mon–Sat, 17.00–23.30 Sun. With exposed ventilation ducts, pop culture posters, row upon row of imported condiments & even a swinging kitchen door, this is a stunningly convincing carbon copy of an upmarket American burger joint. If you're feeling nostalgic or just want a juicy (imported) beefburger with no eggs, chips or other unexpected surprises on top, this is your place. They do fried chicken, hot dogs & soft-serve ice cream too, and prices start at around 3,000F.

✗ **Espirit Sushi** Blvd Djily Mbaye; ☎ 33 821 7000; m 77 623 7177; ⊕ 11.00–15.00 & 19.00–23.00 Mon–Fri, 11.00–15.00 & 19.00–midnight Sat–Sun. With the clean, minimalist styling you'd expect of a high-end sushi house & barely a dozen tables, this bit of Zen, part of a French sushi franchise, is tucked into a nondescript Plateau office block near the Hotel de Ville. They do a full complement of *sashimi*, *nigiri* & *maki* rolls, as well as *tempura* & *brochettes*. A simple roll goes for about 3,000F, & they do lunch specials too.

✗ **Feel Juice** 88 Rue Felix Faure; ☎ 33 821 5400; www.facebook.com/feeljuice.dakar; ⊕ 09.00–19.00 Mon–Sat. Given the number of Senegalese expats in New York City, it must have been only a matter of time before you could get lox & bagels in Dakar, & even though the franchise is originally from France, the bagel bar here would satisfy the *choosiest* of New York breakfasters. (OK, maybe not the choosiest, but New Yorkers are a notoriously hard-to-please bunch & it's superbly done regardless.) The spotless interior smells of freshly squeezed fruits & you've got an enticing variety of bagels, wraps, salads, smoothies & desserts to choose from for 3,000F–5,000F.

✗ **La Fourchette** 4 Rue Parent; ☎ 33 821 8887; www.fourchettedakar.com; ⊕ noon–14.30 & 19.30–midnight Mon–Sat, 19.30–midnight Sun. On the shortlist of Dakar's ritziest addresses, the fusion menu here goes from Mexico to Japan & back again via Paris. Both the dress & the décor are elegant, so shine up your dancing shoes, because they've got live music every Thursday night. At dinnertime you're unlikely to make it out the door for under 20,000F per person; if you're a bit more strapped but still want to give it a try, their 3-course lunch *menu* is a more approachable 9,000F.

✕ La Parilla 6 Rue Emile Zola; ☎33 822 1500; www.groupelaparrilla.com; ⏰ noon–15.00 Mon, noon–15.00 & 19.30–midnight Tue–Fri, 19.30–midnight Sat–Sun. In a cute little cottage hidden away behind some office blocks near the presidential palace sits one of Dakar's most unlikely restaurants, an authentic Argentine steakhouse. Your taste buds will notice that the meat comes straight from South America, & your wallet will notice the same shortly afterwards.

☕ Pâtisserie La Royaltine Av du Président Lamine Gueye; ☎33 821 9994; ⏰ 06.30–20.30 daily. La Royaltine is *pâtissier* to the stars here in Senegal, & even if you don't want an ornate birthday creation shaped like a pirate ship or a smoochy pair of lips, this is *the* address to go on a sugar binge in Dakar. Cheesecake, tiramisu, macaroons of all kinds & even gingerbread houses at Christmas time are but a few of the frosted temptations on offer at this sparkling institution in Plateau. Stop by their *salon de thé* in the morning for an *espresso* & *pain au chocolat*.

✕ Le Bideew 89 Rue Joseph Gomis; ☎33 823 1909; www.facebook.com/lebideew; ⏰ 09.00–23.00 daily. In the gardens of the French Cultural Centre (Institut Français Léopold Sédar Senghor), this outdoor resto-bar is a well-loved hangout for expats & locals alike, & makes for a very welcome retreat from the freneticism of Plateau. The menu has plenty of options & the bar does an array of juices & cocktails with & without alcohol. The burgers & grills are especially good & seem to have a way of changing your mind just as you've decided to try something new for once. What's more, there are concerts almost every evening.

✕ Le Cozy 8 Rue Ramez Bourgi, Plateau; ☎33 823 0606; 📱 77 466 2861; www.facebook.com/LeCozydakar; ⏰ 11.30–15.00 & 19.30–midnight daily. Sleek & modern with world cities on the walls & world flavours on the plates, Le Cozy is a fine destination for anyone seeking innovative gastronomy in Plateau. The meals & cocktails are artfully prepared, with the former averaging around 11,000F. They often have DJs & dancing at weekends as well, so dress sharp.

✕ Le Kermel 7 Rue Aristide le Dantec; ☎33 822 4970; ⏰ 08.00–23.00 daily. A wood-panelled wonder with the heart of a Marseillais rugby club, this unassuming place is hidden away behind Marché Kermel & the simple exterior belies the sophistication of the menu – it's not many places in Dakar you can get fondue (8,500F), steak tartare (6,000F) & a full menu of salads, fish & meat dishes while keeping one eye on the game. Or just belly up to the bar for a cold *bière à la pression* (draft beer).

✕ Le Lagon Rte de la Corniche Est; ☎33 821 5322; www.lelagondakar.com; ⏰ 09.00–midnight daily. A Dakar institution for nearly 60 years, if for one reason or another you can't presently afford a yacht, eating here is just about the next best thing. From the moment you step inside (err... aboard), you feel as if you're on the water, & on the 25m dining pier overlooking Gorée, you actually are. As you might imagine, seafood is the name of the game here & you can stay in the shallows with Senegalese fish *yassa* for 9,500F or plumb the depths of your wallet with rock lobster for 32,000F. Sink another 3,000F & enjoy access to their private beach.

✕ Le Mokai 69 Rue Carnot; ☎33 823 1623; www.facebook.com/mario.kaf.5; ⏰ lunch & dinner daily. Cool, curated & often touted as Dakar's best restaurant despite being barely 3 years old, Le Mokai is an exercise in decorative restraint & culinary indulgence. They do everything from steaks to sushi, & their *fondant au chocolat* sets mouths watering & tongues wagging. Plates start around 12,000F, but their crispy brick-oven pizzas go for half that.

✕ Le Seoul 75 Rue Amadou Assane Ndoye; ☎33 822 9000; ⏰ 11.30–15.00 & 18.30–22.00 daily. The *bibimbap* here doesn't disappoint, & the outdoor terrace & pool certainly don't either. Dakar is actually home to a surprising number of Korean restaurants, & dinner at Le Seoul is a fine way to take a quick detour out of West Africa & into East Asia for the evening. All the tantalising accoutrements of Korean barbeque are in effect, & you know you're in for a treat the moment your server fires up the table-top grill. Hotter still is the Korean *soju* rice wine served alongside. Main dishes are around 5,000F.

✕ Le Toukouleur 122 Rue Moussé Diop; ☎33 821 5193; ⏰ noon–15.00 & 19.00–01.00 Mon–Sat. You'd hardly know it from the street, but the refined French cuisine at this quietly sophisticated expat favourite draws plenty of repeat visitors to sample their weekly rotating menu. The *banco* mud walls & canvas accents of the serene courtyard evoke Senegal's windswept north & open on to the busy exposed kitchen, where all manner of culinary feats are under way. The 3-course lunch menu is 7,000F, while dinner mains can easily double that.

✕ Le Zaouli 90 Rue Moussé Diop; ☏33 823 2803; **m** 77 149 1149; ⏰ 09.00–midnight daily. With tables named after Abidjan & Yamoussoukro, & posters of Didier Drogba on the walls, it becomes quite clear you've hopped a few countries to the south as soon as you walk into this Ivorian hangout just off Avenue Pompidou. The *alloco* (fried plantains), *attiéké* (shredded cassava) or *foutou* (cassava dumpling) are fantastic starch alternatives for the rice-weary, & dishes with chicken or fish start around 2,500F.

✕ N'ice Cream 97 Av Peytavin; ☏33 823 3545; www.nicecream.sn; ⏰ 11.00–22.30 Mon–Fri, 11.00–23.30 Sat, 11.00–21.30 Sun. In a building that looks like a cross between a marshmallow & a complicated board game, N'Ice Cream has been dishing up Dakar's favourite gelato for some years now. With a gobsmacking 75 flavours on offer, ranging from the safe (vanilla, caramel, mint chocolate) & the local (soursop, mango, passion fruit) to the esoteric (rock, jazz, Obama), you won't go home with an empty cone.

✕ Presse Café 108 Rue Carnot; ☏33 821 0579; www.pressecafe.sn; ⏰ 07.00–23.00 Mon–Fri, 07.00–midnight Sat–Sun. With several dozen locations around Quebec, this Canadian coffee shop chain first came to Dakar in 2014 & brought their bagels, lattes, muffins, cappuccinos, iced coffees & toasted sandwiches with them. It's spacious, thoroughly modern & a good place to camp out with your laptop & do some emailing. A bagel & cream cheese goes for 1,500F, while omelettes, crêpes, waffles & sandwiches start around 2,500F.

✕ Restaurant Farid 58 Rue Vincens; ☏33 823 8989; www.restaurant-farid.com; ⏰ noon–23.00 daily. Fast-food *chawarmas* are a dime a dozen in Dakar, but for a truly indulgent selection of freshly prepared Lebanese *mezze*, Farid is in a class by itself. The wide & vegetarian-friendly menu is a tour of Levantine cuisine from *arayess* (grilled pita stuffed with ground meat & herbs) to *zaatar* (quintessential Middle Eastern spice mix)

& everything in between. Small plates start at 3,500F, mains at 5,500F, & the memorable tasting menu is a splurgeworthy 14,000F per person. Desserts, cocktails, & shisha are all on offer as well, & the elegant outdoor terrace makes it hard not to linger.

POINT E
Map, pages 96–7.

✕ B'Food Rue Louga & Rue 7; ☏33 825 7551; www.facebook.com/BfoodDakar; ⏰ 11.00–16.00 & 20.00–23.00 Mon–Sat. A real lifebuoy for anyone who just can't bear to see another fried meal, the brief menu here boasts toasted sandwiches & burgers, crisp salads & fresh smoothies in a bright, fast casual setting. With standards like salade Niçoise (2,800F) & croque-monsieur (1,000F) served up alongside chlorophyll smoothies (1,500F) & fresh fruit desserts, it's a refreshing break from the norm, & your stomach (or waistline) might just thank you.

✕ Jardin Thailandaise 10 Blvd de Ziguinchor; ☏33 825 5833; ⏰ dinner only, Mon–Sat. Universally regarded as the best Thai in Senegal, this may not seem quite so impressive given that it's pretty much a one-man race, but the food here stands up on its own, & so do the tranquil garden surroundings. Inside you'll find more tables & an atmospheric collection of Thai art, & either way you get a range of noodle dishes & fine Technicolor curries (veggie among the options) in the 4,000F–7000F range.

✕ L'Ortolan 3 Rue de Kaolack; ☏33 825 3964; **m** 77 644 0362; www.facebook.com/restolortolan.dakar; ⏰ lunch & dinner daily. With a black & white mosaic floor reminiscent of a geometric Portuguese *calçada* & a polished wooden bar draped in *Marseillais* football scarves & rugby shirts, this backstreet Point E hangout has a vintage vibe, despite only opening in 2009. The menu is chalked up on a board & firmly within the French canon, with *escargot* & *foie gras* both making appearances, as well as more accessible favourites like *moules frites* & occasionally even *raclette*. They've got beer on tap & also do a Senegalese *plat du jour* for 2,500F.

✕ Lalibela Rue Louga; **m** 77 510 1569; ⏰ noon–15.00 & 18.00–midnight Mon–Sat, 18.00–midnight Sun. Pungent notes of *berbère* & fermented *injera* bread waft skywards from the spacious rooftop terrace at this unexpected

Ethiopian joint tucked away in Point E. Serving up authentic specialities from some 8,000km across the continent, the *doro wat* (chicken in berbere sauce), *tibs* (sautéed meat & veg), & *shiro* (chickpea stew) here are all rare treats & go for around 4,500F–6,000F. Ethiopian food is known to be vegetarian-friendly, & the same holds true here.

✕ **Le Must** Rue 1, Point E; ☎ 33 824 5224; m 77 489 4648; ⊕ noon–02.00 Sun–Tue, noon–03.00 Fri –Sat. Billed as a 'restaurant-bar-lounge', it really is a bit of all three, & renowned Senegalese musicians like Cheikh Lô, Orchestra Baobab & Baaba Maal all regularly grace the stage here, but with cover charges up to 10,000F for the shows it attracts a more genteel crowd than some of the other venues in town. The restaurant side of things does artfully presented meat & fish dishes starting at around 6,000F & a daily menu that might include anything from Moroccan *tagines* to Ivorian *kedjenou* stew. Cocktails start at a hefty 5,000F.

✕ **O'Good Food** Av Cheikh Anta Diop & Rue A; ☎ 33 825 3339/40; ⊕ 08.00–midnight daily. Encompassing the triumvirate of O'Pizza, O'Café & O'Burger, this is corporate fast food top to bottom, so if you've had one too many bowls of *thieboudienne*, this may just be the antidote. The terrace out front overlooks a busy intersection & is a great spot to people-watch over a beer or a milkshake. Combos with a drink start around 3,000F.

NGOR AND LES ALMADIES

If you're staying in **Yoff**, there are plenty of simple eateries to be found, along with a few fast food & *chawarma* joints, so you're not going to starve, but there's not so much worth mentioning in a city with as stiff culinary competition as Dakar, so head over to Ngor & Les Almadies when you want to give your taste buds a treat.
Map, page 94.

✕ **Alkimia** Rte des Almadies; ☎ 33 820 6868; www.alkimiadakar.com; ⊕ noon–16.00 & 19.30–23.30 daily, later at w/ends & no lunch on Sat. If your last washing was in a hotel sink & you did the smell test getting dressed this morning, just stop reading here. If you *did* pack some finery, though, & some of it might even be clean, then this mega-swish bar & restaurant could be the place for you. The whole place sits atop a water feature, with wood & glass panels arranged over the illuminated

micro-canals below. Up on deck, everything is draped in a modern B&W colour scheme with gunmetal accents & stands of bamboo providing some greenery. The bar does caipirinhas & other cocktails for 5,000F a pop, while the sophisticated menu will have you reaching for the phrasebook along with the fork: *carpaccio de poulpe* (octopus carpaccio), *calamars tandoori* (tandoori squid) & *côtelettes d'agneau* (lamb chops) are just one letter's worth of the offerings, which start at about 10,000F.

✕ **Annapurna** Rte de Ngor; ☎ 33 868 2222; m 77 394 1590; ⊕ noon–16.00 & 18.00–23.00 Mon–Sat. Just opposite Ngor stadium, the newest member of Dakar's Indian food canon & rapidly becoming a fan favourite, this place isn't particularly fashionable, but it's got all the curries & flatbreads you could want, alongside no less than a dozen vegetarian standbys like *palak paneer, chana masala* & *daal makhani* for 4,000F–6,000F.

✕ **Bayékou** m 77 681 3888; ⊕ 11.30–01.00 Sun–Thu, 11.30–03.00 Fri & Sat. On a gorgeous shaded rooftop terrace overlooking Ngor Island, this place opened at the tail end of 2014 & has earned the good graces of Dakar's foodie community almost overnight; their Peruvian ceviche might be a good clue as to why. The rest of the brief menu skews Italian, & after your penne or aubergine parmigiana you can finish off with a cocktail & a bissap *panna cotta*. Most dishes fall in the 5,000–9,000F range. Open late at w/ends (when there's also occasionally live music).

✕ **Charly's** Rte de Ngor; m 77 438 0350; www. facebook.com/charlydakar; ⊕ 07.30– late daily. Next to the swimming pool at the Sunugal Village Hotel, this well-loved spot has something going on just about every day, from a copious Sunday brunch to a DJ or live band almost every night of the week. Pitch up at the bar or billiard table for rotating happy hour specials (from 18.00) during the week, or grab a chair & indulge in the classy menu. Burgers start at 5,500F, pizza & fajitas are around the same, & prawns or entrecôte will see you parting with 6,500F–8500F. It's mostly an evening joint & the party goes on until late, but they do b/fast & lunch as well, & it's usually possible for restaurant clients to use the pool. Check their Facebook for the latest events.

✕ **La Cabane du Pêcheur** Plage de Ngor; ☎ 33 820 7675; m 77 712 9653; www.facebook.com/

cabanedupecheurngor; ⏲ 09.00–15.00 & 19.00–23.00 daily. First of all, they do Sunday brunch. One that involves bacon, eggs & pancakes. Now that that's out of the way, this place chalks up the latest catches on a board out front, & even has a lobster tank (rowboat-cum-aquarium, actually) inside, so you know it's barely been hours since your meal was underwater (& some taxidermied swordfish on the walls would also attest to that). It's right on the beach & they've got more seafood & crustaceans for 6,500F–9500F than you can shake a fin, pincer or shell at. There's also a handful of nice enough rooms for rent upstairs.

✗ La Cabane du Surfeur (Chez Abdou) Corniche des Almadies; ☎ 33 868 1017; m 76 590 0587; ⏲ 09.00– 21.00 daily. If a plastic picnic table in the sand with a cold beer & grilled fish on top of it sounds like your thing, you could do a lot worse than whiling away some hours here. Beyond the warm welcome, cold drinks (cocktails too!), & the fish, there's a short menu of brochettes, prawns, calamari & even lobster, most of it in the 4,000F–6,000F range.

✗ Layu Café Rte des Almadies; ☎ 33 868 1332; www.ilovelayu.com; ⏲ 08.00–21.00 Mon–Sat, 09.00–20.00 Sun. Half café, half fair-trade boutique, this glimmering new coffee shop serves a small but impressive selection of hot & cold beverages, sandwiches & pastries in a tranquil, air-conditioned dining room with designer jewellery, clothing & décor made in West Africa sold at the back, as well as a good selection of African books & music (in French). They've also got a smaller location on Rue Mohammed V in Plateau.

✗ Le Lodge des Almadies ☎ 33 869 0345; www.facebook.com/lelodgedesalmadies; ⏲ noon–14.30 & 19.30–22.30 Wed–Mon. Tucked away inside the eponymous hotel, this place appears a bit stuffy from the outside, but inside it's more casual & serves an excellent continental menu, with fish carpaccio, lamb shoulder, seafood ravioli & beef in peppercorn sauce all represented, alongside rarer options like goat cheese & foie gras. It's fine cuisine but unpretentious & they do a 5,000F *plat du jour*, a 9,500F 3-course menu, & most of the other mains come in between 7,000F & 9,000F.

✗ Le Ngor Corniche des Almadies; ☎ 33 868 2514; m 77 504 3006; www.lengor-restaurant. com; ⏲ 09.00–midnight daily. The French phrase '*pieds dans l'eau*' (feet in the water) is no rhetorical flourish at this offbeat beachside restaurant just off the Route des Almadies. Looking every bit the outsider art project from the street, old-car-turned-*calèche* & all, walking in reveals a parrot-wielding mermaid (a statue, unfortunately), seashells plastered all over the place, & most importantly an impressive Spanish-inspired menu. They've got all the seafood you'd expect of the location, plus the unexpected bonus of tapas & paella.

✗ Le Ryad Rte des Almadies; ☎ 33 820 9469; m 76 669 4817; ⏲ noon–15.00 & 19.00–23.00 daily. With all the tagines & couscous your little traveller's heart could desire & a setting fit for a sheikh, the Moroccan menu here would make a fitting reward after arriving in Dakar from the dusty interior. The indoor seating is alright, but the outdoor terrace is divine, with seating on plush floor cushions surrounded by flickering lanterns & a babbling fountain. There's a full bar & they put on belly-dancing nights once a month (20,000F, drinks excluded). Other mains go for 6,000F–8,000F, & there's sorbet for dessert.

✗ Noflaye Beach Corniche des Almadies; ☎ 33 820 3032; ⏲ noon–20.00 Mon–Thu, noon–23.00 Fri–Sun. This restaurant & *crêperie* on the Corniche des Almadies is an endearingly simple & effortlessly stylish seaside setup that would look every bit at home in a décor magazine. The short menu boasts a handful of fish & meat dishes starting at 6,000F, but the sweet & savoury crêpes (1,500F–4,000F) are the real stars of the show here, with fillings ranging from curried mussels to caramelised bananas.

✗ Pâtisserie Graine d'Or Rte de l'Aéroport; ☎ 33 859 9000/820 8573; ⏲ 06.30–20.30 daily. One of the leading lights in Dakar's surprisingly competitive patisserie scene, this is a gem by any measure, with several metres of glass cases stuffed with too many cakes, waffles, pies, pastries, muffins & cookies to list here. Inside, it's hyper-clean, freezing cold & does take-away only, while out front they occasionally set up a griddle & sell fresh crêpes to passers-by.

✗ Planet Kebab Rte de Ngor; ☎ 33 848 1176/7; ⏲ 11.00–03.00 Sun–Thu, 11.00–06.00 Fri–Sat. With high-end fast food, pastries & coffee in a scrubbed-till-it-shines glass & steel building on the Almadies strip, this place stays open until the wee hours to make sure no late-night punter goes kebabless. They're equally busy for lunches, & their Plateau location is just as slick.

✗ Restaurant La Marée (Chez Adji) Pointe des Almadies; m 77 550 7358; ☾ 08.00–late daily. In the little warren of shops & restaurants at the end of the road & the very edge of the Pointe des Almadies, this place grills up just about anything with gills, & does a damn fine job of it too. The dining room is just a big covered terrace overlooking the ocean, & it faces straight west so sundowners here are almost mandatory. Prices vary from a 4,000F grilled *dorade* (sea bream) to a full-on *fruits de mer* (seafood) platter with everything they've got including lobster, clams, mussels & prawns for 20,000F.

✗ São Brasil Rte de Ngor; ☎ 33 820 0941; ☾ 11.00–midnight daily, later at w/ends. Brazilian it's not, but the crispy, wood-fired pizzas (starting at 4,500F) here are in the running for best in town & will put your impertinent questioning of the nomenclature to bed with the first bite. On a covered terrace built around a circular bar that reliably has some fresh music playing, this is a funky & unpretentious hangout that attracts locals & ex-pats alike. They've got meat & fish dishes too, but those looking for meats on parade should make a beeline for Churrascaria Brasil (see below) instead.

✗ Sweet Coffee Rte des Almadies; ☎ 33 820 9009; ☾ 09.00–01.00 Tue–Sun. If the teenage-girl's-bedroom colour scheme doesn't send you running straight away, then you're in store for a long menu of panini, pasta, salad & pizza, as well as some (very apropos) sugary coffee creations. There's a full bar & you can get a shisha pipe to smoke on the terrace out front as well. Sandwiches start at 3,000F & other dishes are closer to 5,000F.

ELSEWHERE IN TOWN
Map, pages 84–5, unless otherwise noted.

✗ Churrascaria Brasil 7 Rue Fila, Fann Hock; ☾ dinner Mon–Sat, lunch Sat–Sun; ☎ 33 821 0032; m 77 523 0492. With fine cuts of grilled meats served at your table in an all-you-can-eat *rodízio* style, this ought to be the first stop in Dakar for carnivores weary of the Senegalese fish & rice parade. There's a buffet selection of salads & hot & cold side dishes as well, & the whole shebang goes for 7,900F–8,900F, depending on the day.

✗ La Calebasse Mamelles; ☎ 33 860 6947; m 77 332 0583/639 9500; ☾ noon–22.30 Tue–Sun. For upscale West African cuisine in an impeccable, boldly African setting, go no further than this restaurant connected to the Art Afrique gallery, just south of the Route des Almadies in Mamelles. They've got kora players & other live music every night of the week, & meals are served surrounded by masks & local artwork under a high thatched roof overlooking the ocean. Give yourself some extra time to check out the gallery & the new lounge space open since the end of 2014.

✗ Little Buddha [96 A5] Sea Plaza Mall; ☎ 33 859 9380; www.littlebuddhadakar.com; ☾ noon–midnight Mon–Thu, noon–02.00 Fri–Sat. This hyper-cool lounge in the Sea Plaza mall sparkles with dark wood & dim lanterns in a pseudo-Asian style, with a proper sushi bar on one side & a long bar with sake & plenty of cocktails on the other. They do a range of curries, stir fries & soups, sashimi tastings go for 6,500F–10,000F, & if you're feeling splurgey, their 3-course menu is 20,000F. They bring in DJs at the weekends & house beats pump into the night as Dakar's chattering classes look on.

✗ Trio Toque Rotating location; e triotoque@gmail.com; www.triotoque.com. Once a month since 2012, three Dakar gourmands assemble a one-night-only pop-up restaurant in a private home or other venue around the city where they serve experimental 5-course dinners of *haute cuisine* made with a focus on local inspirations & ingredients. Depending on the month, you could be eating anything from squid ink pasta to *vol-au-vents* with asparagus & morels; the whole affair goes for about 30,000F. Check the website to see the date of their next event & email them early – the location is only divulged to confirmed guests.

✗ Yum Yum Rte de Ouakam; ☎ 33 865 6262 (Ouakam) 822 65 65 (Plateau); www.yumyum.sn; ☾ 07.00–23.00 Mon–Thu, 07.00–01.00 Fri, 09.00–01.00 Sat, 11.00–23.00 Sun. Pizza & doughnuts under one roof. Does this review really need to be any longer? Really, it's just about all they do. (OK, there's some pasta & stuff too, but that's not why you're here.) In an unsubtle red building on the way to Almadies (Ave Cheikh Anta Diop), pizzas here can be mixed & matched with your choice of toppings & crust, & prices range from 2,500F–7.000F, while the glazed & frosted doughnuts go for 500F. Naturally, they deliver, & they've just opened a 2nd location in Plateau at Avenue Lamine Guèye & Rue Bugnicourt.

NIGHTLIFE AND LIVE MUSIC

Many of the restaurants mentioned above double as relaxed venues for music or a drink, particularly **Le Kermel** and **Le Bideew** in Plateau, **Le Must** in Point E, **Little Buddha** at the Sea Point mall in Fann, and **Le Ngor, Charly Bar, Bayékou** and **Alkimia** in Ngor/Almadies.

Whether you want to *mbalax* until morning in a sweaty concert hall, sip top-shelf cocktails and strut your stuff with the sparkling Dakar elite, belly up to the smoke-filled bar for one more round, or simply get your toes into the sand and watch the twinkling coast fall away, Dakar's got something for you after dark. The champagne set mostly heads straight for Les Almadies, there's rootsier dancing and drinking in Point E, and Plateau is home to drinking holes both coarse and classy.

If it's music and dancing you're after, particularly live, it's rare for a place to get cracking before 01.00 at the earliest, and there's no stopping until at least sunrise, so time your afternoon nap accordingly. For the latest in concert listings, many clubs and bars are starting to jump on the Facebook bandwagon; also Au Sénégal and Le 221 (*www.le221.com*) have a well-updated cultural calendar that covers everything from literature to music to sport. Some more concert listings are available at www.dakarmusique.com.

BARS AND NIGHTCLUBS

♀ Chez Sam [90 D4] Rue Joseph Gomis. With bare concrete walls daubed in a festive institutional beige, this place near the French Cultural Centre has all the ambiance of a prison cell & is about the same size too. Still, it's difficult to take issue with what is probably the cheapest beer in Plateau. Save some cash on a Gazelle & some local gin (NB: Bradt Guides not responsible for crippling hangovers) here so you can sip your bissap mojito guilt-free up in Almadies later on.

♀ Le Viking [91 E3] 21 Av Pompidou, Plateau; m 77 244 8056; ⏰ 08.00–02.00 daily. Almost as much of an institution as Ali Baba across the street, this beery pub is perennially busy & the upstairs is a good spot to grab a booth with friends. The crowd here takes all kinds & makes for some fascinating people-watching, though don't be surprised when the objects of your gaze pull up a stool & stay a while. Drinks here aren't particularly cheap, but there's beer on draft & a live band downstairs at weekends.

♀ Siège de Gorée [91 F2] Blvd de la Libération, Plateau; \ 33 822 7569; ⏰ 08.00–midnight daily, later at w/ends. With picnic chairs aplenty, a *plat du jour* by day & a bouncing open-air dancefloor by night, this place hidden behind the Hôtel de Ville is a fine spot in Plateau to knock back some cheap Gazelles & convince yourself you'll be able to stay up for the late night *mbalax* across town.

☆ Calypso [91 E3] 42 Rue Wagane Diouf, Plateau; \ 33 823 73 29; ⏰ 19.00–late daily. The seemingly pan-African nightclub tradition of dancing with yourself in front of a mirror is elevated to an artform at this popular joint in Plateau. It's literally & figuratively miles from the painfully trendy places up in Almadies (dress codes be damned!), but the crowd here is youthful enough & you'll know all the tunes if you've been travelling around West Africa for a while. The VIP tables will make you feel like a petty tyrant at best, but the bottle service is surprisingly economical & you'll definitely be in for more fun & less hassle here with a group.

☆ Duplex [94 D4] Rte de Ngor; \ 33 820 9646; \ 77 354 2954/532 0053; www.twitter.com/duplexclubdakar; ⏰ 23.00–05.00 daily. White parties, black parties, ladies' nights, house nights, dancehall vibes, mask parties & 'the ultimate hip hop affair' are just a few of the themed nightly soirées going on at this too-cool-for-school nightclub on the west side of the Almadies strip. It's mostly DJs moving the acutely stylish butts that pack this club, but once in a while a *mbalax* singer makes an appearance, guaranteeing occasional flying knees & elbows on the dancefloor as well. Expect cover charges around 10,000F & it doesn't get any cheaper inside. Check online to make sure you don't show up in black to the white party – perish the thought!

☆ Five [94 D3] Rte de Ngor; \ 33 820 4006; m 77 755 5555; www.facebook.com/complexefive;

🕙 10.00– 07.00 daily. Fanta here costs 3,500F & alcoholic drinks are pricier yet. Still reading? This place on the main strip in Almadies is open all the time, but looks & feels like a hangover during daylight hours. By night it's full of dancers & drinkers in designer clothes ogling the VIP room upstairs & buying those expensive Fantas & bottles of champagne. Order a shisha pipe & grab a couch out front to watch the world go by.

☆ **Just 4 U** Av Cheikh Anta Diop, Point E; 📞33 825 9925; 📱 77 236 1174/715 9295; 📧 justdakar@gmail.com; 🕙 19.00–late daily. Across from the university, this open-air venue might be the most reliable party in town, hosting Senegal's biggest names every night of the week. Depending on the night, you're just as likely to catch Senegalese hip hop pioneers Daara J here as you are *mbalax* royalty like Omar Pene or the peerless Cheikh Lô. As with anywhere else in town, the headliners won't be on stage until well into the night.

☆ **Le Patio** [94 D4] Rte de Ngor; 📞33 820 5823; www.lepatio-dakar.com; 🕙 19.00–05.00 daily. In a vaguely casbah-esque courtyard with wire-frame tables & thatched awnings, this restaurant-bar-nightclub combo slowly becomes less restaurant & more nightclub as the night wears on. It draws a diverse crowd, but the long wooden bar is usually packed with perfectly-coiffed young Senegalese ladies & their considerably older (and less perfectly coiffed) *toubab* male companions. Bring a group along & the outdoor bar can be nice enough for a few drinks & some fascinating people-watching; come alone & you're likely to spend the night getting chatted up.

☆ **King's Club** [91 E4] 32 Rue Victor Hugo; 📞33 842 8787; www.kingsclubdakar.com; 🕙 23.00–dawn Tue–Sun. The nightclub sibling of Alkimia & La Fourchette, the couches here are low, the heels are high, the prices are steep & the disco lights are set to stun. The music selection, much like the place itself, is aggressively modern, with 'Cuba electro' & 'deep lounge' nights on the calendar. Check the website for upcoming events & come dressed to impress or don't expect to get in.

☆ **Nirvana (High Life)** [94 D4] Rond-point des Almadies; 📱 77 816 4560/70 403 1919; www.facebook.com/nirvanadakar; 🕙 23.00–06.00 Wed–Mon. Maybe the best-known of the several über-chic nightclubs on the strip, they were working on a rebrand at the end of 2014 & will probably be called High Life by the time you read

this. Still, the glitz of their previous incarnation hasn't gone anywhere, & here you get something strictly *verboten* at the aggressively youthful clubs down the street: retro nights! Which in Senegal means soul & disco, classic *mbalax* & live shows from Pape & Cheikh, Orchestra Baobab & newer crooners like Pape Diouf. As with just about everywhere on the strip, dress to impress.

☆ **Sunset Sahel** [85 E6] Centre Commercial Sahm, Blvd Gueule Tapée, Medina; 📞33 821 2118. Dakar nightspots don't get much more venerable than this Medina landmark, here since 1972, where the 70s house band, *Le Sahel*, is credited with creating the Cuban-African fusion that would grow into the *mbalax* rhythm inescapable in Senegal today. Age has done little to dull its edge, so be ready for a rough & ready crowd with a raging case of *mbalax* fever.

☆ **The Box Super Club** [94 D4] Rte de Ngor; 📱 77 546 4636; 🕙 23.00–dawn Thu–Sun. With strobes, fog machines & lasers fit to send an epileptic to the hospital, the dancefloor here pulsates to a selection of top DJs from Dakar & abroad, but they ostensibly screen for a 25+ up crowd (men, anyway), so it feels less like a school leaving party than some of the other clubs on the strip. If it all gets to be a bit too much & you've got money to burn, check out the 1st-floor booths with balconies overlooking the action. The cover charge fluctuates, but expect to pay 5,000F or so.

☆ **Thiossane** [97 G1] Rue 10, SICAP; 📞33 824 70 78. Youssou N'Dour's place is known to all Dakarois, & while the club itself isn't especially long on charm, it's exactly where you want to be if Youssou himself is in town, as he still belts out the *mbalax* late Saturday nights when he's here, to the general adulation of the crowd, raised on the tunes of this hometown hero. When it's open, the fast & furious dance moves go well into the night, but the hours here can be irregular (for instance when Youssou isn't around), so have a plan B if you're headed this way (Just 4 U isn't too far away – see left).

CASINOS

☆ **Casino du Cap-Vert** [94 E2] Rte de Ngor; 📞33 869 7878; www.anfa-group.com; 🕙 noon–04.00 daily. This hangout for monied Dakarois & expats has roulette, 70 slots, & regular poker tournaments. It's attached to L'Airport Hotel if you stay up too late & need a nice place to crash out and tally up the night's results.

☆ **Casino du Port** [91 H2] Av de la Libération; ☎ 33 849 0649; www.casinoduport.com; ⊕ noon–04.00 daily. You can gamble here in 4 different currencies, and with a full complement of blackjack, poker, table games, slots, buffet restaurant & sports bar, you'll probably need at least a couple of them. Leave the flip-flops at home.

ARTS AND ENTERTAINMENT

CINEMA At the moment, your best bet for catching a flick in Dakar is at one of the international cultural centres. Despite Senegal having one of Africa's most venerable film traditions, the industry suffered much neglect after losing the guaranteed support enjoyed under the Senghor administration, and has today yet to recover from its steep decline. There is a multiplex under construction at the Sea Plaza Mall, which will in all likelihood start screening Hollywood blockbusters (and maybe some Bollywood selections as well) during the lifespan of this edition.

Thus, movie buffs would do well to check out the calendar at the **Institut Français** [91 E4] (*89 Rue Joseph Gomis;* ☎ *33 823 0320; www.institutfrancais-senegal. com*), where there are screenings of African, French & other films, usually at least twice a week, though for the most part they'll all be either in French or subtitled in French. Alternatively, the **Goethe Institut** [91 E4] (*Rue de Diourbel;* ☎ *33 869 8880; www.goethe.de/senegal*) in Point E screens films on Wednesdays at 19.30, with a focus on Senegalese films & world cinema, often (in the case of the former) with the directors in attendance.

FESTIVALS Dakar's cultural calendar is always busy, but a few times a year it really heats up, when the city hosts a series of national and international music, art and culture festivals. Starting at the beginning of the year, there's **Ribidion** (*www. ribidionfestival.com*) and the **Joko Festival** (*www.facebook.com/jokkongor*), both of which take place in December/January, often over the New Year. Ribidion puts on some star-studded concerts (they managed to get Nigerian megastars P-Square in 2013), while Joko is a more down-to-earth mix of music, drumming, dance and painting at the little bars & restaurants of Ngor island. A few weeks later, **Dakar Restaurant Week** (*www.facebook.com/dakarrestaurantweek*) kicks off, running for (you guessed it) a week at the end of January and beginning of February, when Dakar's finest eateries (Le Toukouleur, Le Cozy, Alkimia, etc) pull out all the stops and put on tastings of their most innovative cuisine.

From here on there's a lull until a deluge of festivals that starts in May with the **Dak'Art Biennale** (*www.dakart.org*) which runs for a month every even-numbered year. Art takes over the city from Plateau to Pikine, with a bounty of music, dance, theatre and fashion on display in dozens of galleries, museums, theatres and impromptu spaces around the city. A must-see if you happen to be in town. On the odd years, there's another biennial, **Kaay Fecc** (*www.kaayfecc.com*), in town around the same time to pick up the slack. While it doesn't match Dak'Art in size, this dance festival celebrates Senegal's dancers no matter the style, with traditional performances, *mbalax* and break dancing all on the bill.

June offers a glut of culture by any measure, even in a city as artistic as Dakar. Among Dakar's youth, you won't top **Festa2H** (*www.facebook.com/FESTA2H*), which runs workshops on all the elements of hip hop, whether it's DJing, dancing or producing your own records, and rappers from around the world are invited to perform. The more refined **Festival de cinéma image et vie** (Cinema Festival of Image and Life) (*www.imagetvie.org*) showcases cinema from Africa and the

4

Caribbean in partnership with the Institut Français. While all this is going on, the **Dakar Fashion Week** (*www.dakarfashionweek.com*) also takes place in June, and is here to make your threadbare traveller's outfit feel even grubbier. It's an absolute who's who of African fashion & design and, while getting tickets to marvel at the catwalk might be a challenge, you can still spruce up your look with a piece from one of the designers.

Finally, in December there's the **FILDAK Book Fair** (*www.cices.sn*), which is a series of readings, book sales and soirées around the city, but it may unfortunately wind up being of little interest to Anglophones unless you've got a patient translator along.

MUSIC AND DANCE Most live music in Dakar goes on at restaurants, bars and nightclubs, which are listed in the relevant sections. Beyond these, the international cultural centres typically have impressively busy cultural calendars; **Institut Français** (see page 109) has music several nights a week, while the **Goethe Institut** (see page 109) and the **Instituto Cervantes** [97 F5] (*Camp Jeremy, UCAD, Rue Cheikh Anta Diop;* \ *33 825 0669;* e *aula.dakar@cerevantes.es; www.dakar.cervantes.es* or *www.facebook.com/aulacervantes.dakar*), in partnership with their **Cultura Dakar** project (\ *33 821 3081/889 6580;* e *cultura.dk@gmail.com; www.culturadakar.es*), have occasional soirées as well.

The home of the dramatic arts in Senegal was for decades the 1,100-seat **Théâtre National Daniel Sorano** [90 C4] (*45 Blvd de la République;* \ *33 822 3879 www.theatrenationaldusenegal.com*), the *Troupe Nationale Dramatique, l'Ensemble National de Ballet (La Linguère)* and *l'Ensemble Lyrique Traditionel* are all based here and have been since the theatre's opening in 1965. Their repertoire is wide-ranging, and you're just as likely to catch a Senegalese historical epic like *L'exil d'Alboury*, the tale of the last king of Djolof (see page 245), or a play by Ousmane Sembène as you are Shakespeare or Paul Claudel. All of the troupes are actively performing and in some cases touring internationally, but shows here can be infrequent so check the website or the notices out front to get an idea of what's happening when you're in town.

Despite the fact that the Théâtre National Daniel Sorano is in considerable need of modernisation and renovation, 2012 saw the opening of another grandiose Wade-era project, the six-storey, €30 million, Chinese-built **Grand Théâtre National** [85 F6] (*Autoroute Seydina Limamou Laye;* \ *33 822 5700; www.facebook.com/grandtheatrenational*). It is indeed an impressive, if somewhat hulking, structure and, with its double-decker balconies and 1,800 seats, it is reckoned to be the largest theatre in West Africa. It was originally slated to be only the first part of a seven-building campus, the *Parc Culturel de Dakar*, better known as *Les Sept Merveilles de Dakar* ('The Seven Wonders of Dakar'), but, following Macky Sall's ascent to the presidency in 2012 and his considerably smaller appetite for monumental prestige projects, it looks as though the Dakarois will have to make do with fewer wonders for the time being. It's already been host to comedies, choirs and cinema screenings, and a fair few of Senegal's leading musical lights have performed here as well. Unfortunately they don't keep an online events calendar, so you'll have to drop in to see what's on.

Considerably more modest, but still having undergone a spot of renovation in 2014, the **Centre Culturel Blaise Senghor** (*Blvd Dial Diop;* \ *33 824 6600; www.facebook.com/centreculturel.blaisesenghor*) in Grand Dakar is a nucleus for dozens of local artists, actors and musicians. There are usually some low-key exhibitions going on, along with any number of creative young folks polishing their craft.

Naturally, Dakar can't stay so svelte and fashionable without at least a bit of effort, and sporting types will have no trouble at all finding their niche here. The Corniche Ouest is constantly packed with joggers, walkers and press-up fanatics of all stripes making their way up and down the coast, and everything from karate to kitesurfing is a short hop away. The **Olympique Club** [96 A3] (*Rte de la Corniche Ouest*; \ *33 864 5655; e olympique@orange.sn; www.olympique-club.com*) has been offering tennis, squash, fitness, martial arts, basketball, swimming and more since it opened here in 1982. Tariffs vary depending on the activity, but a session at the fitness centre goes for 5,000F, joining a taekwondo class is 3,000F, and pool use is 5,000F/6,000F week/weekend and half price after 15.00. Another good spot for swimming is the enormous **Piscine Olympique** [97 F4] (\ *33 869 0606;* ⊕ *09.00–13.00 & 15.00–18.00 Wed, Fri–Sun*), which has a rather irregular opening schedule but is otherwise probably the most economical swim in town at 1,000F/2,000F weekday/weekend.

If you'd rather be beachside than poolside, scuba, surfing and fishing are all easily arranged from here. The various surf schools in Ngor and Yoff listed under accommodation (Malika, Ngor Island, and Oumar surf camps – see pages 95, 98 and 99) should be your first stop if you're looking to hang ten, and all offer individual lessons as well as multi-session introductory courses. Check their websites for package details. Conditions here are also ideal for kitesurfing, and the camps can point you in the right direction if you'd like to give it a try. The **Rip Curl Surf Shop** [94 D2] (*Rte de Ngor;* \ *33 868 1920; www.ripcurlsenegal.com;* ⊕ *09.00–20.00 Mon–Sat*) can also arrange lessons, or sell you any wax or kit you need.

Under the breakers, there are more than 50 scuba-diving sites scattered around the peninsula and both **Nautilus Diving** (*www.nautilus-diving.com*) based at Maison Abaka in Ngor, and **Oceanium** [91 F6] (*www.oceaniumdakar.org*) on the Route de la Corniche Est know the wrecks, reefs and drop-offs around Dakar like the backs of their flippers. Both offer PADI certifications for new divers, but if you'd rather stay above water, Oceanium has kayaks for hire – explore the coast and take in Dakar from a new perspective, or head for Gorée if you're a strong paddler.

There's no shortage of fresh seafood in Dakar, but if you'd like to take things a step further and catch some for yourself, either for sport or dinner, the folks at **La Cabane Du Pêcheur** in Ngor (see pages 104–5) are experts in all things piscine (whether on hook or plate) and do customisable fishing trips in their own boats around the peninsula. **Le Lagon** (see page 102) also arranges fishing excursions, often accompanied by their world-champion guide.

Back on land, golfers are well catered for at the stunningly located 2,300m, nine-hole course at the **King Fahd Palace** (see page 93) (*www.kingfahdpalacehotels.com/golf*) on the Pointe des Almadies. They've got golf pros if you need some coaching and a driving range for practising your swing or getting some energy out, but don't count on any of it being cheap.

The **Hann Poney Club** [84 G3] (*Parc forestier de Hann;* \ *33 832 0652;* m *77 638 9058; www.poneyclubdakar.com*) in the northeast corner of the Hann Forest Park is Dakar's equestrian refuge, catering to both adults and children with single rides, lessons in riding, jumping and all aspects of horsemanship, or horseback excursions from an afternoon to a week in length. The grounds here are also home to Dakar's only paintball club, **Paintball Mariste** (m *77 638 9058; www.facebook.com/PaintballMariste*). They've got a course set up and all necessary equipment, but you'll need six people to play.

Back indoors, fans of tenpin will assuredly be bowled over by the 12 brand-new lanes at **Red Bowl** [96 A5] (*Sea Plaza;* ☎ *33 859 8998; www.redbowl.sn;* ⊕ *noon–02.00 Sun–Thu, noon–03.00 Fri–Sat*), where you can try to stay out of the gutters in a red- and-black lounge that feels more nightclub than bowling alley. They've got billiard tables, a video arcade and a café-bar, and even more surprisingly it's non-smoking. It's 3,500F per person per game during the week, and 5,000F at the weekends. Don't forget to wear socks!

And if you're finally ready to give it a rest and watch someone else do the sporting, the **traditional wrestling** (*la lutte*) season runs from November to about July. The biggest matches take place at the newly-renovated Stade Demba Diop on Boulevard Président Bourguiba in Grand Dakar, while smaller competitions are sometimes held at Stade Iba Mar Diop on Avenue Blaise Diagne in Medina. Keep your eyes out for hyperbolic promo posters hyping the muscle-bound combatants and their upcoming matches. The events can be packed, chaotic and a great place for pickpockets, so do not bring any valuables and consider getting a VIP ticket if you can.

STUDY

Created as a partnership between Senegal- and US-based academics, the **West African Research Centre** [96 E6] (WARC) (*Rue E, Fann Residence;* ☎ *33 865 2277;* e *warc_croa@warc.sn; www.warccroa.org*) is an excellent resource for scholars interested in the region, and is a particularly good starting point if you're hoping to make contacts at **Université Cheikh Anta Diop** [97 E6] (☎ *33 825 0530;* e *rectorat@ucad.edu.sn; www.ucad.sn*). They host occasional events and lectures, and their canteen does a budget-friendly *plat du jour* that's available to the public.

If you're here to learn a language, the **ACI Baobab Center** [96 B7] (*Fann;* ☎ *33 825 3637/824 8338;* e *rsow@acibaobab.org; www.baobabcenter.org*) does customisable courses in an impressive variety of languages; French and Wolof are their primary curriculum, but they also arrange lessons in Pulaar, Diola, Mandinka, Serer and even Portuguese, Kriol or Arabic. The Institut Français offers scheduled French courses at several levels, while the Goethe Institut does German, and the Instituto Cervantes offers (you guessed it) Spanish – see page 110 for more on these institutions.

SHOPPING

Several malls have popped up around Dakar in the past few years and, aside from speciality items like camping goods, they carry everything from high fashion to hamster food. **Sea Plaza** (*www.seaplazadakar.com*) is the newest kid on the block, the glitziest mall in town, and soon to have Senegal's only multiplex. It's got several dozen stores, including international brands like Aldo, United Colors of Benetton and a bunch more that are too fashionable for the likes of this author. There's an impressively stocked Casino supermarket, kids' boutiques, the Librairie des 4 Vents bookshop and a pet store; the food court has sandwiches, Lebanese food, pizza, pasta, fajitas and a fancier bar and grill as well.

Dakar City Mall on Route de Ngor is considerably smaller, but also superbly stocked with a Casino supermarket, fashion labels like Guess, sporting goods, eyeglasses/spectacles shop, and kid's stuff.

SELF-CATERING The supermarket selection here is phenomenal and you won't want for much, even though most goods are imported so prices tend to be high. The French **Casino** chain has several large outlets with full produce, butchers and packaged goods sections, including at Sea Plaza Mall, Dakar City Mall on Route de Ngor and on Avenue Hassan II near the Place de l'Indépendance. The Spanish-owned **CityDia** (*www.facebook.com/citydiasn*) is another good option, and there are a half-dozen or more of them scattered around the peninsula.

Brands for sale tend to reflect the origin of the chain and such products are nearly all European. For North Americans with a food itch they just can't scratch, the aptly named **American Food Store** [94 B3] (🕿 33 868 3839; m 77 787 7507; ⊕ *09.00–21.00 Mon–Sat, 10.00–20.00 Sun*) has everything from salsa to saltines.

BOOKSHOPS Senegal in general offers rather slim pickings for the Anglophone reader, but Dakar is miraculously home to a speciality bookshop dedicated to just that. **Chez Alpha** [84 C3] (*Mamelles, Cité des Magistrats No. 10*; 🕿 33 820 6359; m 77 642 6383; *www.chezalphabks.com*; ⊕ *noon–17.00 Mon, 09.00–17.00 Tue–Sat*) is as much a community centre as it is a bookshop, which, in addition to its collection of African and world literature for sale, offers English courses, assistance for young people applying to university, and a lending library. The next-best choice would be **Librairie aux 4 Vents** [85 D5] (🕿 33 825 5514; *www.librairie4vents.com*), which has three locations around town (Plateau, Mermoz and Sea Plaza) but only a handful of English-language books in each.

MARKETS Dakar may be home to umpteen glamorous nightclubs and some of the most fabulous fashionistas this side of Paris, but it's still a West African city through and through, and nowhere is this more apparent than in its raucous, crowded markets. Long the beating heart of the city, **Marché Sandaga** [90 D3] suffered a massive fire in October 2013 and the casbah-style central building has been closed since then. Renovations have not been forthcoming (it's understood the city government wasn't too enamoured with Sandaga's aesthetics and isn't in much hurry for it to reopen), so it's likely to remain shuttered for some time to come. Most of the merchants have relocated to the area around Lat Dior bus terminus, as well as spilling out into the streets and alleyways surrounding the market. A trip to Sandaga is still a worthwhile venture and you can still buy just about everything under the sun here, but it's nonetheless a shadow of its former self.

Considerably more manageable than even today's Sandaga is **Marché Kermel** [91 G3], some blocks away in Plateau. Set in an immensely attractive round Victorian building with wrought-iron trimmings, Kermel, too, suffered a great fire and was entirely rebuilt in 1997 as a replica of the original, which was approaching 90 years old when it burned. Inside, the sellers are arranged in concentric circles and, in a Dante-esque touch, the more pungent the item, the closer it is to the centre. Stay on the outer rings for okra, aubergines, peppers and potatoes, then make your way into the core for glassy-eyed fish, symmetrical piles of prawns and bloody butcher's cuts. A few dozen craft sellers have set themselves up as sort of an addendum to the main building, and it's a pretty low-hassle place to pick up souvenirs. Whatever you do, don't miss the awesome wall of masks just outside the market on Rue Aristide le Dantec. From here it's a 10-minute walk to the *gare ferroviaire*, where the **Marché Malien** [91 E1] trades in goods from over the border – shea butter, Touareg jewellery and mud-dyed *bogolan* cloth are among the specialities brought here on the train from thousands of miles inland. With the demise of the train service, the selection might be slimmer than it once was, but it's worth stopping in to have a look and learn a few words of Bambara while you're at it.

Just a touch north of Sandaga on the way to Medina lies the unassuming *Cour des orfèvres* [90 B2] (goldsmiths' court), where you ought to make a stop if you're in the market for hand-hammered bracelets, rings, charms, amulets and more

Pierre Thiam, Chef, Author of Yolele! Recipes From the Heart of Senegal and Senegal: Modern Recipes From The Source to the Bowl *(www.pierrethiam.com)*

Visiting open markets in Senegal, or anywhere in Africa for that matter, is one of my favourite activities. There is no better way to immerse yourself in the pulse of the community and get a good insight into the culture, food, smells and sounds of Senegal than inside its markets. Regardless of the region, Senegalese markets are exciting, vibrant, colourful, noisy and fun.

Since cooking is still a gender-based activity in Senegal, markets are naturally full of women – beautiful women, elegantly dressed in flowing, brightly coloured fabrics. Some sport architectural headscarves, while others carry heavy loads precariously balanced on their heads – often with a baby wrapped up and sleeping comfortably on their backs.

They move about graciously between the crowded and narrow alleys, which are overflowing with food and other domestic items. The atmosphere feels like a carnival: the animated noises of bargain, laughter, haggling and the occasional music seamlessly blend with the smells of *thiouraye* incense, dozens of spices, and of course food.

Indeed, all sorts of foods are to be found: sweet mangoes, sour tamarinds, bitter eggplants, briny clam relish, spicy peppers, fermented conch, salted fish, smoked catfish, fresh fish, all kinds of green leaves, plantain, fried plantain, skinned lamb hanging on hooks, and a bountiful diversity of fresh ingredients. Senegalese markets are a feast for the senses!

Depending on what you're looking for, my personal favourites in Dakar are the historic **Marché Kermel** in Plateau (see page 113) and the perpetually busy **Marché Tilène** in Medina (see pages 114–15). If it's fish you're after and you've got the time, a trip to the **Marché Aux Poissons** up the peninsula in Kayar (see pages 136–7) is absolutely unforgettable, but the fish market at **Soumbédioune** (see page 115) in Dakar typically has an excellent selection as well. For fashion plates rather than dinner plates, there's nowhere better than **Marché HLM** (see below), the ideal place to buy fabrics. Wherever you go, don't be intimidated by the hassle – as anywhere, take good care of your personal belongings, but don't be afraid to stop and chat! After nearly three decades of cooking professionally, I still pick up tips from the vendors every time I go.

made from silver, gold, bronze, copper and other semi-precious metals. Once you've got the bling, head northeast until you hit Dakar's most soignée speciality market, **Marché HLM** [85 F5]. Within the walls of this unlikely den of fashion lie a world of wax prints, hand-hammered Malian *bazin,* delicate embroidery, and all the tailors you could need to help you suit up in the grandest of *grands boubous* or in the traditional three-piece women's *complet* (matching bodice, skirt and wrap). Garments from the modest to the opulent can be measured, cut, sewn and ready for pickup in a matter of hours or days and, if you've got an article of clothing you particularly like, it's no problem to get a replica made out of new material.

While your new *boubou* is at the tailor's, get the unvarnished market experience at the teeming **Marché Tilène** [85 E6] in Medina. Set up for 400 vendors and today hosting an estimated 1,500 and serving 50,000 daily customers, it's a manic slice of life as authentic as the neighbourhood surrounding it, and you won't find any of the craft sellers or anyone else making their living from tourism here. Expect local goods for local needs: fruit, veg, household goodies, kitchen stuff, spices and plenty of roots, herbs and powders for traditional medicine. Look in the right places and you might even come across some real esoterica (think snake skins and dried chameleons) destined to make their way into a *gris-gris* (see box, page 326).

In Soumbédioune on the Route de la Corniche Ouest two markets are worth a stop: the **Marché Artisanal de Soumbédioune** [85 E6] and the **Marché du poisson** [85 E6] next door. The Marché Artisanal has been here since 1961; it consists of a warren of workshops selling leatherwork, statuary, *car rapide* replicas and all manner of Africa-themed painting and batik. Unfortunately it's got a reputation for rather strong-armed sales pitches and general shopping-related hassle, and you should come prepared to bargain. The fish market down the beach (where there's a Moroccan-funded pier going in as of 2015) only kicks into gear when the pirogues come back in the evening, starting around 16.00 – it's a frenzy of commerce as an army of fishmongers descends on to the beach to inspect the catch. The real treat, though, is the *dibiterie* stands nearby – bring them a fish or let one of the women choose for you, and they'll grill it up for you on the spot. Another ideal vantage point to see the boats come in and the feverish hauling in of the catch is up north at the **Marché du poisson à Yoff**, where dozens of pirogues hit the beach around the same time.

If you're curious but hesitant to attack the market scene on your own, all the tour agencies in town can arrange day trips to the markets of your choosing. Another good person to know is the trilingual **Patricia Attiba** (m 77 631 7437), who for 5,000F/hour will take you and two friends to the market of your choice and help you navigate the stalls, find what you're looking for, and make sure you get a decent price.

GALLERIES, WORKSHOPS AND MUSEUMS From larger-than-life renditions of Ahmadou Bamba on any available surface to *sous-verre* street scenes and audaciously colourful *car rapides*, it's nigh on impossible to go anywhere in Dakar without being surrounded by art. There are artists working in dozens of media, and their works, as well as those from around West Africa and beyond, can be seen at galleries and museums across the city.

Among the best known is **Galerie Antenna** [91 F4] (*9 Rue Félix Faure;* \ *33 821 1751; www.galerieantenna.com;* ⊕ *09.30–13.00 & 16.00–19.30 Mon–Sat*), which sits adjacent to the Place de l'Indépendance behind a striking latticework façade carved with Mauritanian Soninke geometric motifs and South African Ndebele colours reminiscent of the Alliance Française in Ziguinchor. A few blocks from here is the **Galerie Le Manège** [91 G3] (*3 Rue Parchappe;* \ *33 823 0320;* ⊕ *11.00–19.00 Mon–Sat*) which is under the watchful curatorship of famed Senegalese sculptor Ousmane Sow and associated with the Institut Français. Set in a delightfully repurposed 19th-century armoury, it runs six rotating exhibitions per year. Media vary, but the focus is on contemporary collaborations between Senegalese and European or other African artists. The **Galerie Nationale d'Art** [91 F4] (*19 Ave Hassan II;* \ *33 821 2511/842 7592; www.galerienationale.gouv.sn*) first opened in 1983 and is a bit dustier than the galleries previously mentioned, but their exhibitions are up-to-date and eminently worth a look. **Galerie Arte** [91 E4] (*5 Rue Victor Hugo;* \ *33 821 9556; www.arte. sn;* ⊕ *09.00–13.00 & 15.00–19.00 Mon–Sat*) near the presidential palace showcases experimental wood and furniture designs made by carvers from Casamance. Heading south from here to the much calmer streets around Place Soweto, you'll find the **Musée Théodore Monod d'Art Africain** [90 D6] (*1 Place Soweto;* \ *33 823 9268; www.ifan.ucad.sn;* ⊕ *09.00–18.00 Tue–Sun*), named after the French naturalist but often known simply as the IFAN museum after its parent organisation, the

HOT COUTURE   *Juliana Peluso*

When you need an outfit for a special occasion and you need it pronto, nothing, even geographic isolation, should stop you from procuring your dream vestment – especially in a country where most mid-sized towns, however far-flung, employ at least one tailor. Having crudely elucidated, haggled and nitpicked my way into several traditional holiday outfits, a pair of American flag overalls, a satin onesie and a few pantsuits, I here present a reasonably credible guide to getting your very own custom-made Senegalese garb.

To start, you'll need fabric. Walking through any Senegalese market is a kaleidoscopically colourful occasion that some might say borders on the hallucinogenic, due in large part to West Africa's iconic textile known as 'wax', bundles of which are stacked high on the makeshift shelves that line innumerable fabric stores. It is named not for its stiffness (and indeed, the first several wears of any new outfit may leave you walking somewhat Tinman-like) but rather the process with which it was traditionally made – via a printing system involving beeswax, originally called 'batik'. Wax is increasingly imported from China, though it is still made artisanally within the West African region. In Dakar (and pretty much only Dakar; everywhere else has to wait a while to update their stock), you can find the season's newest, hottest wax imports – and yes, wax patterns do go out of style, and fashion-prescient folk do notice if you're still wearing last year's 'disembodied rooster heads floating in a sea of pinwheels and beans' print. Typical African imagery – the animals, foods and home goods of daily life – and characteristic whirls, spirals and geometric shapes pop up each year, but always with a fresh twist and new psychotropic colour combinations.

If you're lucky, you may run across a unique wax that's just too good to pass by, despite the guaranteed novelty mark-up (disguise your excitement and you stand a greater chance of getting it at a reasonable price). Recently reported finds include wax printed, singly, with images of lime-wedged highball glasses, the Great Mosque at Touba, pills, Catholic saints, lawn chairs and Barack Obama. Other fabrics, including lace, satin, velvet and heavy 'fancy occasion' material are usually available, but wax is far and away the choice for semi-formal and everyday Senegalese couture.

Institut Fondamental d'Afrique Noire. Set inside a fantastic colonial neo-Sudanese building (which looks a lot like Art Deco to this author) from 1932, the exhibits here got a sprucing up in 2010 and today the collection of masks, carvings and ceremonial items from Senegal and the wider region are looking good, though it's worth noting that the information panels are only in French. The ground floor holds their permanent exhibitions, while upstairs are an assortment of temporary exhibits. The entry is a somewhat pricey 5,000F/2,000F foreigner/resident, but it goes towards maintaining this venerable institution. Just south of the place you'll find the jewellery workshop of **Florence de la Peschardière** [90 D6] (*4 Av Pasteur;* ☏ *33 823 4808; www.fdelapeschardiere.com*), which does intricate ladies' pieces out of amber, coral, shells, lapis lazuli and other semi-precious stones. Up towards the *gare ferroviaire*, the **Musée des Civilisations Noires** [85 D6], next to the Grand Théâtre National (see page 110) and part of the *Parc culturel de Dakar* campus, is slated to open in 2016 and will be one of Africa's largest museums when it does.

Heading north, Point E and its surrounding neighbourhoods are home to several compelling galleries, many of which double as cultural centres, hosting film

Once you've selected your fabric, the next step is to take it to a tailor (ask around for an earful on who's the best) and work out what design you'd like. No idea? No problem. Flip through one of several dog-eared copies of outfit catalogues on hand in the shop, or drag in a live model from the street who embodies your conception of chic. It's also possible, in theory, to recreate Western articles of clothing; if your Wolof is lacking (and even if it isn't), bring a picture of the design, preferably both front and back, and gesticulate until you think your point has been made.

After a few (one might think too few) measurements, some of which may need to be gently corrected (women are advised to request a size up on the bust, as darting is rarely employed, and furthermore skirt hems on Western garments are usually stealthily lengthened by several inches), a price far higher than any self-respecting Senegalese person would ever pay (but far lower than you'll ever again pay for a custom-made wardrobe) will be quoted, with the expectation that you will haggle it down. As with many other goods and services, tailoring in the Sine Saloum, Dakar, Thiès and St. Louis areas will cost a premium, especially for tourists. There is, however, a better chance that what will be made will resemble what you actually asked for.

Depending on the season and proximity of any major holiday or event, your garment(s) could take anywhere from two days to two months to complete – asking for a timeline in advance is advised, as are periodic check-ins, but neither guarantees a set date of completion. Don't be afraid to request alterations to your garments once they're done, because you're almost guaranteed to need them; tailors, especially far from the coast, are often unfamiliar with both Western clothing designs and Vitruvian proportions.

Most importantly of all, don't be intimidated by the process. Many tailors enjoy the challenge (and surplus income), and are by and large capable of copying basic clothing patterns – if occasionally adding a certain Senegalese touch to the finished product. The only thing you should really fear? The regret of never making that Obama-wax tuxedo.

Mbaye Ndow (📞 33 825 9790) is a recommended designer in Point E who speaks English and is happy to take custom orders of all types.

screenings, concerts and more. Most have a website where you can check out what's on, and they all keep daily hours whether there's a special event on or not. Behind a mysterious red door at the end of a short cul-de-sac, **Galerie Agora** [97 E5] (*Rue D, Point E;* 📞 *33 864 1448;* m *77 653 9872; www.agora-dk.jimdo.com;* ⏰ *10.00–18.00 Mon–Sat*) has regular exhibits from resident artists who take on Senegalese motifs with a decidedly modern bent, and their checkerboard courtyard makes for a most welcome retreat after some urban hiking. **Galerie Kemboury** [97 G6] (*Rue du Canal IV, Point E;* 📞 *33 825 4843;* e *kembouryart@orange.sn;* ⏰ *10.00–18.00 daily*) is just down the street and has been cultivating and promoting the work of Dakar's young artists since 1996. The **Raw Material Company** [97 G2] (*4074 bis Sicap Amitié 2;* 📞 *33 864 0248; www.rawmaterialcompany.org;* ⏰ *10.00–18.00 Tue–Sat*) is a baby by comparison, open in its current unmissable olive green compound since 2011. They've kept impressively busy since then, organising more than 15 exhibitions and symposiums, including the growing *Partcours* festival (*www.facebook.com/partcours.dakar*). The art here is modern and dynamic, and so is the cuisine on their rooftop restaurant. Another energetic gallery just nearby is **Éspace Timtimol**

[97 H4] (*Zone B, Rue Sans-Soleil No. 2A;* m 77 646 4119; *www.espacetimtimol.org*), which is more of a freeform artistic space than a formal gallery. Drop in here and you'll catch anything from concerts to debates to fashion shows. Finally, though it's a bit out of the way in Liberté II, **Kër Thiossane** [84 D4] (*Villa No 1695, Sicap Liberté II;* ❦ 33 868 5309; m 77 113 6843; *www.ker-thiossane.org* or *www.facebook. com/ker.thiossane*) is worth mentioning for its innovative approach to performance and gallery space, incorporating new technology, education, an organic garden and performances of all types, particularly during their *Afropixel* festival.

Continuing up the Corniche Ouest towards Les Almadies and Ngor, you'll pass **Les Petites Pierres** [84 C3] (*Cité Comico, Villa No. 118, Ouakam;* ❦ 33 860 7701; *www.lespetitespierres.wordpress.com* or *www.facebook.com/lespetitespierres*), a young and über-hip arts collective with a residence and boutique in the backstreets of Ouakam; they eschew the gallery format and have been bringing art and design into Dakar's neighbourhoods since their inception in 2005. Once you reach the Mamelles neighbourhood and just past the African Renaissance Monument, **Art Afrique** [84 B4] (❦ 33 860 6947; m 77 749 7978; e *art.afrique@orange.sn*), connected to La Calebasse restaurant (see page 106), has a collection of paintings, carvings, statuary and metalwork that would make many museums blush. Be sure to check out the larger-than-life wooden politicians out front! After all this gallery-hopping, stop for a well-earned rest and an iced coffee at **Layu Café** [94 C3] (see page 105), where you'll still be happily surrounded with gorgeous local goods. High end and African-made, the jewellery, bags, clothing and home goods here exude style. Tucked away on a side road, **Céramiques Almadies** [94 D4] (*off Rte des Almadies;* ❦ 33 820 0338; e *cmp@orange.sn;* ⊕ *11.00–18.00 daily*) is Mauro Petroni's personal workshop (*atelier*), and there's usually another artist or two exhibiting alongside his ceramics. Heading towards Ngor village, **Maam Samba** (see page 98) is a welcoming boutique with exquisite hand-woven and naturally dyed textiles made in their partner village Ndem, in Diourbel region, and also provides some of the most comfortable accommodation in the area and is a perfect place to hit the (handmade) sheets after a long day on Dakar's art circuit.

Of course, it would be completely remiss to leave out the **Village des Arts** [84 E2] (*Rte de l'Aéroport;* ❦ 33 835 7160; m 77 648 9964/552 1980; *www. levillagedesarts.com* or *www.facebook.com/VillageDesArtsDeDakar;* ⊕ *10.00–20.00 daily*), and it's absolutely worth the trek out here to see the 52 workshops and dozens of artists and artisans painting, sewing, carving, hammering and welding their latest works, from sculpture to *sous-verre*. Stroll the leafy grounds between workshops and chat with the artists before touring the gallery, then head over to the artists' canteen for a snack.

DAKAR FOR CHILDREN

While it's unquestionably the case that children are cherished in Senegalese society, Dakar wouldn't top many lists of destinations for a holiday with kids. Navigating this frenetic metropolis can take a lot of patience and even a bit of agility on your own, so having kids in tow requires some determination on the part of both children and parents. Still, the payoff for navigating the chaos together is a complement of bespoke children's activities like nowhere else in the country. **Magic Land** [85 E6] (❦ 33 829 5061; m 77 093 7171; e *contact@magiclanddakar.com;* www. *magiclanddakar.com; 2,500F amusement park, 3,000F/4,000F pool and waterslides week/weekend*) has a gorgeous location on the Route de la Corniche Ouest, but more importantly an impressive selection of things to spin, drop and twirl you in all different directions: carousels, Ferris wheels, pirate ships and waterslides, to start. If that all sounds like a parental day in purgatory, take heart, as they've got food, drink and concerts to keep the adults happy as well. Just up the corniche at Sea Plaza, **Red Bowl** [96 A5] (see page 112) has bowling, disco lights and a video game arcade large enough to guarantee at least one bout of screaming for more tokens. Continuing up the coast, the indoor-outdoor play area at **Zippyland** [94 F1] (*Rte de Ngor;* \ *33 820 0308;* m *76 639 1292;* e *zippylandplay@gmail.com; www. zippydakar.com;* ⊕ *09.00–19.00 Tue–Fri, 10.00–20.00 Sat–Sun*) is more or less the non-motorised equivalent to Magic Land, with swings, trampolines, ball pits, slides and a cinema screening nothing but kids' movies. They've also got a good café on site for weary grown-ups. In Plateau, **Sun Park** [90 D4] is a significant step down from either of the above, but this timeworn collection of bumper cars and carnival games next to the cathedral will still put smiles on faces. And finally, at the northeastern corner of Hann Forest Park is the **Hann Pony Club** [84 G3] (*Parc forestier de Hann;* \ *33 832 0652;* m *77 638 9058; www.poneyclubdakar.com*), where equestrians of all ages can ride, take lessons or organise horse rides ranging from an afternoon to five days in length. The park itself is also great for a stroll and is home to a **zoo** [84 G4], but the exhibits here largely consist of listless animals in cramped conditions, so it tends to be considerably more depressing than it is exciting.

SAFETY AND SECURITY

Much has been made of the prevalence of street crime in Dakar and, while it certainly does exist and is worth being aware of, Dakar is generally safe, particularly for a city of its size, and anyone who takes some common-sense precautions is very likely to have an incident-free visit.

The two types of ne'er-do-wells to be careful of in Dakar are pickpockets and muggers. The former tend to operate in the exact places you'd expect them to – packed bus stations, chaotic markets and crowded streets where they're able to get in and out of your pockets without detection. It should go without saying that if you're headed to any of these places, keep valuables safely stashed or – better yet – don't bring them at all. For the essentials you are carrying, simply work to make them less accessible – think money belt, front pockets and buttoned pockets. The streets around Marché Sandaga (and most markets) have a reputation for nimble-fingered rapscallions, but most visits are trouble-free.

There's less you can do to guard against a mugger, and if confronted you should always give up the goods. These incidents (occasionally at knifepoint) tend to happen on the corniche roads (east or west) at twilight or after dark, perpetrated by thieves on the hunt for cash and mobile phones. Just as with the pickpockets, don't carry unnecessary valuables and back up all those photos! If you're planning to go out on the town for an evening, taxis are always advisable (and since distances between venues tend to be long, very welcome as well). Beaches after dark are inadvisable too.

When you're wandering around Sandaga and some of the other markets, it's almost inevitable that someone will attach themselves to you as a so-called guide, new best friend and general pest. A firm no, *non* or *dedet* (or more likely all three, repeated a few times) will usually do the job. If someone comes up to you with the 'remember me' ploy (usually pretending to be the security guard from your hotel), don't feel obliged to engage them; it's more than likely they're a scammer. (Introducing yourself to your hotel security is an excellent way to inoculate yourself against this scam, as well as to be a courteous visitor.)

OTHER PRACTICALITIES

COMMUNICATIONS

Post The main post office (*www.laposte.sn*) is in Plateau at the eastern end of Boulevard El Hadji Djily Mbaye, just up from the *gare maritime*. They've got a small philatelic selection and still offer *poste restante* services, should you be feeling nostalgic.

Internet Nearly all hotels listed offer Wi-Fi (with one or two possible exceptions), and a large and steadily increasing number of restaurants offer it as well. You'll find a fair few cyber cafés, or *télécentres*, dotted around town, but they're not as plentiful as they once were, as many people now get online at restaurants or on their phones. Because of the ubiquity of Wi-Fi and the short shelf life of most cyber cafés, we've opted not to list individual cafés in Dakar. If you're having trouble getting online, your hotel will be able to point you in the right direction.

Alternatively, getting your phone set up with mobile internet is relatively painless and provides basic internet access in all but the remotest parts of the country. See page 65 for details on the various service providers and how to set this up.

Telephone As mobile technology proliferates, *télécentres* are not the one-on-every-street-corner affair they once were, but are still reasonably simple to locate if needed. They'll have internet access and phone services but, unless you've got a particular need for a landline telephone, the benefits over Skype, Viber or similar services are probably marginal.

Thus, many travellers opt to get a local SIM card for their unlocked mobile. These cost 1,000F–2,000F at most (though the guys outside the airport will be happy to charge you five times this) from any service provider (Orange, Expresso or Tigo) or they can be purchased from street vendors as well. All offer voice, SMS and mobile data services on a prepaid basis, and you'll rarely be more than 100m from the nearest top-up credit seller – indeed, it's more likely they'll be the ones finding you.

MEDICAL FACILITIES Hospital facilities in Dakar are perhaps the best in West Africa and, while you should consider evacuation to Europe for serious illness, minor injuries and illnesses can usually be comfortably dealt with here.

Laboratories

✚ **Institut Pasteur** [85 F8] 36 Av Pasteur; ☎33 839 9200/10; e pasteurdakar@pasteur.sn; www.pasteur. sn. Good for all manner of lab tests; specialises in rabies – go straight here if you suspect you've been exposed.

✚ **Bio-24 Lab** [91 E2] 13 Rue Saint Michel; ☎33 889 5151; e bioxxiv@orange.sn; www.labobio24. sn. Centrally located lab that can test for malaria & other ailments.

Clinics

All of the following are well-staffed clinics in the city centre.

✚ **Clinique Casahous** [91 F3] 5 Rue de Thiong; ☎33 889 7200/821 7630; e casahous@arc.sn; www.cliniquecasahous.com. English spoken.

✚ **Clinique du Cap** [85 F8] Av Pasteur; ☎33 889 0202; e cliniquducap@orange.sn

✚ **Clinique de la Madeleine** [90 D7] 18 Rue des Jambaars; e cmd@cliniquedelamadeleine.com; ☎33 821 9470/6; www.cliniquedelamadeleine.com

Hospital

✚ **Hôpital Principal** [91 E6] 1 Av Nelson Mandela; ☎33 839 5002/3; e communication@hpd.sn; www. hopitalprincipal.sn. Dakar's main hospital since 1884.

Ambulance services

All those below provide home consultations as well as transport to hospitals, & are available 24/7.

Service d'Assistance Médicale et d'Urgence (SAMU); Mermoz Sud; ☎800 881 881 (toll-

free)/33 869 8252; e samu@samu.sn;
www.samu.sn
SOS Médécin Rue 62 (@ Rue 64), Soumbédioune;
☏33 889 1515; e sosmeddk@sentoo.sn; www.
sosmedecinsenegal.org
SUMA Assistance Imm Hermes, SICAP Sacré-
Cœur Pyrotechnie;☏33 824 2418/6030;
e sumassistance@gmail.com;
www.sumassistance.net

Optometrist
Dr Erick Roth ☏33 823 9365; m 77 638 5475;
e dr.roth.erick@gmail.com. Dr Roth speaks English
and practises at the Clinique du Cap (info on page 120).

Dentist
There are a number of reputable dentists in town,
but Dr Anta Marie Anne Diop (27 Rue Mohamed V
(@ Félix Faure), First Floor;☏33 821 5203; m 77 455
5535; e drantadiop@orange.sn; www.antadiop.com) is
centrally located & English-speaking.

MONEY Getting cash is rarely a problem in Dakar. The banking network is well-developed, with dozens of (usually guarded) **ATMs** in all areas of town, including at Léopold Sédar Senghor International Airport and the *gare maritime*. You can draw CFA Francs against both Visa and Mastercard/Maestro at BICIS, CBAO, Ecobank and SGBS ATMs. Machines will occasionally be out of service or quite simply out of cash, but this is far from frequent.

If you're arriving with **hard currency**, bank branches will change money at reasonable rates and there are a few private bureaux de change around the city, though they don't offer a significant advantage over the banks. Private moneychangers hang out in front of the airport and sometimes the *gare maritime*, but keep your wits about you and don't hand over a cent until you're absolutely certain you've got the right amount; scamming is a real possibility. It's worth noting that the euro exchange rate is fixed to the CFA Franc at roughly €1 = 655F, so it's much better to carry euros than either US dollars or pounds sterling, which are subject to fluctuations in value and less advantageous exchange rates.

You could try **travellers' cheques**, but we certainly wouldn't advise it. If you go this route, keep the proof of purchase from when you bought the cheques – you may be asked for it when trying to cash them. They'll probably only be accepted at major bank branches in Dakar and at a hefty commission, or it's entirely possible you'll just end up stuck with them. If you're in a jam and need a **wire transfer**, Western Union has dozens of agents at banks, post offices and elsewhere, but fees can be high.

BEAUTY TREATMENTS Most of the top-end hotels have a salon and spa on-site, but in this most fashionable of capitals, you've got plenty of other options if your coiffure is in need of some attention. Le 5 Sens [85 E6] (☏ 33 822 0302; m 77 222 0627; e les5sens@arc.sn) comes recommended, and they do cuts, dyes and massages for both men and women. There's a little café to snack at while you wait.

If you're back in Dakar but still feeling a bit grungy after too much time in an upcountry *sept-place*, **Ryad al Sultan** [96 B4] (☏ 33 824 9928; m 77 474 3333; www.ryadalsultan.com) will scrub you six ways from Sunday with their Moroccan-inspired hammam treatments. Eucalyptus scrubs in the sauna, essential oil massages, facials and clay body wraps are all on offer, starting at 30,000F.

WHAT TO SEE AND DO

PLATEAU While not exceedingly long on traditional sightseeing opportunities, a walk around central Dakar gives you a chance to scope out some of the more intriguing buildings and soak up the frenetic street vibe. Starting at the bone-dry fountains

Dakar WHAT TO SEE AND DO

4

and bare flagpoles of the **Place de l'Indépendance** [91 F3], you're surrounded by an architectural hodgepodge of colonial administration buildings and modern-in-that-70s-kind-of-way office blocks. Take a moment to check out the ornate colonnaded 1910 **Chambre de commerce**, comparatively modest **Préfecture** and the bright red arches of the 1906 **Ministère des Affaires Étrangères** arranged around the northern half of the plaza, known in colonial times as *Place Protet* after former governor and French navy admiral Auguste Léopold Protet. To the west, the 17-storey cheese grater is the **Hôtel de l'Indépendance,** one of Dakar's first high-rises, boasting a rooftop pool that was *the* place to see and be seen in its heyday. Today it stands dormant and neglected, casting a glum shadow over the otherwise-frenetic plaza. A couple of blocks downhill towards the port lies the elegant **Hôtel de Ville** [91 F2], which dates from 1914 and has served continually as Dakar's city hall since that time. It's fine to poke your head in and check out the garden oasis surrounding the building. Another few blocks up the road, the appealing 1912 **Gare ferroviaire** [91 E1] was slated to meet the wrecking ball as part of Abdoulaye Wade's *Parc culturel de Dakar* urban renewal project (of which the neighbouring **Grand Théâtre National** [85 F6] is a part), but with Macky Sall's ascension to the presidency in 2012 it was given a stay of execution and is now set to undergo a full restoration in 2015-16.

On the south side of the Plateau is the **Cathédrale du Souvenir Africain** [90 D5], inaugurated in 1936 in an extravagant week-long ceremony led by Cardinal Verdier of Paris and a coterie of French bishops. Once envisioned as both a cathedral and a quasi-political memorial to Frenchmen who died in the colonies, the inscription above the doors originally read: 'For those who died in Africa, a grateful France' which was quite understandably changed after independence and today is more sacred in message: 'For the Virgin Mary, mother of Jesus the Saviour'. The obelisk bell towers and protruding drainpipes are an architectural homage to ancient Egyptian and local architectural styles. Continuing south, when you reach Place Soweto things are somewhat quieter, the streets clear out a bit and you can actually take something resembling a stroll (savour this feeling). Facing Place Soweto is the 1932 **Musée Théodore Monod d'Art Africain** [90 D6] (see page 115) and the 1956 **Assemblée Nationale** [90 C6], which is the seat for Senegal's 150 parliamentarians. Hop on any DDD bus headed south or walk 1,200m to the old mid-century **Palais de Justice** [90 A3], declared structurally unsound and abandoned in 1998 and today used as one of the city's main bus termini. (The new Palais de Justice was inaugurated further north along the Corniche Ouest in 2008.) Push on another 500m south and you're at the end of the road; here the double-towered **Phare du Cap Manuel** [85 F8] awaits, patiently beaming its message 20 miles off shore. On the way back up to the Place de l'Indépendance, have a look through the gates of the Neo-Classical **Palais de la République,** where first French governor-generals and today Senegalese presidents have been living since 1907. The presidential guard on duty out front in their red *burnous* tunics are a fair bit more relaxed than your average West African palace guard, and might even let you get away with some photos.

SUBURBS AND THE CORNICHE OUEST As you head north out of the former colonial centre into districts like Medina, created in colonial times to house the capital's African population separately from the Europeans in Plateau, the unequal patterns of investment become apparent as pre-independence landmarks are all but absent. Planned neighbourhoods like Medina eventually give way to the once-scattered fishing villages that have been sucked into Dakar's ever-growing perimeter, but which retain their independent flair. Entering Medina, the enormous minaret of the **Grand Mosque** [85 F6] went up in 1964 in partnership with Moroccan king

Hassan II, and it's done in a suitably Moroccan style, with a green and white geometric filigree over the whole of the building. There are no official tours but, if you ask for the caretaker at a quiet time and are appropriately dressed, he might show you around. Nonetheless, the Mourides and their taste for monumentality are on course to dwarf the Grand Mosque with their own construction in Grand Dakar. The **Massalikoul Djinane Mosque** [85 F5] is scheduled to open at the end of 2015, and it already boasts five minarets. The tallest of them clocks in at 78m, besting the Grand Mosque by nearly a dozen metres.

Back on the Corniche Ouest, the **Porte du Troisième Millénaire** [85 E7] was built to commemorate the new millennium and consists of three doors, each increasing in size, representing growth and openness to the world, while a golden woman atop the second gate announces a gathering on her traditional horn. Designed by Senegalese architect Pierre Goudiaby, it won't change your life, but the views from here are nice, and the ball-topped minarets at the **Seydou Nourou Tall Mosque** [85 F7] are worth a glance as well. Further along, next to the Sea Plaza Mall is the **Place du Souvenir**, built to commemorate the 1,863 people drowned in the sinking of the previous Dakar–Ziguinchor ferry, the *MV Le Joola,* off the coast of Gambia in September 2002. It's a windswept spot and sometimes the host of outdoor concerts and other events. Just before you reach the twin peaks of the Mamelles, the **Mosquée de la Divinité** [84 C4] is set in a steep-walled cove to your left, where you're treated to an eye-level view of the bulbous minarets from the Route de la Corniche Ouest. The mosque itself sits steps from the beach among a cluster of buildings and dozens of pirogues at the bottom of the cove.

As for that statue visible before you even land in Dakar, it's the hugely controversial **Monument de la Renaissance Africaine** (⊕ *10.00–13.00 & 15.00– 19.00 Mon–Fri, 10.00–13.00 & 15.00–19.45 Sat–Sun; entry 6,500F non-residents, 1,000F (lower floors)/3,000F (viewing deck) residents*). Perched atop one of the two *mamelles* (literally 'breasts', because well, duh) this enormous North Korean-built statue is either an eyesore or a triumph depending on who you ask. Designed by Pierre Goudiaby (who also did the *Porte du Troisième Millénaire* mentioned above, though this too is the subject of some controversy), the statue is 52m high (150m if you count the hill it's sitting on), with a base area of 1,154m², and outdoes Lady Liberty and her pedestal in New York by 10m, but these numbers are irrelevant to most Senegalese, who are more concerned with the amount of cash that went into its construction (€20 million), where all those entry fees are going (Wade has claimed 'intellectual property' rights to 35% of all income generated), and how many metres of uncovered bronze flesh the shirtless man and his short-skirted accomplice are showing. Even so, it's become something of a 'must-visit' on the Dakar tourist circuit and, while it's worth stopping in for the views over town if nothing else, the statue is hardly a masterpiece (Senegalese master sculptor Ousmane Sow has lambasted it as 'aesthetically childish and banal in the extreme'), and it's hard to shake the feeling that you're standing under one massive missed opportunity. Inside, the first several floors have informational panels about the monument's construction (primarily in French) and some works by local artists are showcased on the floors above. The viewing deck is a claustrophobic doughnut set around the elevator shaft inside the man's hat, and you're allowed no more than a couple of minutes at the top before your guide ushers you back downstairs. If you're saving money, just enjoy the views from the base and think about how good your calves are going to look after climbing the nearly 200 stairs each way up and down the hill. If you're still in a climbing mood afterwards (or instead), head over to the *mamelle* next door, where you'll find one of the oldest extant buildings in Dakar, the whitewashed **Phare des Mamelles** [84 D4], built here way back in 1864. It's rarely crowded up here, so pack a lunch and enjoy the view and maybe even a little bit of solitude – not easily done in Dakar.

Continuing up the peninsula brings you to Les Almadies, where there isn't much in the way of conventional sightseeing, but it's a great place for a stroll. The Route des Almadies is the main drag and, combined with the nearby Route de Ngor, this is without question Dakar's flashiest neighbourhood. Bars, nightclubs and boutiques line the street, along with a healthy sprinkling of offices for international agencies working in Senegal. Just a few blocks south and running parallel along the **Corniche des Almadies** (map, page 94), the mood changes completely. Surfer haunts, crêperies and views over the rocky Atlantic coast without four lanes of traffic whipping by behind you (as on the Route de la Corniche Ouest) make it one of Dakar's best places to slow down with beer in hand and feet in water. Head all the way west and you reach a warren of little restaurants serving nothing but seafood at the Pointe des Almadies, the westernmost edge of the African continent, and the Old World as a whole. Slurp some fresh oysters here and wish the sun well on its long journey to the Americas.

North of here is Ngor village and the **Île de Ngor** (map, page 94). The former is a sandy, overgrown fishing village that, once you leave the main route and enter the village, feels very far indeed from the shopping malls and nightclubs barely a kilometre back. As for the island, if you come to Dakar and don't make the time to get across for at least a meal, you've undoubtedly missed a trick. Finally, heading east past the airport along the northern coast, you enter Yoff, one of the peninsula's most conservative communities, and the spiritual home of both the Layenne brotherhood and the Lebou community that makes up most of their membership. Yoff is officially autonomous, and nearly all policing and governance is handled strictly within the village. Bars and smoking are *verboten*, and residents would greatly appreciate you dressing more conservatively than you might in the rest of Dakar while wandering the village. Aside from the beach (see below), the distinct atmosphere of this self-sufficient community is the real draw, and the heart of the community is the **Seydina Limamou Laye Mausoleum and Sacred Well** (map, page 99). The mausoleum holds the founder of the Layenne order, who, in sharp contrast with mainstream Islamic tradition, is worshipped as a reincarnation of the Prophet Muhammad. The sacred well is the source of what Layennes believe to be holy water, much like the Zamzam well in Mecca. The wind-battered village beach is basically a dumping ground for fish guts, but head a bit further east and you'll come upon a long row of **beach shacks** with food, drink and sturdy umbrellas for hire, from where you can kick back and watch the surfers do their best as the breakers roll in.

BEACHES Dakarois love a day at the beach, and while the *plages* here don't stack up as Senegal's finest, any excuse to pack up the family and head out for a day picnicking on the sand is happily taken. Thus on weekends (particularly Sundays), the beaches around town can be teeming as residents from all over the city flee their stuffy apartments in search of a cool breeze. As a rule, the best beaches in the area are on the north side of the peninsula, but these are also exposed to the heaviest currents, so be cautious and heed local advice. Around Plateau, your only real choices are either at either **Plage de l'Anse Bernard** [85 F8] or the private beach at **Le Lagon** [91 G4]. Anse Bernard is a nice enough little bay, but it's rather unkempt and not exactly the stuff of tropical fantasies. The beach at Le Lagon is much nicer, and the day-use fee is 3,000F for non-guests, so if you're determined to spend a day swimming in Plateau this is likely to be a more comfortable option.

The Corniche Ouest is home to a couple of beaches, notably **Plage de la Voile d'Or** [85 G5], which is private and attached to an eponymous hotel. It's well maintained and there's an entry fee, but the industrial surrounds and military base next door don't make it the most attractive option in town. Plage de Hann is little more than a rubbish tip and unsuitable for much, let alone bathing.

On the western shoreline rocks abound and the surf can be heavy, so swimming spots are few and far between. The five-star option is obviously the sandy, chaise-longue-laden **Plage Terrou-Bi** [85 D6], privately owned by the hotel and accessible to non-guests (along with the swimming pool) for 6,000F/8,000F during the week/weekend. Further north, the **Plage de Ouakam** [84 C4] is home to dozens of fisherman and the Mosquée de la Divinité (see page 123), while the superbly well-hidden **Plage des Mamelles** [84 B4] is something of a local secret, tucked away behind a sheer rock face (the edge of one of the *mamelles*) and only accessible by a footpath starting at the Mamelles roundabout (near La Calebasse restaurant). There are usually a couple of beach shack restaurateurs at work down here as well, and it's rightfully popular with surfers.

The Corniche des Almadies is too rocky to really call any of it a beach, but there's an ingenious ocean-fed saltwater swimming pool at Surfer's Paradise restaurant here. At the **Pointe des Almadies** [94 A3], there are two beaches: one inside the Hôtel des Almadies and a much smaller *plage* next to all the little restaurants at the point. The hotel beach costs 5,000F/10,000F week/weekends, and is a beautiful little spit of sand, while the small beach next to the restaurants is a reasonably clean and casual spot for a swim, with food and drink close at hand.

Along the north coast, the **Plage de Ngor** [94 D2] is a hugely popular spot for young people and families alike; it faces Ngor Island, and is protected from the southbound waves by the same. It's something like 500F per person to swim, which goes towards the very appreciable beach cleanup, or you could also hop across to the island where there are a couple of perfectly pleasant beaches as well. A touch further east, the **Plage Sunugal** [94 E1] charges 4,000F for non-guests to swim at their beautifully kept and fully sheltered beach. After this is the surfer-happy **Plage du Virage** [94 F1], where umbrellas are for hire. Depending on the winds, swimming might be a challenge. Finally, the **Plage du Yoff** (map, page 99) is Dakar's longest beach by, well, *miles*; it starts across from the diminutive Yoff Island and carries on and on eastwards until it eventually merges with the beaches of the Grande Côte, stretching well past the horizon, up to Saint-Louis and beyond. The first kilometre or so facing Yoff-Tonghor is given over entirely to fishing and its attendant refuse but, continuing eastwards to the Djily Mbaye neighbourhood, the rubbish clears out and the wide sandy coast plays host to dozens of beach shacks with chairs for rent, fish to grill and drinks on ice. Waves are often too high for swimming here, but it's a great spot to watch the surfing acrobatics.

AROUND DAKAR

ÎLE DE GORÉE *Population: 1,500*
Built from old walls, populated by old ghosts, and wrapped in the folds of old silences, the past, unvarnished in all its glories and horrors, is within easy grasp on Île de Gorée, barely 20 minutes and 3km from the monuments and motorways of forward-looking Dakar and its shimmering, shape-shifting landscape across the water. Without a car or tarred road on the entirety of the island, Gorée's 36 hectares are as striking an antidote to its younger sibling across the water as can be imagined. Narrow sand-and-cobblestone streets shaded with palms and baobabs wend their way between the thick pastel walls of centuries-old homes, some bright and newly restored, others assuming the cracks and imperfections of venerable old

age, all of them home to a close-knit village of families, some of whose roots on the island go back centuries.

Gorée's tranquillity today belies a sordid and tortured history, and the island has long been synonymous with the slave trade. It remains among the best-preserved of hundreds of major and minor entrepôts along the West African coast, where abducted Africans were imprisoned to await the detestable prison ships that would periodically arrive to haul them off yet again, this time to either their deaths on the Atlantic during the Middle Passage or, for the survivors, slavery in the Americas. As such, a visit to Gorée can be deeply contemplative and intensely emotional. The quietness of the island allows those so inclined a space for meditation on the raw wounds of a human tragedy that are far from fully healed.

Many visitors come to Gorée on a day trip from Dakar but, if you have the time, it's absolutely worth spending a night on the island and absorbing the hush that descends on the streets after each departing ferry takes more visitors, souvenir sellers, and would-be tour guides back across the water for the night. Locals promenade on the streets and go visiting from house to house, and the quayside here is as fine a place to feel the day slip into darkness as there is anywhere in Senegal.

History For centuries visited by Lébou fisherman from the Cap Vert peninsula but never permanently occupied thanks to a dearth of fresh water, Gorée was first sighted by Europeans when Portuguese mariner Dinís Dias rounded (and christened) the Cap Vert peninsula in 1444, and a trading post was built on the island, then known as Palma or Beseguiche. The Portuguese ran a minor trading network here until the Dutch forced them out in 1617, building two forts and calling the island *Goede Reede* or 'good bay', which eventually became Gorée. Over the next centuries, Gorée would change hands some half a dozen times, with the Portuguese returning from 1629 to 1645, when the Dutch reasserted control until being evicted by the English between 1664 and 1667. After this the Dutch returned yet again, only to be routed by the French in 1667, never to return. From here on, the English and French were content to fight it out, and while the British occupied the island on several occasions in the intervening years, most notably from 1804 to 1817, Gorée remained largely in French hands and developed as an economic and political centre second only to Saint-Louis.

A small métis community developed during the 18th and 19th centuries, and the métis women, known as *signares*, wielded considerable economic influence on the island. By the 1780s the free population on Gorée was 1,840, with an estimated several hundred captives awaiting export on the island at any given time. It was during this era, in 1786, that the now-infamous Maison des Esclaves was built as a residence for a powerful *signare* woman known as Anne Pépin. Just how major a rôle Gorée ultimately played in the slave trade is a subject of considerable and occasionally acrimonious debate, however, with some scholars dismissing the island as a marginal entity in the trade and putting forth estimates of 200 to 500 individuals exported annually, while others point to records from the port of Nantes indicating that 103,000 slaves left Gorée for a single destination over a 12-year period from 1763 to 1775. The true figures may never be fully known and, while it's up to visitors to weigh the numbers themselves, what is abundantly clear is that from 1536 to at least 1848, when France abolished the trade, Gorée was deeply invested in the export of human misery.

Despite being granted *commune* status (along with Saint-Louis) in the wake of France's 1848 revolution, and reaching its peak population of 4,000 around the same time, the island's decline in importance began shortly after in 1857 when the

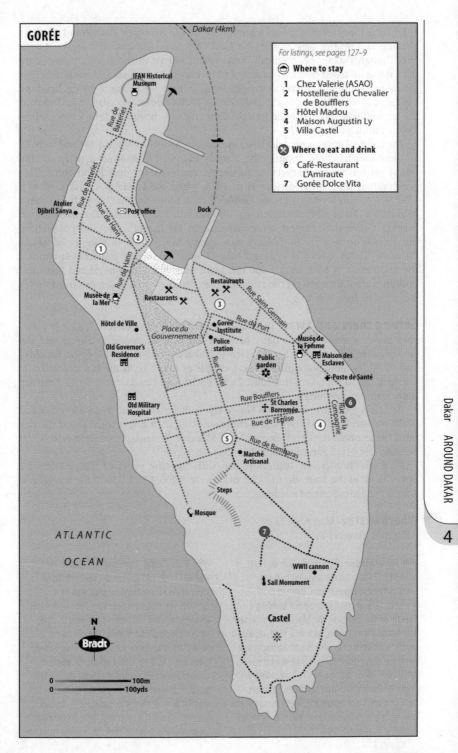

GORÉE

Dakar (4km)

IFAN Historical Museum

Rue de Batteries

Rue de Batteries

Atelier Djibril Sanya

Rue de Hann

Post office

Dock

② ①

Rue de Hann

Musée de la Mer

Restaurants

Restaurants

③

Rue Saint-Germain

Hôtel de Ville

Place du Gouvernement

Gorée Institute

Police station

Rue du Port

Musée de la Femme

Maison des Esclaves

Old Governor's Residence

Public garden

Poste de Santé

Old Military Hospital

Rue Castel

Rue Boufflers

St Charles Borromée

Rue de la Compagnie

⑥

④

Rue de l'Église

⑤

Rue de Bambaras

Marché Artisanal

Steps

ATLANTIC

OCEAN

Mosque

⑦

WWII cannon

Sail Monument

N

Bradt

Castel

0 — 100m
0 — 100yds

For listings, see pages 127–9

⌂ **Where to stay**

1 Chez Valerie (ASAO)
2 Hostellerie du Chevalier
    de Boufflers
3 Hôtel Madou
4 Maison Augustin Ly
5 Villa Castel

✖ **Where to eat and drink**

6 Café-Restaurant
    L'Amiraute
7 Gorée Dolce Vita

Dakar AROUND DAKAR

4

colonial authorities established a settlement on the mainland that would go on to become Dakar. The new city on the Cap Vert peninsula quickly outgrew Gorée and, though Dakar was politically subservient as part of the Gorée municipality until it was awarded *commune* status of its own in 1887, the colonial administration would gradually migrate on to the peninsula in time for Dakar to be declared the capital of French West Africa in 1902. By the 1920s, Gorée's population had sunk to the triple digits, and the once-independent city was subsumed into a reorganised Dakar municipality in 1929.

The colonial government declared the island a historical site in 1944 and forbade all new construction, stalling the already-marginal economic activity on the island yet further but preserving its unique character for decades to come. This preservation paid some dividends in 1978, when the island was inscribed as a UNESCO world heritage site, and Gorée's fortunes took another happy turn when a ballooning Dakar administration was divided into 19 *communes d'arrondissement*, making Gorée the smallest *arrondissement* by far in both size and population, but serving to reopen the island's municipal council after an absence of nearly 70 years. Today Gorée is among Senegal's most important tourist destinations, the population is back over 1,000 residents, and many long-neglected historical buildings are starting to get the attention they deserve – though on this front there's still a rather long way to go.

Getting there and away The Liaison Maritime Dakar-Gorée (📞 *33 849 7961*) runs about a dozen ferries daily between the *Gare Maritime* in Dakar and the *embarcadère* in Gorée. The first boat leaves Dakar at 06.15 from Monday to Saturday and 07.00 on Sundays, running every couple of hours until the last departure *to* Gorée at 22.30 Monday–Thursday, 23.30 Friday and Sunday, and 00.45 Saturday night (Sunday morning).

Returning, the first boat from Gorée takes off for Dakar at 06.45 Mon–Sat and 07.30 on Sundays, and they again run every couple of hours throughout the day until the last boat back to Dakar at 23.00 Monday–Thursday, midnight Friday and Sunday, and 01.15 Saturday night (Sunday morning).

It's a wholly pleasant 20-minute trip with fantastic views of Dakar from the upper deck of the boat. Round-trip tickets are 5,200/2,700/1,500F for foreigners/ Africa residents/Senegal residents.

Where to stay *Map, page 127.*
All hotels have Wi-Fi.

Hôtel Madou (5 rooms) 1 Rue du Port; 📞 33 842 77 09; e hotelmadou@gmail.com; www.hotelmadougoree.com. Opened in 2012 in a painstakingly restored colonial building directly on the quayside, this place is the smartest accommodation in town, with airy, high-ceilinged rooms done up in crisp whites with wrought iron furniture, glass-door showers & all mod cons (AC, telephone, fridge & flatscreen TV), including what might be Gorée's first-ever swimming pool on their gorgeous rooftop terrace. There are some nice *sous-verre* pieces for sale downstairs, & meals are available on request. **$$$**

Villa Castel (3 rooms) Rue Castel; m 77 263 6075/523 0453; e oliviercogels@hotmail. com; www.villacastelgoree.com. Run by a Belgian-Senegalese couple who live on-site, this lovingly restored old home is dripping in style, with individually decorated 1st-floor rooms with terracotta floors, flatscreen TVs, big canopy beds, nets, AC & en-suite bathrooms, all set around a fantastic central courtyard draped in plants & bougainvillea. One of the rooms has its own balcony, & there's a shady rooftop terrace accessible from the courtyard. It's a friendly & unpretentious setup, & they can arrange massages, spa treatments & nautical excursions on their own boat. Good value, with prices at the lower end of this range. **$$$**

⌂ **Chez Valérie** (ASAO) (5 rooms) Rue Saint Joseph `\` 33 821 8195. This is definitely the best budget option on the island, with a handful of idiosyncratic rooms sleeping up to 4. All the bright 1st-floor rooms here have fans & nets but are otherwise completely different. The double is daubed with fat green polka dots & has an en-suite bathroom directly underneath the lofted bed, while the triple is big & open, with hardwood floors & big, built-in bookshelves full of artwork. All rooms but the polka-dot double & one of the 2 4-bed rooms use shared ablutions, but there's hot water for all. The ground-floor gallery shop is worth a look as well. **$$**

⌂ **Hostellerie du Chevalier de Boufflers** (5 rooms) `\` 33 822 5364; e boufflers@live.fr. Named after a minor author & short-term colonial governor, this perennially popular place opposite the main beach is Gorée's longest-serving accommodation, & coming in the front door feels like walking into your favourite restaurant, the one you know hasn't changed so much as the wallpaper in decades. The whitewashed rooms in the next building are simply furnished & en suite with fans & nets, & the 1st-floor rooms come with balconies for an extra 5,000F. It's all a bit creaky, but still pleasant, & the restaurant, where meals start around 4,500F, is often ranked the finest table in town. **$$**

⌂ **Maison Augustin Ly** (4 rooms) m 77 657 0087/76 123 8180; e maisonaugustinly@gmail.com; www.maisonaugustinly.com. Down the east side of the island in the centre of town, this restored colonial house is warm & colourful, offering simple en-suite rooms with fans & nets decorated in tapestries & *sous-verre*. Showers are hot, & the leafy rooftop terrace is a perfect spot to while away the afternoon. Meals are available by request, & they can also set up tours of the artisans' workshops on the island. **$$**

✕ Where to eat and drink *Map, page 127.*

✕ **Ann'Sabran** `\` 33 826 9429; m 77 557 3389; ⊕ 08.00–midnight daily. One of the handful of eateries strung along the beach, this place does seafood, grills & Senegalese dishes starting around 4,500F, as well as cheaper sandwiches for 1,000F & up. The beachside restaurants are all broadly comparable, but other options include the Taverne des Boucaniers (`\` *33 824 3371;* m *77 574 1579*) & Chez Tonton (`\` *33 821 9200;* m *77 657 0087/515 6282*).

✕ **Café-Restaurant L'Amiraute** Rue Saint-Germain & Rue de Boufflers `\` 33 823 0035; m 77 630 7269/414 0166; ⊕ 09.00–20.30 daily. On a covered terrace facing the rocky shore, the waves break just steps from your table at this tranquil seafood joint on the east side of the island. Mains start around 4,000F & there's a gallery & workshop to check out while waiting for your food. Also, there's a resident pelican that walks around the restaurant (really).

✕ **Gorée Dolce Vita** `\` 33 842 7726; m 77 556 0203; ⊕ lunch & dinner daily. This cheerful terrace restaurant is an excellent stop on the way down from the castel for pizza, drinks (hot or cold) & views over the island. Chicken *yassa* or steak go for 4,000F, while a grilled *thiof* (white grouper, a Senegalese speciality) or seafood spaghetti is more like 5,000F. They've got live music some Sat nights as well.

Other practicalities

Communications
There's a post office near the boat dock & Wi-Fi at all the hotels, but no public *télécentre* that we could find.

Money
There are no ATMs on the island, so bring cash from Dakar.

What to see and do It's worth mentioning straight away that all of the museums are closed on Mondays, so plan your trip for another day of the week if at all possible. The main landmark and reason for many people's visits is the haunting **Maison des Esclaves** (⊕ *10.30–noon & 14.30–18.00 Tue–Sun*) and door of no return. Built in 1786 by a wealthy métis *signare*, it became a museum in 1962, and the dank corridor into the dungeons below framed by artful dual staircases leading to the upper residences is one of Senegal's most evocative and enduring images. A place of pilgrimage for politicians of all stripes, it's been host to a stream of dignitaries ranging from Yasser Arafat to Pope John Paul II and the last three sitting US presidents. There are French-only informational panels tracing the history of the slave trade and resistance to it in the rooms above, along with a selection of iron restraints, antique rifles and other devious-looking period artefacts. The dungeons below are a silent and powerful indictment of man's inhumanity to man, and the 'Bob was here 2004' style graffiti carved into the walls here are not exactly a ringing endorsement of man's capabilities either.

Across the street, the **Musée de la Femme** (✆ 33 825 2151; *www.mufem.org* or *www.facebook.com/MuseeDeLaFemmeHB*) has been dedicated to promoting Senegalese women's voices of today and yesteryear in this spot since 1994 and, while it was unfortunately closed for renovations when we checked in, you might find Pap Nguer or another artist at work on some paintings inside regardless. Up towards the island's central plaza, the **Musée de la Mer** (*entry 500F;* ⊕ *10.00–13.00 & 14.30–18.00 Tue–Sun;* ✆ 33 821 5066) pays tribute to the long maritime history of Gorée and its environs, with exhibits on fishing and navigation traditions, ships, and row upon row of preserved fish and crustaceans on display.

At the northern end of the island, the **IFAN Historical Museum** (*entry 500F;* ✆ 33 822 2003; ⊕ *10.00–17.00 Tue–Sun*) is housed in the Fort d'Estrées, which was completed in 1856 and named for Vice-Amiral Jean d'Estrées, the French naval officer who prised Gorée from the Dutch once and for all in 1677. Inside, the information panels cover a lot of ground, starting with the Palaeolithic era and running all the way up to Senegalese independence. The fort itself is an impressive structure and, when you're done inside, climb up to the perimeter wall for views over the harbour and Dakar.

Beyond the official museums, Gorée boasts an active creative scene that belies its tiny population. Much of what's sold on the island is the usual tourist kitsch, but there are some unique pieces available if you know where to look. To start with, sculptor **Djibril Sagna** (*Rue des Batteries;* m 77 734 9611), whose gallery space consists of a mostly roofless building, designs using nothing but found objects – driftwood, old teapots, rusty nails, you name it. His sculptures are by turns avant garde and strangely evocative, and absolutely worth a look. There's no sign, but a giant blue graffiti-style bird is painted on the wall near the entrance. There are also artists working in sculpture, *sous-verre* and other styles at the old military hospital and in a few spots up at the **castel**, where the sight of enormous WWII-era cannons used to prop up artworks is heartening indeed.

The castel itself, also known as Fort Saint-Michel, traces its origins to 1892 and isn't much of an architectural marvel – the Fort d'Estrées across the island is much more interesting for that – but the climb up is worth it for the views alone, and some of the art for sale up here is really excellent and of a better quality than the stuff for sale at the **Marché Artisanal** at the base of the path up. Also at the top is a rather incongruous and very tall sail-shaped monument to the victims of the slave trade, erected here in 1999.

For a swim, the **beach** up near the IFAN museum is well-suited and popular, and some enterprising locals have even set up a kiosk with umbrellas and such for hire. And if a quick dip isn't the challenge you're looking for, the **Dakar–Gorée swim** is exactly what it says it is, attracting hundreds of competitors to the event held here every October. If that seems a bit much, you can also get here at any time of year with a kayak hired from Oceanium in Dakar (see page 92).

Another festival you'd be lucky to catch here is **Regards Sur Cours** (*www.goree-regards-sur-cours.org*), which takes place every year on Pentecost weekend, when all of Gorée's historic homes fling open their heavy wooden doors and invite visitors into their bougainvillea-draped courtyards in a weekend of impromptu concerts and art exhibitions. Though they mostly put on conferences, symposiums, and the like, you might also poke your head into the **Gorée Institute** (*Rue du Jardin;* ❱ *33 849 4849; www.goreeinstitut.org*) as it's housed in a beautifully restored old building, and they've been known to occasionally sponsor artists working on the island as well.

Finally, **Gorée Cinéma** (*www.goreecinema.com*) puts on open-air film screenings on the first Saturday of the month during May, June, July and August, with a focus on young and promising filmmakers from Senegal and around Africa.

ÎLES DE LA MADELEINE NATIONAL PARK From the Route de la Corniche Ouest in Dakar, these two jagged, weather-beaten volcanic rocks look about as inhospitable as it gets, and indeed the 15ha Îles de la Madeleine are uninhabited and have been for hundreds of years. Today the Lébou believe the islands are home to *Ndoek-Daour*, protector spirit of Dakar, to whom they bring offerings of food & drink in the hope of keeping peace in the city. A smattering of pot shards and iron-age artefacts excavated here point to at least seasonal occupation perhaps a millennium ago; since then, the only trace of human habitation is the foundation of a ruined building, usually explained away with apocryphal tales of misbehaving army sergeants sent into exile on the island or missionary hermits taking up residence here in centuries past. The inaccessible rocky outcrop forming the second isle is occasionally referred to as *Île Lougne*, while the main island is commonly known as *Île aux Serpents*, possibly derived from *Île Sarpan*, the supposed surname of the legendary rule-breaking sergeant once held on the island, since the snake population here is entirely unexceptional. These names have changed a fair bit over the centuries, but the Catholic Portuguese are thought to be the originators behind *Ilha de Madaleña*. Best of all, though, and thanks to the impressive numbers of seabirds and their attendant guano found on the islands, they were once marked on some delightfully blunt 17th-century French maps as *Isles de Merde*, while the equally irreverent Dutch opted for *Bescheiten Eylands* – the shitten isles.

These unbecoming appellations were short-lived, however, and these wild islands – now officially under their ecclesiastically approved name – were designated a flora and fauna reserve by the colonial authorities in 1949, gazetted as a national park in 1976, recognised by BirdLife international as an Important Bird Area in 2001, and finally have been on the tentative list of UNESCO world heritage sites since 2005. Their undulating sea cliffs reach 35m at their highest point and taper down into several small coves, one of which protects a rocky pool where you can swim. The centre of the main island is a grassy plateau that is home to some tortured, low-growing baobabs bent double by the oceanic winds, the ruins of that mysterious old building, and a whole bunch of seabirds, including breeding colonies of Great Cormorant (*Phalacrocorax carbo*), Black Kite (*Milvus migrans*), and Southern Red Bishop (*Euplectes orix*). It's also the only place in mainland Africa to see the Red-billed Tropicbird (*Phaethon aethereus*), which primarily lives on islands further out to sea in places like Cape Verde and the Galapagos. The islands here are home to an estimated 30 breeding pairs.

To get here, you need to call or visit the **National Parks Office** (❱ *33 832 2309*) on the west side of the Route de la Corniche Ouest, where they will arrange a boat and guide to take you over. It's best to do this either the day before, or a few hours in advance of when you'd like to set out, as they can be a bit disorganised getting everything together. Allow yourself a few hours on the island, keeping in mind there are no facilities or shelter whatsoever so you'll want to be back before dark. Pack all the food, drink and sun cream you think you'll need, along with bathing gear if you want to swim. With a group of four or more, the boat over should be 5,000F per person, with an additional 1,000F per person for the park entrance fee, and 5,000F overall for the guide. Alternatively, most of the places offering nautical excursions around Dakar can arrange trips here as well. The conservation-minded guides at Oceanium (see page 92) are among the best, and can also introduce you to the dive sites surrounding the island.

LAC ROSE Named after its striking pink hue, the 3km² Lac Rose (sometimes known as Lac Retba) lies some 35km northeast of Dakar towards the base of the peninsula and, depending on the season and the light, the waters here range from a disorienting Pepto-Bismol sherbet pink during the dry season (November to June) to a murkier, less alien but still noticeably amaranth shade once the rains start to fall and dilute the waters. Backed by an incongruous cluster of sand dunes, the scene here can take on a truly sci-fi hue when the lake is in full bloom. The explanation for the otherworldly fuchsia waves lies in the lake's hypersalinity. With concentrations of up to 40% in parts, it's in a league with Djibouti's Lac Assal and the Dead Sea as one of the saltiest bodies of water anywhere on the planet, and you're equally buoyant when trying to go for a swim. Such conditions are ideal for halophilic (salt-loving) cyanobacteria like *Dunaliella salina*, which nourish themselves on a combination of salt and energy from the sun, turning a rich shade of magenta in the process. The high densities of salt and minerals also whip themselves into soapy foam with the water's movements, and tumbling puffs of bubbles reminiscent of an enormous washing machine disaster float across the lake, winding up on the shores and eventually crystallising into a highly prized speciality, *fleur de sel*.

Most of the lake's produce is far from *haute cuisine*, however, and the estimated 1,000 people who make their living here harvesting and processing salt can expect to be paid just over €40 for every *tonne* of salt they extract from the lake. It's backbreaking work, and labourers – men dredging up the salt from the lake bottom and women hauling it ashore – have to coat their bodies in shea butter to protect their skin from the salt's deleterious effects. After it's dredged off the lake bottom, loaded into a pirogue and brought ashore, it's arranged into tall heaps, jealously looked after by their producers. It's eventually sold on around the region, and now the salt processing on-shore includes running it through a basic iodisation facility, giving this artisanal product a fighting chance of competing with the factory-produced table salts promoted by health agencies and common throughout the region.

Until its cancellation and subsequent move to South America in 2008, Lac Rose was also home to the finish line of the Dakar Rally, where the winners (and losers) would annually take over the village for a few days of post-race jubilation. With the rally now gone, there's no big annual event to draw you here, but it's a consistently popular weekend retreat for *Dakarois* in need of a respite from the peninsula's chronic congestion. It's an equally good escape for tourists; even if the aquatic pyrotechnics aren't on full display, the swimming, boat trips, camel rides and horse safaris on offer here are hardly less compelling. It can easily be visited in either a day trip or overnight, though plan for a solid couple of hours each way if you intend to get here by bus.

Getting there and away All Dakar tour agencies and many hotels arrange day trips to Lac Rose.

By bus From Plateau, catch DDD 11 from Terminus Lat Dior or AFTU-Tata 56 from Terminus Petersen, both of which terminate at Keur Massar, from where you can pick up the AFTU-Tata 73 which goes between Thiaroye Poste on the RN1 and Lac Rose, via Keur Massar. Coming from Ngor, Yoff or Les Almadies, AFTU-Tata 61 runs from Terminus Mamelles (near the African Renaissance Monument) all the way (via Route de Ngor and Route de l'Aéroport) to Keur Massar.

You can of course also connect to the AFTU-Tata 73 at Thiaroye Poste; the advantage of changing at Keur Massar is that it's a line terminus for DDD 11 and AFTU-Tata 56 and 61, so you can ride to the end without worrying about missing your stop. To get back, just do the same thing in reverse.

By car Take the toll road to get in and out of Dakar, exit for the route between Niaga and Rufisque and turn left towards Niaga. It's an easy ride of about 35km, reasonably well signposted, and surfaced the entire way.

Getting around Lac Rose village sits at the southwest edge of the lake, and most accommodation is within a few hundred metres of here. The Esprit d'Afrique complex, which includes Gîte du Lac, Bonaba Café and Chevaux du Lac, is the exception, located on the northern shore. To get here, the road around the east side of the lake is approachable with a sturdy 2x4, while the track through the dunes at the west end is strictly 4x4 only.

Where to stay *Map, page 78; see point 4 on the map for all hotels except Gîte du Lac.*

Hôtel Le Palal (22 rooms) 33 836 2414/30 113 6791; m 77 633 5477; e ibalacrose@ hotmail.com; www.lac-rose-palal.com. Something of a Lac Rose standby, the lakeside bar (where *pieds dans l'eau* is not an exaggeration) & restaurant here is consistently popular, but the rooms are nothing to write home about. They're tiled & clean but a bit plain & under-decorated. The rambling compound is studded with banana trees & lazy cats & dogs napping in the shade. They've got their own 4x4 for trips around the lake. **$$**

Campement Tool-Bi (12 rooms) m 77 522 9654; e toolbi2003@yahoo.fr; www.toolbi. viens.la. With a warm welcome, clean rooms, a blue swimming pool & lots of hammocks scattered about, this locally run campement right across the street from the lake is a stellar budget option. The thatched bungalow rooms are spick & span, with fans, nets & TV, & the casual restaurant out front does good Senegalese dishes. **$$**

Le Trarza (18 rooms) 30 106 8852; m 77 108 4704/300 9156; e le.trarza@gmail.com; www.hotel-le-trarza.com. The most characterful place in town & only slightly more expensive than some of the others in this range, so mid-range travellers should make a beeline here when they arrive at the lake. The grounds are decadently green & colourful, with bright mosaics in the

rooms & even at the bottom of the swimming pool. Eat at the terrace bar-resto or on their viewing deck over the water, lit with lanterns by night. The en-suite rooms are built from natural materials & have AC, nets & flatscreen TVs. **$$**

Campement Lac Rose (Chez Salim) (50 rooms) 33 836 2466; m 77 632 6185/572 9962; e manager@campement-lacrose.com; www.campement-lacrose.com. Even though this place is huge, it's also hugely popular, so often fills up in advance. Once upon a time the party spot for Dakar Rally drivers when they reached the end of the road (check out the bar for plenty of their graffiti), today it's busy with school & company groups & weekending Dakarois. There's a big pool, plenty of activities, & the thatched bungalow rooms are comfortably equipped. Rates in the middle of this range. **$$**

Hôtel Arc En Ciel (46 rooms) m 77 574 4812; e hotelarcenciel-lacrose@hotmail.fr; www. hotelarcenciel-lacrose.com. About 800m removed from the action (if you can call it that) on the lakeshore, this feels a bit like a resort hotel from Saly transplanted up to Lac Rose. The VIP rooms are done up to the nines (think Italian bath fixtures), while standard rooms are set in comfortable bungalows with earth-tone walls, AC, nets & little terraces out front. Their 3-course French menu goes for 9,500F, & you can expect some drinking & dancing at the poolside bar. The turnoff is to the right before you reach the lake. Rates in the top half of this range. **$$**

🏠 **Les Cristaux Roses** (34 rooms) m 77 634 0468/524 0787; e contact@lescristauxroses. com; www.lescristauxroses.com. The AC & fan rooms here are something of a Dr Jekyll & Mr Hyde scenario; AC rooms are cute & thoughtfully appointed with wrought iron features, 4-poster beds & TVs, while the fan rooms feel a bit unkempt & lack any of the décor that makes the AC rooms charming. Still, even if you cheap out on the room, gardens here are full of birds, the pool is the right colour & the restaurant is prim & proper. **$$**

🏠 **Étoile du Lac** (50 rooms) 📞 33 836 2450; m 77 512 9213; e etoiledulac@etoiledulac. com; www.etoiledulac.com. This huge new resort is much better suited to conference-goers than to travellers; if you don't mind the rather

characterless surroundings, the rooms are well-appointed with fridge, nets & TV. There's a big diamond-shaped swimming pool, 2 restaurants, a disco & some coin-operated grocery-shop rides for the kiddies. **$$**

🏠 **Gîte du Lac** 📞 33 860 92 93; m 77 452 8344; e gdl@espritdafrique.com; www.gitedulac. com. The only accommodation on the remote northern side of the lake, the high-ceilinged thatched bungalows here are cool & comfortable, with 4-poster beds, nets & en-suite ablutions. Situated between ocean & lake, there's a little sandy beach for swimmers who want to brave the saline waters of Lac Rose, or the windswept beaches of the Grande Côte are only 900m away, accessible by an easy walk, horse ride or even on their quad bikes. You can get here with a normal vehicle by going east around the lake, & it's also home to Bonaba Café & Chevaux du Lac (see below). Rates in the top half of this range. **$$**

✕ **Where to eat and drink** *Map, page 78.*

✕ **Bar-Restaurant Au 212** m 76 582 2570/666 4663; ⏱ 08.00–19.00 daily. Food options outside of the hotels here are few & far between, but pitch up under one of the lakeside gazebos & nosh on fish & Senegalese dishes for an affordable 3,000F if you're feeling stir-crazy back at the ranch. It's right on the water & there are a handful of laid-back craft sellers hanging around here as well.

✕ **Bonaba Café** 📞 30 108 1720; m 77 633 5201; e bnc@espritdafrique.com; www.bonabacafe. com; ⏱ 10.00–18.00 daily. Serving refined cuisine on a shaded lakeside terrace on the north side of the lake, it's absolutely worth the trip out here to luxuriate over one of their 3-course lunches (6,500F weekdays, 8,000F w/ends) for the afternoon. Hang around & play some pétanque after eating, or just enjoy the view of the village on the other side.

What to see and do Most of the hotels here can arrange the full array of lacustrine activities, including pirogue trips and 4x4, camel or quad bike excursions into the dunes. The best place to go for horse rides is **Chevaux du Lac** (m *77 572 8452/452 8344;* e *cdl@espritdafrique.com; www.chevauxdulac.com*) at Gîte du Lac/Bonaba Café on the northern lakeshore; they do a customisable range of trail rides in the dunes, on the ocean beaches opposite the lake or in the fishing villages beyond.

RUFISQUE *Population: 462,741* Recognised as a *commune* by the colonial government in 1880 (predating even Dakar, which didn't enjoy this status until 1887), Rufisque was once one of Senegal's most important ports and settlements, but as Dakar's star rose, that of Rufisque fell, and its decline has been steep. Today it's an industrial centre, home to a cement works and a handful of other light industries. Most of the colonial buildings remaining in the old city centre are in a state of deep disrepair, and for most Senegalese, Rufisque is largely associated with little more than traffic-choked streets and hawkers taking advantage of their captive audiences wishing they were in Dakar already. In the old centre and along the quayside, a string of old warehouses and commercial buildings sport toothless wooden shutters dangling from their hinges and Marseillais terracotta roof tiles hanging on to their sagging structures for dear life. Many of them sit disused, often themselves colonised around their perimeter by vendors' stalls attached to what remains of the old walls like barnacles. Many of the buildings are still in use as well: the *gare ferroviaire*, done in a similar style to the other stations along the line, still sees two trains a day between Dakar and Thiès, while the Église Sainte Agnès dates to 1885 and the active parish celebrated their 130th anniversary in 2015. The *gare routière* and livestock market are conveniently right next to each other at the roundabout (*rond-point Rufisque*), so you might as well pick up a goat for the ride home while you wait. DDD bus 15 runs between here and the Place de l'Indépendance in Plateau.

🛏 **Where to stay, eat and drink** *Map, page 78.*
The new toll road means it's now possible to fly through here without a second thought, but if you're on public transport your fellow passengers might be unwilling or unable to pay the toll, so you very well might end up sitting in Rufisque anyway. (Of course you could offer to pay the tolls yourself if you've got more means than patience.) Thus, for most travellers, the little of Rufisque they see from the RN1 is more than enough, so unless you're a determined urban explorer with a taste for colonial decay (and not always the picturesque kind), there's really not much to detain you here. If you do find yourself in the area and in need of a night's kip, escape to the **L'Oustal de L'Agenais** (*14 rooms;* ✆ *33 836 16 48;* e *moniquegaye@ yahoo.fr;* $–$$) just off the RN1 at the west end of town, which has pleasant enough air-conditioned rooms for 25,000F, fan rooms for half that, and meals starting around 3,000F.

KEUR MOUSSA MONASTERY Founded in 1963 by nine Benedictine monks from Saint-Pierre Abbey in the French village of Solesmes, the Monastère de Keur Moussa (✆ *33 836 3309;* m *77 617 0517/375 1667; www.abbaye-keur-moussa.org*) between Dakar and Thiès has been perfecting a unique fusion of Gregorian chant and West African instrumentation for over 50 years now. In a modest church adorned with 16 striking red, black and gold panels depicting the life of Mary, the chorus of French and Senegalese monks sing original and traditional compositions in French and Wolof, accompanied by kora, calabash drums and balafon. Catch one of their masses to hear them play; they're held daily at 11.15, and at 10.00 on Sundays. When the brothers aren't attending to sacred duties, they're tending the gardens or in their instrument workshop where they manufacture their own koras.

They cut their first record in 1967 and have put out dozens of albums since then, many of which are available for purchase at their shop next to the church (or online). It's open for a couple of hours after each mass, as well as from roughly 15.00 to 17.00 in the afternoons. You can buy their music here, along with agro-products from the orchards like jams, juices and their famous goats' cheese. Their handmade koras are also for sale, and unlike in many tourist markets, the quality here is guaranteed. If you're going to be in the area for a while, kora lessons can also be arranged. The grounds and gardens around the church are pleasant and appropriately contemplative, if unspectacular, and it's possible to get a tour around them – ask at the shop when you arrive.

Getting there and away The monastery itself is about 45km from Dakar and 25km from Thiès, and is not to be confused with Keur Massar, which is the town where you would change buses to get to Lac Rose. Keur *Moussa* village is on the road to Kayar, 1.5km north of the RN2 towards Thiès on the road to Bayakh and Kayar. The monastery itself is 1.5km west of the village along a surfaced road. (The only surfaced turnoff in the village.) To get here on public transport, you can get a Thiès-bound vehicle at Baux Maraîchers (or Dakar-bound if you're coming from Thiès) and hop out at the junction for Kayar (a tiny village called Mbirdiamm), from where you can either walk the roughly 3km to the monastery; equally you shouldn't have much trouble getting a lift. Alternatively, bus DDD 15 goes from the Place de l'Indépendance in Plateau all the way to Rufisque, from where you can find transport to Kayar, but be careful to mention you want to get off in Keur Moussa, as there are two routes to Kayar from Rufisque, only one of which passes there. Getting back to Dakar shouldn't pose too much of a problem: catch a *ndiaga ndiaye* passing through Keur Moussa, or if you don't feel like waiting just walk the 1.5km to the RN2, where there's plenty of passing traffic.

VILLAGE DES TORTUES (☏ *33 836 3632;* e *diattabenoit@yahoo.fr;* ⊕ *09.00–18.00 daily; entry 3000/2000F foreigner/resident*) On the 16ha Réserve Spéciale Botanique de Noflaye just north of Sangalkam village and about 30km from Dakar, this unexpected sanctuary is home to over 350 tortoises, ranging from abandoned pets to animals forced out of their habitats by building developments. The stars of the show here are the African spurred tortoises (*Centrochelys sulcata*), which can weigh up to 100kg and live over 100 years. Native to the Sahelian belt stretching from here clear across the continent to Ethiopia, these burrowing tortoises are the world's third-largest, second only to the giant tortoises resident on the Galápagos Islands and Aldabra Atoll. If you're here at the right times, you can witness the tortoises breeding and feeding, and the laying or hatching of eggs in their underground burrows. In their nursery you can get up close with the newest additions to the sanctuary, who weigh in at a paltry 40g when they're born. Many of the tortoises raised here are eventually released into larger reserves in the north as they mature into young adults.

You can walk around the grounds alone, but the guides here know their stuff, and for the price of a tip it's worth taking one along (assuming you share a common language). The information panels are all in French, but the grounds are verdant, with many of the trees and their practical or medicinal uses labelled as well. It would be easy to spend a relaxed hour strolling through the gardens and taking in the various enclosures, and there's a little café and boutique at the end with cold drinks and a handful of souvenirs. From Dakar, you can check if there's a Kayar-bound *ndiaga ndiaye* that goes via Sangalkam at Baux Maraîchers, or try the AFTU-Tata 66 (towards Terminus Gorom II) which you can pick up at the Yoff terminus or along the Route de l'Aéroport, which stops in Sangalkam, from where it's a short walk up the road to the sanctuary, signposted on the left-hand side (or you can ask them nicely to drop you at the entrance).

KAYAR At the base of the Cap Vert peninsula where the Grande Côte begins its windswept journey up to Saint-Louis, the fishing port of Kayar is an overgrown Lébou village of entirely outsized piscatorial importance. For the length of the town, the beach is packed to the (and with some) gills with teams of fishermen hauling in their catches or heaving their pirogues into the water. During high season (November to June), nearly 1,200 boats set out from here every day to reel in the fish destined for millions of bowls of *thieboudienne* eaten daily across the country. The riot of brashly coloured pirogues, each fighting to one-up their neighbours' catch and their cachet, is a feast for the eyes, but the heaps of fish guts and football fields' worth of fish drying racks can be equally vivid on the nose. The catch is barely on shore before an army of fishmongers starts sorting, gutting, and selling to the waiting distributors – the catch is put on trucks and is back in Dakar before you can say *thiof*. Meanwhile, a troop of boat builders sand away throughout the day, patching up leaky hulls in need of attention and building replacements for the timeworn vessels which have made their last trips out to sea.

Kayar can make for a fascinating day trip and some fantastic photo opportunities, but don't expect to do any swimming or much beachside relaxing; this is a working town through and through, not to mention that the ocean currents here are strong. When you've had enough of the beachside madness and start to feel like one of the unlucky fish gasping for fresh air, head east a few blocks and climb one of the sand dunes for a view over the feverish proceedings below. To get here from Dakar, see if there's a vehicle leaving from Baux Maraîchers, or take DDD 15 to Rufisque and get a *ndiaga ndiaye* from there to Kayar. There used to be a couple of campements in town and you still might be able to get a basic bed at Auberge des Cocotiers [map, page 78](❧ *33 953 5006*), but it's much preferable to combine a visit here with a trip to Lac Rose and stay on the lake, about 25km away.

FOLLOW BRADT

For the latest news, special offers and competitions, subscribe to the Bradt newsletter via the website www.bradtguides.com and follow Bradt on:

f www.facebook.com/BradtTravelGuides
🐦 @BradtGuides
📷 @bradtguides
📌 pinterest.com/bradtguides

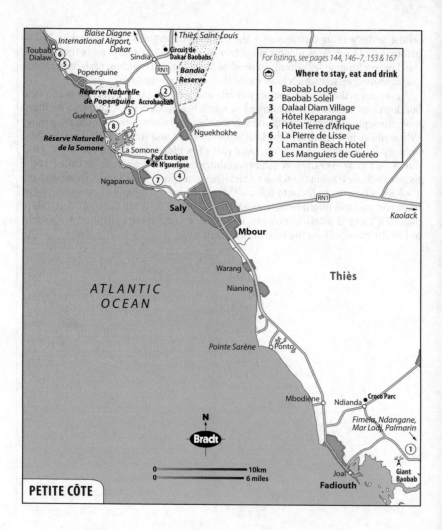

For listings, see pages 144, 146–7, 153 & 167

⊜ **Where to stay, eat and drink**

1 Baobab Lodge
2 Baobab Soleil
3 Dalaal Diam Village
4 Hôtel Keparanga
5 Hôtel Terre d'Afrique
6 La Pierre de Lisse
7 Lamantin Beach Hotel
8 Les Manguiers de Guéréo

Blaise Diagne
International Airport,
Dakar

Thiès, Saint-Louis

Toubab
Dialaw

6
5

Popenguine

Sindia

Circuit de
Dakar Baobabs

**Bandia
Reserve**

RN1

*Réserve Naturelle
de Popenguine*

2

Accrobaobab

Guéréo

3

8

Nguekhokhe

*Réserve Naturelle
de la Somone*

La Somone

Parc Exotique
de N'guerigne

Ngaparou

7

4

RN1

Saly

Kaolack

Mbour

Warang

Nianing

Thiès

*ATLANTIC
OCEAN*

Pointe Sarène

Ponto

Mbodiène

Ndianda

Croco Parc

*Fimela, Ndangane,
Mar Lodj, Palmarin*

1

N

Bradt

0   10km
0   6 miles

Joal

Giant
Baobab

PETITE CÔTE

Fadiouth

5

The Petite Côte

At the very heart of Senegal's tourism industry, the sun-soaked shores and gentle blue waters of the Petite Côte are prime postcard material, and tens of thousands of visitors flock here annually, tracing the countless wingbeats of their avian neighbours also headed south for some winter sun. The coast is home to an eclectic cluster of settlements, but this is the one part of Senegal where package tourism is truly king, and many visitors see no more of the country than their resort and the route to the airport. (And even this trip is set to shrink with the opening of Blaise Diagne International Airport, positioned barely 30km from Saly, with exactly these visitors in mind.) Still, there are something like a dozen easily accessible settlements scattered along the shore here, and while all enjoy their own slice of the dazzling waterfront for which the coast here is famous, they are otherwise an incongruous and enticingly eclectic mix, offering everything from djembe dance lessons and *dibiterie* to hot stone massage and charcuterie. Thus, whether you're seeking authenticity and starry nights or indulgence and laser lights, there's room enough for all on the sands of the Petite Côte.

In sharp contrast to the windswept Grande Côte to the north, the waterfront here is protected from strong ocean currents by the Cap Vert peninsula; the Petite Côte traces a white sand arc for nearly 100km southeast from Dakar, until it finally trails off into the serpentine channels and mangrove islands of the Sine-Saloum Delta at Joal-Fadiouth. Between these two points, life for both tourists and locals largely revolves around one thing: the beach. Every morning in Mbour, sinewy, sure-footed fisherman hurl their pirogues into the water and manhandle their shimmering, fish-laden nets back out by night, while a few kilometres up the sand in Saly, well-oiled Europeans bronze themselves (or attempt to), try their hands at all variety of watersports, or sip drinks whose colours compete with the landscape for the title of most tropical.

Starting in the north, Toubab Dialaw is home to an afro-bohemian arts scene, while Popenguine, just a stone's throw south, is pious, unspoilt and serene. Continuing across the lagoon to La Somone and Ngaparou, things get a bit busier, and signs of major tourist development start to appear, growing in frequency as you inch closer to Saly. Considered the Petite Côte's crown jewel by some and a hopeless tourist trap by others, Saly is, love it or hate it, the centrepiece of the Petite Côte, and an unapologetic mélange of quad bikes, golf, four-star bungalows, four-course meals, throbbing discotheques and without question the highest density of souvenir shops anywhere in Senegal. Continuing south, Mbour is a bit dusty and workaday, but nonetheless has a big-city buzz; while it's rather short on conventional attractions, it's home to some excellent accommodation and a surprisingly fine beach. Warang and Nianing both fall somewhere in between Saly's overdevelopment and Popenguine's tranquillity, and make for a happy middle ground for sun seekers who still want to soak up a little bit of the local vibe. Sleepy and isolated, the low-key resorts at Mbodiène mark the last stop before the road heads inland at Joal, gateway town to the otherworldly island of Fadiouth, worth seeing if only to witness for yourself the seemingly fanciful reality of a whole town built on, and of, little more than millions upon millions of discarded seashells.

And while the beach is rightfully the star of the show along most of the coast, there's an assortment of land-based activities to keep you occupied as well. Start with a big-game fix at Bandia Reserve before checking out the high-flying zip lines and ropes courses across the road at AccroBaobab, where you're guaranteed to get your heart pumping to make up for all those days lounging on the beach. The Réserve Naturelle de Popenguine offers good rambling opportunities, and keen ornithologists (and those that love them) will be happy to know that the entirety of the Petite Côte has been recognised as an Important Bird Area, making it a perfect compromise if you and your travel buddy can't decide if you're going for the water or the weavers.

Towns here are listed here from north to south, and visitors should be aware that the only banking facilities on the Petite Côte are in Saly and Mbour.

TOUBAB DIALAW

Only 45 km by road from Dakar, the sprawling fishing village of Toubab Dialaw has developed into something of a low-key vacation colony for affluent Dakarois and expats seeking a beachside retreat close to the city, but without the tourist buzz of Saly or the big-city bustle of Mbour. It's also a magnet for the Bohemian set, in part thanks to Haitian Renaissance man Gérard Chenet and his lodge-meets-cultural-centre Sobo Badè, which acts as the village's cultural anchor and has been drawing artists, musicians and creative types of all sorts to Toubab Dialaw since it opened here over 30 years ago. The internationally renowned Jant-Bi dance school is based in the village as well, and if your aim is to study or practise your art, drumming, dance, music or theatre, and to do it within metres of the beach, you could hardly choose better than Toubab Dialaw.

The town itself is a bit hodgepodge, with all manner of opulent, though not particularly tasteful, vacation homes in various stages of completion spilling haphazardly over the hilltops and crowding up to the rocky, ochre cliffsides at the water's edge. Even with the vacation villas, it somehow remains refreshingly unpretentious and, though Senegal lacks a backpacker's mecca in the mould of Mozambique's Tofo beach or Malawi's Nkhata Bay, Toubab Dialaw in many ways fits the bill, and functions as something of an off-beat antithesis to the industrial holidaymaking of Saly. As with the rest of the coast, life here revolves around the water, and it's one of the absolute finest places on the coast to sit back and watch the tide come in, the boats go out, and life go by.

GETTING THERE AND AWAY Toubab Dialaw is just about the furthest flung destination reachable on Dakar's **bus** system, and this is a reliably cheap (and reliably slow) way to get here. DDD line 228 serves Toubab Dialaw from Rufisque, and it's most easily caught at either Rufisque or Diamniado. The Dakar Dem Dikk terminus in Rufisque is reachable by a number of lines, including DDD15, which you can pick up at Place de l'Indépendance in Plateau. If you're coming from Ngor-Almadies, you'll have to first get to Gare routière Baux Maraîchers via AFTU-Tata 61, from where you can pick up the DDD15 a few metres away at Croisement Bountou Pikine. Once at the Rufisque DDD terminus, DDD228 (direction Yenné) goes to Toubab Dialaw via Diamniado. If you're changing buses at the Gare routière Baux Maraîchers/Croisement Bountou Pikine, it's equally possible to get the AFTU-Tata 64 from there all the way to Diamniado, and pick up the DDD228 at Diamniado. (Check out www.talibi.net for a very useful route planner.) It's also possible to take the standard assortment of *sept-places* or *ndiaga ndiayes* from Gare routière Baux Maraîchers to Diamniado, and a similar vehicle from here to Toubab Dialaw.

Coming **from the south**, there are two turnoffs from the RN1 to Toubab Dialaw (one surfaced, one not so much) that you could try and catch a lift at, but your best bet on public transport would be to head a few kilometres further north to Diamniado and get a vehicle (or the DDD228) from there. Getting here with private transport is a no-brainer and can be approached in any vehicle. The paved route branches west from the RN1 between Diamniado and Mbourouk, and continues 10km into town.

WHERE TO STAY, EAT AND DRINK

La Source Ndiambalane (14 rooms) **m** 77 635 7888/556 7978; **e** ndiambalane@yahoo.fr. Clinging to the cliffs like a barnacle above the breaking surf, this seashell-studded retreat boasts uninterrupted views over the water & ocean breezes that are nothing short of revelatory. Rooms come with either private or communal balconies & all are en suite with fans & nets. The resto-bar whips up meals on request, & while the standard rate is bed only, a full-board stay can be arranged for a trivial 5,000F extra per person. It doesn't have the active social scene of Sobo Badè, but you could hardly be closer, & with prices barely scraping the bottom of this range, it's really excellent value. There's no Wi-Fi, though. **$$**

La Mimosa (10 rooms) **** 33 836 0015; **m** 77 354 1988/148 3454; **e** lamimoza@gmail.com. Compared with the superbly characterful places around the corner, the step down in quality here is considerably larger than the step down in price, but penny-pinchers will be happy to save the cost of a couple of beers (though the dorm at Sobo Badè is still the cheapest sleep in town). Rooms are decidedly no-frills, but all are en suite with fans & nets, & there are a few with AC as well, but these will nudge you into the next price category. The resto-bar does pizzas, fish & a selection of Senegalese staples for 2,000–3,000F, & you can catch a djembe drumming session here most Sat nights. No Wi-Fi. **$**

Sobo Badè (36 rooms) **** 33 836 0356; **e** sobobade2012@gmail.com; www.sobobade.com. The idiosyncratic oceanside domain of Haitian-born artist-architect Gérard Chenet had its origins here in the late 1970s, & it's been shapeshifting & expanding ever since. The rambling, mosaic-adorned complex takes a big page from Gaudí (and maybe even a bit of one from Dalí), with a mad architectural farrago of towers, parapets, archways, seashells, thatched domes & cupolas, serpentine balustrades & surprises around almost every corner, making for a thoroughly inimitable architectural experience, all stuck atop the sea cliffs a few metres from the beach. It's as much cultural centre as it is hotel & restaurant, & there's a rotating range of activities here depending on who the artists-in-residence are at the time. They also operate the **Théâtre de l'Engouement** nearby (see page 142), & you can expect possible lessons in kora, djembe or balafon; clay sculpture, batik & sous-verre; or dance, drama & fashion. There is a variety of room options, starting with a 5,000F dorm bed & ranging up to an en-suite double with sea view for 23,000F. There's Wi-Fi & a good resto-bar on site. Recommended. **$$**

Centre Mampuya (18 rooms) **m** 77 569 3773; **e** contact@mampuya.org; www.mampuya.org. Surrounded by 40ha of protected land in the hills above town, this eco-conscious hideaway was set up in 2001 as a Swiss-Senegalese centre for sustainable development & acts as an incubator for numerous ecological projects around Toubab Dialaw. The bright & airy rooms are built to blend in with the surroundings & come in a variety of en-suite constellations – the largest being a split-level family suite sleeping up to 5. They're occasionally booked up with seminars, so it's best to call ahead to check availability or arrange a pickup from town. If you're trekking out here yourself, take the middle road at the 3-way junction at the south end of town & continue just under 2km into the hills. Given the out-of-the-way location, all guests are accommodated on a half- or full-board basis, & prices are squarely in the middle of this range. **$$$**

✕ Le Rocher (Chez Nabou) m 77 657 1790; www.naboulerocher.wix.com/rocher; ⏰ 08.00–23.00 daily. Smack dab on the beach, this amiable local joint is the place to go to fill up on Senegalese staples without taking your toes out of the sand. The dishes have an appropriately oceanic flair (think fish *yassa*), & you can sit inside or take advantage of one of their umbrella-shaded chaise longues while you wait (preferably with a cold Gazelle).

✕ Chez Paolo m 77 532 3189; www.facebook.com/chezpaolotoubabdialaw; ⏰ 07.00–22.00 daily. This Toubab Dialaw standby does crispy, Italian-style pizzas baked over a wood fire for around 4,000F, & serves them up on a breezy terrace with fabulous views over the water. Extravagant it ain't, but the pizza menu is surprisingly sophisticated, with capers, artichoke hearts & *saucisson* all making an appearance.

☆ Black and White m 77 052 2300/572 1220; thiampo@gmail.com; www.blackandwhitesn.com. Taking an everything-under-one-roof-approach, this locally run place, painted up in colours you might expect & set just along the main road through town, has a restaurant, dancefloor & stage for live music, along with a swimming pool & even a clutch of neatly kept thatch bungalows out back, (though you can expect these to be noisy at weekends).

WHAT TO SEE AND DO The beach exerts a nearly irresistible pull for locals and tourists alike in Toubab Dialaw; you'll probably share the sand with a local football side or two practising in the surf, and some lovestruck couples out for a bit of privacy and a barefoot stroll. Besides the myriad opportunities here in art, music and dance, relaxation really is *de rigueur*. Pull up a picnic chair from one of the beachside watering holes and watch the world go by. When this gets too strenuous, take a dip. Repeat.

If you absolutely must do something besides building sandcastles and eating grilled fish, there are good opportunities to explore the hills behind town, either on foot from the trails around **Centre Mampuya**, or on horseback with the equestrians at **Les Cavaliers de la Savane** (m *77 569 0365/333 3323*; e *daoflorence@hotmail. com; www.facebook.com/Cavaliersdelasavane*), who arrange rides for people of all skill levels in the bush outside of town, starting at around 15,000F.

Artists and performers should already have made a beeline for Sobo Badè, but while you're there, be sure to ask what the latest program at the **Théâtre de l'Engouement** (*www.facebook.com/TheatreDeLEngouement*), which consists of workshop space, bedrooms and a theatre all set 2km away from Sobo Badè in 3ha of gardens. Here they also offer an array of lessons and creative programming depending on who's in town; the architecture is equally unorthodox and otherworldly, and worth a visit in itself. If dance is your thing, be sure to get in touch with **Jant Bi (L'École des Sables)** (✆ *33 836 2388*; e *jantbi@gmail.com; www.jantbi.org* or *www.facebook.com/ JantBicompagnie*). Owned by Benin-born choreographer Germaine Acogny, their dance troupes tour worldwide, and visitors can look in and see the working stages of their next performances. It's set south of the central village, 1.4km from the main route as it heads south out of town. Follow the dirt road that branches to the right just before the turning to Ndayane and Popenguine.

POPENGUINE

Site of the community-based Réserve Naturelle de Popenguine and home to the most important shrine in the country for Senegal's Catholics, the mixed Wolof and

Serer village of Popenguine is a thoroughly agreeable oceanside escape, situated 60km south of Dakar on a rise overlooking one of the most ruggedly picturesque stretches of coastline in the country (but with plenty of not-so-rugged beach for swimming), and much like its neighbour Toubab Dialaw to the north, it's remained refreshingly free of the mass-market tourist development and mushrooming resorts to be found further down the coast. Popenguine will easily satisfy both water babies and dedicated ramblers, and there's a handful of charming accommodation to choose from, all situated some metres above the beach at the south end of town.

GETTING THERE AND AWAY Popenguine sits 10km west of the RN1 at the end of a surfaced feeder road from the junction town of Sindia. All transport between Dakar or Thies and Mbour passes this junction, so it's easy to find a lift here from pretty much any direction. From Sindia itself, vehicles zip back and forth to Popenguine throughout the day for a few hundred CFA, and there will surely be a few *djakarta* drivers angling to give you a lift as well.

WHERE TO STAY, EAT AND DRINK All hotels listed below offer Wi-Fi.

In Popenguine

Auberge de Popenguine (7 rooms) `33 957 8599; m 77 384 0998; e daborosemarie@ gmail.com; www.auberge-popenguine.com.` Welcoming, bright & cheerfully festooned with colourful décor & oceanic accents, this tranquil family-run guesthouse has a clutch of freshly whitewashed en-suite rooms & a cosy ground-floor restaurant. The upstairs rooms have their own terraces, & all rooms come with fans & nets. It's less than 100m to the beach, & they can arrange trips to the nature reserve, Somone lagoon & beyond. It's good value, with rates at the low end of this range, & they'll even knock a couple of thousand CFA off the price in the off-season. **$$**

Campement Ebène (6 rooms) `33 957 7166; m 77 658 2701; e sokhna@ campementebene.com; www.campementebene. com.` Artsy & earth-toned, this pretty little campement sits in a leafy compound south of the town centre & is almost assuredly the most relaxing accommodation in Popenguine. The cool & comfortable en-suite bungalows come with beds & nets, & each is individually decorated with murals, sculpture & tapestries of Malian *bògòlanfini* mud cloth. There's a 2-bedroom family house as well. All activities & trips throughout the region are easily arranged, French-inspired meals are available on request & there's a rooftop terrace above the restaurant. Rates are at the upper end of this range. **$$**

Kër Cupaam (14 rooms) `33 956 4951; m 77 575 4174; e rnpopenguine@gmail.com.` Also sometimes known as the *campement des femmes* or 'women's campement', this friendly compound is run by the Regroupement des Femmes de Popenguine pour la Protection de la Nature (RFPPN), & also serves as the headquarters for the Popenguine Nature Reserve, making it the cheapest & most convenient accommodation in town if your aim is to visit the park. Sharing a compound with a plant nursery (part of their reforestation efforts) at the south end of town, the tidy rooms here are bereft of any frills, but all are en suite with fans & nets, & proceeds support conservation initiatives. They offer dorm beds, en-suite rooms and 2-room houses, the latter of which are much newer & brighter but are only rented out as a unit. A night in the dorm goes for 6,000F, the double is 12,000F, and the 2-room house (sleeping 4) goes for 30,000F. Good Senegalese meals are available on request. **$**

Le Balafon Café m 77 562 6254/608 5053; e agnesmalicktop@gmail.com; www.balafon. wordpress.com; ⊕ lunch & dinner daily. This low-key terrace restaurant lies behind a *banco* mud archway on the beach side of the road, & the multi-coloured interior is home to a pool table & some fantastic views over the ocean. There's a rotating selection of continental & African meals for 3,000–5,000F covering everything from warthog to *lotte* (monkfish), & occasional live music in the evenings.

l'Echo-Cotier `33 957 7172; m 77 637 8772; www.facebook.com/echocotier.popenguine; ⊕ 08.00–21.00 daily.` At the juncture of fine white sand & crisp white tablecloths lies this unexpectedly stylish eatery down a long flight of steps on the beach opposite Kër Cupaam. The easy grace of the indoor-outdoor dining area belies the sophistication of the menu, & meals start with carefully crafted amuse-bouches & appetisers, followed by an eclectic selection of mains including duck confit, chicken tikka, spring rolls & a wide range of seafood for about 6,500–9,500F. And to top it off, they make their own ice cream, so the desserts are equally extraordinary.

Around Popenguine

Hôtel Terre d'Afrique and La Pierre de Lisse are directly next to each other on the beach just north of Ndayane village, accessible from the coastal laterite road between Toubab Dialaw & Popenguine, while Les Manguiers de Guéréo & Dalaal Diam Village are more remote – call to arrange a pickup or to get directions. All have Wi-Fi.
Map, page 138.

🏠 **Les Manguiers de Guéréo** (15 rooms) Guéréo; ✣ 14.510864, −17.081927; m 77 276 9010; e info@lesmanguiersdeguereo.com; www. lesmanguiersdeguereo.com. With a fabulously isolated location on the north side of Somone's lagoon, this upmarket escape caters largely to family groups of Europeans & weekending *Dakarois*, so the en-suite bungalows are sizeable & comfortably equipped. It's got a swimming pool of its own, but is also spitting distance from the lagoon & about a kilometre from the beach, should you feel like venturing out. The kitchen turns out continental delicacies, the management speaks English, & they can arrange activities anywhere on the Petite Côte. Accommodation is all-inclusive, with prices at the top of this range. **$$$$**

🏠 **Dalaal Diam Village** (10 rooms) Thiafoura; ✣ 14.522015, −17.056432; m 77 691 4677; e info@dalaaldiam-village.com; www. dalaaldiam-village.com. In an 8ha patch of savannah somewhere between Popenguine & La Somone, the fantastical architecture alone is worth the trip out here. Accommodation ranges from simple rooms with the usual fans & nets to luxurious 'Bio-Climatique' villas built from *banco* that wouldn't look out of place in Timbuktu, and it's all spread out along a quiet riverbend in the bush. The resto-bar overlooks the swimming pool, they arrange the usual activities, & prices start at the very bottom of this range. **$$$**

🏠 **Hôtel Terre d'Afrique** (18 rooms) m 77 236 3141/643 9666; e hotelterreafrique@ gmail.com; www.hotelterreafrique.com. A touch downmarket from its next-door neighbour, the bungalows here are modern & bright, though lacking a bit of the character found next door. Still, the grounds are serene & finely manicured, facilities are built to a high standard, & all the rooms are en suite with AC. There's a large pool, terrace resto-bar, & all the usual aquatic activities can be arranged. Unusually, it's also accessible for those with reduced mobility. The B&B rate is at the bottom of this range, & HB is smack in the middle. **$$**

🏠 **La Pierre de Lisse** (21 rooms) Ndayene; ☎33 957 7148; e pierredelisse@orange.sn; www. itinerairelisse.net. With accommodation in cool stone-and-thatch cottages scattered throughout a large beachside garden, rooms at this quiet resort are tastefully furnished & well equipped, & all come with AC, TV & en-suite ablutions. There's a large pool, covered terrace resto-bar, spa, volleyball, pétanque & a variety of other activities on offer. Guests are accommodated on a HB or FB basis, & the HB price hovers near the top of this range. **$$**

WHAT TO SEE AND DO

Basilique Notre-Dame de la Délivrance (✆ 33 957 7106) This basilica enjoys pride of place up at the centre of town. It is a logical starting point for exploring Popenguine and makes for a rewarding short visit, even for those of a determinedly secular outlook. The basilica began its life in 1888 when Mathurin Picarda, then the apostolic vicar of Senegambia, visited Popenguine and ordered a shrine to be built to the Virgin Mary. The installation of the black Madonna figure, a replica of a centuries-old sculpture found in the Norman village of Douvres-la-Délivrande, took place later the same year. Construction went on in fits and starts and the building eventually took the shape of a church, though it wasn't officially completed until a whopping 100 years later in 1988. It was declared a minor basilica (of which there are only 21 in Africa) in the run-up to Pope John Paul II's 1992 visit to Popenguine.

Thus, despite its diminutive size, Popenguine packs a storied religious history, and is an enormously important site for Senegal's Catholics – some even claim to have witnessed Marian apparitions here, though no sightings have been confirmed by Rome just yet. For most of the year, Popenguine unhurriedly ambles along much like Senegal's other coastal villages, but it balloons in size over the annual **Pentecost** holiday, when it hosts the Christian equivalent of Touba's Grand Magal (see page 249), and thousands of Catholics from around the country and beyond stream into town to commemorate the feast. Numerically speaking, it's a quaint gathering compared with the Grand Magal's million-plus throngs (only about 5% of Senegalese are Christian, after all), but the significance is much the same, and there's certainly no shortage of fervour or enthusiasm among the pilgrims.

Réserve Naturelle de Popenguine (✆ 33 957 7251; 2,000F entry, 8,000F guide)
South of town lies this award-winning 1,009ha reserve, which occasionally goes by its Wolof name, Kër Cupaam – house of Cupaam, a deity thought to be resident on the reserve's cliffs – and was gazetted in 1986. It's been managed since shortly after that by the women of Popenguine and surrounding villages, as part of the Collective of Women's Groups for the Protection of Nature (COPRONAT), which today consists of over 1,500 women in eight villages surrounding the reserve. Their efforts in reforesting and revitalizing what was once a denuded patch of land have earned them accolades throughout the country and throughout the world. They were the 2006 winners of the Equator Prize, awarded biennially by the UNDP-affiliated Equator Institute for excellence in community-based poverty reduction through conservation and sustainable management of biodiversity. Since they've been managing the park, the women have planted a hugely impressive 11,000 trees within the reserve and a surrounding buffer zone, and a staggering 50,000 mangroves in and around the reserve's lagoon and maritime areas.

The reserve itself is slung over a series of low, baobab-studded hills, which rise to peak of 74m above the beach. The protected zone continues into the ocean, covering a 2km stretch of coast and water down to a depth of 800m offshore. Some 600m south of the village and beyond a small seasonal lagoon, you'll find *Cap de Naze* (Cape Naze), the reserve's highest point, better known as the *Falaises de Popenguine*, a 300m-long wall of cliffs that rises nearly 75m from the sandy beach below. These cliffs briefly marked the furthest extent of European exploration of the West African coast when Portuguese slave-trader Álvaro Fernandes reached here in 1445 before turning back towards Madeira. He would return and sail further south the next year, but the precise terminus of this next expedition remains unclear, so these cliffs remained the furthest uncontested marker of European exploration for over a decade. Today, the sheer cliffs and heaps of boulders at the bottom make for a stunning backdrop to Popenguine's already gorgeous and delightfully unspoilt beach.

The reserve is a great destination for ramblers, and certainly makes for the best hiking opportunities on this stretch of coast, but if it's big-game spotting you're after, this isn't the place to do it – head for Bandia or Fathala instead. Though it was once home to elephant, African wild dog and even leopard, these have unfortunately long been locally extinct; under the stewardship of the women, however, the reserve has witnessed the return of numerous species long thought to have disappeared locally. So while it may not be the Serengeti, visitors here still have a reasonable chance of spotting some of the resident bushbuck (*Tragelaphus scriptus*), common duiker (*Sylvicapra grimmia*), African civet (*Civettictis civetta*), golden jackal (*Canis aureus*), spotted hyena (*Crocuta crocuta*), serval (*Leptailurus* serval), pardine genet (*Genetta pardina*), crested porcupine (*Hystrix cristata*), patas monkey (*Erythrocebus patas*), marsh mongoose (*Atilax paludinosus*) and savannah monitor (*Varanus exanthematicus*), among others.

Birders have a checklist of nearly 200 species to get through here, including Palaearctic migrants like the blue rock-thrush (*Monticola solitarius*) and common rock-thrush (*Monticola saxatilis*). In the hills above the beach, there are resident numbers of long-tailed glossy starling (*Lamprotornis caudatus*), yellow-crowned gonolek (*Laniarius barbarous*) and Senegal parrot (*Poicephalus senegalus*), along with game birds like stone partridge (*Ptilopachus petrosus*), helmeted guineafowl (*Numida meleagris*) and double-spurred francolin (*Pternistis bicalcaratus*). Gulls, terns and other waterbirds are also common, including the grey heron (*Ardea cinerea*).

CIRCUIT DE DAKAR BAOBABS

An unlikely Mecca for petrolheads, this racetrack signposted 2.5km east of the RN1 at Sindia is the first permanent auto-racing track in West Africa. The 4.7km circuit here hosts races throughout the year, including the vintage-vehicle Dakar Historic Grand Prix, and attracts pro racers, fans and amateur participants alike. Check out *www.circuitdedakar.com* for an up-to-speed calendar of events.

RÉSERVE DE BANDIA

As the closest 'safari' destination to Dakar and the beaches of the Petite Côte, the privately owned **Bandia Reserve** (❨ *33 958 2023;* m *76 685 5885/77 556 5927;* e *bandiareserve93@yahoo.fr; www.reservedebandia.com;* ⊕ *08.00–18.00 daily*) is a perennially popular destination for well-to-do locals and tourists alike, who come for the reliable wildlife encounters and the genuine bush atmosphere. At 3,500ha, the reserve is not especially large (which explains the reliable sightings), and the collection of animals found here is a bit of a hodgepodge of species native to Senegal as well as some imported crowd-pleasers like giraffe, buffalo, rhino and zebra, but if you can get over some of the illogical ecology and the slightly zoo-ish vibe, the baobab-studded savannah inside the reserve is without question a spectacular backdrop for photo safaris. Some replica Serer burial *tumuli* have also been built within the park in a nod to the history of the region.

Once inside, you're likely to spot the previously mentioned giraffe, buffalo, rhino and zebra, along with a bevy of antelope, including two types of eland (cape and Derby), roan, kudu, kob, dama gazelle, red-fronted gazelle and waterbuck. Primates include vervet and patas monkeys, while Nile crocodiles and the giant tortoise represent the reptile contingent. Other mammals include mongoose, jackal and warthog, and there are more than 120 species of birds here, including ostrich.

The driving circuit around the park takes about two hours (walking is not allowed), and can be approached in your own car if you've got a 4x4 or high clearance. They have 4x4s (with driver) for hire at the entrance if you don't. The price structure breaks down as follows: entry is 10,000/5,000F per person for adults/children, and each vehicle is required to take a guide along for 5,000F. If you bring your own vehicle, the fee is 10,000F, but to hire one of theirs it will cost you 40,000F. Thus, an outing for two in your own vehicle would add up to 35,000F.

Once you're done, the restaurant out front entices with views over a popular watering hole (for animals, not you), and a highly refined selection of meat, fish, grills, pizzas and a 12,000F *menu du jour*. There's no accommodation at the park, but the closest hotel is just across the street at **Baobab Soleil** [map, page 138] (m *77 175 4238;*

e *baobab_soleil@yahoo.fr; www.facebook.com/baobab.soleil;* **$$**), it has 14 rooms, and a swimming pool at the turnoff for Accrobaobab.

ACCROBAOBAB

About 2km west of the RN1 opposite Bandia Reserve, Accrobaobab (✆ *33 865 0555;* **m** *77 638 7474/637 1428;* **e** *espasaccro@gmail.com; www.accro-baobab.com;* ⏲ *08.00–noon & 15.00–19.00 Tue–Sun, closed Sep*) and its custom-built treetop playground easily ranks among Senegal's most unique attractions. With a series of high rope courses full of ziplines, tightropes, monkey bridges, vines and even a flying canoe, the sky's the limit on fun here, and the joy of making your way between the tops of centuries-old baobabs (and sneaking a peek at the savannah around you) is a difficult feeling to replicate. One of the baobabs has even been equipped with handholds and turned into a climbing wall. All of their climbing courses are built to European safety standards, and there are rope courses closer to the ground that are suitable for young clamberers as well. A go-round on the main ropes course is 17,500/15,000F for non-residents/residents, and 5,000F less for kids.

If you're interested in climbing again, hanging around for more than a few hours, or just a good deal on accommodation in the area, they've also got drinks for sale, self-catering facilities and two dorm rooms in their *Gîte de courtoisie,* where climbers can put up for a night or two at 10,000F/person and relive memories of summer camp.

LA SOMONE AND NGAPAROU

Hemmed in to the west by the ocean and to the north by the delightfully tropical lagoons and mangrove creeks of the Réserve Naturelle d'Intérêt Communautaire de la Somone (see page 150), La Somone (not to be confused with Sokone in the Sine-Saloum Delta) sits in a cul-de-sac at the northern end of the coastal road from Saly, while Ngaparou is directly south, occupying the liminal space between Saly and La Somone. The junction towards the RN1 at Nguékhokh serves as the centre of commerce and transport for both towns and, though most of the action is up in La Somone, both towns have a good range of facilities for visitors and feel like something of a happy medium between the sleepy villages to the north and the fast-paced development just a few miles south. The undulations of the beach form an uninterrupted fringe to both towns and, no matter where you stay, you're rarely more than a few minutes' walk (or *calèche* ride) from the sparkling waters of the Atlantic or the tangled mangroves of the lagoon.

GETTING THERE AND AWAY Ngaparou and Somone are centred around a three-way junction where the coastal road between Saly and Somone meets the feeder road to the RN1 junction village of Nguékhokh, 7.5km away. On public transport, any vehicle heading between Dakar/Thiès and Mbour will drop you at Nguékhokh, from where you can easily pick up a connection to Somone or Ngaparou for a few hundred CFA, or hire a taxi/*djakarta* directly to your hotel. There are also minibuses and informal shared taxis known as *clandos* that ply the coastal road between Saly and Somone.

If you're village hopping, keep in mind that even though Somone is less than 10km from Popenguine as the crow flies, the lagoon between them means getting between the two, which involves trekking out to the RN1 and back to the coast for a journey of nearly 30km.

WHERE TO STAY

Le Phénix (14 rooms) Somone; 33 957 7517/7433; m 77 643 2585; e phenixsomone@ orange.sn; www.facebook.com/cantinemamieflo. More or less opposite Keur Pelican on the beach side of the road, this Somone standby is built around a central courtyard with swimming pool & has an excellent location right on the beach. Rooms here are rather plain, however, & while there's nothing wrong with them per se, they do suffer from an acute lack of character. Still, they all sleep 3–4 & come with their own kitchen, so it's a solid option for groups & self-caterers. A block of new rooms opened here at the end of 2014, & these ought to have a bit more pizazz than their counterparts. The restaurant, apropos of nothing, specialises in Vietnamese cuisine, so be sure to pass by if you're craving a bowl of *pho*. **$$$**

Keur Pélican (9 rooms) Somone; m 77 667 5937; e olivier@keur-pelican.com; www. keur-pelican.com. On the main road just as you enter central Somone, this Belgian-run place has plenty of colour & cheer, with a clutch of nicely equipped & warmly decorated en-suite bungalows surrounding the pool, & a popular resto-bar serving Senegalese & seafood meals. There's often live music at weekends & a projector for screening movies in the evenings. They can help arrange all activities, & the beach is a few dozen metres away. Room rates range from 18,500F to 32,500F. **$$**

Africa Queen (48 rooms) Somone; 33 957 7435; m 77 577 1898; e africa.queen@orange.sn; www.africaqueen.net. With a fantastic beachside location on the main road towards the Decameron Baobab, this small resort boasts a wide oceanfront terrace with a very pretty swimming pool & restaurant surrounded by ping pong, pétanque, billiards & a bar. The rooms are comfortable if uninspired, many have private terraces, & all are smartly equipped with AC, TV, fridge & safe. They run regular fishing trips, & it's a good place to arrange such an outing, whether or not you're staying here. If you are, ask for a room on the upper floors to take full advantage of the indulgent sea breezes. **$$$**

Auberge l'Orangeraie (8 rooms) Ngaparou; 33 958 5183; m 77 659 3376; e hotel.orangeraie@gmail.com; www.hotel-orangeraie.com. On the main road 1.5km north of the main roundabout just as you enter Somone, this homey lodge feels a bit like a European country cottage plonked down 50m from the beach. Rooms are simply furnished & comfortable, & all are en suite with nets & AC. The 1st-floor rooms have their own rooftop terraces with ocean views, & there are splashes of African décor throughout. There's a casual resto-bar & the gardens have plenty of space to stretch out in the sun next to the pool. It's good value, with prices at the upper end of this range. **$$**

Royal Decameron Baobab (259 rooms) Somone; 33 939 7171; m 77 363 7613; e commercial@decameron.sn; www.decameron. com. Undoubtedly the most prestigious address in town, this luxury resort faces several hundred metres of private beach at the end of Somone's cul-de-sac where the coastal road meets the lagoon. The clientele here is almost exclusively fly-in tourists from Europe on package tours, & all guests are hosted on an all-inclusive basis. They have everything you'd expect: 2 swimming pools, 2 restaurants, 4 bars, fitness centre, kayaks, spa, nightly shows, the works. Rooms are equally smartly equipped with AC, satellite TV, minibar, safe, etc. They'll accept walk-ins, but reservations are the done thing. **$$$$**

Gîte l'Anacardier (10 rooms) Ngaparou; 33 954 9448; m 77 370 4075; e giteanacardier@ yahoo.fr; www.gite-anacardier-senegal.com. Named after the cashew trees dotting the large green compound, this pleasant owner-managed lodge, signposted 500m north of the main roundabout, has accommodation in self-contained duplex bungalows that share a kitchen between the 2 units, making it an excellent choice for families & self-caterers (though they can also provide meals). The rooms are all tastefully appointed, come with nets & AC, & there's a big pool, BBQ facilities & lawn games aplenty. Prices on the lower end of this range. **$$$**

Le Tamarin (8 rooms) Somone; 33 958 5691; m 77 570 9674/456 6437; tamarinformica@ yahoo.fr; www.letamarin-somone.com. On the main road smack in the centre of Somone, this place doesn't look like much from the outside, but inside it's a friendly & unpretentious retreat with a 'Cheers'-esque vibe & a host of colourful regulars propping up the bar (which has music Sat nights) or lounging by the pool. They've got en-suite rooms & studios, the latter of which sleep 4 & come with fridge & AC, while all are clean & comfy with a sprinkling of African textiles & décor. The resto does good meals & there are some craft sellers set up across the street if you're itching to go shopping. Prices in the bottom half of this range. **$$**

⌂ Domaine de la Mangrove (8 rooms) Somone; ✆ 33 957 7265; m 78 162 9942; e domaine.mangrove@gmail.com; www.domainemangrove.com. Opened in 2013, this place has quickly become a favourite in Somone & it's not too hard to see why. In a carefully landscaped compound 800m up the lagoon road (towards the walking trail & oyster beds), the duplex bungalows here come with bright designer interiors (each in a different colour), 2 terraces (upstairs & downstairs) & can be rented individually or as a unit with kitchen that sleeps up to 5. The poolside bar, '*ndanc ndanc*', is Wolof for 'slowly slowly', & its exhortation to relax is persuasive indeed. If you are feeling active, though, they've also got kayaks & arrange activities with Secret Bay across the lagoon. It's something of a cultural space as well, & they occasionally host art exhibitions, fashion shows, live music & other events. Prices in the bottom half of this range. **$$$**

✕ WHERE TO EAT AND DRINK The far side of the lagoon, just across the water from the Royal Decameron Baobab, is home to a handful of very chilled-out beach-shack restaurants. In addition to Teranga Paradie listed below, **Le Thiokaam (Chez Bouba)** (m *77 197 3286*) and **Paradise Rasta** (m *77 557 63 31*) both fully embody the beachside vibe and come recommended for a meal or a cold drink. Any of the *piroguiers* will punt you across for no more than a few hundred CFA, or call ahead and they'll send somebody to fetch you, often gratis.

✕ Teranga Parade m 78 162 9978; ⏲ lunch & dinner daily. Facing the oceanfront at the west end of the row of beach-shack bar-restaurants across the lagoon from the Baobab hotel, the patchwork thatch gazebos here are strung up with seashell garlands & Senegalese flags, & the menu is exactly what you'd want from such a place – fish, lobster, mussels & prawns are all in evidence, starting at around 3,000F. Ring them to arrange pickup from the Somone side of the lagoon, or better yet, call beforehand to place your order, unless you fancy a leisurely spell on one of their bamboo loungers.

✕ Le Coin Gourmand ✆ 33 958 5246; m 77 553 0259; ⏲ 11.00–15.00 & 18.00–23.00 Tue–Sun. With the longest & most sophisticated menu in town, this is the table of choice in Somone if you're looking to impress a date. The menu is displayed right out front of their location on the main road, so you'll have some time to decipher the possibilities before sitting down & ordering. Steak tartare, foie gras & fondue are all well represented, & they do some Thai-inspired curries as well. Most mains fall within the 5,000–10,000F range.

✕ Chez Jean Marie m 77 428 2113; ⏲ lunch & dinner daily. This local landmark on the main road through Somone draws a crowd of locals & foreigners alike to their street-facing terrace for their heaped portions of grilled fish (*lotte, sole, capitaine*) & meat (*steak, osso buco*) that start at a very reasonable 4,000F. The menu changes by the day & will be chalked up out front, & it's a popular spot for evening drinks as well.

✕ Chez Norbert m 77 561 9756/777 0540; ⏲ Sun lunch. If you're in town on Sun, save the excuses & just get yourself over here to Somone's ultimate insider's hangout. Directly facing the *parc à huitres* (oyster beds) at the end of the lagoon road (past Domaine de la Mangrove), Norbert & his fellow oystermen here put on a fabulous feast, with raw & grilled oysters served at long tables just steps from the lagoon. There's often some live music too, & fresh oysters will set you back an easy-to-stomach 5,000F/dozen.

✕ L'O à la Bouche ✆ 33 957 7161; m 77 145 0672; www.traiteur-loalabouche.com; ⏲ 19.00–midnight Mon, noon–15.00 & 19.00–midnight Tue–Sat. Opened in 2014, this new place sits on the main road at the very south end of Ngaparou *en route* to Saly, just shy of 2km from the main Somone roundabout. The menu covers a lot of (mostly continental) ground, with pizza, paella, tapas, gnocchi & even a lobster tartare all at your command, starting at around 5,000F. The indoor-outdoor seating area is classy & colourful, with a minimum of fuss, & they put on themed menus & soirées for all kinds of holidays.

WHAT TO SEE AND DO Covering 700ha at the north end of town, the **Réserve Naturelle d'Intérêt Communautaire de la Somone** (☎ *33 832 2309/958 4998; entry 1,500F*) is Somone's biggest draw, save for the obvious magnetism of the waters offshore. It was gazetted in 1999, making it among the newest of Senegal's officially protected areas, and it seems that conservation plans are really starting to show results. There's no shortage of would-be piroguiers here who will take you out on the water, but put your bargaining face on. Conversely, Secret Bay (see below) or any hotel in town can easily arrange a trip out here for you. Opened in 2011, the newest addition to the reserve is the *Sentier Écologique de la Somone*, an easy walking trail that loops through the mangroves on a narrow footpath for around 1km. There are several (French) informational panels and a lookout tower where birders and others can sit and enjoy the views over the mangroves and the quiet of the lagoon. The trailhead is poorly marked from town, coming from the south, it can be reached from the main road by branching right on to the unpaved road towards the lagoon at the diagonal intersection just before Africa Queen. Follow this for five blocks and make a right turn just before Domaine de la Mangrove. The trailhead is at ✪ 14.494552, –17.078934.

Somone isn't known as one of Senegal's surfing hotspots, but for that very reason **Secret Bay** (m *76 687 3467*; e *surfshareafrica@yahoo.fr; www.surf-somone-senegal. com*) is a fabulous place for beginners to get their board skills down without worrying about getting knocked down by a roller. It's right next to the restaurants on the far side of the lagoon, and private lessons go for 23,000F for two hours, with deals to be had for longer courses. They've also got canoes, kayaks and the like, and are a great destination for most any water-based activity around Somone. You can even do a standing paddleboard trip (and lesson, if needed) through the mangroves! If you want to go fishing, head over to Africa Queen (see page 148) and they can tell you about this week's trips.

Back on land, the **Centre Équestre l'Hippocampe** (☎ *33 958 5060*; m *77 647 5091; www.xhipp0campe.skyrock.com*) is the place for horse rides in the bush, through nearby villages or on the beach, any of which start at 18,000F per person for two hours. They're signposted just off the road to Nguékhokh a few hundred metres from the main junction in Ngaparou.

A couple of km further towards Nguékhokh lies the **Parc Exotique de N'guerigne** (☎ *33 958 5030*; m *77 572 1504*; e *parc.exotique@gmail.com; http://perroquets.voila. net;* ☉ *09.00–18.00 daily; entry 5,000/3,000F adults/children, includes a drink*), a private bird sanctuary with large gardens and ponds, an aviary and a breeding centre that's home to dozens of colourful local and exotic bird species like parrots, macaws and others. It's diverting enough for a visit, and they might even have some food on offer by the time you read this.

SALY-PORTUDAL AND SALY-NIAKHNIAKHAL

The beating heart of Senegal's package tourism industry, Saly is polarising to say the least. A place in the sun to its fans and an irredeemable tourist trap to its detractors, Saly offers all the sun and fun you could ask for and then some, but most independent travellers opt to steer well clear of this resort city. Still, even for those allergic to all-inclusive, if you're itching for a bit of pampering and immoderation – or simply a couple of days in a *chaise longue* after one too many days in a *sept-place*, it's a fine place for an indulgent weekend; just leave your qualms and traveller snobbery at the door.

Though the geographical divisions have mostly disappeared and it's today more or less part of one big conurbation with Mbour, Saly's two halves are more fraternal

above left The once-grand Château du Baron Roger in Richard Toll is still impressive in its decrepitude (SC) page 222

top right There's no better Casamance experience that pushing out onto the water in a pirogue from the steamy river town of Ziguinchor and disappearing into the mangroves beyond (MM) pages 286–94

above right Diourbel's Ottoman-inspired grande mosque was the first major Mouride landmark to be built in Senegal (BP/DT) page 248

·SERVICE TRAITEUR ·PLATS À EMPORTER ·CUISINE LIBANAISE

FARID

RESTAURANT - TERRASSE

58, RUE VINCENS - TÉL: 33 823 61 23 - HOTELFARID@ORANGE.SN - WWW.HOTELFARID.COM

above In Mbour the catch of the day dictates the daily schedule, and the city has a staggeringly busy fish market as a result (AVZ) pages 158–61

below The maze of mangroves and islets around Palmarin is best explored by *pirogue* (SC) pages 183–6

bottom The windswept beaches of Mboro-Sur-Mer see sprited and impromptu games of football at the edge of the surf (SC) pages 241–2

above Christians and Muslims are buried side by side in the island cemetery of Fadiouth, built on seashells (SC) pages 164–6

right Just off Dakar's corniche, the Parc National des Îles de la Madeleine covers 45ha of rocky islets, making it Senegal's smallest national park (D/DT) pages 131–2

below The riverfront is the hub of Matam life, as the place where the city's residents come to do their washing, have a bath or haul in catches of fish (AVZ) pages 230–1

top   The habitats found in the Niokolo-Koba National Park range from Sudan/Guinea savannah to riverine stretches of gallery forest, floodplains, marshes and even some of Senegal's few hills (EH/DT) pages 258–63

above left   The UNESCO World Heritage Site of Siné Ngayène comprises 1,102 megalithic carved stones arranged in 52 circles (SC) pages 174–7

below left   Lompoul is an unexpected 20km² patch of towering sand dunes; visitors can get a feel for the Sahara by staying in a traditional Mauritanian tent (E/DT) pages 242–3

bottom   The long, narrow islet that makes up the Langue de Barbarie National Park is home to thousands of seabirds (AVZ) pages 211–13

top   A tailor's shop in Ziguinchor
(AVZ) pages 293–4

above left and right   There is no shortage of brightly decorated
shopfronts and stalls in Senegal (SC and
AVZ) pages 63–4

right   An artist's atelier in Saint-Louis; Senegal's
visual art scene is one of the foremost on the
continent (AVZ) pages 30–2

Luxury...

out of your comfort zone

The perfect mix of high-end comfort at a *luxury lodge* in Senegal's most beautiful bay protected by UNESCO and *out of your comfort zone* excursions, cultural encounters and adventure.

www.lespaletuviers.com
info@paletuviers.com
+221 33 948 77 76 | +221 77 884 45 61

than identical twins, and there's a noticeable difference in feeling between the two. Saly-Portudal is a beach scene worthy of any tourist boardwalk around the world: a higgledy-piggledy assortment of roaring quad bikes, thumping tunes, speeding jet skis, decidedly un-Islamic swimwear, and certainly the best sun cream selection anywhere in Senegal, just in case you've run out. (It's also home to a lively trade in short-term boyfriends and girlfriends, if that's your thing.) Saly-Niakhniakhal, even though it's just steps down the beach, looks positively sedate by comparison, with a grid of sandy streets running between the city's many vacation homes and a number of smaller hotels that feel a bit better connected to their surroundings than the resorts further north. The beach is equally fine, and it's a good place to base yourself if you want to be within striking distance of the main drag, but still with a bit of breathing room.

On a more practical level, it's also got the only banking facilities on the Petite Côte outside of Mbour and excellent supermarkets, so it's quite possible you'll wind up here for some necessities and stick around for a quick dip or a drink; there are plenty of fine places to do so, even for the most dedicated of tourist trail naysayers. Since the amenities here are mostly geared towards fly-in package tourists, however, the listings in this section aren't an attempt to be authoritative. There are dozens upon dozens of hotels and restaurants in Saly, and many of them are quite good, so below is just a collection of highlights – there's plenty more to explore should you decide to sink your teeth into this beachside Mecca.

It's also worth noting that beach erosion has become an acute problem here in recent years, which has led to the closure of some businesses made vulnerable by their seafront location, including the well-regarded Hotel Espadon in 2014. An ongoing programme of breakwater construction seeks to stem the proverbial tide and reverse the destruction of Saly's beaches, and it's had some success so far, but this is an ongoing issue and you could well see changes (for the better or worse) during the lifespan of this edition.

GETTING THERE AND AWAY Saly's central roundabout is signposted 3.5km west of the RN1, and all transport **from the north** (ie: Dakar) will pass this turnoff *en route* to Mbour. **From the south** (ie: Kaolack) most transport will terminate in Mbour unless it's continuing on to Dakar. Saly doesn't have a bus station of its own, so if you don't drop at the turnoff, you'll arrive at the *gare routière* in Mbour, 6km from Saly's roundabout. From here to Saly, there's no public transport as such, but an informal network of *clandos* (from *clandestines*), private cars that take passengers on an ad hoc basis. You'll find them on the RN1 outside the *gare routière*, and a seat shouldn't cost more than a few hundred CFA. Alternatively, there are plenty of taxis and you shouldn't pay more than around 2,000F (and less for a *djakarta*).

If you've got a plane of your own or feel like chartering one, there's an **airstrip** (*www.saly-aerodrome.com*) at the edge of town and a **heliport** on the road leading to the RN1.

SALY ONLINE

Atcha lene! (*www.atchalene.com*), which means 'Let's go!' in Wolof, is a fantastic source of (French-language) information on La Somone, Ngaparou and Saly, and if you plan to spend any time in the region it would be eminently worth checking out, if only for their up-to-date events calendar. Additionally, www.salysenegal.net has good information (also in French) on everything from recommended guides in the area to tips on buying real estate.

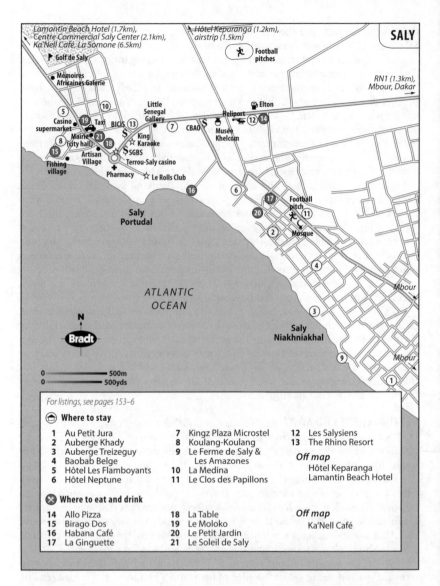

For listings, see pages 153–6

Where to stay

1	Au Petit Jura	7	Kingz Plaza Microstel	12	Les Salysiens
2	Auberge Khady	8	Koulang-Koulang	13	The Rhino Resort
3	Auberge Treizeguy	9	Le Ferme de Saly &		
4	Baobab Belge		Les Amazones		*Off map*
5	Hôtel Les Flamboyants	10	La Medina		Hôtel Keparanga
6	Hôtel Neptune	11	Le Clos des Papillons		Lamantin Beach Hotel

Where to eat and drink

14	Allo Pizza	18	La Table		*Off map*
15	Birago Dos	19	Le Moloko		Ka'Nell Café
16	Habana Café	20	Le Petit Jardin		
17	La Ginguette	21	Le Soleil de Saly		

Both Saly-Portudal and Saly-Niakhniakhal are easy enough to get around on foot, but there are always plenty of *djakartas, clandos* and *calèches* around to give you a lift.

FESTIVAL DES VIEILLES PIROGUES

FESTIVAL DES VIEILLES PIROGUES Since 2013, the Festival des Vieilles Pirogues (m *77 833 1515; www.vieillespirogues.com*) has put on a weekend-long bash of music, dance, art, theatre and food once a year at the heliport in Saly, though the dates seem to rotate – it's been held in December, February and May so far. Their website has all the info, and even if you don't make it to the festival itself, all the bars and restaurants in town put on special performances and after-parties throughout the weekend.

WHERE TO STAY   *Map, page 152, unless otherwise noted.*

All the hotels listed below have Wi-Fi.

Saly-Portudal

🏠 **Lamantin Beach Hotel Resort & Spa** [Map, page 138] (148 rooms) ☎ 33 957 0777; e reservation@lelamantin.com; www.lelamantin.com. Long a favourite of winter sunseekers & expats alike, this Saly institution suffered a catastrophic fire in 2011 but was rebuilt from the ground up & opened its doors again the next year. As a result, just about everything is new here & the accommodation is some of the finest for miles around. There are 3 different restaurants, a 400m² swimming pool, hot tubs, tennis courts, putting green, marina & indulgent spa centre with Turkish-style hammam & a range of Senegalese body products. Individually decorated with African sculpture & textiles. All rooms here come with AC, TV, minibar, safe, double sinks, bathtub & a private terrace or balcony. A dbl room HB starts at €200. **$$$$$**

🏠 **Hôtel Neptune** (69 rooms) ☎ 33 957 2320; e neptune@orange.sn; www.saly-hotel-neptune.com. At the south end of central Saly just before you hit Niakhniakhal proper, this venerable resort has been offering high-standard accommodation in Saly for years now. Set in a green compound overflowing with palms & bougainvillea & centred around an expansive 400m² pool, the rooms here are all suite style, with a separate sitting room with fold-out sofa & fridge. They're quite comfortable though not extravagant, & all are equipped with AC & TV. (There are some larger family villas as well.) Guests are accommodated on a HB or FB basis, & there's an in-house band that plays poolside every night at dinner. The hotel itself is set 150m back from the beach, but they've got their own serviced stretch of sand where you can kayak, windsurf or just kick back on a chaise longue. Prices are in the bottom half of this range, & during low season they dip into the price category below. It's good value, so no surprise that it's often full. **$$$$**

🏠 **The Rhino Resort** (41 rooms) ☎ 33 957 3744; e info@therhinoresort.com; www.therhinoresort.com. The new kid on the block when it comes to Saly's big-name resorts, this glitzy Asian-inspired address opened in 2011 & missed out on snagging an open slice of oceanfront, but goes a long way towards making up for it with an artificial beach (59 tons of sand!) facing one of their 3 swimming pools. Set in a 2-storey building with colonial-style wraparound balconies, rooms here are serene, breezy & luxuriously appointed in dark wood, linen & stone, & all come with en-suite bathtub, king-sized bed, safe, minibar, AC & flatscreen TV. The spa may be the star of the show here, with hot & cold pools, hammam, massive indoor waterfall, beauty salon & at least 4 dozen different massages & treatments on offer. The 2 restaurants have developed a reputation for their seafood, though beachwear will get you a frosty reception at dinnertime. Rates towards the centre of this range. **$$$$**

🏠 **Hôtel Keparanga** [Map, page 138] (16 rooms) ☎ 33 957 8000; m 77 315 0502; e info@keparanga.com; www.keparanga.com. Down a dirt track next to the airstrip in the Saly-Joseph neighbourhood, this new place is about as off the beaten track as it's possible to get without leaving Saly altogether, & while that may not be saying a whole lot in terms of remoteness, it still feels refreshingly far from the hustle & bustle of the main drag. The motif here is clean lines & minimalist design, & all rooms come with AC, TV, canopy beds, glass-walled showers & private terrace. The continental restaurant has been cultivating a loyal following since opening here in 2012, & the boulder-flanked pool & garden will have you wondering whether you really have to go into town after all. B&B rates are near the top of this range. **$$$**

🏠 **Hôtel les Flamboyants** (36 rooms) ☎ 33 957 0770; e lesflamboyantsaly@gmail.com; www.hotelsenegalflamboyant.com. Smack dab on the main drag through town, this place has been a decent mid-range option in the city centre for years now, & while it's starting to show its age a bit, the facilities are still comfortable & prices (at the bottom of this range) are about as low as you're likely to get without heading some blocks off the strip. Rooms are tiled & en suite, with wire-frame furniture, TV, AC & a smattering of African décor. The resto-bar does pizzas & paninis starting around 2,000F, & there's a large pool, hammam & massage parlour on site. **$$$**

🏠 **Koulang-Koulang** (5 units) ☎ 33 957 0434; m 77 651 4944; e koulang@gmail.com; www.saly-koulang.com. Tucked between the main drag & the ocean in the fishing neighbourhood of Saly-Koulang, this pretty little place caters mostly to groups, with 4 villas sleeping up to 6 & a studio sleeping 2, all set in lush gardens around the bean-shaped swimming pool. Decorated in cool earth tones & bold African patterns, rooms here come with AC & mozzie nets, & meals can be arranged either here or at their partner restaurant Bigaro Dos (see page 155), which is just around the corner. It feels a bit more integrated than most options in Saly, & rates for a dbl scrape the bottom of this range. **$$$**

🏠 **Kingz Plaza Microstel** ↘33 957 73 40; e info@kingzplaza.com; www.kingzplaza.com. With dorm beds available at 8,000F a pop, this place could reasonably claim to be the nearest thing to a backpackers' lodge in Saly, though it lacks any of the feel or character normally associated with such places. There is, however, a pleasant garden & sizeable pool, & sterility aside, penny-pinchers will take comfort in knowing this is the cheapest sleep in town. If you're going to spring for a self-contained room, however, the rates are comparable with more interesting options in town like Baobab Belge, Auberge Khady or La Ferme de Saly. **$$**

🏠 **La Médina** ↘33 957 4993; m 77 567 6469; e lamedina@orange.sn; www.facebook.com/lamedina.saly. A few blocks east of the main drag, this well-loved place in the Saly-Tapée neighbourhood has a vaguely Moroccan vibe (try the couscous), regular live music around the central swimming pool, & simple, well-tended en-suite rooms with mosquito nets & fan or AC (for an extra cost) set on two floors around the pool & restaurant. Rooms are good value, with rates at the upper end of this range. **$$**

🏠 **Le Salysiens** (5 rooms) m 77 569 9424/285 9898. In a storey building just opposite the Elton filling station on the road into town, this unassuming place can't claim much in the way of scenery, but with a well-equipped fan dbl for 15,000F or AC for 20,000F, the prices are close to the best in town. Rooms are scrupulously clean & come with en-suite bath, fridge & flatscreen TV. The fan rooms are more modest, but still comfortable. There's no food on-site, but Allo Pizza is right next door (see page 155). **$$**

Saly-Niakhniakhal

🏠 **Au Petit Jura** (6 rooms) ↘33 957 3767; e aupetitjura@yahoo.fr; www.aupetitjura.ch. The very last stop in Saly as you head down the coast towards Mbour, this Swiss-run auberge is actually closer to Mbour than central Saly (it's only about 700m to Tama Lodge), & as such it feels well removed from Saly's more frenetic side. Less than 100m from the beach, the carefully manicured gardens here are home to a troop of happy dogs, an inviting pool, yard games, sun loungers & a well-regarded terrace restaurant. The en-suite rooms aren't particularly fashionable, but are fastidiously kept & all come with AC, nets & safe. Prices at the lower end of this category. **$$$**

🏠 **Le Clos des Papillons** (8 rooms) m 77 174 0755; e ericpyl@orange.sn; www.leclosdespapillonssenegal.com. This new place along the Piste des Charrettes connecting Saly-Niakhniakhal and Mbour has an array of different rooms, all of which are en suite with walk-in mozzie nets & a subtle but alluring Afro-Moroccan vibe throughout. There's no shortage of carving & sculpture around, & their comfortable tearoom has echoes of a kasbah courtyard. There's an infinity pool surrounded by fruit trees, a massage parlour & a French-inspired terrace restaurant with a 3-course menu for 13,000F. Prices span either end of this range depending on the room. **$$$**

🏠 **Auberge Khady** (8 rooms) ↘33 957 2518; e auberge_khady@hotmail.com; www.aubergekhady.com. Barely a block in from the water, this homey *auberge* offers good-value accommodation & a quiet base that's well suited for individuals or groups. The en-suite rooms sleep 2 or 4, & the latter come with lofted beds. The 1st-floor terrace restaurant is covered in mosaics & masks, serves good continental food, and is a prime spot to soak up views of the pool, gardens & neighbourhood beyond. Rates at the upper end of this range. **$$**

🏠 **Auberge Treizeguy** (7 rooms) ↘33 957 0509; m 77 821 5128; e info@autreizeguy.com; www.autreizeguy.com. The name of their place might be a bit cryptic, but the warmth of the owner-managers, Thérèse & Guy (hence the name), could hardly be clearer. It's easy to feel like part of the family here, & the kids, dogs & lawn games make every day feel like a picnic. There's a large pool, beachside bar, a restaurant with its own vegetable garden, plenty of space for a round of *boules*, & the beach couldn't be closer. The ground-floor rooms are all en suite & come with nets, fans & private terraces overlooking the gardens or the beach. Prices at the top of this range. **$$**

Baobab Belge (5 rooms) 33 957 0222; m 77 597 5292; e baobabbelge@gmail.com; www.baobabbelge.com. In the heart of Saly-Niakhniakhal, this small Belgian-run guesthouse has 5 mosaic-studded, individually decorated rooms, all of which are en suite with fans & nets, & have access to a kitchen where you can cook your own meals (though they have a restaurant as well). There's a small hot tub for a quick dip or a soak, but no full-sized pool. Good value with prices at the upper end of this range. **$$**

La Ferme de Saly & Les Amazones 33 957 1670; m 77 638 4790; e farmsaly@yahoo.fr; www.farmsaly.com. Accommodation in Saly doesn't get much more venerable than this seaside retreat, where Jean-Paul has been welcoming travellers for more than 2 decades now. La Ferme has simple terracotta-tiled rooms with nets & fans & it's long been the destination for travellers who want to check out Saly but wouldn't be caught dead wearing a resort wristband. Les Amazones is its younger & more luxurious sibling, offering rooms & apartments with AC. Either way, they've got a garden full of monkeys & birds, a big swimming pool, & can arrange all manner of land & water activities. Low season prices at La Ferme are towards the bottom of this range & high season towards the top, while rooms at Les Amazones are in the neighbourhood of €45 per person HB, with a smaller seasonal variation. **$$**

✖ WHERE TO EAT AND DRINK *Map, page 152.*

Self-caterers should aim for either the **Supermarché Casino** at the very centre of Saly-Portudal, or the new **Le Supermarché Saly Center** at the Centre Commercial Saly Center on the coastal road at the northern edge of town as you approach Ngaparou. Both are very well stocked with meat, veg, cheese, wine and other staples.

All hotels in Saly have restaurants, many of which are quite good, but below are some places worth checking out if you start getting cabin fever. There's also no shortage of drinking holes in Saly; again, this is small selection. Do bear in mind that anybody unaccompanied (and even those who are) can expect a lot of attention at either of the nightclubs listed below, as well as other bars in town – Saly has a somewhat deserved reputation for sex tourism.

✖ Allo Pizza 33 957 0910; m 77 450 0780/569 3593; ⊕ 11.00–23.00 daily. Opposite the Elton station on the way out of town, this place serves up good wood-fired pizzas in a thatch-roofed dining room facing the road. It's a friendly & unpretentious spot to hang out for a slice & a beer, but just in case you're glued to a sun lounger somewhere, they also do delivery. Pizzas start at around 4,000F.

✖ Bigaro Dos m 77 884 1883; www.facebook.com/bigaro.dos; ⊕ lunch & dinner Wed–Mon;. Though it's only a couple hundred metres from the Saly strip, this congenial hideout in Saly's fishing quarter, Saly-Koulang, feels a world away. Seafood & seasonal produce are *de rigueur* on the rotating menu here, & a 3-course meal goes for a very friendly 6,000F. Food & drink are served in the shaded gardens, they've got a swimming pool for clients, & if you're stuck for something to do on a Sunday, their midday BBQ buffet & evening film screenings are just the ticket.

✖ Habana Café 33 957 1730; www.bloghotel.org/habanacafe; ⊕ lunch & dinner Tue–Sun. This has been a reliable Saly meeting point since 2002, & it's not just the ocean views from the terrace that keep the place humming along. They cover some culinary ground you're unlikely to find elsewhere, & *parmentier de queue de bœuf* (shepherd's pie with oxtail) & *filet de bar à la crème d'oursins* (bass fillet in a sea urchin sauce) are both counted among the specialities of the house. They usually have a *plat du jour* for slightly less, but expect to pay 7,000F and up.

✖ Ka'Nell Café m 78 162 7086/77 681 3321; www.ka-nell-cafe.com; ⊕ bakery: 07.30–19.30 Mon–Sat, 09.30–17.30 Sun, tearoom: 09.30–17.30 Mon–Sat. This über-modern place in the Centre Commercial Saly Center is the local answer to Dakar's scrubbed-'til-they-sparkle cafés, & has rapidly become the go-to spot in town for pastries, cakes, crêpes, coffee, juices, sandwiches & light meals. There's terrace seating & it's a certified hit for brunch.

✖ La Guinguette m 77 158 0808; www.laguinguettedesaly.e-monsite.com; ⊕ 11.30–14.00 & 19.30–midnight Thu–Tue. This purple-walled paradise tucked away in Saly-Niakhniakhal gets rave reviews from visitors & locals alike, & it's not hard to see why. With a rotating French-inspired menu on the chalkboard & garden seating surrounded by art pieces & coconut palms, it's an eminently pleasant place to spend an evening, & there's often live music to boot. Depending on the day, you could get bruschetta, baked camembert, zebu steaks, thiof (white grouper) fillets & maybe even a mint chocolate iced macaroon for dessert. Plan to spend around 15,000F per person with drinks & appetisers.

✖ **La Table** m 77 537 4242; www.facebook.com/latablesaly; ◷ 18.30–02.00 Mon–Sat. Opened in 2012, this Belgian-run restaurant & bar has a rather rowdy location on the strip, but once you step inside it's pure refinement. The menu is peppered with fine French & Belgian comfort food like *carbonade flamande* (Belgian beef & onion stew), *souris d'agneau façon grand-mère* (lamb shank, grandma's style) and *blanquette de lotte* (monkfish ragout), & either the ground floor restaurant or bar-lounge upstairs would make a fine destination for a romantic night out in Saly. The vibe may be soigné, but the prices are surprisingly down-to-earth: most mains go for 6,000–8,000F.

✖ **Le Moloko** m 77 648 1115; ◷ 18.00–01.00 Mon–Sat;. Opened in late 2014, this stylish new tapas bar on the main drag is the newest addition to Saly's fast-moving restaurant scene, & it comes warmly recommended for its Spanish-inspired small plates. The décor is thoroughly contemporary, but rather than sleek & minimal, it's warm & earthy, with bògòlanfini mud cloth & mangrove accents throughout. There's occasional entertainment, & cocktails on the upstairs terrace would make a great way to kick off the evening.

✖ **Le Petit Jardin** m 77 463 5825; www.facebook.com/lepetit.jardinsaly; ◷ lunch & dinner daily. Just as you enter Saly-Niakhniakhal, this place has indoor-outdoor seating in the namesake garden, a stage for the bands that play here throughout the week, & a laid-back, genuine air – sometimes a rarity in image-conscious Saly. Grills are the name of the game here, fish especially, & the catch of the day is marked on a blackboard, always next to a deliciously reasonable price. Steaks, brochettes, sole, *capitaine* (rather unflatteringly known as hogfish *en anglais*), *lotte* & more all make appearances for 3,000–5,000F.

✖ **Le Soleil de Saly** m 77 541 25 26; www.lesoleildesaly.com; ◷ 11.00–late daily. On a 1st-floor roost smack dab in the centre of the action, the opening hours here ('from the noon aperitif to the end of the night') give you a pretty good idea of what Mamadou Basse & his team get up to here. There's live music 3 times weekly, & it acts as one of several raucous nuclei along the strip that you're likely to at least pass through (whether you remember it or not) on any given night in Saly. The long menu boasts an assortment of fish, meats & pizzas, starting around 3,000F.

☆ **King Karaoke** ☏ 33 957 27 27; m 77 443 52 62; www.facebook.com/kingdiscotheque.kingsaly; ◷ 22.30–05.00 daily. One of Saly's infamous discotheques, this place is a guaranteed party, & in addition to their revolving door of theme nights (white party, pool party, you name it), they do karaoke until about 01.00, & afterwards DJs pump the tracks until the faithful are waking up to pray. You can also occasionally catch some big names performing here – *mbalax* stars like Assane Ndiaye & Alioune Mbaye Nder have been known to make appearances, along with Senegalese hip-hop heavyweights Daara J.

NIGHTLIFE

☆ **Le Rolls Club** m 77 279 3863; www.facebook.com/saly.lerolls; ◷ 23.00–06.00 daily. Along with King Karaoke, this is the epicentre of Saly nightlife, & merrymakers shake their asses here until dawn every night of the week. The impossibly slim waitresses work the floor in vertiginous heels & seasonally themed miniskirts, & they've got a similar array of dress-up nights ('sexy famous party night' being a personal favourite) to choose from. Resident DJs *aux platines* (on the turntables) keep the bass to a steady roar.

☆ **Terrou-Saly** ☏ 33 939 7272; m 77 434 7870; www.facebook.com/terrousaly; ◷ noon–late daily. With pride of place on Saly-Portudal's main roundabout, this new complex can very convincingly present itself as the most luxurious place in town. Consisting of a restaurant, bar-lounge & casino with all the trimmings, it's a place to see & be seen, & certainly no place for your grungy traveller flip-flops. Wear a shirt with buttons & make sure there's some cash (or cards) in your wallet – aside from the Sunday buffet, it's unlikely you'll make it out the door for under 10,000F. There's seating inside & outside, & reservations are recommended.

OTHER PRACTICALITIES

Money All the major banks (BICIS, CBAO, SGBS, etc) have ATMs within a few hundred metres of the main roundabout in Saly-Portudal.

Health Both **Urgences 24** (*main roundabout;* \ *33 957 4747;* e *laminedr@yahoo. fr*) and **SUMA Assistance** (*opposite BICIS;* \ *33 957 5624;* e *sumassistance@gmail. com; www.sumassistance.net*) offer 24/7 ambulance and clinical services, and some of the larger resorts have a medic on their staff.

WHAT TO SEE AND DO Life and leisure in Saly all revolve around the sea, regardless of which side of town you find yourself on, and pretty much every hotel arranges all manner of nautical activities or can point you to someone who can. A good place to start, though, is **Sénégal Loisirs** (\ *33 957 0343; www.senegal-loisirs.com*), based at the Lamantin Beach Hotel. They hire out kayaks (*3,000F/1hr*), pedalboats (*5,000F/30mins*), windsurfers (*10,000F/1hr*) and jet skis (*36,000F/30mins*), along with terrestrial toys like quad bikes (*40,000F/1h15mins*) and dune buggies (*50,000F/1h30mins*).

There are also a few addresses worth knowing for more specialised pursuits: Sailors will want to get in touch with the **Saly Sailing Club** (m *77 651 4944;* e *infos@saly-voile.com; www.facebook.com/SalySailingClub*), where you can meet fellow mariners and arrange trips or participate in one of their periodic competitions. There are a fair few places in town catering to fisherfolk, but **Gildas Espadon** (\ *33 957 1949; www. gildas-espadon.com*), also based at the Lamantin, offers a wide range of trips with itineraries and prices detailed on their informative website.

Back on land, there's also no shortage of firms offering quad bikes and dune buggies, but **Esprit Evasion Quads** (m *77 370 4050; www.espritevasion.fr*) is conveniently located in the town centre and does quad trips starting at 28,000F, and it's 36,000F for a half-day trip up to the lagoon at La Somone and back. Golfers are well taken care of at **Golf de Saly** (\ *33 957 2488; www.golfsaly.com*), where they've got 18 holes (seven with a water hazard), and it costs 32,000F for a round including caddy but not clubs (around 4,000F extra).

Finally, if land and water grow tiresome, you can even take to the skies – **Saly Sénégal ULM** (m *77 259 2310;* e *aerociel@gmail.com; www.senegal-ulm-christophe. com*) offers ultralight aircraft tours from the aerodrome in Saly-Joseph.

Art lovers are also surprisingly well catered for here, and there are a handful of shops, galleries and museums worth checking out once you've tired yourself out swimming, golfing or flying. On the way into town, **Musée Khelcom** (m *77 574 3584;* ⊕ *09.00–18.00 daily*) may look a bit dusty, but the collections of metal sculpture and artwork here are surprisingly compelling. Further down the road, **Little Senegal** (m *78 185 9987; www.little-senegal.com*) specialises in contemporary art of all types – photography, sculpture, beadwork and painting are all well represented. Heading north towards Ngaparou, **Galerie Mémoires Africaines** (\ *33 957 0401;* m *77 457 0665; www.memoires-africaines.com*) is the place to go for historically inspired masks, bronzes, clay, jewellery and metalwork. Finally, if your art needs are a step down from the fine goods found in the galleries, the **village artisanal** sells all the usual manner of masks, carvings, paintings, jewellery and textiles, usually at highly inflated prices–don't be afraid to bargain!

History buffs and those on the hunt for historical relics are likely to leave Saly disappointed, but the Portuguese were indeed known to have had a trading presence here from the 15th century on, and Saly-Portudal's suffix is not a simple corruption of Portugal as is sometimes believed, but actually originates from the original Portuguese name for the area, Puerto Dali or Porto d'Ale. There are a few buildings of some historicity (including a fort apocryphally dated to the Portuguese era) hidden away south of the centre near the fishing village in Saly-Koulang, though none are open to the public.

MBOUR

Often visited as a day trip from Saly or simply in transit, it's true that Mbour is considerably rougher of a gem than its glitzy northern neighbour, but there's still plenty to occupy a couple of days in this workaday city where the catch of the day dictates the daily schedule and the din of commerce provides the aural backdrop. In addition to its utility as a transport and banking centre, Mbour is home to a couple of good stretches of beach, a staggeringly busy fish market and a big-city vibe that's totally absent anywhere else on the Petite Côte. It's unlikely to be the most exciting stop on your trip, but you're probably going to wind up here at some point anyway, so there's no sense in not diving right in and embracing the seaside bustle.

Even though there are few concessions made specifically to tourists here the way they are down the road in Saly, the facilities in Mbour are surprisingly good. There isn't a glut of hotels, but the ones that are here are actually for the most part very pleasant and good value for money. So if you want a beach holiday but don't fancy cocooning yourself in a vacation colony, Mbour might be just the thing. Much of the beach here is given over to fishing pirogues, which are a sight in themselves, but the places that aren't are every bit as pretty as the beaches in Saly, and you're always within easy walking or *calèche* distance from market madness, street snacks from roadside shacks, and a genuine slice of city life that lacks all the flash of Dakar or Saint-Louis, but pays ample dividends in authenticity.

GETTING THERE AND AWAY The RN1 leaves the coast and turns inland towards Kaolack at Mbour, and it's relatively easy to get transport in most directions from here. After the RN1 hooks east, a good surfaced road continues south serving Warang, Nianing, Mbodiene and Joal-Fadiouth. The *gare routière* is conveniently located on the main road, and direct *sept-places* are available to Dakar (1,500F), Kaolack (2,500F), and points beyond. To Joal, you're more likely to be hopping on an *ndiaga ndiaye* that stops every 200m, but it won't cost you more than 1,000F.

FESTIVAL DES CULTURES DE MBOUR (FESCUM) If you're here in April, check if the Festival des Cultures de Mbour (🕿 30 114 4015; *www.festivaldembour.com*) is going on, when parades of dignitaries, drummers, musicians and artists take over the town's streets and stadiums for the weekend.

🏠 **WHERE TO STAY** *Map, page 159.*

🏠 **Tama Lodge** (See ad, page 167) (9 rooms) 🕿 33 957 0040; e contact@tamalodge.com; www.tamalodge.com. Not just the finest accommodation in Mbour, but among the most enchanting hotels anywhere in the country, this beautifully designed & lovingly managed boutique lodge easily sets the bar for characterful luxury accommodation anywhere on the Petite Côte. The stunning *banco* & thatch bungalows sit directly on the sand, & their décor reads like a finely curated African art museum, with textiles, handicrafts & furnishings from Congo, Mali, Mauritania & beyond in every room. The interiors are finished in the Moroccan *tadelakt* technique, & each comes with en-suite ablutions, beds hewn from a tree trunk, AC & a ceiling fan. The main building here, home to an opulent 1st-floor suite, evokes the elegant earthen curves of the great mosque at Djenné, while the open-air thatch shelter of the restaurant below is beach chic at its finest. The menu rotates

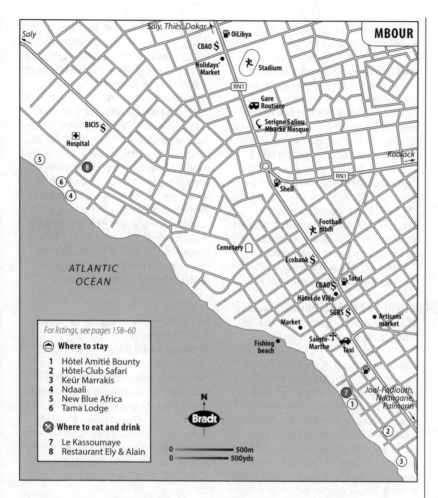

The map labels:

- Saly, Thiès, Dakar
- Saly
- OiLibya
- **MBOUR**
- CBAO
- Holidays' Market
- Stadium
- RN1
- Gare Routière
- Serigne Saliou Mbacké Mosque
- BICIS
- Hospital
- Kaolack
- Shell
- RN1
- Football pitch
- Cemetery
- ATLANTIC OCEAN
- Ecobank
- CBAO / Total
- Hôtel de Ville
- SGBS
- Market
- Artisans' market
- Fishing beach
- Sainte-Marthe
- Taxi
- Joal-Fadiouth, Ndangane, Palmarin

For listings, see pages 158–60

Where to stay
1. Hôtel Amitié Bounty
2. Hôtel-Club Safari
3. Keür Marrakis
4. Ndaali
5. New Blue Africa
6. Tama Lodge

Where to eat and drink
7. Le Kassoumaye
8. Restaurant Ely & Alain

N

Bradt

0 ———— 500m
0 ———— 500yds

daily, & its sophisticated seafood offerings are a rare treat & available to guests only. It's all directly on the water, & the fabulous (& popular) *Plage des Cocotiers* out front is where Mbour comes to swim, jog, play & preen. Rates are in the bottom half of this range for low season, & the upper for high. **$$$$**

Hôtel-Club Safari (18 rooms) Rte de Joal; 33 957 1991; e info@hotelclubsafari.com; www. hotelclubsafari.com. Set in a rambling compound a block in from the waterfront, this bright & popular place is festooned with all manner of rather touristy African-style artwork. There's a bright blue swimming pool, pleasant terraces & gardens, & the rooms are well equipped with canopy bed, fridge & AC. The resto-bar does the usual assortment of continental fish & meat dishes, & discounts are

available for Senegal residents. Prices towards the upper end of this range. **$$**

Keür Marrakis (11 rooms) 33 954 7454; m 77 277 8718; e reservations.keur@marrakis. com; www.marrakis.com. On a rise just above the beach at the very south end of town, this tranquil Moroccan-themed guesthouse is lit with calabash lanterns & has cool, breezy rooms with ceiling fans, hand-carved canopy beds, mozzie nets, en-suite ablutions & a touch of Afro-Arab décor. Some also have ocean views & prices are the same, so ask if one is available. There's also an Italian-inspired resto-bar, swimming pool & a fantastic stone terrace with sunset views. Prices near the top of this range. **$$**

Ndaali Hotel (8 rooms) 33 957 4724; m 76 683 6632; e contact@ndaali.com; www.

ndaali.com. From the moment you enter the seashell-strewn grounds here, this place feels every bit the secret garden, with a clutch of split-level thatch bungalows covered in local murals & surrounded by all manner of greenery. Most of the rooms are split level, with a sleeping area upstairs & lounge space below. They're all individually decorated & come with fan or AC (5,000F extra for AC), nets & en-suite bath. The Plage des Cocotiers, the nicest beach in Mbour, is right out front, & the restaurant does Senegalese & continental standards. Excellent value, with prices near the top of this range. **$$**

🏠 **New Blue Africa** (19 rooms) 📞33 957 0993; m 76 689 3634. As close to the beach as it's possible to be without getting wet, this place at the very northern edge of town (indeed it's only 300m from Au Petit Jura in Saly-Niakhniakhal) has more than earned the French appellation *pieds*

dans l'eau, & it's a particularly fine stretch of beach to boot. The rooms are pleasant if unspectacular, & all come with AC, nets & en-suite ablutions. The restaurant serves up Senegalese favourites, & the staff are friendly & attentive. Prices towards the upper end of this range. **$$**

🏠 **Hôtel Amitié Bounty** (18 rooms) m 77 203 6201/634 2613. A few dozen metres from the beach on the south end of town, it feels that the bar-resto here is slightly more of a focus than the hotel, but the rooms are kept immaculately clean nonetheless. Big & covered in bold artwork (check out that elephant mirror!), the décor won't be to everyone's tastes, but the prices certainly will be – a dbl room with fan goes for as little as 10,000F (15,000F with AC). Expect these to rise a bit in peak season, but it's an excellent budget option either way, leaving you plenty of cash to splurge on a meal at Le Kassoumaye down the street. **$**

✖ **WHERE TO EAT AND DRINK** *Map, page 159.*

✖ **Le Kassoumaye** 📞33 957 3524; m 77 691 4960; http://le-kassoumaye.vefblog.net; ⏰ 17.00–midnight Thu–Fri, 10.00–midnight Sat & Sun. Gastronomes of Mbour, rejoice! Though this owner-managed restaurant on the beach keeps rather limited hours, if you can make it work with your schedule, it's probably the finest table in town. The cuisine is rooted firmly in French & broader continental traditions, & meals can be taken either in the swanky indoor lounge or under the stars on the lantern-lit beachfront terrace. The menu rotates, but you can expect standbys like *filet mignon* & *foie gras* alongside the catches of the day

& a selection of exquisite desserts, mostly in the 7,000–10,000F range.

✖ **Restaurant Ely & Alain** m 77 550 1742; ⏰ 10.00–midnight daily. There's certainly no shortage of identikit roadside restaurants in Mbour, but most are nothing to write home (or in a book) about. This one, on the other hand, stands head & shoulders above the crowd. It's nothing flashy, but for good grilled chicken, fish brochettes or a zebu filet, this festive, palm-fringed little spot is the best address in town. Prices clock in around 3,000–5000F, & there's a range of house cocktails too.

OTHER PRACTICALITIES

Money All of Senegal's major banks are represented here with ATMs scattered throughout town on the main roads.

Communications There aren't too many options for getting online here outside of the hotels, but there should be a *télécentre* or two along the main road.

Health The Hôpital Departemental de Mbour (📞 *33 957 3739*) is on the north side of the road just up from the Plage des Cocotiers.

WHAT TO SEE AND DO As in Saly, the beach is quite simply the raison d'être for tourism here, but unlike in Mbour's northern neighbour, the ratio of fishing to recreation space on the beach here is decisively skewed in favour of the fishermen, so you've got to be a bit more careful choosing your spot unless you fancy picnicking between pirogues or getting caught up in a discarded net. Thus, there's no better place in town to sprawl out in the sand than the ***plage des cocotiers*** in front of

Tama Lodge and Ndaali Hotel, which is popular with locals and tourists alike for its clean sands and phenomenal people-watching. Stretch out here for a while and see the whole town pass by to do their calisthenics or canoodle with their *copains* and *copines* (boyfriends and girlfriends).

And while all that fishing (nearly 3km of pirogues!) might not do wonders for the beaches, the **fish market** here is in a class all to itself. By some reckonings it's the second largest in Senegal, and if you end up here when the pirogues come in for the evening & the catch is hauled in, you'll be incredulous that there could be a bigger, noisier, smellier, more frenetic pile of fish and humanity anywhere, let alone somewhere up the same beach. If you're starting to feel agoraphobic, or just afraid the fish smell is never going to leave your clothes, make a dash a few blocks over to the **artisans' market**, where you can do a considerably more relaxed bit of shopping between the little boutiques and workshops selling a rather standard souvenir selection of carvings, clothes, jewellery, sculpture, masks, and more. As usual, make sure that you bargain.

For the religiously minded, the **Serigne Saliou Mbacké mosque** next to the *gare routière* is an impressive Mouride structure modelled after the grand mosque in Touba. Feel free to have a look outside, but you'd have to make special arrangements to visit the interior. If you've got the time, it would also be worth having a gander at the multi-storey bell tower and church at the **Église Sainte Marthe de Mbour**, which dates from the 1950s.

WARANG

Things start to slow down again here once you've run the gauntlet of Saly and Mbour, and, though Warang is a bustling village in and of itself, it's easily a few dozen notches slower than either of its frenetic northern neighbours. Barely 6km south of Mbour, the small-town feel here is both a surprise and a welcome change, and will be a breath of fresh air for anyone who was sold one too many bracelets in Saly or dodged one too many minibuses in Mbour. Most importantly, the beach continues to shamelessly flaunt its charms all along Warang's shoreline, but the dune buggies and fishing boat chaos are a distant memory.

GETTING THERE AND AWAY There are occasional direct vehicles from Dakar to Joal that can drop you off here, but you're much more likely to change vehicles in Mbour. To leave, stand by the road and flag a *ndiaga ndiaye* heading north to Mbour or south to Joal, neither of which will be more than 500F. A taxi from Mbour should be around 2,000F.

⌂ WHERE TO STAY, EAT AND DRINK

⌂ **Maison La Paresse** (4 rooms) m 77 627 3910; e maisonlaparesse@gmail.com; www. maisonlaparesse.com. About 500m east of the main road at the north end of Warang (the turnoff is more or less opposite the one for Le Warang), this aptly named new lodge (*paresse* is French for laziness) sits in a 6,000m² garden & is sure to bring out the sloth in even the most active of travellers. The thoroughly modern bungalows are 45m² & each is decorated based on a different aspect of Senegalese culture or geography. All come with AC, safe, 4-poster beds,

dual sinks & private terraces looking out on to either the gardens or the sizeable swimming pool. Meals can be taken on the terrace or in the dazzling ochre central building, where you can take advantage of the lounge-bar, set up a massage or pop back outside for a game of pétanque in the grass. It's a bit far from the beach, but it's no fuss for them to arrange you a *calèche* ride over. Prices dip into the price category below in low season. **$$$$**

⌂ **Teranga Belge** (6 rooms) m 77 121 2557; e terangabelge@gmail.com; www.terangabelge.

com. In the centre village, not far from Le Manguiers, this new Belgian-run guesthouse has a handful of trim en-suite rooms set around a small shady courtyard & swimming pool, all of which come with canopy beds, mozzie nets, AC & ceiling fan, along with some nice African touches like linens trimmed with wax print & lamps shaded with carved calabashes. They can arrange all the usual Petite Côte activities including djembe & dancing, & meals are available on request. Rates towards the centre of this range. **$$$**

🏠 **Le Kakatar du Sénégal** (4 rooms) m 77 262 2227/704 9113; e lekakatardusenegal@voila.fr; www.kakatar-location.com. Named after the Wolof word for chameleon, the colour-coded 1st-floor rooms at this charming little place at the north end of Warang each come in a different hue, & each one is perfectly simple & meticulously kept, with fans, nets, en-suite bath & a terrace out front. There's a pool & Jacuzzi, a fully equipped kitchen for guests, & satellite TV in the lounge. It's signposted 200m west of the main road & a further 400m to the beach. Excellent value, with prices in the bottom half of this range. **$$**

🏠 **Le Kenkeni** (6 rooms) m 77 646 9561; e lekenkeni@gmail.com; www.lekenkeni.com. In a rather nondescript 2-storey building 450m off the main road (follow signs for Le Warang), this is probably the best budget option in town. Both en suite & rooms with shared ablutions are available, & all of them are comfortably equipped & scrupulously clean (& the shared bathrooms are only between a couple of rooms). B/fast on the mural-adorned rooftop terrace is delightful, & they can arrange other meals on request. It tends to be quiet, & a nap in one of the rooftop hammocks is probably the most exciting part of the day around here, though they can arrange activities & massages as well. Rates for an en-suite room are at the bottom of this range, & rooms with shared bath are one below. **$$**

🏠 **Les Manguiers** (24 rooms) ☎ 33 957 5174; m 77 529 1001; lesmanguiers@orange.sn; www. lesmanguiersdewarang.com. Right in the centre of town, this reliable place sits in large leafy grounds

signposted about 400m off the main road. The en-suite rooms are simply equipped with fans & nets, or they'll even fix you a bed under the stars up on one of the roof terraces. There's a pool & perennially popular restaurant, & the whole place is occasionally booked out with groups. They arrange courses in batik, drumming & dancing, & in case you pull a muscle on one of your moves, they do massage treatments as well. Rates are scraping the bottom of this range, but don't forget to tack on an extra €3.50 for b/fast. **$$**

🏠 **Le Warang** (30 rooms) m 77 571 0530; e contact@hotel-lewarang.com; www.hotel-lewarang.com. Just above the beach & well signposted off the main road through Warang, this place is a bit of a local institution, & though the bungalows here are reasonably well equipped (AC, nets, en suite), they're a bit too closely-spaced & it feels as if they tried to cram as many on to the property as was possible without much regard for the aesthetics. Still, the resto-bar has a lovely beachfront perch, & there's a big swimming pool as well. They cater largely to groups, & it's middling value with rates near the top of this range. **$$**

🏠 **Auberge du Soleil** (6 rooms) m 77 289 6674/448 2743; e louloulete@gmail.com. On the east side of the road at the south end of Warang, this place looks rather unassuming off the bat, but the simple en-suite rooms come with nets & fans & the prices are a steal (though we got the sense that these may vary – we were quoted 10,000F/room; don't be afraid to negotiate). There's a pool, resto-bar with standard meals around 3,000F, & it all feels new & well kept, if not exactly dripping with character. **$**

✖️ **La Pirogue** m 77 114 4702; ⏰ 11.30–00.00 Thu–Tue. On the main road at the north end of Mbour, this relaxed outdoor eatery has shaded seating & an enticing little menu with standards like steak & brochettes, some slightly more rarefied selections like beef bourguignon, & a hard-to-resist banana flambé for dessert. They've got Louis Armstrong on the stereo & a fully stocked bar. Mains start around 3,500F.

WHAT TO SEE AND DO Beyond the obvious beach activites which all the hotels in town can arrange, Warang is best known for the delightful **Liqueur de Warang** (m 77 524 5416; e ldw.usinewarang@gmail.com; www.liqueursdewarang.com; ⏰ 11.00–13.00 & 15.00–19.00 Mon–Sat), where you can taste more than a dozen seasonal, locally produced liqueurs made from corossol (soursop), cashew apples, madd, mango, ginger, bissap and more. They do (generous) tasting sessions at the garden bar replete with koi pond at their whitewashed colonial-style headquarters on the main road at the north end of Warang. A bottle to take home costs about 8,000F and does make a good souvenir.

NIANING

Continuing south, the Serer fishing village of Nianing shares a similar small-town feel with Warang, but is perhaps just a whisker busier, with a few very pleasant restaurants & bars clustered around the town centre giving things a more cohesive feel. Its most famous address, the vast Domaine de Nianing, closed its doors in 2014, but it's still home to a good selection of accommodation and, once again, a lovely stretch of beach, though there's a fair bit more fishing going on here than in Warang.

GETTING THERE AND AWAY There are occasional direct vehicles from Dakar to Joal that can drop you off here, but it's much more likely that you'll change vehicles in Mbour. To leave, stand by the road and flag a *ndiaga ndiaye* heading north to Mbour or south to Joal, neither of which will be more than 500F. A taxi from Mbour should be around 4,000F.

WHERE TO STAY, EAT AND DRINK

🏠 **Casa Coco (8 rooms)** 📞33 957 3536; e casacoco@orange.sn; www.casacocosenegal. com. In a bougainvillea-draped compound at the very centre of Nianing, the duplex bungalows here are decorated in mosaics & African textiles, & all are comfortably equipped with AC, nets, safe & en-suite bathrooms. They've got direct beach access & serviced sun loungers both on the sand & around the illuminated swimming pool, which is probably the nicest in town. The terrace resto-bar does French-inspired meat & fish dishes starting at around 4,000F. They close for a portion of the low season, so call ahead if you'll be travelling mid-summer. Most guests are accommodated on a HB basis, which puts you at the upper end of this range. **$$$**

🏠 **La Maison Couleur Passion** (12 rooms) m 77 556 3938; e contact@maison-couleur-passion.com; www.maison-couleur-passion.com. While the name may be a bit over the top, the designer rooms at this beachside boutique hotel are undoubtedly fetching, & would make a fine destination for a romantic getaway. It's right on the beach & rooms are arranged around an alluring courtyard with terrace seating, 2 swimming pools, & abundant greenery. Each room comes with flatscreen TV & DVD player, wrought-iron canopy beds, AC, bathtub, dual sinks & eclectic Afro-European décor, & the luxury bungalow rooms have ocean views. Spa treatments & all manner of land & water activities are easily arranged. Rates span the bottom half of this range, depending on room & season. **$$$**

🏠 **Le Ben'tenier** (14 rooms) 📞33 957 1420; e bentenier@gmail.com; www.lebentenier.org. In the centre of town & long a Nianing institution, this easygoing spot with deep roots in the community has simple & pleasant bungalows with shaggy thatch roofs & mosaic floors. They're all en suite with fans & nets, & the family rooms sleep up to 6. The staff are amiable & attentive, the pool is a bright blue & the restaurant does the usual range of Senegalese classics & seafood. It's also the base of the Africa Touki travel agency, which arranges all manner of trips including special women-only events. Prices towards the upper end of this range. **$$**

🏠 **Akwaba** (7 rooms) m 77 378 3745/175 4869; e akwabanianing@yahoo.com; www. akwaba-lescasesdelaplage.com. Right on the beach at the very north end of Nianing (actually in Nianing II, 800m north of the main village, to be precise) & signposted about 400m from the main road, this prim little guesthouse has a clutch of neat tiled bungalows with AC & canopy beds. There's a small swimming pool, beachfront terrace, seashell décor aplenty, & the kitchen does tasty Ivorian cuisine like *poulet attiéké* starting around 3,000F. It's also pretty difficult to argue with the price. **$**

✕ **Le Coco Diop** m 77 570 9404; www. cocodiop.com; ⏰ 19.00–22.00 Tue–Sun, noon–15.00 & 19.00–22.00 Sun. Just east of the main road through central Nianing, this perennially popular restaurant serves up a diverse menu of meat, fish, pizza, pasta & more (available on their website, unusually) in a shaded garden courtyard. It's popular with good reason & a fabulous spot for a casual dinner out, but they deliver to both Nianing & Warang for a nominal fee. Mains start around 3,000F, but save room for a crêpe or chocolate fondant for dessert.

✗ **Le Petit Bonheur** m 77 054 1043/616 9881; ⏱ 10.30–23.30 daily, live music on Mon & Thu.

Generously adorned with mirrors & mosaics, this roadside restaurant in the centre of town sparkles despite its dusty locale. The welcome is warm & it's perilously easy to come here for a meal & wind up watching the town go by over a few drinks. Pizzas start at 2,500F, meat & fish dishes (even steak tartare!) are more like 4,000F, & they've got sweet crêpes for dessert. There's Wi-Fi too.

WHAT TO SEE AND DO In short: go to the beach! All the hotels can arrange excursions on water and land, but Nianing is first and foremost a place to kick back and soak up the vibe. Chat with the fishermen, head up to the road to grab a cold drink and see if there's any live music on, and repeat.

MBODIÈNE

Something of a town in two parts, this rather haphazard roadside village eventually gives way to an oceanfront strip of vacation homes facing an 8km spit of dunes protecting a small lagoon to the north. Unique on the Petite Côte, there's a sandy barrier peninsula between Mbodiène and the oceanfront here, forming a long brackish lagoon to the north. Hire a pirogue to punt you the 100m over to the other side, and you'll have the entirety of this magnificently isolated beach all to yourself.

GETTING THERE AND AWAY There are occasional direct vehicles from Dakar to Joal that can drop you off here, but it's much more likely that you'll change vehicles in Mbour. To leave, stand by the road and flag down a *ndiaga ndiaye* heading north to Mbour or south to Joal, neither of which will be more than 500F. A taxi from Mbour should be around 8,000F.

⌂ WHERE TO STAY, EAT AND DRINK

⌂ **Laguna Beach** (86 rooms) \ 33 957 8811; e laguna@orange.sn; www.lagunabeach. sn. With dozens of rooms arranged in various combinations of suites, duplexes and standard enisuite rooms, this huge place on the south side of Mbodiène can feel more than a bit drowsy in the off-season, but when visitors are in town you can expect their beach, 3 swimming pools, 2 restaurants, windsurfers, mountain bikes and tennis courts to be getting some good use. All rooms come with AC, minibar, hairdryer, Wi-Fi & TV. Fishing excursions are arranged in

partnership with the Sarene Beach Club just up the road. **$$$**

⌂ **Auberge Plein Soleil** (9 rooms) \ 33 957 8823; m 77 015 1515; e pleinsoleilmbo@ orange.fr; www.afriquesenegal.com. In a shell-strewn compound not too far from the beach, the understated thatch bungalows here exude calm & quiet. There's a pool in the centre, breezy resto-bar up front, & the rooms all come with fans, nets, Wi-Fi & en suite ablutions. They do excursions around the village and the Petite Côte, & have discounted rates for stays of a week or longer. **$$**

JOAL-FADIOUTH

Stretched out along the end of a peninsula some 30km or so south of Mbour, the twin town of Joal-Fadiouth marks the end of the Petite Côte and the beginnings of the Sine-Saloum Delta. On the mainland, Joal holds a revered place in Senegalese history as the boyhood home of Léopold Sédar Senghor, and today it's a major fishing centre. As such, it comes pretty low on the list of Petite Côte beaches, and while Joal is also home to most all of the accommodation, transport, and other services in town, its smaller neighbour Fadiouth is undoubtedly the star of the show.

The island of Fadiouth, linked to Joal by a 500m footbridge (there are no cars on the island), is the largest and most impressive of the various seashell islands found in the Sine-Saloum Delta. Quite literally just a massive pile of oyster, mussel, clam, and any other mollusc you can name's shells collected over hundreds of years, Fadiouth is a strikingly unlikely city, and is not only a physical but a cultural island as well. Nearly all the residents here are Catholic – the sheer number of pigs raised on the island is a dead giveaway – and the myriad passageways and streets all converge on a large church at the centre of the island. A second footbridge connects Fadiouth to the island's cemetery, a hilly, baobab-studded patch of even more seashells where Christians and Muslims are buried side by side – a poignant tribute to the coexistence that so defines Senegal today. Either island is an enchanting place for a wander, and though there seem to be more craft sellers per capita on Fadiouth than anywhere else in the country, this doesn't especially mar what is without question an otherworldly experience.

GETTING THERE AND AWAY Joal sits at the end of the tarmac road from Mbour, and it's regularly served by *ndiaga ndiayes* from there for 800F. There may occasionally be a direct vehicle to Joal from Dakar, but you'll probably have to change vehicles in Mbour. A taxi from Mbour should be around 12,000F.

Joal is also the jumping-off point for Palmarin (for which you may have to change in Samba Dia), Fimela and Ndangane in the Sine-Saloum Delta, to which tickets should all be 1,500F or less.

WHERE TO STAY, EAT AND DRINK

Keur Seynabou (3 rooms) 33 957 6744; m 77 540 5461. Subtle, stylish & right on the water (though separated by from the beach by a wall), the earth-tone stucco buildings here are set in a garden of bougainvillea, palms & aloes, and home to 3 handsomely appointed 1st-floor rooms overlooking the swimming pool & gardens. With canopy beds, private terraces, fans, nets & airy white canvas trimmings, the rooms here are probably the nicest in Joal. They close annually from 15 Jul to 15 Oct. 40,000F dbl. **$$$**

Auberge Le Thiouraye (3 rooms) m 77 531 8707/515 6064; e relais114yacinebalde@yahoo.fr; www.relais114joal.overblog.com. This family-run place faces the lagoon on the east side of Joal. It has a pretty restaurant area right over the water & some rather basic rooms with fans & nets. The accommodation is much better value for a couple than for single travellers, but Joal is unfortunately somewhat short on alternatives. Bicycles, pirogues & guides to Fadiouth can be arranged here & they're connected to Keur Bintou next door (under the name 'Relais 114', indicating their distance from Dakar), so you can shop around for a room you like. Prices at the lower end of this range. **$$**

Campement Le Palétuvier (7 rooms) Fadiouth; 33 957 6205. Rather dank, dismal & timeworn, this is unfortunately the only campement on Fadiouth itself. It has a pretty location overlooking the mangroves, otherwise it's quite difficult to recommend the place. Some rooms are en suite while others use the grimy shared ablutions, but the price is the same either way. Meals are available on request. The price is at the very bottom of this range, but all but the most dedicated of penny-pinchers will have a better stay on the other side of the water. That being said, their rate for single travellers is by far the cheapest in town. **$$**

Joal Lodge (9 rooms) 33 954 8248; m 77 590 7909; e joallodge@gmail.com; www. joallodge.wordpress.com. In a small, ochre-coloured compound just up from the beach, this newish place has comfortable en-suite rooms, a rooftop terrace, small swimming pool & a resto-bar serving up the usuals. Rooms are large & come with AC & nets, the staff are warm & helpful, & it's good value for the price, which is in the top half of this range. **$$**

Hôtel de la Plage (15 rooms) 33 957 6677. With a similar sand-coloured motif to Keur Seynabou down the beach, the en-suite rooms

5

here are on the smaller side, but are still smartly appointed with fans & terrace & painted with African-style murals. Clearly signposted off the main road. Dbl 25,000F. $$

✕ La Taverne du Pêcheur ✆ 33 249 4483; ⏰ lunch & dinner daily. Right at the end of the footbridge with views over to Fadiouth, this pretty little restaurant is eminently worth a stop for a meal or a drink after you've finished touring Fadiouth. There are plenty of cushions to plant yourself on & watch the tide come in, & they do a good selection of seafood & meat dishes in the 3,000–5,000F neighbourhood.

WHAT TO SEE AND DO Activities here tend to draw you down to the bridge for Fadiouth almost immediately, but in Joal itself it's worth first stopping by the **Musée Mbind Diogoye** (m 77 541 3961; ⏰ 09.00–13.00 & 15.00–18.00 Mon–Sat; admission 1,000F), which is set in Léopold Sédar Senghor's boyhood home and means 'house of the lion' in Serer. It's loaded with photos and artefacts from Senghor's life and works and will be of interest to fans of African history and politics, but as usual the information is French-only.

It's been obligatory to bring a guide when visiting Fadiouth since 2014, so head over to the **Syndicat Bureau d'accueil et d'information du Tourisme** (⏰ 08.30–18.00 daily; ✆ 33 954 8295) at the foot of the bridge and request an English-speaking guide. It's a reasonably well-run operation, and they've got several different ways you can explore the island. A walking tour of Fadiouth is 5,000F for up to four people; 6,000F for a pirogue journey through the mangroves around the island to see the traditional stilted granaries over the water used to store the year's harvests; 11,000F for both; and 15,000–20,000F for longer pirogue journeys through the creeks and channels of the nearby mangrove swamps.

Wandering the island itself is a joy, and the guide structure is actually rather helpful, if only to help you avoid the attentions of persistent craft sellers. The island is centred around the **Église Saint-François-Xavier de Fadiouth**, which is lovingly adorned with local artworks – check out the mangrove scene behind the altar! Several blocks over is a monument to a different tradition altogether, the local **sacred baobab**, which is purported to be more than 800 years old. It's a lovely tree and there's something especially pleasing to see it growing out of the shells, but if it's sheer size you're after, its counterpart in Fadial (see below) is several times larger. From here, you'll head over another 200m footbridge to the **cemetery**, which is quite simply one of the most magical spots in Senegal, both for its symbolism and its physical beauty. Even though it's a diminutive speck of land, barely 200m across, the landscape undulates in little hills sprouting with baobabs, and a field of metallic crosses and crescents stand like terracotta warriors, in stark relief against the bleached-white mounds of shells they overlook.

AROUND JOAL

In Ndianda village, 6km off the main Mbour-Joal road towards Nguéniène, lies the **Croco Parc** (✆ 33 849 5200; m 77 297 2741; e crocoparc@gmail.com; www. crocoparcsenegal.com; entry 3,000F), where you can check out the 12,000m² gardens, home to dozens of plant species as well as lizards, crocodiles, giant tortoises, snakes, mangabey monkeys and more. It's a private park, but they've partnered with the local community to promote conservation efforts in the area. Entry includes a free drink at the resto-bar, and there's a pool if you're feeling hot-blooded.

After leaving Joal on the way towards Samba Dia and just before you hit Fadial village (about 8.5km), there's a **giant baobab**, apocryphally but rather convincingly regarded as the largest baobab in all of Senegal, and said to be 33m in diameter.

There are lots of craft sellers camped out in its shade (and there's lots of that), but they're quite low pressure. There are guides who can give short tours and (for a small fee) take you inside the hollowed-out core of the tree, where, according to Serer tradition, griots were once buried. It's worth going inside simply to get a feel for how enormous the tree really is.

If it's late in the day, or you're just particularly enamoured with the tree, **Baobab Lodge** [map, page 138] (**m** *77 255 0564;* **e** *babalodje@gmail.com; www.baobab-lodge.sn*) is right next door and has a swimming pool and well-kept double rooms at €84.

Welcome to a world apart...

TAMA LODGE

Beach lodge - Mbour

Website : www.tamalodge.com
E-mail : contact@tamalodge.com
Instagram : @tama_lodge
Phone : 00 221 33 957 00 40

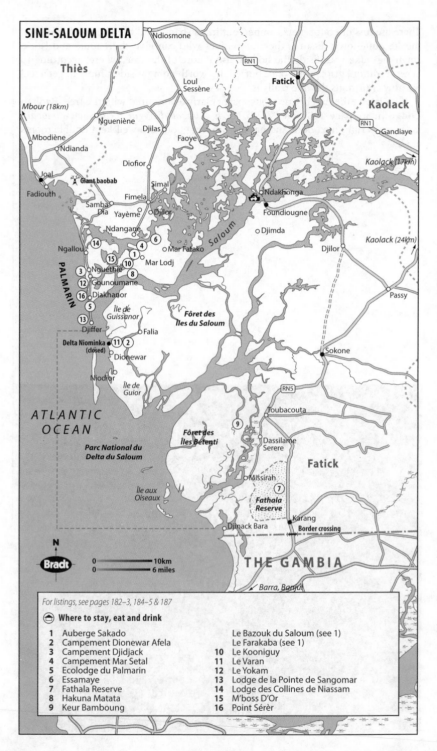

SINE-SALOUM DELTA

Ndiosmone

Thiès

RN1

Loul
Sessène

Fatick

Kaolack

Mbour (18km)

Nguenière

Djilas

Faoye

RN1

Gandiaye

Mbodiène

Ndianda

Diofior

Kaolack (17km)

Joal

Giant baobab

Simal

Fimela

Fadiouth

Ndakhonga

Samba
Dia

Yayème

Djilor

Foundiougne

Djimda

Ndangane

④ ⑥

Kaolack (24km)

Ngallou

⑭

Mar Fafako

Djilor

⑮

① ⑩

PALMARIN

Nguethie

⑧

Mar Lodj

③

⑫ Gounoumane

⑯ Diakhanor

*Fôret des
Îles du Saloum*

Passy

⑤

*Île de
Guissanor*

⑬

Djiffer

Falia

Delta Niominka
(closed)

⑪ ②

Dionewar

Sokone

*Fôret des
Îles du Saloum*

RN5

Miodior

*Île de
Guior*

*ATLANTIC
OCEAN*

*Fôret des
Îles Bétenti*

⑨

Toubacouta

Dassilame
Serere

Fatick

*Parc National du
Delta du Saloum*

Missirah

⑦

*Île aux
Oiseaux*

**Fathala
Reserve**

Karang

Border crossing

N

Bradt

0   10km

0   6 miles

Djinack Bara

THE GAMBIA

Barra, Banjul

For listings, see pages 182–3, 184–5 & 187

☺ **Where to stay, eat and drink**

1	Auberge Sakado		Le Bazouk du Saloum (see 1)
2	Campement Dionewar Afela		Le Farakaba (see 1)
3	Campement Djidjack	10	Le Kooniguy
4	Campement Mar Setal	11	Le Varan
5	Ecolodge du Palmarin	12	Le Yokam
6	Essamaye	13	Lodge de la Pointe de Sangomar
7	Fathala Reserve	14	Lodge des Collines de Niassam
8	Hakuna Matata	15	M'boss D'Or
9	Keur Bamboung	16	Point Sérèr

6

Kaolack and the Sine-Saloum Delta

As you head south from the well-trodden beaches and resorts of the Petite Côte, the palm trees get thicker and the coast itself begins to shapeshift; the land swirls, twists, and eddies back around on itself, tying an ever-tighter series of knots in the brackish ribbons of three rivers here, all desperately seeking the sea which lies somewhere on the other side of this impossibly circuitous, riotously green, fractal-like entanglement of land and water.

This, then, is the Sine-Saloum Delta. It's home to the traditionalist Serer people who navigate these creeks like the backs of so many proverbial hands, earning their livings on water or land from villages hidden behind mangroves deep within the delta with fish, salt, trade and, today, a little bit of tourism. There's a fair bit of tourist infrastructure here, but you'd hardly notice it as hotels and campements are almost universally low-key; the mega-resorts to the north are nowhere to be found down here.

Recognised as a UNESCO world heritage site in 2011, the delta is an intoxicating place to get lost for a few days, a few weeks, or a lifetime, if many of the campement owners are any indicator. Roads here are few and far between, and though getting around by boat is a bit of a splurge, it's undeniably the best (and sometimes the only) way to see this region – you can bring costs way down if you find a few friends to tag along.

The region's remoteness also means that the modern conveniences that are quickly becoming a given in much of the rest of Senegal are often greatly restricted or entirely absent in the delta. Many villages have only solar electricity. Wi-Fi, when available, requires monastic amounts of patience, land transport in the islands is almost exclusively by horse-cart, and, perhaps most importantly, the nearest banks are all back on the Petite Côte in Mbour, or in the unloved and ill-starred regional centre of Kaolack.

KAOLACK *Pop. 466,421*

Poor Kaolack. Senegal's most maligned city by a mile, it's widely regarded as the armpit of the country and derisively nicknamed *Foulack* by the Anglophones and *Kradolack* by the French, both striking at much the same idea – quite frankly, the city is a mess. Still, just as an actual armpit is a critical bodily juncture, Kaolack is also among the most important crossroads in the country, and as such it's likely you'll pass through at some point whether you like it or not. Facilities here are for the most part quite good, and while it's not going to be the highlight of anyone's trip, it's also not nearly as bad as the naysayers around the country will have you believe.

Set along the Saloum River, Kaolack has been an active inland port for centuries and, while its largely polluted waterfront doesn't offer a whole lot in the way of recreational possibilities, the constantly growing and disappearing mountains of salt across the river make for an oddly scenic, if rather industrial backdrop –

particularly enthralling if viewed from poolside with a cold beverage in hand at one of the city's two riverside hotels.

Kaolack is also of huge significance to the Tijani brotherhood, as one of their most revered *marabouts*, Ibrahima (Baye) Niass, moved here in the 1930s and began building the mosque and surrounding neighbourhoods that bear his name to this day – Medina Baye. It was from here that he led his spiritually and politically influential branch of the Tijani brotherhood until his death in 1976, after which leadership passed to his various sons.

HISTORY As with much of north-central Senegal, Kaolack and the lands surrounding it were a part of the Djolof Empire from around the 12th century until its fragmentation into separate kingdoms starting in the late 1400s. With the collapse of the Djolof Empire, the Saloum Kingdom formed around a new capital at Kahone, just a few kilometres upriver from (and today definitively eclipsed by) Kaolack. As opposed to the primarily Wolof kingdoms further north, Saloum was ruled by a Serer military elite, and the kingdom definitively claimed its independence in the late 16th century. In the centuries following, Kaolack became an important centre for the slave trade, counting French and British traders along with Moors from the north among their clientele.

As commercial slave trading began to dry up in the 19th century, Tijani warrior Ma Ba attacked the Saloum Kingdom and its neighbour to the south, Rip. He declared a short-lived empire with a capital at Nioro du Rip in 1862 (see pages 174–7), but was dead within five years and the resultant instability allowed the French and British to ratchet up expansionist pressure on the Saloum and Rip Kingdoms, resulting in the takeover and partition of both kingdoms by the close of the 19th century. Along with French expansion came the expansion of groundnut cultivation, which was already a significant cash crop in the Wolof heartlands to the north, and Kaolack quickly became one of the most significant ports in colonial Senegal. The early 20th century saw Kaolack's prosperity continue; a rail spur that opened in 1912 connected the city to the soon-to-be-completed Dakar–Niger railway line, and it was even the second-largest city in Senegal for a short period.

With the deterioration of the railway and the diminishing economic importance of both the groundnut and the port (the latter superseded by Dakar), Kaolack entered a slow decline from which it has yet to really recover. It remains an important transport hub, but its glory days feel long ago indeed.

GETTING THERE AND AWAY Kaolack is pretty much the most important road transport hub in the country, so it's easy to get here from pretty much any direction. There are two *gares routières* serving the city: Garage Nioro, which handles all destinations to the south and east (ie: Tambacounda (*6,500F*), Toubacouta/Karang (*2,500F*), Ziguinchor (*6,500F*)), and Garage Dakar, which handles traffic to the north and west (Mbour (*2,500F*), Dakar (*3,500F*)). Garage Nioro is just south of the city centre and is quite simply an unmitigated shambles: changing vehicles here, though usually quick enough, is typically accompanied by a fair bit of shouting, hawking and begging, while Garage Dakar, about 2.5km from town on the road to Mbour, is a bit more sane. A taxi between the two should cost 800F.

For **self-drivers**, Kaolack is easy of access, and despite all of them being at least nominally surfaced, the roads approaching town are highly variable. Coming from Dakar, the stretch of the RN1 between Fatick and Kaolack is more suitable for a game of whack-a-mole than it is driving, and the RN5 between Kaolack and Sokone is much the same. Other than that, most of the tarmac is decent, if not great.

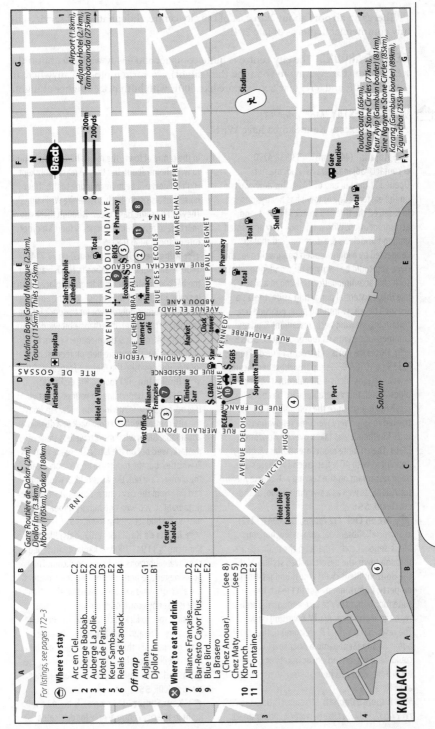

KAOLACK

For listings, see pages 172–3

Where to stay
1 Arc en Ciel.....................C2
2 Auberge Baobab.............E2
3 Auberge La Jolie.............D2
4 Hôtel de Paris.................D3
5 Keur Samba....................E2
6 Relais de Kaolack............B4

Off map
Adjana...............................G1
Djolloff Inn.......................B1

Where to eat and drink
7 Alliance Française............D2
8 Bar-Resto Cayor Plus.......F2
9 Blue Bird........................E2
La Brasero
  (Chez Anouar)..............(see 8)
Chez Maty.....................(see 5)
10 Kbrunch..........................D3
11 La Fontaine......................E2

Gare Routière de Dakar (2km),
Djolloff Inn (3.3km),
Mbour (105km), Dakar (180km)

RN 1

RTE DE GOSSAS

Medina Baye Grand Mosque (2.5km),
Touba (115km), Thiès (145km)

Airport (1.8km),
Adjana Hotel (2.1km),
Tambacounda (275km)

Saint-Théophile
Cathedral

AVENUE VALDIODIO NDIAYE

Pharmacy

Total

BICIS

Ecobank

Hospital

Village
Artisanal

Hôtel de Ville

Post Office

Alliance
Française

Internet
café

RUE CHEIKH IBRA FALL

Pharmacy

RUE DES ECOLES

RUE MARECHAL BUGEAUD

RUE MARECHAL JOFFRE

RN4

Stadium

Clinique
Sarr

CBAO

Star

BCEAO

RUE DE FRANCE

AVENUE MERLAUD PONTY

RUE CARDINAL VERDIER

RUE DE RESIDENCE

Market

Clock
tower

AVENUE J F KENNEDY

Taxi
rank

SGBS

Superette Tmam

AVENUE EL HADJ ABDOU KANE

RUE PAUL SEIGNET

Pharmacy

Total

RUE FAIDHERBE

Port

Total

Shell

Total

Gare
Routière

Saloum

AVENUE DELOIS

RUE VICTOR HUGO

Coeur de
Kaolack

Hôtel Dior
(abandoned)

Toubacouta (66km),
Wanar Stone Circles (77km),
Keur Ayip (Gambian border) (81km),
Sine Ngayene Stone Circles (85km),
Karang (Gambian border) (89km),
Ziguinchor (255km)

Bradt

N

200m
200yds

0

171

There's an **airport** about 2km east of the city centre, though it wasn't serviced by any commercial flights as of late 2015.

GETTING AROUND The city centre is quite compact and easily walkable, but if the heat and dust are getting to you (and they might), a *jakarta* moto-taxi anywhere in town is 500F, and a regular taxi is more like 800F, with both prices higher at night.

WHERE TO STAY *Map, page 171.*
All hôtels except Keur Samba have Wi-Fi.

Adjana (44 rooms) 33 938 4290; e contact@adjana.net; www.adjana.net. Opened at the tail end of 2014, this new place on the eastern edge of town has neatly muscled in & seized the title of Kaolack's highest-end accommodation. With numerous fully appointed garden bungalows & a dozen stilted chalets connected by a long wooden boardwalk over the river, you could be forgiven for wondering what such chic accommodation is doing in a place like this. Existential pondering aside, there's a seashell beach, swimming pool, poolside bar, restaurant, viewing deck, restaurant & prices commensurate with its top-end status. **$$$$**

Hôtel de Paris (37 rooms) Rue de France; 33 941 1018/19/20; e paris@hbsenegal.com; www.horizons-bleus-senegal.com. Kaolack's oldest hotel, this venerable place has been receiving guests since the colonial era & was treated to some very welcome renovations in 2013 when it was taken over by Horizons Bleus. The en-suite rooms are spotless & nicely appointed with AC & flatscreen TV. There's a good restaurant on site serving a 3-course menu for 7,000F, as well as a swimming pool in the courtyard. **$$$**

Arc en Ciel (12 rooms) 33 941 1212; e arcenciel@hbsenegal.com; www.horizons-bleus-senegal.com. Smack on the main road through town, the desert kasbah styling of this, the Horizons Bleus chain's most budget-friendly property, unfortunately doesn't reach the en-suite rooms, but they're nice enough regardless, with terracotta tiles, AC, TV & writing desks. The resto-bar is casual & welcoming, the travel agent on site (Senegambia Agence de Voyage) could be of use arranging air tickets or regional excursions, & guests here are free to use the pool at Le Relais. **$$**

Auberge Baobab (9 rooms) 33 942 2725; m 77 532 6737. Set in a 3-storey building smack in the centre of town, the rooms here are nothing to write home about, but they're reasonably kept. Higher floors will be more immune to the street noise, but also more likely to lose the Wi-Fi signal. They can do some basic meals (though there's no shortage of restaurants around) & there's a cyber café on the ground floor. **$$**

Auberge La Jolie (6 rooms) m 77 714 1400; e aubergelajolie@yahoo.fr. Hidden around the backside of another building, this place doesn't look like much from the outside, but the en-suite rooms are surprisingly decent for the price (at the bottom of this range), if perhaps a bit windowless. They have AC or fan, & the managers claim to be able to rustle up mosquito nets on request. Well located just opposite the Alliance Française. **$$**

Djollof Inn (21 rooms) Rte de Fatick; 33 941 9360. Depending on your perspective, this no-nonsense joint's location a few km from the city centre is either a drawback or a distinct advantage. Given what most travellers think of Kaolack, we'd bet on the latter. There are no bells & whistles, but the rooms are impeccably clean, the showers are hot, the AC is cold, & while it is a taxi ride from the city centre, there's an attached restaurant so you won't go hungry. Probably the best-value budget spot in town. **$$**

Relais de Kaolack (50 rooms) Plage de Kundam; 33 941 1000; e kaolack@hbsenegal.com; www.horizons-bleus-senegal.com. The poolside terrace here overlooking the Saloum & the ever-growing salt mountains on the other side is a serious contender for Kaolack's most pleasant spot to kick back & relax. The en-suite rooms are tiled and well appointed, but the leafy grounds are the real star of the show here; birders will notice that it's an avian oasis in the city as well. Non-guests can swim for a rather steep 5,000F. **$$**

Keur Samba (13 rooms) 33 942 4480. Right in the city centre & only for dedicated barrel-scrapers, this is the cheapest dive in town. Rooms here are rather dank & cave-like, & the bathrooms are on the pungent side of things. Still, if you do take the plunge, the 1st floor rooms are much more pleasant than those downstairs. No Wi-Fi. **$**

✖ WHERE TO EAT AND DRINK *Map, page 171.*

✖ Alliance Française ☎33 941 1061; www.afkaolack.org or www.facebook.com/alliancefrancaisedekaolack; ⏱ 10.00–midnight daily. Accessed through the gate to the right of the alliance's main building, this is their combination outdoor concert venue & bar-restaurant, where you can catch the many musicians they bring into town (listings on website) or just kick back with a no-hassle beer. They also do simple meals & grills starting around 2,000F.

✖ Blue Bird ☎33 941 5350; m 77 300 3068; ⏱ 07.30–02.00 Mon–Thu, 07.30–03.00 Fri-Sat. It doesn't look like much from the outside, but step inside & this might just be the nicest eatery in town. The menu runs the gamut from panini sandwiches to the usual grills & pizzas, with the very noteworthy addition of falafel & some Lebanese specialities, all for somewhere around 3,000F. There's a pool table, Wi-Fi, full bar & waffles for dessert.

✖ Chez Maty m 77 359 3880; ⏱ 07.30–02.00 daily. The fantastically friendly ladies whisking between the always-busy tables here are reason enough to stop by, but the 1,000F *plat du jour*, cold beer & range of tasty *chawarmas*, chicken & steaks seal the deal nicely. There's no sign, but look out for the bright orange place on the corner.

✖ Kbrunch ☎33 941 1716; m 70 450 7355; www.facebook.com/www.kbrunch.sn; ⏱ 07.00–midnight Mon–Sat. In the mould of the slick cafés & patisseries found in Dakar, this newish place in Kaolack isn't exactly cosmopolitan but it's modern enough, with aggressive AC, & does a range of pizzas & pastas for around 3,000F, with omelettes, snacks & a *plat du jour* for closer to 1,500F. Espresso too.

✖ Le Brasero (Chez Anouar) Ave Valdiodio; ☎33 941 1608; m 77 637 8898/721 4622; ⏱ 07.00–22.00 daily. A Kaolack staple if there ever was one, Anouar (who speaks some English) has been easing the minds & filling the bellies of weary travellers in this unpretentious courtyard hideout on the main road for years. Grills, pizzas, Senegalese dishes, a full bar, Wi-Fi & usually some action classics on the TV all await you here. Expect to pay in the neighbourhood of 3,000F for a main course.

☆ Bar-Resto Cayor Plus m 77 479 6530; ⏱ 08.00–midnight daily, later at w/ends. Despite the name, there's only liquid nutrition to be had at this dive in the town centre. The anthropomorphic alien-frog beast on the façade beckons in to an equally colourful interior, where rheumy eyes squint through the clouds of boozy air & conversations are shouted over the wheeze & the rumble of the terminal sound system.

☆ La Fontaine ☎33 942 2115; ⏱ 09.00–01.00 daily. Come for the rooftop terrace, stay for the rooftop terrace. The downstairs here is cramped & dismal, but upstairs it's all breezes (dusty though they may be) & a refreshingly removed perspective on the streetside madness below. They supposedly have live music on occasion as well.

OTHER PRACTICALITIES

Money If you're headed south towards Toubacouta and the Sine-Saloum Delta, Kaolack is your last opportunity to draw cash. Heading for Casamance, your next Senegalese ATM is in Bignona. All the major banks are represented with branches and ATMs in town.

Communication There's a cyber café next to Auberge Baobab and Wi-Fi at Le Brasero and Blue Bird, as well as almost all of the hotels. The post office is on Rue de France [171 D2].

Health The Centre Hospitalier Régional El Hadji Ibrahima Niass [171 D1] (☎ 33 938 4151; *www.hopital-kaolack.org*) is easily accessible in the centre of town, and Clinique Sarr [171 D2] (☎33 941 1921) on Rue de France looks quite modern as well.

WHAT TO SEE AND DO Despite its unbecoming reputation, it's surprisingly easy to spend a pleasant day in Kaolack if you've got the time. On your way into town from Mbour, the first things you'll notice are the razor-sharp and rather cartoonish minarets of the **Ndiouga Kèbè mosque**, about 3km from the city centre. Built in the 1980s, it sits empty and forlorn, the peeling paint on its garish domes giving it the look of a long-abandoned theme park. There are a few stories behind its rejection, but many say it was a vainglorious prestige project built with money from questionable sources; as such, the congregation found it unbecoming to pray in such a building and thus here it stands, condemned as a shrine to material wealth rather than spiritual enlightenment.

The city centre is equal parts rundown and frenetic – burnt-out buses and popular boutiques line the roads just metres apart, and the **central market** is often touted [171 D2] as among the largest in West Africa. Given the number of markets this author has seen awarded such a title, the distinction is probably rather spurious, but it's quite an impressive market nonetheless, whether or not it's earned any superlatives. Give the old **clock tower** [171 D3] and its paralysed timepiece on Avenue Kennedy a look and dive in to the warren of stalls underneath. The nucleus of the market has been swarmed with traders of all stripes since the colonial era (though parts suffered a fire in recent years), and once inside, the stopped clock looming overhead seems oddly apt. The goods may have changed – there are a whole lot of Chinese plastics bouncing around – but the traders still sit under crumbling arches and sip *attayah*, still haggle with their gimlet-eyed clients, and still roll up the shutters in time for prayers at the nearest mosque. It's the most rewarding place to explore in Kaolack and the vendors inside can cater to every fetish, whether they involve *gris-gris*, g-strings or both.

To the north across Avenue Valdiodio Ndiaye, the **Village Artisanal** [171 D1] is home to a dozen or so workshops with a surprisingly good selection of leatherwork, carving and sculpture, masks, silverwork, jewellery, clothing and other accessories. Tourists aren't exactly coming out of the woodwork around here, so you can expect plenty of invitations to 'visit my shop', but it's quite laid-back on the whole.

On the cultural front, the **Alliance Française** [171 D2] (see also page 173) is the place to be. Their calendar of concerts, movie screenings, lectures, art exhibitions and language courses is always packed, and members get access to library and computing facilities as well. It's an admirable set-up, and even more so given Kaolack's rather stunted cultural landscape. Check their website or drop by to see what's on while you're in town.

Finally, about 2.5km from the centre on the north side of town is the **Medina Baye Great Mosque** [171 D1]. As you pass through the archways leading into this Tijani neighbourhood, all roads lead to the mosque and the change in feeling from the city centre is palpable. Construction of the mosque began under Ibrahima (Baye) Niass in the 1930s, and it's been expanded multiple times in the years since. There are no tours or visits as such, but you're sure to strike up a conversation with one of the legions of worshippers or religious paraphernalia sellers if you hang around in the courtyard, and the mosque's stout minarets, enormous green domes, tiled facades and stained-glass windows are all worth a look. The atmosphere is quite pious, so dress conservatively. There's a fair bit of English-language information on the Tijani brotherhood and the Medina Baye neighbourhood at www.iammedinabaye.com.

AROUND KAOLACK

NIORO DU RIP AND THE MEGALITHIC SITES Lying 55km south of Kaolack, Nioro du Rip is the only settlement of any size before reaching the Gambian border and Farafenni. Once an important trading centre as part of the Rip and Saloum kingdoms, it was conquered by the Tijani warrior Ma Ba in 1862 and declared the capital of his putative empire. A contemporary of El Hadj Omar Tall, Ba named the city Nioro du Rip as a counterpart to Tall's base at Nioro du Sahel, in present-day Mali. Ba's rule was to be a breathless one, however, and he died in battle five years later, leaving behind a succession crisis eagerly exploited by expansionist French and British forces; the kingdom's lands were incorporated into their respective colonial spheres of influence in the years that followed.

Today the town is still a busy trading centre for the agricultural hinterlands surrounding it, and the Tuesday *loumo* (weekly market) here buzzes with activity. Facilities for visitors are decidedly limited, however (the nearest banks are in Kaolack), and it's mostly known as the jumping-off point for Senegal's two UNESCO-inscribed megalithic sites, the stone circles at Siné Ngayène and Wanar. Despite being internationally recognised for their significance, these are some of the least-visited attractions in Senegal, and decidedly off the beaten track. While the sites themselves are an intriguing relict of the ancient past that would thrill any archaeology lover, navigating a miles-long web of criss-crossed village paths to reach them makes for a worthwhile adventure in itself.

Getting there and away Any transport headed between Kaolack and The Gambia will drop you at Nioro du Rip. The road from here to Kaolack is surfaced and in decent shape, while between Nioro and the border is atrociously potholed and very slow going. A seat from Kaolack to here should be 1,500F.

The megalithic sites at Siné Ngayène and Wanar are difficult to access, and local knowledge of them is slim, particularly in the case of Wanar (our driver got hopelessly lost despite repeated assurances that he knew the site). Thus, if you're determined to get out here and you've got GPS capability on your phone or otherwise, it would be wise to mark the coordinates listed below.

To **reach Siné Ngayène** (✛ 13°41'42.7"N 15°32'07.5"W), you head south out of Nioro du Rip until a left-hand turning on to an unmarked track near the village of Keur Sièt. The turning is exactly 17.2km from Guantanamo bar in Nioro. From the turning, it's a further 12.5km on unimproved tracks – approachable in the dry season with 2WD and a bit of skill, but certainly 4x4 only if it's wet – through several villages (Keur Bamba, Payama) to the site itself.

To **Wanar** (✛ 13°51'23.1"N 15°37'03.4"W), the turnoff is in Nioro du Rip itself, on to a reasonably well-graded road that runs 23km to Sinnitou Wanar (or Sinnitou Vanar). This is a larger and better-maintained road than the one to Siné Ngayène, so there's even a signpost or two. From Sinnitou Wanar, it's another 4.5km of unimproved tracks that circle slightly back towards Nioro via the closest settlement, Wanar village, to get to the site.

The two sites are about 20km from each other as the crow flies and, with some skilful navigation and driving, it's possible to make a loop and visit both without doubling back to the RN4, though the way between the two is little more than a weaving web of bush paths. The two sites are separated by the Bao Bolong, a tributary of the Gambia River, so anyone heading this way will have to cross it using the causeway at Kabakoto, where you'll also find **Campement Kabacoto** (m *78 104 1058*; e *ludovic@kabacoto-safari.com; www.kabacoto-safari.com*), an upmarket hunting camp with well-equipped bungalows and swimming pool. It's more common to connect between the two on the main road, but if you've got the wheels, it's doable either way.

If you're on public transport and you want to get out here, hiring a car and driver is by far the easiest way, and a day trip from Kaolack can be arranged for about 40,000F. If that sounds a bit steep, you could head for Nioro du Rip on public transport and try to arrange a car to either of the sites from there, or cheaper yet, a *jakarta* or *calèche*. For Siné Ngayène, the small town of Medina Sabakh is about 15km away from the site near the Gambian border, so if you're coming from the south you could try to hire a *calèche* here as well.

🏠 **Where to stay** Neither hotel has Wi-Fi, and for food you'll probably have to head into the centre of town, where you'll find a couple of basic eateries. The nearest other accommodation is Campement Kabacoto (see page 175), about 19km from Nioro in the village of Kabakoto. It's considerably more luxurious than either of the following, and reasonably well signposted.

🏠 **Guantanamo** (6 rooms) m 77 504 3574/369 2044. While it's not nearly as grim as its American namesake, this place is more drinking hole than anything else. The tiled en-suite rooms are set around a courtyard in the back, and they're decent for a night's kip if need be. Given that a dbl room goes for 5,000F, it's hard to complain too much, & thankfully you're allowed to leave whenever you please. **$**

🏠 **ONG Ker Yaakaar** (8 rooms) m 76 475 1269. Across the road from Guantanamo, this place offers similar standard accommodation at the same price, though given that it's part of an NGO rather than a bar, there's probably a smaller likelihood of any late-night shenanigans here. **$**

What to see and do There are actually hundreds of minor megalithic sites scattered throughout Senegal and Gambia in a 100km band north of the Gambia river on both sides of the border as far east as Tambacounda, and it's understood that this region represents the highest concentration of stone megaliths anywhere in the world. Indeed it's quite likely you'll see a few stray examples of these mysterious stones poking out of fields here and there as you make your way to and from Siné Ngayène and Wanar. These two Senegalese sites have been UNESCO-inscribed since 2006, along with two others, Wassu and Kerbatch, that lay in present-day Gambia and are somewhat better developed for tourism, though both are considerably smaller than their Senegalese counterparts.

Considered to be a complex of pre-Islamic necropolises used over an extended period of time, the stone circles are little understood, even today, and truly represent remnants of a lost civilisation. The sites are thought to date from the 12th and 13th centuries, and excavations at both sites have revealed numerous burials performed according to a diverse set of protocols. Some consist of multiple bodies within one circle, which are either arranged side-by-side or stacked at varying depths. Spears, jewellery, pottery and other grave goods have been excavated along with the bodies. Whether these were natural deaths, victims of epidemics or warfare, or even possibly ritual sacrifices, remains unknown. The information on offer at either site is nearly non-existent, but the established facts are so scant that these places are perhaps best simply enjoyed for their mystery.

The 5ha **Siné Ngayène** site sits just outside a village of the same name, and is the larger of the two Senegalese UNESCO sites, with 1,102 carved stones arranged into 52 distinct circles, including one concentric double circle known as the 'royal tomb'. These circles usually consist of between eight and 14 pillars each, set at a diameter of 4m to 6m, and range up to nearly 2m high, but most measure somewhere between waist and shoulder height. The quarry where the laterite stones were excavated and carved sits about 1km to the east, and one of the stones used to grind and shape the pillars is visible here too, though the quarry site is not under formal protection. The

complex is fenced, and a small entrance fee is theoretically charged, th
are scarce here so it's just as likely the caretaker won't be around when
the fence is more of a railing so you can just head in regardless. If th
around, you might be able to check out the small visitor centre.

At just over 2ha, **Wanar** is the smaller of the two Senegalese sites, anu is nome to
21 circles (one of them also a double circle), and nine 'lyre stones', consisting of two
pillars carved from one stone, bridged near the top with a narrow strip of laterite.
It's understood to date from the same era as Siné Ngayène and was also used as a
funerary complex. It's also fenced and likely to present a similar caretaker situation.
You're highly likely to have either site all to yourself, aside from some curious
villagers coming by when they see you arrive. Pack yourself a lunch in Kaolack and
revel in the silence and enigma of either site.

THE SINE-SALOUM DELTA AND NATIONAL PARK

Recognised in various overlapping permutations as a national park, Important Bird
Area, UNESCO world heritage site *and* RAMSAR wetland, it's safe to say the Sine-
Saloum Delta is nothing short of spectacular and that you should make your way
down here post haste – any visit to Senegal without at least a peek into this wild
and disorienting expanse of saline *bolongs* (creeks), lofty palms, gnarled baobabs,
surreal shell islands, ancient burial mounds and a bewildering expanse of mangroves
larger than the world's 25 smallest countries would be woefully incomplete. This is
where the Sine, Saloum and Diombos rivers meet the ocean, and is the heartland
of the fiercely independent Serer people, who, despite making up less than 15% of
Senegal's population, count among their ranks both of Senegal's first two presidents,
'the father of African cinema' Ousmane Sembène and global superstar musician
Youssou N'Dour. As with the rest of Senegal, Islam plays an important rôle here, but
in the delta Christianity and traditional beliefs predominate, and Sunday morning
mass is often even busier than Friday afternoon prayers.

The countless islands of the delta are home to dozens of fishing villages ranging
from decently sized to downright diminutive, but outside of these settlements, a
patchwork of uninhabited land, tidal flats, rivers, and ocean is protected as a part of
the 76,000ha Sine-Saloum National Park (✆ *33 832 2309; admission 2,000F*). Most
trips into the delta offered by tour operators or hotels will end up in the national
park, so it's usually not necessary to liaise with the park authorities directly. The
northern sector, including the Pointe de Sangomar, is most easily accessed from
Palmarin, Mar Lodj or Ndangane, while the southern bit, including the Île aux
Oiseaux and surrounds, is better reached from Toubacouta or Missirah. More
information on the delta and the park is available at www.deltadusaloum.com.

Along with Djoudj National Park in the north, the Sine-Saloum is one of the best
birding sites in Senegal and an important destination for Palearctic migrants crossing
the Sahara. The Île aux Oiseaux alone has been recorded as hosting a staggering
40,000 nests of royal tern (*Sterna maxima*), making it the largest royal tern breeding
colony anywhere in the world. The coastal and marine environments on the outer
edge of the delta are host to many gull and tern species including Audouin's gull
(*Larus audouinii*), lesser flamingo (*Phoenicopterus minor*) and mangrove sunbird
(*Anthreptes gabonicus*), while the expanses of swamps, *bolongs* and tidal flats inland
are a key feeding and breeding habitat for herons and waders, including the great
egret (*Casmerodius albus*), grey heron (*Ardea cinerea*) and Goliath heron (*Ardea
goliath*). Significant numbers of whimbrel (*Numenius phaeopus*), Senegal thick-knee
(*Burhinus senegalensis*), Eurasian oystercatcher (*Haematopus ostralegus*) and black-

6

winged stilt (*Himantopus himantopus*) are also present in this zone. Further upriver, the salt marshes towards Kaolack serve as a breeding area for American flamingo (*Phoenicopterus ruber*) and slender-billed gull (*Larus genei*), and also host the largest wintering populations of osprey (*Pandion haliaetus*) in Senegal.

Underwater, besides the barracudas so prized by fisherman in the area, lucky visitors have a decent chance of spotting the African manatee (*Trichechus senegalensis*) or the African humpbacked dolphin (*Sousa teuszii*), both of which are IUCN-listed as vulnerable but continue to be present in the delta, though population figures are uncertain. The sandy beaches and flats of the delta are also an important turtle breeding ground, with the critically endangered hawksbill turtle (*Eretmochelys imbricata*), endangered loggerhead (*Caretta caretta*) and green turtle (*Chelonia mydas*), vulnerable leatherback sea turtle (*Dermochelys coriacea*) and olive Ridley sea turtle (*Lepidochelys olivacea*) all known to dig their nests here.

FIMELA, DJILOR AND SIMAL

The triplet villages of Fimela, Djilor and Simal sit on a lazy, lush bend in the river a handful of kilometres north of Ndangane. As the largest of the three, Fimela takes pride of place in the centre, while Simal lies across a scenic 2km causeway to the northeast, and Djilor is 2km south, following the curvature of the riverbank. All three villages would pretty readily be described as backwaters, but Djilor is forever immortalised in the minds of schoolchildren nationwide as the birthplace of Senegal's first president, Léopold Sédar Senghor. Outsized historical importance aside, the village still trods along with the tides as it always has, and the only evidence of Senghor's presence here is his preserved boyhood home which is now a small museum. To his great credit, the poet president wasn't much for the palaces, airports and other prestigious flotsam that so often litters the hometowns of African leaders, and Djilor is all the more charming for it.

Any of the three villages would make for a fantastic getaway, and they're home to some of the best accommodation in the delta. Don't come here expecting to do much at all – a dip in the river and a wander in the village would count as an action-packed day around these parts. That being said, the hotels happily arrange all riverine activities, so water babies, birders, paddlers and explorers can all get their fixes here as well.

GETTING THERE AND AWAY The turnoff for Fimela, Djilor and Simal is at Ndiosmone *carrefour*, just as for Ndangane. Fimela sits about 35km south of the junction, and any vehicle heading between Mbour and Kaolack can drop you there. From Ndiosmone, vehicles trundle back and forth to Ndangane throughout the day, and they'll drop you at Fimela, about 35km away, for under 1,000F. The road is surfaced all the way through Fimela, but the roads in and between the three villages are not.

GETTING AROUND The three villages are tiny and no more than a couple of kilometres apart, so most opt to walk. Still, getting between the villages in the heat of the day can be a real chore, and Simal to Djilor would be quite a hike, so there are plenty of *calèches* around to be hired for inter-village trips should you so desire.

⌂ WHERE TO STAY, EAT AND DRINK

⌂ **Ecolodge de Simal** (7 rooms) Simal; ☎ 33 957 0057; m 77 957 0057; e reservation@ ecolodge-senegal.com; www.ecolodge-senegal. com. The huge mud & straw domes lining the

water at this newly refurbished place on the edge of Simal village are nothing less than striking, modelled after traditional Fulbe pastoralists' dwellings & feeling at once both comfortable &

alien, with the red clay & rounded edges recalling the domes of Tataouine, only with the languid waters of the delta lapping at their feet. Inside, the rooms are pleasant & simple as can be, with private terraces, built-in seating & attached outdoor ablutions. Yard games, canoeing, kayaking, fishing, boat trips into the mangroves, *charette* excursions into the villages & a host of other activities are all included in the price, while massages, 4x4 hire & excursions further afield can all be arranged at a cost. The resto-bar does excellent seafood under the stars, & there's Wi-Fi available for more earthly concerns. It's under the same management as the also-excellent ecolodges in Palmarin & Lompoul. All guests are accommodated on a HB or FB basis, & this fact is reflected in the price category. **$$$$**

🏠 **Souimanga Lodge** (8 rooms) Fimela; m 77 638 7601/511 4912; e dmenciere@ souimanga-lodge.com; www.souimanga-lodge. com. In a fantastically beautiful setting just outside of Fimela village, this charmer of a lodge consists of 8 standalone luxury bungalows built from locally sourced wood & clay, set in forested grounds along the river. The high-ceilinged rooms all come with canopy beds, Wi-Fi, dual sinks, eucalyptus trim & full-length mirrors, & all open on to either a terrace or private pier set between the mangroves. The infinity pool attracts both sunbathers & a flurry of birdlife, & activities run the gamut from kayaking & horseback riding to massages on a platform over the water. The cosy restaurant & lounge has an impressive wine list & only a few competitors for finest gastronomy in the delta. **$$$**

🏠 **La Source aux Lamantins** (6 rooms) Djilor; ☎ 33 949 5008; m 77 241 2303; e resasourceauxlamantins@hotmail.com; www.lasourceauxlamantins.com. A touch more conventionally resort-like than its neighbours, the thatched rooms here are clean & well kept, with AC, large mosquito nets, & private terraces. Meals can be taken opposite the library in the huge central *case d'impluvium* or on the shaded pier over the river, & they do a weekly brunch buffet on the pier every Sun. There's Wi-Fi in the restaurant, a pool, & the usual array of activities

can be arranged. Prices are towards the bottom of this range. **$$$**

🏠 **Fagapa Village** (10 rooms) Djilor; ☎ 33 949 5058; m 78 158 7327; e senegaldjilorsaloum@ gmail.com; www.fagapavillage.wordpress.com. Low-key & carefully manicured, this symmetrical green space on the water has trim, comfortable en-suite bungalows that are pleasant but not overly characterful, & a well-positioned resto-bar overlooking the river. The management is helpful & happy to assist with any arrangements you need to make, & it's conveniently located directly opposite Miam Miam restaurant. **$$$**

🏠 **Le Domaine du Cajou** (6 rooms) Djilor; ☎ 33 948 4946; m 77 648 2217; e lecajou@ aliceadsl.fr; http://domaine-du-cajou.chez-alice.fr/ index_064.htm. Though it was closed for the season when we passed through, it's worth mentioning that the fan rooms at this easy-going campement will be your cheapest option in the area. **$$**

🏠 **Boundao Lodge** (6 rooms) Yayème; m 77 700 0788; e olivier.servanin@gmail.com; www.boundaolodge.com. Situated 2km west of Fimela in Yayème village, this beautiful new owner-managed lodge opened at the tail end of 2014, & has been getting rave reviews ever since. The superbly stylish *banco* & thatch standalone bungalows here are built with sustainable techniques & an artist's eye, & all are arranged in a lush compound centred on their curvaceous swimming pool. Rooms come with private terraces, shaded outdoor showers, canopy beds & either fan or AC. All guests are accommodated on a HB basis, with meals at the Mediterranean-inspired restaurant. Prices at the upper end of this range. **$$$**

✖ **Miam Miam** Djilor; m 77 172 7426; www. restau-miam-miam.com; ⊕ 09.00–22.30 daily. Not only a restaurant, but a multipurpose space with organic gardens, a pirogue for hire & an African art museum in the works, this ambitious homestead is the best address to stop in for a bite & to then wind up lost in the gardens or signed up for an excursion. The menu rotates but always includes plenty of seafood to be had. There's a full bar, espresso coffee, Wi-Fi, & they make their own ice cream.

WHAT TO SEE AND DO Aside from riverine excursions into the mangroves, be sure to pass by the childhood home of Léopold Sédar Senghor, known locally as *Mbin Diogoye* or 'house of the lion' in Serer. Built in 1880, Senghor was born here in 1906, and today it's home to a small museum about the life and times of Senegal's first president.

Unfortunately, it was closed for renovations when we stopped in, but should be open again by the time you read this, so stop by and let us know what they've done to the place at our updates website, www.bradtupdates.com/senegal.

FAOYE

At the end of a 10km feeder road that connects to the main route between Ndiosmone and Ndangane that varies in condition depending on the season, Faoye village is barely five blocks squared, and given its location at the end of a long cul-de-sac, it's one of the least-touristed villages in the mainland delta. The Serer inhabitants here primarily make their living from fishing, farming and gathering salt, and it's a great place to get a feel for village life thanks to its community-run campement. You shoud be able to pick up transport here from Ndiosmone, or at the Faoye turnoff north of Fimela in Loul Sessène.

▲ WHERE TO STAY, EAT AND DRINK

▲ Ecocampement Solidaire de Faoye (8 rooms) m 77 432 0116; e famarafaye63@yahoo. fr; www.campamentos-solidarios.org. Part of the Spanish Campamentos Solidarios organisation, these architect-designed wood & thatch huts sit on stilts overlooking the river from their private terraces. It's rustic indeed – kerosene or solar lanterns are your only source of light – but all rooms do have their own basic ablutions & beds are kitted out with mozzie nets. Senegalese meals are served on request in the equally simple thatched resto-bar, & pirogue excursions should be easily arranged. **$**

NDANGANE

Split into two sections and connected by a causeway, the bifurcated town of Ndangane sits on the water at the end of the road from Ndiosmone and Fimela, just opposite the island of Mar Lodj. The road drops you off in Ndangane-Campement, which is home to all of Ndangane's tourist infrastructure, while Ndangane-Sambou, despite being barely 700m away, only really sees visitors who are making transport arrangements with the boatmen's collective located here.

It's a pleasant spot, if perhaps more noteworthy as a jumping-off point to destinations deeper inside the delta than a destination in itself. Still, facilities here are among the best on offer anywhere in the delta, nautical excursions of all stripes set sail from here, and the several-hundred-metre strip of campements in the very aptly named Ndangane-Campement gives it the feel of a minor travellers' hub.

GETTING THERE AND AWAY The junction for Ndangane is at Ndiosmone *carrefour* and any vehicle on the RN1 between Mbour and Kaolack can drop you here, where you'll change for a *sept-place* or *ndiaga ndiaye* covering the 41km to Ndangane for under 1,000F. The road is surfaced all the way to Ndangane.

The piroguiers in Ndangane-Sambou have a union, the **GIE Dioubo des Piroguiers** (m 77 459 2671), with an office near the port and fixed prices listed. A transfer to Djiffer from here costs 40,000F.

▲ WHERE TO STAY

All hotels except Le Barracuda have Wi-Fi.

▲ Hôtel le Pélican du Saloum (60 rooms) ✆33 949 9320/30; e resa-pelican@senegal-hotels. com; www.senegal-hotels.com. In forested grounds overlooking the river, this long-serving place has the somewhat outdated but not altogether unpleasant feel of an aging resort. It's the biggest hotel in town & is well taken care of: the en-suite rooms come with nets, AC & a bit of Senegalese décor, & all the features you'd expect – swimming pool, tennis courts, etc – are here as well. Most guests stay on a HB or FB basis, but the restaurant can also arrange individual meals. **$$$**

🏠 **Les Cordons Bleus** (12 rooms) ☎ 33 949 9312; m 77 403 8056; e cordons-bleus@orange. sn; www.lescordons-bleus.com. Here for over 20 years, this beachside place is the top choice in town. The en-suite thatch bungalows come with canopy beds, nets & AC, & they do vary in size – ask to see a couple as they're all the same price. The bar has football shirts of victorious teams on the walls, & the poolside terrace restaurant hosts occasional DJs & other events. All the usual activities like fishing, pirogues & pétanque are available here, with the notable terrestrial additions of quad bikes & mini-golf. **$$$**

🏠 **Auberge Bouffe** (7 rooms) ☎ 33 949 9313; m 77 786 5448; e info@aubergebouffe. com; www.aubergebouffe.com. Bright & bold, with busy colours & art all around, this little place offers super value with a super vibe. Rooms are simple & lovingly tended; none have AC but all are en-suite & come with nets & a ceiling fan. The flowery grounds are home to an enormous baobab, inviting swimming pool & terrace restaurant-bar. The multilingual owner-managers extend a warm welcome & will happily help plan your time in the delta. It's signposted about 400m from the main road & across from Les Cordons Bleus. **$$**

🏠 **Campement Le Cormoran** (9 rooms) ☎ 33 949 9316; m 77 619 4584; e contact@ lecormoran.net; www.lecormoran.net. At the base of the road from Fimela just before it hits the water, this friendly place has long been a popular hangout. Rooms are simply equipped but all have nets & AC, & there are some nicer new rooms that go for the same price as the others. The terrace restaurant-bar is a reliable gathering spot in season & serves the usual assortment of seafood & Senegalese meals. **$$**

🏠 **Couleur Café** (10 rooms) ☎ 33 949 9999; m 77 553 2703; www.facebook.com/ CouleurCafeAuSenegal. Known more for the restaurant out front than the rooms at the back, this place down the road towards Auberge Bouffe does a variety of Belgian & French dishes in their comfortable roadside restaurant. The thatch bungalows at the back are reasonably well equipped & come with either fan or AC, though prices are on the high side for what you get & AC will bump you up into the next price bracket. **$$**

🏠 **Le Barracuda** (10 rooms) m 77 077 5771/559 3229; e salioudiouf2014@live.fr. Cheap & reasonably cheerful, this unremarkable place opposite Le Cormoran is the most economical option in town. Rooms all have nets & come with either fan or AC, & there's a restaurant & bar on the 1st floor dishing up hot *thieboudienne* & cold Gazelle. There's a room that sleeps up to 4 for 20,000F. They can arrange all the usual pirogue excursions. **$**

✗ **WHERE TO EAT AND DRINK** There are probably half a dozen restaurants scattered along the road from Fimela into town and along the riverside at the end of the road, all of which serve Senegalese basics like *thieboudienne* and *yassa*, and a variety of grilled fish and meat mains. **Le Flamant Rose** and **Le Ganalé** are good bets on this road, along with **Le Piroguier** on the riverfront; they all serve lunch and dinner daily.

WHAT TO SEE AND DO Getting out on the water is the primary goal of most visitors here; all hotels run the usual array of pirogue, fishing, birding and other excursions into the delta. **Afrikayak** (m *77 646 0914/523 5710*; e *afrikayak@hotmail.fr*; *www. afrikayak.com*) provides kayaks for hire at 10,000F for a half-day; punt yourself over to Mar Lodj and explore the coast, or sign up for one of their guided trips. **Voile-Sénégal** (m *77 972 7223*; *www.voile-senegal.com*) runs fully customisable sailboat tours around the delta, ranging from a two-hour guided tour for 10,000F per person (four person minimum) to crewed boat hire, or just the boat if you've got sailing experience. There's a full price schedule on their website, but a full day on a crewed boat goes for 90,000F per person, including fuel and drinks.

With no cars and no electricity, the baobab-studded island of Mar Lodj makes Ndangane look positively like the big city. The island itself is home to four villages and a few thousand souls; most of the action happens in the village that's given the island its name. Like much of the delta, most people living on Mar Lodj are Serer, and as such the island is heavily Catholic – indeed, Sunday mass on the island is a tourist attraction in itself.

Mar Lodj has all the allure of the delta's remotest islands but the boat trip from Ndangane isn't even 15 minutes long, making it the best of both worlds – easy of access and distant in character, and the moment you step on to the island, the rest of Senegal melts away behind you. Wander the villages, exchange bashful smiles with the locals, swim, fish, catch a *calèche,* set sail deeper into the delta or get lost on the island for way longer than you planned – it's all easily done on Mar Lodj.

GETTING THERE AND AWAY All campements here will arrange pickup from Ndangane, so give them a call when you know you're coming – their transfer rates are more or less the same as the *piroguiers* on the beach in Ndangane, and some will throw in a free transfer if you're staying a few nights. Otherwise, there are a few irregular public boats making the crossing from Ndangane to Mar Lodj village throughout the day for a few hundred CFA.

Le Bazouk du Saloum, Le Farakaba and Auberge Sakado are all next to the Mar Lodj village boat launch, while the other campements can be reached by either hiring a pirogue to drop you off directly, or by disembarking at Mar Lodj village and hiring a *calèche* to carry you the rest of the way by land. Hiring a pirogue from Ndangane to Mar Lodj village costs 12,500F.

WHERE TO STAY, EAT AND DRINK *Map, page 168*
All accommodation operates on solar and sometimes generator power, so electricity is typically limited.

Hakuna Matata (16 rooms) m 77 637 2473; e hakuna_matata_fr@yahoo.fr; www.campement-hakunamatata.net. In a densely forested 10ha compound at the southern end of the island, this isolated spot has all the ingredients of a lost idyll. The widely spaced wood & thatch bungalows are simply appointed with fans & nets, but large & lovingly kept. They're all en-suite & have outdoor showers. Fishing is the order of the day here, but kayaks, hammocks & a sandy beach will keep non-fisherfolk equally happy. A pirogue transfer direct from Ndangane takes 35 minutes & costs 30,000F, or you can take a cheaper pirogue trip to Mar Lodj village and arrange a calèche from there for 5,000F or so. The location is magnificently isolated; thus all guests are on a full-board basis, which includes 3 meals daily, purified water, coffee & the house cocktail of *kinkeliba* tea & rum. **$$$**

Le Bazouk du Saloum (12 rooms) m 77 333 1952; e bazoukdusaloum@hotmail.fr; www.

bazoukdusaloum.com. Near the boat launch at the west end of the island, this place has had energetic new managers since 2012, & under their stewardship it's rapidly become one of the prettiest options on the island. The shell-studded en-suite thatch bungalows are spread around the beachside gardens & all come with mozzie nets & private terraces overlooking the water. There's Wi-Fi in the breezy resto-bar, a trampoline for the kids & free kayaks, & all activities around the delta can be arranged here. Guests are hosted on a HB or FB basis, & this is reflected in the price category. Free transfer from Ndangane. **$$$**

Campement Mar-Setal (Chez Kurt) (8 rooms) m 77 637 2531; e mar-setal@hotmail.com; www.marsetal.blogspot.com. Directly across the water from Ndangane, this clutch of cosy en-suite bungalows is the closest accommodation on Mar Lodj to the mainland. Kurt, an Austrian expat who has lived on the continent since the early

1980s, is *le patron* around here, & he's happy to arrange all the usual fishing, birding & excursions around the delta. The *piroguiers* in Ndangane will ferry you over here for 5000F, or it's a 30min walk from Mar Lodj village. As with most places on the island, HB/FB accommodation is the norm. **$$$**

🏠 **Le Kooniguy** (8 rooms) **m** 77 647 3741; **e** kooniguy@gmail.com; www.lekooniguy-senegal.com. On the west coast of the island just south of Mar Lodj village & the main cluster of accommodation, the swimming pool here tips this place into the upper echelon of accommodation on the island, & the gastronomic French-inspired cuisine serves to confirm that impression. The en-suite thatched bungalows here are tiled & spacious, with big beds, nets, wrought-iron furnishings & hints of African décor. Fishing & pirogue excursions are easily arranged, & it's 13,000F for a direct transfer here from the Ndangane *piroguiers*. HB rates put you towards the top of this bracket. **$$$**

🏠 **Essamaye** (10 rooms) ****33 930 9006; **m** 77 555 3667; **e** info@senegalia.com; www.senegalia.com. Set in a grand Casamance-style *case d'impluvium* on the north side of the island, the ochre rooms here are simply equipped with big beds, nets & fans; all use common ablutions & the whole place is kept scrupulously clean. The dynamic owner is originally from Casamance, & can arrange activities from here to his hometown

& everywhere in between. Trekking, kayaking & all the island usuals are on offer, & the chef is happy to share her expertise on how to cook the perfect plate of *mafé*. The price category listed below is based on their B&B rate, while HB will just barely bump you up into the next bracket. Camping possible. **$$**

🏠 **Le Farakaba** **m** 77 564 6883; **e** farakaba@hotmail.com. One of the handful of campements slung along the western shore between the boat launch & Mar Lodj village, this locally run place is known for its warm hospitality, homecooked meals & reasonable prices. The en-suite rooms are simple with nets & fans, & it's a good place to stay if you want to get a feel for the pulse of the village. It's equally good if you want to hop in a pirogue & catch some fish or go exploring. **$$**

🏠 **Auberge Sakado** (5 rooms) **m** 77 593 7729; **e** aubergesakado@hotmail.fr; www.aubergesakado.e-monsite.com or www.facebook.com/aubergesakado. A few steps back from the water, the beds at this friendly hostel are the cheapest on the island, with options ranging from a sheltered hammock with mozzie net to basic 2-, 3- & 4-bed rooms using shared ablutions. The bar serves cold drinks, meals & barbeques are done with prior arrangement, & there's a kitchen for guest use (a rarity in Senegal)! There's also a paid internet connection, & all kinds of island excursions can be arranged. Camping possible. **$**

WHAT TO SEE AND DO Mar Lodj doesn't have a whole lot in the way of structured activities going on, but taking some time to explore the villages and soak up the island vibe is pretty much the order of the day. The island is home to a number of **artisans** and craft sellers, and the hard sell that's so quick to drive away tourists elsewhere is refreshingly absent here, in keeping with the island's lackadaisical modus operandi. Hang around and chat and they might show you around their workshops as well. Whether or not you're religious, the **Catholic mass** on Sunday mornings has a well-deserved reputation for its drumming and song, and if you're here on a Sunday you'd be missing a trick not to at least look in – dress conservatively though. *La lutte* matches – Serer-style, of course – are popular in the first couple months of the year; ask your campement if there's anything going on while you're around.

On the water, the assortment of kayak, pirogue, fishing and other excursions is just as enthralling as what's on offer in other parts of the delta. Every campement will happily set up a full range of aquatic activities, or refer you to someone who can.

PALMARIN AND DJIFFER

Consisting of a long string of villages slung along the Sangomar Peninsula, which stretches some 15km between the ocean to the west and the tangled mangrove *bolongs* to the east, Palmarin's five villages, north to south, are Ngallou, Nguethie, Gounoumane,

Diakhanor and Djifer. If it feels like the end of the road when you get here, that's because it is; the one dirt road that travels the length of the peninsula passes through some fantastically windswept coastal scenery here before dead-ending in Djiffer, which, since a flood in 1987 broke the peninsula in half, has been the end of the peninsula – previously it stretched some 15km further south! Today the true Pointe de Sangomar is an uninhabited island, separated from the mainland by 5km of open water.

It would be hard to get much sleepier than Palmarin without descending into a vegetative state, so if it's peace and quiet you're after, there aren't many better choices in Senegal. The bouncy red-earth road might see a car every hour on a busy day, and the roving goats fully enjoy the right of way around here. The beach runs parallel to the road along the western shore, and, except in Djiffer, is usually nigh on deserted and ripe for a run, a nap under the palms and pines, or just some much-needed hours in the sunshine. The Palmarin villages are considerably more scenic than their counterpart to the south – unfortunately Djiffer is a bit of a trash pit. Much like other places in the delta, Serer traditions remain strong here; adherents to Catholicism and animist cosmologies outnumber Muslims, and the most traditional form of Senegalese wrestling, or *la lutte* – originally a Serer tradition – is regularly performed (see page 32).

GETTING THERE AND AWAY Palmarin is many things, but a transport hub isn't one of them. Visitors on public transport should arm themselves with a bit of patience, or be prepared to shell out for some extra seats to get things moving. To get here, you first have to aim for Joal, south of Mbour on the Petite Côte. From Joal, look for a *sept-place* or *ndiaga ndiaye* to Samba Dia – it's possible you'll get lucky and find a car all the way through to Palmarin from Joal, but don't count on it. From Samba Dia, there are occasional vehicles making the 25km trip to Djiffer, but expect to wait. Tell the driver where you're planning to stay and he'll drop you at the turnoff.

Self-drivers should be fine in a 2WD, but note that the tarmac ends in Joal; from there on out it's all reasonably well-maintained laterite.

GETTING AROUND The best way to get up and down the peninsula is to hire a *calèche*: not only is it more fun, but there aren't many cars around to hire (though there are a few – a taxi from the northern end of the peninsula to Djiffer is around 2,500F).

⌂ WHERE TO STAY, EAT AND DRINK *Map, page 168.*

⌂ Lodge des Collines de Niassam (13 rooms) Ngallou; m 77 639 0639; e resa@niassam.com; www.niassam.com. Built in perfect harmony with the natural environment, the 3 types of rooms here are inspired by the elements air, water & earth. Air rooms sit high in a gnarly baobab, water on isolated platforms over the lagoon, & the rounded *banco* earth rooms rise organically out of the terra firma. All are en-suite & handsomely appointed with big beds, nets & fans. The restaurant serves some of the finest cuisine this side of Dakar, based on a fixed menu that rotates daily. It's accessible by a 1,900m track through the salt ponds that branch east from the main road at Palmarin-Ngallou; all guests here are accommodated on a HB or FB basis. **$$$$**

⌂ Ecolodge de Palmarin (18 rooms) Diakhanor; ☏ 33 957 00 57; m 77 957 00 57; e reservation@ecolodge-senegal.com; www.ecolodge-senegal.com. With orange walls & archways rising out of the earth like an overgrown sandcastle, this beachside *banco* chateau about 800m south of Palmarin-Diakhanor has an Africa-meets-Alice-in-Wonderland appeal, & would appease sun-seekers & surrealists just the same. All rooms are en-suite & equipped with nets & fans, & the *banco* keeps temperatures low. There's Wi-Fi in the restaurant, lawn & board games for the kids, & quite possibly the best range of activities on the peninsula, with fishing, massage, pirogue trips into the national park & tours to go see the fearless palm wine tappers all easily arranged.

It's under the same umbrella as the excellent ecolodges in Simal & Lompoul, and all guests are accommodated on a HB or FB basis, which is reflected in the price category. **$$$**

🏠 **Campement Djidjack** (16 rooms) Gounoumane; 📞 33 949 9619; 📱 76 669 0371; ✉ info@djidjack.com; www.djidjack.com. Between the central Casamançaise *case d'impluvium* & the Mauritanian *khaïma* tent, this place about 1km north of Palmarin-Gounoumane has both sides of the country neatly covered. The *case d'impluvium* hosts the resto-bar & library, where you can read French comics, have a drink or use the Wi-Fi, while the *khaïma* tent sleeps up to 8 at a budget-friendly 6,500F a pop. All the bungalows are en-suite, the usual activities are on offer, & there's a swimming pool too. Prices for the bungalows are at the top end of this range. **$$**

🏠 **Le Yokam** (20 rooms) Gounoumane; 📞 33 958 4383; 📱 77 567 0113/614 7182; ✉ leyokam@gmail.com. In an isolated spot on the beach about 1km south of Palmarin-Gounoumane, the reed bungalows at this friendly campement are basic, breezy & mostly en-suite, with high ceilings, mozzie nets & terraces overlooking the water. Hikes, horse rides and pirogue excursions can all be arranged, & the restaurant has Senegalese meals at request & cold Gazelles at the ready. **$$**

🏠 **Lodge de la Pointe de Sangomar** (14 rooms) Djiffer; 📱 77 536 4425; ✉ pointesangomar@gmail.com. All the way at what is today the end of the peninsula, this is the only accommodation in Djiffer, & it's surprisingly nice, given Djiffer's rather raggedy façade. In a large, eucalyptus-studded compound between the 2 halves of the village, this has the feel of a sleepy & rather timeworn resort, but it's still very pleasant & a good place to stay if you want to get a feel for how a real workaday African village operates. The

2 main fishing beaches are metres from the gate, & while the area around the lodge is kept clean, there are still better swimming options further up the peninsula. The reed & thatch rooms have either en-suite or shared ablutions & are equipped with fans & nets. Pirogue trips are easily arranged. **$$**

✕ **Point Sérèr** Gounoumane; 📱 77 614 7582; ⊕ lunch & dinner daily. This shiny new place in Palmarin-Gounoumane wears many hats, with restaurant, bar, cyber café, cultural centre & nightclub foremost among them. Palmarin in general is sorely lacking in these types of spaces, so Catalan singer Lluís Llach & his eponymous *fundació* most certainly had the right idea when they helped set this place up. They do a Senegalese *plat du jour* daily for a couple thousand CFA, there are several computers where you can get online for a fee, & there's usually football on the telly. By night the bar takes over, & there's live music at the weekends – expect an eclectic mix of reggae, salsa, *mbalax* & more.

Near Palmarin
🏠 **M'boss Dor** (4 rooms) Île M'Boss Dor; 📱 77 541 9683; ✉ mbossdor@yahoo.fr; www.mboss-dor.com. If the words 'private island' set your heart aflutter, this retreat nestled deep in the mangroves between Palmarin & Mar Lodj ought to be cause for a few palpitations, & if that doesn't do it, their ultralight aircraft tours over the delta surely will; manager Frederick's aerial photography of the region has even been published in a coffee table book. The en-suite wooden chateaux are widely scattered & elegant in their simplicity. You can't exactly nip out to a restaurant around here, so everyone stays on a full-board basis, which includes water & wine – no miracles needed. Advance booking is required & pickup is at the mosque in Palmarin-Ngallou. **$$$$**

WHAT TO SEE AND DO The **beach** is the obvious choice, but look to the east and you'll find the 10,480ha **Réserve Naturelle Communautaire de Palmarin** (entry 2,000F), which covers the maze of mangroves, islets, and bolongs east of the peninsula. The best way to explore the reserve is in either a pirogue or a kayak, and all the campements in Palmarin will arrange trips.

Alternatively, the **Maison de l'Éco-tourisme** (📞 33 949 4195; 📱 77 265 1765/445 8636/435 6665; www.ecotourisme-palmarin.com; ⊕ 08.00–12.30 & 15.00–18.30 Mon–Sat) in Palmarin-Gounoumane can do the same. They also can arrange plenty of land-based activities, including visits to the **salt ponds** east of Palmarin-Ngallou (5,000F), **hyena spotting** every evening (15,000F) and, for those aerially inclined, can help arrange ultralight aircraft flights in conjunction with M'boss Dor (see above).

mar Kayak (m *77 535 5011;* e *senegal.kayak@gmail.com; www. rkayak.com*) in Palmarin Diakhanor is another warmly recommended that can arrange all of the above, in addition to fully customisable and absolutely magical **kayak excursions**.

For the first half or the year, Palmarin is also a reliable spot to see **Senegalese wrestling**, *la lutte,* in its most traditional form. *La lutte* is a national obsession, but it's well known that the wrestling practised in the rest of the country and at the packed stadiums in Dakar has evolved a great deal from its Serer roots. Here, striking your opponent, expected in Dakar, will get you ejected from the match straightaway – Serer wrestling is all technique. Drop your opponent into the sand and the proverbial bell rings; you're the victor, ready to move on to the next match. There's a stadium in Palmarin-Gounoumane – ask at your campement to see if there are any matches on.

OTHER PRACTICALITIES The nearest bank is in Mbour, so don't forget to take out money before you head down here.

ÎLE DE GUIOR (DIONEWAR AND NIODIOR)

Known by a few names, but often just called Niodior, after its largest town, the Île de Guior is home to a handful of villages including Falia, Dionewar and Niodior, and a couple of good hotels. It's a fantastic spot to get a feel for everyday life in a fishing village undeveloped for tourism, and you're very likely to be the only visitor for miles if you venture down to Niodior (or any of the villages) from the hotels, both of which sit in a beautifully isolated spot at the north end of the island. It's also the birthplace of author Fatou Diome, the most popular Senegalese writer in decades, and is the setting of her 2003 novel *The Belly of the Atlantic* (Serpent's Tail, 2003, translated by Lulu Norman and Ros Schwartz):

> Over there, people have been clinging to a scrap of land, the island of Niodior, for centuries. Stuck to the gum of the Atlantic like bits of leftover food, they wait resignedly for the next big wave that will either carry them off or leave them their lives. This thought hits me every time I retrace my path and my memory glimpses the minaret of the mosque, rigid in its certainties, and the coconut palms, shaking their hair in a nonchalant pagan dance whose origin is forgotten.

Indeed, the minarets and coconut palms here do compete for vertical superiority, and both keep careful watch over the scores of fisherman that heave their pirogues into the waves every morning; baobabs and kapok trees complete the skyline with their unimaginable heft. Take a *calèche* down here to see the whole process draw to a close every evening as the nets are hauled in, and witness one of the timeless island sunsets immortalized by Diome, when 'The sun seemed to flee human questioning and threatened to plunge into the Atlantic.' If you're crossing the delta by boat and want to stretch the journey over a few days, Île de Guior makes for an enchanting place to break the journey.

GETTING THERE AND AWAY Going by pirogue is the only way, and Djiffer, south of Palmarin, is the jumping-off point. There may be a couple of public pirogues crossing throughout the day, but Campement Dionewar Afela also arranges cheap transfers in either direction for 2,000F. To continue onwards from here, you'll have to negotiate a boat transfer to your next stop.

WHERE TO STAY, EAT AND DRINK *Map, page 168.*

🏠 **Le Varan** (10 rooms) m 77 278 2512;
e levarandionewar@gmail.com. In a brand new
compound at the north end of the island right next
door to Dionewar Afela, this French-run place is a
prim & geometric little resort built around a central
courtyard & swimming pool. It's rather conventional
& not long on local character, but the facilities are
high quality. All the tile & thatch rooms come with
TV, AC, Wi-Fi, tea/coffee facilities & nice en-suite
ablutions. The resto-bar was still under construction
when we checked in, but expect lots of local seafood
with a French twist. **$$$**

🏠 **Campement Dionewar Afela** (5 rooms)
m 77 378 1725; e madioufo1@gmail.com.
Newly opened & in a gorgeous spot on the water,
this locally run campement has super clean

accommodation in either shared-bath bungalows
or en-suite rooms, all of which are equipped with
nets & fans. The larger en-suite rooms get a desk
& couch as well. They can arrange guided trips to
the villages on the island, excursions out into the
mangroves, or you could just stick around – the
beach out front is clean & swimmable. Guests are
accommodated here on a HB/FB basis, & even then
prices are an absolute steal. **$$**

🏠 **Delta Niominka** Closed and in the process
of being bought out as of early 2015, it's likely that
this high-end resort will come back under different
ownership during the lifespan of this edition, but
it's impossible to say when this will be or what it
will be called. Check the Bradt updates site at www.
bradtupdates.com/senegal for the latest.

FOUNDIOUGNE

A reasonably active river port during the colonial era, Foundiougne today is a
somnambulant collection of old French warehouses and colonial homes, many of
them in the process of being devoured by strangler figs. Though its importance
as a port may have faded, life here still very much revolves around the water;
colourful pirogues still ply the river as they've done for centuries, and the town
schedules its days around the car ferry that chugs its way between the banks ten
times a day.

A recent development will see the town reclaim some of its mercantile glory,
however, as a South Korean firm has been contracted to build all-new port facilities
on the northern bank of the river at Dakhonga. Well under construction as of early
2015, it should be finished within the lifespan of this edition, and seems likely to
shake the town out of its decades-long slumber. Thus, the next few years are poised
to be an exciting time for Foundiougne economically, but visitors should consider
stopping over right now, while the half a dozen cars waiting for the ferry are still
the only traffic in town.

GETTING THERE AND AWAY If you're coming by **public transport**, be aware
that longer-haul vehicles typically go via Kaolack to avoid the ferry crossing at
Foundiougne, so you'll typically have to change vehicles at least once to get here.
Approaching from the south, any transport between Karang and Kaolack will drop
you in Passy, from where vehicles cover the remaining 30km to Foundiougne. From
the north, you first have to get to Fatick, where you'll change for a Dakhonga-bound
vehicle, which will take you the 25km to the riverbank opposite Foundiougne.

The **river ferry** here runs according to a set schedule. The boat runs daily,
departing Foundiougne at 07.30, 09.30, 11.30, 15.00 and 17.00, and returns from
Dakhonga at 08.30, 10.30, 12.30, 16.00 and 18.00. It costs 100F for foot passengers
and 1,500F per vehicle.

As elsewhere in the delta, there are plenty of **piroguiers** happy to ferry you
between the islands, and a transfer from Foundiougne downriver to Ndangane or
Mar Lodj would be in the neighbourhood of 60,000F for up to seven passengers.
Baobab sur Mer or Baobab sur Terre are fine places to set this up.

WHERE TO STAY, EAT AND DRINK

Hôtel Foundiougne (40 rooms) ↘33 948 1212; **m** 77 566 5013; **e** papsakante@live.fr. The only thing missing to complete the picture of decay at this longstanding hotel would be angry vultures circling overhead. Rooms are frozen in the 1970s, & the abandoned outbuildings don't do much to combat the air of neglect. Somehow, it just about still functions, & there is a nice pier over the river, a few scattered loungers near the green swimming pool, & meals available on request. All this, & it's still considerably more expensive than anywhere else in town. For emergencies only. **$$**

Le Baobab sur Mer (Chez Anne Marie) (10 rooms) ↘33 948 1262/3; **e** baobabmer@ yahoo.fr. In a lovingly tended, seashell-strewn compound right on the riverbank, the warm welcome & Instagram-worthy meals alone make breaking the journey here worthwhile. The en-

suite rooms are simple, spotless & freshly painted, come with fan or AC, & it's the only place in town with Wi-Fi. And while there isn't much to do in Foundiougne but to sit back and watch the river slink past, this is undoubtedly the best place to do it. **$$**

Le Baobab sur Terre (16 rooms) **m** 77 538 0911/946 1692; **e** baobab77@ymail.com; www. baobab-terre.sitew.com. A bit more downmarket than its nautical competitor across the road, this earthy place has simple detached rooms with nets & fans. They're kept clean & freshly painted, & the English-speaking manager is a certified guide & excellent resource if you're looking to set up boat transfers or other activities in the region. The resto-bar here was being remodelled when we checked in, & it's got nice river views from across the street. Prices are at the bottom of this range. **$$**

SOKONE

Not to be confused with Somone on the Petite Côte, Sokone is on the RN5 between Kaolack and Toubacouta, and most travellers breeze right through here without a second look. It's a pleasant enough little town, however, and can actually make a decent base from which to explore the delta. It's also less developed for tourism than Toubacouta, if you're looking for ways to get off the *toubab* trail (though it's perhaps a busier town generally speaking). It's home to a couple of good accommodation options, and it comes to life every Wednesday, when buyers and sellers from across the region stream into town for the weekly *loumo*.

If you're thinking about staying here, the excellent community-run **Campement Fadidi Niombato** (\ 33 948 2792; **m** 77 215 6860; **e** niombato@orange.fr; www. niombato.com) on the riverfront just opposite Sokone proper has 18 well-equipped en-suite rooms, while **Le Caïman** (\ 33 948 3140; **m** 77 638 2841; **e** contact@hotel-caiman-senegal.com; www.hotel-caiman-senegal.com) is on the main road on the north side of town and offers comfortable en-suite accommodation. Both hotels can arrange all excursions, though Le Caïman's clientele is mostly hunters & fishermen. **Le Cailcedrat** (**m** 77 430 4685; ⊕ 08.00–23.00 daily), named after the enormous *Khaya senegalensis* out front, is the place to go for a bite or a beer.

TOUBACOUTA

Taking full advantage of the happy coincidence of being both among the easiest of access of communities in the delta and the most pleasant, the chronically sleepy Mandinka village of Toubacouta is probably the biggest tourist centre in the delta (which still isn't saying much), and far from being spoiled by it, still putts along at its own languid pace. One of a number of Senegalese towns with dangerously similar names, Toubacouta is not to be confused with the dusty eastern capital of Tambacounda; they're several hundred kilometres and several worlds apart.

Indeed, Toubacouta is little more than a clutch of dirt roads and twisting footpaths sandwiched between the RN5 and the Saloum River. There are two turnoffs into town – the northern one leads west down a largely residential street until it hits the river, while the southern one (at the Total filling station) follows the main drag past dozens of tiny shops and restaurants until it hits the hotels and riverside at the end. The facilities here are excellent and cater to all budgets, and it's a great spot from which to explore the delta, whether you just want to dip a toe or two into the bioluminescent water, hook a barracuda, or hop in a kayak or pirogue for an expedition to little-visited traditional villages and age-old deserted islands offshore.

GETTING THERE AND AWAY Approaching by land, Toubacouta sits along the surfaced RN5 between the Gambian border at Karang, 23km to the south, and Kaolack, some 65km northeast. Regular *sept-places* ply the route between Kaolack and Karang for 2,500F, and these will drop you in Toubacouta on request. From Kaolack you'll be charged the full fare, but only a portion if you're headed north from Karang. Getting out of town can be a bit trickier, though, as there's no *gare routière* in the village. Stand by the road and hop on whatever's going. If you're not quite satisfied with that arrangement, all hotels can rustle up a car for you.

By water, **pirogue transfers** can be arranged to and from all corners of the delta, but they don't come especially cheap. Expect to pay about 70,000F for a boat transfer between here and Palmarin with up to seven passengers, which is a gorgeous excursion in and of itself – if you do go this way, negotiate a few stops (ie: Dionewar, Pointe de Sangomar) and some grilled fish with the skipper and make a day out of it. All of the hotels here can arrange this for you.

GETTING AROUND A *jakarta* or *calèche* are pretty much your only two options besides the ones at the ends of your legs to get across town, and neither should cost you more than a few hundred CFA to do so.

WHERE TO STAY, EAT AND DRINK All hotels listed below offer Wi-Fi except Keur Youssou, though it may be on the way here as well.

Les Palétuviers (See ad, 2nd colour section) (34 rooms) \33 948 7776; m 77 639 2630; e info@ paletuviers.com; www.paletuviers.com. The most luxurious spot in town, this resort has a long history in Toubacouta but would be almost unrecognisable to anyone who stayed here in years past. The last few years have seen aggressive & impressive updates here, today it's a superbly stylish retreat, & thankfully altogether lacking in the pretension that often plagues such resorts. Rooms are chic & airy, with canopy beds, nets, AC, modern en-suite ablutions, wood floors & contemporary décor. Their private dock stretches almost 200m into the river, & boat trips to Sipo Island, the shell islands & around the delta run daily. They've also got a fabulously isolated campement on Djinack Island, which is only bookable as an excursion for Paletuviers guests. You, accompanied by a personal chef, spend 2 days in complete solitude in a private beachside bungalow on the island – truly one of the delta's most indulgent experiences. **$$$$**

Club de Vacances Kairaba (21 rooms) \33 948 7770; m 77 687 2939/718 1095; e commerciale@clubdevacanceskairaba.com; www.clubdevacanceskairaba.blogspot.com. In the bush adjacent to Soukouta village, this well-equipped resort is about a kilometre north of central Toubacouta & feels considerably more isolated from the goings-on of the village than the other hotels in town. There's a nice pool & restaurant, & the bungalows here have the trimmings you'd expect – AC, nets, reading lamps, writing desk, TV, etc – but it all feels a bit characterless & seems a better choice for groups than individual travellers. Prices are at the bottom end of this range. **$$$**

Keur Saloum (54 rooms) \33 948 7715; e keursaloum@orange.sn; www.keursaloum. com. With a troupe of tortoises as the welcoming committee, this spacious & well-manicured riverside resort has been a Toubacouta institution for over 40 years now, & its Belgian managers ensure it wears that age with an admirable charm & grace. The side-by-side pool & restaurant are eminently attractive, their private dock cuts deep into the mangroves, & they've got one of the best selections of activities in town; excursions on land & water are easily arranged using their mountain bikes, 4x4s or fleet of 14 pirogues. The bungalows are recently renovated & come with AC & all the modcons, & low season prices scrape the very bottom of this price range. **$$$**

🏠 **Africa Strike** (6 rooms) 📞33 948 7740; m 77 575 6651; e yayakikia@hotmail.fr; www. africastrike.com. Fisherfolk arriving in Toubacouta ought to cast their lines here straight away, & even though fishing seems to be first priority, it's a pleasant enough option for guests whose interests lie above water as well. The en-suite rooms are clean, high-ceilinged & cool, though the décor feels a bit behind the times, & the sleepy bar-resto by the swimming pool offers a good assortment of meals & drinks. **$$**

🏠 **Keur Billy Teranga** (2 rooms) m 77 409 0533/228 8521; e billy16@live.fr or vernaillenlydie@ hotmail.com; www.facebook.com/teranga.bily. With just a couple of rooms in front of their bright blue swimming pool, this low-key place a few minutes' walk from the centre of the village is simple, clean & good value for money. Rooms are big, bright & airy, with canopy beds, fans, nets & writing desk. There are a couple of gazebos under which to lounge. All kinds of trips in the delta can be arranged, & meals are available by request. **$$**

🏠 **Keur Thierry** (5 rooms) m 77 439 8605/015 1155; e thierrytillieu@orange.sn; www.keurthierry. com. In a green, seashell-strewn compound near the town centre, this friendly place has quad bikes for hire along with all the usual fishing & nautical excursions. Rooms are en-suite & come with fans, nets, TV & hot water; prices are at the low end of this range & it's quite good value. AC is an option for 2,500F more per room, & the popular restaurant-bar here specialises in grills. **$$**

🏠 **Keur Youssou** (6 rooms) 📞33 948 7728; m 77 634 5905; e keuryoussou@yahoo.fr; www.keuryoussou.com or www.facebook.com/ campement. In a family compound near the village centre, the en-suite rooms here are basic but kept impressively tidy & are really quite difficult to beat for the price. They sleep 2–5 & all come with mozzie nets. The ladies of the house can whip up Senegalese favourites, & they arrange the usual set of excursions & activities. No Wi-Fi. **$**

✖ **Chez Ass Senghor** m 77 652 0960/133 6152; www.ass-senghor-campement-toubacouta. blogspot.com; ⏰ 10.00–23.00 daily. In an unmissable yellow building (with an unmissable name) in the village centre, this low-key standby serves good meat & fish dishes for around 3,000F, as well as *chawarmas* & sandwiches for less. There are a few bungalows around the back for hire, & they've theoretically got Wi-Fi as well.

Near Toubacouta

🏠 **Keur Bamboung** (7 rooms) Île Sipo; m 77 510 80 13; e ckbamboung@gmail.com; www.keurbamboung.wordpress.com or www. oceaniumdakar.org. Magnificently isolated on the far side of Île Sipo, this community campement is run by island residents & operates in partnership with Oceanium in Dakar. The sizeable mud & thatch rooms are slung along the edge of the *bolong* (creek), completely bereft of frills, & sleep 2–6. They do all have mozzie nets, private ablutions, open-air showers & solar lanterns for light. Family-style meals are taken in the central meeting space, & a pirogue trip from here into the islanders' community reserve, the 6,800ha *L'aire marine protégée Bamboung*, where all fishing, oyster harvesting & firewood gathering are strictly verboten, is an absolute must. For a glimpse of the delta at its purest, this place is hard to beat. Prices include all meals (HB/FB) & activities, & are towards the bottom of this range. **$$$**

OTHER PRACTICALITIES The nearest bank is in Kaolack. The upmarket hotels typically take cards, but it's still safest to bring cash. The village is home to a health post and **pharmacy** (📞 *33 945 8769*) should you need some basic medicines. Almost all of the lodging offers Wi-Fi.

WHAT TO SEE AND DO Much like in the other towns of the delta, Toubacouta serves primarily as a jumping-off point for **pirogue** or **kayak trips** around the myriad creeks and islands. It's among the easiest places to make arrangements for trips anywhere in the estuary, and it's a quick jaunt to the **Île aux Coquillages**, where baobabs grow directly out of the millions of oyster shells that form the island, **Île aux Oiseaux**, where up to 40,000 pairs of royal terns have been known to nest, or the traditional fishing village on **Île Sipo** (also home to Keur Bamboung, see page 190). Plage d'Or on Djinack island, the villages of Niodior and Dionewar, and dozens of other specks of land hidden deep within the mangrove forests are all also accessible. All of the hotels here offer both standard itineraries and customisable trips tailored to your interests, and birdwatchers will have a field day in Toubacouta. The waters off of the village are one of the best places in the delta to see and experience **bioluminescence**, the milky glow aroused in marine plankton, known as dinoflagellates, when they're disturbed. Take a dip by night to see the surreal, swirling, sparkling trails of light that follow each of your limbs through the water, and soak up the meditative stillness of nighttime in the delta.

Back on land, Toubacouta is home to a new **village artisanal centre** and **cultural centre** facing each other along the main road through town. Both were still in the process of opening when we visited, so have a look to see if they've kicked off yet. Otherwise, there are plenty of **craft sellers** lining the streets of the village centre near Les Palétuviers and Keur Saloum (some of these may migrate to the **new market** near the entrance to town when it eventually opens, but probably not all). *Calèche* trips to neighbouring settlements or Toubacouta village tours are also easily arranged.

MISSIRAH

Most often visited as a side trip from Toubacouta, Missirah village, home to a couple of thousand Serer and Mandinka farmers and fisherfolk, sits in a spectacular corner of the delta, right up against the bolong about 12 km south of Toubacouta. The shoreline here is lined with thousands upon thousands of discarded shells, dozens upon dozens of pirogues, and a wide field of fish smoking and drying racks at the base of a long pier sprawling 250m out into the bolong. Stretching about a kilometre inland, the village itself is a workaday collection of homes and shops, but its central tree, a magnificently gnarled and unthinkably old *fromager*, whose drooping wizard's-sleeve branches and buttressed roots splay out regally in all directions, is a sight to behold.

Like Toubacouta to the north, Missirah is a great place to launch boat trips out into the delta, and the nature lovers at Campement Fannabara can set them up for you with ease.

GETTING THERE AND AWAY There's precious little transport that comes this way, but you've got the best chance of getting a lift here from Toubacouta, where vehicles wait near the big *fromager* tree. No more than a couple of *taxis brousses* trundle back and forth between the two each day, so if you don't manage to catch one (or just don't feel like waiting) you can hire a car for about 5,000F each way, less on a *djakarta*.

🏠 WHERE TO STAY, EAT AND DRINK

🏠 **Campement Fannabara** (5 rooms) **m** 77 537 2230; **e** fannabara@gmail.com; www.fannabara.blogspot.com. Set about 1km north of Missirah in Caltoupoto, this eco-friendly campement is run by former rangers at the national park, so they're deeply invested in environmental protection & know the lay of the land around here like the backs of their hands. Rooms are set in a row of simple en-suite bungalows, & it's a great place to arrange visits to all corners of the national park & its surrounding villages & islands (see their website for details on their various excursions). Rates in the bottom half of this range. **$$**

FATHALA RESERVE

Once a rather unremarkable forest reserve, an enclosure was built here in 2006 to accept translocations of the critically endangered western giant eland, and since that time the forest here has been developed into a full-fledged wildlife reserve and tourist attraction. The reserve itself consists of 6,000ha of densely wooded Sudano-Guinean savannah, and a 2,000ha fenced area at the core of the reserve where the animals reside. As the reserve matures, plans exist to eventually fence the remaining 4,000ha, but this is probably some way off.

The lion walks here are rapidly becoming a fixture on the Senegalese tourist trail, and while they're undoubtedly exhilarating and sure to get your heart pumping one way or the other, the domesticity of the lions isn't everyone's cup of tea. In the main reserve (the lions have a separate enclosure), you'll find southern and eastern African transplants like zebra, giraffe and rhino as well as local antelopes and primates. Fathala Reserve is considerably easier to access than Niokolo-Koba National Park and, if your primary goal is to spend a day seeing some animals rather than to have a wilderness expedition, you'll have a considerably more satisfying visit here than you would at the national park out east. Fathala seems to have struck a healthy balance – it's small enough that game sightings are quite reliable (though not guaranteed), but large enough and wild enough that it never feels like a drive-in zoo.

GETTING THERE AND AWAY On the RN5 between Toubacouta and the Gambian border at Karang, the Fathala Reserve is easily accessed by any transport headed between Kaolack and the Gambia. The welcome centre and lion enclosure are both just off the main road, while the accommodation is several kilometres into the reserve and accessible by a free transfer for guests.

WHERE TO STAY, EAT AND DRINK

Fathala Wildlife Reserve (20 rooms) m 77 840 1420/70 590 2430; e reception@ fathala.com; www.fathala.com. This glowing new place, a down-to-the-studs replica of a South African tented camp, is the only accommodation within the reserve & will feel very familiar to anyone who's spent time in the national parks of southern & eastern Africa. One-of-a-kind in Senegal, it offers a luxury tented safari experience, common on the other side of the continent but almost entirely absent here in the west. Granted, Fathala Reserve is no Kruger National Park, but the facilities here are top-notch & a visit here would rightly rank among the highlights of any trip to Senegal. The standing tents sit on platforms overlooking a seasonal waterhole where the animals come to drink. The tents themselves are spectacularly appointed, & come with dual sinks, bathtub, dual outdoor shower, AC, canopy bed, mozzie nets, reading lamps, hardwood floors, safe, hairdryer, coffee/tea facilities & private terrace. There's a pool overlooking the waterhole & an impressive tree-root chandelier at the open-air lounge & restaurant.

WHAT TO SEE AND DO The game drives here manage to feel remarkably remote, despite the fact that the whole reserve is within 10km of the RN5, and they're unquestionably the most reliable game-viewing experience in Senegal, if not the most authentic (a number of species here are non-native introductions). Though their rhino, giraffe, buffalo, and zebras might steal the show, the real rarity here is the critically endangered western giant eland (*Taurotragus derbianus derbianus*). Also known as the Derby eland, it's the largest antelope on earth, weighing up to 1,000kg and standing nearly 2m high. Its coat is striated with narrow white bands, its enormous furry dewlap swings freely under its chin, its intimidating spiral horns can themselves be over a metre long, and there are fewer than 200 of them anywhere in the world – this is one of a *very* small handful of places you can see them in a semi-wild habitat. You're also sure to encounter more common antelope like red-flanked duiker (*Cephalophus rufilatus*), bohor reedbuck (*Redunca redunca*), roan antelope (*Hippotragus equinus*) and waterbuck (*Kobus ellipsiprymnus*), along with primates like Temminck's red colobus (*Procolobus badius temminckii*) and the pig family's most iconic member, *Phacochoerus africanus*, better known as the common warthog.

The **lion walks** take place in a separate enclosure, where you stroll through the bush with walking sticks, and the guides have a nice bit of donkey meat on a spike. The lions here aren't from the wild, but have been bred in South Africa, and as such haven't had the wilderness experience necessary to recognise prey in the same way as a wild lion would; regardless, the meat keeps their attention a lot better than you and your camera do. The walk has plenty of time for photo ops and even a chance to pet the lions. Some have criticised the walks as rather exploitative and zoo-like, and that's a decision you'll have to make on your own, but the rangers are professional, the lions are well cared for, and it's an undoubtedly thrilling experience to be in their company.

Whether or not you stay at the lodge, the game drives and lion walks are open to all (not quite all, actually – for the lion walks you *must* be at least 1.5m tall). A two-hour game drive with guide will run you €27/30pp in your/their vehicle, and there are two departures a day, at 11.00 and 14.00, if you want to go in theirs. Lion walks are €39pp, last about 45 minutes, and run throughout the day at the top of every hour. It's very possible to do both in an afternoon, and the combo package goes for €59/62 in your/their vehicle.

A wider range of activities is on offer for lodge guests. The lion walks are the same as far as duration and cost, but game drives (€40, their vehicle) operate on a different schedule, are an hour longer, and include snacks and drinks. The game drive and lion walk combo costs €71. Guests can also take a boat trip for sundowners in the mangroves (€35), walking and birding safaris (€20), boat trips to Djinack with a village tour (€70), and there should be massages and other spa treatments available soon.

DJINACK

Home to a stunning crescent stretch of beach, this barrier island is about 12km long and primarily Gambian territory, but the northern kilometre or so falls north of the border in Senegal, and the villages of Djinack Bara and Djinack Diatako are both on the Senegalese side of the line. All accommodation, with the exception of Les Palétuviers' exclusive beach campement on the Plage d'Or (see page 189), is in either of the two Gambian villages, Jinack Kajata and Jinack Niji, and while there are no controls between the two sides of the island, it would be worth keeping this in mind if you intend to do some exploring. Any *piroguier* will take you out here, but it's a bit of a hike from most of the jumping-off points within Senegal, so prepare to pay for it.

SENEGAL ONLINE

For additional online content, articles, photos and more on Senegal, why not visit www.bradtguides.com/senegal.

7

Saint-Louis and Surrounds

SAINT-LOUIS

Dripping with balconies and bougainvillea, the stately ochre homes and warehouses of old Saint-Louis, with their toothless wooden shutters and Marseillaise clay roof tiles, are the steadfast and picturesque guardians of one of the most intensely atmospheric and densely historied places in all of West Africa. Known as Ndar in Wolof, the tiny city-island sits protected by the Langue de Barbarie peninsula to the west and lapped on either side by the calm waters of the Senegal River as they make their final approach to the Atlantic.

As the crossroads of Senegal's north, the population here is as diverse as the history, and the island's grid of sandblown streets are home to Wolof merchants in perfectly starched *boubous* and Moroccan slippers, Mauritanian shopkeepers forever adjusting their impossibly large blue robes, scarified Toucouleurs proudly sporting their beauty marks, Baye Fall devotees piled high with leather *gris-gris*, and the island's *indigènes*, the mixed-race descendants of the Métis *signares,* who can occasionally be spotted in their traditional flowing white gowns.

The orderly streets here radiate history, and perhaps never more visibly than in the early evening, when the thick clay walls of the city glow with the accumulated heat of the day, insulating against the cool ocean winds that whip in from the west. Doors are flung open, televisions switched on, and residents hiding from the afternoon sun once again dare to come out on to the streets and take their evening promenade, making the rounds from family to family, tending friendships that trace their roots not only to childhood, but sometimes two, three and even more generations back amongst the old families of the island. Listen out for drums – it's not uncommon for a family to simply close off one of the back streets in front of their home to celebrate a wedding or other event with an impromptu street party and – naturally – a band.

Saint-Louis is in many ways the feather in Senegal's cap, and a startlingly lucid window into the long and difficult history of this rapidly modernising country, where traces of the past can and do disappear by the day. Any visitor who doesn't make the trip up here is missing out not only on one of Senegal's most fascinating destinations, but on a chance to physically and intellectually engage with the places and events that have shaped the Senegal of today.

HISTORY The mouth of the Senegal River had been frequented by Portuguese traders since the 15th century, but was never settled by Europeans. It wasn't until 1638 that a number of French slave traders, including the navigator Thomas Lambert, built a small outpost on Bocos Island; 21 years later in 1659, after flooding made operations on Bocos Island untenable, Louis Caullier, a Norman trader with the Compagnie du Cap Vert, erected the first permanent buildings on the previously uninhabited Ndar Island, ceded to the French by Djambar Diop (also known as Jeanne Barre), son of the *brak* (king) of Waalo. It was renamed after the reigning French monarch, Louis XIV, a little while later.

Early on, the settlement was managed by the various mercantile companies based here trading in slaves and gum arabic sourced from the hinterlands, and they forbade European workers from bringing their families to the settlement, thus setting the stage for the growing class of free Métis *signares* who would eventually come to be a powerful social and economic force on the island. The settlement continued to grow, inhabited by slaves, traders, sailors and a number of free Africans who had moved over from Gandiol. But like Gorée and as with other colonial possessions in West Africa, Saint-Louis was subject to the territorial ambitions of competing European powers, and in 1758 the island fell to the British who occupied it for more than 20 years, eventually being forced out during the American Revolution. The French took direct control (rather than through their commercial representatives) in 1779. The insult was not forgotten, however, and the British returned to occupy Saint-Louis during the Napoleonic Wars, from 1809 to 1817.

In 1848, Saint-Louis and Gorée became the first two of what would eventually become the four Senegalese *communes*, cities in which the African residents theoretically enjoyed equal rights as Europeans and were recognised as full French citizens. In practice this was often far from the case, but 1848 also saw all slaves in the city given their freedom, which by some estimates represented a staggering 75% of the island's population at emancipation. Saint-Louis remained on the ascendant through the mid-to-late 1800s, and many of the historic homes and landmarks seen on the island today were constructed in this period. However, the coming decades and the growing importance of the groundnut trade further south, along with the

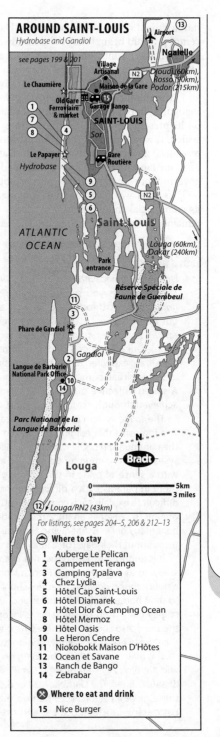

AROUND SAINT-LOUIS
Hydrobase and Gandiol

see pages 199 & 201

For listings, see pages 204–5, 206 & 212–13

🛏 **Where to stay**
1 Auberge Le Pelican
2 Campement Teranga
3 Camping 7palava
4 Chez Lydia
5 Hôtel Cap Saint-Louis
6 Hôtel Diamarek
7 Hôtel Dior & Camping Ocean
8 Hôtel Mermoz
9 Hôtel Oasis
10 Le Heron Cendre
11 Niokobokk Maison D'Hôtes
12 Ocean et Savane
13 Ranch de Bango
14 Zebrabar

✖ **Where to eat and drink**
15 Nice Burger

development of the superior ports at Dakar and Rufisque towards the end of the century, would begin to lay the groundwork for the city's slow decline.

The Dakar–Saint-Louis railway reached here in 1885, but by 1902 the decision was made to move the capital of French West Africa from here to Dakar, though Saint-Louis remained the administrative capital for the territories of Senegal and Mauritania. The real *coup de grâce* for Saint-Louis came in 1923, at the inauguration of the rail line linking Dakar and Bamako, when Dakar began to take on its present-day importance in earnest and Saint-Louis's fate as an also-ran was sealed. It would remain the administrative capital of Senegal until 1958 when the territorial government also moved to Dakar in preparation for independence, and of Mauritania until their own independence in 1960, when their newly formed government was seated in the purpose-built capital, Nouakchott.

Thus what was once the most important city in French West Africa, stripped of its commercial and administrative duties, became little more than a backwater, and remained so for the next 40 years. The relative lack of investment in the city meant,

SENEGAL'S STREET CHILDREN

Hadiel Mohamed with Hattie Hill and Timothy Van Vliet

The little boys you see begging on streets and shaking old vegetable tins in *gares routières* throughout Senegal aren't simply orphans or poverty-stricken, but rather students sent away by their families to receive a religious education. Known as *Talibés*, from the Arabic word for student, they study the Quran at a *daara* (Quranic school) under a *marabout* (Quranic teacher), and many, though not all, are expected to pay their way through begging. Their religious education is a long spiritual journey led by their *marabout*, who acts as their *de facto* guardian. A stated objective of the *talibés'* spiritual journey is to acquire humility; this is achieved through extensive begging.

The *talibé* system in Senegal is deeply rooted within the religion and culture. The intensive rôle religion has within the country's politics is a leading factor in the continuation of the current practice you see today. When discussing the *talibé* system, it is common for Senegalese adults to reminisce on their own *talibé* days with a sense of pride in the suffering they endured, believing Allah will reward them in paradise. It's a difficult concept to grasp as an outsider and even more difficult to explain each complex facet. As one of the five pillars of Islam, the giving of alms, or *zakat*, is an important tradition in Senegal, often practised daily, and here many believe that giving alms early in the morning will help ensure calmness throughout their day. Thus, *talibés* serve as an opportunity to deliver these alms.

It is important to note that not all *talibés* will beg on the streets. Some children studying at a government/French-language school will study the Quran at their neighborhood *daara* as an after-school religious education. These *talibés* will return to their home after their studies and will not be forced to beg. This opportunity is largely influenced by the family's income. Girls can also study the Quran and are therefore also considered *talibés*. It's considered improper for a girl *talibé* to beg on the streets, however, acknowledging the potentially greater risk to their safety.

The *talibés* you will see begging on the streets are roughly five to 14 years old, and are typically sent by their families into Senegal's urban centres from Guinea-Bissau, Guinea, The Gambia, Mali or distant Senegalese regions. Once in the cities, these *talibés* are forced to beg on the streets for a combination of money and basic staples including sugar and rice, commonly having strictly enforced daily however, that much of the colonial architecture remained intact, albeit often dilapidated, as there was little means or appetite to modify it to any great extent. This was the situation in the year 2000, when the old city was recognised as a UNESCO World Heritage Site. Since then, efforts to safeguard and restore the physical and cultural history of the island have gathered pace, and today the city is a compelling architectural hodgepodge of the restored and ruinous, with ranks of the former category happily growing by the day.

GETTING THERE AND AWAY

By car The RN2 in either direction from here is surfaced and in good shape, and it's about a four-hour journey from Dakar. The road to Gandiol is unpaved for part of the way, but it's approachable in a 2WD, including the alternate route between Saint-Louis and Louga via Gandiol, Potou and Leona.

By bus and *sept-place* The main *gare routière* is in Sor, about 5km south of Saint-Louis island on the west side of the RN2. There are regular *sept-places* to Dakar

quotas. Human Rights Watch has condemned the practice as an example of human trafficking, and indeed the personal enrichment of *marabouts* on the back of forced *talibé* labour is widespread and acknowledged, though punishments or prosecutions are fleetingly rare. These trafficked *talibés*, of which there are an estimated 50,000 in Senegal, will also sleep at the *daara* in a small room normally severely overcrowded with *talibés*. These sleeping arrangements lead to the spread of contagious diseases, ringworm, malaria, common colds, staph infections and other preventable ailments.

The *talibé* situation is undoubtedly heartbreaking; it is difficult to know our place as outsiders. During your time in Senegal, don't forget that these ragged *talibés* persistently asking you for money are **children**. They are young children who, through no choice of their own, have been sent away and entrusted to the religious leader to receive a prideful religious education.

When encountering *talibés*, follow the respectful Senegalese tradition of shaking one's hand, and engage in a conversation with them (you don't have to speak the same language to make a child laugh). When buying fruit or shopping at a boutique, give the vendor an extra 500F and ask him to give *talibés* fruit or a treat; the distribution will be less chaotic if the Senegalese is delivering the items. Be mindful that giving the *talibés* money doesn't address the problem, but you can still have a positive impact on these children's lives by respecting them.

If you'd like to have a more hands-on experience with the children, get involved with local NGOs. There are organisations in Dakar, Saint-Louis and most other major cities that provide assistance to talibés. The **Empire des Enfants** (*www.empiredesenfants.com*) in Dakar provides *talibés* with a diverse range of services including psychological and medical care, technical skills classes and a safe environment for the children to play. **Maison de la Gare** (*www.mdgsl. com*) in Saint-Louis has been assisting *talibés* since 2007 and offers the children medical care and French classes, and has a dormitory to house runaway children discovered during their frequent night rounds.

As mentioned previously, the *talibé* system is multifaceted and problematic, but remains a deeply significant institution in Senegalese society; if you'd like to learn more, please visit www.talibes.org.

throughout the day for 5,000F, or to Thiès for 3,500F; while heading east, vehicles go regularly to Rosso and Richard Toll for 2,200F. Further along the northern route, it's possible to get a *sept-place* to either Podor (4,000F) or even as far as Ourossogui (9,500F), but aim for an early start, as these aren't nearly as common.

By air There is an airport some 7km northeast of town towards Bango, but there were no scheduled flights here at the time of writing.

By boat The undisputed *grande dame* of the Senegal River, the 52m *Bou el Mogdad*, was for decades a lifeline for communities as far upriver as Matam until its 40-odd years of service came to a halt in the 1980s. Road transport in the river region has since rendered these once-remote communities more accessible than ever, but more than 20 years after its premature retirement, the *Bou el Mogdad* was bought and returned to the river by the Saint-Louis family behind Sahel Découverte and La Résidence. Today it plies the waters between Senegal and Mauritania once more, this time as a tourist boat, connecting Saint-Louis and Podor on what is without question Senegal's quintessential boat journey.

It makes the run between Saint-Louis and Podor every two weeks from October to May. The week-long cruises start at €910/1,460 for a single/double cabin all-inclusive, and you can embark in Saint-Louis, Podor or any of the stops in between, including Djoudj, Richard Toll, Dagana and others. Bookings are possible through Sahel Découverte (see page 37) or www.compagniedufleuve.com.

ORIENTATION The centre of all tourist activity is the rectangular Saint-Louis Island, which is contiguous with the original colonial city. To the west, the Langue de Barbarie peninsula is connected to Saint-Louis Island by a short bridge, and is home to the fishing villages of Guet Ndar and Ndar Toute, and the resort area known as the Hydrobase a few kilometres to the south. On a tidal island east of the colonial city across the Faidherbe Bridge is the bustling modern quarter of Saint-Louis known as Sor, which is primarily of interest to travellers as the site of the *gare routière*.

GETTING AROUND Saint-Louis is probably the most walkable city in Senegal, but it's still worth knowing that all taxis charge a fixed rate of 500F by day and 600F by night, so there's no need to bargain. A taxi from the *gare routière* to the island should be 600F, and a ride to the Hydrobase from anywhere in town should be 1,500F.

TOURIST INFORMATION AND TOUR OPERATORS With pride of place at the entrance to the island, the **Syndicat d'Initiative** [201 C2] (❧ *33 961 2455;* m *77 572 1353;* e *stltourisme@orange.sn; www.saintlouisdusenegal-tourisme.com;* ☉ *09.00–13.00 & 15.00–18.30 Mon–Fri, 09.00–13.00 & 15.00–18.00 Sat, 09.30–17.30 Sun)* is efficiently run and a worthwhile stop whether you'd like to arrange a trip to the nearby national parks, a tour around the island, or simply to get some literature or a map of the city (though these are likely to be on the outdated side).

There is also a handful of tour operators based in town, and they can arrange trips to the Langue de Barbarie or Djoudj National Park, city tours, canoe trips, 4x4 excursions, car hire and more. **Sahel Découverte** [201 C1] (*Rue Blaise Diagne;* ❧ *33 961 5689;* e *jeanjacques@saheldecouverte.com; www.saheldecouverte.com)* is the best-known of the bunch, and in addition to all of the above, this is also the place to get your tickets for the *Bou el Mogdad*. **Senegalib'Tours** (*Rue Khalifa Ababacar Sy;* ❧ *33 961 0103;* m *77 556 6322;* e *contact@senegalibtours.sn; www. senegal-lib-tour.sn)* offers a similar range of services.

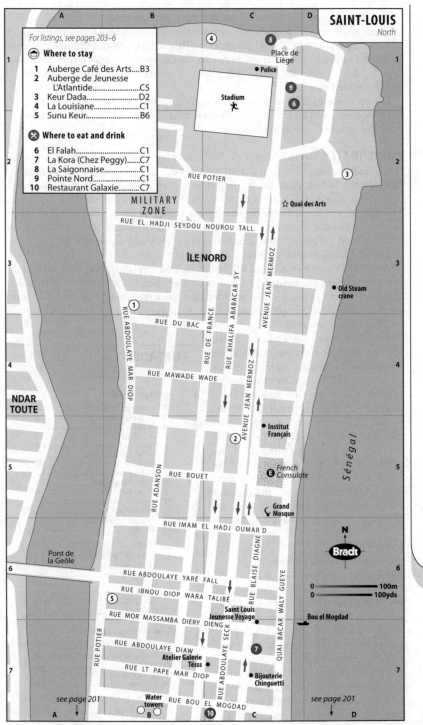

SAINT-LOUIS
North

For listings, see pages 203–6

⌂ **Where to stay**

1 Auberge Café des Arts....B3
2 Auberge de Jeunesse
    L'Atlantide........................C5
3 Keur Dada...........................D2
4 La Louisiane......................C1
5 Sunu Keur..........................B6

✕ **Where to eat and drink**

6 El Falah................................C1
7 La Kora (Chez Peggy).......C7
8 La Saigonnaise...................C1
9 Pointe Nord........................C1
10 Restaurant Galaxie..........C7

Place de Liège
● Police
Stadium 🏃

RUE POTIER

MILITARY ZONE
☆ Quai des Arts
RUE EL HADJI SEYDOU NOUROU TALL

ÎLE NORD

● Old Steam crane

RUE DU BAC

RUE ABDOULAYE MAR DIOP
RUE DE FRANCE
RUE KHALIFA ABABACAR SY
AVENUE JEAN MERMOZ

NDAR TOUTE

RUE MAWADE WADE

AVENUE JEAN MERMOZ

● Institut Français

RUE ADANSON
RUE BOUET

E French Consulate

Sénégal

☪ Grand Mosque

RUE IMAM EL HADJ OUMAR D

Pont de la Geôle

RUE ABDOULAYE YARÉ FALL
RUE IBNOU DIOP WARA TALIBÉ

RUE BLAISE DIAGNE

N
Bradt

0 ———— 100m
0 ———— 100yds

RUE MOR MASSAMBA DIERY DIENG
Saint Louis Jeunesse Voyage ●

QUAI BACAR WALY GUEYE
Bou el Mogdad ⚓

RUE POTIER
RUE ABDOULAYE DIAW

RUE ABDOULAYE SECK

Atelier Galerie Tësss ●

7

RUE LT PAPE MAR DIOP

● Bijouterie Chinguetti

Water towers ○ ○ RUE BOU EL MOGDAD

see page 201
see page 201

7

Smaller operations include **Saint-Louis Découverte** (m *77 572 1837*; e *saintlouisdecouverte@yahoo.fr; www.saintlouisdecouverte.blogspot.com*), which is owner-operated by the English-speaking Pape Dieye and can arrange day tours in Saint-Louis or custom trips anywhere in the country, and **Djiby Tourisme** (m *77 535 1546*; e *mbayes60@yahoo.fr; www.djiby-tourisme.com*) comes recommended as well.

For **up-to-date info**, www.saintlouisdusenegal.com is a good resource for further tourist information and history, while www.ndarinfo.com covers all the latest news from the city; both are in French.

WHERE TO STAY On the Langue de Barbarie a few kilometres south of town, the **Hydrobase** was once home to a landing strip for Jean Mermoz and the pilots of the Aéropostale. While today the landing strip is long gone and you won't see much being built here as the island's very existence is threatened by erosion (see pages 211–12), it's still home to the frenetic fishing village of Guet Ndar, where the day's rhythm is dictated by the hauling in of the nets and sorting of the catch – some of it destined for plates a few hundred metres away and some of it heaped on to lorries and trucked hundreds of kilometres inland. Heading south from here, the pirogues start to peter out and a kilometres-long stretch of gorgeous sand, pine and palms opens up, fronted by a row of low-key beachside hotels. So if your aim is indeed to hit the beach rather than wander the streets, the Hydrobase has some good accommodation options, none more than 4km from the city, so it's equally possible to base yourself here and make forays into town as you wish. The hotels here are often booked out in blocks for Senegalese corporate retreats in the off-season, but they're so close to one another you won't end up stranded if you show up and they're full. *Car rapides* trundle back and forth to the Hydrobase *carrefour* (near Le Papayer) throughout the day for a few hundred CFA per person, while a taxi ride to any of the hotels here shouldn't cost much more than 1,500F, though expect to be quoted wildly inflated prices to start with. See pages 204–5 for Hydrobase listings.

Saint-Louis

All hotels listed for **Saint-Louis** have Wi-Fi. Map, page 201, unless otherwise noted.

Fil du Fleuve (3 rooms) Rue El Hadj Malick Sy; m 77 379 9534; e camara.mariec@ yahoo.fr; www.fildufleuve.com. In a fabulously restored 19th-century gum Arabic warehouse once owned by a *métis* merchant, this new boutique hotel is nothing short of a gem. The 3 en-suite rooms here have AC & mozzie nets, & are each individually appointed with works by different Senegalese artists, including pieces designed by

---

SAINT-LOUIS *South*
For listings, see pages 200 & 202–6

Where to stay
1	Auberge Chehama	C2
2	Fil du Fleuve	C5
3	Hôtel de la Poste	D2
4	Hôtel du Palais	C2
5	Hôtel La Palmeraie	A7
6	Hôtel La Résidence	C1
7	Hôtel Le Ragniat	C2
8	Hôtel L'Harmattan	C2
9	Hôtel Pointe Sud	B7
10	Hôtel Sindone	C6
11	Jamm	C1
12	La Maison Rose	C1
13	Ô Sésame	C4
14	Siki Hôtel	C1

Off map (see map, page 195)
Auberge Le Pelican	A7
Chez Lydia	A7
Hôtel Cap Saint-Louis	A7
Hôtel Diamarek	A7
Hôtel Dior & Camping Ocean	A7
Hôtel Mermoz	A7
Hôtel Oasis	A7

Where to eat and drink
15	Aux Délices du Fleuve	C2
16	La Crêpe Saint-Louisienne	C3
17	La Linguère	C1
18	Le Reveil	C2
19	Patisserie La Rosa	C2

Off map (see map, page 195)
Nice Burger	D3

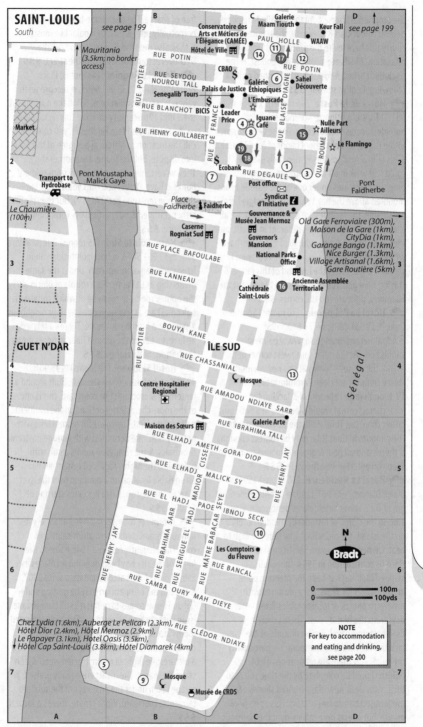

SAINT-LOUIS
South

A

Mauritania
(3.5km; no border
access)

B

Conservatoire des
Arts et Métiers de
l'Élégance (CAMÉE)
Hôtel de Ville

RUE POTIN

RUE SEYDOU
NOUROU TALL

Palais de Justice
Senegalib' Tours
RUE BLANCHOT BICIS

RUE HENRY GUILLABERT

Market

RUE POTIER

RUE DE FRANCE

CBAO $

Galérie
Éthiopiques
L'Embuscade

Leader
Price

Iguane
Café

C

Galerie
Maam Tiouth

PAUL HOLLE

14

RUE POTIN

RUE BLAISE DIAGNE

Sahel
Découverte

D

Keur Fall

WAAW

see page 199

11

17

12

6

1

15

Nulle Part
Ailleurs

Le Flamingo

QUAI ROUME

4

8

19

18

Ecobank

7

RUE DEGAULE

1

3

2

Transport to
Hydrobase

Pont Moustapha
Malick Gaye

Le Chaumière
(100m)

Place
Faidherbe Faidherbe

Caserne
Rogniat Sud

RUE PLACE BAFOULABE

RUE LANNEAU

Post office

Syndicat
d'Initiative

Gouvernance &
Musée Jean Mermoz

Governor's
Mansion

National Parks
Office

Cathédrale
Saint-Louis

Pont
Faidherbe

Old Gare Ferroviaire (300m),
Maison de la Gare (1km),
CityDia (1km),
Garange Bango (1.1km),
Nice Burger (1.3km),
Village Artisanal (1.6km),
Gare Routière (5km)

16

Ancienne Assemblée
Territoriale

3

GUET N'DAR

RUE POTIER

BOUYA KANE

ÎLE SUD

RUE CHASSANIAL

Centre Hospitalier
Regional

Maison des Sœurs

Mosque

13

RUE AMADOU NDIAYE SARR

RUE IBRAHIMA TALL

Galerie Arte

Sénégal

4

RUE ELHADJ AMETH GORA DIOP

RUE ELHADJ MADIOR MALICK SY

RUE EL HADJ PAOE SÈYE IBNOU SECK

RUE HENRY JAY

2

RUE HENRY JAY

RUE IBRAHIMA SARR

RUE SERIGUE EL HADJ

RUE MATRE BABACAR SÈYE

10

Les Comptoirs
du Fleuve

RUE BANCAL

5

6

RUE SAMBA OURY MAH DIEYE

Chez Lydia (1.6km), Auberge Le Pelican (2.3km),
Hôtel Dior (2.4km), Hôtel Mermoz (2.9km),
Le Papayer (3.1km), Hotel Oasis (3.5km),
Hôtel Cap Saint-Louis (3.8km), Hôtel Diamarek (4km)

RUE CLÉDOR NDIAYE

5

9

Mosque

Musée de CRDS

N

Bradt

0   100m
0   100yds

NOTE
For key to accommodation
and eating and drinking,
see page 200

7

Saint-Louis and Surrounds   SAINT-LOUIS

the proprietress herself. All thick-walled archways, neutral colours, art & greenery, the terraces & courtyards here invite the profoundest sorts of relaxation. Meals are available on request, & the (included) b/fast & cocktails have gained quite a following. English spoken. **$$$**

🏠 **Hôtel de la Poste** (36 rooms) \33 961 1118/48; e htlposte@orange.sn; www. hoteldelapostesaintlouis.com. At the very entrance to the island, this old school haunt of Jean Mermoz & his fellow Aéropostale airmen feels like they could still walk in off the airstrip at any minute & drop their suitcases under one of the gazelle heads mounted above the bar. While the nostalgia here is palpable, the facilities are decidedly modern; all the en-suite rooms are a bit different in layout, but they're all bright & airy, with AC, TV, & many have wrought-iron balconies as well. The courtyard is verdant, prices are at the low end of this range, & staying here gets you free access to the pool at the Flamingo, right around the corner. **$$$**

🏠 **Hôtel La Palmeraie** (30 rooms) Southern Quai; \33 961 8888; m 76 640 5598; e ndpalmeraie@orange.sn; www.palmeraie-stlouis.com. At the quiet southwest corner of the island, the en-suite rooms at this newish multi-storey complex are clean & comfortable with AC & TV, though rather ahistorical & lacking the nods to local character that would place you in Saint-Louis rather than, say, Thiès. Still, the views overlooking the pirogues in Guet Ndar may be context enough, & there's a small pool & ground-floor restaurant to keep you entertained otherwise. **$$$**

🏠 **Hôtel La Résidence** (36 rooms) 159 Rue Blaise Diagne; \33 961 1260; e hotellaresidence@gmail.com; www.hoteldelaresidence.com. Even among the clutch of historically minded hotels on the island, the old school vibe here is tough to beat. Owned by the same Saint-Louisian family since its construction in 1954, this nautically inspired building has been *the* meeting point in Saint-Louis for years, & it's plastered with timeworn photos of local notables & red letter days from the island's past. There's more here than nostalgic navel-gazing though, as the facilities are trim & contemporary – particularly the suites – & there are renovations afoot (which should be complete by the time you read this), with sleek new glass-fronted showers & modernised bathrooms to start. There's no pool on site, but guests here can swim at the Flamingo

free of charge. The restaurant-bar downstairs is perpetually busy & host to regular live music, & they also own the *Bou el Mogdad* & Sahel Découverte tour agency across the street. **$$$**

🏠 **Hôtel Le Rogniat** (48 rooms) Place Faidherbe Nord; \33 961 9595; e recerogniat@yahoo.fr; www.rogniat.com. Set in the northern of the 2 mid 19th-century *casernes* (barracks) facing each other across Place Faidherbe, you could hardly call the location or historical pedigree of this hotel into dispute, but the rooms are another story. They've certainly come a long way from soldiers' bunks & have all the mod cons you'd expect in this range (en-suite bath, AC, TV), but they're still rather cramped & not particularly compelling for the price. **$$$**

🏠 **Hôtel Pointe Sud** (15 rooms) Rue Ibrahima Sarr; \33 961 5878; e hotelpointesid@yahoo.fr; www.hotelpointesud.com. Under the same ownership as La Palmeraie a couple of blocks away, the homey rooms here (some of which come with balconies) are as well-equipped as their neighbour & perhaps a bit more intimate. There's a relaxed little resto-bar on the ground floor, & prices are at the bottom of this range. **$$$**

🏠 **Hôtel Sindone** (40 rooms) \33 961 4244/5; e hotelsindone@yahoo.fr. Built around a lantern-lit Moroccan-style courtyard, this is one of the more characterful options on the southern half of the island. The colourful rooms come with nets, TV & AC, are decorated with vintage postcards & mosaics, & the river view rooms come with balconies. The highly regarded restaurant has an enviable location on a pontoon over the river & serves meat, fish, pasta & tajines starting at 5,000F. **$$$**

🏠 **Jamm** (4 rooms) m 77 443 4765; e yves.lamour@gmail.com; www.jamm-saintlouis.com. This elegantly restored 1848 home in the heart of the city has been drawing accolades as Saint-Louis's finest accommodation since 2007, & though the competition may be getting stiffer (Fil du Fleuve comes to mind) it's still hard to take issue with such an assessment. The high-ceilinged rooms are calm & spilling over with art; all have canopy beds, AC & mozzie nets, & are connected by a picturesque flight of reconstructed wood & iron stairs & terraces. The meals are equally praised, & can be taken under the archways of the sublime terracotta courtyard. What's more, there's a Jacuzzi. **$$$**

⌂ **Keur Dada** [Map, page 199] (16 rooms) Pointe Nord; ✆33 961 4412; m 77 477 5522; e keurdada@gmail.com; www.keurdada.com. Tucked away near the northwest corner of the island, the building here is new but it's built in a classic style with wood & metal accents & earth-toned walls, opening on to a wide river terrace home to the 2 swimming pools & waterfront restaurant. Opened in 2010 & done up in jazz motifs (rooms bear the names of luminaries from Fats Waller to Fela Kuti), the rooms here are spacious, & all come with flatscreen TV, minibar, safe, nets, AC & rainfall showers. They've got a boat & can arrange excursions as well. $$$

⌂ **La Maison Rose** 40 Rue Potin; ✆33 938 2222; e lamaisonrose@orange.sn; www.lamaisonrose.net. In a restored colonial home with a colour befitting the name, this is a comfortable mid-range option with a teeming courtyard garden & a rooftop terrace restaurant boasting excellent views over the river. The décor is tasteful, with wooden furnishings & typically colourful African accent pieces; all rooms are en suite with AC & TV but they're not all created equal – some are a bit lacking in natural light – so ask to see a few before you decide. They've got spa treatments & their suites are spacious & well appointed, but they'll also bump you up into the next price category. $$$

⌂ **Siki Hotel** (8 rooms) Rue Abdulaye Seck; ✆33 961 6069; m 77 529 9684; e info@sikihotel.com; www.sikihotel.com. Set in the former home of Battling Siki, the flamboyant 1920s Senegalese boxing champ with a Jack Johnson-esque flair for the extravagant, this place has been meticulously restored with a style & finesse that would be certain to appease its past owner. Rooms are chic & thoroughly modern, with balconies, hardwood floors, whitewashed walls, & designer wood & wax print accessories. It's Spanish-owned, & the phenomenal tapas bar downstairs is proof. Excellent value. $$$

⌂ **Auberge Chehama** (7 rooms) ✆30 100 6716; e auberge-chehama@hotmail.com. Next to Hôtel de la Poste, this simple Mauritanian-run place is clean & functional, though rooms (both fan & AC) are a bit on the dark side & not quite as cheap as you'd expect them to be. There's a simple restaurant on the roof that whips up a Senegalese *plat du jour* for 1,500F, though. $$

⌂ **Hôtel du Palais** (9 rooms) ✆33 961 1772; e robert.dupas@orange.sn; www.hoteldupalais.

net. Though it looks like it hasn't had a refresher for awhile, the high-ceilinged rooms here are a reliable budget option, & all are en-suite with bed nets & either fan or AC. There's a bar & their own patisserie on site, & prices for ground-floor rooms are towards the bottom of this range. $$

⌂ **Hôtel L'Harmattan** (6 rooms) Rue Guillabert ✆33 961 8253; e philip1155@hotmail.com; www.hotelharmattan.com. If your old aunt Agnes spent 40 years in the merchant marine then decided to open a hotel & bar, it might look something like this. The restaurant-bar downstairs is all dark wood & cigarette smoke, with ship's wheels & stallion portraits on the walls, while upstairs in the rooms it's an uncanny Golden Girls-meets-Senegal scene, with rattan peacock chairs jostling for space with cow horns & frilly lampshades. Rooms are all en suite with either fan or AC, & both the roof terrace overlooking the city & the leafy sidewalk seating down below are good places to laze away some hours. The Iguana Café next door kicks out the jams until late, which may be good or bad, depending on your perspective. $$

⌂ **La Louisiane** [Map, page 199] ✆33 961 4221; m 77 637 1741; louisiane@orange.sn; www.aubergelalouisiane.com. At the very northern tip of the island, this place overlooking the river has thoughtfully appointed en-suite rooms decorated in bright tapestries with wrought-iron canopy beds, nets & AC. Upstairs rooms are better for catching the river breezes, as otherwise the restaurant (pretty though it might be) is between you & the water. Said restaurant is the picture of tranquillity, & does a French-African melange of flavours; you'll find brochettes of *lotte* fish, tagines & *crème de bissap* on the sophisticated menu starting around 5,000F. $$

⌂ **Ô Sésame** (4 rooms) ✆33 961 0856; m 77 336 2082; www.facebook.com/osesamedesaintlouissenegal. Relocated from the northern half of the island to a beautifully restored red & white *maison* on Quai Henry Jay at the end of 2014, this combination tea house–auberge has fantastic views over the Pont Faidherbe from the balconies off the airy & comfortably appointed rooms or from the open central corridor. Good meals & the aforementioned tea are served in the pebbled garden, where all manner of humanoid & other salvaged-metal sculptures keep watch while white canvas sunshades flap overhead. $$

🏠 **Sunu Keur** [Map, page 199] (8 rooms) Quai Giraud-Nord; 📞33 961 8800; 📱 77 524 2732; 📧 chaffoisjeanjacques@yahoo.fr; www.sunu-keur. com. Inside the ochre walls of this restored colonial building at the base of the new Pont de la Geôle is a gorgeous terracotta courtyard restaurant surrounding a water well & covered in planters, ringed by a series of bright stucco en-suite rooms on the first floor with original wide-plank floors, wrought-iron bedposts, nets, AC & balconies. Above it all is a west-facing roof terrace that could very well be the finest place on the island for a sundowner. Recommended. **$$**

🏠 **Auberge Café des Arts** [Map, page 199] (6 rooms) 📞33 961 6078; 📱 77 613 8914; 📧 aubergecafedesarts@yahoo.fr. The 5-bed dorm here is without a doubt your cheapest sleep on the island, but the en-suite doubles (with hot shower!) will hardly break the bank either. Fan rooms are small, colourful & kitted out with mozzie nets, & the 5-star views from the westward-facing roof terrace are worth the price of admission alone. **$**

🏠 **Auberge de Jeunesse L'Atlantide** [Map, page 199] 📞33 961 2409; 📧 gijeunesse@ yahoo.fr; www.aubergedelajeunesse.com. This long-serving budget option was closed when we visited in 2014 because of some kind of kerfuffle with the city over permits. It's hard to say whether they'll reopen or close down permanently, but if the former, they've got simple rooms with fans & nets set around a central courtyard. **$**

Hydrobase
Map, page 195.

🏠 **Hôtel Cap Saint-Louis** (35 rooms) 📞33 961 3939; 📧 hotelcap@orange.sn; www. hotelcapsaintlouis.com. The most upmarket option on the hydrobase, this place is also among the most conventionally resort-like. That being said, the rooms are in neat thatched bungalows set around the large swimming pool & restaurant, & they've all got nets, AC, & small flatscreen TVs. They've got volleyball, pétanque & ping pong, along with mountain bikes, body boards & a boutique if you run out of suncream. **$$$**

🏠 **Chez Lydia** (5 rooms) 📞33 961 6969; 📧 francine.bolomey@bluewin.ch; www.lydia-sn. com. Hidden away in a modern villa a few blocks off the main road & right on the beach, this homey new Swiss-run place is impressively equipped with all European fixtures & appliances, & the big, bright

en-suite rooms come with AC, are packed with local sculpture & artwork, & some have balconies. There's a swimming pool, open kitchen, & common rooms with flatscreen TVs for lounging. Unusually for Senegal, it's also designed to be accessible for people with disabilities. Good value. **$$**

🏠 **Hôtel Diamarek** (21 rooms) 📞33 961 5781; 📧 hoteldiamarek@orange.sn; www. hoteldiamarek.com. Today this place stands in a somewhat perilous position as southernmost hotel on the hydrobase, but potential erosion aside, this friendly spot is set in 3ha of gardens with tennis & badminton courts, pétanque pitches, a swimming pool, boutique & small French-language library all on-site. The bungalows are exactingly neat, with AC doubles & communicating rooms sleeping up to 4 people. The restaurant serves a range of dishes from sandwiches to multi-course meals. **$$**

🏠 **Hôtel Dior & Camping Ocean** (19 rooms) 📞33 961 3118; 📧 hoteldior@orange.sn; www.hotel-dior-senegal.com. With spacious high-ceilinged bungalows on one side & basic bamboo & thatch camping huts on the other, there's a bit of something for everyone here. The bungalows are comfortable & well maintained, if a bit plain in terms of décor, while the camping huts come with beds, nets & not a whole lot else, but that's alright for the price. There's a resto-bar & pool on site, as well as some (rather brusque) English-speaking staff. **$$**

🏠 **Hôtel Mermoz** (40 rooms) 📞33 961 3668/5269; 📧 hotelmermoz@arc.sn; www. hotelmermoz.com. If you're after a mud bath, French manicure or even a Brazilian wax, the spa & hammam here have got you covered – or uncovered, as it were. The widely-spaced bungalows here are equally well equipped, with nets, TV & AC, & for fun you can sun yourself at the beachside swimming pool or hop on one of their jet skis. The red-walled restaurant serves an array of continental meat & fish dishes starting around 4,000F, and a 3-course menu for 8,500F. It's also home to the Belgian honorary consulate. **$$**

🏠 **Hôtel Oasis** (14 rooms) 📞33 961 4232; 📧 hoteloasisfishing@gmail.com; www.hotel-oasis-saintlouis.com. Smaller and less resort-like than its neighbours, this laid-back fishing camp is crisscrossed by sandy pathways connecting their two types of rooms: upmarket thatch beach shacks with fans, nets & en-suite bathrooms, or larger bungalows sleeping up to four with higher ceilings & optional AC for an extra 5,000F. There's a nice pool

& bar-resto in front, & while fishing excursions are their bread & butter, the usual range of trips & tours around Saint-Louis are all on offer as well. **$$**

🏠 **Auberge Le Pélican** (11 rooms) ☎ 33 961 8837; m 77 508 5449; e aubergepelican@gmail. com; www.auberge-pelican.com. The cheapest place in town is also (not coincidentally) the closest thing Saint-Louis has to a backpacker's mecca, and this unassuming place has colourful & comfortable rooms sleeping up to four people (some en-suite, some not) slung over 3 floors & a few basic straw huts in the sandy courtyard below. The amount of mismatched furniture they've assembled is almost impressive in itself, & there's a simple resto-bar on the top floor with divine breezes coming off the ocean a few steps away. **$**

Bango
Map, page 195.

🏠 **Ranch de Bango** (41 rooms) Bango; ☎ 33 961 1981; e ranchbango@orange.sn; www. ranchdebango.com. In the barracks town of Bango 10km northeast of Saint-Louis, this unexpected getaway caters more to families & groups than it does to individual travellers, but the expansive grounds are carefully manicured & they've got a very stylish new fitness centre to go with their 2 swimming pools. Rooms are meticulously clean & nicely decorated (their standard room is in this price category but all others are in the one above). They do lots of fishing, horseback riding & quad trips, & while it seems well run, the reception staff were unexpectedly abysmal. **$$**

🍴 **WHERE TO EAT AND DRINK** *Map, page 201, unless otherwise noted.*

Nearly all the hotels in Saint-Louis either have a full-fledged restaurant on site or can arrange simple meals on request, so the selections below focus on stand-alone eateries. It should be noted that in addition to the listings below, **La Résidence**, **La Louisiane** and **Hôtel Sindone** are all warmly recommended for their restaurants.

Self-caterers can aim for the reasonably well-stocked Lider Price supermarket on Rue de France, or potentially head off the island to the Spanish CityDia chain's new outlet on Avenue Général de Gaulle in Sor.

🍴 **Aux Délices du Fleuve** Rue Guillabert; ☎ 33 961 4251; ⏰ 07.30–13.00 & 15.00–midnight Mon–Sat, 07.30–13.00 & 17.00–midnight. Saint-Louis's most famous patisserie, the fresh croissants, pain au chocolat, tea, coffee & ice cream here have made this unassuming café a regular feature on Saint-Louis's culinary map. They do simple meals as well, & they've got Wi-Fi so you can catch up with the world over your morning cuppa.

🍴 **El Falah** [Map, page 199] Av Jean Mermoz; m 77 657 2751; ⏰ 11.00–23.00 daily. For a quick séjour into the Sahara without ever leaving the comfort of the island, trek over to this welcoming address at the north end of Ave Jean Mermoz, where, in a bout of permanence that would surely unsettle any nomad, they've been serving up heaping Moroccan *tajines* (for a thoroughly reasonable 3,000F) since 1999. Dine under their impressively large red & green *khaïma* tent & stop to linger over a mint tea before diving back into the city.

🍴 **La Crêpe Saint-Louisienne** Rue Maitre Babacar Seye; m 77 808 0228; ⏰ 09.00–midnight Mon–Sat. In the cathedral's library, of all places, this cheerful little café serves up sweet & savoury crêpes that are just the antidote for anybody who

can't stand another plate of rice & fish or steak-frites. They've got crêperie standbys like honey, bananas & chocolate along with mango, fish, omelettes, chicken & curry sauces done with a local flair. The sweet crêpes go for around 1,000F & savoury ones creep closer to 2,000F.

🍴 **La Kora Chez Peggy** [Map, page 199] 402 Rue Blaise Diagne; ☎ 33 961 6179; m 77 637 1244; www.facebook.com/lakorachezpeggy; ⏰ 11.30–15.00 & 18.00–23.30 Tue–Sat, 18.00–23.30 Sun. Served with style & sophistication, the food here is quite possibly the most refined on the island, with a smart *salle à manger* to match. The eclectic French menu rotates, but tartare at the bar or burgers under the baobab are both a distinct possibility. Mains come in at around 6,500–9,000F, & since you're splurging already, take our advice & don't even think about skimping on dessert.

🍴 **La Linguère** Rue Blaise Diagne; ☎ 33 961 3949; ⏰ 08.00–midnight daily. This central canteen opposite Hôtel La Résidence has been dishing up Senegalese favourites for years now, & the old-school Coca-Cola signboard out front is proof. It's one of the most reliable stops on the island for a generous afternoon bowl of thieboudienne or mafé, & their yassa is known to be better still. Plates start around 2,000F.

✖ **La Saigonnaise** [Map, page 199] 33 Place de Liège; 📞33 961 6481; m 77 644 0031; ⏰ noon–22.00 daily. The irrepressible Vietnamese proprietress at this pretty restaurant on the water prides herself on serving 'the best pho in the world', as she carefully simmers the homemade beef broth for more than 4 hours every day before the first bowl is served. Whether or not it'd top a global ranking is a discussion you can take up with her yourself, but you'd be hard-pressed to find a better bowl of the stuff in Senegal. Curries, noodles & other southeast Asian specialities are on the menu here as well, starting at around 3,500F.

✖ **Le Reveil** Rue Abdoulaye Seck; m 77 701 9682/044 2001. With some of the kindest & most welcoming management on the island, a stop in here is good for the stomach & the soul. Every inch of the inside is covered in bright murals painted by local artists, & the menu does local specialities, sophisticated seafood dishes (the coconut shrimp is divine) & more starting at around 2,500F. You may be asked to sign the sign the guestbook when you leave – it's already heaving with praise; you'll be glad to join the chorus. There's no bar, but they're happy to pop out & get you some beer.

✖ **Nice Burger** [Map, page 195] Rue Moustapha Malick Gaye, Sor; 📞33 961 4493; m 77 644 5909; ⏰ always open. This mainland institution is a bit removed from most of the tourist action on the island, but it's a solid bet for all things grilled & greasy, with burgers, chawarma & big bowls of thieboudienne & other Senegalese standbys on offer all day & all night, all starting around 1,500F.

✖ **Pâtisserie La Rosa** Rue Khalifa Ababacar Sy; 📞33 961 1950; ⏰ 07.00–01.00 Sun–Thu, 24hrs Fri–Sat. With a mouth-watering selection of pastries & seating in an air-conditioned dining room, this casual café has the feel of a classic diner & is a stellar place to break for a cold coke or hot espresso if your feet start to lose interest in your plan to circumambulate the island. They've got a full menu, & you can get green salads for 2,500F, a variety of meat & fish dishes starting at 4,000F, & their plat du jour (which even comes with a dessert) for 3,000F. They also keep some of the longest hours in town.

✖ **Pointe Nord** [Map, page 199] Av Jean Mermoz; 📞33 961 8716; m 77 518 9851/514 2923; ⏰ 11.00–16.00 & 19.00–midnight Mon–Sat, 19.00–midnight Sun. The ownership of this happy little joint at the north end of the island hails from Côte d'Ivoire, & the flavours here are as much Saint-Louis as they are Grand-Bassam, the similarly faded Ivorian colonial capital some 2,000km down the coast. Drop in here for some grilled fish or chicken served with attiéké (shredded cassava) or alloco (fried plantains) starting around 3,500F.

✖ **Restaurant Galaxie** [Map, page 199] Rue Abdoulaye Seck; 📞33 961 2438; ⏰ 11.00–15.00 & 19.00–23.00 daily. No frills, but a full bar & solid choice of seafood & Senegalese dishes keeps hungry Saint-Louisians & visitors coming back to this standby day after day. There's a small courtyard, & while it's not the fastest restaurant in town, the bar & Wi-Fi ought to keep you entertained in the meantime. Meals average around 3,000F.

NIGHTLIFE

☆ **Iguane Café** [201 C2] Rue Abdoulaye Seck; 📞33 961 0660; www.facebook.com/iguaneslsn. The truck smashing through the wall out front makes this place look more spring break than Saint-Louis, but it's been a favourite late-night party spot on the island since 1997. Give in to the Cuba-themed murals on the walls & belly up to the long wooden bar for a mojito before hitting the dance floor (or one of the tabletop dance poles should the mood – or the mojito – strike you).

☆ **L'Embuscade** [201 C1] Rue Abdoulaye Seck; 📞33 961 8864; ⏰ 10.00–03.00 daily. For a cold beer, maybe a pizza & a night out without pretence, this corner tavern fits the bill nicely. It's

nothing fancy, but if you've had it with riverside views & would rather go prop up a bar for awhile & not break the bank, this might be the place. There's often live music at weekends.

☆ **Le Chaumière** [Map, page 195] Place Pointe à Pitre, Guet Ndar; 📞33 961 1980; ⏰ 22.00–late daily. The grande dame of Saint-Louis nightspots, a laundry list of dance moves & hairstyles may have come & gone with the years, but the party hasn't moved on from this ocean-side staple for decades. There's a cover charge of a few thousand CFA, & leave the beachwear at the hotel – this is the place where Saint-Louis's smartest dressers come to preen for the crowd (& the mirrors).

☆ **Le Flamingo** [201 D2] Quai Roume; m 77 655 1723; ⊕ 10.30–02.00 daily. The view, the pool & the music are the things to come here for. The bar here is perennially busy & host to live bands several nights a week, & the poolside crowds will have you contemplating any number of films where everybody somehow winds up swimming fully dressed. It's a gorgeous spot overlooking the bridge, & they also serve a long menu of meat & fish dishes starting around 5,000F, though for a nice sit-down meal the restaurants at Hôtel Sindone or La Résidence are a better bet. Guests at La Résidence or Hôtel de la Poste can swim here for free, but for others in need of a dip, it's 4,000F.

☆ **Le Papayer** [Map, page 195] Hydrobase; ☎ 33 961 8687; ⊕ noon–late Mon–Sat. Just over 3km from the island at the Hydrobase carrefour, the restaurant here serves food from noon onwards, but the nightclub doesn't open until 23.00, & doesn't get cracking until after midnight at least. It's another venerable party spot & convenient for a night out if you're staying on the Hydrobase (see pages 204–5), but it might be worth checking what's on in advance if you're coming from town.

☆ **Nulle Part Ailleurs** [201 D2] Quai Roume; ☎ 33 961 0418; m 77 403 5748; www.facebook.com/NulParAilleurs; ⊕ 11.00–04.00 daily. The stage here is home to an ever-changing assortment of bands, DJs, & dancers, but the packed bar, billiards, & disco lights are a constant. Mondays are Senegalese night, Thursdays see the crowd rocking to some dancehall, & there's often live music at the weekends. The crowd here is diverse & they make sure to screen the latest football too.

☆ **Quai des Arts** [199 C2] Rue Jean Mermoz; ☎ 33 961 5656; ⊕ 18.30–03.30 daily. With a theatre that can hold up to 1000, this is far & away the largest venue in town, & while it gets its biggest workout annually for the jazz fest, bands will come & shake the rafters here throughout the year as well. Drop by to see what's on the schedule, & even if there's no concert, the outdoor bar next door is a reliable party too.

OTHER PRACTICALITIES

Communication All of the hotels have Wi-Fi, and many restaurants offer it as well. The post office is at the foot of the Faidherbe Bridge as you arrive on the island.

Money Several banks are represented here with ATMs and money-changing facilities, including CBAO, Ecobank and BICIS. Larger hotels will also generally change euros for CFA.

Medical The **Centre Hospitalier Régional** [201 B4] (☎ 33 938 2400) is on Boulevard Abdoulaye Mar Diop on the southern half of the island, while Suma Assistance (*Rte de Dakar;* ☎ 33 961 0204/1125; *www.sumassistance.net*) in Sor offers ambulance service and home visits. Basics can be taken care of up here, but as with anywhere in Senegal, serious problems should be taken to Dakar.

Embassies and consulates The French honorary consul (m *77 815 0660;* e *acfsaintlouis@gmail.com;* ⊕ *08.30–12.30 Mon–Fri*) is based at Hôtel La Résidence (see page 202).

FESTIVALS Saint-Louis hosts a glut of arts and music festivals from about April to June, and the centrepiece of the island's cultural calendar is undoubtedly the Saint-Louis Jazz Festival (☎ *33 961 2455; www.saintlouisjazz.org*), which has been happening here every June for nearly 25 years. Doors are flung open, dusty corners swept out and brought to life, and musicians from as far afield as Turkey and the US come and take over the island for nearly a week of concerts & celebration. Don't fret if you're not a jazz addict – the line-up (published in advance online) is reliably eclectic. The new Saint-Louis Fashion Week (m *77 261 6257/634 1718*) was inspired by its better-established cousin in Dakar, and timed its first edition in 2014 to coordinate with the jazz fest – look out for fashion shows around the

7

island showcasing the latest in modern and traditional couture. Also held over May and June is the gallery festival Le Fleuve en Couleurs (↳ 33 961 6026; www.lefleuveencouleurs.com), where a series of openings are held featuring the works of contemporary Senegalese sculptors, painters, photographers and others in hotels and galleries around town. Around the same time, but usually a touch earlier than the ones mentioned above, Festival International Rapandar (m 77 596 8281; www.rapandar.com) takes place over April and May and runs a series of cultural exchange and music production workshops that lead up to several days of hip hop with dozens of artists on the bill; the majority are Senegalese, but musicians from Gabon, Guinea and even Sweden have made appearances in the past.

Very ably picking up the wintertime slack after the crush of springtime events, the growing **Festival Métissons** (m 77 698 1644; www.facebook.com/FestivalMetissons) was founded in 2010 and livens up November with several days of concerts in bars and clubs across the island, mostly by Senegalese and French artists. Finally, **Les Fanals** is a beautiful New Year's tradition that dates from the 1700s, when the wealthy Métis *signares* would make their way to midnight mass on Christmas Eve. Meticulously coiffed, draped in jewellery and fine white gowns, they navigated the night-time streets with the aid of servants carrying lanterns to light the way and thus from all corners of the island a glowing procession was formed, reaching its apex at the cathedral. Today, the lantern-carrying tradition has become a week-long celebration of competitive float building – these rice-paper creations can reach up to 5m high, and are all the more impressive for their calm glow and ephemeral delicacy. The processions are marked by music and dance, and can be tracked down most days during the week between Christmas and New Year, and they're always out for a New Year's celebration as well.

ACTIVITIES Hotels on the Hydrobase and several of the ones in Gandiol have swimming pools & the ocean within a couple of hundred metres of each other, so avid swimmers will be spoiled for choice at any of these. Ranch de Bango is a good spot for several different activities, with quad bikes, horseback riding and fishing trips all readily available, while quads can also be booked at Campement Teranga in Gandiol, and Hôtel Oasis remains the obvious choice for fishing excursions.

STUDY For courses in French or Wolof, the **Institut Français** [199 C5] (*Ave Jean Mermoz*; ↳ 33 938 2626; e chrystelle.lafaysse@institutfrancais-senegal.com; www.institutfrancais-senegal.com) has long been the go-to destination, but **Waaw** (↳ 33 961 0779; m 77 143 8890/1; e info@waawsenegal.org; www.waawsenegal.org) offers customisable courses in both languages as well.

WHAT TO SEE AND DO Saint-Louis, more than perhaps anywhere else in Senegal, invites easy, aimless strolling (or perhaps touring in a *calèche*) and soaking up the artful atmosphere of the town without a particular destination in mind. There is a fair bit of street hassle that goes on – the usual 'come see my shop', 'take a tour with me', etc. – but it's not particularly aggressive and a firm 'no thanks, next time' is usually enough to send would-be sellers on their way. But don't be dissuaded entirely, there *is* a fantastic variety of art on display and often for sale here, and no visit would be complete without stopping into at least a few of the numerous galleries dotting the island.

Galleries Starting near the centre of the island, **Galérie Éthiopiques** [201 C1] (*Rue Khalifa Ababacar Sy*; m 77 143 8890/1; www.facebook.com/ethiopiques; ☉ 10.00–14.00 & 16.00–18.00 daily) is associated with the Waaw centre (see above) and exhibits works by their own artists-in-residence from all over the world alongside, and sometimes in collaboration with, local artists. Exhibitions usually run for a few weeks, so it's always worth poking your head in to see what's new. A few blocks northeast is the phenomenal **Keur Fall** [201 D1] (*Quai Roume;* ⊕ *09.30–13.00 & 15.00–19.30 Mon–Sat;* ☎ *33 961 6238; www.facebook.com/keurfall. stlouis*), which deals in an impressive assortment of fair-trade goods, including many produced in partnership with Maam Samba and their textile workshop in Ndem (see page 98). It's a lively and welcoming space, with fine clothing, sculpture, *sous-verre* paintings, and all manner of repurposed tin can and bottlecap creations. The Reiki healing centre here is sure to be the only one for at least a few kilometres as well.

Right around the block from here is **Galerie Maam Tiouth** [201 C1] (*Rue Blaise Diagne;* ☎ *33 961 3611;* m *77 070 3531;* ⊕ *09.00–18.00 daily*), set in the cave-like ground floor of a restored colonial building, the assortment of painting, sculpture, jewellery and photography here is carefully curated and of excellent quality. They do rotating exhibitions as well. Continuing north from here, you should make a point to stop in and see what the Mauritanian jewellers at **Chinguetti** [199 C7] (*Rue Blaise Diagne;* ☎ *33 961 5059;* m *77 648 2907*) are up to; the Saharan silverwork here is divine.

Another couple of blocks inland leads to **Atelier Galerie Tësss** [199 C7] (*Rue Khalifa Ababacar Sy;* ☎ *33 961 6860; www.tesss.net or www.facebook.com/GalerieTesss;* ⊕ *09.00–13.30 & 15.00–20.00 Mon–Sat*), where the centuries-old and remarkably intricate traditional weaving techniques of the Manjack people, native to Guinea-Bissau and Senegal, are on display. Just down the street is the affiliated **Conservatoire des Arts et Métiers de L'Élégance (CAMEE)** [201 C1] (*Rue Paul Holle;* ☎ *33 961 6860; www.lecamee.wordpress.com;* ⊕ *10.30–13.30 & 15.00–17.30 Thu–Sat*), which also specialises in textiles. They keep rather short hours, but if you happen upon them when they're open, there are guided visits for a somewhat pricey 2,500F, though the fees go towards workshops and materials for the artisans. In addition to the artists on site, they host rotating exhibits – a showing of traditional Saint-Louisian *signare* dress was taking place at the end of 2014.

Moving on to the south side of the island, **Galerie Arte** [201 C5] (*252 Quai Henry Jay;* ⊕ *09.00–13.00 & 15.00–19.00 daily;* ☎ *33 961 60 26; www.arte.sn*) is a branch of their main location in Dakar, and they host a similar array of experimental furnishings and Casamançais carvings as their Dakar gallery. Just down the quay, **Les Comptoirs du Fleuve** [201 C6] (*Quai Henry Jay;* m *77 553 7777; www. facebook.com/lescomptoirsdufleuvesaintlouisdusenegal;* ⊕ *09.00–19.00 daily*) is an all-but-mandatory stop for their impressively restored colonial warehouse location and their admirable collections of sculpture, painting and photography by some of Senegal's leading artistic lights.

Leaving the island altogether and heading northeast from town towards Richard Toll, the **Village Artisanal** is run down and doesn't offer much for the souvenir hunter that can't be found on the island itself. Finally, some 10km northeast of town lies **Chez Ismaël** (*Ranch de Bango;* ☎ *33 961 9956;* m *77 639 0974; www.chezismael. com*), which deals in rare Mauritanian Kiffa beads and precious beadwork artefacts from as far afield (and as long ago) as ancient Rome, Mesopotamia and early Islamic empires. Prices can and do reach into the millions of francs. If that all leaves you feeling a bit skint, they've got a great (and considerably more approachable) collection of old postcards and prints of Senegal that are suitable for framing and won't have more than three zeroes in the price.

Sights
The city's most famous icon also happens to be among its most useful: the 507m **Pont Faidherbe** [201 D2] was inaugurated here in 1897, after demand steadily outstripped the capacity of the river ferries and pontoon bridge contraptions

that were previously the only connection between Saint-Louis and the mainland. An engineering marvel at the time, and still pretty marvellous today, the seven-spanned bridge is noteworthy for its rotating second arch, which, though almost never used today, simply turns out of the way when a ship needs clearance. As the bridge pushed 110 years of age and beyond, the creaks and groans when crossing it grew ever more unsettling; it underwent a much-needed overhaul in 2011, which very thankfully left the bridge's iconic silhouette reinforced and fully intact.

The densest cluster of sights sits just opposite the island's entrance, where the small **Musée Jean Mermoz** [201 C2] (❨ *33 961 2455;* ⊕ *09.00–13.00 & 15.00–18.30 Mon–Fri, 09.00–13.00 & 15.00–18.00 Sat, 09.30–17.30 Sun; admission price 1,500F*), next to the Syndicat d'Initiative in the old whitewashed **Gouvernance** building (built on the site of an earlier ruined fort and worth a look in itself) has three rooms of photos and exhibits chronicling the history of the Aéropostale mail-delivery service between Europe and South America, for which Saint-Louis was an important stop, and the last before the long Atlantic crossing to Natal, Brazil, first completed by Jean Mermoz in 1930. A few steps south of here is the generously balconied **Ancienne Assemblée Territoriale** [201 C3], where Senegal's territorial parliament met in the lead-up to independence.

Rounding the bend as you continue to head west, **Place Faidherbe** [201 B2] opens up in front of you, at the end of which a oxidised-copper green and rather self-satisfied looking Faidherbe regards his eponymous *place* from atop a stone pillar. On either side of you when locking eyes with Faidherbe are the two *casernes*, former colonial army barracks named after one General Rogniat. **Rogniat Sud** was built in 1830 and today is under renovation, though it's unclear what exactly the building will be used for once works are complete. Its younger sibling across the *place*, **Rogniat Nord**, was completed in 1843 and is today home to the Hôtel Le Rogniat (see page 202). Bordering the east side of the square are the leafy grounds and imposing façade of the **Governor's Mansion** [201 C3], which also dates from the mid 19th century.

From here, the island divides into two unequal halves. To the south is the old Christian quarter, known as Sindoné, while heading north will take you into the former Muslim quarter, Lodo. Today these divisions aren't particularly salient, and people of both faiths live in all parts of the island, but the vast majority of the action in terms of food, drink, art and accommodation takes place in the ten or so blocks north of the Place Faidherbe. Heading up Rue Khalifa Ababacar Sy, you'll pass the 1841 **Palais de Justice** [201 C1] and 1888 **Hôtel de Ville** [201 C1]. Head to the Quai Henry Jay (where you can get a fabulous meal aboard the *Bou el Mogdad* [199 C7] if it's in town) and continue north for a look at the 1847 **Grand Mosque** [199 C5], built by the French as a concession to the overwhelmingly Islamic local populace, one has to suspect that the utterly incongruous clock face embedded in the minaret was intended as a not-entirely-subtle reminder by the French as to who was really running the show. At the end of the quay a few blocks further north is an intriguing **steam crane** [199 D3] (*grue à vapeur*) built from French parts and assembled here in 1883. Capable of lifting 20 tonnes until it was mothballed in 1954, it's one of a very few such engineering artefacts that have managed to avoid the scrapheap worldwide. It's only a few blocks from here along Avenue Jean Mermoz to the northern tip of the island, from where you can see the beginnings of Mauritania and the rarely visited Senegalese island of **Bopp Thior**, where the bricks for nearly all of Saint-Louis's grand buildings were sourced, and the island's dead were buried until the mid 20th century. (Indeed, *Bou el Mogdad*, advisor to the colonial government and namesake for the famous riverboat, was buried here in 1880.) Today it's almost completely forgotten, home to some 800 farmers and fisherman and little else.

On your way back to the centre of the island, cross over to the Hydrobase on the brand new **Pont de la Geôle** [199 A6] and have a wander through the villages of **Ndar Toute** and **Guet Ndar**, both entirely given over to fishing and commerce and feeling much, much further away than the not-even 150m that separate them from the old colonial town. This is the place to dodge overloaded *charettes* and their over-eager prepubescent drivers, watch the fisherman heave their pirogues through the surf, dive into the crowded market and generally revel in the village atmosphere until you're ready to cross back over to the comparatively tame colonial centre on the unremarkable but quite old Pont Moustapha Malick Gaye, built in 1856. If you're still feeling the village vibe and aren't ready to head back yet, the net-covered graves at the fisherman's cemetery south of the bridge are a unique and surprisingly poignant memorial to the departed members of this seafaring community.

The smaller south end of Saint-Louis island is home to a handful of intriguing buildings as well, starting just south of the governor's palace with the neoclassical **cathedral** [201 C3], consecrated in 1828 and rather functionally also named after St. Louis, producing the rather circular French appellation of *Cathédrale Saint-Louis de Saint-Louis-du-Sénégal*. If you haven't yet stopped at La Crêpe Saint-Louisienne (see page 205), it's next door in the church libraries and there's really no good reason not to do so immediately. Once you're sufficiently crêpe'd, take Rue El Hadj Madior Cisse south about six blocks, where you'll encounter the **Maison des Soeurs de Saint-Joseph de Cluny**, a former nunnery home to the iconic dual staircases featured in Bertrand Tavernier's Oscar-nominated 1981 drama *Coup de Torchon*. Today the building is home to some sort of (presumably also action-packed) tax office. Finally, at the very southern tip of the island is the **Musée du Centre de Recherche et de Documentation du Sénégal (CRDS)** [201 B7] (\ *33 961 1050;* ⊕ *09.00–noon & 15.00–18.00 daily; admission 1,000F)*, which, here since 1956, traces the history of Senegal from prehistoric times, the ways of life and traditions of Toucouleur and other Senegalese ethnic groups, and the history of Saint-Louis in particular. There are displays of jewellery, pottery, and other artefacts, a replica *Fanal* lantern and numerous old photos. Upstairs they host rotating art and photography exhibits, but you'll have to pop in to see what's on. Head back north on the Quai Henry Jay and stop for a classy riverside dinner at the Hôtel Sindone – you've earned it.

PARC NATIONAL DE LA LANGUE DE BARBARIE

The Langue de Barbarie itself is a narrow, sandy peninsula that once stretched between Senegal and Mauritania for an uninterrupted 50km, separated from the mainland by the Senegal River as it empties into the ocean and providing a barrier against the ocean waves for Saint-Louis, Gandiol, Mouit and other low-lying coastal settlements. Thus, flooding has long been an issue here, and in 2003 the Senegalese government cut a 2m gap in the peninsula itself just south of the Hydrobase area as part of what was intended as a flood-alleviation scheme. Instead, things rapidly went pear-shaped and it's become nothing short of an unmitigated environmental disaster in the dozen years since. As soon as the artificial channel was opened, the ocean currents began to erode its edges, the waves and tides steadily churning away and forcing the gap wider almost daily. What began as a 2m channel is, as of early 2015, more than 5.5km of open ocean where the former peninsula has disappeared completely. As recently as 2013 there were hotels on the Langue de Barbarie itself, but they've since been overcome by the advancing waves and left to their Atlantean fate.

Gazetted in 1976, the **national park** (m *77 545 8331/70 458 9813; entry 2,000F;* ⊕ *08.00–sunset daily)* is still, for the time being, intact. Covering 2,000ha at the southern end of the Langue de Barbarie and a portion of the river delta and facing mainland, the erosion has yet to reach the park boundaries, but this is likely to happen in the future, possibly even during the lifespan of this edition. The long, narrow island, barely 500m at its widest point, consists of sand dunes to the west, and is vegetated in the east by some pine trees and low, creeping vines like goat's foot and sea purselane. It was recognised as an Important Bird Area by Birdlife International in 2001, and keen ornithologists, particularly between November and April, will spot seabirds in their thousands, including a notable variety of wintering gulls and terns, including the gull-billed tern (*Gelochelidon nilotica*), Caspian tern (*Hydroprogne caspia*), royal tern (*Thalasseus maximus*), little tern (*Sternula albifrons*), grey-headed gull (*Larus cirrocephalus*) and slender-billed gull (*Larus genei*), all of which have breeding sites here.

GETTING THERE AND AWAY The primary jumping-off points for the Langue de Barbarie are from either the park office in Mouit, the Gandiol lighthouse, or any of the mainland hotels facing the island, all of which are discussed below. All of the aforementioned spots are accessible with a 2WD vehicle, but if you're on public transport taking a taxi to get down here from Saint-Louis is likely to be your best bet; you can negotiate a cab ride from the city to Mouit (park office, Zebrabar) for around 3,500F, and perhaps a bit less to Gandiol (Niokobokk, 7palava). It's also possible that you'll find a *taxi-brousse* to Gandiol, but don't bank on these being at all frequent.

All of the hotels and campements in and around Gandiol can quickly and easily arrange trips to the Langue de Barbarie, and some even offer canoes and kayaks so you can punt yourself over and back at your leisure. At the park office in Mouit, they arrange 90-minute pirogue trips for one to three people for 7,500F, with an extra 2,500F per person for parties larger than three, and a 3,000F guide fee per party.

You can also still get a lift to the island from long-time *piroguier* Jules (also known as Souleyman) (m 77 656 4633) at the Gandiol lighthouse (*phare de Gandiol*), though given that the hotels that were once on the shore opposite here have since washed away, today it's more common for people to arrange a visit with their hotels on the mainland or at the park office. Budget travellers should note well, though, that Jules will take a party of up to five people across from here for a bargain-basement 4,500F, with an extra charge of 1,000F per person for parties larger than five, and he can arrange a grilled fish lunch on the island for a few thousand CFA more.

WHERE TO STAY, EAT AND DRINK *Map, page 195.*
There is no longer any accommodation on the Langue de Barbarie itself, but a number of choices directly facing it on the mainland.

Niokobokk Maison d'Hôtes (4 rooms) Gandiol; 33 962 0562; m 77 790 7399; e niokobokk@gmail.com; www.niokobokk.com. About 2km north of the Gandiol lighthouse & accessible via a signposted turnoff, this casbah-esque ochre *maison* is among the more soigné establishments on Saint-Louis' southern shores. All the rooms here have terraces or balconies overlooking the swimming pool & the ocean, & come equipped with modern fixtures & contemporary African décor. They can arrange all the usual host of activities, or you can just give in

to the delicious temptation of an afternoon spent reading in a hammock. **$$$**
Océan et Savane (40 rooms) Sowène; 33 961 1260; m 77 637 4790; e oceanetsavane@orange.sn; www.oceanetsavane. com. Formerly on the Langue de Barbarie itself, this lovely upmarket campement had to up stakes and relocate to the mainland in 2013 due to the shocking pace of erosion on the island – its former location today sits underwater. But they've handled the change with aplomb & the new location on the mainland 30km south of Saint-Louis is a

thoroughly charming escape. They've got standing tents with open-air ablutions & duplex bungalows (which unfortunately have rather thin walls), all ornithologically christened & perched on platforms on the sand with views over the water. Activities range from sport to spa, & you can grab a kayak & paddle over to explore the island at your leisure. There's no food for miles, so accommodation here is typically on a HB/FB basis. **$$$**

🏠 **Campement Teranga** Gandiole; (7 rooms) ✆ 33 962 5853; m 77 636 0209; e reservation@ gandiole-teranga.com; www.gandiole-teranga. com. With a repurposed *car rapide* serving as the bar, this lovely riverside campement is a cheerful spot to go nowhere fast & kick off your flip-flops by the pool & play some pétanque, unless of course you're keen to hop on one of their boats or quads. Either way, the en-suite thatch bungalows here are comfortable, come with AC or fan & mozzie nets, & the river-facing ones have sizeable windows to take in the view. **$$**

🏠 **Le Heron Cendre** (6 rooms) Mouït; ✆ 33 962 8736; m 77 545 8331/70 458 9813; e mniang1@hotmail.com. At the Langue de Barbarie National Park office, there are some simple rooms here, but it might be a challenge to find a compelling reason to stay here given that Zebrabar only a couple hundred metres away & the prices are broadly comparable. Still, the tiled en-suite rooms have nets & fans & are kept clean, there's a nice terrace overlooking the floodplain, & it's (naturally) easy to arrange trips into the park from here. No Wi-Fi, meals on request. **$$**

🏠 **Zebrabar** (14 rooms) Mouït; ✆ 33 962 0019; m 77 638 1862; e info@zebrabar.net; www. zebrabar.net. In the same spot since 1996, this is Senegal's unchallenged overlander's Mecca, & it really is something of a backpacker wonderland, particularly if you've just hauled yourself across the sands of Mauritania. With accommodation ranging from light & colourful en-suite bungalows with solar shower & reading lamps to a hollowed-out camper shell-cum-miniature room using shared ablutions (also with solar shower), or plenty of space to pitch your tent, there's some kind of funky accommodation here for all but the fussiest of tastes. There's a lookout tower, kayaks (free for guests), a playground for kids, & a bar where travellers actually swap stories & not just status updates. It's technically within the Langue de Barbarie National Park, so the 2,000F park entry fee applies to guests. **$$**

🏠 **Camping 7palava** (5 rooms) Gandiol; m 77 123 6326; e info@7palava.com; www.7palava.com. Opened in 2013, this sandy German-run campground north of the Gandiol lighthouse has lots of space to pitch a tent, Mauritanian *khaïma* tents if you forgot to bring your own, & a couple of simple rooms with shared or en-suite ablutions. The *khaïma* tents are one of the best deals in town (starting at 4,000F per person), & there's plenty of good food & drink to be had on their platform overlooking the beach. They closed due to flooding in May 2015, but were intending to reopen – call ahead to get the latest. **$**

RÉSERVE SPÉCIALE DE FAUNE DE GUEMBEUL

Gazetted and fenced in 1983/4, declared a Ramsar wetland of international importance in 1986, and recognized as an Important Bird Area in 2001, the 720ha *Réserve Spéciale de Faune de Guembeul* (✆ 33 961 8621; m 77 351 9986; ⊕ 07.00–18.00 daily; entry 1,000F, guide 3,000F) seems unassuming at first glance, but can make for a worthwhile detour, especially since it's directly on the route between Saint-Louis and Gandiol.

Consisting mostly of a large rain-fed saline lagoon surrounded by thorny acacia scrub, the biggest attraction here is the breeding enclosure for the scimitar-horned oryx (*Oryx dammah*), IUCN-listed as extinct in the wild, the critically endangered dama gazelle (*Nanger dama*) and the vulnerable dorcas gazelle (*Gazella dorcas*), all of which are here as part of a long-running breeding and reintroduction program which has been slowly translocating animals to an exponentially larger enclosure at the truly remote Ferlo Nord and Ferlo Sud reserves in the east of the country (see box, page 247). There's also a breeding program here for the vulnerable African spurred tortoise (*Geochelone sulcata*), and you're likely to spot a handful of reasonably common mammals on a walk around the reserve, like Crawshay's hare (*Lepus microtis*), desert hedgehog (*Paraechinus aethiopicus*), desert warthog (*Phacochoerus aethiopicus*), Egyptian mongoose (*Herpestes ichneumon*), patas monkey (*Erythrocebus patas*), Libyan striped weasel (*Ictonyx libyca*), and crested porcupine (*Hystrix cristata*).

Visits usually begin with a stop in the museum at the entrance, which has a large display of well illustrated information panels that offer diagrams of the various species to be found here and unusually, captions in both English and French. After that, the walk around the reserve lasts between one and two hours, and it's easy to forget just how close you are to Saint-Louis once you're out on the paths to the lagoon. In the lagoon there are two diminutive islands used as avian breeding grounds, and birders should be on the lookout for wintering populations of greater flamingo (*Phoenicopterus roseus*), Eurasian spoonbill (*Platalea leucorodia*), pied avocet (*Recurvirostra avosetta*), grey-headed gull (*Larus cirrocephalus*) and slender-billed gull (*Larus genei*). If you've got your own 4x4, it may be possible to arrange a drive around the reserve as well.

FOLLOW BRADT

For the latest news, special offers and competitions, subscribe to the Bradt newsletter via the website www.bradtguides.com and follow Bradt on:

🄵 www.facebook.com/BradtTravelGuides
🄵 @BradtGuides
🄵 @bradtguides
🄵 pinterest.com/bradtguides

8

Senegal River and the North

The arid yin to steamy Casamance's yang, northern Senegal is one end of Senegal's two extremes, a world away from the southern swamps and forests, and a palpable spiritual and physical distance from its freewheeling and fashionable coastal centres. The most conservative region of the country, here tradition reigns supreme. Its Toucouleur inhabitants were among the first groups in West Africa to convert to Islam as it spread from the north, and even today their religious achievements are a visible point of pride; Toucouleurs account for more than their share of *marabouts*, *qadis* (judges) and *imams* throughout Senegal.

Once a major trade route for French West Africa, the Senegal River today forms the boundary between Senegal and Mauritania, and has long since seen its arterial status slip away with the current. Indeed, today the river route is almost an archetypal backwater, with long-neglected colonial towns and their riverside forts keeping watch for ships and raiders that no longer arrive. In the thorn scrub between the towns, Fulbe herders follow the rains while Soninke farmers wait for them to recede, so as to plant their crops along the riverbanks and tap the residual moisture, a most valuable resource in this parched and unforgiving land.

Indeed, the Senegalese government is staking much on the agricultural potential of this valley, and leaving Saint-Louis today you're met with a schizophrenic landscape: neatly delineated patches of glowing green rice and sugar cane besieged by seed-snatching egrets and herons, while the surrounding landscape of crusty, baking acacia scrub remains unchanged, watched over by birds of prey cruising silently on the roasting updrafts. This new flurry of investment means the region is easier to access than ever, with a beautiful tarmac road as far as Ndioum, three new bridges connecting to the Île à Morfil, and even the occasional flight to Matam. So leave the heels and designer jeans in Dakar, pack a change of *boubou* for those sweaty *sept-place* rides, and come kiss the edge of the Sahara in this, Senegal's least forgiving and most enigmatic region.

DIAMA

Looking out over a wide expanse of the Senegal River held back by its eponymous dam, Diama is little more than a pleasant riverside backwater, but has been of interest to travellers (particularly those with vehicles) as an alternative border crossing to and from Mauritania since the dam's completion in 1986, as it represents the only road bridge between the two countries. The 16km between here and the RN2 are now covered by an excellent new road, so crossing here and avoiding the scrum at Rosso is easier than it's ever been, though a good vehicle is advised to tackle the considerably less modern road on the Mauritanian side. There's typically not much transport here, but with the new tarmac this stands to improve, and travellers on foot ought to have a decent chance of getting a lift from the RN2 junction, if not

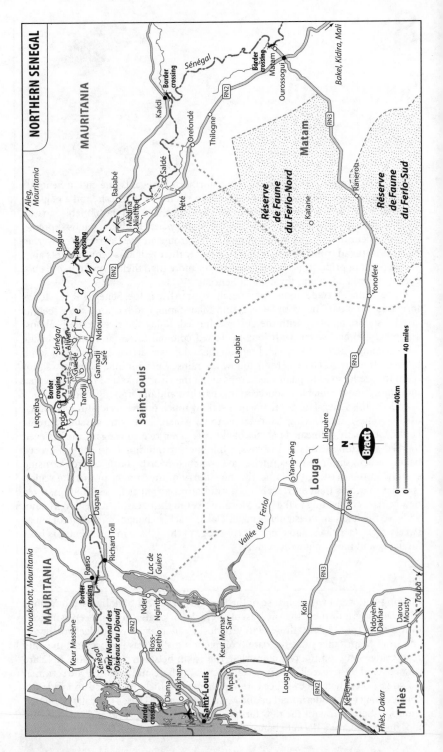

NORTHERN SENEGAL

from Saint-Louis itself. If you want to cross here, allow time to cover the 100km on the other side of the border between the dam and Rosso-Mauritania. If for some reason you get stuck or just feel like spending the night here, you could pitch up at either of the two riverside camps catering for hunters, both located between Diama and its neighbouring village 2km to the east, Maka. **Campement Maka Diama** (◗ *33 961 1233;* m *77 511 2267; www.facebook.com/maka.diama*) is the more upmarket of the two, with air-conditioned bungalows and a swimming pool, while **Le Mirador** (◗ *33 961 5152/4632;* e *sljv-safarisow@orange.sn; www.safarisow.com*) has simple thatch bungalows with fans in a beachy compound.

PARC NATIONAL DES OISEAUX DU DJOUDJ

On an inland delta southeast of the Senegal River, this 16,000ha park was gazetted by the Senegalese government in 1971, listed as a Ramsar Wetland of International Importance in 1977 and declared a UNESCO World Heritage Site in 1981. Across the river in Mauritania, Diawling National Park is has been contiguous with Djoudj since its gazetting in 1991, bringing over 32,000 uninterrupted hectares under protection.

Situated on an inland delta just southeast of the Senegal River, the multiple layers of recognition and protection afforded to the park are indicative of its massive importance to African and European birdlife, particularly Palearctic migrants. The first permanent water source south of the Sahara, Djoudj is the destination for hundreds of thousands of birds as they depart Europe and cross the wastes of the Sahara in search of more amenable climes both here and further south. Seasonally inundated, the park is crisscrossed by a lush, labyrinthine network of brackish marshes, lakes and tidal streams that are visited by 3,000,000 birds annually, with no less than 350 different species represented among them. The terrestrial fauna here isn't quite as exciting, but you're still very likely to spot at least a few warthogs (*Phacochoerus africanus*), possibly some red-fronted (*Eudorcas rufifrons*) or Dorcas gazelles (*Gazella dorcas*), and with a real stroke of luck, perhaps an African manatee (*Trichechus senegalensis*) gliding silently by.

GETTING THERE AND AWAY The park entrance gate and both accommodation options are located together and accessible via two possible routes from the RN2. The primary route starts at a clearly signposted turnoff in Ross-Bethio, 50km from Saint-Louis, from where 18km of well-kept laterite (manageable in a saloon car) lead to the park. Your other option is to first aim for Diama, from where there's 27km of rougher road between you and the park gate.

Public transport options are slim, though there is reputedly a once-daily *ndiaga ndiaye* that departs from garage Bango in Saint-Louis at 13.00 and stops at the village of Diadem III, 800m from the park entrance. It departs Diadem III for the return trip to Saint-Louis around 07.30, and each way costs about 2,000F. A **taxi hire** from Saint-Louis will start around 25,000F, or you could potentially take public transport as far as Ross-Bethio and hire a cheaper lift from there. Easier yet, all tour agencies and larger hotels in Saint-Louis arrange day trips to the park; Sahel Découverte (page 198) and Saint-Louis Découverte (page 200) are both recommended.

The *Bou el Mogdad* (see page 198) also calls here on its way between Saint-Louis and Podor.

WHERE TO STAY, EAT AND DRINK *Map, page 218.*
If you don't mind being slightly further from the park and the added travel times that entails, **Lampsar Lodge** (see page 219), between Ross-Bethio and Makhana, is another good option for park visitors.

8

PARC NATIONAL DES OISEAUX DU DJOUDJ

Rosso (48km)

MAURITANIA

Diadiam II

Sénégal

Debi

Tiguèt

Lac Lamantin

Canal du Crocodile

N

Bradt

Grand Lac

Diadiam I

Marigot de Diar

Parc National des Oiseaux du Djoudj

Lac Khar

Gorom

Park office & Station Biologique

②
①

Diadiam III

Diama (27km), RN2 (43km), Saint-Louis (60km)

Ross-Bethio (RN2) (18km), Rosso (66km), Saint-Louis (70km)

| 0 | 5km |
| 0 | 3 miles |

For listings, see below

⊖ **Where to stay, eat and drink**

1 Campement Njagabaar
2 Hôtel Djoudj

🏠 **Campement Njagabaar** (6 rooms) Diadem III; ✆ 33 962 7147; m 77 563 2208/541 9941/656 4790; e lenjagabaar@yahoo.fr; www. djoudjvillages.sn. Diadiem III about 800m from the entrance to the park. They technically close at the same times as the park, but you can still get a room here in the off-season – just call ahead so they can prep for your arrival. The en-suite thatched bungalows here are tidy & simply equipped with fans & nets, sleeping up to 4 and facing a lily-pad-covered pond. Meals & drinks are available on request, & they can arrange all pirogue, hiking & horse-cart (*calèche*) trips within

the park, as well as excursions to see the tanners, weavers & rice fields of the surrounding villages. You can pitch a tent here for 2,500F as well. **$$**

🏠 **Hôtel Djoudj** (60 rooms) ✆ 33 963 8702; e contact@hotel-djoudj.com; www.hotel-djoudj. com. Open Nov–May, this has long been the go-to for Djoudj accommodation. The pool is blue, & the en-suite rooms are trim, comfortable & named after different species of birds you can find in the park. The restaurant does fine meals on the terrace. Boat, 4x4 or walking trips into the park can be arranged daily. Unlike the campement, it's not possible to stay here during the off-season. **$$**

WHAT TO SEE AND DO The park (✆ *33 961 8621; e parcdjoudj@yahoo.fr*) is technically open from November to May, and it's still usually possible to gain entry at other times, though the sightings are less spectacular. The population of Palearctic migrants peaks over the new year, and over 400,000 individuals are typically present in January. Entry costs 2,000F per person per day, while vehicle access is 5,000F per trip. A half-day pirogue tour costs 4,000F per person, plus 6,000F for the guide. The half-day tour consists of a visit to several viewpoints within the park, flamingo nesting sites, and the jaw-dropping pelican breeding island, where an incredible

15,000 great white pelicans (*Pelecanus onocrotalus*) stand beak-by-jowl with their young on a diminutive scrap of land surrounded by the river.

For the dedicated ornithologist, custom tours by pirogue, 4x4, foot or even *calèche* can be arranged to all corners of the park, including Lac Lamantin, the Grand Lac and the Canal du Crocodile. This can be set up with any of the tour agents in Saint-Louis, or at either of the hotels in Djoudj. A few of the species that can be reliably found wintering here in their thousands include purple swamphen (*Porphyrio porphyrio*), pied avocet (*Recurvirostra avosetta*), ruff (*Calidris pugnax*), slender-billed gull (*Larus genei*), sand martin (*Riparia riparia*), great white pelican (*Pelecanus onocrotalus*), great white egret (*Ardea alba*), black-crowned night-heron (*Nycticorax nycticorax*), Eurasian spoonbill (*Platalea leucorodia*), greater flamingo (*Phoenicopterus roseus*), ferruginous duck (*Aythya nyroca*), garganey (*Spatula querquedula*), northern shoveler (*Spatula clypeata*), white-faced whistling-duck (*Dendrocygna viduata*) and northern pintail (*Anas acuta*). Arabian bustards (*Ardeotis arabs*) and lesser kestrels (*Falco naumanni*) have been known to make an appearance as well, and Djoudj is a year-round home for the river prinia (*Prinia fluviatilis*). Serious birders should plan to spend a couple of nights here, and get a copy of *Birds of Senegal and The Gambia* by Nik Borrow and Ron Demey, published in 2012, which has excellent illustrations and in-depth info on all of the above.

MAKHANA

Travelling from the foot of the Faidherbe Bridge in Saint-Louis, after 16.5km you reach Mbarigo village, where there is an almost unnoticeably signposted left-hand turnoff for a forgotten engineering marvel. Conceived in 1859 during Governor Faidherbe's riverine expansion into the region, the Kassak Creek and Toucouleur village of Makhana were designated as the site of a reservoir and pumping station that eventually took shape here in 1882 with the arrival of a steam engine that came online in 1885, providing Saint-Louis and the wider region with fresh water. A second pump was built here in 1901, and they were in near-constant use until 1952. Today they stand as rusting, derelict hulks, but the size of the equipment is still impressive: metres-high wheels and thousands of kilos' worth of tanks, cranks and pumps, all frozen in place here for over 60 years, the buildings housing them long since having lost their roofs and doors.

To get here, once you've found the correct junction, follow the dirt road for 1.8km and you'll be right on top of the stations. It's likely that the whole village (or at least all of its children) will come out and greet you, so if you want any pictures of the equipment without kids crawling all over it, get them as soon as you roll up! It's possible that a small fee will be requested for the adjacent village, but this wasn't the case when we visited. It's worth the detour if you're heading this way already, but unless you're an engineering buff, it makes for a short stopover at best.

There's no accommodation in Makhana itself, but it sits almost equidistant between Saint-Louis and the highly regarded new **Lampsar Lodge** (*4 rooms;* ✆ *16.204680, –16.261243;* m *77 733 6609;* e *lampsarlodge@gmail.com; www. campement-senegal.com;* **$$**), set 15km east of Makhana (and 15km shy of Ross-Bethio and the turnoff for Djoudj) in the tiny roadside village of Ndioungue Mberess. Open from October to July, they've got a waterfront location on the Lampsar River, green gardens, eclectically appointed en-suite rooms with AC or fan, a French-inspired kitchen and – most importantly in this part of the country – a swimming pool. It's excellent value, and a good base for visits to Djoudj as well, which they can help arrange.

For such a small place, Rosso really has a lot of people who hate it, and they're not entirely unjustified. Sharing a name with the Mauritanian city across the water, it's a disorganised and tiresome place, and often a waterlogged mess during the rains. It's also the primary border crossing between Senegal and Mauritania, and the river crossing can make for an interesting place to hang around and observe the border goings on (indeed, you'll very likely have time for just this while waiting for the ferry), but there's precious little else to do here but get your stamps and move on. If you're in a hurry, there are plenty of pirogues happy to take you across for 1,000F or so.

GETTING THERE AND AWAY Rosso is easy of access at least, connected to the RN2 by a surfaced 5km feeder road. The *gare routière* is on the left-hand side as you enter town from the south, and the river and Senegalese border facilities are a walkable 1,100m beyond at the port. The border operates from 08.00 to 13.00 and 15.00 to 19.00 daily, taking a decidedly unhurried two-hour lunch break in between. The crossing is relatively straightforward for travellers on foot, but has a reputation for hassle for travellers with vehicles (though this is reported to be improving). The Mauritanian government-owned ferry makes its way back and forth across the river all day; it's officially 5,000 Ouguiya (€15) for cars, and either nothing or a nominal fee for foot passengers. Ignore all the self-appointed 'helpers', and be vigilant with the black market moneychangers. Heading into Senegal from the *gare routière*, transport leaves to Richard Toll (350F), Saint-Louis (2,200F), Podor (3,500F) or Dakar (7,500F). To head east towards Ourossogui, you'll have to do the trip in stages, starting in Richard Toll.

WHERE TO STAY, EAT AND DRINK The only place to stay is the decidedly less-than-ideal **Auberge Le Walo** (*7 rooms;* \ *33 963 6250;* m *77 611 3401;* $), which should only be considered if for some reason you can't get across the border or onwards into Senegal for the night. (Richard Toll is only 15km from here and has far better accommodation.) Coming from the south, it's a few metres down the last left turnoff before the border gate. The nicest room here goes for 25,000F and is en-suite and does have AC, but it also had a broken sink hanging off the wall and a generally decrepit air about it. Cheaper options include a handful of differently sized and shaped fan rooms with aromatic shared bath, and the bottom of the barrel is hiring a grungy mattress on the common room floor for 3,000F. The bar out front does simple dishes and blasts the tunes from here to Mauritania.

If you get stuck on the Mauritanian side of the border, head for the new **Hôtel Mauritour** (❂ *16.512374, –15.804843; Lot 78, Medina 1;* m *(+222) 46 41 34 30 (Mauritania);* e *info@mauritcom.com; www.mauritcom.com;* $$), which sits atop the Place d'Italie Market just under 2km from the border crossing. The frilly rooms here go for around €50 for a double and represent the most reliable option in town, with the added perk of a rooftop terrace from which you can take in Rosso's panoramic chaos in peace.

OTHER PRACTICALITIES Unfortunately, there's no ATM in town (the nearest are in Richard Toll or Saint-Louis), but many of the little boutiques along the road will change CFA for Ouguiya and vice-versa, and you're at less risk of being cheated here than on the street. There's petrol, a post office and a *poste de santé* in town as well.

RICHARD TOLL

'Toll' means garden in Wolof, and while today it's more plantation than botanical garden, it still seems strangely appropriate that one of Senegal's busiest agricultural centres should carry such an appellation. It's named after the colony's head botanist, Jean Michel Claude Richard, who was tasked with founding a botanical garden to study the cultivation of introduced species of fruits, vegetables and medicinal plants here during colonial governor Baron Jacques-François Roger's 1821–27 tenure. Baron Roger so liked these gardens that he built his none-too-subtle château here at the same time.

Today Richard Toll is very much a company town, where the sticky-sweet air flows in heavy, syrupy puffs and the 10,000ha of fields and factories of the Compagnie sucrière sénégalaise (CSS) dominate the skyline. The town itself is slung haphazardly between river and road along a few kilometres of the RN2, and is home to migrants from all over Senegal seeking work at the factory and its associated jobs. More functional than fabulous, the town isn't a must-see in and of itself, but the roads are heaving with commerce of all kinds and the facilities here are good. Several banks are represented (these are the closest ATMs to the Rosso border), the hotels have Wi-Fi and there is a string of reliably stocked petrol stations.

GETTING THERE AND AWAY Richard Toll is a primary jumping-off point for cities east along the RN2, including Podor (2,500F), Ourossogui (7,000F), and Bakel (11,000F). It's also easy enough to head back to Saint-Louis (2,200F), and there are direct *sept-places* to Dakar (7,500F) as well. The RN2 was resurfaced in 2014 and is in great shape in either direction.

The 130km track to Louga via Lac de Guiers' eastern shore meets the RN2 here, and while you could try to hitch or find the odd *taxi-brousse* passing the villages on this route, it's not to be counted on, and self-drivers will need a 4x4.

WHERE TO STAY, EAT AND DRINK *Map, page 222.*

Gîte d'Étape (19 rooms) 33 963 3240; e alaingite@arc.sn. With 'feet in the water' as the French expression goes, this place smack on the riverfront is Richard Toll's most prestigious address, & while that may not be saying a whole lot, the rooms here are well-kept with AC & flatscreen TVs, though the furnishings aren't exactly modern. Still, the swimming pool is a tempting aquamarine, the pier over the river is the best vantage point in town, & the restaurant does meals on white tablecloths starting at around 5,000F. **$$$**

La Taouey (12 rooms) 33 960 2941; m 77 531 4010; e hotellataouey@yahoo.fr. Winning the prize for both most vowels in a single word & the friendliest management to help you pronounce it, this laidback place opposite the river is a perfectly pleasant stopover in Richard Toll. The en-suite rooms are neat & tidy with AC & some homey, cobbled-together décor, & meals in the restaurant-bar (with billiard table) are surprisingly good.

Richard Toll in general is middling when it comes to value for money, but this is probably your best bet. **$$**

Auberge de la Cité (11 rooms) 33 963 3361. The fan rooms with shared bath here are the cheapest in town, but if you're planning on springing for AC anyway, you get considerably more bang for only a couple bucks more at La Taouey. First-floor rooms will be a bit airier, & they sleep anywhere from 1 to 5. The shared ablutions are a squat toilet & cold shower – just the thing to get you up & out to the *gare routière* across the street for an early morning start. **$**

Burger City 33 963 3030; ⏲ 06.00–03.00 daily. A safe bet for a quick bite whether you're staying in Richard Toll or just passing through, this place does a Senegalese *plat du jour* for 1,300F, along with fast-food standbys like burgers, charwarma & fattayah. It's clean, open almost all the time, & even serves ice cream.

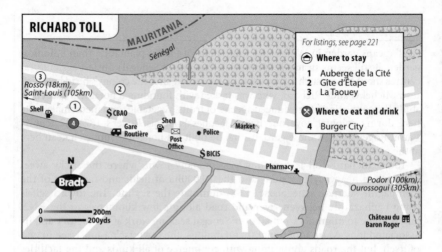

RICHARD TOLL

MAURITANIA

Sénégal

Rosso (18km), Saint-Louis (105km)

Shell

CBAO

Gare Routière

Shell

Post Office

Police

Market

BICIS

Pharmacy

Podor (100km), Ourossogui (305km)

N

Bradt

0 — 200m
0 — 200yds

Château du Baron Roger

For listings, see page 221

Where to stay
1 Auberge de la Cité
2 Gîte d'Étape
3 La Taouey

Where to eat and drink
4 Burger City

WHAT TO SEE AND DO The elephant in the garden and more or less *the* thing to see in Richard Toll is the **Château du Baron Roger**, perhaps more often (or more accurately) known as the *Folie* ('folly') *du Baron Roger*. The ostentatious mansion is perhaps more often (or more accurately) known as the *Folie* ('folly') *du Baron Roger*. Built in the 1820s, it still dwarfs everything else in town save the sugar factory, and though it's in rough shape cosmetically, the archways and buttresses are still solid as rock. There have been various ideas floated as to how to bring the building back to life, but so far no action has been taken to restore the property and it's occupied by a handful of people somewhere on the continuum between caretaker and squatter. Someone will be happy to show you around, and the high-ceilinged rooms are still impressive in their decrepitude, as much for their architectural grandeur as for their overweening lunacy. The city's namesake gardens that once surrounded the château have been long ignored, so that whatever exotic botanicals were once raised here today blend seamlessly with the surrounding bush. It's also generally possible to tour the **CSS sugar factory** (\ *33 938 2322;* e *direction.generale@css.sn; www.css. sn*), but it would be best to try to set this up in advance.

LAC DE GUIERS

Senegal's only freshwater lake, Lac de Guiers is 35km from top to bottom and nearly 8km wide, covering nearly 17,000ha all told. Mostly known as the source of Dakar's fresh water, it also waters much of the sugar cane grown at the lake's north end near Richard Toll, and with the exception of **La Teranga du Lac de Guiers** (*dbl from €38;* m *76 282 0999/77 646 6231;* e *laterangalacdeguiers@yahoo.fr; www.teranga-guiers.com*) north of Nginth village on the west coast of the lake, there's no tourist development whatsoever. Nder village (a few km north of Nginth) on the western shore was the last capital of the Waalo Kingdom until its fall to the French in the 1850s.

The shores are swampy and the banks are commonly used for agriculture, largely rice and sugar cane. It's an important permanent water source for pastoralists in the area. It was designated an Important Bird Area in 2001, and is a winter breeding location for Eurasian spoonbill (*Platalea leucorodia*), glossy ibis (*Plegadis falcinellus*), lesser flamingo (*Phoeniconaias minor*), African spoonbill (*Platalea alba*), white-winged tern (*Chlidonias leucopterus*), and a year-round home for the river prinia (*Prinia fluviatilis*).

You'll probably need your own 4x4 to get here; if you're on public transport you'll need a lot of patience and a bit of luck with a *taxi-brousse* from Richard Toll or Louga, but assuming you find one, make sure which side of the lake it's headed down – there are two routes. In addition to the only hotel, the west side of the lake is home to two water treatment facilities at Keur Momar Sarr and Nginth villages, and the road here alternates between variable tarmac and laterite. Keur Momar Sarr (at the lake's southern tip) holds its weekly *loumo* on Saturdays, so you'll have an easier time finding transport (probably from Louga as it's much closer) around then.

DAGANA

Another former trading outpost for the French and centre of the Waalo Kingdom, today most travellers pass right by Dagana without noticing, and it hasn't been privy to any of the restoration works that are raising the profile of nearby Podor (see below). Still, there's a modest fort and some colonial-era warehouses on the quay that are of some interest, and an impressively large bronze of Ndaté Yala, the last *brak* (queen) of Waalo, the northernmost of the former Wolof kingdoms. If you want to stay in town, ask for **Auberge le Walo** (↘ *33 962 7155;* e *adamafallkane@ hotmail.fr;* **$$**), which has AC rooms. The *Bou el Mogdad* (see page 198) calls here on its way to and from Podor.

PODOR

At the edge of the Sahara and at the same latitude as Timbuktu, Podor, Senegal's northernmost town, looks like another planet, feels like an oven and sounds like the hush of a forest after fresh snow. The buildings, laid out along the river in a neat colonial grid, share the burnt saffron tones of the surrounding lands, and it feels more like an organic, earthen village than it does a district capital, only one located on Mars, perhaps. Sweltering and silent, you can hear for blocks around when one of the few resident vehicles starts cranking its timeworn motor, or when a stifling Mauritanian wind comes calling with its wholly predictable gift of sand and dust.

It's also a place of some antiquity, by turns part of the Tekrour state at the turn of the last millennium, then falling under the influence of the Denanke Kingdom for some centuries until the Imamate of Fouta Toro took hold of the region in 1776. The French established a trading post here in the mid 18th century, and many of the venerable quayside buildings now being restored are former traders' homes and warehouses dating to the late 1700s. The fort didn't take its modern shape until 1854, when it was expanded and reinforced as part of Faidherbe's drive to solidify French control over river trade.

Today there's little to do in Podor but soak up the atmosphere, and perhaps there's something about its otherworldly, meditative air that acts as an incubator for the creative, as Podor punches well above its featherweight population when it comes to the arts. Singer and guitarist Baaba Maal is a hometown hero, and next to Youssou N'Dour, is probably the most famous Senegalese in the world. He sings in Pulaar and has released dozens of albums, including collaborations with fellow *Podorois* musician Mansour Seck. Award-winning fashion designer Oumou Sy is another of Podor's native daughters; she launched the now-indispensable Dakar Fashion Week, opened boutiques in Paris and Geneva, and designs outfits for film and stage productions, as well as for her contemporaries like Baaba Maal himself. Behind the lens documenting it all and with a growing cult following is Podor's resident photographer, Oumar Ly, whose studio portraits and decades-long documentation

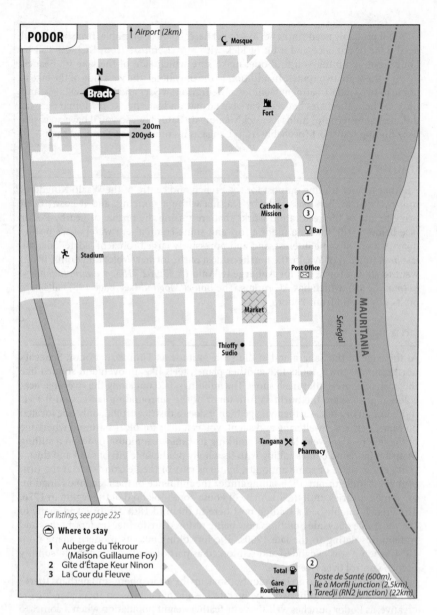

PODOR

↑ Airport (2km)

ᘓ Mosque

N

Bradt

0 ———— 200m
0 ———— 200yds

᛭ Fort

Catholic ● ①
Mission ③

♀ Bar

大 Stadium

Post Office ✉

Market

Thioffy ●
Sudio

Sénégal

MAURITANIA

Tangana ✕ ✚
Pharmacy

For listings, see page 225

🏠 **Where to stay**

1 Auberge du Tékrour
   (Maison Guillaume Foy)
2 Gîte d'Étape Keur Ninon
3 La Cour du Fleuve

Total ⛽ ②

Gare
Routière 🚐

Poste de Santé (600m),
Île à Morfil junction (2.5km),
↓ Taredji (RN2 junction) (22km)

of life in the community have recently found wide acclaim and exhibition in Dakar, Europe and beyond.

GETTING THERE AND AWAY A handful of **vehicles** leave Podor early in the morning, but after that the *gare routière* starts to look more than a little deserted. It's 4,000F for a *sept-place* to Saint-Louis from here, and 2,500F to Richard Toll, but to go east, you need to first get to Taredji, 22km away at the RN2 junction (where you'll have to head anyway if you miss the early-morning cars). It's 500F for a lift between the two and cars go back and forth throughout the day. The RN2 from here to Saint-Louis is 220km of bitumen bliss, while the route eastbound is considerably less dreamy.

Pirogues dart across the river to Lexeiba II in Mauritania throughout the day; be sure to track down the immigration officer before you go. There's an airport 2km north of town, but the only flights here will be one you charter yourself.

Podor is also the eastern terminus for trips on the *Bou el Mogdad* (see page 198), and if you've got the cash, this is without question the most interesting and comfortable way to get here.

WHERE TO STAY, EAT AND DRINK *Map, page 224.*

If you'd rather avoid the potentially long nights of music & alcohol-fuelled shenanigans at the rough and tumble **Keur Ninon**, the **Catholic Mission** has been known to occasionally offer spare rooms for visitors – worth an ask, anyway.

La Cour du Fleuve (6 rooms) 33 965 1712; m 77 492 5415; e courdufleuve@orange.sn; www. lacourdufleuve.com. From the moment you walk inside, you could be forgiven for pinching yourself that such a place exists in Podor. The gorgeous *banco*-style rooms in this restored quayside building are set around a courtyard filled with art & sculpture by the likes of Ousmane Sow, Mauro Petroni & Podor's own Oumar Ly, & all come with AC, big mosquito nets, designer trimmings & mosaic accents, while the suites sleep 3 & have private terraces overlooking the river. There's a library with a book collection & flatscreen TV, canoes & bicycles for hire, & your choice of terraces (roof or garden) for dining, sunbathing or both. **$$$**

Auberge du Tékrour (Maison Guillaume Foy) (6 rooms); 33 965 1682; m 77 526 5200/249 8665; e maison-guillaumefoy@podor-rivegauche.com; www.aubergedutekrour.net. Podor's simmering renaissance began here nearly 10 years ago, and this lovingly restored 200-year-old mansion on the quay remains an immensely welcome sight after the long journey to Podor, whether you've come by land or water. Enter through the heavy wooden doors into a pastel garden courtyard ringed by a 1st-floor balcony providing access to all the rooms. The thick-walled historic rooms overlook the river, some from their own private terraces, while the new rooms face north with views over the fort. All the rooms but one are en-suite with AC. There's a phenomenal display on the ground floor with maps, artefacts & Oumar Ly photos cataloguing Podor's long history, & a library with several hundred volumes as well (all in French, though). They arrange all kinds of trips to neighbouring villages, artisans' workshops & excursions along the river & to Île à Morfil. Rates start in the middle & continue to just beyond the top of this range, depending on the room. **$$**

Gîte d'Étape Keur Ninon (6 rooms) 33 965 1642; m 77 651 8313; e kitekeurninon@ yahoo.fr. At the south end of town across from the *gare routière*, the indifferent rooms here are basic, but so is the price. All are en-suite with nets & fans & are configured to sleep 2 to 4 people. The complex is also home to a rather unglamorous bar where you could probably rustle up a bowl of *thieboudienne*. **$**

WHAT TO SEE AND DO The **fort** at the north end of town has gone through countless ups and downs in its long existence, but it's recently retired from the military life and today it's been patched up and converted into a modest museum. The panels delve into the history of Podor and the region, but only in French. Still, the building itself is fully worth a visit, and there are usually some Oumar Ly photos on display here as well. If nobody's around when you come knocking, try calling the guardian, Mr Ibrahima Sy (m *77 447 4457/618 3111*), and he'll come to open it up for you. A bit south of here, the historic **quay** is only a few blocks long, but its quietness is mesmerising; don't be surprised if the hours here slip past like so much water.

When you're done on the waterside, head inland a few blocks to the **market**, which stocks all the essentials, even if some of the fruits and veg look like they've had a rough go of it out here in the desert. Next door is Oumar Ly's **Thioffy Studio**, where if he's open you can have a chat, pore over some of his thousands upon thousands of portraits, or even get one taken of yourself – a truly one-of-a-kind souvenir.

On the far side of Podor's wide meander in the Senegal River lies **Ngawlé** village, a tiny *banco* wonder of a village 3km west of town. It's easy as can be to set up a guided trip here at Auberge du Tékrour (see page 225), or you could just hire a *calèche* yourself to take you over. They can also arrange pirogue trips on the river, including custom journeys further afield on the 24m *Reine du Fleuve*.

If you happen to be here during December, don't miss the annual **Blues du Fleuve** festival (*www.festivalbluesdufleuve.com*). The brainchild of Baba Maal himself, the festival takes over Podor with music, art and dance ever year, bringing in both Senegalese luminaries and groups from as far afield as Malawi and the UK.

NDIOUM

Remarkable mostly for the fact it's now home to a brand new bridge over the Doué to Île à Morfil, Ndioum is an important crossroads and market town for Senegal's extreme north, and is generally better connected than nearby Podor. If you're coming from the west, the skating rink tarmac comes to an abrupt halt here, but if you're headed to the coast, the journey is a lot more comfortable from here on. Sandwiched between the Doué River and the RN2, Ndioum is busy with all manner of traders and travellers passing through town, especially on Mondays for the weekly *loumo*, when blue Mauritanian *boubous* and Toucouleur pointed hats might even outnumber knockoff football shirts. If you've come up short on cash, there's a CBAO with ATM here – the only one you'll see for a while in either direction. If you decide to break the journey here rather than pushing on the additional 45km to Podor, the **Auberge Macina Toro** (✆ *33 965 3272*) offers basic fan and AC rooms in town for about 15,000F, but for a more comfortable stay, head 7km west to the hamlet of Gamadji Saré, where you'll find **Auberge Les Jardins du Fouta** (8 rooms) (m *77 533 2664*; e *jardindufouta@ gmail.com*) just north of the road, which offers spotless en-suite rooms in a family compound with AC, mozzie nets, Wi-Fi and Senegalese meals. They also arrange trips to neighbouring pastoralist villages and the Île à Morfil just across the river.

ÎLE À MORFIL

Between the Senegal River to the north and its tributary the Doué to the south, the Île à Morfil is Senegal's largest island, sandwiched between these two waterways and separated from the mainland for nearly 150km. *Morfil* is an antiquated French term for raw ivory, and the island got its name in the mid-17th century from French colonialists who would come here for, believe it or not, elephant hunting. Once home to not only elephants but lions and more long-gone big game, the island today is better known for its string of traditional *banco*-constructed villages, with several buildings dating back to the times of Île à Morfil's most famous resident, El Hadj Omar Tall, who was born in Alwar (sometimes *Halwar*) village when the island was part of the Futa Toro Imamate sometime around 1797. Around 1850 he went on to found and lead the Toucouleur Empire, which at its greatest extent stretched from the eastern shores of the Senegal River all the way to Timbuktu and, though he recruited many of his followers from Île à Morfil and surrounds, French expansion along the river meant that his home village of Alwar and the island as a whole would never fall under his rule.

It's one of the least-visited places in Senegal, and if Podor feels like you've reached the end of the earth (though technically it's on the island as well), then the rest of Île à Morfil is a few steps into the ether beyond. Pocked with diminutive Toucouleur villages that live by the dictates of the seasons and their herds, it's a journey into a traditional landscape that's rapidly disappearing in Senegal and throughout the region. Incredibly, Sudano-Sahelian style *banco* mosques from the days of Omar Tall's presence here still stand in Alwar, his home village, and Guédé village, some kilometres to the west. Closer to Podor on the north side of the island, Donayé was abandoned after catastrophic floods hit the village at the turn of this century, and the empty buildings of the village are an eerie testament to the durability of their mud brick construction. There's a 19th-century mosque here as well, and the few families hanging on in the village tend to it.

SHEEP SHOPPING IN THE SAHEL: TABASKI EDITION   *Juliana Peluso*

Livestock are a big-ticket item in Senegal, and one does not commit with abandon. Traditionally acquired by families as a kind of investment/ insurance of capital (which provides some insight as to the etymology of the very word 'live-stock'), most animals, to the confusion of Westerners, are herded to and fro for the majority of their lifespans, dropping dead only of old age or exposure. While families will occasionally dip into their supply to furnish the thieboudienne bowls of a wedding or baptism, animals are kept alive and grazing primarily because they represent theoretical wealth, like a highly visible financial portfolio. There is, however, one large and important exception to this rule: the Tabaski ram.

Snow-white Tabaski sheep, the caviar of the ungulate world, are fattened *à la perfection* for the biggest Islamic holiday of the year and can run in the hundreds of thousands, and occasionally thousands of thousands, of CFA (that is, roughly, at least a few hundred euros for your standard, no-frills model). Herders and breeders of these animals are usually careerists and look to do as much business as possible during the Tabaski timeframe, unloading their product in a seller's market. Supply and demand as well as tradition are the cause for seasonal markups, as according to the Koran, every able family is obligated to purchase an animal of sufficient size to feed themselves as well as share with relatives and donate to the needy during the festivities. Known as Eid al-Adha in the Islamic world outside West Africa, the holiday varies in date in accordance with the lunar Islamic calendar and commemorates the willingness of Ibrahim to sacrifice his only son, Ismail, on God's command.

Smaller, cheaper designs, usually somewhat battered in appearance and lacking a certain majesty (as well as the appealingly flawless white coat), can be found for, at minimum, around 60,000 CFA (€90). One would be well-advised to start sheep-seeking early if frugality is the goal; cheap sheep sell like hot cakes. Furthermore, if at all possible, it would be prudent to bring a trusted local companion to aid in the linguistic and cultural aspects of the haggling process, which can be of unprecedented fierceness. French is not sufficient and will most likely result in the purchase of Toyota sheep at BMW prices.

If you should decide to take the plunge, guard your new purchase with care, because despite the reason for the season, livestock theft reaches its height in the period before the holiday. It's not uncommon to see Tabaski sheep tethered to beds indoors, literally chained to their owners, or stashed on rooftop balconies, safe from would-be kidnappers as they blithely await the inevitable.

GETTING THERE AND AWAY The island's isolation has been long-standing, and it wouldn't be uncommon to hear an islander headed for the mainland say that they're 'going to Senegal'. This is changing fast, however, and the past several years have seen the construction of three different bridges facilitating access to the island. The easiest way to get on to the island is from the turnoff just south of Podor, where there's a helpful signpost listing distances to the villages. Also at the island's west end, there's the new bridge at Ndioum or the ferry near Guédé village. From the turnoff near Podor, it's 10km to Donaye, at which there's a turnoff leading to either Alwar (left) or Guédé (right). From the junction south of Podor, it's 24km to Guédé village and another 1,500m after the ferry crossing until you're back on the RN2. To reach Alwar, it's 43km from the junction south of Podor, and to continue from here back to the RN2, there's a small ferry crossing of yet another tributary of the Senegal River 3km beyond Alwar, after which it's just over 5km to the new bridge at Ndioum.

The only improved roads on the island are at either end. West to east, these consist of the route from Podor to Guédé Village and the ferry crossing back to the mainland, or from Podor to Alwar and the new bridge at Ndioum. At the east end of the island there is a bridge at Madina Ndiathbé (3.5km from the RN2), which follows a roughly 60km loop via Cascas, Thioubalel and Saldé (where Matam-born author Cheikh Hamidou Kane's 1961 semi-autobiographical novel *Ambiguous Adventure* is thought to be set), crossing another new bridge over the Doué River at Ngouye, from where it's another 6km until you rejoin the RN2 at Pété. In the centre of the island between these two loops, there are plenty more villages connected by rough tracks, as well as access to the Mauritanian city of Boghé via the border village of Diemet Tienel. You'd need a vehicle to get here, but unless you're brave enough to strap your 4x4 on to a homespun ferry made of some lashed-together pirogues, crossing the river with it may prove a challenge. (The other Mauritanian border crossing near here is just beyond the island's eastern tip; the turnoffs for Kaédi, Mauritania are at either Orefondé or Agnam Goly, and it's about 30km on rough tracks to the remote pirogue crossing by either route.)

OUROSSOGUI

Just as the river dictated the fortunes of its neighbour Matam, the road has done so with Ourossogui. The most important transport junction anywhere along the northern river route, Ourossogui's profile has risen as Senegal's road network has improved and river transport largely disappeared. Today it's subservient to Matam politically, but in terms of transport, trade, facilities, population and nearly every other aspect except charm, it's the dominant of the two interlinked cities. More a place to break your journey than anything else, Ourossogui is home to several functioning ATMs, a post office, decent hotels with internet, reliable petrol stations, a hospital and a decently stocked supermarket.

GETTING THERE AND AWAY Ourossogui is where the river route from Saint-Louis (RN2) intersects the new road from Louga via Linguère (RN3), and as such is the locus for all road transport in northeastern Senegal (such as it is). From here, it's 215km of beautiful new tarmac to Linguère, but you're looking at something of a potholed mess in either direction along the RN2. Daily *sept-places* go in all directions, including a few direct vehicles to Dakar (13,000F), Saint-Louis (9,500F), and Bakel (3,000F). For Tambacounda, you'll have to transfer in Bakel; start very early if you aim to do this in a day, and ignore maps that say there's a direct route between Ourossogui and Tambacounda; it's a track at best and all traffic goes via

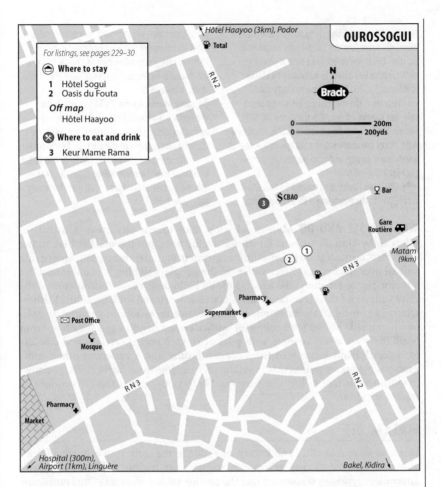

For listings, see pages 229–30

Where to stay
1 Hôtel Sogui
2 Oasis du Fouta

Off map
Hôtel Haayoo

Where to eat and drink
3 Keur Mame Rama

Hôtel Haayoo (3km), Podor

Total

N

Bradt

0   200m
0   200yds

RN 2

Bar

$ CBAO

Gare
Routière

Matam
(9km)

RN 3

Pharmacy

Supermarket

Post Office

Mosque

RN 3

RN 2

Pharmacy

Market

Hospital (300m),
Airport (1km), Linguère

Bakel, Kidira

Kidira. With the exception of Bakel, it's a fair old distance to anywhere from here, so you'd be well advised to get down to the *gare routière* early, particularly if you're aiming for Saint-Louis.

If you've found yourself out here short on patience but flush with cash, **Groupe Transair** (\ *33 865 2565/991 6774;* **e** *sales@groupetransair.sn; www.groupetransair. sn* or *www.facebook.com/groupetransair*) runs two flights a week from Dakar for around 90,000F one-way.

WHERE TO STAY, EAT AND DRINK *Map, above.*
All hotels offer Wi-Fi.

Hôtel Sogui (45 rooms) \33 966 1536. This 3-storey hotel in the town centre primarily caters to travellers on business whose expense accounts won't cover the Haayoo. There's a bunch of rooms with balconies out front overlooking the road (equal parts interesting vantage point & obnoxious traffic noise), or a selection of standalone

bungalows set around the back gardens. All have TV & AC, & they offer a standard assortment of meals. Prices towards the middle of this range. **$$**
Hôtel Haayoo \33 966 3730; **m** 77 542 99 59/514 0504; **e** hotel.haayoo@yahoo.fr; www. hotel-haayoo.com. Boasting what is almost certainly the only swimming pool for a couple of

229

hundred kilometres, this shiny new business oasis 3km from town towards Saint-Louis would be a worthy stop if you've got road dust in places you didn't realise you could. Inaugurated by Macky Sall himself in 2013, it isn't particularly long on character & the rooms are a bit on the small side, but they've all got AC & flatscreen TV, & it's winning the contest for smartest digs in town by a mile. Prices are around the top of this range, there's a restaurant on site, and non-guests can use the pool for 2,000F. **$$**

🏠 **Oasis du Fouta** (10 rooms) 33 966 1294. Just opposite the much larger Hotel Sogui, this place offers well-kept en-suite rooms with AC & TV, & the manager will happily go out of his way to make sure you're taken care of. Food & drink are available by request, & it's the most affordable sleep in town. **$$**

✗ **Keur Mame Rama** 🌂 30 118 0102. On the surface it doesn't look much different to any other picnic table restaurant, but this local standby serves some of the best chicken in town & a daily selection chalked up on the board out front that might include burgers, yassa, steak, fish, omelettes or fattayah; it all goes for a very palatable 1,500F.

WHAT TO SEE AND DO More truck stop than tourist attraction, Ourossogui offers wafer-slim pickings as far as sightseeing goes, but the **market** here draws craftsmen, farmers and a multi-ethnic assortment of traders from Mali, Mauritania and all over the Senegal River valley, so the people-watching is phenomenal. It's a major centre for the Fulbe herders of the Ferlo desert and Toucouleurs of the river valley, and their traditional dress is widely worn and sold, including leather-trimmed conical straw hats quite reminiscent of those worn in southeast Asia, and handmade knives with colourful leather-bound handles and sheathes. From Mali, there are a few vendors with piles of rings, bangles, earrings and amulets for sale, all hand-hammered from copper, bronze and a variety of other semi-precious metals, as well as others selling metres of lustrous *bazin* cloth, pounded to within an inch of its life with cartoonishly large wooden mallets to produce its trademark shine.

MATAM

Home to several families and known as Tiaïdé in the early 17th century, the city of Matam adopted its current name during the slave-trading era, when the town's Toucouleur residents demanded that the passing raiders *matama* – Toucouleur for 'pay in cash'. The name stuck, and the town became an important outpost during inveterate fort-builder and colonial governor Louis Faidherbe's drive to pacify the upper reaches of the Senegal River in the 19th century. A fort was in fact constructed here in 1857, but early 20th-century flooding destroyed it completely. Still, Matam remained an important stop along the river route for many years, and the *Bou el Mogdad* called here starting in the 1950s, when it was still one of the most important modes of trade & transport on the river.

In the years since, Matam's fortunes have been on the decline, as much of the action has moved from the river to the road and to its young upstart neighbour Ourossogui. It remains the regional capital, but any glory here is definitely of the faded variety and time has long since passed Matam by. For residents, this lack of development despite the town being the regional capital is a chronic complaint (there isn't a single bank here, for instance), but for a visitor, the *banco* architecture in the old quarter, frozen-in-time colonial warehouses and car-free streets can make for an enchanting visit.

GETTING THERE AND AWAY All transport to Matam goes via Ourossogui, 9km across the floodplain to the west on the RN3. Rattletrap *ndiaga ndiayes* make the journey throughout the day for a few hundred CFA. Pirogues make the river crossing to Toufunde Civé in Mauritania throughout the day; don't forget to get your passport stamped in town.

WHERE TO STAY, EAT AND DRINK
Map, right.

Résidence du Fleuve (9 rooms) \33 966 2083; m 77 658 0234. Pretty much the only game in town when it comes to hotels, the handful of rooms here are clean & simple, all with en-suite bath & AC. There's Wi-Fi, & they do a standard range of food options on request. Matam's tourist office is also based here, and can arrange a variety of tours and visits around the town or the region (see below). Rates at the centre of this range. **$$**

✗ **CRETEF** m 77 645 60 52; ⊕ lunch daily. The canteen at this NGO does a Senegalese *plat du jour* for around 2,000F; otherwise your best bets for a meal will be to poke around near the market or eat at the Residence du Fleuve.

WHAT TO SEE AND DO Matam can be a bit coy when it comes to revealing its charms, but it's eminently manageable to walk the whole city in an afternoon (or a morning to avoid the wilting heat). The town is

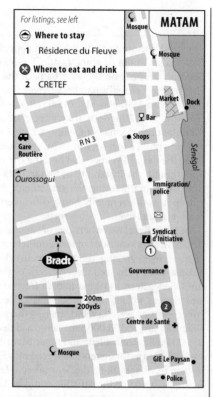

largely split into two halves, with the old quarter north of the road from Ourossogui and the colonial district to the south. (Both of these could justifiably be called old, but so is pretty much everything in Matam.) Hidden between more workaday buildings in the old town is one of the biggest concentrations of Sudano-Sahelian architecture anywhere in Senegal, with several dozen venerable *banco* structures with fat, rounded columns, and irregular triangular windows still standing along the narrow streets or within compounds that have grown around them in the years since they were built. It's obviously impossible to know which compound walls are hiding these gems, so architecture buffs may be interested in chatting with the **Syndicat d'Initiative** (m *77 502 5832;* e *syndimatam@yahoo.fr; www.tourismematam.com*) as they know exactly where all the historic homes are and can set you up with a guide to help you gain access. They can also set up pirogue trips, visits to local carvers, tanners, weavers and more.

The waterfront market is small but dependably lively, and the riverfront is a great place to look up close at the riverine agriculture that's sustained residents here for centuries, though sadly it's trash-strewn to a shocking degree. You'll also meet hundreds of *Matamois* out to do the washing, have a bath, or haul in their catches at the pier. The colonial *gouvernance* and some of the warehouses at the south end of town are worth a look, and you'll have the dusty streets largely to yourself down here. If you've got the time, stop by and see Mr Mustafa Ndiaye at his nursery, **GIE Le Paysan** (\ *33 265 5679*), which is also in the neighbourhood. It's a shady oasis in a town where these are sorely lacking, and you'll hardly believe the bounty of fruits and vegetables he coaxes out of his riverfront patch of land.

BAKEL

The most remote and possibly most appealing of all the towns along the river route, Bakel is set amongst some gentle, baobab-studded hills (very gentle – this is still Senegal, after all) on the west bank of the Senegal River, the last settlement of any size before Senegal's namesake river leaves the country entirely at the tri-point border with Mali and Mauritania. It was founded in the 18th century by migrants from the Jolof Kingdom; they were granted a concession of land at Bakel from the Soninke *tunka* (king) of Galam, which ruled the area until the French negotiated rights to build a fort here in 1820, eventually exerting control over the entire region. Over the next 30 years Bakel became the most important trading centre in the area and, though the instability of Omar Tall's neighbouring Toucouleur Empire led to difficulties maintaining the settlement, it remained the region's primary trading entrepôt until eventually being overtaken in importance by Kayes in Mali, where road, rail and river all converged.

In 1989, Bakel was where one of Senegal's most serious crises outside of Casamance began, when a localised but fatal conflict between Mauritanian herders and Senegalese farmers over grazing rights touched off a diplomatic feud and ethnic pogroms against those perceived to be citizens of the opposing country, typically along racial lines. Senegalese and Mauritanian interests in Nouakchott and Dakar were torched and dozens killed, the border was closed, and diplomatic relations between the two countries were severed. In less than two months' time, an estimated 170,000 Mauritanians and 75,000 Senegalese had fled to their country of origin, and as many as 53,000 Fulbe, Toucouleur and other Mauritanian citizens of black African ethnicities were labelled as foreigners and forced into Senegal. Some 13,500 Mauritanian refugees remain in villages along the Senegalese side of the river as of 2015.

Today, however, the situation could hardly be calmer. Pirogues laden with cement, cooking oil and other goods where there's a significant price differential between the two countries do a brisk trade – sometimes openly, sometimes clandestinely – and there's a functioning immigration post at either side of the river. The impressive fort still stands guard over a magnificent bend in the blue-green river, but today the long-rusted cannons guarding the gates serve as a drying rack for the local washerwomen. It's one of Senegals' remotest and hottest towns, but even though its time as the upper Senegal's major hub is long consigned to the days of yore, Bakel today still looks and feels a lot more active than crumbling Matam or otherworldy Podor.

GETTING THERE AND AWAY The RN2 in either direction from Bakel passes through some appealingly hilly terrain, but the road itself is nowhere near as pretty. Count on some serious pothole-dodging in either direction from town. There are *sept-places* to Kidira (1,500F) throughout the day, and more occasional vehicles to Tambacounda (6,000F) (via Kidira) or Ourossogui (3,000F). Arriving in Bakel, it's possible that your vehicle will drop you at the RN2 junction 5km from town, where local vehicles will ferry you into town for a few CFA. **Niokolo Transports** (❨ 76 639 1884; www.niokolotransports.com) has direct buses to Dakar (via Tambacounda) every Monday, Wednesday, and Friday for 11,000F, departing at 17.00 and arriving in Dakar in the early morning. You can also jump off in Tambacounda for 3,500F.

Pirogues laden with goods and passengers cross the river between here and the Mauritanian village of Gouraye throughout the day; passport control is just up from the beach where the pirogues land. There's also an airport about 10km from town towards Kidira, but there were no scheduled services here at the time of writing.

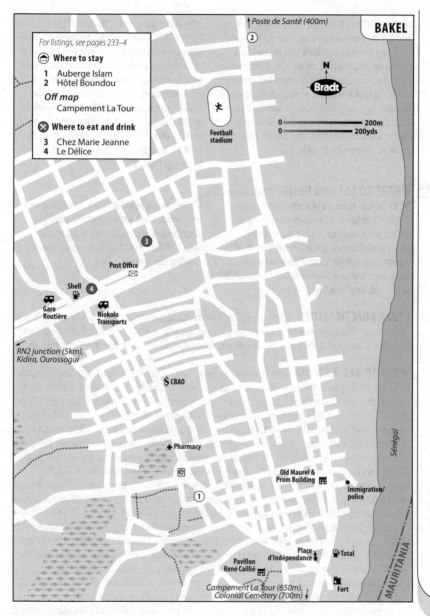

For listings, see pages 233–4

⌂ Where to stay
1 Auberge Islam
2 Hôtel Boundou

Off map
Campement La Tour

✖ Where to eat and drink
3 Chez Marie Jeanne
4 Le Délice

BAKEL

↑ Poste de Santé (400m)

②

N

Bradt

0 ———————— 200m
0 ———————— 200yds

★
Football
stadium

③

Post Office ✉

Shell ④
🚌
Gare
Routière

🚌
Niokolo
Transports

↙ RN2 junction (5km),
Kidira, Ourossogui

$ CBAO

✚ Pharmacy

ℯ

①

Old Maurel &
Prom Building 🏛

● Immigration/
police

Sénégal

Place
d'Indépendance 🕯
🚏 Total

Pavillon
René Caillié 🏛

🏛
Fort

*Campement La Tour (650m),
Colonial Cemetery (700m)* ↓

MAURITANIA

Senegal River and the North   BAKEL

8

⌂ WHERE TO STAY *Map, above.*

⌂ **Auberge Islam** (9 rooms) ☎ 33 937 9029;
📱 77 937 6938. In a several-storey building
smack in the city centre, rooms here have either
fan or AC, & all rooms use shared ablutions &
come with mosquito nets. The fan rooms here are
the cheapest digs in town by half, but if you're
going to spring for AC, the other two places have

en-suite rooms for the exact same price. And
there's no bar (duh). **$$**

⌂ **Campement La Tour** (3 rooms) 📱 77
523 3033; ℯ sambao@hotmail.fr. Perched at the
top of a hill at the south end of town, the three
standalone chalets here have far & away the best
location in Bakel, overlooking a spectacular bend in

the Senegal River & offering views in all directions, which is the exact reason they share the hill with a military lookout tower built here in years past. Rooms are simple but all are en-suite & come with AC, & there's a covered terrace where self-caterers are free to cook if they like, or meals & drinks are available by request. The manager speaks English & can arrange pirogue trips up & down the river. It's possible there'll be no one on the hill when you arrive, so call ahead if possible. **$$**

Hôtel Boundou (18 rooms) ☏ 33 980 3184; m 77 655 2565; e hotelboundou@yahoo.fr. This place unfortunately takes almost zero advantage of its pretty riverside location, but it's a nice quiet spot on the edge of town nonetheless. Rooms all come with Wi-Fi, AC, TV & en-suite bath, & you could probably get away with a bit of negotiation on the prices as well. There's some outdoor seating, meals & drinks on request, & apropos of absolutely nothing, what seems to be a homemade helicopter in the courtyard. **$$**

WHERE TO EAT AND DRINK *Map, page 233.*

✘ **Le Délice** Bakel is a little thin on restaurants that aren't set up on the kerbside every morning, but this place would be a solid choice even if it wasn't almost the only game in town. They do all the Senegalese usuals like yassa & mafé, sandwiches & snacks like chawarma & fattayeh, & if the menu is to be believed, they've got 'humberger' too.

♀ **Chez Marie Jeanne** The local drinking hole, which won't get any Michelin stars, but is surprisingly pleasant. (A good thing, because Bakel's climate won't take long to send you crawling over here for a nip.)

OTHER PRACTICALITIES There's a CBAO with ATM on the main road in town, a post office near the *gare routière*, and you can get online at either Hotel Boundou or the first-floor internet café a few blocks down from the ATM (look for the 'Canalsat' logo).

WHAT TO SEE AND DO The imposing **fort**, began in 1820 and expanded under Faidherbe in the 1850s, is the obvious starting point for exploring Bakel. At the top of the entrance ramp is the porticoed prefecture building, which dates from the same era but has been kept in remarkably good shape (even the teal shutters remain) and still functions as the seat for local governance. The gardens aren't quite as inspiring, but there are a few baobabs hanging about, and the views from up here over the river and out to the dusty horizon in Mauritania are stellar. Barely 200m away on another hill just inland sits the derelict **Pavillon René Caillié**, built here as a staging post for the renowned French explorer's journey to Timbuktu in the 1820's. At the top of a hill with a few footpaths leading up to it and a whole lot of rusted-through bowls and other detritus on all sides, it's been abandoned, squatted, and abandoned again in recent years, and it's in thoroughly lamentable shape, though that does little to diminish the excellent views over Bakel from here.

At the south end of town near the Campement La Tour is an old military **watchtower** – the staircase is no more, so you can no longer get to the top, but it's on the same hill as the campement, and worth a look for its imposing thick walls and narrow slit windows that seem to make a rather ironic smiley face when seen from the right angle. At the base of the hill lies the **colonial cemetery**, which holds the remains of French administrators and soldiers, with burials from 1850 to 1900. It's in rather poor shape as well, but the epitaphs are worthy insight into the vainglorious colonial madness that led so many to lose their lives here.

Pirogue trips from an hour to a day in duration can be arranged through the campement, as well as visits to local artisans and neighbouring villages.

9

Central Senegal and the Grande Côte

Heading west from Dakar, you leave the spectacular oceanic scenery of Cap Vert behind and make your way into the baking, dust-blown interior – it may not be the most compelling scenery in the country, but if you've got any chance of understanding what makes Senegal tick, here is the place to find out. The cities of central Senegal are not only the geographic but also the spiritual heart of the entire country, and this is particularly true of the Mouride capital of Touba. What happens here is figuratively and literally shouted from the rooftops in all corners of the country, and the wealth and influence of the brotherhood becomes starkly apparent when you realise they both own and manage the second-largest city in the country.

Thiès is the region's most appealing city for visitors, and while not exactly teeming with attractions, its tree-lined centre, easy vibe, and lively music & arts scene might just convince you to slow down for a day or two, especially as a calming provincial counterpoint to Dakar's non-stop action just down the road. Further inland, Diourbel, Dahra, Louga, and Linguère factor into vanishingly few tourists' itineraries, and while they won't bowl you over with their dozens of landmark attractions (hope you packed your selfie stick), each played an important rôle in the several Wolof kingdoms that controlled the area before the *bourbas*, *damels*, *teignes* and kings of these historic states were toppled and replaced by a French governor in Saint-Louis after French annexation in the late 1800s. Diourbel is also an important Mouride centre, and is home to a grand mosque predating Touba's.

Meanwhile, on the coast you'll find a jaw-dropping 150km of uninterrupted beach that runs all the way from Yoff on the Cap Vert peninsula to the Langue de Barbarie just south of Saint-Louis. The geography of this stretch of coast leaves it exposed to strong ocean currents from the north, which means it's largely been left the domain of fishermen and has seen almost none of the tourist development you'll find on the Petite Côte south of here. So while sun-seekers may want to consider looking elsewhere, the incredible power and raw beauty of the ocean is on full display here, and towns like Mboro or Lompoul make excellent bases for checking out this unexplored stretch of coast.

THIÈS *Population 636,000*

Thiès (pronounced *chess*) is probably Senegal's most alluring urban centre away from the coastline, and it makes for a worthwhile escape if you've had a few too many days dodging traffic and staying up all night out on the peninsula in Dakar. And while it's most certainly tranquil when compared with Dakar, Thiès lacks the religiously inspired strictures of its more pious neighbours to the east, and as such there's a good enough chance you'll find yourself out dancing all night here as well. The city centre is refreshingly – and almost uniquely for Senegal – covered in old, beautiful trees, making it a pleasurable, low-hassle place to stroll, even in the heat

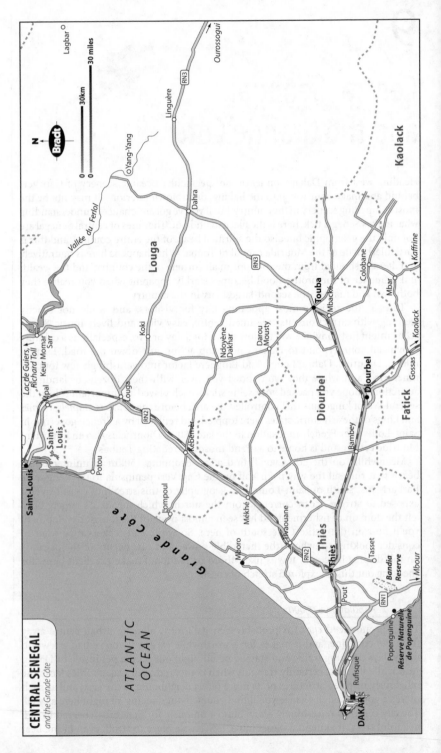

CENTRAL SENEGAL
and the Grande Côte

of the day. The arts scene here is also surprisingly active, and it's home to a weaving operation unique in West Africa, though its work tends to be well out of the reach of most traveller's budgets.

HISTORY Thiès's moniker as Senegal's 'railway city' is perhaps somewhat less appropriate today given the much-reduced state of the rail network, but still it remains, and indeed, even in its diminished state Thiès is still Senegal's most significant rail centre. The railway was a source of pride for many in the region, but Thiès has always had a complicated relationship with it. The still-revered *damel* (king) of Cayor (the Wolof kingdom of which Thiès was a part), Lat Dior, was fervently opposed to the construction of the railway, as he very accurately foresaw that it would lead to the downfall of his kingdom and the loss of independence from the French. While based some kilometres north in Tivaouane, Lat Dior and his men fought here and made attempts to sabotage the railway's construction. Ultimately, the collapse of Cayor, the completion of the railway, and the violent death of Lat Dior all came to pass as Dior himself predicted between 1885 and 1886.

The *Thièsois* never lost their independent streak, and the city was a crucial support centre during the great railway strike of 1947–8, when under the leadership of Ibrahima Sarr the railway union downed tools, crippling rail transport across French West Africa for nearly six months and extracting pay raises, family benefits and a number of other concessions from the colonial authorities in a dramatic climb-down, immortalised in Ousmane Sembène's 1960 novel, *God's Bits of Wood*, much of which takes place in Thiès.

Before taking the reins as the first president of a newly independent Senegal, Léopold Sédar Senghor was mayor of Thiès for several years in the late 1950s. And while Sembène's description of mid 20th-century Thiès was rather less than charitable ('a vast, uncertain plain where all the rot of the city has gathered...a place where everyone – man, woman, and child – had a face the colour of the earth'), the state of the city today is considerably more cheerful.

GETTING THERE AND AWAY
By bus and *sept-place* Just 60km east of the capital, Thiès forms the gateway to Dakar and the Cap Vert peninsula, and as such could hardly be easier to access. Transit from here goes in all directions, with *sept-places* regularly departing the *gare routière* for Dakar (1,500F), Saint-Louis (3,500F), Kaolack (3,000F), Mbour (1,200F), Tambacounda (9,000F), Touba (2,300F), and Banjul (5,500F).

By car The RN2 to Saint-Louis and RN3 towards Touba meet in Thiès, and anyone heading north/northwest from Dakar will certainly pass through here. Roads in all directions are tarmac and in fair to good shape. There's even some talk of extending the Dakar toll road to Thiès eventually, but this is a long way off. With its wide boulevards and total lack of Dakar-style congestion, Thiès would also have to rank among Senegal's easier cities for self-drivers.

By train Train enthusiasts rejoice! There is still one passenger train service running in Senegal, and it's a daily run between Dakar and Thiès, affectionately known as the *petit train bleu* (little blue train) or the *petit train de banlieue* (little suburban train). It leaves Thiès every morning at 06.55 and arrives in Dakar about two hours later, after which it turns around and heads back to Thiès at 17.15, passing through Colobane, Hann, Thiaroye, Rufisque, Bargny, Sébikotane and Pout *en route*. There's a first class car with AC and soft seats for 1,250F, or second class and benches for 500F.

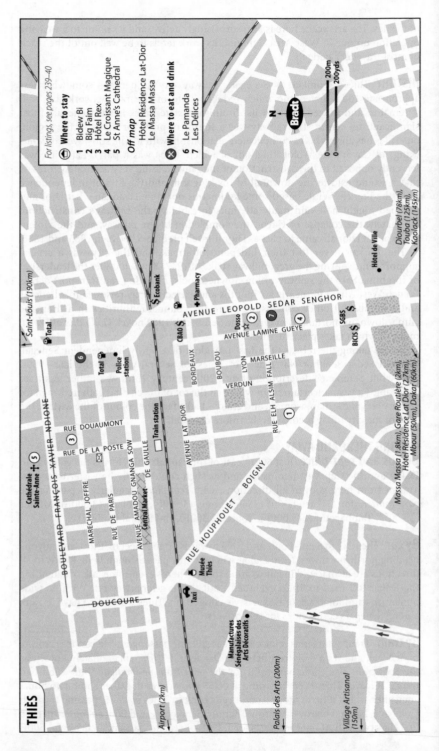

THIÈS

For listings, see pages 239–40

Where to stay
1 Bidew Bi
2 Big Faim
3 Hôtel Rex
4 Le Croissant Magique
5 St Anne's Cathedral

Off map
Hôtel Résidence Lat-Dior
Le Massa Massa

Where to eat and drink
6 Le Pamanda
7 Les Délices

Saint-Louis (190km)

Cathédrale Sainte-Anne

BOULEVARD FRANÇOIS-XAVIER NDIONE

RUE DOUAUMONT
RUE DE LA POSTE

MARECHAL JOFFRE
RUE DE PARIS

AVENUE AMADOU GNANGA SOW
Central Market
DE GAULLE

Train station

Police station

Total
Ecobank
Pharmacy
CBAO
Dosso

AVENUE LEOPOLD SEDAR SENGHOR

AVENUE LAMINE GUEYE

BORDEAUX
BOUBOU
LYON
MARSEILLE
VERDUN

RUE ELH ALSIM FALL

AVENUE LAT DIOR

RUE HOUPHOUET – BOIGNY

DOUCOURE

Taxi

Musée Thiès

Manufactures Sénégalaises des Arts Décoratifs

Palais des Arts (200m)

Village Artisanal (150m)

Airport (2km)

SGBS
BICIS

Massa Massa (1.8km), Gare Routière (2km),
Hôtel Résidence Lat Dior (2.7km),
Mbour (50km), Dakar (60km)

Diourbel (78km),
Touba (125km),
Kaolack (145km)

Hôtel de Ville

N
Bradt

0   200m
0   200yds

By air Given that it's only 60km from Dakar, it's a bit unclear what purpose Thiès airport is intended to serve, but whatever it is, it's not passenger flights. In fact, Thiès will be even closer, some 35km, from the new Blaise Diagne International Airport (see page 79) once it opens, which should be during the lifespan of this edition.

WHERE TO STAY *Map, page 238.*

Hôtel Résidence Lat-Dior (37 rooms)
\33 952 0777/8; m 77 569 6767; e dioufmoctar@hotmail.com; www.hotel-residencelatdior.com. At the edge of town on the road towards Mbour, this is a rather large complex with a fitness centre, swimming pool & restaurant. It's a bit more expensive than other offerings in town, & while it's comfortable, the rather gaudy furnishings & artistically bankrupt Chinese murals don't so much convey luxury as they do a loose approximation of it. **$$$**

Bidew Bi (15 rooms) Av Houphouet-Boigny; \33 952 2717; e bidewbi@orange.sn. Upstairs from the action at the all-in-one bar-restaurant-nightclub below, the tiled en-suite rooms here are neat & trim, with AC, fridge, flatscreen & and some abstractly modernist décor. It's a few bucks cheaper than its neighbours closer to Av Senghor. **$$**

Big Faim Av Léopold Sédar Senghor; \33 952 0622; e bigfaim@orange.sn; www.bigfaimhotel.com. Clean, shiny & behind one of Thiès's most popular restaurants, the en-suite rooms here aren't exactly characterful, but well appointed with AC, TV & fridge, & some even have a balcony for the same price. The restaurant out front hums along no matter the hour, serving an impressive selection of pizzas, pastries, grills & crêpes on a decidedly pleasant streetside terrace. **$$**

Hôtel Rex (32 rooms) \33 951 1081; www.facebook.com/HotelRestaurantRex. In the same leafy spot since 1992, this is an old Thiès standby & offers clean & quiet en-suite rooms (with fan or AC) set around a central courtyard. They're somewhat less modern than their counterparts south of the tracks, but still very pleasant & good value. There's

a full restaurant & bar downstairs, as well as some crafts & artwork for sale. **$$**

Le Croissant Magique Av Lamine Guèye; \33 951 0606; e croissant.magique@hotmail.fr; www.croissant-magique.com. While it may be named after a magic croissant, the facilities here are somewhat less psychedelic than their namesake. The spick & span rooms have the usual comforts like AC, TV & hot water, & some open on to small balconies overlooking the courtyard. There's a restaurant-bar-patisserie downstairs that serves a solid selection of pizzas, cakes, sandwiches & drinks. It's mostly aimed at the business market, but is centrally located & good value overall. **$$**

Le Massa Massa (10 rooms) \33 952 1244; e massamassa@orange.sn; www.massamassa-senegal.com. Around the corner from the gare routière, this cosy Belgian-run hotel is probably the most characterful accommodation in town, with a keen eye for detail & tourist sensibilities (as opposed to the business clientèle that predominates in Thiès). Rooms are done up in warm pastels with a touch of African décor & all have AC, canopy beds & nets. It's known for its restaurant, serving up heaped portions of haute cuisine (everything from chicory au gratin to beef bourguignon) that start around 4,500F a plate. **$$**

St Anne's Cathedral \33 951 2732; m 77 617 6467. The sisters at St. Anne's usually have some basic rooms available, & while they're the cheapest in town & taken care of with the careful attention you'd expect of a cloister, don't plan on going out & dancing the night away if you're staying here – they've little patience for late-night shenanigans. **$**

WHERE TO EAT AND DRINK *Map, page 238.*

Le Pamanda Av Coumba Ndoffène Diouf; \33 952 1550; e lepambox@gmail.com; ⊕ 10.00–midnight daily, later at w/ends. Something of a one-stop shop for food & entertainment, this place on the main drag has a billiard table, bar, air-conditioned dining room & a shady terrace out front. Dishes run the gamut from

chawarma, pizza & paninis starting around 1,000F to beef in Roquefort sauce for closer to 5,000F. Wash it down with an ice cream & check in at the weekend to see if there's any live music on.

Les Délices 60 Av Léopold Sédar Senghor; \33 951 7516; e restaurantlesdelicesthies@gmail.com; ⊕ 06.00–01.00 daily, later at w/ends.

The core of the menu here is similar to the continental offerings you'll also find at Big Faim or Le Pamanda, but they switch things up with a good few Lebanese & Asian dishes starting around 2,500F.

NIGHTLIFE

☆ **Dosso** ↘33 951 2640. If DJ hits & the latest in Naija R&B & hip-hop are more your speed, head over to Dosso where there's a swimming pool, but everyone is definitely too cool to use it. It was being remodelled when we checked in, but seems set to be the hippest place in Thiès to hear the beat drop for some time to come.

☆ **Palais des Arts** ↘33 951 7010; ⊕ 18.00–late daily. Owned by & musical home to local *mbalax* heroine Ma Sané & her band Waflash, they reliably get the rafters shaking here every Sat night. If your legs recover in time, there's more *mbalax* every Mon, while the party crosses the Atlantic on Fri for what is surely Thiès's one & only salsa night.

OTHER PRACTICALITIES

Money All the expected banks are represented; **CBAO** and **Ecobank** are on Avenue Senghor near the train tracks, while **BICIS** and **SGBS** are further south near Place de France.

Communications All the hotels & most sit-down restaurants offer Wi-Fi.

WHAT TO SEE AND DO Aside from soaking up the laid-back vibe and having a wander around town, Thiès has a few diverting historical and artistic ports of call for the visitor. It's emphatically worth stopping in to the **Manufactures Sénégalaises des Arts Décoratifs** (*entrance fee 1,000F exhibition hall, additional 1,000F artisan's workshop*; ⊕ 08.00–13.00, 15.00–17.00 Mon–Fri; ↘ 33 951 1131; m 76 534 7429/70 771 0847; e msadthies@gmail. com; www.culture.gouv.sn), where artisans have been weaving meticulously detailed tapestries based on Senegalese paintings and motifs since the centre was opened by Léopold Sédar Senghor in 1966. Since then, the acclaimed artists have woven pieces that adorn such rarefied halls as the White House and AU headquarters in Ethiopia, but in almost 50 years, none has been larger or more elaborate than the 24m^2 *Magal de Touba*, which after three years of toil by two artisans was completed in 2012 and today hangs at UN headquarters in New York. Each design forms the basis for no more than eight tapestries, and while they do sell to the public, you'd better bring your wallet; prices start at €800 for a square metre, and can easily be double that. Given the stratified clientele, the centre has in the past struggled to support itself, but today it's hoping to raise money by developing programmes in batik, *sous-verre*, and other, more affordable, disciplines. If your heart's set on a souvenir but you're priced out of the market here, the nearby **Chambre des Metiers and Village Artisanal** (↘ *33 951 1773*) has a somewhat more conventional array of artwork; the sprawling **central market** isn't exactly an art hotspot, but all kind of goods spill into the streets here east of the train station between avenues Général de Gaulle and Ahmadou Gnanga Sow. A few blocks north lies the impressively large **Cathédrale Sainte-Anne de Thiès**, which was consecrated in 1945 and makes for a relaxing pause on any perambulation of Thiès.

Housed in a French-built fort dating to 1864, the **Musée Thiès** (↘ *33 951 3074*; m *76 588 1531*; e *info@museethies.org; www.museethies.org*) was inaugurated in 1975, once again by Senegal's cultural champion, the poet-president Léopold Sédar Senghor. The exhibits here are something of a smorgasbord of *Thièsois* history; everything from Palaeolithic artefacts and early tools to exhibits on the Cayor and Baol kingdoms, the slave trade, the railroad, Lat Dior and modern politicians as well, though it's worth noting that information is in French. Be sure to drop by the attached *sous-verre* workshop next door as well. They might close up if there are no visitors, but you can usually ask someone to fetch the key for you.

TIVAOUANE

The status of Tivaouane (*tiva-wan*) today as a rather unprepossessing junction town belies its outsized historical significance. After the 16th-century breakup of the Jolof Empire, the Cayor Kingdom ruled the lands around Tivaouane, successfully sabotaging the construction of the Dakar–Saint-Louis railway and fighting off French encroachment under the leadership of the revered Cayor *damel* (king) Lat Dior for several decades until the deaths of both Lat Dior and Cayor's final *damel*, Samba Laobe Fall, at the hands of the French in 1886.

After the fall of Cayor, Tivaouane became an important transit point along the Dakar–Saint-Louis line for groundnuts grown further inland, but the town took on its modern-day significance when Senegal's preeminent Tijani brotherhood leader (see box, page 23) El Hadji Malick Sy took up residence and established his *zawiya* (religious school) here in 1902.

Today the town remains the most important Tijani shrine in Senegal and is home to several moderately captivating mosques, but you'll probably breeze right through town unless you're here for the annual *gamou* pilgrimage, which attracts over one million participants every Mawlid (the prophet Muhammad's birthday): see page 63 for dates. The total number of pilgrims is second only to Touba's Grand Magal (see page 250), but given Tivaouane's much smaller size, pilgrims here can outnumber residents by an unbelievable ten- or even 20-to-one during the *gamou*.

Tivaouane is the road junction for nearby Mboro, and battered *sept-places* ply back and forth between the two all day for about 600F, passing the enormous phosphate mine at Darou Khoudoss on the way.

MBORO

A few kilometres after you pass the unmistakeable mountains of phosphate tailings at Darou Khoudouss on the way from Tivaouane you come to the market town of Mboro (not to be confused with Mbour, some 90km south on the Petite Côte). And while it won't be first on anyone's must-see list in Senegal, the surroundings are studded with palms and surprisingly lush for northern Senegal, and it's a short hop to its windswept beachside counterpart of Mboro-Sur-Mer, where you'll find dozens upon dozens of fiercely colourful fishing pirogues, and an army of fishermen heaving the boats into the water every morning and hauling up the catch at the end of the day. As soon as it hits dry land, the catch is picked, sorted, and spirited away by a cadre of waiting fishmongers. It's a picturesque spot to people-watch, and you'll surely see (or potentially be invited to play in) some spirited football matches at the very edge of the surf. Mboro is a good place to see the wild and working Grande Côte, especially if the pirogue madness further south at Kayor sounds like a bit too much.

▲ WHERE TO STAY, EAT AND DRINK

▲ **Hôtel Amaya** (14 rooms) ☎ 33 955 7817; m 77 566 0913; e jeansar2@hotmail.com. In the centre of Mboro proper, this unassuming place has clean & tiled en-suite rooms with high ceilings, nets, AC, hot water & views overlooking the small hotel garden. The restaurant on site does simple meals with enough notice, & the helpful manager speaks good English. **$$**

▲ **Campement Waou** (8 rooms) ☎ 33 955 4121/01; e daniel@waousenegal.net; www. waousenegal.net. Set 500m off the road from Mboro to the beach & run by a French-Ivoirian couple, this place has a handful of basic en-suite rooms clustered around a dusty but pleasant courtyard. Food is the real focus here, & they take great pride in their menu – if you feel like splurging, a veritable feast of lobster & prawns is available for 12,000F. **$$**

🔺 **Fayene** (3 rooms) Mboro-Sur-Mer; m 77 691 6346. There are a number of private cottages for rent on the oceanfront in Mboro-Sur-Mer, & while they mostly orient themselves to Senegalese families or other groups, they can be a good option for individual travellers who like to self-cater & represent the only Mboro-area accommodation directly on the beach. Fayene has a cute enough handful of double rooms; make a left when you get to the beach to find it. **$$**

🔺 **La Tiarangal** (4 rooms) m 77 436 3295; e latiarangal@free.fr; www.latiarangal.com. Sharing a compound with a bunch of palm trees & a notably enormous baobab, this tranquil spot is about 3km from the oceanfront along the road from Mboro. The house is decorated in red earth tones & pastels, & opens on to a shaded garden with fish pond & a large rooftop terrace with views over the surrounding bush. The rooms are simply furnished and each 2 share a bath. **$$**

OTHER PRACTICALITIES The nearest bank is 50km away in Thiès, so bring some cash. The RN2 at Tivaouane is 22km from here and regular *sept-places* do the trip for 600F. If you want to head between Mboro proper and Mboro-Sur-Mer, there are battered shared taxis running back and forth all day for small change. Alternatively, you could clop-clop-clop your way there in a *calèche* for a few hundred CFA more.

LOMPOUL

Like a little chunk of Sahara that got separated from its mother, the Lompoul desert is an incongruous 20km^2 of dunes hidden away several kilometres inland from the ocean but, from the moment you arrive here, it's as if you've been magically transported miles north (by flying carpet, perhaps?), to the enormous sand seas, known as *ergs*, of Morocco and Mauritania. And while much of northern Senegal sizzles and bakes as you'd expect of any good desert, this is the only place in the country (and for hundreds of miles beyond) that you'll find true sand dunes, towering above the low *khaïma* tents, the traditional Mauritanian domicile of choice, set up beneath them. Stoic dromedaries ponder the sands with nonchalance and ferry visitors up and down the windswept mountains dunes at the age-old, unhurried pace of the desert. Lompoul is truly one of Senegal's greatest escapes, and if you're going to splurge somewhere this would be an excellent place to do it.

GETTING THERE AND AWAY There are three more-or-less distinct entities that are often referred to as 'Lompoul': the eponymous village, the busy fishing settlement at Lompoul-Sur-Mer, and the nearby desert. Many visitors to Lompoul arrange their trip through a tour agency, but it's quite possible to get here on your own as well.

Lompoul village is 26km west of the RN2 junction at Kébémer, and the road is surfaced all the way through. A handful of *sept-places* make the trip back and forth from Kébémer throughout the day, though Lompoul is a small place so you might wait a bit for the car to fill. You'll be dropped off in Lompoul village, from where the surfaced road continues to Lompoul-Sur-Mer, on the beach a further 7km west. You might have some luck getting a lift to Lompoul-Sur-Mer, but otherwise you can always hire a *calèche* or *jakarta* to carry you the rest of the way.

The dunes are 3–4km north of Lompoul village and while the distance isn't especially far, there's no transport and you should make arrangements with your hotel to pick you up from here, which most will do for a small fee (transfers are of course also available from Kébémer or further afield). The tracks into the desert are (unsurprisingly) sandy and not to be approached without a 4x4 and some driving skill.

WHERE TO STAY AND EAT The trio of rather confusingly named tented camps are all located in the dunes north of Lompoul village, while VITEL & Africa Roots are on the beach in Lompoul-Sur-Mer. The desert camps typically operate on a HB/FB basis, as there aren't exactly many places to pop out for a quick bite over the next sand dune. Prices for the three are broadly similar, ranging from about €75 to €100 for a HB double, with low season and resident discounts also possible.

Le Camp du Desert m 77 705 5695/76 387 0011; e cdd@espiritdafrique.com; www.campdudesert.com. The most traditional of the 3 camps, the wide Mauritanian *khaïma* tents here are pitched on the sand in true nomadic style & meals are taken at a long, low table surrounded by cushy Moroccan leather ottomans & lanterns. Endless cups of sweet tea & camel rides here are a must. They're affiliated with the Origin Africa tour agency, so trips here can be arranged in Dakar through them as well. **$$$**

Ecolodge de Lompoul (Le Gîte Africain du Lompoul) ☎33 957 0057; m 77 957 0057; e reservation@ecolodge-senegal.com; www.ecolodge-senegal.com. Newly renovated in 2014 and tucked away in 3 separate clusters at the base of a metres-high dune, the tents here are bright & airy with attached ablutions. Activities include everything from 4x4 safaris to massage, or a late-night bonfire under the desert stars. It's associated with two other camps in Simal & Palmarin, and done up with the same localised flair & careful attention to detail as the others. **$$$**

Lompoul Desert Lodge (15 rooms) ☎33 869 7900; m 77 650 2280/76 335 3639; www.lompouldesertlodge.com. Perched 40cm above the sands on wooden platforms, the tents here are decorated with a safari-chic elegance, and represent the most luxurious accommodation on offer in Lompoul. All the tents come with a terrace & private outdoor ablutions, & meals are served at wrought-iron tables surrounded by hanging Moroccan lanterns. Camel rides, market trips & dancing workshops can all be arranged. **$$$**

Africa Roots (25 rooms) Lompoul-Sur-Mer; m 76 586 8066; e info@atlanticnaturesenegal.com; www.atlanticnaturesenegal.com. Right on the beach about 1.5km north of where the fisherman haul in their nets, this little village of prim stone bungalows is set in a carefully manicured garden. The tiled rooms are all en-suite with nets & solar panels, & they can arrange a host of land & water activities including horseback riding. There's a big open-air restaurant with bar & pool table overlooking the waves, & the whole place is done up in murals by local artists. It's popular with groups, but they can cater to individual travellers as well. **$$**

VITEL (9 rooms) Lompoul-Sur-Mer; m 76 470 6190; e info@vitel-lompoul.com; www.vitel-lompoul.com. The reed-&-thatch huts at this small, locally-owned campement are set around a sandy compound in a stand of pine trees a short walk from the ocean in Lompoul-Sur-Mer. They're about as basic as it gets, but well maintained, & the engaged management can set up tours into the dunes, market visits & drumming lessons. **$**

WHAT TO SEE AND DO The various lodges all offer a similar range of possibilities, but you won't have any trouble setting up camel rides through the dunes, boat trips from Lompoul-Sur-Mer, market visits during the *loumo* on Thursdays, drumming and dancing lessons, or simply chilling out and disconnecting in the silence of the desert.

Every April the **Festival du Sahel** (*www.festivaldusahel.com*) comes to town, and just like a desert mirage, a massive, weekend-long concert of West African and international stars rises from the shifting sands. In years past, luminaries like Baaba Maal, Ismaël Lô, Tamikrest, Habib Koite and artists from as far afield as Israel and Brazil have come to perform.

LOUGA *Population 355,000*

Central Louga sits barely 2km east of the RN2 linking Saint-Louis and Dakar, but most travellers pass by entirely unaware of the town's existence. (Driving past on the RN2 you'd really have little idea how substantial the city actually is.) And while it's far from a must-see, Louga is an important regional hub and offers a dusty, windblown slice of urban African life in the Sahel. There's nothing here specifically aimed at travellers, but accommodation and facilities are surprisingly good nonetheless.

GETTING THERE AND AWAY The most substantial settlement between Thiès and Saint-Louis, Louga is well served by public transport, and you can get here either by a direct *sept-place* from Dakar (3,500F) or Saint-Louis (1,500F), or any vehicle heading along the RN2 can drop you at the one of the four junctions for Louga. The *gare routière* for Dakar & Saint-Louis is at the southwest edge of town on Ave Djily Mbaye (about 1.2km from the RN2), while eastbound traffic to Touba (2,500F), Linguère (3,500F) or Ourossogui (8,000F) arrives and departs from a separate *gare routière* at the east end of town, where the R31 heading east begins.

It's also the beginning of some 345km of tarmac (designated as R31/D309 until Dahra, where it becomes the RN3) that eventually rejoins the RN2 in Ourossogui after passing through Dahra, Linguère, and the twin wildlife reserves of Ferlo North and Ferlo South (see box, page 247). Crossing some of Senegal's remotest countryside, the road from Linguère onwards was once a shambles, but today it's a breeze (a hot one, but still) and many vehicles headed between Dakar and Ourossogui will use this route rather than the northerly RN2.

If you've got your own (4x4) wheels, the Lac de Guiers (see pages 222–3) is an eminently worthwhile diversion from Louga. Heading north for 50 km, the road splits at the base of the lake, a village known as Keur Momar Sarr. The route to the east of the lake hugs the coastline and rejoins the RN2 in Richard Toll, while the western route strays further from the shores, meeting the RN2 8km west of the Rosso turnoff.

WHERE TO STAY, EAT AND DRINK Just why Louga is home to two Italian-themed hotel-restaurants barely a block away from each other is as good a question as any, but mysteries aside, they're both friendly and comfortable, with restaurants (naturally also Italian-inspired) attached. They're 500m from the RN2 at the northwest edge of town, near the *Palais de Djily Mbaye*.

Casa Italia (15 rooms) ✆33 967 3879/987 0205; e casaitalialg@yahoo.fr; www.facebook. com/casa.it.lg. Rooms here are clean & probably even a bit overfurnished, with couch, writing desk, wardrobe, fridge, full-length mirror & TV all sandwiched into the homey interior. All rooms but one have AC & hot water, so ask for that one if you're bargain hunting. The halls are decked with needlepoint, there's a shady courtyard with swimming pool, & the restaurant boasts an enormous faux-waterfall fountain & a menu with pizza, gnocchi & more. **$$**

Il Pellicano (12 rooms) ✆33 987 0227; m 77 130 0350; e pelicanhotel@live.fr; www. hotelilpellicanosn.com. A touch less sophisticated than its cousin down the street but equally comfortable, rooms here all have AC, TV, hot water, fridge, nets & a sitting area. The real draw here is the 6 upstairs rooms with big private terraces; get one of these and you're winning. The restaurant here is more Dakar than it is Rome, but there's a small selection of Italian dishes available as well. **$$**

WHAT TO SEE AND DO As a route focus and important market centre, there's no shortage of hubbub and commerce going on in Louga, and if markets are your thing you won't be disappointed. The heart of the city lies east of the railway tracks, and the main **market**, French-built **cathedral**, and all banking facilities

(CBAO, Ecobank, SGBS, BICIS) lie no more than 500m from the old **train station** building. It's occupied by squatters but still clings to some of its former elegance, wrought iron railings and all. Be sure to ask permission if you'd like to explore inside.

If you're here in December, it's absolutely worth checking out the annual **International Festival of Folklore and Percussion (FESFOP)** (m *33 967 43 79; e fesfoplougasn@gmail.com; www.fesfop.org*). Every year performers from all over West Africa and beyond congregate in Louga to take part in an ambitious week-long agenda of music, drumming, art, dance, and theatre.

DAHRA AND LINGUÈRE

The dust-blown twin towns of Dahra and Linguère are miles from anywhere at the edge of what's known as the Ferlo, a sparsely populated desert region stretching east from Linguère to the Senegal River valley. The Djolof Kingdom, successor to the fallen Jolof Empire, had its capital here in the village of Yang-Yang, some 35km north of Dahra.

As with the other Wolof states, it fell afoul of late 19th-century French territorial ambitions, but unlike his uncle Lat Dior who died in a desperate, last-gasp battle with the French, the last independent Djolof *bourba* (king) Alboury Ndiaye mounted a mass exodus to the east in 1890 with several hundred of his subjects ahead of a rapidly advancing French army. Many Djolofs eventually returned to their lands, but Alboury Ndiaye never did. The *bourba* and some loyal followers continued their trek eastwards; he was never captured and died in Niger in 1902.

Dahra is a surprisingly busy market centre and relatively important crossroads between Louga, Touba and Ourossogui, while Linguère is home to the district administration and feels every bit the one-street outpost, seemingly in danger of being swallowed up by the desert wilds ahead. Now that the road is surfaced, crossing the Ferlo is hardly as arduous as Alboury Ndiaye might've had it, but the end-of-the-world feel remains.

GETTING THERE AND AWAY Dahra and Linguère are 40km apart and absolutely shattered *ndiaga ndiayes* clatter their way back and forth throughout the day for 500F, though they can take ages to fill up. Dahra is the more important of the two in terms of transport, as it sits at the crossroads where the RN3 from Touba turns east for the long run to Ourossogui. *Sept-places* run from Dahra to Louga (85km, 2000F), Touba (70km, 1500F), and Ourossogui (260km, 5500F). Traffic volumes are low out here, so waits can be long and you should start early if you want to get to Ourossogui.

The road from Louga is in decent shape, between the two towns is a mess of potholes, and eastwards from Linguère is tarmac you could skate on.

A branch line of the Dakar–Saint-Louis railway was built to Dahra and Linguère in the 1920s, but there hasn't been a train in either town since the early 1980s.

WHERE TO STAY, EAT AND DRINK In an entirely unexpected twist, Linguère is actually home to some of the finest local dairy products in Senegal. There's a cooperative here run by a Lutheran NGO that tries to take advantage of the huge numbers of milk-producing cattle raised in the region, despite dairy not traditionally being a part of the local diet. They sell cold milk, yogurt and *lait caillé* (sweetened curdled milk) out of an unassuming white building at the west end of town, and it all goes down quite nicely in the heat.

🏠 **Auberge WSD Ker Gan** (14 rooms) Dahra; m 77 428 6818; e wsd.gana@yahoo.fr. Opposite the stadium on the road towards Linguère, this place is aimed squarely at visitors in Dahra on business, so they've got very decent air-conditioned rooms with Wi-Fi, some of them in stand-alone bungalows behind the main building. The restaurant rustles up a standard variety of Senegalese meals. **$$**

🏠 **Centre Amadou Seck** (8 rooms) Linguère; 🕿 33 968 1255; m 77 551 3450/70 881 2654; e centreamadouseck@gmail.com. Behind the Hôtel de Ville, this new community-run place has proper rooms with AC & Wi-Fi. They can arrange the usual variety of Senegalese meals, & the fact that much of the produce is grown in their very own garden is particularly impressive in a sizzling climate like Linguère's. **$$**

OTHER PRACTICALITIES

Money There are no banks along this stretch of road; the nearest ATMs are in Louga or Ourossogui, so bring enough cash to get through.

Communications There's at least one cyber café in both towns, but your best bet for getting online out here will probably be using the Wi-Fi at either of the hotels.

WHAT TO SEE AND DO Dahra holds its weekly *loumo* (market) on Sundays, and since this is pastoralist country, an impressive mass of livestock are driven in from the hinterlands for the day – massively horned cattle, harried sheep and the ever-present goats all descend on Dahra for the day in a scrum of hooves and fur – if you're lucky you'll spot some camels as well.

The *gare ferroviaire* (train station) in Linguère is mostly disused, but still grandiose in its own decrepit way, with two identical two-storey buildings with vaulted tile rooftops and wide, arched porticoes. You can find it about four blocks south of the 'main' road junction, while the station in Dahra is gone and there are plans to build a hotel on the former site.

For history obsessives, the former Djolof capital of **Yang Yang** is on a rough track 34km north of Dahra. Today it's a village of no more than a few hundred, but there's a homespun museum in the century-old former home of Alboury Ndiaye's son, Bouna Ndiaye, who was known for having fought to develop the Djolof region after his father's exile and French annexation. There are a handful of artefacts on display and a scattering of defensive ruins around the village. The occasional *taxi-brousse* may pass this way, especially for the Sunday market; ask around at the Dahra *gare routière*.

DIOURBEL

After the 16th-century breakup of the Jolof Empire that created the handful of Wolof kingdoms that would rule north-central Senegal until French annexation in the late 19th century, Diourbel (*Joor-bell*) became capital of the Baol kingdom, which ruled the surrounding lands under a series of leaders known as *teignes* until it was finally overwhelmed and annexed by the French at the end of the 19th century, after which it became the Baol regional capital in 1903. The railroad arrived in 1908 and, under Mouride leadership, the hinterland around Diourbel became one of Senegal's most important centres for peanut production, enriching the brotherhood and financing construction of their landmark mosques and other facilities. Reliance on the crop has waned in recent decades, but the area around Diourbel and beyond continues to be known as Senegal's 'peanut basin', and Diourbel is still regional capital, only now of its own eponymous region.

Gazetted in 1971 and 1972 respectively, the 6,000km² *Réserve de faune du Ferlo Nord* and 6,337km² *Ferlo Sud* are together (despite being bisected by the RN3) among the largest protected areas in the Sahel, and encompass a dry and unforgiving terrain of flat, semi-desert thorn savannah surrounded by equally wild grazing lands where the handful of Fulbe (Peul) residents eke out a living with their cattle and sheep.

A refuge for under-protected ungulates, most of its residents have been reintroduced after a disappearance of years or decades, but it's also home to a remnant population of Red-fronted gazelle (*Eudorcas rufifrons*), which are classified as vulnerable by the IUCN. Within the reserve, a 12km² fenced enclosure was set up near Katané village & expanded several times to accommodate reintroductions of scimitar-horned oryx (*Oryx dammah*), Dama gazelle (*Nanger dama*), and Dorcas gazelle (*Gazella dorcas*). The scimitar-horned oryx is completely extinct in the wild, Dama gazelle is critically endangered and was locally extinct in Senegal until its reintroduction here in 2003, and the vulnerable Dorcas gazelle was also locally extinct until its reintroduction. Numbers are small but growing, with an estimated 120 oryx and smaller numbers of the two gazelle present in 2014. The reserve works in partnership with the Guembeul Special Reserve near Saint-Louis (see pages 213–14), where many of the animals are first introduced after being sourced from zoos and sanctuaries abroad, and before being relocated to Ferlo.

Both halves of the reserve are also designated as Important Bird Areas (IBAs) and 184 species have been recorded between the two, many of them palearctic migrants. Among them are two types of bustard (Arabian and Sevile's), the Sahelian woodpecker, golden nightjar, Sudan golden sparrow, and a number of raptors.

The ranger camp (⊕15.486511,–14.110174) and enclosure at Katané village are some 30km of rough bush tracks northwest of Ranérou. There are no facilities here for guests; the reserves are entirely undeveloped for tourism (or much else), and this is about as remote as it's possible to get in Senegal. Thus, you should prepare to be self-sufficient with all food, water and other supplies, and it's highly recommended that you contact the Guembeul Special Reserve (m *77 351 9986*) if you'd like to plan a visit.

Diourbel's most famous resident is Shiekh Ahmadou Bamba, founder of the Mourides and their holy city of Touba, who was forbidden from returning there by a colonial government deeply suspicious of his growing power. Kept near the colonial administration in Diourbel rather than in Touba where the French had little control, Bamba lived here under house arrest from 1912 until his death in 1927, when he finally made the 45km journey to Touba for burial.

Today Diourbel is a sleepy and rather humdrum administrative town, mostly of note for being home to the Mouride's first grand mosque, and typically visited in conjunction with Touba to see its more famous counterpart there.

GETTING THERE AND AWAY The *gare routière* is about 3 km east of the centre on the RN3, and there are frequent *sept-places* that run to Thiès (78km, 1,500F), Dakar (140km, 3,000F), Touba (45km, 1,000F), and Kaolack (65km, 1,500F). Roads are in good condition in all directions.

⌂ WHERE TO STAY, EAT AND DRINK You're not exactly spoiled for choice when it comes to your culinary options in Diourbel, but **Complexe Borom Gaware** (m *77 926 7036*) and **Khadim Rassoul Fast Food** (m *77 554 9279*) serve up simple meals in the town centre.

⌂ Keur Dethie (Auberge du Baol)
(10 rooms) Quartier Chiekh Anta; ☏33 971 5190; m 77 535 5672; e boalhotel@yahoo.fr. Signposted just north of the RN3 on the east side of town, this family-run place is all frilly curtains & carved headboards, & the big en-suite rooms come with AC, TV & Wi-Fi. It's modest but done up with some nice murals & a fresh coat of paint, & the friendly owner speaks some English as well. They can arrange Senegalese meals for 2,000–3,000F. **$$**

OTHER PRACTICALITIES

Money BICIS, CBAO, Ecobank and SGBS are all represented with ATMs on the RN3 (*Av Léopold Sédar Senghor*).

Communications There's Wi-Fi at Keur Dethie, but other than that your options for getting online are pretty slim.

WHAT TO SEE AND DO Tourist hotspot it isn't, but Diourbel's history as a French administrative centre and its deep significance to Mourides as the former home of Ahmadou Bamba means there are a few diverting sights, and it's easily coupled with a trip to Touba.

The Ottoman-inspired **grand mosque** is resplendent under its blue domes, and its construction is distinguished as the first major Mouride landmark to be built, predating its more famous cousin in Touba by more than 40 years. It was completed during WWI while Ahmadou Bamba was under house arrest in his compound next door, known as **Keur Gou Mak** (the master's house) in Wolof and still occupied by the Bamba family. To visit the mosque, you'll have to ask around for the caretaker; so long as prayers are not in session he'll usually oblige you with a short tour, but don't forget to dress conservatively.

Ker Gou Mak is set behind enormous walls that measure even longer than the 313m they are sometimes claimed to be (a sacred number referring to how many Muslims fought under Muhammad at the battle of Badr in 624CE), and it's impossible to miss as you head towards Touba on the RN3. It's not open to casual visitors, but inside are a number of mosques and other shrines to the departed sheikh.

The 1908 *gare ferroviaire* (railway station) still stands, and like most of these underutilised structures it's looking a bit forlorn, but the stopped clocks, French postboxes, and anachronistic 'no spitting' signs give the place an out-of-time air that's worth soaking up for a moment.

TOUBA-MBACKÉ

Eric Ross, PhD, author of Sufi City: Urban Design and Archetypes in Touba *(www. ericrossacademic.wordpress.com)*

Touba is Senegal's greatest and most celebrated Sufi city. It is home to the Murid order, Senegal's largest single Sufi institution, with about three million adherents. Murids often refer to Touba as their 'capital', a good indication of the importance of this city in their eyes. Touba is where Cheikh Ahmadu Bamba Mbacké (1853–1927), the founder of the Murid order, lies buried, along with the former residence and resting place of all of his successors (the current Caliph-General is Cheikh

Ahmadu Bamba's grandson, Cheikh Mokhtar Maty Lèye). It is where all Murids – no matter where they live – congregate once a year for the Grand Magal (18th day of the Muslim month of Safar, see page 63 for dates), and where many wish to be buried when they depart this world.

Touba is the name of the tree of paradise in Islamic tradition. It represents the promise of eternal bliss in the Hereafter for those who live a righteous life on earth. In the Sufi vocabulary of symbols, this tree also represents the epitome of ascension to Divine light, the tree at the extremity of creation, beyond which is only God. Cheikh Ahmadou Bamba founded Touba in a moment of spiritual illumination while on his Path. The year was 1887 and Touba was a lonely spot in the uncultivated savanna just outside his ancestral home, the town of Mbacké. Though Cheikh Ahmadou Bamba had wanted to settle there and devote himself to God, his path proved tortuous. Exiled twice by the French colonial authorities, he was never allowed back to Touba and died under house arrest in 1927. It was left to the Murids to fulfil their founder's wish to see Touba rise as a city.

Touba refers to both the city and the mosque. For Murids, God has blessed Touba and it is the greatest of Cheikh Ahmadou Bamba's legacies. The Murids built Touba, starting with the mosque, and the Murid order manages all urban amenities, from allotments, roads and waterworks to schools, markets and hospitals. Described as a 'marabout village' of 5,000 people 50 years ago, Touba is now Senegal's second largest city, with about 700,000 inhabitants.

Touba has a concentric layout. At the city's centre is the Great Mosque, towards which all its main avenues converge. About 2km from the Mosque is a wide circle road called the Rocade. The concentric city plan this produces, akin to a mandala, is seen in Sufi terms as expressing Touba's blessed status. The city is renowned for religious instruction and Sufi recitation. It has also developed as a major transportation, agribusiness and retail hub. Touba has autonomous administrative status and the sanctity of the blessed city is energetically maintained by the order. For example, alcohol and tobacco are banned in Touba; visitors to the city must not bring these products with them.

GETTING THERE AND AWAY Touba is centrally located and within several hours' drive of most north-central Senegalese cities, and accessible on fair to good tarmac roads in all directions. Dakar is just under 200km away and Saint-Louis about 175km, so with your own vehicle (or with an early enough start on public transport), it's very possible to start your day in Dakar, visit the mosque, and continue on to Saint-Louis or another city. *Sept-places* from Touba depart throughout the day, with runs to Dakar (3,500F), Saint-Louis (4,000F), Kaolack (2,500F) or Tambacounda (7,500F). If your goal is the eastbound RN3 to Ourossogui, you'll probably have to first aim for Dahra (1,500F) and change vehicles there.

A 1931 rail line extension built with Mouride assistance once connected Touba to the Dakar-Niger line at Diourbel, but it's long since been out of service.

WHERE TO STAY AND EAT

Campement Touristique Le Baol (19 rooms) Mbacké; 33 976 5505; m 77 516 0199; e hotelbaol@gmail.com. In Mbacké 9km from the grand mosque on the RN3 towards Diourbel, this is the closest accommodation to Touba proper & your only option save getting invited to someone's home. The en-suite bungalows here aren't exactly modern, but they're well enough equipped to be reasonably comfortable & come with TV & Wi-Fi. The restaurant does meals around 3,000F & doesn't serve alcohol, but you didn't come to Touba for the party scene, did you? **$$**

OTHER PRACTICALITIES

Money There is no shortage of banks in Touba; Ecobank, CBAO, BICIS, and SGBS all represented with one or more ATM-equipped branches in Touba (most along the RN3 into town from Diourbel) and/or Mbacké.

Health About 3.5km west of the grand mosque, Hôpital Mathlaboul Fawzaïni (↘ *33 974 05 29*) serves Touba.

Communications There's Wi-Fi at Campement Le Baol, and there are a handful of cyber cafés scattered around both Touba and Mbacké.

WHAT TO SEE AND DO It's obligatory to have a guide to visit the mosque, but unfortunately there isn't much of a system to determine who is and isn't an actual guide, nor where you should pick one up. Would-be guides are likely to approach you around the mosque or elsewhere in town, but you should head for the **Bibliotheque Cheikhoul Khadim** (m *77 558 4857*) across the street from the mosque, where the knowledgeable Mamadou Diabaye (m *77 345 0374/76 663 8916*) and a number of other well-informed guides speaking a variety of languages can be found. Women are allowed to visit the mosque but should cover themseves up well.

The text on all of the following sights was written by Eric Ross.

Touba's Great Mosque Touba's Great Mosque is the most important Murid monument. It lies on a great square at the centre of the city. Avenues converge on it from all directions and its tallest minaret can be seen from far and wide. Construction began in 1931 but was interrupted in 1939 by the war. It resumed in 1948 and the mosque was inaugurated in 1963. It has three large domes; the one in the northeast corner rises above Cheikh Ahmadou Bamba's tomb. The mosque originally had five minarets; two more were added in 2014. The towering central minaret (87m), known as 'Lamp Fall', is a popular Murid symbol. The mosque was extended in 1987–88 when prayer galleries were added, and it was entirely resurfaced in white and pink marble in 1996–97.

On the mosque's eastern side are the Mausolea of Cheikh Ahmadou Bamba's sons and successors: Sëriñ Mamadou Moustapha (Caliph: 1927–45), Sëriñ Falilou (1945–68), Sëriñ Abdou Khadre (1989–90), Sëriñ Saliou (1990–2008) and Sëriñ Murtada (d. 2004). The eastern esplanade is a main entrance for pilgrims, who can reach Cheikh Ahmadou Bamba's tomb directly from the mosque's large eastern door. Many also visit the adjoining tombs of the caliphs.

The library Across the street to the east of the Mosque is the Bibliotheque Cheikhoul Khadim. It was built in 1977–82 by Sëriñ Abdoul Ahad (Caliph: 1968–89), whose mausoleum stands in its courtyard. The library contains many of Cheikh Ahmadou Bamba's manuscripts, as well as collections of Qurans and religious scientific texts.

The cemetery Touba's main cemetery lies directly to the east of the mosque. It was established by Cheikh Ahmadou Bamba at Touba's foundation and harbours the tombs of many important members of the Murid order, starting with the founder's wives, and those of his daughters, sons and disciples. The mausoleum of Cheikh Ibra Fall (1855–1930) and his sons is the largest. The cemetery is frequently visited by pilgrims but is now closed to new burials due to lack of space. The new cemetery lies 3km further east.

THE GREAT GREEN WALL

Since 2008, Senegal has been the starting point of a project that is perhaps as audacious as it is necessary – the Great Green Wall. Though the concept was first mooted by naturalists in the 1950s, the accelerating rates of desertification across the Sahel led the idea being picked up in earnest, and this time adopted by a series of 11 national governments, in the mid-2000s. Beautiful in its simplicity, the crux of the initiative involves planting a 15km wide and 7,100km long belt of trees along the Sahara Desert's southern fringe, which will eventually run all the way from Dakar to Djibouti and form a massive, natural bulwark against the Sahara's expansion, which has been aggravated by ongoing deforestation across the region and seriously threatens the livelihoods of millions of farmers and herders across the continent.

At the forefront of the initiative, Senegal has been planting nearly two million seedlings per year since 2008, and these today cover more than 30,000ha, mostly in the villages around Louga. The Agence Nationale de la Grande Muraille Verte (\ 33 859 0531; e contact@angmv.sn; www.angmv. sn) oversees the project's implementation in Senegal, and while it doesn't currently offer much to see for a tourist, it's early days yet, and in the future you'll hopefully be able to tour the protected forests of northern Senegal and imagine that someone, 7,100km away on the shores of the Indian Ocean in Djibouti, is doing the same.

Aïnou Rahmati Aïnou Rahmati, the 'Well of Mercy', lies one block north of the mosque. It was dug at the behest of Cheikh Ahmadou Bamba at Touba's foundation. The well's water is considered to be conducive to spiritual purification. Set in a garden, it receives a steady stream of pilgrims.

Darou Khoudoss Mosque A few blocks north and west of Touba's Mosque is Darou Khoudoss, the oldest settlement in central Touba. It commemorates another key moment of illumination on Cheikh Ahmadou Bamba's Path. Known as the 'Pact of Exile', his visionary encounter with the Prophet Muhammad there in 1894 led to his subsequent exile from Touba for the remainder of his life. This mosque, in front of Caliph Mamadou Moustapha's residence (called 'Bayti'), was Touba's only functioning mosque while its Great Mosque was under construction. It has been rebuilt several times since then; in the latest expansion it was surfaced in green tile.

Other mosques in central Touba

Sëriñ Souhaïbou's Mosque Cheikh Ahmadou Bamba's son Sëriñ Souhaïbou (1921–91) lies buried in this mosque, which is still under construction. It stands on a square four blocks west of Darou Khoudoss Mosque.

Darou Minam Mosque This mosque lies half a kilometre west of Touba's central square. Next to it are the mausolea of Sëriñ Bassirou (1895–1966) and of his sons. Sëriñ Bassirou was a son of Cheikh Ahmadou Bamba and wrote a well-known biography of his father. The mosque has been completely rebuilt, enlarged and greatly embellished since the early 2010s.

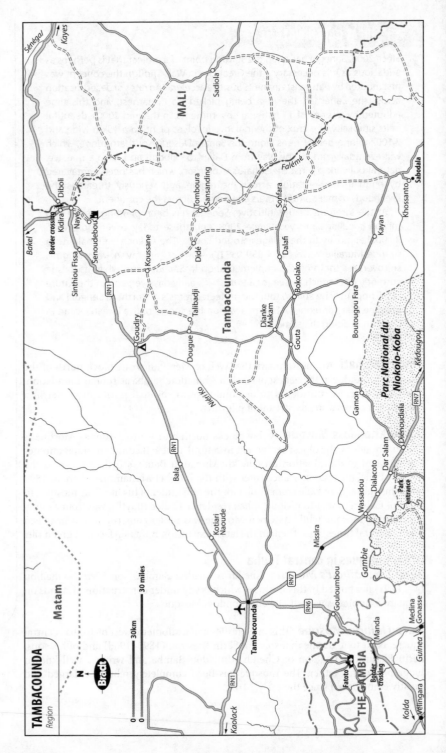

10

Tambacounda and Niokolo-Koba National Park

TAMBACOUNDA *Population 284,000*

It's just 'Tamba' to its friends, though this scorcher of a junction city doesn't exactly go out of its way to make them. Lines of heaving lorries stretch in all directions, the end of each queue obscured by blazing-hot asphalt mirages that shimmer and undulate in the distance. The daily ritual of loading and unloading this panoply of people and cargo is Tamba's *raison d'être*, and if you plan to spend any time in eastern Senegal, you'll be changing vehicles here at least once, so you might as well make the most of it.

Tambacounda is originally a Bambara name meaning 'house of Tamba', but some Wolof wisecrackers have since derisively dubbed it *Tanga*counda, which in their own language roughly comes out as 'house of heat', and they've rather got a point. During the day, you'd be forgiven for thinking you might melt into the dust as you make your way around town, but in the cool of dusk, Tamba crawls out from under the sun's merciless yolk and hits the street. Youths chow down at the innumerable *dibiteries,* muezzins wail, TVs blare, chairs appear, *attayeh* is brewed, mats are unrolled and tired legs are stretched. Tamba shines best when the lights are dimmed, so be sure to take an evening stroll to see this unvarnished city in its best light.

HISTORY Tambacounda was a small Mandinka village before the Dakar-Niger railway reached it in 1915 and it began to assume its position as eastern Senegal's transport hub, which, despite the demise of passenger services on the railway, it still holds today.

GETTING THERE AND AWAY
By air Tambacounda's airport is about 5km south of town, set just before the road junction to Kédougou and Kolda. As of early 2015, **Groupe Transair** (\ *33 865 2565/991 6774;* e *sales@groupetransair.sn; www.groupetransair.sn or www.facebook. com/groupetransair*) flies to Tamba from Dakar once a week on Saturdays for 100,000/190,000F single/return.

By car Roads in all directions from here are tarmac, but the condition of said tarmac varies from skating-rink smooth to something approaching the lunar surface. The **RN6** to Kolda is nothing short of bipolar, with a gorgeous new road as far as Manda, an endurance-testing litany of potholes from there to Vélingara, and a mishmash of roadworks, tarmac, and laterite the rest of the way to Kolda. The Vélingara-Kolda section is being actively improved, however, and should be better by the time you read this. The **RN7** to Kédougou is fair to good tarmac all the way, and the **RN1** in either direction towards Kaolack or Kidira is surfaced, but a decidedly mixed bag as far as quality.

By bus and *sept-place* Tambacounda is the hub on which all transport in eastern Senegal turns, and if you're spending any time in the region, prepare to get acquainted with the Tambacounda *gare routière*, where a seemingly never-ending file of *talibés* (see box, pages 196–7) will politely seek to separate you from your change. *Sept-places* are regularly available in all directions from here, including to Kédougou (*6,000F, 4hrs*), Kaolack (*6,500F, 4hrs*), Dakar (*9,500F, 8hrs*) and Ziguinchor (*9,500F, 10½hrs*). You might also have some luck finding a vehicle to Koundara (Guinea) here, via the Tijânî city of Madina Gounass. Eastbound transport to the Malian border at Kidira (*3,500F, 3hrs*) or onwards to Bakel (*5,000F, 4½hrs*) leaves from a separate *gare routière* about 1.7 km along the **RN1** to Kidira.

   Niokolo Transports (\ *30 113 8839*; m *77 529 5665/76 639 1891*; e *niokolotamba@ nt-sa.com; www.niokolotransports.com*) has an office around the corner from Auberge Sadio (ex-Gadec), and offers a reliable daily (except Saturdays) service to Dakar (*8,000F, 7 hrs*) departing from their office at 22.00 and arriving in Dakar sometime around 05.00. They also serve Kédougou (*3,000F*) and Bakel (*3,500F*), with daily departures at 14.00, except on Saturdays. It's best to buy tickets a day in advance.

   The **Al-Azhar** (*car mouride*) (\ *33 981 0109*; m *77 433 7693*) service is also represented in Tambacounda, and has a central office where you can sort out domestic tickets to Dakar (*5,000F, daily at 22.00*) and international ones heading anywhere from Bamako to Conakry and beyond. They run a daily service to Dakar (*5,000F*) departing at 22.00, and another to Bakel (*3,500F*) that leaves at 14.00 every day but Friday.

By train The legendary Dakar-Bamako line sadly ground to a halt sometime around 2009; today only cargo passes through the town, and even that irregularly. You could always ask around the station building for an update, but it seems highly likely that this once-iconic service will be out of commission for the foreseeable future.

ORIENTATION AND GETTING AROUND Tambacounda is built on an easily navigable grid, with a few exceptions for the seasonal watercourse that wends its way through town. The main market, *gare routière* and old administrative quarter are all just north of Boulevard Demba Diop, while much of the accommodation is in or near the Quartier Abattoir at the south end of Avenue Léopold Sédar Senghor. Banking, groceries, and fuel are all available near the junction of Boulevard Demba Diop and Rue Amadou Ndiaye Dionewar. A taxi ride anywhere in town should cost 500F, and closer to 300F if you take a *jakarta*.

TOURIST INFORMATION There are several places in town where you can arrange visits to Niokolo-Koba National Park, but the best way to do this may be through the campements closer to the park, ie: Wassadou, Dar Salam or Keur Annick in Mako. Further information is available at www.destination-senegaloriental.com as well.

Bureau des Guides Touristiques Av Léopold Senghor \ 33 981 0049; m 77 655 1481/70 791 1341. Unfortunately this place was looking pretty derelict when we checked in, but it still seems to just about function.

National Park Office Rte de Kidira; \ 33 981 1097; m 77 555 0578. They don't organise their own trips as such, but they can advise you on current park conditions and connect you with drivers, guides & the like.

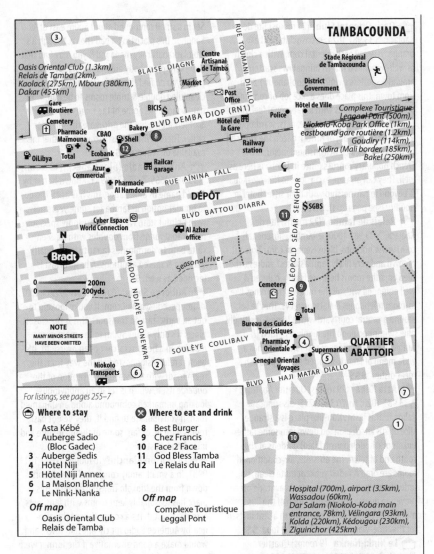

TAMBACOUNDA

Oasis Oriental Club (1.3km),
Relais de Tamba (2km),
Kaolack (275km), Mbour (380km),
Dakar (455km)

Centre Artisanal de Tamba

BLAISE DIAGNE

RUE TOUMANI DIALLO

Market

Stade Régional de Tambacounda

District Government

Post Office

Gare Routière

BICIS

Hôtel de Ville

Cemetery

BLVD DEMBA DIOP (RN1)

Pharmacie Maïmouna

CBAO

Bakery

Hôtel de la Gare

Police

Complexe Touristique
Leggal Pont (500km),
Niokolo-Koba Park Office (1km),
eastbound gare routière (1.2km),
Goudiry (114km),
Kidira (Mali border, 185km),
Bakel (250km)

OiLibya

Total

Shell

Ecobank

Railway station

Azur Commercial

Railcar garage

Pharmacie Al Hamdoulilahi

RUE AÏNINA FALL

DÉPÔT

BLVD BATTOU DIARRA

SGBS

Cyber Espace World Connection

Al Azhar office

BLVD LÉOPOLD SÉDAR SENGHOR

N

Bradt

Seasonal river

Cemetery

0 ——— 200m
0 ——— 200yds

Total

NOTE
MANY MINOR STREETS
HAVE BEEN OMITTED

AMADOU NDIAYE DIONEWAR

SOULÈYE COULIBALY

Bureau des Guides Touristiques

Pharmacy Orientale

Supermarket

QUARTIER ABATTOIR

Niokolo Transports

Senegal Oriental Voyages

BLVD EL HAJI MATAR DIALLO

For listings, see pages 255–7

🛏 **Where to stay**
1 Asta Kébé
2 Auberge Sadio (Bloc Gadec)
3 Auberge Sedis
4 Hôtel Niji
5 Hôtel Niji Annex
6 La Maison Blanche
7 Le Ninki-Nanka

Off map
Oasis Oriental Club
Relais de Tamba

✖ **Where to eat and drink**
8 Best Burger
9 Chez Francis
10 Face 2 Face
11 God Bless Tamba
12 Le Relais du Rail

Off map
Complexe Touristique
Leggal Pont

Hospital (700m), airport (3.5km),
Wassadou (60km),
Dar Salam (Niokolo-Koba main
entrance, 78km), Vélingara (93km),
Kolda (220km), Kédougou (230km),
Ziguinchor (425km)

10

Senegal Oriental Voyages Quartier Abattoir
📞33 981 0084/5; e s.orientalvoyages@yahoo.com;
www.facebook.com/SenegalOriental. Across the
street from and affiliated with Hôtel Niji, this place
can arrange 4x4 hire, guides & trips into the park.
Don't be afraid to negotiate.

WHERE TO STAY *Map, above.*

🏠 **Hôtel Niji** (68 rooms) Quartier Abattoir;
📞33 981 1250/2902; e nijihotel@sentoo.sn or
nijihotel@orange.sn; www.hotelniji.com. While
it's a step down from either the Oasis or Relais in
terms of quality, Niji's location in the city centre
helps make up the difference, particularly if you
don't have your own transport. The serviceable
en-suite rooms come with AC, TV & Wi-Fi, & there

is a swimming pool, albeit one that oscillates
between moderately murky & seriously swampy.
The desk staff are usually quite helpful – they're
affiliated with the travel agency across the street
– & the on-site restaurant-bar does a selection of
the usual European-inspired dishes. The annexe
around the block offers cheaper rooms with fans.
$$$

255

Oasis Oriental Club (21 rooms) Rte de Kaolack; ☎ 33 981 1824; e oasisclub.tamba@orange.fr; www.oasisoriental.com. With a clutch of well-appointed thatch bungalows scattered around a spotless swimming pool about 1.3km from town, this place does a nice job of combining up-to-date amenities with a traditional feel. All rooms come with AC, TV, fridge, nets, wardrobes & a low-key smattering of African décor. The cheerful restaurant does a French-inspired menu, & the French honorary consul's office in Tamba is here as well. They can arrange excursions to Niokolo-Koba & beyond in partnership with their sister hotel in Goudiry (see page 264). **$$$**

Relais de Tamba (22 rooms) Rte de Kaolack; ☎ 33 981 1000; e tamba@hbsenegal.com; www.horizons-bleus-senegal.com. 2km out of town and very likely Tamba's nicest address, the tiled en-suite rooms here are freshly painted & well equipped with all the modern trimmings like in-room telephones & flatscreen TVs. They're set around a central courtyard with a large & invitingly blue swimming pool. The highly regarded (& furiously air-conditioned) restaurant-bar has a wide menu of French-inspired salads, plus fish & meat dishes. **$$$**

Asta Kébé (29 rooms) Quartier Abattoir; ☎ 33 981 1028; m 70 306 0225; e socihota@yahoo.fr. This institution-like place is a strange slice of 70s kitsch plonked down into some rather unkempt (though parrot-filled) gardens at the south end of town. The en-suite, air-conditioned rooms are drab & faded yet kept quite clean, but unfortunately the swimming pool's avocado green proves an unwelcome continuation of the 70s motif. The restaurant is almost worth a visit in itself for the time-warped décor, if not the food. **$$**

Le Ninki-Nanka (9 rooms) Quartier Abattoir; ☎ 33 980 1992; m 77 613 5976; e info@ninki-nanka.com; www.ninki-nanka.com.

Set in a small compound about 500m east of Av Senghor, this place isn't a bad choice, though it's a bit lackadaisically managed & you may find that there's simply nobody around to open the gate for you. If you do find the elusive keeper, there are clean tiled double & triple rooms to be had, with nets & fan or AC. Some of the rooms are en-suite & others aren't, but the prices are the same for either. There's Wi-Fi, b/fast included, & other meals available on request. **$$**

Auberge Sadio (Bloc Gadec) (13 rooms) ☎ 33 981 0665; ☎ 77 531 8931. Known better by its old name of Bloc Gadec, this has been the go-to budget option in Tamba for some years now, with helpful staff, Wi-Fi & surprisingly spacious rooms that range from doubles with AC & en-suite bath to dormitories (a rarity in Senegal!) with fan & shared ablutions. A basic b/fast is included as well. **$**

Auberge Sedis (6 rooms) m 77 511 4007; e groupesedis@gmail.com. If you're looking to get an early start on transport, this is the closest place; it's only about 500m to the main *gare routière*. In a head-scratcher of an oversight, it's been carefully signposted all the way from the main road, with the startling exception of the *auberge* itself, which is set in an anonymous-looking unmarked compound along an unnamed road. If you manage to find it, they've got basic rooms with AC or fan, some of them en-suite and including b/fast. **$**

La Maison Blanche (6 rooms) m 77 161 0981. In a small family compound a few doors down from the Niokolo Transports office, this place has reasonably kept rooms with fans, nets & that's about it. It's a competitor of the also-nearby Auberge Sadio for cheapest in town, and would make a good alternative if the former were full. **$**

✖ WHERE TO EAT AND DRINK *Map, page 255.*

All of the better hotels have good sit-down restaurants serving a variety of European and Senegalese fare in comfortable, if not inspired, surroundings. For a nice night out with a bottle of wine or two, Relais de Tamba (see above) probably has the widest menu and best kitchen in town.

✖ **Best Burger** Blvd Demba Diop; ☎ 33 981 5703; m 77 447 3927; ⊕ lunch & dinner daily. Despite the name, your chances of actually getting a burger here (be it the best or otherwise) are quite

small, but it's still a good sit-down option for rice & the usuals near the *gare routière*.

✖ **Face 2 Face** Av Léopold Senghor; ☎ 33 981 5560; m 77 578 9853; ⊕ lunch & dinner daily.

At the southernmost end of town in the *quartier abattoir*, the brochettes here take a while but are unequivocally worth the wait. There's also a rotating *plat du jour* if you're in more of a hurry.

✖ **God Bless Tamba** Av Léopold Senghor; m 78 151 4483/77 577 7092; ⊕ lunch & dinner daily. The *crème de la crème* of Tamba's street stalls, this place offers what might be the only pizza in town; never mind the fact they're made on a griddle with ketchup & mayo, they're as close to divine as you'll get around these parts.

✖ **Le Relais du Rail** Av Amadou Ndiaye Dionewar; ✆ 33 981 0196; m 77 552 7096; ⊕ 09.00–23.00 daily. This festive little place is done up in bright blue with a covered terrace in front well-suited to watching the traffic race by. They mostly do fast food standbys like chawarmas, fattayahs, burgers & omelettes, while trying their hand at a few other dishes like couscous & pizza.

⚲ **Chez Francis** Av Léopold Senghor; ✆ 33 981 4923; ⊕ 18.00–late daily. The most hassle-free bar in town, where the beers are frigid, the service is warm, & there's football on the TV out back. The owner (not Francis, actually) speaks some English & they also do a nice steak/chicken & chips, but it's not always available.

⚲ **Complexe Touristique Leggal Pont** Rte de Kidira; ✆ 33 981 1756; ⊕ 23.00–04.00 daily. Whether you're on the hunt for a 'Bar Americain' (which looks suspiciously like most other bars in Senegal), all-night dance club, or some surprisingly reasonable-looking rooms out back, this place ought to have you covered, though it's a pretty smoky affair & probably best enjoyed in a group. And while the rooms are trim enough, you'll need a good set of earplugs or a good number of drinks before getting much shuteye.

SHOPPING For groceries, **Azur Commercial** (⊕ 08.00–23.45 Mon–Sat, 10.00–21.00 Sun) is the place to go. They've got a good selection of packaged and frozen goods including ice cream, which you'll want if you stay in Tambacounda long enough. Fruit and vegetables abound at the **central market** nearby. There's another small supermarket across from Hotel Niji. Craft shoppers will want to head for the **Centre Artisanal de Tamba** (see page 258). You'll also find a couple of fantastic jewellery sellers in the market and along Blvd Demba Diop, who carry traditional bangles, rings, and amulets handmade from bronze, copper and other semi-precious metals.

OTHER PRACTICALITIES
Banking and foreign exchange All the major banks are represented in Tambacounda, with most branches (CBAO, Ecobank, BICIS) clustered around the intersection of Boulevard Demba Diop and Avenue Amadou Ndiaye Dionewar, with the exception of SGBS, which is on Avenue Léopold Senghor. There's at least one private bureau de change in town, but its advantage over the banks is questionable.

Hospital The **Centre Hospitalier Régional** (✆ 33 981 1218) is about 2.5km south of town along Avenue Léopold Senghor. Care here is adequate, but as with all of Senegal's regional hospitals, serious problems are best dealt with Dakar.

Internet Cyber Espace World Connection (⊕ 09.00–22.00) on Avenue Amadou Ndiaye Dionewar has a handful of computers, 250F/hr.

Police At the main roundabout where Avenues Demba Diop and Léopold Senghor meet (✆ 33 981 1317).

Post office In the administrative quarter north of Boulevard Demba Diop near the market.

Swimming The Oasis Oriental Club (see page 256) allows visitors to use its clean & blue swimming pool for 3,000F per person.

WHAT TO SEE AND DO There isn't much in Tamba that you would call 'sightseeing', or not with a straight face, anyway, but if you've got a couple of days in town, there are a few spots worth a gander. That being said, the old **train station** ought to be any visitor's first stop. Built in the 1910s, it's still a functional office and stationmaster's residence so you can't go inside, but it's worth poking around the station grounds anyway. The **station hotel** next door is a fantastic old red-and-yellow building, but it's in lamentable shape today and home to several families of squatters, so be sure to ask permission and be respectful if you choose to go exploring.

The **Centre Artisanal de Tamba** had also fallen into disrepair in recent years, but was somewhat revamped in early 2014 and is now a welcome addition to the rather short list of attractions in Tamba. Its offerings may not exactly be bountiful, but it has a worthwhile collection of a dozen or so workshops belonging to local sculptors, painters, jewellers, shoemakers and more.

The **central market** is where you'll find all manner of fruit, veg, fabric, tools, cosmetics, clothing, bits, bobs and everything in between. This is where the locals come to do their provisioning, and while it's not tourist-oriented in the slightest, it's the beating heart of Tambacounda and the various jewellers and tailors either carry or can whip up some one-of-a-kind pieces if you've got time to wait.

If you're suffering from some post-market exhaustion, the hushed streets of the former administrative quarter north of Boulevard Demba Diop are a welcome retreat from the frantic traffic and commerce endemic to the rest of town. Home to leafy old trees and modest colonial villas, it won't make it on to any top ten lists, but it's about the most diverting place in Tamba for a stroll.

NIOKOLO-KOBA NATIONAL PARK

Inscribed as a UNESCO world heritage site in 1981 and ignominiously added to the list of endangered world heritage sites in 2007, Niokolo-Koba National Park extends over 9,130km^2 of river, savannah and gallery forest southeast of Tambacounda, and represents the largest and wildest area of protected and uninhabited land in Senegal. The habitats here vary between wide expanses of Sudan-Guinea savannah punctuated by riverine stretches of gallery forest, floodplains, marshes and even a few hills towards the southeast of the park, which peak at the rarely visited 311m Mount Assirik. Most of the easily accessed areas of the park lie along the Gambia River, but the park also takes in the rambling watercourses of several tributaries, including the Koulountou and the park's namesake river, the Niokolo-Koba. Since 1985, Niokolo-Koba has also been contiguous with Guinea's much smaller (382km^2) Badiar National Park, which lies just across the border to the south (though there are no legal crossings or roads between them).

Cut into two uneven halves by the RN7, nearly all tourist activity in the park takes place in the southern section, and the main hotel and ranger station are both located at Simenti (no prizes for guessing the etymology), which sits between an impressive lagoon (*mare de Simenti*) and the Gambia River, just over 30km into the park from the entrance gate at Dar Salam. Unfortunately, no matter which side of the reserve you're on, illegal hunting and poaching are a serious problem here, and wildlife numbers here have been on the decline for many years now. Compounding the problem, increased traffic and the growing importance of the Tambacounda-Kédougou artery don't bode well for the future of the park. Still, all is far from lost and Niokolo-Koba certainly remains a wild and enchanting place, and a worthy destination for any visitor with an interest in what a less densely populated Senegal might have looked like once upon a time.

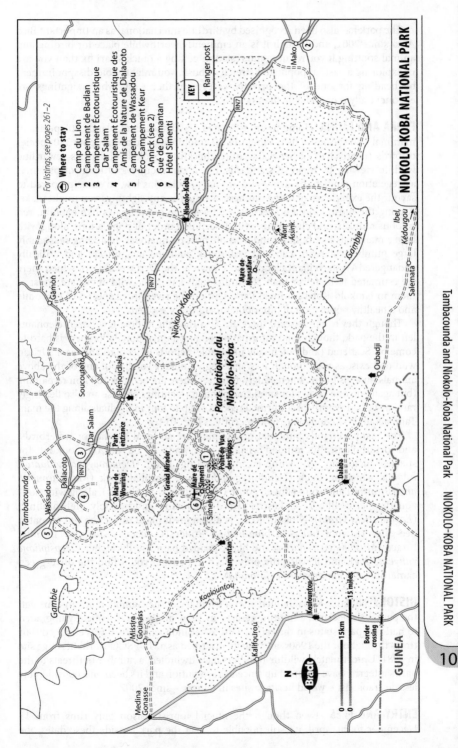

NIOKOLO-KOBA NATIONAL PARK

For listings, see pages 261–2

Where to stay
1 Camp du Lion
2 Campement de Badian
3 Campement Écotouristique
    Dar Salam
4 Campement Écotouristique des
    Amis de la Nature de Dialacoto
5 Campement de Wassadou
    Éco-Campement Keur
    Annick (see 2)
6 Gué de Damantan
7 Hôtel Simenti

KEY
🛖 Ranger post

GUINEA

Parc National du
Niokolo-Koba

The park has also been recognised by BirdLife International as an Important Bird Area since 2001, and though it is an eminently worthwhile place for birding and animal spotting if you're more interested in getting a quick safari fix than you are in exploring a vast, unpopulated stretch of bush, you might avoid disappointment by heading for one of the private reserves further west, where sightings are exponentially more reliable than here.

FLORA AND FAUNA Home to an estimated 1,500 species of plants, 80 species of mammals, 60 species of fish, 38 reptile, 20 amphibian, and a whopping 330 species of birds (nearly half of Senegal's entire checklist), Niokolo-Koba has rewarding wildlife viewing by regional standards, but it can require a little bit of patience, as vegetation tends to be dense and animal populations low, so come prepared to savour the experience of being out here as much as any sightings you might make. Among the most common species you'll see here are primates like baboon, red colobus monkey, and chimpanzee (in descending order of population), along with larger mammals like buffalo, and a whole host of antelopes, including reasonably large numbers of roan, kob and waterbuck, and the magnificent and critically endangered Western giant eland (also known as the Derby eland), of which there are estimated to be fewer than 200 individuals left in the wild anywhere, most of them in Niokolo-Koba National Park. Out on the river, three species of crocodile and a healthy population of hippopotami are easily spotted.

Though they're rarely seen, there are also thought to be a few dozen elephants left in the park, though solid information on any animal population here is hard to come by. Scattered (and potentially unreliable) reports of leopard and even African wild dog exist as well, though it's vanishingly unlikely you'll spot any of the above animals on a visit here. Interestingly, however, there are perhaps 100 lion remaining (but again, no one knows for sure), and although sightings of these are also fleetingly rare, we've had reports of confirmed reports of up to four individuals along the main Tambacounda–Kédougou road as recently as late 2014.

The many wetlands punctuating the park are an ideal habitat for waterbirds, and ornithologically minded visitors will want to be on the lookout for species including the white-faced whistling duck (*Dendrocygna viduata*), fulvous whistling duck (*Dendrocygna bicolor*), marbled duck (*Marmaronetta angustirostris*) and spur-winged goose (*Plectropterus gambensis*), along with non-aquatic species like lesser kestrel (*Falco naumanni*) and possibly Mali firefinch (*Lagonosticta virata*). Niokolo-Koba is also a great place to see the red-throated bee-eater (*Merops bulocki*), blue-bellied Roller (*Coracias cyanogaster*), violet turaco (*Musophaga violacea*) and black-headed paradise-flycatcher (*Terpsiphone rufiventerthe*), and it's also the only place in Senegal you'll find the olive-green camaroptera (*Camaroptera chloronota*).

HISTORY Niokolo-Koba, named after a tributary of the Gambia that runs through the park, was declared a hunting reserve in 1926, and was subsequently upgraded to national park status in the early 1950s. After independence, it was enlarged four times throughout the 1960s, and finally inscribed as a UNESCO world heritage site in 1981. Unfortunately wildlife numbers have dwindled, a number of threats to the park's integrity have cropped up since its recognition and it's been on a considerably less desirable list – world heritage sites in danger – since 2007.

ENTRY AND FEES Even though the official tourist season only runs from 15 December to 30 April, it's still possible to visit the park outside these dates; the entry gate at Dar Salam is open ☉ 07.00–18.00 daily, all year round. Regardless of whether it's in or out of season, visitors are required to pay a daily park use fee of 2,000F, a one-time entry fee of 5,000F per vehicle (no walking is allowed), and an additional 10,000F per day for your obligatory guide. If you don't have a vehicle of your own, a 4x4 hire including petrol for a trip into the park will usually start in the neighbourhood of 90,000F per day.

GETTING THERE AND AWAY

By car The tarmac **RN7** between Tambacounda and Kédougou bisects the park, though most visits take place in the larger section south of the road, which is host to the majority of the park's road network and all accommodation. In the dry season, the road from the entrance gate to Simenti and a handful of other tracks nearby are doable in most vehicles, but any other road in the park will require at least high clearance and preferably a 4x4 to get through. Your guide will be able to advise you as to the latest condition of the roads.

By bus and *sept-place* There is no public transportation within the park and hiking is not allowed within its boundaries, so travellers on public transport will have to arrange a vehicle of some kind. Any transport going between Tambacounda and Kédougou can drop you at the Dar Salam entrance gate, but you may have to pay the full fare (6,000F) regardless of where you get off. It's worth at least asking about a dedicated vehicle to your destination as there will be occasional *sept-places* and *ndiaga ndiayes* serving the intermediate towns and villages along the way (Wassadou, Dialacoto, Dar Salam and Mako), but as always the *ndiaga ndiayes* can be desperately poky. Be aware that getting onward transport to Kédougou or Tambacounda from any of the intermediate villages on the RN7 can be time-consuming, since most traffic on the road is going all the way through so vehicles are often full when they pass.

By transfer Trips to Niokolo-Koba can be arranged through almost any tour operator in Senegal, including all of the campements around the park, as well as agents based in Dakar and the Petite Côte, who often run trips to Niokolo-Koba that also incorporate visits to nearby Kédougou and the Bassari country. Starting in Dakar and using private road transfers (as opposed to chartering a flight to Tambacounda, which is also theoretically possible), most excursions last between four and eight days. The following are some recommended Dakar/Saly operators, and in Tambacounda **Senegal Oriental Voyages** (see page 255) is a good first port of call.

Africa Travel Group 📞33 869 7900; e info@ africatravel-group.com; www.africatravel-group. com

Origin Africa 📞33 860 1578; e info@origin-africa.sn; www.origin-africa.sn

---

🏠 **WHERE TO STAY, EAT AND DRINK** *Map, page 259.*
In the park

🏠 **Hôtel Simenti** (20 rooms) 📞33 984 1136/985 9696; m 77 107 8630; e ndewanne@ yahoo.fr. While the facilities have the aura (& all the charm) of a repurposed mental institution, the fantastic terrace overlooking the Gambia River goes a long way towards making up for the dated

interiors. All the rooms are well maintained & en-suite with AC & nets, & the newer bungalows behind the main building are a bit more expensive but less likely to touch off any unwelcome nostalgia. It's open all year round & can arrange a range of activities within the park from 4x4 game drives (starting at 24,000F) to hikes & pirogue trips. There's a swimming pool too, but it was dry when we checked in.

Camp du Lion (6 rooms) m 77 711 1994. The bamboo & thatch huts here were in a deplorable state when we visited, but renovations were promised for next year. It's in a lovely spot overlooking a bend in the Gambia River & shaded by enormous borassus palms and kapok trees though, so it would make a fantastic place to stay if the renovations go forward. All inquiries go through the main park gate anyway; ask there as to the state of the camp. **$**

Gué de Damantan (8 rooms) m 77 711 1994. With stone & thatch bungalows that feel a fair bit more established than their counterparts at Camp du Lion, this place could be considered a more reliable option, even if it might take second place in the scenery stakes. The bungalows are basic with 2 or 3 beds with nets in each, & little more. The river is about 100m away, & this is also the home of an orphaned panther found in the park in 1995 & cared for here in a reasonably large enclosure ever since. Rates in the middle of this range. **$**

Accommodation outside the park itself, in north-to-south order

Campement de Wassadou (20 rooms) Wassadou; ↖33 982 3602; m 70 910 7325; e wassadou@niokolo.com; www.niokolo.com. With perhaps the prettiest location & the most comfortable rooms of any campement in or around Niokolo-Koba, this is the first you'll encounter heading down from Tambacounda, & an eminently enjoyable stop whichever direction you're heading. There are plenty of activities on offer, including 4x4 & motorboat trips, canoeing, fishing, swimming & cultural tours. Rooms are in tastefully decorated tiled bungalows, & the commended restaurant-bar sits on a lazy bluff overlooking the river. **$$**

Campement Écotouristique des Amis de la Nature de Dialacoto (12 rooms) Dialacoto; ↖33 984 0245; m 70 107 3636/77 984 3737; e gieamisdelanature@yahoo.fr; www. campementdedialacoto.overblog.com. This is an

admirable community-based set-up with rooms in very pleasant en-suite thatch bungalows with nets & fans. It's a good starting point for hikes in the surrounding Fulbe (Peul) & Mandinka villages, & the usual trips into the park can be arranged. **$**

Campement Touristique Dar Salam (10 rooms) Dar Salam; ↖33 984 4275; m 77 805 6292; e ecovillage@fallou.org; www.fallou.org. At the very beginnings of a complete overhaul when we checked in, this was once something of a fallback for visitors, but with the scheduled improvements & new partnership with Spanish NGO Fallou, it's poised to become a prime launch pad for exploring the park & surrounding regions. Rooms are in en-suite bungalows, it's spitting distance from the entrance gate, & they can arrange boat trips, 4x4 excursions, village visits & outings to their various community projects. **$**

Éco-Campement Keur Annick (11 rooms) Mako; m 76 667 8500/77 300 8599; e niokolovoyages@yahoo.fr; www.sites.google. com/site/keurannick. Signposted 1km off the main road on the south bank of the Gambia River, this spacious compound is home to basic but comfortable whitewashed bungalows with en-suite bathrooms & terraces just steps from the river. The kitchen here whips up a high standard of French-inspired cuisine, & it's a fantastic place to set up excursions into Niokolo-Koba, as well as to the waterfalls & Bédik or Bassari villages to the south. **$$**

Campement de Badian (9 rooms) Mako; ↖33 957 5839; m 77 555 1873; e makhan. camara@ymail.com or asociacion@campamentos-solidarios.org; www.campamentos-solidarios.org. In a shady compound about 500m beyond Keur Annick & also on the south bank of the Gambia River, this rootsy campement has a cluster of basic bamboo & thatch huts with attached outdoor bathrooms. The huts are starting to show their age a bit, but it's a homey set-up with good meals on offer & superbly welcoming staff. They can arrange boat & 4x4 excursions into the park, & it's associated with the Spanish Campamentos Solidarios organisation, so profits benefit the local community. **$$**

WHAT TO SEE AND DO Most trips here take the form of vehicle safaris, and there's a good network of shaded hides overlooking a series of lagoons, floodplains and watering holes where you can take in the surroundings and any animals that might happen by. Most of these are arranged within a few kilometres of either Simenti or the two camps, and the most commonly visited viewpoints include the *Grand Mirador, Mare de Kountadala, Mare de Dalafourounté, Mare de Woëni* and *Mare de*

THE BACK ROUTE THROUGH NIOKOLO-KOBA

If you've got a 4x4 and are self-sufficient on food and shelter, it's even possible to make a loop between Simenti and Salemata (from where there's a good road to Kédougou) without backtracking to the main RN7, via remote tracks on the west side of the park.

Starting from the south, continue west from Salemata to the Bassari village of **Oubadji** (✪ *12.673032, –13.051512*) (occasionally marked on maps as Edale) where you'll find **Campement Dunya (Chez Ousmane et Aminata Diallo)** (m *77 599 46 20/78 304 6789; http://dunyavoyage.free.fr*) and the park's southern entrance. Here's where you can pay your park fees and get information about conditions ahead. Oubadji is also noteworthy for occasionally hosting the Bassari initiation ceremony, the *Koré* (see box, pages 272–3).

From Oubadji you'll head west and then north past two more ranger posts, **Dalaba** (✪ *12.751709, –13.275646*) and **Damantan** (✪ *12.997150, –13.402481*), after which you'll turn eastwards towards the gué (meaning river ford – built from logs in the dry season and crossed by a hand-pulled ferry in the wet) across The Gambia at the Gué de Damantan campement/ranger post.

From here it's spitting distance to Simenti, and though the trip is only about 100km overall, allow at least a couple of days as the roads are atrocious (and probably impassable during the wet season). If you don't have your own 4x4 but would like to set this up, any of the tour agencies running trips into the park should be able to make it happen.

Simenti, where there are two hides, one on each side of the lagoon (one of which is accessible by foot from the hotel). While you're driving around, you might also notice a few signs for the *pont suspendu* (suspension bridge), which was once a rather exhilarating footbridge stretched over the Niokolo-Koba river, but has long been out of service.

Another, potentially superior, way to tour the park is by boat, and while it's already a pleasure to cruise the glassy surface of the Gambia, the wildlife viewing along the riverbanks is also often better than what you'll see around the densely vegetated roadsides, and you're almost certain to catch hippos, crocodile, antelope and plenty of birds.

Since walking isn't allowed, keen hikers will be glad to know that the Dialacoto-based **Groupement d'Intérêt économique (GIE) of Niokolo-Koba National Park Guides** (m *76 336 2640;* e *info@niokolo-safari.com; www.niokolo-safari.com*) is developing a number of trails on the peripheries of the park (currently between 9km and 25km) that can be approached on foot either alone or with a guide. They're hoping to have trail markers posted by the end of 2015, but until that happens a guide would prove very useful. Check their informative English-language website for details of the routes.

EAST OF TAMBACOUNDA

GOUDIRY Along the N1 about 115km east of Tambacounda and a further 70km to Kidira and the Mali border, Goudiry was once a stop on the Dakar-Niger railway line; today it is not particularly memorable, other than being the access point for the **Boundou Community Nature Reserve** (*Réserve Naturelle Communautaire du Boundou*) (✆ *77 713 9279;* e *corena.tamba@hotmail.com; www.reserve-boundou.*

Tambacounda and Niokolo-Koba National Park   EAST OF TAMBACOUNDA

10

com), an ecotourism and sustainable development project launched by 21 villages in the area along and south of the N1, including Koussane, Dougué, Toumboura, Didé, Talibadji, Sansanding, Goundafa and Sintiou Fissa. The project is in its early stages, but birding, trekking, historical tours, boat trips on the Falémé and village visits can all be arranged.

The only accommodation here is at the **Savane Safari Club** (\ *33 983 7165/981 1825;* m *77 644 06 68;* e *contact@savanesafari.com; www.savanesafari.com*), sister hotel to the Oasis Oriental Club in Tambacounda (see page 256) and of a similar standard. They've got ten fully equipped en-suite bungalows along with a restaurant-bar and swimming pool; they can also provide up-to-date information and arrange excursions into the Boundou Reserve and throughout the region.

KIDIRA The only reason you're likely to end up in Kidira is if you're *en route* to Mali, or travelling between Tambacounda and Bakel. Either way, there's little reason to spend any longer here than it takes to change vehicles and move on, though you could give the old railway station a glance if you felt like it. If you get here after the border closes (late evening), the **Hôtel Boundou** [map, below] (m *77 969 7495*) is close to both the border and the main *gare routière*, and has decent en-suite rooms

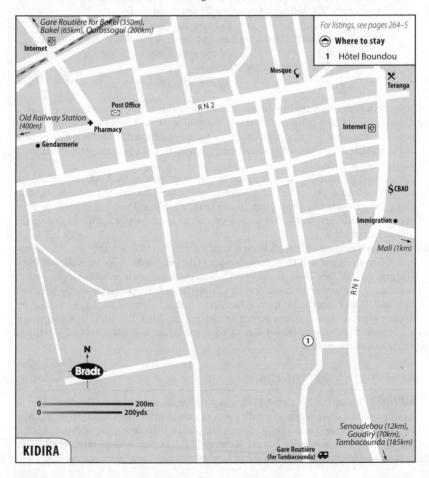

Gare Routière for Bakel (350m),
Bakel (65km), Ourossogui (200km)

Internet

For listings, see pages 264–5

⊖ **Where to stay**
1   Hôtel Boundou

Mosque (

✗ Teranga

Post Office   RN 2

Old Railway Station (400m)
Pharmacy

Internet

Gendarmerie

$CBAO

Immigration ●

Mali (1km)

RN 1

N

Bradt

0 ━━━━━━ 200m
0 ━━━━━━ 200yds

①

Senoudebou (12km),
Goudiry (70km),
Tambacounda (185km)

KIDIRA

Gare Routière
(for Tambacounda)

with fan or AC starting at 15,000F and an attached restaurant/bar with meals on request. Transport to Bakel (*75mins, 1,500F*) leaves from a separate *gare routière* a few hundred metres up the road towards Bakel. There are several *sept-places* to/from Tambacounda (*3hrs, 3,500F*) throughout the day, and it's also possible to get a direct *sept-place* to Dakar from here if you're up for the 11-hour trek.

If you've got some time here, your own 4x4, and want some history without heading all the way up to Bakel, the little-known and less-visited **Fort Senoudebou** (✪ *14.358701, –12.244969*) lies 12km south of Kidira on the west bank of the Falémé, in the village of the same name. Building began when the French purchased the land in 1845 but they abandoned the fort shortly afterwards, sometime in the 1860s. Despite occasional occupation by local regents after the French lost interest, it fell into deep disrepair and today only a handful of stone walls, archways and parts of the corner ramparts remain standing. Still, it's an atmospheric site in a traditional village along the Falémé and has to be among Senegal's least-seen colonial relicts. Coming from Kidira, take the **N1** towards Tambacounda for 5km and turn left onto an unmarked dirt track at the village of Nayé, from where there's an 8km tangle of crisscrossed sandy tracks between you and Senoudebou.

SEND US YOUR SNAPS!

We'd love to follow your adventures using our *Senegal* guide – why not send us your photos and stories via Twitter (@BradtGuides) and Instagram (@bradtguides) using the hashtag #senegal. Alternatively, you can upload your photos directly to the gallery on the Senegal destination page via our website (*www.bradtguides.com*).

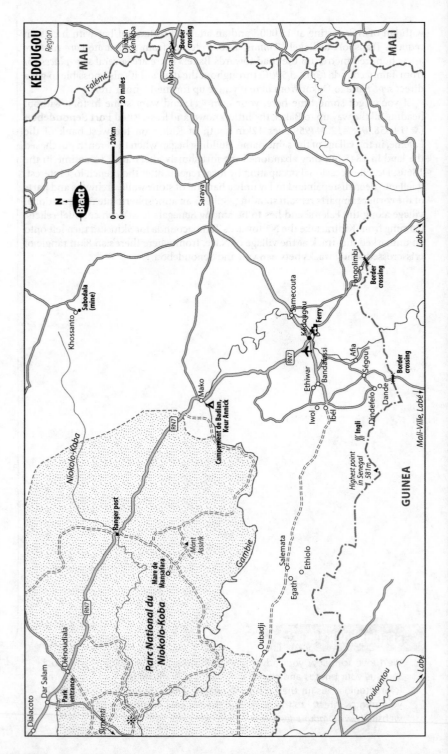

11

Kédougou and Around

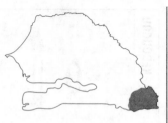

In the far southeastern corner of Senegal lies perhaps the country's most incongruous and beguiling region. Breaking with Senegal's relentlessly flat topography, the Kédougou region encompasses the northernmost foothills of the Fouta Djallon highlands that continue into neighbouring Guinea, and is home to Senegal's highest point. And while its 581 unnamed metres aren't likely to set mountaineer tongues wagging, the region is still host to the best hiking, trekking and rambling to be found anywhere in Senegal, and is practically a riot of greenery with its rolling forested hills, making a most welcome respite from Tambacounda's baking plains to the north.

KÉDOUGOU

Kédougou itself is a thoroughly agreeable provincial capital with a diverse and growing population. Long a sleepy river town at the end of the road and the very edge of the country, Kédougou is expanding rapidly, spurred on since the early 2000s by a global spike in gold prices that has brought massive commercial investment to the once-artisanal mining that has taken place here for hundreds of years. Add to this the recently completed tarmac routes to Tambacounda and Mali, and Kédougou is looking more and more like a boomtown every day. That being said, it's still an easygoing place where horse-drawn *calèches* and house-sized mining equipment jostle for position on the few tarmac roads through town. There isn't a whole lot to detain a tourist in the city itself, but it has banks, internet and a good selection of accommodation, and it's the obvious base to arrange trips throughout the region.

HISTORY Before the founding of Kédougou itself, the area was seasonally occupied by Bediks, who came to harvest the Borassus palms native to the area. The first permanent settler was a Fulani (Peul) migrant from near Bakel by the name of Massiré Ba who, after a year-long sojourn around the region, set up shop in what was to become Kédougou in 1825. The first European visitors passed here in 1880 and the French established an administrative post here in 1904, but for most of its history Kédougou was little more than an outpost, counting only 2,665 residents as recently as 1965. Today 76,242 people call Kédougou district home, but the region, with 152,134 residents, remains Senegal's least populated by far.

GETTING THERE AND AWAY
By air There is an airport 4.5km from the centre of town on the road to Tambacounda, but there were no scheduled flights at the time of research. It's not out of the question that Groupe Transair (*www.groupetransair.sn*) or Senegal Airlines (*www.senegalairlines.aero*) might start serving Kédougou during the lifespan of this edition.

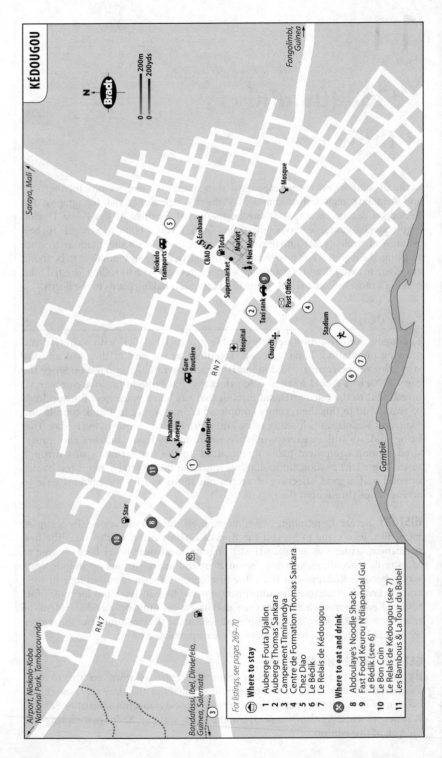

KÉDOUGOU

Saraya, Mali

Airport, Niokolo-Koba
National Park, Tambacounda

Bandafassi, Ibel, Dindefelo,
Guinea, Salemata

Fongolimbi,
Guinea

Gambie

Niokolo
Transports

Ecobank

CBAO

Total

Supermarket

Market

A Nos Morts

Taxi rank

Post Office

Hospital

Church

Stadium

Mosque

Gare
Routière

Pharmacie
Keneya

Gendarmerie

Star

RN7

For listings, see pages 269–70

Where to stay
1 Auberge Fouta Djallon
2 Auberge Thomas Sankara
3 Campement Timinandya
4 Centre de Formation Thomas Sankara
5 Chez Diao
6 Le Bédik
7 Le Relais de Kédougou

Where to eat and drink
8 Abdoulaye's Noodle Shack
9 Fast Food Keurou N'diapandal Gui
   Le Bédik (see 6)
10 Le Bon Coin
   Le Relais de Kédougou (see 7)
11 Les Bambous & La Tour du Babel

By car Kédougou is the terminus of the RN7, situated 230km from Tambacounda, 78km from Salemata, 107km from the Malian border at Moussala, 32km from the Guinean border at Fongolimbi, 40km from the Guinean border past Ségou (32km from the lesser-used crossing at Fongolimbi) and an even 700km from Dakar. The road to Tambacounda is surfaced and in generally good shape with a few pot-holed stretches. Self-drivers should be able to get through in about three hours. The road to Mali and bridge over the Falémé River were recently surfaced in an effort to ease congestion for goods traffic between Bamako and Dakar, which could previously only cross the border further north at Kidira. Note that this is the only official crossing to Mali from Kédougou; but many maps have yet to mark the new section of road from Saraya to the border at Moussala, and instead include unsurfaced and little-used bush roads to the villages of Satadougou or Farincounda. All routes to Guinea are unsurfaced, and the road up the escarpment to Fongolimbi should not be attempted without a strong 2x4 with high clearance, and preferably a 4x4.

By bus and *sept-place* Kédougou's *gare routière* is among Senegal's least orderly, and a minor catastrophe of mud or dust depending on the season, but it's reasonably well-served and getting to and from town is quite straightforward. *Sept-places* from Tambacounda (*6,000F, 5hrs*) leave throughout the day, and you'll have to change vehicles here for all other destinations.

If your goal is Dakar, Niokolo Transports (*www.niokolotransports.com*) runs a direct service (*11,000F*) three times weekly, departing from their ticket office (where you should buy your tickets in advance) opposite Chez Diao at 17.00 on Tuesdays, Thursdays, and Sundays, and arriving in Dakar about 12 hours later. There are the usual *car Mouride* and other anonymous buses scattered about the garage, but Niokolo is the most reliable by far.

ORIENTATION AND GETTING AROUND Kédougou sits north and west of a lazy bend in the Gambia River, although the town itself doesn't take much advantage of this riverside location. Most shops, businesses and restaurants line either the RN7 into town from Tambacounda or the first stretch of the D509 to Saraya, where both of the banks can be found. The junction of these two routes is more or less the centre of town, and the best place to find a taxi. There's really nowhere in town that isn't walking distance, but if you're tired or in a hurry, rides in town cost 500F.

WHERE TO STAY *Map, page 268.*

Le Bédik (24 rooms) ☎ 33 985 1000; e kedougou@hbsenegal.com; www.horizons-bleus-senegal.com. Part of the well-regarded Horizons Bleus chain, the rooms here aren't exactly oozing with character, but they're comfortable enough & the facilities on offer are among the best in town. Rooms are spotless & all have TVs, Wi-Fi & hot water, while the pool & restaurant overlooking the river are both prime candidates to while away a few hours. The restaurant does a wide range of meat & fish dishes, & religiously screens the latest football on a new flatscreen. Rates at the bottom half of this range. **$$**

Le Relais de Kédougou (20 rooms) ☎ 33 985 1062; e fhuard480@gmail.com; www. relais-de-kedougou.com. Probably Kédougou's most venerable accommodation, the grounds here are draped in bougainvillea & the restaurant has the best views in town. The en-suite thatched rooms have high ceilings, a fresh lick of paint & a smattering of African art to liven them up. All the usual amenities are on offer & it's good value, but be prepared to rub elbows with some people who are in town for bloodsport – the bulk of their clientèle is here to hunt. That being said, you won't find warthog on the menu anywhere else. Rates at the bottom half of this range. **$$$**

Budget

🏠 **Auberge Fouta Djallon** (8 rooms)
📞 33 985 1892; m 77 060 1695; e alphadouc@
hotmail.com. Rooms here are reasonably cool &
comfortable with all the expected amenities, but
aside from some flourishes in the furniture & a few
other flowery pretensions, it's not a whole lot more
for your money than at the other options in this
category. Rates in the middle of this range. **$$**

🏠 **Centre de Formation Thomas
Sankara** (16 rooms) m 77 555 9026;
e dansokhomoussa@yahoo.fr. Mostly used for
conferences & the like, this low-key hotel doesn't
bother with frills, but has quiet rooms at eminently
reasonable prices. First-floor rooms are breezier,
but all are tiled & clean, with fan, Wi-Fi & en-suite
bathroom. Rates at the lower end of this range. **$$**

Shoestring

🏠 **Auberge Thomas Sankara** (8 rooms)
m 77 622 9192. The rather haphazard sibling of
the Centre de Formation Thomas Sankara around
the corner, this place offers basic ground-floor
rooms with twin beds, en-suite bathrooms, fans

(1 room has AC) & not a whole lot else. On the
plus side, it's smack in the centre of town & there's
supposed to be Wi-Fi as well. **$**

🏠 **Campement Timinandya** (9 rooms)
📞 33 984 1515; m 77 552 6121; e timinandya72@
yahoo.fr. In a compound on the edge of town
about 600m down the Salemata road, this is every
bit the rural *campement*, & while the rooms, set in
thatched rondavels around a central restaurant-
bar, are far from special, they're almost certainly
the cheapest in town. The amenable owner can
help set up hiking trips & transport into the
villages, & though the rooms don't have them at
the moment, he can probably rustle up a mosquito
net or two as well. Meals by request. **$**

🏠 **Chez Diao** (5 rooms) 📞 33 985 1124;
m 77 238 1130. In a surprisingly green compound
for a town-centre location, this place has a handful
of colourful & welcoming thatch bungalows with
nets, fans & Wi-Fi. The on-site restaurant does basic
meals & usually has some beers on ice as well.
It's the best place in town to set up hikes around
the region, & is right across from the Niokolo
Transports office as well. Excellent value. **$**

✗ WHERE TO EAT AND DRINK Map, page 268.

The restaurants at both Le Relais and Le Bédik (see page 269) are the best in
town, and both offer sit-down dining with river views, full bar and long menus of
brochettes, fish, steak, and even warthog in-season at Le Relais, with dishes starting
at about 4,000F.

✗ **Abdoulaye's Noodle Shack** ⏲ dinner
daily. In an unmarked shelter of corrugated
tin typically hidden behind some overnighting
lorries or car parts, this is about as basic as it gets,
but Abdoulaye still draws a nightly crowd for
his sizzling spaghetti creations. You pay by the
ingredient & can pick from an assortment of eggs,
meat, onions, mustard, mayo & the like; it usually
adds up to around 1,500F.

✗ **Fast Food Keurou N'diapandal Gui**
m 77 869 9090/76 338 4141; ⏲ lunch & dinner
daily. Kédougou's most reliable shawarma &
sandwich joint, this place dishes up greasy but
satisfying *fattayas*, burgers & chicken, & even takes a
stab at pizza as well, all starting at around 1,500F.

🍷 **Le Bon Coin** ⏲ afternoon–late daily. This rough
& ready roadside bar has cold Gazelles, a covered
terrace & plenty of picnic furniture to go around.

☆ **Les Bambous & La Tour du Babel**
📞 33 980 6667; m 77 816 9295; e lesbambous@
sunumail.sn; ⏲ lunch & dinner daily. While it's no
Babylonian ziggurat, this one-storey nightclub &
restaurant is certainly among Kédougou's liveliest
nightspots, & given the recent influx of migrants,
there's probably more than a few languages
spoken here on any given night as well. The music
stays turned up to 11, though, so body language
tends to be the *lingua franca*. During the day,
they've got grilled meats & fish, but order early.
Meals go for around 4,000F.

SHOPPING There are two unnamed supermarkets with a good selection of
packaged foods, as well as some frozen items and alcohol. One is a couple of blocks
north of the main junction on the road towards Saraya, and the other is opposite
Ecobank along the same road. Chez Diao (see above) is more or less the only

address for craft shopping in Kédougou, but they've got a nice little selection of paintings, carvings and jewellery.

OTHER PRACTICALITIES
Banking and foreign exchange Ecobank and CBAO are both represented, and sit within a block of one another along the east side of the road to Saraya. Both have 24-hour ATMs and money-changing facilities. There are no private bureaux de change, but there are some gold buyers scattered around town in case you've brought your money in precious metal form. If you've come over the border with Guinean francs, you might try asking near the Guinea-bound transport at the *gare routière*.

Hospital The District Sanitaire and NGO-sponsored Clinique CMRA-SARL (*www.pistesantekedougou.com*) are both on the main road from Tambacounda, but care options here are likely to be limited, so as with anywhere in Senegal, get to Dakar if it's serious.

Internet Both Le Relais and Le Bédik offer Wi-Fi at their respective restaurants, and there's a small internet café on the connector road near Le Bon Coin.

Police The police station is on the Tambacounda road, opposite the gendarmerie.

Post office The post office is few blocks south of the main junction towards Le Relais and Le Bédik.

Swimming The only swimming pools in town are at Le Relais and Le Bédik. The pool at Le Bédik is for guests only, but Le Relais allows restaurant customers to swim. It's also possible to wander to the edge of town and swim in the Gambia River; while there aren't supposed to be many crocodiles or hippos near town, this does carry the potential risk of contracting schistosomiasis.

WHAT TO SEE AND DO Kédougou's charms mostly lie in the surrounding villages and forests, but the city itself is a hassle-free and pleasant enough place to while away a few days between excursions. Little evidence of its history is apparent on a walk around town, with most of the buildings and infrastructure being of thoroughly modern provenance. There are a handful of early 20th-century colonial buildings, but they're of decidedly limited interest. The market is a sprawling den of knockoff Chinese goods, traditional medicines, pesticide sprayers, metal detectors, second-hand clothing and a wider selection of fruits and vegetables than pretty much any market further north. The restaurants at Le Relais and Le Bédik are the best places in town to kick back and see the river, but down on the banks, the hand-pulled ferry crossing to Fongolimbi is a fine place to watch the world go by as well. There's supposed to be a bridge built here soon, but it was still a way off when we visited. Find a patch of shade and watch as fishermen, traders and travellers wend their way across the water.

AROUND KÉDOUGOU

The area surrounding Kédougou is populated by a unique ethnic mix of Fulbe (Peul), Bassari and Bédik people (see page 21), the latter two of which only live here and in nearby villages across the border in Guinea, and the cultural landscape here is so unique it's been protected as a UNESCO World Heritage Site since 2012. The natural environment is equally spectacular, and several of the Fulbe (Peul),

11

Simon Fenton (www.thelittlebaobab.com), author of Squirting Milk at Chameleons *(Eye Books, 2015; www.eye-books.com)*

On an April morning at home in Abéné, I received an unexpected call from Batta, a Bassari lad, who explained to me that the *Koré* was coming up. This is the boys' initiation ceremony, a major event that usually, but not always, happens once a year. So, *gris-gris* strapped in place, off we went: mile after mile of potholed roads and corrugated red mud tracks, hot diesel fumes circulating the cabin, sweat dripping. Outside: bleached out landscapes, burnt scrub, donkeys, carts and lonely villages of small thatched roundhouses. After a day or so of this, we finally arrived in Kédougou, where the temperature was 41°C. The sun was going down as we reached Salemata, and after some fish and rice, a couple of mercifully cold Gazelles, and a decent night's kip, we set off the next morning to walk across the 'mountain range' to Ethiolo, the Bassari village where the *Koré* was to take place. After catching a lift part of the way on a truck, we continued on foot across a landscape of very dry grass slopes and shea butter trees.

Along the way, we stopped at a Bassari compound of simple round huts made from lumps of rock and thatched with grass. Lined up outside were some long bows. A grandma came out and offered us a dirty plastic cup of millet beer, which was delicious. Before long we'd arrived in Ethiolo and went to hang out at Balingo's, the main campement. It was about 11am and the sun was brutal.

At about 15.00 we set off up the hill to check out the *Koré* ceremony. The Bassari are a small tribe who live as hunters and farmers in the foothills of the Fouta Djalon in southeastern Senegal. In Bassari society, roles and responsibilities are defined by a person's place in a very strict chronological hierarchy – far more so than most traditional societies. Order is enforced by the older level. There are seven stages for men and *Koré* is the most important ceremony, marking the passage into adulthood. The boys are separated from their families and live in communal houses for several months, separated from females. For the initiation, older initiates take them to the sacred forest where legend states the boys are killed and eaten by Numba, a chameleon deity who then regurgitates them as young adults.

Before they enter the forest, they are washed and rubbed with palm oil by older women who then braid their hair and tie in feathers from sacrificed chickens. They endure a series of harsh rituals and emerge from the forest acting like infants. Their guardians – older initiates – must wash, feed and even put them to sleep. From this state of regression, they emerge as mature adults. I later read that throughout the ritual, boys must not smile, laugh, talk or even look from side to side, or else they'll be seriously punished.

Up on the hill the initiation huts sat around a clearing amongst some large trees. The entire area was bustling with activity: ladies selling drinks, snacks, goats and some tack. Cauldrons bubbled on fires and many people gathered to socialise. Young men who were being initiated wore their hair plaited and, for reasons unknown to me, football outfits. There were some delicious local drinks available: the palm wine was fantastically rich and the honey wine was sublime.

Bassari, and Bédik villages surrounding Kédougou are working together as part of the Dindefelo Community Nature Reserve (RNCD), an ecotourism collective founded in cooperation with the Spanish branch of the Jane Goodall Institute (*info@ecosenegal.org; www.ecosenegal.org, www.janegoodall.es*) and recognised as

Youngsters were constantly blowing whistles, some chanting was heard and a procession of young men arrived down a slope and circled around the ceremonial area, shuffling along as someone played a local flute. A couple of cows and many a goat were slaughtered before us as well, and the dead cows were hung in a tree. Darkness began to fall, and all the while the dancers trooped around chanting. It was fantastic – fires lighting the area, dancers conga-ing at least until midnight, and an increasingly inebriated atmosphere. We eventually made the trek back the campement and flopped down for a few hours of rest before we were woken at 06.00 for breakfast.

After a few coffees we walked back up the hill for the main event of the *Koré*. Each initiate stood with an older man as a chicken was waved around his head. Then it was stretched out and its head cut off – the chicken's, not the initiate's. The headless chickens fell to the ground and ran in circles as the initiates impassively chased and beat them with a stick. The chickens' testicles were then examined – white is a good omen, black bad – and then the chickens were hung in trees. A gun occasionally boomed, making everyone jump.

The next part of the ceremony was something I'd seen previously in photographs and was eagerly awaiting. A procession of dancers moved slowly down the mountain wearing distinctive cartwheel masks. Their bodies were painted with ochre and their faces hidden by gauze. We could hear whistles, chanting and screams as they appeared at the top of the ridge across a valley. Slowly, they wound their way down the track, mimicking the movements of a chameleon. At the head of the procession was a masked creature with a ring of leaves tied around its chest, similar to the Diola *Essamye* mask. Shortly after they'd passed me they whooped and started running down the mountain.

The next phase of the ceremony was forbidden to females and cameras. A little way down the mountain was a large open space around which the audience formed a circle. The dancers removed their cartwheel masks but continued to wear the bark hoods and visors. They formed a line along one edge of the circle. After some time the next phase began – *la lutte*, or Senegalese traditional wrestling. Here, the young initiates took turns to fight the older and much bigger hooded creatures as a measure of their courage and virility. The small boys – some looking about 13 years old – approached the giants, who were holding heavy sticks and shields. You could hear the thud of wood on flesh before they locked bodies and wrestled in the more traditional sense. It's not necessary for the initiate to win, as long as he fights like a man. Following this, he receives a new name and status before being presented back to his parents as a stranger with a similar appearance to the boy who'd left months earlier.

Most of the initiates were beaten, but eventually one little Scrappy-Doo-like character went in quickly and knocked the opponent off balance, landing him on his back. The arena exploded with everyone dancing into the circle and whooping for joy as the initiate was carried away on shoulders.

Finally, that was it – the initiates would return to the forests that night for further training and presumably celebration of their first night as Bassari men, and we would shuffle down to Salemata, melting and dripping in the midday heat.

an Important Bird Area in 2015. All offer rustic accommodation in bungalows typical of the region, most without running water or electricity (though many have limited solar options). All can arrange meals, waterfall visits and a large number of circuits through the region.

All attractions associated with the RNCD (waterfalls, etc) charge an entry fee of 1,000F, which goes towards conservation and community projects in the associated villages. If you plan on visiting a number of the attractions or staying around for a while, a monthly pass can be purchased for 3,000F.

LOCAL GUIDES Almost all of the campements in this section have affiliated guides, but unfortunately relatively few of them speak English. Below is a selection of English-speaking guides and the villages in which they are based. Regardless of their home village, guides work throughout Kédougou region and can arrange visits to any village in the area. Guiding fees are typically between 10,000F and 15,000F per day depending on the activity (ie: driving versus hiking), and most are members of the communities themselves and can therefore offer insights far beyond what meets the eye in these often-enigmatic communities.

Doba Diallo (Dande) m 77 360 6401; e dobadiallo@yahoo.fr
Cheikh Tidiane Diallo (Dindefelo/Afia) m 77 554 6574; e afiacheikh@hotmail.fr

Souleymane Ba (Ibel) m 77 574 54 48; e souley90@yahoo.fr

GETTING THERE AND AROUND Transport around the region can be sporadic, so if you can't bear the thought of another hour of waiting in the Kédougou *gare routière*, it's possible to privately hire a *sept-place* and driver to just about any village in this section, or a *jakarta* (moto taxi) if you'd rather save some cash and feel the wind (and dust!) in your hair. Chez Diao or Le Bédik are good places to make these arrangements, particularly if you'd prefer to arrange a 4x4 (starting at 70,000F/day), but if you're feeling confident you can always try to set it up at the *gare routière* yourself. If you do this, make sure to be very clear with the driver about how much time you expect to have at your destination before returning.

WEST OF KÉDOUGOU

BANDAFASSI As you set out along the red earth road to Salemata, the rocky green hillsides to the north and south edge closer and closer to the roadside, creating a wide valley settled by a mix of Fula (Peul), Bédik and Bassari people (see page 21), though the latter two typically live in their own villages on the surrounding hillsides rather than in the largely Fula villages along the road. Situated under just such an escarpment, Bandafassi is the jumping-off point for trips to the Bédik village of Éthiwar, a 90-minute hike into the hills above.

Getting there and away Almost 15km west of Kédougou and 4km beyond the turnoff for Ségou & Dindefelo, Bandafassi is the first larger village you'll reach heading west. There are a few *ndiaga ndiayes* from Kédougou that pass this way daily, or, alternatively, all traffic (this is not saying much, mind you) headed to/from Salemata or other villages further up the road passes here, so you can try to flag a lift on the roadside as well.

⌂ Where to stay, eat and drink

⌂ **Campement Le Bédik (Chez Leontina)** (10 rooms) m 77 554 9915. Along the main road about 600m west of the village centre, this is the only accommodation in Bandafassi, & while it's poorly signposted, the en-suite thatch rondavels are bright yellow & everyone knows where it is anyway. Inside, the rooms are slightly more modern than most village campements, with tiled floors, electricity, fans & nets. The proprietress, Leontina, a Bédik herself, is a fantastic source of information on the area, & has all the connections to set you up with a guide to Éthiwar, or through to Iwol & the entire string of Bédik villages along the escarpment north of the road. **$**

What to see and do The biggest reason to visit Bandafassi is not so much the village itself, although it's an atmospheric slice of African village life with a reputation for fine basketry, but what's above it. Situated under a dramatic forested escarpment, Bandafassi is the jumping-off place for trips to the Bédik village of Éthiwar, a 90-minute hike into the hills above. Éthiwar offers views over the valley below all the way to Kédougou, and across to the Fouta Djallon mountains of Guinea to the south. It's also the starting point for longer treks in the hills to the enigmatic and little-visited Bédik villages of Andyel, Iwol (see below) and Ethiés, returning to the road at Ibél or as far west as Ninefécha. Guides and all other practicalities can be arranged at Le Bédik (Chez Leontina).

IBÉL As with Bandafassi, its neighbour just up the road, the low-slung agricultural village of Ibél sits under a rocky, forested escarpment, on top of which the neighbouring Bédik village of Iwol is situated. As with most of the lowland villages in the area, Ibél is predominantly Fulani (Peul), and residents here are typically farmers or cattle herders. Aside from the occasional sonic punctuation of a vehicle sputtering through town, Ibél still moves to the sounds of stomping hooves, creaking bicycles and laughing children. You'll only find silence more complete if you take to the hills above town and make the trek to Iwol.

Getting there and away Ibél is 23km from Kédougou and 9km past Bandafassi, so any transport headed for Salemata will serve Ibél as well. As with Bandafassi, there are a few *ndiaga ndiayes* from Kédougou that pass this way daily, and all traffic headed to/from Salemata or other villages further up the road passes right through the village, so you can usually flag a lift on the roadside as well.

Where to stay, eat and drink

Campement Croisée de Cultures
m 77 616 0583/574 5448; e souley90@yahoo.fr. Souleymane is both guide & owner here, he speaks some English, & he's happy to set up everything from day hikes up to Iwol to multi-night excursions through the villages. Rooms are in basic thatch bungalows with shared ablutions, & meals are arranged on request. **$**

Campement Le Bande (4 rooms, 7 under construction) m 77 060 1697/653 1538. A new addition to the Ibél accommodation 'scene', the pointy-roofed bungalows here feel fresh & bright, & they've got the usual offerings in terms of meals & guided treks as well. Friendly management, clean ablutions & a breezy compound on the edge of the village make this a welcoming option. **$**

What to see and do Like Bandafassi up the road, visitors to Ibél are typically here for the vertiginous hike up the hills behind the village, on which you find the seemingly timeless Bédik hamlet of Iwol. Depending on your speed, you can reach the top in about an hour, but it's a proper calf-burner. Either campement can arrange a guide for something like US$4–US$6, and your time in Iwol will be very much enriched by having one along. The land here is steeped in legend, but these can be as impenetrable as the Bédik tongue without the right introductions.

SALEMATA *Population 21,000*
Cut off on the west by the remote southern reaches of the Niokolo-Koba National Park (and its Guinean counterpart, Badiar National Park, to the south), Salemata sits more

11

or less – for transport purposes anyway – at the end of a cul-de-sac, but it's without question one of Senegal's most enchanting drives, the road tucked into a wide valley of farms and savannah by steep, rocky hills on either side of the road. The whole journey is a riot of greenery cut through by the fiercely red road, particularly if there's been any rain recently; it's among the most archetypally African landscapes to be found anywhere in the country.

Salemata itself is a small regional centre with little in the way of services (take money out in Kédougou), simple but well-kept tourist facilities and a positively languorous atmosphere. Most visitors come here for chimpanzee trekking and visits to the surrounding Bassari villages, but it's just as worthwhile to spend a day watching the Fulbe (Peul) herdsmen driving their charges down from the hills into town. And given the paucity of transport connections here, you might have no choice!

Getting there and away 77km west of Kédougou at the end of a well-maintained laterite road that can be easily tackled in a saloon car, Salemata is the jumping-off point for trips to the main Bassari village of Ethiolo. There are no more than a couple of *ndiaga ndiayes* that make the two-hour run between Kédougou and Salemata daily (2,500F), but more on Thursdays, when Salemata holds its weekly *loumo* (market).

Heading west, the road gets rougher still, and the truly isolated Bassari village of Oubadji sits along the route 28km beyond Salemata. Oubadji marks the southern entrance to Niokolo-Koba National Park and the beginning of a potential circular route through the park for self-sufficient travellers (see box, page 263 for details). There might be a very occasional *taxi-brousse* or *ndiaga ndiaye* from here to Oubadji, but best pack a book, as you'll no doubt be in for a long wait.

Where to stay, eat and drink

Campement Chez Gilbert \33 985 1400; m 77 654 4935. Salemata's most venerable campement has been hosting visitors since 1985, & was for many years the only game in town. Even with the newfound diversity of options available, Chez Gilbert is still an excellent choice with simple thatch bungalows, good meals & a warm welcome. It's also a solid bet for trips around the region; after 30 years in the business, Gilbert knows the area like the back of his hand. **$**

Auberge Walo Bassa (Chez Kamara) (5 rooms) \77 578 1122. Kamara's place is right in the centre of town & about as simple as it gets. Thatch bungalows jostle for space with the shared bucket ablutions in a small compound centred on the open-air bar & restaurant where the ladies of

the establishment whip up some excellent plates of rice & meat or fish. Kamara is a helpful host and can set up multi-day guided hikes to Ethiolo & beyond, through Bassari villages where visitors are a rare sight indeed. **$**

Campement Le Peluun (8 rooms) \33 985 3315; m 77 680 7536; e peluun@orange.sn. Perched on a little hillside at the entrance to the village, this is the most upmarket accommodation in town. Still, the rooms here are simple thatch bungalows, but the new furnishings, fans, nets & baobab-studded compound with views over town go a long way towards making it the pick of the litter in Salemata. They can arrange good meals, hikes, guides & even bicycle hire. **$**

What to see and do Salemata draws the most visitors in May, when the Bassari coming-of-age rites (see box, pages 272–3) take place in nearby Ethiolo. It's the best base for hikes to Ethiolo and other Bassari villages in the area, and all of the campements can help set up excursions ranging from an afternoon to several days in length. In addition to cultural expeditions, the hills around Salemata are among the few places in Senegal where you'll have a chance to spot the threatened western chimpanzee (*Pan troglodytes verus*). If you can't make it here for the Bassari initiations in May, there are also a number of smaller festivals to commemorate the harvest season from November to February; ask at your campement for the latest. Barring that, most of the campements are happy to arrange traditional dance performances for guests when given enough notice.

ETHIOLO Etiolo is only about 9km from Salemata along a rough earthen track, but makes the latter seem like a bustling hub by comparison. With no more than a couple of thousand residents, Ethiolo is truly a village, but this belies its true significance as the largest Bassari settlement anywhere in the world. It's a picture of rural tranquillity, a clutch of homesteads with a thatch skyline, punctuated by kapoks, baobabs, curls of smoke from cooking fires, and yes, now a couple of mobile-phone masts as well.

Though few in number, the Bassari have clung tenaciously to their traditions in the face of aggression from all sides, from the French and the Fulbe to globalisation today. They continue to live in their own communities and speak their own language much as they always have, only today visitors from around the world are making the long trek here just to sneak a peek at these ancient traditions, once dismissed by outsiders as so much paganism, but today recognised and protected by UNESCO. And while this newfound protected status is excellent news, the Bassari have been stubbornly living on their own terms for as long as they've been around, and everyone hopes that they'll continue to do so for many years to come.

Getting there and away There's no public transport to Ethiolo, so your options are either to walk or to arrange 4x4 hire or other transport with your campement. The walk between here and Salemata is as picturesque as any in the area, and can be done without a guide in two to three hours. There are also smaller (and more direct) footpaths connecting the two, but you'd probably need to enlist some help to avoid getting lost on these. Either way, the views here are spectacular, you pass through some smaller Bassari settlements along the way, and if you're lucky you might even spot chimpanzees.

Where to stay, eat and drink

🏠 **Chez Balingo** (13 rooms) 📞 33 937 9698; m 77 146 8139. Ethiolo's only accommodation is run by the venerable Balingo, a true Bassari raconteur who has been introducing visitors to the tales & traditions of Ethiolo for years. Accommodation here is in traditional Bassari stone huts, kitted out with beds, nets & little else. Toilets & bucket ablutions are shared & under the open skies. As you might expect, it gets booked solid during the initiations, but there's usually some floor space if you're flexible. The stillness here at night is positively meditative. **$**

What to see and do The obvious draw here is the Koré, the annual initiation ceremony for young Bassari men that takes place in May every year (see box, pages 272–3), which is a fantastic multi-day affair of masks, pageantry, marching, dancing, wrestling, homebrew, lots of plastic whistles, the firing of ceremonial rifles, and – so the squeamish are warned – a whole lot of animal sacrifice. If you're in Senegal around the time it's not to be missed. From November to February there are a number of smaller harvest festivals that take place, and no matter the time of year Balingo can always arrange a variety of fascinating cultural excursions in and around town. It's worth noting that while the Koré's location is often in Ethiolo, it does sometimes rotate, and it took place in nearby Egath (or Égatyé) village in 2015. Amazingly enough, you can find more information on the next ceremony's timing and location online at www.facebook.com/PaysBassariSenegal.

11

SÉGOU The last major village in Senegal before entering Guinea, Ségou is situated in a palm-studded agricultural valley at the foothills of the Fouta Djallon mountains, which continue to undulate their way hundreds of kilometres south into Guinea and beyond. The setting is stunning, but still sees few tourists, so you're quite likely to have the *cascade*, or even the campement, all to yourself.

GETTING THERE AND AWAY 28km from Kédougou, the turnoff for Ségou is 10km down the road towards Salemata. Something like three or four *ndiaga ndiayes* serve Ségou from Kédougou daily, charging 1,300F, with more on Sundays for the *loumo*. There's an immigration post here, and Guinea-bound buses to Mali-*ville* and Labé pass through two or three times weekly, but you'd be very wise to make arrangements in Kédougou if you fancy getting a seat.

WHERE TO STAY, EAT AND DRINK

Campement Luuro Pelle (4 rooms) 33 985 3230; m 77 604 7940/987 3766/233 7650. The bungalows here are built into a rocky hillside, each with two double beds, nets & en-suite bucket shower (toilets are shared). The rooms are quite spacious & are hooked up to solar panels. There's a small menu of meals to choose from in the covered lounge area, & a percentage of all proceeds goes into community projects in the village. They arrange the usual variety of day hikes to the falls & chimpanzee spotting, as well as longer circuits. **$**

What to see and do The main attraction here is the waterfall, accessible by a 7km hike that begins in peanut plantations on the outskirts of the village, continues into thick groves of bamboo, palm and gallery forest, and eventually into a wild, boulder-strewn riverbed where you hop, skip and clamber your way to the cascade. The pool at the base is too small for any particularly aerobic swimming, but it makes for a heaven-sent cool dip after the two-hour hike to reach it. As an added bonus, a trip to the waterfall can easily double as a chimpanzee trek, though sightings are far from guaranteed and the thick vegetation means getting a good view of them can be a challenge. Still, this is one of the best places in the country to spot them, and the campement can also arrange dedicated chimpanzee-spotting treks. For either the falls or chimp spotting you can arrange a guide at the campement, and while these are quoted at 10,000F and 15,000F respectively, you can probably get away with some negotiation, particularly if you're alone or in a couple.

AFIA Of villages with accommodation in the region, Afia is perhaps the least-visited, so even though the tourist trail around Kédougou is still faint, if you're looking to get off of it anyway, a few days on the Gambia River in Afia might just be the thing.

Getting there and away Though it's only about 2km off of the road to Ségou, Afia isn't served by public transport and as such is comparatively isolated, but any Ségou-bound vehicle can drop you off at the signposted turnoff, from where it's an easy walk, though you should prepare for mud if it's been raining!

Where to stay, eat and drink

Campement d'Afia 33 982 3602; m 77 758 4596. In the centre of Afia village just up from the river, this offers a similar standard of accommodation to the other camps in the area, with basic thatch bungalows & local meals on request. Despite being just up the road from Ségou, only the determined make it this far & it's quite likely that you'll be the only tourists in town. **$**

What to see and do The Gambia River is the only game in town here, and Afia faces a particularly scenic stretch of water, where the wide flow of the Gambia is broken into countless little streams and pools by a clutch of rocky islets. It's not uncommon to see monkeys or warthogs drinking at the river, as well as a wide variety of birds. Ask around for safe places to go swimming (though bear in mind schistosomiasis may be a risk here), or set up hikes to Ségou, Dindefelo or the even-less-visited Cascade d'Affia, where the creek that feeds Ségou's waterfall forms a natural pool suitable for bathing before heading over the cliff's edge into the falls.

DINDEFELO Without question the premier natural attraction in the area and also namesake for the community reserve surrounding it, Dindefelo village is host to the eponymous waterfall, a 115m rock face where a year-round stream plunges over the edge into a wide pool below perfectly suited for bathing. The village itself sits in the shadow of an enormous outcrop of red rock and cliffside forest known as *Barra Lande*, atop which you'll find Dande village (see pages 281–2).

Getting there and away 6km from Ségou, there are typically three or four clapped-out *ndiaga ndiayes* from Kédougou serving Dindefelo and Ségou daily for 1,300F, with more on Sundays for the weekly *loumo*. Private *sept-places* or *jakartas* for a half-day return journey from Kédougou go for about 30,000F and 7,000F, respectively – bargain hard.

Where to stay, eat and drink

🏠 **Campement Africa Cascade** (8 rooms) m 77 029 6703/435 8540; e camaracascade@ yahoo.fr. A bit less well kept & ever-so-slightly cheaper than its neighbour below, this place offers similar stone bungalows with shared bathrooms and can also arrange meals & hikes. The owner here, Djibril, also works at the RNCD visitors centre across the road. **$**

🏠 **Campement Le Dogon du Fouta** (10 rooms) \33 985 2187; m 77 552 3831/789 4002; e moktardiallo@hotmail.com. The nicest option in town, here you can choose between either Bassari-style stone bungalows or bouncy-floored reed huts, the latter of which have a private outdoor

bathroom (bucket showers) attached. It's simple but very nicely kept, & they can arrange basic meals for 2,500F. **$**

🏠 **Campement Villageois** m 77 516 5875. Another fine choice with basic rooms, shared ablutions & meals by arrangement. A portion of the proceeds benefits the village school & clinic. All the usual excursions can be coordinated here. **$**

✕ **Restaurant Chez Alpha** m 77 437 7522. While the fare is similar to what's dished up at any of the campements, this is Dindefelo's only bespoke restaurant & thus represents your only real opportunity for anything approaching a night on the town.

What to see and do The Cascade de Dindefelo is a 30-minute, not particularly strenuous hike from town, and while with a little luck (and some pantomimed questions along the way) you'd probably be able to find it without a guide, any of the campements can arrange one for about 3,000F. The rocky pool at the bottom of the falls is Senegal's best swimming this side of the Atlantic, though it might get a bit shallow at the height of the dry season. You could very happily pack a lunch and spend an afternoon here, but be aware if you want to get back to Kédougou that transport options in the evening are quite slim indeed.

Dindefelo is also probably the best jumping-off point for the truly remote Cascade de Pélél and Vallée de Nandoumary along the Guinean border. The Cascade de Pélél is a completely wild and rarely visited waterfall situated in a narrow gorge beneath the village of Nandoumary. The eponymous valley nearby

Pierre Thiam, chef and author of Yolele! Recipes From the Heart of Senegal *and* Senegal: Modern Recipes From The Source to the Bowl *(www.pierrethiam.com)*

Fonio was the main reason for our journey to Kédougou. In this dry region, fonio is king. This drought-resistant grain matures within two months and is therefore the ideal food against famine.

But fonio is more than just a famine food. It was once a major crop across Africa and was always considered the food of kings because of its delicate taste. In ancient Egypt, fonio was found in burial grounds as the grain chosen to accompany the souls in the afterlife. The Dogon people of Mali call it *po* or 'the seed of the universe'. Fonio is more than 5,000 years old and is arguably the longest-cultivated grain in the world. It's also one of the most nutritious of all grains – it is rich in methionine and cysteine, both amino acids that are vital to human growth and deficient in today's major cereals like wheat, barley, maize, rice and rye.

When my car drove in to Kédougou, which was a chaotic 14-hour ride from Dakar at 43°, I experienced three flat tyres in a row with my travelling buddies photographer Evan Sung, his wife Jeanna, a seven-person crew from GLP Films (on assignment from *National Geographic*) and our driver Ousseynou. Needless to say, the drive had taken a toll on our crew.

However, all the pain seemed to dissipate from our aching bodies when Mrs. Aya Ndiaye – and the 25 founding members of her cooperative, the Koba Club – greeted us with songs, dance and a feast fit for kings.

For the past two years, Evan and I have been coming to Senegal regularly in preparation for my next book. Our mission is simple: to crisscross Senegal, my country, in order to meet and document the experience of food producers, farmers, fishermen and other people involved in food production so that we can follow the food process from the source to the bowl.

The book hit shelves at the end of 2015, and this one last trip was dedicated to the Kédougou region in general, and one of its most enterprising daughters, Mrs. N'diaye, in particular. N'diaye started the Koba Club cooperative more than 20 years ago. Her goal was to promote the production of local ingredients, such as fonio, baobab fruit, palm fruit oil and shea butter. Today, their work is paying off and the Koba Club is now helping other women to organise. In fact, their cooperative has been recognised as an example across Kedougou, and N'diaye even received a special prize from the President of Senegal.

Using fonio, the Koba Club prepared a banquet for us, displaying several variations of the classics of Senegalese cuisine on a low bamboo table. First, there was *thieboudienne*, where, in a twist on the Senegalese national dish, the rice was substituted with fonio and slowly simmered in an intensely rich tomato

forms part of both the natural and political border between Senegal and Guinea, is home to the highest concentration of baobabs anywhere in the reserve, and sunsets here are rumoured to be among Senegal's finest. There's no campement in Nandoumary, so you'll have to either camp, stay with a local family, or time your visit so as to be back in Dindefelo by night. The campements can advise you as to the best way to do this. Dindefelo would also be the best jumping-off point for the Cascade de Ingli, an extremely isolated waterfall accessible by some 20km of footpaths to the west.

broth flavoured with fermented conch, root vegetables, eggplant, cabbage and a *thiof* (the country's favourite fish), stuffed with a parsley and spice mixture called *rof*.

We also had *yassa poulet*, which is chicken grilled over wood charcoal and served with onion-lime confit over steamed fonio. For dessert, they served us fonio pound cake and *thiakry*, with fonio replacing the traditional *lacciri*, or coarse millet couscous, and served with a homemade sweet milk curd called *sow*. For drinks, we were served a mint-scented hibiscus infusion and a thick, sweet and sour baobab fruit juice that reminded us of lassi.

Fonio is great for its versatility, and as the Bambara saying goes, it 'never embarrasses the cook'. But even though it's been eaten here for centuries and is becoming more and more widely recognised (both in Senegal and elsewhere) for its praiseworthy nutritive properties, it's still rarely served in restaurants in Senegal, so you'll have to either pick some up yourself at the market in Kédougou (or most others) and get cooking, see if you can make a special request at your hotel, or – best of all – find a Senegalese friend to help you whip up a special dinner.

Here's one of my favourite fonio recipes to get you started:

FONIO SALAD (VEGAN, GLUTEN-FREE)
Ingredients
180g fonio
1 tbsp salt dissolved in 60ml water
juice of 2 lemons
1 tsp salt
½ tsp freshly ground black pepper
240ml peanut or canola oil

1 bunch parsley, finely chopped
1 bunch mint, finely chopped
1 cucumber, peeled and diced
2 plum tomatoes, diced

Wash the fonio with cold running water and drain well. Place the fonio in the top of a steamer lined with cheesecloth. Set over simmering water, cover, and steam the fonio about 15 minutes. Remove from the heat and fluff up the grains with a fork. Drizzle with the salted water and steam again until the grains are tender. (Alternately, fonio can be prepared in a microwave by adding enough water to cover in a bowl and cooking until tender, six to eight minutes.)

In a small mixing bowl, combine the lemon juice with the salt and pepper and whisk to dissolve. Slowly pour in the olive oil while still whisking to emulsify.

Place the cooked fonio in a large bowl and add parsley, mint, cucumber, and tomatoes. Pour enough dressing over the fonio mixture to coat the grains well. Toss and serve.

DANDE On the plateau high above Dindefelo, the village of Dande enjoys an enviable perch over the savannah below and is home to two fantastic rock formations, the caves (*grottes*) and teeth (*dents*) of Dande, both a short hike from the village.

Getting there and away Only accessible by foot, Dande sits on the plateau 400m above Dindefelo. Most visits to Dande are in connection with a trip to the Dindefelo waterfall, so ask the guide who directed you to the falls to point you the way up the mountain to Dande.

⌂ Where to stay, eat and drink

⌂ Chez Doba m 77 360 6401/729 6008; e dobadiallo@yahoo.fr; www.sites.google.com/site/chezdobadande. With a complement of facilities & services much like the campements in neighbouring villages, what really sets this place apart is its location & its management. Run by the engaged & English-speaking Doba, you get the usual thatch bungalows & good local meals, & Doba is a thoroughly knowledgeable guide to the sites atop the plateau & beyond. **$**

What to see and do Dande is blessed with a stunning location atop the plateau to begin with, but apart from the views across the savannah or from above the Dindefelo waterfall, there are two other noteworthy sites on the plateau. The caves (*grottes*) are rather low-key, but are a site that ought to satisfy everyone from hikers to historians to geologists. The series of large caves, probably hollowed out by water over thousands of years, were once the scene of warfare; they were valued for their defensive capabilities during battles between the original Bassari and Bédik inhabitants of the area and the more recently arrived (and now numerically dominant) Fulbe (Peul). They were also valuable, then as now, for their plentiful fresh water, as the stream that feeds the Dindefelo waterfall has its source here.

The teeth (*dents*) are isolated pillars of rock at the edge of the plateau, long since separated from the main section by erosion. They make for a hugely dramatic dropoff, and rock hyraxes also make their homes here. You've a pretty good chance of spotting them as they fearlessly traverse the cliffsides, particularly if you've brought binoculars along.

A number of hamlets on the plateau are also home to artisanal pottery and textile makers whose products can be purchased at reasonable prices, but remember you've got to carry them down the hill! Steep drops abound up here, so do be aware of hidden drop-offs and/or make your trips with a guide.

FONGOLIMBI Known throughout Senegal for its inaccessibility, the mixed Peul-Jalonké village of Fongolimbi has a Timbuktu-esque reputation among Senegalese, as it sits high on a ridge only 2km from the Guinean border and is about as far from Dakar as it's possible to get without leaving the country. It's actually only 30km from Kédougou, but remains difficult of access as it's on the other side of the Gambia River (spanned only by a diminutive hand-operated ferry) and sits at the top of a rough, switchbacked earthen track up the ridge, which is only suited for the toughest of vehicles. As with many such far-flung locales, much of the reward is in the journey here (the road up the mountain is equal parts stunning and nerve-wracking), but the nearby Lombel waterfall and views from the top make it eminently worth the detour. Unlike the previous villages in this section, Fongolimbi is not part of the RNCD, and tourist development here is non-existent.

Getting there and away Public transport options are decidedly limited, but there's one daily *taxi-brousse* that departs Kédougou in the afternoon and makes the return journey from Fongolimbi early the next morning. It departs from near the fire department (*sapeurs-pompiers*) behind the market in Kédougou rather than the *gare routière*. If you miss this, you can also try your luck hitchhiking at the ferry crossing. Bridge construction was in its nascent stages in late 2014, so there may or may not be a new crossing by the time you read this; if so, expect transport options to improve significantly.

Fongolimbi is also home to an immigration post and, while it's possible to cross into Guinea here, it's best to try on *loumo* day or to be prepared for a long wait.

Don't attempt the trip up here in a hired or private vehicle unless it's a 4x4 or very strong pickup with high clearance.

Where to stay, eat and drink There's no accommodation in Fongolimbi, so you'll either have to camp or make friends and try to stay at someone's house. With a private vehicle or a bit of luck and some hitchhiking, it's possible to make a day trip here from Kédougou as well, especially on the day of the *loumo*.

What to see and do There's precious little to do in Fongolimbi itself, save perhaps the weekly *loumo* on Thursdays where you'll find a wide selection of fresh produce from Guinea, but the 30-minute walk to Lombel village and the Cascade de Lombel are not to be missed. The falls are dry for much of the year, but even without water, the sweeping views from the top (where the village sits) are nothing short of breathtaking. Ask anyone in Fongolimbi for '*cascade*' or Lombel and they'll point you in the right direction, but you can start by making a left at the Poste de Santé as you enter Fongolimbi. The walk to Lombel takes you through some gratuitously bucolic fields and meadows, where if not for the sweat soaking through your shirt, you might be forgiven for thinking you were in Switzerland for the briefest of moments. Once in Lombel, just ask again to be shown the falls and someone will be happy to show you the way. There are no fees or any sort of formalised visit structure, but it wouldn't go unappreciated if you brought a small gift for either your guide or the village chief, who you're likely to meet as well.

EAST OF KÉDOUGOU

SARAYA *Population 55,000*

Situated 60km from Kédougou on the new road to Mali, the only reason unrelated to mining (Saraya is the closest city to Senegal's largest gold mine at Sabodala) that you're likely to stay in Saraya is if you are *en route* to/from the Moussala border crossing with Mali. It's easy enough to do this journey directly from Kédougou and with the new road it only takes a couple of hours, but if you arrive late or want to get the earliest possible start, this is the closest accommodation to the border. When in town, ask for **Chez Mamady** (m *77 146 9211/944 7178*; e *mamadydanfa@yahoo.fr*), where there are decent rooms for US$14 per person.

SENEGAL ONLINE

For additional online content, articles, photos and more on Senegal, why not visit www.bradtguides.com/senegal.

11

12

Ziguinchor and Basse Casamance

For travellers with a penchant for the faraway, Basse (lower) Casamance and its agreeably dishevelled capital at Ziguinchor are quite simply an embarrassment of riches. With seemingly endless tracts of spiralling mangrove labyrinths playing host to rare river dolphins, manatees and dozens of hidden traditional villages, this is quite simply the best place in Senegal to disappear right off the map, and it's got absolutely nothing to do with rebels. While today it's easier to get around the compact region than it's ever been, in its further reaches it would be possible to spend days travelling Basse Casamance on nothing but footpaths and bolongs, let alone a surfaced road. Still, if your idea of a vacation is more piña colada than canoe and paddle, Basse Casamance has you covered as well. Home to nearly 30km of powder-fine beaches centred on Cap Skirring, Senegal's largest resort colony outside of Saly, and a wilder but equally dazzling 30km stretch north of the river from the Presqu'Île aux Oiseaux to the Gambian border at Niafourang, Casamance has something for sun worshippers and adventurers of all stripes.

Lush, tropical and covered in a bewilderingly dense maze of forest, mangrove, and an uncountable number of creeks, Basse Casamance both looks and feels a very long way from the baking plains and wide expanses of Senegal's north. Cut off from the rest of the country by The Gambia, Basse Casamance is not only a geographical place apart, but a cultural and political one as well and, as a traveller here, it's easy to feel you've arrived in an entirely different country. Indeed, today it's also a religious anomaly in overwhelmingly Islamic Senegal, as Animism is practised openly and comparatively widely, and Catholics represent a higher percentage of the population here than in any other region, though neither Christianity nor Islam made significant inroads here before the late 1800s, already centuries after Islam established itself in the north of the country.

Homeland to the Diola people, the pre-colonial political and state structures here were, in sharp contrast to their neighbours, comparatively egalitarian, and lacked the rigid social hierarchies and permanent warrior, priestly and ruling classes of Wolof and Fulbe societies to the north and east. As such, a centralised Diola state never emerged in Basse Casamance, and the area remained a pastiche of small traditional chieftancies operating at the village level, and a few small kingdoms like Blouf, Bandial (Mof Awi) and Floup, all of which retain some ceremonial relevance today, particularly Floup, centred in Oussouye.

Thus, Basse Casamance's status as a place apart derives from a long tradition of rejecting outside influence and outside rule. For centuries the area has been a hotbed of social and political resistance, first in a centuries-long competition with Mandinkas from the north and west who sought (sometimes successfully, sometimes not) to rule and convert the region's inhabitants to Islam (in fact, *Kassa Mansa*, from where Casamance gets its name, derives from the Mandinka for 'king of Kasa', a 15th-century kingdom in the area), followed by fierce opposition to the French colonial presence

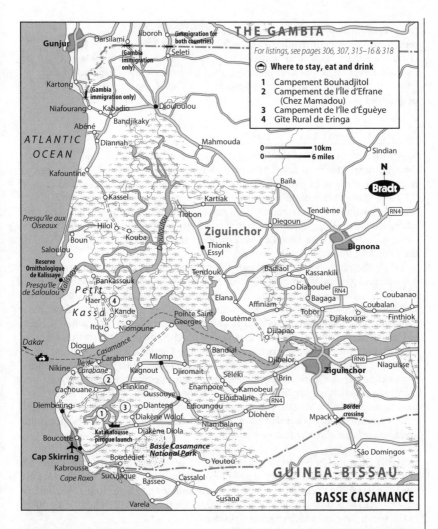

THE GAMBIA

For listings, see pages 306, 307, 315–16 & 318

🏠 **Where to stay, eat and drink**

1 Campement Bouhadjitol
2 Campement de l'Île d'Efrane
   (Chez Mamadou)
3 Campement de l'Île d'Éguèye
4 Gîte Rural de Eringa

Gunjur · Darsilami · Jiboroh · (immigration for both countries) · Seleti · (Gambia immigration only)

Kartong · (Gambia immigration only) · Kabadio · Dioufoulou · Niafourang · Bandjikaky · Abéné · Diannah · Mahmouda · Sindian

ATLANTIC OCEAN

Kafountine · Baïla

Kassel · Kartiak · Tiobon · Diegoun · Tendième · RN4

Hilol · Kouba · **Ziguinchor** · Thionk-Essyl · Badiaol · Kassankili · **Bignona**

Presqu'île aux Oiseaux · Boun · Saloulou

Reserve Ornithologique de Kalissaye · Bankassouk · Tendouk · Elana · Diaboubel · RN4 · Bagaga · Coubanao

Presqu'île de Saloulou · Petit · Haer · Kande · Affiniam · Tobor · Djilakoune · Coubalan · Finthiok

Kassa · Itou · Niomoune · Pointe Saint-Georges · Boutème · Djilapao

Dakar · Diogué · Casamance · Bandial · Djibelor · RN6 · Niaguisse

Nikine · Île de Carabane · Mlomp · Djiromait · Séléki · Brin · **Ziguinchor**

Cachouane · Elinkine · Oussouye · Enampore · Kamobeul · RN4

Diembéring · Diantene · Edioungou · Diohère · Mpack · Border crossing

Boucotte · Diakène Wolof · Nlambalang

Katakalousse pirogue launch · Diakène Diola

Cap Skirring · Boudédiet · **Basse Casamance National Park** · Youtou · São Domingos

Kabrousse · Sucujaque · Basseo · Cassalol · **GUINEA-BISSAU**

Cape Roxo · Varela · Susana

BASSE CASAMANCE

0 ⟶ 10km
0 ⟶ 6 miles

N

Bradt

(the region was the last in Senegal to be fully 'pacified' by French forces in 1920), and finally against the independent Senegalese state itself, which the Mouvement des forces démocratiques de Casamance (MFDC) has been fighting in a low-level, on-again-off-again independence war since 1982 (see *History*, pages 14–15).

The rationale for the war was in part based on the central government's long-standing neglect of the region, and for a visitor it only takes a few shuddering minutes on Ziguinchor's abysmal roads to lend some credence to the argument. Things have improved a great deal since Macky Sall's 2012 inauguration, however, and with three boats now serving the region from Dakar, an aggressive road-surfacing programme stretching from Diembéring to Thionk-Essyl to Kolda, and with the foundation stone laid in February 2015, even some progress on the long-mooted but never-realised Trans-Gambia bridge over the river at Farafenni, Basse Casamance is better integrated with Senegal today than it's ever been in the past. (Though you'll still hear residents casually mention that they're 'going to Senegal' when planning a trip to Dakar.) After years of nervous tourists keeping their distance,

Ziguinchor and Basse Casamance

12

the proudly independent residents of the region are once again ready to share the charms of their homeland with visitors, and, whatever their political leanings, to show off that most inherently Senegalese of qualities, *teranga*.

ATMS

The only ATMs in the region are in Bignona, Ziguinchor and Cap Skirring.

ZIGUINCHOR (CITY)

Set on the south bank of the Casamance, arriving here from the north you pass through nearly 10km of tidal mangrove swamps before reaching the 600m bridge over the river where Ziguinchor first spills into view. Steaming, slinking and centred on a low-slung clutch of buildings that seem moments or days from simply giving up and sinking into the riverbank, Ziguinchor is a stereotypically tropical river port where the thick, sluggish air smells of peanut oil, and trucks heaped with peanuts, cashews, fish and more line the roads on their way to and from Guinea-Bissau or the long haul inland to Tambacounda.

While the city's crumbling infrastructure, legacies of conflict and government neglect, and generally tumbledown feel only add to the sense of equatorial torpor that takes hold of you here, there's also an ebullient air that's as difficult to escape as it is to pin down, and if you ask Senegalese anywhere in the country about their favourite places, Ziguinchor is almost always high on the list. Much like the rest of Casamance, arriving here feels that you've touched down not only in a different country than the one you left behind north of The Gambia, but in a different world altogether from the parched and parochial desert towns of the north. For visitors, Ziguinchor can be a polarising place, with many people breezing through and dismissing it as little more than a run-down backwater, but if you give the city some time to reveal itself and tease your nostrils with its heady tropical musk, you'll find an open and friendly place that pays few dividends to those in a hurry, but holds great rewards for those who take their time.

HISTORY Ziguinchor is actually a settlement of some antiquity, but there are few visible signs of this history dating beyond the 19th century. The Portuguese operated a trading post here from 1650, and a military garrison from 1696, both of which were subordinate to the larger Portuguese settlement at Cacheu, some 40km to the south in what is today Guinea-Bissau.

French, British and Dutch traders all spent considerable blood and treasure jockeying for position in and around the Casamance in the intervening centuries, but the tables began to turn decisively in favour of the French with the 1836 occupation of Carabane, followed shortly by the occupation of Sédhiou in 1837, hemming in the Portuguese at Ziguinchor on both sides. It would seem, however, that the fortunes of the Portuguese *presidio* (garrison town) at Ziguinchor had long since begun their decline, as in the same year the commandant of Gorée visited Ziguinchor and waxed poetic regarding '…the town, if one dares use the term for such a pitiable grouping of miserable huts…'.

The situation had clearly not improved by 1874 when a Father Sène of the Holy Ghost Fathers visited and said that 'nothing could be sadder than the appearance of Ziguinchor… Along the *quais*, in the streets, everywhere is complete chaos.' Thus, control of Ziguinchor seems to have long been slipping out of Portuguese hands, and it was decisively handed over to the French following negotiations at the 1884–5 Berlin Conference with the signing of the Luso-French Convention of

1886, which remains the basis for the Senegal–Guinea-Bissau border today. Thus, the French took possession of Ziguinchor in 1886 and began to develop the city as a river port and centre for trade in peanuts, cashews, cotton and rice, before its status as Basse Casamance's most important centre was confirmed with the colonial administration's move from Carabane to Ziguinchor in 1901.

TOURIST INFORMATION AND TOUR OPERATORS Ziguinchor is the somewhat unlikely home to what is probably the best tourism office in the country. The **Office de Tourisme de Casamance** [289 C2] (\ *33 991 7777;* m *77 544 0332;* e *tourismeoffice.casamance@gmail.com; www.casamance-tourisme.sn*) has an excellent selection of brochures, maps and other information on flora, fauna, artisans, history and more. They can help set up transport, advise you on their suggested itineraries or help you plan a custom one, and liaise with the *campements villageois* (see box, page 336) throughout the region.

In addition to the Office de Tourisme de Casamance, **www.voyagerencasamance. com** is an excellent website with profiles of Ziguinchor and the region's many villages and accommodation options.

Alternatively, both **Diambone Voyages** [289 C2] (\ *33 991 6774;* m *77 641 5132;* e *diambone@orange.sn; www.diambonevoyages.com*) and **Diatta Tour International** [289 C2] (\ *33 992 0648;* m *77 517 5895/721 3316;* e *diattatour@yahoo.fr; www. casamance-ecoparc.com*) are reputable agencies that can arrange car hire, tours and more.

CONSULATES The French honorary consulate (\ *33 991 2223;* m *77 641 8830;* e *acfziguinchor@gmail.com*) in the centre of town can offer emergency services to EU citizens, while Guinea-Bissau's consulate (m *77 512 6497*) is a low-hassle place to get visas for travellers continuing to Bissau (see box, pages 302–3 for details).

FESTIVALS Ziguinchor and Casamance more generally are known for their festivals – both traditional celebrations and modern events – so it's definitely worth keeping your eyes out for anything going on while you're around. The Office de Tourisme de Casamance keeps tabs on the cultural calendar, so drop by to see what's coming up. They'll also know if any villages in the region are putting on the traditional Diola coming-of-age ceremony, known as *bukut*, this year.

A couple of reliable bets of a more secular bent include **Casamance en Scène** (\ *33 991 28 23;* m *77 531 94 42;* e *casamance.en.scene1@gmail.com; www. casamance-en-scene.org*), which brings together theatre companies from across West Africa and Europe for a week of performances, workshops and exhibitions every December, and the **Boukout Festival** (m *77 543 1887/635 7490;* e *contact@ boukoutfestival.com; www.boukoutfestival.com*), also in December, which sets up shop in both Ziguinchor and Bignona with concerts, expositions and a parade of traditional masks and costumes.

GETTING THERE AND AWAY
By air Both **Groupe Transair** (\ *33 991 0105;* m *77 563 7827;* e *sales@groupetransair. sn; www.groupetransair.sn* or *www.facebook.com/groupetransair*) and **Senegal Airlines** (\ *33 991 1111/865 8881;* m *800 800 888 (toll-free);* e *relations.clients@ senegalairlines.aero; www.senegalairlines.aero*) fly once or twice daily to Dakar, with a twice-weekly connection to Cap Skirring (though the connection to Cap doesn't always operate in low season). Tickets cost about 70,000/120,000F one-way/return, and you can book either directly at the **Ziguinchor Airport**, or through Diambone Voyages or Diatta Tour International (see *Tourist information and tour operators,*

page 287) in town. The airport is on the southern edge of town, 3km south of Rond-Point Jean-Paul II and 1km south of the Alliance Franco-Sénégalaise. It's served by Tata bus line 1, and it shouldn't be hard to get a taxi either.

By road As the southern terminus of the rather aspirationally named (but reasonably well surfaced) Trans-Gambia Highway, Ziguinchor is well served by public transport in all directions and it's perfectly possible to get to Dakar (via The Gambia, 9,500F) or Tambacounda (9,500F) in a day from here. Allow about ten hours for either destination, though going to Dakar you have to contend with two border crossings and the ferry across the Gambia River at Farafenni, where waits can sometimes be hours long. Also be aware that the RN4 (Trans-Gambia Highway) and RN5 in Basse Casamance are closed to through traffic from dusk till dawn, so it's important to get a reasonably early start when coming in or out of the region so as to reach your destination before the roadblocks go up. Departing Ziguinchor, the earliest cars will often fill up before sunrise and queue at the roadblock outside town until the soldiers give them the go-ahead. It's unclear whether the rehabilitated RN6 to Kolda will be subject to similar restrictions when it opens, but it's certainly a possibility. The road to Oussouye (1,500F) and Cap Skirring (2,300F) is open 24/7 and served by *sept-places* and *ndiaga ndiayes* throughout the day.

By boat The German-built *MV Aline Sitoé Diatta* has been plying the waters between Ziguinchor and Dakar twice weekly since 2008, and it was joined in 2015 by two new South Korean vessels, the *Diambogne* and *Anguène*, for a total of four departures weekly. All the boats are run by COSAMA (	33 991 7200/821 2900/984 3190; e *cosama@orange.sn; www.cosamasn.com*), and there are departures from Ziguinchor every Tuesday, Thursday, Friday and Sunday at 13.00, and from Dakar on the same days at 20.00. (See box, pages 292–3, for boat details and prices.)

Many of the surrounding riverine villages are served by regular public pirogues that depart from the boat launch (alternately known as the *ancien bac* or *Embarcadère de Boudody*) between Le Perroquet and Hôtel Kadiandoumagne, and you can charter a pirogue directly from the captains here as well. Schedules and prices tend to be a bit nebulous, but they're listed where available in the sections for each town.

GETTING AROUND Central Ziguinchor is eminently walkable, but if you don't feel like hiking down to Marché Boucotte or the Alliance Franco-Sénégalaise, there's now a small fleet of **Tata buses** clattering across the potholes of Zig. Line 1 serves Marché Boucotte, the airport, and the Hôpital Régional from Rue du Commerce; Line 2 serves Rond-Point Jean-Paul II, Marché Boucotte and Hôtel Néma Kadior/Alliance Franco-Sénégalaise from the *gare routière*; line 3 will take you past Hôtel Diola and Camping Casamance on the RN6 before circling back to Rond-Point Jean-Paul II and its terminus at the *gare routière*; and line 4 will take you out to Colobane (for Auberge Aw-Bay) and the Djibelor checkpoint (1.5km before Ferme de Djibelor) from the Rond-Point Aline Sitoé Diatta.

Still, a **taxi** anywhere within Ziguinchor only costs a flat 500F, so unless you're just a fan of public transport, these are more than likely the way to go.

WHERE TO STAY *Map, page 289.*

Hôtel Kadiandoumagne (46 rooms) 33 938 800; m 77 637 7811; e resa@hotel-kadiandoumagne.com; www.hotel-kadiandoumagne.com. The name might be a tongue-twister, but there's no confusion about the appeal: this is arguably Ziguinchor's most prestigious address, & the finely manicured gardens, riverside swimming pool & fashionable

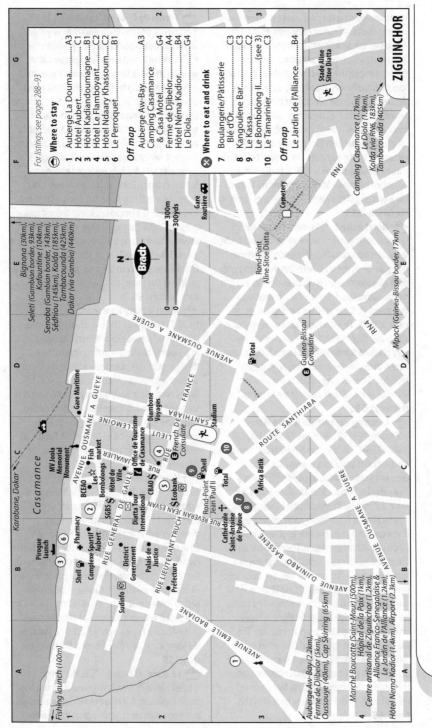

ZIGUINCHOR

For listings, see pages 288–93

Where to stay

1	Auberge La Douma	A3
2	Hôtel Aubert	C1
3	Hôtel Kadiandoumagne	B1
4	Hôtel Le Flamboyant	C2
5	Hôtel Ndaary Khassoum	C2
6	Le Perroquet	B1

Off map

	Auberge Aw-Bay	A3
	Camping Casamance & Casa Motel	G4
	Ferme de Djibelor	A4
	Hôtel Néma Kadior	B4
	Le Diola	G4

Where to eat and drink

7	Boulangerie/Pâtisserie Blé d'Or	C3
8	Kangoulene Bar	C3
9	Le Kassa	C2
	Le Bombolong II	(see 3)
10	Le Tamarinier	C3

Off map

	Le Jardin de l'Alliance	B4

Casamance

Karabane, Dakar

Fishing launch (100m)

Bignona (30km),
Seleti (Gambian border, 93km),
Kafountine (104km),
Senoba (Gambian border, 143km),
Sédhiou (145km), Kolda (185km),
Tambacounda (425km),
Dakar (via Gambia) (440km)

Gare Maritime

MV Joola Memorial Monument

Pirogue launch

Shell

Pharmacy

Complexe Sportif Aubert

District Government

Palais de Justice

Préfecture

Sudinfo

RUE GENERAL DE GAULE

RUE LIEUTENANT TRUCH

AVENUE EMILE BADIANE

SGBS

BCEAO

Les Bombolongs

Hôtel de Ville

fish market

Office de Tourisme de Casamance

Diatta Tour International

CBAO

Ecobank

RUE JAVALIER

RUE LIEUT DEVILLE

RUE REVEREN JEAN ESVAN

Cathédrale Saint-Antoine de Padoue

Rond-Point Jean Paul II

Total

Africa Batik

Diambone Voyages

French Consulate

Stadium

AVENUE OUSMANE A GUERE

RUE DE FRANCE

ROUTE SANTHIABA

AVENUE DJINABO BASSENE

AVENUE OUSMANE A GUERE

Total

Guinea-Bissau Consulate

Rond-Point Aline Sitoe Diatta

Cemetery

RN6

RN4

Mpack (Guinea-Bissau border, 17km)

Camping Casamance (1.7km),
Le Diola (1.9km),
Kolda (via RN6, 183km),
Tambacounda (405km)

Stade Aline Sitoe Diatta

Auberge Aw-Bay (2.2km),
Ferme de Djibelor (5km),
Oussouye (40km), Cap Skirring (65km)

Marché Boucotte (Saint-Maur) (500m),
Hôpital de la Paix (1km),
Centre artisanal de Ziguinchor (1.2km),
Alliance Franco-Senegalaise &
Le Jardin de l'Alliance (1.2km),
Hôtel Nema Kadior (1.4km), Airport (2.3km)

N

Bradt

0   300m
0   300yds

Gare Routière

12

restaurant right on the docks make it a perennially popular choice. All rooms come with AC, TV, nets, & minibar, but be aware that the rather cramped & dated standard rooms are almost certainly the least impressive aspect of the place. If you're spending the money already, the upper floor & deluxe rooms are considerably better value & eminently worth the upgrade, as they're not only more spacious & recently renovated, but the river breezes are more generous up here as well. The restaurant on the pier does a wide menu of French cuisine starting around 5,000F, & their wine list is organised by region. Standard rooms are towards the lower end of this range & deluxe ones firmly in the middle. **$$$**

🏠 **Hôtel Aubert** (34 rooms) ☎ 33 938 8020; e hotelaubert@orange.sn; www.hotelaubert.com, www.facebook.com/HotelAubertOfficiel. It may not quite be all the way there, but this (along with the Kadiandoumagne) is about as close as you'll get to international-standard accommodation in Ziguinchor, & the spacious tiled rooms all come with AC, TV, wardrobe, minibar, & en- suite ablutions. They're a bit light on decoration, but very pleasant & with some welcome batik accents here & there. There's a resto-bar, pool, & gym facilities, & guests have access to the sporting complex next door too. Rates at the lower end of this range. **$$$**

🏠 **Camping Casamance & Casa Motel** (12 rooms) ☎ 33 991 9606; m 77 557 3108/220 8645/735 3400; e info@casa-motel.com; www. campingcasamance.com or www.casa-motel. com. In a sandy compound filled with palms & bougainvillea about 150m off of the RN6 & the same distance up the road from Le Diola, this newish place is Ziguinchor's only camping ground, & you can pitch your tent here or stay in their billowy Mauritanian *khaïma*. The resto-bar serves Guinean & Moroccan-inspired fare, but there's a kitchen available for guests as well. For those who prefer a roof over their heads, Casa Motel is in the same compound & has trim, whitewashed rooms with ceiling fans & en-suite facilities, & rather uniquely also offers handicap accessibility. The rooftop terrace on the second floor offers stellar views over the town & nearby bolongs. It's 3,500F per tent for a night at Camping Casamance (about the same in the *khaïma*), & Casa Motel's rooms are agreeably priced at the very bottom of this range. **$$**

🏠 **Ferme de Djibelor** (3 rooms) ☎ 33 991 1701; m 77 644 3914; e mowartraux@yahoo.fr; www.fermededjibelor.com. Easily earning the title of Ziguinchor's most unlikely accommodation, this working crocodile farm sits in densely vegetated grounds (including some fantastic kapok trees) along the road to Oussouye, about 5.5km from the city centre. Accommodation here is in plank-built en-suite cabins that sleep up to 3 & are bound to be nostalgic if you've ever attended summer camp. They're a fair bit more comfortable, though, & all come with fans & a fully equipped kitchenette for self-caterers. The crocodile pools aren't in a particularly edifying state, but this is a farm, not a zoo, after all, & a crocodile plate at the restaurant goes for 7,000F (but you'll have to arrange this ahead of time during low season). They've also got a new 3-bedroom villa right across the street, Le Chato-Banco, that can sleep up to 10. Prices in the middle of this range, particularly good value for a party of three. **$$**

🏠 **Hôtel Ndaary Khassoum** ☎ 33 991 1472; m 77 727 0426/403 1014; e ndaary@hotmail. com; www.facebook.com/NdaaryKhassoum. In a 3-storey block right in the centre of town, this unremarkable place feels a bit on the dated side but is pleasant enough, with both AC & fan rooms available, a good bit of artwork & sculpture scattered around, & a nice little patch of garden with a few gazebos surrounding the building, where meals can be taken by request. Rooms are well priced, with fan rooms near the top of this category & AC about 4,000F more. **$**

🏠 **Hôtel Néma Kadior** (30 rooms) ☎ 33 991 1052; m 77 150 0601/559 5757; e khadygiroux@ yahoo.fr; www.hotelnemakadior.com. Originally opened in 1977 but closed for many years thereafter due to the conflict, this retro resort finally reopened in 2005, & while the grounds are a tad scruffy (the tennis court has seen better days), the tiled en-suite rooms here are anything but, & all come with minifridge, flatscreen, AC, mozzie nets, & natural mangrove wood ceilings. There's a nice pool & resto-bar, & it could hardly be closer to the Alliance Franco-Sénégalaise if you want to see some music or a film. Prices at the top of this range. **$$**

🏠 **Le Diola** (37 rooms) ☎ 33 991 7500; e hotellediola@yahoo.fr. With reception in a huge *case à impluvium* & a range of African-inspired art in the common areas, you'd expect the detached clusters of rooms at this businesslike place on the edge of town to have a bit more character. Still, they're spacious & well-appointed with AC, fridge, king-size beds, & private terraces, even if the grounds surrounding them have something of an unfinished air. There's a pool & terrace resto-bar, & it looked as if a beauty salon was about to open when we checked in. Rates in the upper half of this range. **$$**

🏠 **Le Flamboyant** (32 rooms) 📞33 991 2223; e resaflamboyant@casamance.net; www. flamboyant.info. With a location smack in the centre of town & tidy terracotta-tiled rooms opening directly on to either the gardens or swimming pool, this is a very pleasant option, even if it won't necessarily win any awards for character. Still, rooms come with TV, fridge, safe, & AC or fan, & they run regular discounts on the rooms depending on the season. Across the street, the retro-glam 'Hotel Tourisme' restaurant is under the same ownership & does lunch & dinner daily, with a three-course menu for 7,000F. Rates sit towards the middle of this range, with poolside rooms below & garden rooms above the midpoint, possible discounts notwithstanding. **$$**

🏠 **Auberge Aw-Bay** (12 rooms) 📞33 936 8076/990 0570; m 77 323 8362/323 8362; e dodsgoudiaby@yahoo.fr; www.awbay. wordpress.com. In the Colobane neighborhood about 3km from central Ziguinchor on the road to Oussouye, this cheerful little place is ever so faintly signposted & easy to miss – look out for a tall communications tower on the right hand side & it's about 100m behind that. Once here, you'll find a breezy little compound with a few hammocks scattered about between the mango trees, & a

clutch of surprisingly well-kept en-suite rooms that are an absolute steal for the price. They've all got fans & nets, & some even come with their own (admittedly rather claustrophobic) terraces. The sleepy resto-bar does Senegalese staples for 1,000–2,000F, but otherwise it's a bit of a hike to the nearest food options. **$**

🏠 **Auberge La Douma** (10 rooms) 📞33 991 9978; m 77 515 3350/414 7591; e ladouma@orange.sn; www.sites.google.com/ site/aubergeladouma. In a quiet compound just south of the city centre, this homey place has an old-school vibe & cheery double & triple en-suite rooms with fans, nets, & bright wall murals. There's shady garden seating or a dusky bar inside with plenty of football on the flatscreen, & a surprisingly sophisticated menu at the restaurant, with barracuda brochettes, steaks & even *côtelettes de porc* going for around 3,500–5,000F, plus a rotating *plat du jour* for 1,000F. Fantastic value. **$**

🏠 **Le Perroquet** Rue du Commerce; 📞33 991 2329; e perroquet@orange.sn; www.hotel-le-perroquet.com. For budget digs in Zig, the location doesn't get any better than this tranquil spot on the riverfront next to the pirogue launch. The resto-bar is right on the water & a welcoming place to laze away some hours over a drink or the football, & the meals have earned a loyal following in town. Rooms are simple & well kept, & all come with fans, nets, & en-suite facilities. The river-view rooms upstairs are well worth the 2,000F upgrade for the breezes off the water & tiny balconies; rooms downstairs can feel a bit airless. Either way, it's brilliant value. Riverview rooms nudge the price into the next category. **$**

🍴 WHERE TO EAT AND DRINK *Map, page 289.*

Toto, we're not in Touba anymore – there are drinking dens aplenty in Ziguinchor, and you won't want for places to slake your thirst. They don't tend to be particularly salubrious, but the vibe is relaxed, and that's half the fun anyway. Most of the restaurants double as drinking holes as the night wears on and some do live music on the weekends, but if you're out late enough, phototaxis sets in and all the barflies head for the flashing lights at Le Bombolong II.

🍴 **Boulangerie Pâtisserie Blé D'or** 📞33 991 9999; m 77 063 9636/70 468 4868; ⏰ 08.00–01.00 daily. With cakes, croissants, doughnuts & pastries baked on site, this delightfully air-conditioned new café is cast in the mould of Dakar's shiniest *patisseries*, &

it's a convincing slice of the big city in out-of-the-way Ziguinchor. There's a flat screen TV & some sofa seating inside, espresso coffee on the menu, & a street-side terrace if you'd rather soak up the scenery. In addition to the baked goods, they do a long list of sandwiches, burgers, & pizzas (& a Nutella crêpe for dessert), all starting around 1,500F. Even better, they do delivery.

✕ **Le Tamarinier** m 77 754 8181; ⊕ noon–late daily. The charming proprietress (& bona fide judo master) here will happily chat you up in a mélange of French, Portuguese & English before she goes around back to make you the undisputed best shrimp in Ziguinchor for a delicious 3,000F. The rest of the menu is equally good, & it's a great place to try some Bissau-Guinean & Cape Verdean dishes. The walls are decked out in last year's Christmas ornaments, an out-of-place pair of animal horns & a generous selection of beer posters. The welcome could hardly be warmer, & it's a great spot for live music on Fri & Sat.

✕ **Le Kassa** ✆33 991 1311; m 70 206 3306; ⊕ 07.00–midnight daily, later at w/ends. Directly off the Rond-Point Jean-Paul II, this eclectic open-air restaurant serves as a popular meeting point for *Ziguinchorois* of all stripes. With an aquarium, billiard table & no shortage of potted plants

scattered around the sizeable courtyard, it's an unpretentious hangout where you can get a bowl of *thieboudienne* or the usual array of meat & fish dishes. Mains start around 3,500F & there's a *plat du jour* for 2,000F.

✕ **Le Jardin de l'Alliance** ✆33 991 2823; ⊕ 08.00–22.00 Mon–Sat. In a shady, seashell-covered courtyard at the Alliance Franco-Sénégalaise, this is a great spot for a drink or a meal at the south end of town. The menu covers a range of grills & Senegalese classics in addition to their affordable *plat du jour*. They often do concerts & film screenings on the weekends, so it's possible that there'll be a small cover charge on these nights.

♀ **Kangoulene Bar** m 77 403 1111; ⊕ 08.00–23.00 daily. Though it's billed as a bar, this place is also known around town for its steak & shrimp dishes, both of which clock in right around 3,000F. There's a shaded terrace out front, TV inside for football fans, & a general living-room air about the place that entices you to put your feet up and stay awhile.

CASAMANCE BY BOAT

As of mid-2015, there are now three boats plying the route between Dakar and Ziguinchor, typically with a stop in Carabane *en route*. The largest and most famous of the ships is the *Aline Sitoé Diatta,* named after the anti-colonial heroine who was born in Kabrousse (see page 296).

The other two boats, *Diambogne* and *Anguène*, are considerably smaller and named after two mythological sisters who were travelling together in a pirogue near the Gambia delta when their boat broke in half and the currents swept them apart. Diambogne eventually reached the northern shore, while Anguène was carried to the south, and each remained on her side of the river. Today Diambogne is the spiritual mother of the Sine-Saloum's Serer people, and Anguène the spiritual mother of Casamance's Diola. Built in South Korea, the two boats came into service here in 2015.

All three are run by COSAMA (✆ *33 821 2900 (Dakar); 33 991 7200 (Ziguinchor); 33 984 3190 (Carabane);* e *cosama@orange.sn; www.cosamasn.com*) and tickets have to be purchased in person **in advance** at one of their bureaux at the ports. These very often sell out (though the addition of the two new boats has helped), and it's unfortunately not usually possible to book from afar, though a few tourist agencies may do it for you for a reasonable fee. **Diambone Voyages** (✆ *33 991 6774;* m *77 641 5132;* e *diambone@orange.sn; www.diambonevoyages.com*) in Ziguinchor is one such agency; email ahead to ask, and remember that any issues with the voyage itself have *nothing* to do with your tour agency and everything to do with COSAMA.

Arrive early for boarding, and if you're taking the *Diambogne* or *Anguène* and want to go to Carabane, make very sure to double-check that they'll be calling there, as their schedules are still being ironed out and we've had recent reports that they may not always make the stop.

♀ **Le Bombolong II** 📞 33 938 8001; 📱 77 535 0545; www.hotel-kadiandoumagne.com/nightclub; ⏰ 22.00–late daily. Under the same ownership as the Hôtel Kadiandoumagne, this has been the go-to nightspot in Ziguinchor for some years now, & it doesn't show much sign of slowing down. There's a DJ or a band depending on the night, & the dance steps here are likely to be the fastest you see anyone move in Ziguinchor, full stop.

OTHER PRACTICALITIES

Health President Macky Sall inaugurated the brand new Hôpital de la Paix [289 B4] (📞 33 991 9800) here in Feb 2015, but if you can't get to it for whatever reason, the much older Hôpital Régional de Ziguinchor (📞 33 991 11 54) also operates at the south end of town near the airport.

Communications If the place where you're staying doesn't have internet (though nearly all of them do), Sudinfo on the west side of town has computers, and there's another internet café near Rond-Point Jean-Paul II [289 C2]. Most people with their own devices head to the riverside restaurant at Le Perroquet.

The post office is a block down from the district government building on Rue Général de Gaulle.

WHAT TO SEE AND DO Ziguinchor's premier attraction is simply a wander along the river and through the old colonial centre, where a mélange of colonial and modern buildings are stuffed with small shops and petty traders hawk their

Full-price non-resident rates between Dakar–Ziguinchor on the *Aline Sitoé Diatta* are 30,500/28,500/18,500F for a bunk in a two/four/eight-person cabin and 15,500F for a seat, while the *Aguène* and *Diambogne* only have seats, so these are also 15,500F each. Senegal residents pay 26,500/24,500/12,500F for a two/four/eight-person cabin, and 5000F/seat. Tickets from Dakar–Carabane are the same price as all the way to Ziguinchor, while the fare for the much shorter journey from Ziguinchor–Carabane is half of the full Ziguinchor–Dakar price.

If you're travelling with a vehicle, cars can make the trip for 63,000F each way, and they have to be on the boat the night before departure.

SCHEDULE (JUNE 2015):

Depart Dakar (all arrive in Ziguinchor around 10.00 to 11.00 the next morning with an early morning stop in Carabane)

Tue 20:00	Aline Sitoé Diatta
Thu 20:00	Diambogne/Anguène
Fri 20:00	Aline Sitoé Diatta
Sun 20:00	Diambogne/Anguène

Depart Ziguinchor (all arrive in Dakar around 6-7 the next morning with an afternoon stop in Carabane)

Tue 13.00	Diambogne/Anguène
Thu 13.00	Aline Sitoé Diatta
Fri 13.00	Diambogne/Anguène
Sun 13.00	Aline Sitoé Diatta

12

wares on the crumbling, palm-lined roads out front. In terms of architecture, the *gouvernance, palais de justice, conseil régional* and post office are all worth a look and are clustered within a few blocks of each other in the centre. If you follow Rue de Commerce all the way west of the city centre, you'll wind up at Zig's **fishing beach** [289 A1], a constantly busy patch of sand where you can see pirogues being built and the day's catch being hauled ashore and loaded on to *charettes* and trucks in the afternoon. Dedicated aquaculturists will also want to head for the **Ferme de Djibelor** (⊕ *07.30–18.00 daily; see page 290*), where you can look around their somewhat scruffy but still intriguing gardens and crocodile pools – call ahead if you'd like to sample their croc plate for dinner.

If you're interested in diving into a market or checking out the local artisans, head south of the centre towards **Marché Boucotte** and **Marché Saint-Maur** [289 B4] for the usual array of fabric, buckets, tools, belts, bootleg football kit, produce, paint and all the other goodies you tend to find in markets around Senegal. For souvenirs, the **Centre artisanal de Ziguinchor** [289 B4] is a bit further south near the Alliance Franco-Sénégalaise, and, while it's looking a bit long in the tooth overall, it's still a good place to drop in and see the sculptures of Salif Badiane and a number of other talented carvers, painters, leatherworkers and more. There aren't many customers around, so expect a bit of attention when you arrive, but also the potential to make some good deals. Back up towards the centre and absolutely worth a stop is **Africa Batik** [289 C3] (m *77 653 4936;* e *mamadoucherifafricabatik@hotmail.com*), where Mamadou Cherif Diallo prints all manner and all sizes of dazzlingly colourful batiks, including custom pieces – he'll proudly show you his commissioned rendition of Picasso's *Guernica.*

For music, film, and other cultural events, look no further than the **Alliance Franco-Sénégalaise** [289 B4] (☎ *33 991 2823;* e *afszig@orange.sn; http://ziguinchor. af-senegal.org or www.facebook.com/AllianceFrancosenegalaiseZiguinchor; entry 1,000F*), where there's an impressive schedule of concerts, workshops, language lessons, film screenings, art exhibitions and more, all built in a show-stopping double *case à impluvium* (see page 331) done up in dazzling geometric patterns and mosaics. Check their Facebook page for what's coming up next.

Finally, while Ziguinchor as a whole may move at a decidedly languorous clip, the athletically minded need not give in to the stupor entirely as there are plenty of athletic facilities in town that can help keep your blood pumping. The **Complexe Sportif Aubert** [289 B1] (☎ *33 938 8020*) is free for guests of the Hôtel Aubert, but otherwise anyone can splash around in their pool for 1,000F/day or pump some iron in the gym for 500F. The considerably more scenic Hôtel Kadiandoumagne's pool is also open to non-guests for 2,000F/day (see pages 288–90). Also at the Kadiandoumagne, Bakin Centre (m *77 543 0512/3*) does **yoga classes** and massage on Wednesday evenings.

CAP SKIRRING AND KABROUSSE

Situated just north of Cape Roxo, where the coast finishes its longitudinal course and takes a sharp turn to the southeast as it enters Guinea-Bissau, the twin towns of Cap Skirring and Kabrousse sit at Senegal's extreme southwestern edge, and along what could very easily be the finest beach anywhere in the country. Set beneath a dramatic escarpment (dramatic for topographically challenged Senegal, anyway) with sensational views from the top, the beach arcs its way up the coastline in a series of shallow crescent-shaped coves that are made all the more striking by the riotous vegetation climbing the hillsides behind.

As far as tourist centres go, the *station balnéaire* or seaside resort at Cap Skirring is second only to Saly in terms of its popularity as a European holiday getaway, and the direct flights from Paris to Cap's miniscule airport are proof. It's still much smaller and calmer than its Petite Côte cousin, though, and it continues to get quieter as you head down the beach towards Kabrousse, which is impressively low-key given that it's only a few kilometres down the road from central Cap's quad-happy main drag. As such, Cap Skirring and Kabrousse play something of a happy medium when it comes to resort towns. Yes, you'll see plenty of wristbands, beach buggies and Club Med guests on parole from their private beach at the centre of town, but you'll also find family-run campements, great music, lively bars, a panoply of land and seaborne activities on offer, and even if none of these things fire you one bit, there's still that absolutely magical stretch of beach.

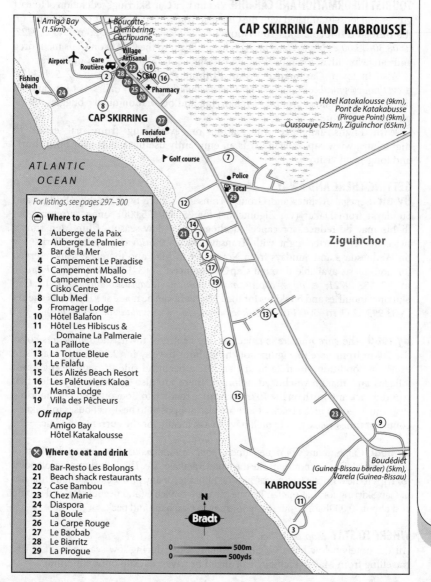

CAP SKIRRING AND KABROUSSE

Amigo Bay (1.5km)
Boucotte, Diembéring, Cachouane
Airport
Village Artisanal
Gare Routière
Fishing beach
SCBAO
Pharmacy
Hôtel Katakalousse (9km), Pont de Katakabusse (Pirogue Point) (9km), Oussouye (25km), Ziguinchor (65km)
CAP SKIRRING
Foriafou Écomarket
ATLANTIC OCEAN
Golf course
Police
Total
Ziguinchor

For listings, see pages 297–300

🛏 **Where to stay**
1 Auberge de la Paix
2 Auberge Le Palmier
3 Bar de la Mer
4 Campement Le Paradise
5 Campement Mballo
6 Campement No Stress
7 Cisko Centre
8 Club Med
9 Fromager Lodge
10 Hôtel Balafon
11 Hôtel Les Hibiscus &
 Domaine La Palmeraie
12 La Paillote
13 La Tortue Bleue
14 Le Falafu
15 Les Alizés Beach Resort
16 Les Palétuviers Kaloa
17 Mansa Lodge
19 Villa des Pêcheurs

Off map
 Amigo Bay
 Hôtel Katakalousse

🍴 **Where to eat and drink**
20 Bar-Resto Les Bolongs
21 Beach shack restaurants
22 Case Bambou
23 Chez Marie
24 Diaspora
25 La Boule
26 La Carpe Rouge
27 Le Baobab
28 Le Biarritz
29 La Pirogue

Boudédiet (Guinea-Bissau border) (5km), Varela (Guinea-Bissau)
KABROUSSE

N
Bradt
0 — 500m
0 — 500yds

12

Political junkies will also be interested to know that Kabrousse is the birthplace of Aline Sitoé Diatta (1920–44), the Diola anti-colonial heroine, often described as the Casamance's Joan of Arc, who rose to fame as a spirit medium who organised a revolt and boycott of the Vichy France regime's heavy taxation and seizure of local farmers' rice crops during WWII. She was quickly identified as a leader of the movement, arrested, and hauled away to exile in Timbuktu, where she was to die less than a year later. Today she is regarded as a foremother of the Senegalese independence struggle, and the ferry linking Dakar and Ziguinchor, the *MV Aline Sitoé Diatta*, is named in her honour.

TOURIST INFORMATION AND CAR HIRE Set up by a Cap Skirring's federation of tourist guides and loosely affiliated with the Office de Tourisme de Casamance in Ziguinchor, the **Bureau d'Informations Touristiques** (✆ *33 993 2721/990 3952;* m *77 653 0427;* ⏰ *08.30–13.00 & 16.00–20.00 daily*) is located next to the CBAO on Cap's main drag and can help with accommodation, excursions, car hire, guided tours and more.

Also in town, **Casamance Vision Éthique** (✆ *33 993 0138;* m *77 541 3472;* e *cvethique@gmail.com; www.casamancevisionethique.com*) offers 4x4 hire and all manner of excursions around Cap Skirring and beyond on quads, buggies, bikes, pirogues and more.

With English-language information on everything from real estate to nightclubs, **www.cap-skirring.fr** is an eminently useful resource for both short- and long-term visitors.

GETTING THERE AND AWAY

By air Senegal Airlines and Groupe Transair fly here twice weekly (Fridays and Sundays) from Dakar (via Ziguinchor) for 75,000/125,000F one-way/return, but flights may be reduced or cancelled altogether in low season. **Club Med** runs a twice-weekly charter flight with Transavia (*www.transavia.com*) from Paris-Orly on Wednesdays and Sundays from November to May, and there are seats reserved for non-guests available through **CapCasamance** (✆ *(+33) 015 341 0050; (France);* m *77 653 9721;* e *infos@capcasamance.com; www.capcasamance.com*). In Cap Skirring, inquiries and bookings for the Paris flight can be made at **Villa des Pêcheurs** (✆ *33 993 5253;* m *77 431 0080;* e *sitoe@orange.sn; www.villadespecheurs.com*).

By road The *gare routière* is smack in the centre of town, and *sept-places* cover the 70km from here to Ziguinchor throughout the day for 2,300F. The road is in excellent condition, open 24 hours, and it's a beautiful ride through sleepy forest villages and mangrove-choked bolongs. There are also occasional vehicles that trundle back and forth on the 10km of tarmac road up to Boucotte and Diembéring.

If you've got to make tracks, there are also supposed to be direct buses to Dakar a couple of times weekly, but you'll have to ask locally for the current schedule.

By boat Cap Skirring's pirogue launch (*pont de Katakalousse*) is about 10km east of town towards Ziguinchor, opposite the Hôtel Katakalousse. This is the jumping-off point for trips to Île d'Ehidje (see pages 306–7), Elinkine, or any pirogue trips originating out of Cap Skirring for that matter. Private hires are available (and negotiable), and should cost about 50,000F for a round-trip journey to Carabane and back.

⌂ WHERE TO STAY Map, page 295.

All the hotels below have Wi-Fi, and many close during low season, so if you're travelling from May to October, call ahead or have a backup option in mind.

Cap Skirring

🏠 **Club Med** (205 rooms) 📞 (+44) 8453 670 670 (UK); 📞 33 993 5222; e reservations.uk@ clubmed.com; www.clubmed.com. Senegal's very own branch of the world-famous all-inclusive chain is recently renovated & has everything you would expect, including 2 restaurants, 3 bars, 9-hole golf course, fishing, tennis, sailing, volleyball, archery, wellness centre & a range of land & water excursions. Prices vary & there are deals to be had, but count on around €300/night for 2 people. **$$$$$**

🏠 **Les Alizes Beach Resort** (17 rooms) 📞 33 993 5288; m 77 554 1358/9; e info@les-alizes-hotel.com; www.les-alizes-hotel.com. At the south end of the coastal road, this expansive lodge bills itself as the only 5-star hotel in Casamance, & while we won't involve ourselves in neighbourly star-measuring contests, it's got every bit of the luxury to back up their sidereal boasts. The cream-&-black patterned 2- & 3-storey bungalows are arranged in 3 rows, with those closest to the ocean perched delicately at the hill's edge and enjoying a truly enviable coastal panorama from their private terraces. All the 80–225m² suites & lofts are beautifully equipped in dark wood & whitewash, with mangrove-&-reed ceilings, local carvings & artwork accents, AC, flatscreen TV, full kitchen, stereo, DVD player & enough bedrooms for a single traveller on up to a group of 8. There's a casual grill on their private stretch of beach, a gourmet restaurant up the hill next to the infinity pool, a couple of bars, wine cellar, spa & massage styles on offer from California to Sweden. For the active or the antsy, a whole list of activities is available, from kitesurfing to calisthenics. All guests are accommodated on a HB or FB basis; a HB dbl starts at €360. **$$$$$**

🏠 **Amigo Bay** (9 rooms) 📞 33 993 5287; e info@amigobaysenegal.com; www. amigobaysenegal.com. On a deserted stretch of beach north of town, these luxury vacation villas are set around a finely manicured estate where you won't find a blade of grass out of place. The villas themselves are pure modern European minimalism, with 2–4 bedrooms, full kitchens, AC, living rooms, flatscreen TV, private terrace & grounds, & some even come with their own infinity pool. All are just metres from the beach & have access to the hotel's on-site restaurant, bar & swimming pool. Nightly rates start around €150

and easily stretch to double that, with weekly & monthly deals available. **$$$$**

🏠 **La Paillote** (30 rooms) 📞 33 993 5151/5252; m 77 529 4719; e paillote@orange. sn; www.paillote.sn. Comfortable in its position as the doyen of Cap Skirring's hotels, this venerable resort has been keeping an eye on the beaches here for over 40 years & shows little sign of slowing down. Hemmed in to the north by a rocky outcrop & stand of trees, the beach here is remarkably private, & the palm-grove restaurant on the sand is a delight. The bungalows are up-to-date & tasteful, & all come with AC, TV, safe, fridge & private terrace. Needless to say, they know the region by heart & can help with all queries & excursions. Oddly, there's no pool. Rates in the bottom half of this range, except over the festive season. **$$$$**

🏠 **Mansa Lodge** (5 rooms) 📞 33 993 5147; m 77 652 8315; e evasion@capsafari.com; www. capsafari.com. Feeling more like a tastefully decorated private home than a guesthouse, this owner-managed lodge has simple bungalows & suites with refined touches of African décor liberally scattered throughout. All the units come with AC, safe, lounge area & terrace, & are available in a 1- or 2-bedroom configuration, making them well suited to families & groups. The garden restaurant has spectacular ocean views, serves a range of dishes from grilled lobster to Moroccan *tagines*, & there are plenty of poolside hammocks to slink away to should you overindulge & need a nap. They run the Cap Safari tour agency, which can arrange tours & transport anywhere in Senegal, as well as pirogues, quads, bicycles, kitesurfing, fishing, & a host of other activities in & around Cap Skirring. Double rooms start around €80 and range up to €220 depending on room & season. **$$$$**

🏠 **Cisko Centre** (29 rooms) 📞 33 990 3921; m 77 549 2215; e cisko@ciskocentre.com; www. ciskocentre.com. As much a cultural centre as it is a hotel, this bustling spot is a major hub for Cap Skirring's arts & music scene, with a sizeable outdoor stage & their own weekend-long jazz fest here every April. They do all kinds of lessons & workshops, including drum, dance, kora, painting & others, as well as a robust range of excursions on bikes, quads & pirogues. Rooms are set up in sparkling new 3-storey bungalows with shaded rooftop terraces, & the modern-feeling rooms come with AC, flatscreen TV, mini fridge, balcony, sofa & writing desk. There's a big swimming pool, billiards, a popular bar & restaurant, & regular events at weekends. Rates at the bottom of this range. **$$$**

🏠 **Hôtel Katakalousse** m 77 776 0838; e infos@katakalousse.com; www.katakalousse.com. Just under 10km east of Cap Skirring on the road to Oussouye, the management of this bolong-side lodge lives & breathes all things piscatorial. Set just across the street from Cap's public pirogue launch, they do a specialised range of fishing excursions, all of which are detailed on their informative website, & can arrange kayaks & dune buggy trips; they do day-long excursions to Carabane on Wed & Fri as well. Their thatched bungalows are nothing extravagant, but comfortably equipped, & the restaurant & pool enjoy fabulous views over the bolong. **$$$**

🏠 **Hôtel Balafon** (24 rooms) ☏ 30 102 6130; m 77 816 0896; e hotelbalafon@yahoo.fr; www.hotel-cap-skirring.fr. With central Cap Skirring in front & a wide, green bolong out back, this comfortable accommodation feels quite a bit different than the beachside resorts nearby, & while it doesn't take fantastic advantage of its location next to the mangroves, the grounds & rooms are thoroughly agreeable nonetheless. The spacious, high-ceilinged rooms are arranged around the swimming pool & courtyard, & all come with AC, TV, mini fridge, writing desk & mozzie nets, & the adjoining rooms are available for families as well. Rates towards the middle of this range. **$$**

🏠 **La Tortue Bleue** (4 rooms) m 77 692 6585; e info@latortuebleue.org; www.latortuebleue.org. Run by a Belgian-Senegalese family & opened here in 2013, this lovingly tended lodge just off the main road between Cap & Kabrousse is a welcome new addition to the accommodation scene & one of the best deals in town to boot. Arranged in an intimate, fruit-tree-filled compound, rooms here are done up in a minimalist European style decorated with eye-catching African batiks & a different colour scheme for each room, all of which come with fridge, fan, canopy bed, mozzie net, reading lamps & a sizeable bathroom. They do meals on request (including vegetarian options grown in their organic gardens), & the English-speaking hosts are experts at rolling out the welcome wagon. The beach is about 500m away,

they can arrange all excursions, & rates are at the bottom of this range. Recommended. **$$**

🏠 **Le Falafu** m 77 513 3185/568 3617; e falafu@gmx.net; www.lefalafu.com. The northernmost stop along the coastal road, this has a fine location overlooking the beach & restaurants below, but feels a bit scruffy & unkempt. The en-suite rooms are acceptably equipped with nets & fans, & could probably do with a sprucing up, though the sea-facing rooms' private terraces go quite a long way towards making up for the uninspiring air about the place. Given the other options available within a few hundred metres, it's a bit difficult to recommend at the price, but it's absolutely worth the 5,000F upgrade to a sea-view room if you do stay. Prices at the lower end of this range. **$$**

🏠 **Les Palétuviers Kaloa** (16 rooms) ☏ 33 993 5210; m 77 575 6177; e paletuviers.kaloa@gmail.com; www.hotel-les-paletuviers.com. Also between town & the bolong, but taking better advantage of the locale than its neighbour Hôtel Balafon, the en-suite rooms here are on the small side but are comfortably kept with AC & TV, & many have views or terraces overlooking the bolong. There's a central swimming pool, well-regarded little restaurant, & they've even got their own discotheque that opens on the weekends. It's nice enough but, with rates at the very top of this range, perhaps a touch overpriced. **$$**

✕ **Villa des Pêcheurs** (7 rooms) ☏ 33 993 5253; m 77 431 0080; www.villadespecheurs.com. Whether you're a die-hard angler or don't know your bait from your barracuda, it doesn't much matter at this charming Afro-Mediterranean abode on the beach. The 2 open-air restaurants specialise in (naturally) all things Neptunian, & a 3-course grilled fish *menu* goes for 7,000F. The tiled rooms are clean & simple with AC & private terraces near the pool. The fishing options are manifold, & they're the local contacts for seats on the flight to Paris. Rates at the upper end of this range. **$$**

🏠 **Auberge Le Palmier** (11 rooms) ☏ 33 933 5109; m 77 511 4404. Though it's barely 100m from Cap Skirring's central roundabout, this is a quiet & reliable budget option with a casual terrace restaurant & bar out front. The en-suite rooms at the back are on the small side with some rather funky floor plans, but they're certainly kept clean & all are equipped with either fan or AC. The closest beach is about 600m away, so you don't get much in the way of views, but the prices are more than reasonable. **$**

🏠 **Auberge de la Paix** (15 rooms) 📞 33 993 5145; 📱 77 651 2431; 📧 aubergedelapaix@yahoo.fr; www.facebook.com/delapaixauberge. In the middle of the row of campements at the northern end of the coastal road, the rooms here aren't much to write home about & the compound is on the dingier side of things, but it is a credible contender for the cheapest en-suite place in town, as their en-suite doubles go for 8,000F in high season & even less at other times of year. They can arrange meals, or the beach-shack restos below are only a few steps away. **$**

🏠 **Campement Le Paradise** (19 rooms) 📞 33 993 5129; 📧 capskirringparadise@hotmail.fr. Certainly the choicest campement on this stretch of beach, this cosy blue-&-white place sits on a rise above a row of rastafied beach-shack restaurants & a sprawling expanse of sand & surf. Rooms range from simple digs in a traditional *case à impluvium* with nets, fans & shared facilities for 7,000F, to tiled en-suite rooms with fan or AC for 12,000–20,000F, depending on the room (the priciest ones have sea views). Whichever you pick, they're all meticulously kept & the staff goes out of their way to make you feel at home. They can arrange pirogue trips, fishing, bicycling, cars, motos & other excursions. **$**

🏠 **Campement Mballo** (10 rooms) 📱 77 447 9250/609 8135. This family-run place is another contender for the cheapest sleep in town, particularly for single travellers. The row of facing accommodation blocks won't inspire any paeans to their inspired design, but the en-suite rooms with nets & fans are surprisingly nice, particularly rooms 8–10, which are newly renovated but go for the same price. The rooms with shared facilities are cramped & airless, but undeniably clean, & it's hard to argue with a 4,000F single bed if you're scrimping. **$**

🏠 **Campement No Stress (Chez Seleck)** (7 rooms) 📞 33 93 5349; 📱 77 614 6450; 📧 diattaeugene2000@yahoo.fr; www.campementnostress.webs.com. With bargain basement rates & luxury penthouse views, this aptly named campement midway down the coastal road does everything you'd hope it would & then some. The compound is grassy with plenty of room for a round of *pétanque*, the veggies grown on site (& more than likely a few of the chickens) are served up at their low-key resto-bar, & the simple rooms are spotless, bright, & en-suite, with

high ceilings, nets & fans. A steep set of stairs takes you down to the beach below, & they'll set you up with the usual range of pirogue & other excursions. **$**

Kabrousse

🏠 **Hôtel Les Hibiscus & Domaine La Palmeraie** 📞 33 993 5273/5136; 📧 immocapcab@yahoo.fr; www.hibiscus.sn. These conjoined twin hotels at the south end of Kabrousse vary in services but are similar in character. Les Hibiscus is a full-service resort with a French-inspired terrace restaurant, eminently attractive swimming pool & comfortable thatched bungalows scattered in their spacious beachfront garden. Next door, La Palmeraie is aimed more at families & consists of larger self-contained bungalows with kitchens that can sleep anywhere from 1 to 10 guests. They're both perfectly comfortable but not exactly oozing with character. Prices for a double span this entire range depending on season & room, & some dip into the category below during low season. **$$$**

🏠 **Bar de la Mer** (9 rooms) 📞 33 993 5280; 📧 resa@hotel-capskirring.com; www.hotel-capskirring.com. *Pieds dans l'eau* is an exact claim at this Miami-Beach-inspired pastel palace smack on the white sand at the very southern end of Kabrousse. Rooms are cool & comfortable with AC, TV, minibar & big beds set on a built-in pebbledash dais. The restaurant does French-inspired fare & seems popular, though the rude ownership leaves something to be desired. A standard double is 20,000/30,000F depending on season, while a deluxe goes for 15,000F more. **$$**

🏠 **Fromager Lodge** 📞 33 993 5421; 📱 77 761 9353/614 6522; 📧 giulioselmi@yahoo.it. With a bar built into their eponymous *fromager* (kapok) tree, a shaded treehouse-terrace directly above, & an inexplicably triangular swimming pool, it's hard not to like this eclectic-feeling place right off the bat. The thatched en-suite bungalows are arranged around the forested compound & draw their inspiration from Diola architectural styles. All come with fans & nets, & each one is individually decorated with West African art & artefacts from Guinea, Côte d'Ivoire & beyond. What's more, the Italian owner is renowned for rolling out some of the best wood-fired pizzas & calzones in town, starting around 4,000F. Rates in the upper half of this range. **$$**

✕ WHERE TO EAT AND DRINK *Map, page 295.*

In addition to the eateries listed below, there's a cluster of **beach shack restaurants** facing the row of campements at the north end of the coastal road. Self-caterers should aim for the well-stocked **Foriafou Écomarket** (🕐 *09.00–13.00 & 15.00–19.00 Mon–Sat*; 📱 *77 452 2138*) where there's a good selection of meat, cheese, frozen foods, packaged goods and alcohol.

✕ Chez Marie 📱 77 532 3798; 🕐 lunch & dinner daily. For local dishes on the cheap in Kabrousse, this roadside eatery dishes up all the Senegalese standards you've come to expect for undemanding prices. If they're closed, there's another hole in the wall just across the street where *thieboudienne* is their stock-in-trade, though don't expect either one to be quick.

✕ Diaspora 📱 77 618 8152; www.facebook.com/diasporas.capskirringwww.facebook.com/diasporas.capskirring; 🕐 08.00–15.00 & 19.00–23.00. Around the block from the city centre, this friendly new place just down from the fishing beach has an ambitious menu, killer prices & a welcoming vibe. Crab ravioli & sautéed shrimp go for a more than reasonable 3,500F, while filet mignon for 4,000F is a deal by any measure. They've got plenty of pizzas starting at 3,000F, a nice open-air dining area, & a handful of brand new & very pleasant little rooms in back for 11,000F/dbl. It could potentially get a bit loud at the bar, but otherwise this is a great choice for a meal or a night's kip.

✕ La Carpe Rouge 📱 77 651 2460; 🕐 10.00–22.00 daily. One of the most reliable options on the Cap Skirring strip, this surprisingly bright & airy place not only does a true Casamançais *caldou* fish stew (with rice, naturally) as their *plat du jour*, but the handful of dishes that get chalked up on the board out front every day are much more than your usual roadside chop. The grilled chicken & *lotte brochettes* are a menu favourite all over the coast, but it's not too many places you'll get a *crabe farci* (stuffed crab) too, & even fewer for 4,000F.

✕ La Pirogue 📞 33 993 5176; 🕐 lunch & dinner daily. Standing opposite La Paillote at the entrance to town, this Cap Skirring institution has been serving up hefty portions of Marseillaise comfort food (think bouillabaisse, stuffed crab, lobster & Provençal stews) alongside Senegalese specialities for ages now – the French owners have been in Casamance for decades. Their *menu* goes for 8,000F.

✕ Le Biarritz 📱 77 933 6075/975 1113; 🕐 09.00–dawn daily. Given its central-as-can-be location, it's little wonder this upbeat spot has become a popular meeting point for tourists, expats & locals alike. With the very welcome selection of crêpes, paninis, salads, pasta, pastries & home-made ice cream in addition to the obligatory Senegalese mainstays & grills, this is a convenient & convivial place for a meal, a drink or dessert, particularly at weekends when there's live music & dancing. It's also got just about the longest hours in town.

♀ Bar-Resto Les Bolongs Directly opposite the bank, the 1st-floor terrace here is a prime spot to pull up a chair, crack open a Gazelle, & watch the ebb & flow of traffic, commerce & life down below. They serve the usual range of Senegalese meals & you'll usually find football on the TV.

♀ La Boule 📞 33 936 2127; 🕐 07.00–late daily. Dark & stylish with live music at weekends, this place is slightly more of a bar (& *rhumerie*) than it is a restaurant, but that doesn't stop them from dishing up one of the best-value *plats du jour* in central Cap for only 750F. There's live music every Sat night, & it's a certified jam session with guitars, djembes, koras & even saxophone all represented.

☆ Case Bambou 📞 33 993 5178; 📱 77 547 9126. Mild-mannered restaurant by day, swinging discotheque by night, this Cap Skirring staple is more known for its nighttime vibes than its daytime fare, but they specialise in lobster & shrimp so you won't go hungry regardless of the time. DJs handle the music most nights of the week except Thu, when they put on a *soirée Sénégalaise*.

☆ Le Baobab 📱 77 407 2070; 🕐 22.00–dawn daily. If you're looking to see sunrise, a stop by here might be a good way to do it, but put on your dancing shoes beforehand. Bass thrums out into the night from this 2-level discotheque, where the latest and not-so-latest top 40, hip-hop & electro jams compete for aural dominance over the youth of Cap. There's a covered roof terrace with tables & chairs upstairs, & down a level is the laser light show & dancefloor. If you can prize your eyes away from the fancy footwork, the big screen usually shows the latest football.

OTHER PRACTICALITIES

Health The nearest hospital is in Ziguinchor, but the pharmacies in town are well stocked, and there is Dr. Mamadou Ndiaye (✆ *33 993 5123*; m *77 659 6022*), if you need to see someone in town.

Communications There's an internet café with computers at Cisko Centre, and Campement Le Paradise is a good place to use the Wi-Fi if you've got your own device. There's a post office on the main road in Kabrousse.

WHAT TO SEE AND DO Cap Skirring is the type of place where you can do pretty much whatever you want, just so long as it involves the beach in some way. Most of the hotels arrange their own activities, so in practice the easiest way to arrange a pirogue trip, windsurfing/kitesurfing class, fishing excursion, quad, buggy or 4x4 trip, or any other land or water activity, is quite simply to ask at your hotel, because if they don't offer what you're looking for, you can bet they know somebody who will. **Cap Safari** (✆ *33 993 5147*; m *77 652 8315*; e *evasion@capsafari.com; www.capsafari. com*) is a recommended operator based at Mansa Lodge, and the Oussouye-based **Casamance VTT** (✆ *33 993 1004*; m *77 377 0566/646 8088/572 1196, 78 206 8143*; e *casavtt@yahoo.fr; www.casamancevtt.com*) runs several half- and full-day mountain biking, pirogue and hiking trips that originate in Cap Skirring.

And while beach-bound activities do rightfully rule the day in and around Cap Skirring, if you're somehow sick of sand in your swimming bottoms, a fresh water dip is easily arranged at Cisko Centre's sizeable **swimming pool** (see pages 297–8). If you opt for a meal in their restaurant you're welcome to backstroke all you like, but if you're of the mind that grandma was right and swimming and eating don't mix, pool use alone is 1,500F for the day. Also, if you're here on a Friday, Bakin Centre (m *77 543 0512/3*) offers **yoga classes** and massage, just in case you pulled a muscle on your windsurfer.

Souvenir shoppers should head for the warren of workshops at the **Village Artisanal** (m *77 515 6797*) at the very centre of Cap Skirring, where nearly four dozen artisans carve, scrape, sew, paint, weld, polish, hammer, bend and bead all manner of sculpture, jewellery, leatherwork, paintings and more. There's an excellent profile on all the artisans here (*www.cap-skirring.fr/village_artisanal_cap_ skirring/art_africain_cap_skirring.html*) if you want to do some window-shopping ahead of time. Also be aware that prices here, as would befit a tourist town, are often seriously inflated – don't be afraid to bargain.

Finally, golfers will be glad to know that **Club Med** (see page 297) (✆ *33 993 5222*) is home to Casamance's only golf course, a ridiculously scenic 9-hole affair that's open to non-guests, but you'll have to call or stop by to enquire about this season's green fees.

BOUCOTTE

If it's the beach you're after but not the party, Boucotte sits on the road just inland from the start of an unbroken and largely deserted 18km strand of beach just as fine as any in Cap Skirring that wends its way up the coast from here, past Diembéring, until it eventually reaches the Casamance River mouth at Nikine. All the hotels listed below, with the exception of Ecolodge Semebene Ousmane, are set in a row within about a kilometre of each other 2km west of the main road and Boucotte proper. Should you need it, they will all typically offer pickup from Cap Skirring or along the road either free or at a small fee. If you're self-driving, the roads get quite sandy beyond Hôtel Maya and 4x4 is strongly recommended.

BONUS TRIP TO GUINEA-BISSAU

Just 15km from Ziguinchor and spitting distance from Cap Skirring, the former Portuguese colony of Guinea-Bissau makes for a worthwhile side trip if you've got some extra time and want to check another country off your list. Though it's never enjoyed the political stability of its northern neighbour and tends to be in the news for all the wrong reasons (narcotrafficking, for one – expect thorough checks coming back into Senegal), it's generally regarded as safe to visit and is home to the 88 marvellously isolated islands of the Bijagós Archipelago (recognised as a UNESCO Biosphere Reserve, and of which only 20 are inhabited), dozens of untouched and Arcadian seaside villages, and the crumbling low-rise capital of Bissau. That's all a bit beyond the purview of this guide, but for a quick taste of the Lusosphere, the seaside village of Varela offers almost comically unspoilt beaches and fabulous budget accommodation just a few kilometres south of the border.

You need a visa to enter, but these are easily arranged at the **Guinea-Bissau consulate** (m 77 512 6497) in Ziguinchor, which opens weekdays at 09.00 and usually does multiple-entry visas on the spot for 20,000F. Bring a photo and copy of your passport. Once you've got your visa, there are a number of border crossings between Senegal and Guinea-Bissau, but the overwhelming majority of traffic uses the RN4 south of Ziguinchor via Mpack (Senegal)–São Domingos (Guinea-Bissau). Regular *sept-places* serve São Domingos and Bissau from Ziguinchor (5,000F), and the journey to Bissau takes three to four hours. Bring some small notes, as the military checkpoint at São Domingos collects 2,000F from all inbound travellers.

Once in São Domingos, you can either continue east to Bissau or turn west towards the beach town of Varela, which sits at the end of a patience-testing and spine-compacting 50km dirt road served by just a couple of vehicles daily. You'll forget all about your transport-induced aches and pains when you see Varela's beach, though – centre of a proposed national park and every bit as heavenly as the sands north of the border, it's fringed with the ruins of hotels past, but the last guests here have long since checked out and there's nary a sun lounger (or towel reserving it) in sight – the acres of beach are quite simply yours to explore.

Boucotte is also home to the community-based **Casamance Ecoparc** (❧ 33 991 2781; m 77 517 5895/721 3316; e *diattatour@yahoo.fr; www.casamance-ecoparc. com*), which was declared here in 2010 and covers a 400ha of primary forest, mangrove swamps, palm groves and a 250m band of the Atlantic coast between Boucotte and Diembéring. The primary mission here is to encourage environmental stewardship and education in the surrounding schools and villages, and visitors are invited to get involved with their reforestation and education programmes along with the guided hiking and biking tours they offer through the reserve and surrounding villages. It's an admirable project and well worth supporting, and the setting could hardly be prettier.

Nearby (the Casamance Ecoparc folks will take you) you'll also find Boucotte's small open-air **Musée Kadioute**, where traditional Diola instruments, tools and ceremonial items are kept in the sweeping folds of an enormous kapok tree. The guardians will lead you around it and shine a light on the sometimes-opaque significance of the objects, and while there's officially no charge, a reasonable tip is expected.

Thus, the only address in town is the über-friendly and totally unexpected **Aparthotel Chez Helene** (⊕ *12.291948, -16.584556*; m *(+245) 530 1373 (Guinea-Bissau)*; e *f.cirell.38@gmail.com; www.chezhelenevarela.com*), where Fatima and her Italian husband Franco will have a cold drink waiting, along with 15 meticulously kept and budget-friendly en-suite bungalows and a restaurant menu befitting the confluence of Mediterranean, Atlantic and West African flavours their little corner of Guinea-Bissau represents.

To get back to Senegal, it's possible to avoid retracing your steps on the Varela–São Domingos road, assuming you're prepared for a solid hike and a serious adventure. From Varela, there's a warren of footpaths that wind their way northwest up the coast (staying within about 1km of the water) for 11km to the Bissau-Guinean village of Sucujaque, from where it's a further 2km to a 250m river crossing (known variously as the Boudédiét, Sucujaque or Essaout bolong) where there are plenty of pirogues to ferry you across to the border village of Boudédiét/Budjedjete, which sits on a laterite road 5km east of Kabrousse and is split right down the middle between the two countries. If you want to go this way, it wouldn't hurt to ask for guidance (or maybe even a guide) at Chez Helene, and be aware there's at least one inlet (aside from Boudédiét) that you'll have to find your way across. Alternatively, you could backtrack from Varela as far as Cassalol and make a left on to the forest track towards Sucujaque for a total of 22 dry kilometres.

It would be equally possible to do this itinerary in reverse, entering Guinea-Bissau at Boudédiét, hiking down to Varela, and returning on the roads to São Domingos and Ziguinchor. Note that neither country has an official immigration post at Boudédiét, but soldiers from both countries will inspect your passport (and check for your Guinea-Bissau visa) here. Whether you're coming or going using this route, you have to handle your Senegalese entry/exit stamps at the Cap Skirring airport, and Chez Helene will help get you stamped and sorted on the Guinea-Bissau side.

Both Ecobank and Banco da África Ocidental (BAO) are represented with several ATMs accepting Visa in Bissau, and BAO also has branches in São Domingos, Canchungo, Bafatá and Gabú.

🏠 WHERE TO STAY, EAT AND DRINK

🏠 **Hôtel Maya** (20 rooms) m 77 616 3307/575 6177; e contact@hotel-maya.com; www. hotel-maya.com. With a fabulous location on a hillside sloping down to the beach, the earth-red stucco rooms at this superbly manicured hotel are staggered along the hillside & set around a serene garden & swimming pool. All come equipped with AC, TV, writing desk, full-length mirror, en-suite ablutions & private terraces. The restaurant offerings are commensurate with the general air of easygoing sophistication about the place, & their terrace is the best sundowners perch for miles around. Rates at the lower end of this range. Wi-Fi. **$$$**

🏠 **Auberge Kibalaou** (6 rooms) m 77 160 4249; e kibalaou@gmail.com; www.kibalaou.com.

About 700m up the beach from the Way Kassala, the duplex bungalows here are colourful & scrupulously clean, with bright textile accents, modern fixtures & high ceilings. It's more or less equidistant between Diembéring & Boucotte villages, & sandwiched between the beach & the rice paddies in a beautifully isolated spot where you're sure to have the beach all but to yourself. They can line up hikes, bikes, kayaks, quads, fishing, drumming, dancing & other cultural activities on request. The restaurant does lots of seafood with a seasonal twist, & it's good value overall, with a single rate at the bottom of this range & double towards the middle. **$$**

🏠 **Oudja Hotel** (16 rooms) ☎ 33 992 0648; m 77 517 5825; e aessibye@yahoo.fr; www.

12

casamance-ecoparc.com. At the end of a track that rapidly devolves into tire-swallowing soft sand for the last 100m or so as you arrive on the beach, this feet-in-the-water place has quite reasonable tiled en-suite rooms in a shady, palm-studded compound just north of Hôtel Maya. The oblong blue-&-white thatched bungalows hold 4 rooms each, & all come with mozzie nets. The usual seafood grills & Senegalese staples are available upon request. The hotel is affiliated with Diatta Tour & Casamance Ecopark, so arranging activities & excursions should be a piece of cake. Rates towards the bottom of this range. **$$**

🏠 **Campement Way Kassala** (7 rooms) ☎33 992 8458; m 78 291 0372/187 8591; e nicole.tour@yahoo.fr; www.way-kassala.fr. Just a couple hundred metres up the beach from the Oudja, this cheerful campement has rooms in a brightly painted case à impluvium with 1 en-suite room & the rest using shared ablutions. They're all bright, simple & well-kept, & there's

a 3-bedroom house for family groups as well. They run trips just about anywhere in Basse Casamance, or you can indulge in a bit of surf fishing, drum lessons or an evening campfire right on their doorstep. Meals consist of fresh-caught fish & vegetables from their large organic gardens. Campers welcome. **$**

🏠 **Ecolodge Sembène Ousmane** (12 rooms) ☎33 991 2781; m 77 517 5895/721 3316; e diattatour@yahoo.fr; www.casamance-ecoparc.com. Signposted to the left about 2km before you reach Diembéring village, this little place sits between the forest & the rice paddies, about 900m from the main road & 500m from the beach. Rooms are no frills & come either in a large case à impluvium or duplex bungalows, & all are en-suite. It's under the same management as the ecopark, so it makes for an easy base if you want to see the outdoor museum or arrange a guided hike or bike through the forests & rice fields. Meals on request. **$**

DIEMBÉRING

Centred around yet another spectacular village kapok at the end of a spiffy new tarmac road from Cap Skirring, this village of a few thousand souls set just in from a jaw-dropping stretch of beach and dunes has managed to capture an outsized spot in Senegal's cultural imagination, both as the setting for Ousmane Sembène's 1971 film, *Emitaï*, and as the subject of hometown-hero-turned-nationwide-star Metzo Djatah's 2005 hit song named after the village, which you'll no doubt hear played or sung if you hang out here long enough. It's not hard to see where the fascination comes from, as Diembéring is an inherently attractive place that very charmingly treads the line between the bustle of a small town like Oussouye or Elinkine and the torpor of the many hamlets lost deep in Casamance's bolongs. Not to mention that the flawless beach that stretches up here from Cap Skirring and Boucotte might be even more striking here thanks to the dunes that fringe its perimeter.

It's also home to the Festival des Rizières (m 77 955 1588/646 9929; *www.festivaldesrizieres.wordpress.com*) every April, when the whole village turns out for a weekend of music, art, dance, film, workshops and traditional wrestling, in which the Diembéringois competitors are renowned for their strength and flair.

TOURIST INFORMATION Set up by the local administrative body, the Communauté Rurale de Diembéring, www.diembering.tripadviseur.com has some good (French-language) information about local traditions, events, history, trade, tourism, and governance.

🏠 **WHERE TO STAY, EAT AND DRINK** In addition to the accommodation options listed below there is another well-known guesthouse in Diembéring, the **Auberge les**

Rizières (*on your left as you enter town*; m *77 504 1621/514 0315*), but it looked thoroughly run down and not entirely operational when we checked in.

🏠 **Akine Dyioni Lodge** (5 rooms) m 77 507 3775; e akinelodge@gmail.com; www. akinelodge.com. Artistic, eclectic & like nothing else in the region, this inimitable place has a cluster of individually decorated rooms built from wood, earth, thatch, shells, stone & just about any locally derived material you can come up with. They're all detached & widely spaced throughout the compound, & all are built in wildly divergent styles, from a 2-storey thatch pyramid vaguely resembling a witch's hat to a loft space built out of mangroves & reeds – check out their website to choose your favourite. Their restaurant comes warmly recommended, & it's also the first destination in Casamance for yogis of all types; they have a variety of yoga & meditation sessions on offer in addition to the usual excursions. Go left right before you hit the fromager – it's about 900m towards the beach along a sand track. Rates at the top end of this range. **$$**

🏠 **Campement Asseb** (16 rooms) 📞 33 992 0526; m 77 541 3472/424 7147; e campementasseb@gmail.com. At the entrance to the village, this long-serving place has thoroughly knowledgeable owners & en-suite rooms scattered around a rather slipshod compound. Some are newer than others but all go for the same price, so ask to see a couple before you commit. They quoted us a laughable 13,000F per person, which is well over what it's worth, so

bargaining is well advised – a fair price would be less than half that. **$$**

🏠 **Bar-Restaurant Sujuwass** (4 rooms) m 77 980 9464. Under construction when we dropped in, the en-suite rooms behind the bar here look poised to be a good & cheap option, & their location right next to the towering fromager could hardly be more central. Up front they do a 1,000F *plat du jour* & you won't be left wanting for reggae jams or cold drinks. **$**

🍴 **La Cour des Grands** m 77 975 0525; ⏰ 08.00–22.00 daily. Named for Youssou N'Dour & Axelle Red's World Cup '98 anthem & set right around the corner from the big fromager, this is a reliable central option & whips up a different *plat du jour* every day for about 2,000F. The interior is quite small, but there's a very pleasant little terrace & tables out front.

🍴 **Restaurant Albert Sambou** m 77 514 0377/318 9978; ⏰ 13.00–evening Tue–Sun. Hidden away along the winding roads of the central village (straight past the kapok, with a few signposts scattered about), the rose-tinted interior of this popular thatch-covered joint is covered in murals of palm-wine tappers, *ekontine* players, rice planting & other cultural themes. The menu covers familiar ground, with grills & rice dishes all well represented for around 2500F, along with a cheaper *plat du jour*, pasta & a couple other nods to European cuisines. There's a full bar & even a cocktails menu.

CACHOUANE

Just a speck of a village opposite the southern shores of Île Carabane, Cachouane consists of barely a few dozen homes and farms – practically the definition of a rural idyll. With a fine, palm-studded bolong-side beach and plenty of hammocks at the campement, this Diola hamlet is the perfect place to disappear for a few days or a few weeks, and may leave you forgetting that you ever owned a watch in the first place. There's plenty of opportunity to fish, paddle and laze, and when it's finally time to go, it's a short hop in a pirogue to Elinkine or Île d'Efrane.

The only way to get here by land is on an intoxicatingly peaceful 9km track heading northeast from Diembéring, which can be tackled on foot, 4x4 or by hiring a *djakarta*. Otherwise, Cachouane is most easily reached by pirogue from Elinkine. Call Auberge Sounka ahead of time and they'll come fetch you for 8,000F. They'll do the same from Carabane for about 20,000F, and either Diembéring or Cap Skirring (Katakalousse) for 30,000F.

WHERE TO STAY, EAT AND DRINK

Auberge Sounka (11 rooms)
✛ 12.504983, −16.711336; m 77 645 3707;
e casa.sounka@free.fr; www.auberge-casamance.
com. If you're making the trek from Diembéring,
trust that there'll be a frosty Gazelle waiting with
your name on it when you straggle in – or better
yet a calabash of palm wine. Set in the central
village just feet from the beach in a bright ochre
case à impluvium, rooms here are basic doubles
or triples painted up in big bright murals. A new

block of 3 en-suite rooms opened in 2015. As
far as things to do, beyond swimming, lounging
& savouring the sounds of village life, you can
participate as well – go scavenging for oysters,
learn to cook *thieb*, accompany a rice farmer or
palm wine tapper for the day (which makes for
some good birdwatching as well), or take one of
their windsurfers out on the bolong. No Wi-Fi, but
surprisingly it's available from a neighbour. $

ÎLE D'ÉGUÈYE

If you've had just one too many days wiping someone else's sweat off your arms in
the back row of a *sept-place*, one too many near-misses with a runaway donkey cart
forcing you into the gutter, or one too many toes stepped on in a crammed market
passage, don't scream, just pack up and come here. On a petite island of forests, fields
and exactly zero villages, this is the place to go if you quite simply want to be alone
with nature and listen to the ripple of the river out front and the chatter of the birds
above. The campement here is the only thing on the island, and the accommodating
staff are happy to help you soak up the silence in any way you see fit.

The best way to get here is from the pirogue launch at Diakène Wolof, which is
3.5km off of the main Oussouye–Cap Skirring road. The junction itself is at Diakène
Diola, where any transport will drop you, and if you call the campement in advance,
they'll send somebody to pick you up from either of the Diakène villages. It would
also be possible to get here without too much difficulty from Elinkine, though you'll
have to either pay for the transfer or negotiate one for yourself at the Elinkine pirogue
launch. To make the journey under your own steam, Casamance VTT (see page 308)
organises kayak and mountain bike journeys here from their base in Oussouye.

WHERE TO STAY, EAT AND DRINK *Map, page 285.*

Campement de l'île d'Éguèye
(17 rooms) m 77 544 8080/649 7900/572 2957;
e iledegueye@outlook.fr; www.iledegueye.com.
In a wooded compound at the edge of a bolong
on its very own island, this is another fabulous
option for aspirant castaways of all sorts. The
tidy thatched rooms are whitewashed, with
mangrove ceilings & colourful accents, & food is
a focus here. B/fast is taken at the water's edge &
features locally made jams & homemade bread,
while other meals are served under the high
thatch roof of their open-air restaurant, & grilled

oyster tastings are always a possibility in season.
When you're done eating, take a guide or paddle
yourself out into the mangroves & search the
creeks for crocodiles or scan the skies for birds.
Back on land, try your hand at traditional weaving
& basketry with some of the women from the
nearest village, Diantème. Given that it's on a
deserted island & you can't exactly pop out for a
snack, accommodation is done on a HB/FB basis.
HB rates for an en-suite room are at the bottom of
this range, while rooms with shared ablutions are
in the category below. $$

ÎLE D'EHIDJE

The blink-and-you'll-miss-it village of Ehidje is barely two dozen buildings perched
on a bulge at the far eastern shore of its namesake hatchet-shaped island, and
it's known throughout the area as a centre for animist worship. As with many of
Casamance's isolated riverine islands, Islam and Christianity have made limited

inroads here as compared with the rest of the country, and the fetish priests of Ehidje are powerful figures indeed. Fortunately, they're also a welcoming bunch, and will take you to a number of sacred trees, shrines and other significant spots around the island. Where they won't take you, however, is to the cemetery. This mystical island is claimed to 'refuse her dead', and funerals for residents who have passed on involve one final pirogue journey to a nearby island for burial. Happily, you can arrange a variety of considerably less macabre pirogue trips with the campement.

Only accessible by water, the pirogue launches at Elinkine and Katakalousse (Cap Skirring) are more or less equidistant from here, so if you ring ahead of time, the folks at Campement Bouhadjitol will fetch you and return you to either where you started or the opposite for 15,000F, making it a very pleasant way to travel the bolongs and potentially cover some ground as well.

WHERE TO STAY, EAT AND DRINK *Map, page 285.*

Campement Bouhadjitol (4 rooms) ✧ 12.461702, −16.694166; m 77 608 9532/454 9432/653 0340; e mardoumbia@hotmail.com; www.ehidj.wordpress.com. Known for its cuisine, this fetching little campement is often used as a stopover on pirogue trips from Katakalousse to Elinkine, sometimes even just for a long, lazy lunch *en route*. It's well worth sticking around for a night or two, though, as it's a decidedly pleasant little corner of the delta & offers all the usual tiny-island activities like swimming, fishing, hikes, hammocks, pirogue trips, farm visits & palm-wine tapping, but also a rarer chance to explore the animist sites unique to the island. The tiled en-suite rooms aren't exactly long on character, but they're undoubtedly shipshape & carefully looked after. Rates start at 7,000F per person for just the room, but considering its isolation, most visitors are hosted on a FB basis for 16,000F. **$$**

OUSSOUYE AND EDIOUNGOU

With a perfectly central location that's an easy trip from most parts of Basse Casamance south of the river, Oussouye and its neighbour Edioungou are pleasant enough towns and worth discovering in their own right, but are perhaps of more interest to the visitor as a strategic locale from which to arrange your excursions in the region. There's good budget accommodation here, and the highly regarded tour agency Casamance VTT (see page 308) can get you out and about anywhere in the area. Calm and welcoming, it makes for an excellent base between excursions, and there's a rich cultural life to explore while you're here.

Traditionally, Oussouye has been of enormous significance to Diolas, as Manne Sibiloumbaye Diédhiou, the king of the region (once upon a time known as Floup, but this appellation is little-used today), maintains his palace here in town and commands great admiration among Diolas throughout the Casamance. It's not unheard of for him to grant tourists an audience, but this has to be arranged through the proper channels in line with the decorum and protocols of the royal court. Ask at your hotel if you'd like to try and arrange it and, while it's no guarantee you'll get to see him, there are plenty of pictures of him in local houses – he's resplendent in red, and you won't catch him in public without his ceremonial ochre gowns.

Life here for the most part rolls along at a rather sedate pace, but that's anything but the case during their two important annual festivals. First on the calendar is the celebration of the palm wine harvest in March and April, when, as you might imagine, many celebratory toasts are made, and calabashes full of the tangy stuff are passed around to all comers. The excitement here pales in comparison to the most important feast of the year, though, and Oussouye is not to be missed when La Fête du Roi (the king's festival), also known as *xulam*, comes around in September. It's among the most important dates for traditional wrestling anywhere in Senegal, and the matches draw huge, excited crowds. The dates shift slightly every year, but the tourism office in Ziguinchor can advise you on when to catch it.

Not even 1km down the road but considered a separate village, Edioungou acts as a smaller counterpart to Oussouye and is primarily known for its traditional pottery made by the women of the village. Handcrafted from clay, the pitchers, pots, jugs, cups and bowls were once sold for the amount of rice that would fill the pot you wanted to buy, but today the women will be much happier with CFA. Any of the campements can direct you here but, since it's in Edioungou itself, Campement des Bolongs is much closer to their workshops.

GETTING THERE AND AWAY Oussouye's *gare routière* is on the main road in the centre of town, and cars go back and forth between Cap Skirring (1,000F) and Ziguinchor (1,500F) from here all day. There are also less frequent vehicles headed north to Mlomp (400F) and Elinkine (600F).

TOURIST INFORMATION Just up the road from Campement Emanaye, **Casamance VTT** (33 993 1004; m 77 377 0566/646 8088/572 1196, 78 206 8143; e *casavtt@yahoo. fr; www.casamancevtt.com*) offers all manner of full-, half- and multi-day itineraries to all corners of the Casamance by bicycle, kayak and on foot. The trips originate here in Oussouye (or occasionally in Cap Skirring) and mostly travel between the various campements in the region, but there are also camping excursions on offer; all their activities and prices are detailed on their informative website.

WHERE TO STAY, EAT AND DRINK All accommodation except for Campement des Bolongs is clustered along the laterite road to Elinkine (not the tarmac route via Mlomp) at the west end of town, starting about 600m after the main roundabout. None of the hotels in town have Wi-Fi except Campement des Bolongs.

Auberge du Routard (10 rooms) 33 993 1025; m 77 228 9393. In a very pretty *case à impluvium* with shapely *banco* pillars & murals depicting all manner of traditional Casamançais scenes, rooms here have all the basics you'd expect from a rustic campement, including mosquito nets & shared ablutions, as well as a rather phlegmatic monkey on a string lazing about the compound. The ladies in charge whip up Senegalese meals on request, & it's a couple of bucks cheaper than its competitors, but a fan for the night will run you an extra 1,500F. **$**

Campement Aljowe (11 rooms) m 77 517 0267/542 4982/222 2722; e joliot@gmail.com. With a handful of happy dogs & a gazelle – yes, a gazelle – living in the gardens here & occasionally poking their noses into the rooms, this place at the edge of town will put a smile on the face of animal lovers before you're even in the front gate. Rooms are in a magnificent *case à impluvium*, large enough to have a full garden in the centre, & come in 2 types: rooms, which use impeccably

clean & cheerful common ablutions, & apartments, which are en suite & come with their own sitting area courtesy of an attached bungalow at the back. Both are lovingly decorated with a bounty of masks & artwork, & the quiet grounds are home to plenty of birds along with their 4-legged companions. All the usual meals & excursions are on offer, & it often fills up in season. Apartments are at the very bottom of this price range; rooms are in the one below. **$$**

Campement des Bolongs (Chez Hortense & William) (18 rooms) Edioungou; 33 936 9018; m 77 910 5241/571 4083/815 1615; e mamanga2907@hotmail.com; http:// patclement.free.fr/william. In Edioungou village about 1km from the main road & 700m east of Oussouye proper, this 2-storey place has a brilliant bolongside locale, & while the simple en-suite rooms (with the usual fans & nets) don't take much advantage of the view, the 1st-floor terrace resto-bar certainly does, & it's an easy place to spend a few hours with feet up & a plate of grilled shrimp to munch on. Pirogue excursions are as simply arranged as stepping out into the water, & they can also connect you to the women potters of the village. **$**

🏠 **Campement Emanaye** (12 rooms) ☎ 33 993 0047; m 77 573 6334/605 9776; e casavtt@yahoo.fr; http://emanaye.free.fr. With a name that means 'rice' in Diola, this traditional *banco* (adobe) *case à étage* (2-storey building) overlooking the bird-filled rice paddies at the edge of town is both aptly named & beautifully built. The family that runs the place is quite expert at rolling out the red carpet, & you're made to feel right at home. The en-suite rooms are simplicity itself, but remarkably pleasant given how basic they are – there's little more than beds & mozzie nets in each one, but they're kept sparkling. The resto-bar does the usual Casamançais meals upon request, & they liaise with Casamance VTT just up the road to arrange all activities. **$**

🏠 **Campement Villageois Sibendoue** (17 rooms) ☎ 33 993 0015; m 77 443 5473; opened 1982; www.casamance-tourisme.sn. The *case à étage* here is undoubtedly the most traditional in town, with everything from the *banco* stairs & pillars to the mangrove pole & beam ceilings made exclusively from local materials & in the traditional Diola style. It's also probably the simplest, & the small rooms have low ceilings &

are a bit short on windows. Still, the ambiance couldn't be any more authentic & it's a beautiful place to get up close & personal with the region's celebrated vernacular architecture. There's even a terrace you could sleep on, should you feel so inclined. Ablutions are shared & prices could hardly be lower, though if you're doing a tour with Casamance VTT they somehow still manage to offer a discount. **$**

✘ **Bar-Restaurant Buwenten** ⊕ lunch & dinner daily. This fine local eatery daubed in epic scenes of duelling traditional wrestlers sits right at the turnoff for Campement Emanaye & makes for an excellent alternative if you're looking to get away from your hotel for a meal or a drink. The co-managing couple, Fone & Maryama, do delightful versions of the usual specialities, & are known for their game dishes, though these have to be ordered in advance.

🍸 **Bar le Rond-Point** m 77 815 1615; ⊕ 08.00–midnight daily. Under the same ownership as the Campement des Bolongs, this was little more than a chilled-out corner compound with cold beverages at the ready when we stopped by, but plans to expand into a full-fledged restaurant were in the works, so it's quite likely they'll be doing simple brochettes, grills & bar favourites by the time you read this.

MLOMP

Roughly midway between Oussouye and Elinkine, Mlomp sprawls a couple of kilometres in any direction from its central (and newly paved) T junction. Notable first and foremost for its architectural achievements, Mlomp is, along with neighbouring Oussouye, perhaps the best place to see the traditional *banco* **cases à étage**, the traditional two-storey buildings made entirely from local materials native to Basse Casamance. A couple of fine examples sit on the south side of the road on the Elinkine side of the T junction, and the families who live there are happy to give you a tour for a small donation. The houses sit next to a cluster of staggeringly large kapok trees, with their sinewy, imposing roots spilling out in all directions and forming canyons easily big enough to fit a human – hide-and-seek players, take note.

Also nearby and housed in Casamance's other traditional architectural treasure, the *case à impluvium*, is the low-key **Musée de la Tradition Diola** (m *77 407 3174/250 3222/040 8700; entry 1,000F*), where the curator Yannick will introduce you to Diola history, culture and cosmology through his collection of traditional items ranging from *bombolong* talking drums to rice cultivation implements and fetish charms.

There was no accommodation here when we passed through but, if you need a quick bite while you flag down a ride, there are a few chop bars lining the road. Any vehicle going between Oussouye and Elinkine can drop you here for around 500F.

BASSE CASAMANCE NATIONAL PARK

Gazetted in 1970 and covering 50km² of low-lying mangrove swamps, mudflats, savannah and the only remaining patch of Guinea-Congo forest anywhere in Senegal, Basse Casamance National Park is a remote tropical wilderness unlike any other in the country, and was recognised as an Important Bird Area in 2001.

Because of its ecological affinity with the Guinea-Congo forests to the south rather than the Sudan-Guinea savannah and Sahelian biomes found in the north of the country, it's the only place in Senegal where a number of species more common to these areas creep up into Senegal. As far as birds go, there are more than 200 species on the checklist here, including the only recorded sightings of the vulnerable yellow-casqued hornbill (*Ceratogymna elata*), near-threatened rufous-winged illadopsis (*Illadopsis rufescens*), and splendid sunbird (*Nectarinia coccinigaster*).

Over 50 species of mammal are also thought to be present, including Temminck's red colobus (*Procolobus badius temminckii*), Campbell's mona monkey (*Cercopithecus campbelli*), African forest buffalo (*Syncerus caffer nanus*), leopard (*Panthera pardus*), Prince Demidoff's bushbaby (*Galagoides demidovii*), Beecroft's flying squirrel (*Anomalurus beecrofti*) and, in the waterways, African manatee (*Trichechus senegalensis*) and dwarf crocodile (*Osteolaemus tetraspis*) representing the reptile contingent.

All that being said, the park has been closed to the public since the 1990s due to the conflict, and remains so at the time of writing, as fears of both landmines and potential MFDC camps hidden away deep in the forest remain unresolved. Thus it's not possible to visit, and this doesn't look likely to change anytime soon, but if the peace holds it will hopefully reopen – if not in the lifetime of this edition, then perhaps in that of the next one. The **park office** (❨ *33 993 0083/832 2309*) is in Oussouye and you can get all the latest updates there.

DJIROMAIT

Less than 5km to the east of Mlomp is the tiny fishing village of Djiromait, and its next-door neighbour, the enormous and utterly inexplicable **Complexe Hotelier Djiromait** (m *77 616 0638*; e *badara.abd@gmail.com*), named after the nearby village it dwarfs in size. Built in 1983 and never opened, there are close to 100 rooms here that have bafflingly never seen a customer, partly because – at least according to one story – the roads to get here were so bad that the VIPs it was built for couldn't be bothered to come all this way. Still, you never know what might happen: in 2014 the son of the original owner appeared on *Great Entrepreneur* – the Senegalese version of *Dragon's Den* – seeking a share of 20 million CFA to kick-start operations here, though ultimately he wasn't selected. There is usually security and other personnel on site who you might be able to talk into letting you have a look around, but it's not officially open in any capacity.

To get to Djiromait village, continue until the tarmac road ends – yes, the road now services the empty hotel but not the village – and continue walking along the shore for 700m. It's little more than a fisherman's hamlet, but it sits on a phenomenally unspoilt sliver of land that juts deep into the bolongs, and is the closest jumping-off point for pirogue trips to Pointe Saint-Georges.

POINTE SAINT-GEORGES

Without a doubt the most remote village on the Casamance mainland, Pointe Saint-Georges sits all by its lonesome at the tail end of a wide peninsula jutting into the river north of Mlomp. It's a wild and wonderful spot on its own, and the chance of time slipping away from you once you get up here is all too real. The conservationists at Oceanium (*www.oceaniumdakar.com*) are very active here, and have helped to institute several fantastic tourism projects in and around the village that would be worth the visit alone.

To the west, the **Forêt de Kanoufa** spreads out for 6km along the river and a marked ecotrail has been set up here, where a trained guide from the village will escort you on anything from a 2.5-hour to a full-day hike, taking you through the forest to several ponds frequented by waterbirds, the ruins of Kouendoum village, a palm-wine tasting, and most unexpectedly, a 25m-high observation tower built into a kapok tree and accessed by a rope ladder – harnesses and safety equipment are provided. Simply put, the 360° views over the forest and river from the top are divine. The guided tour costs 2,000F, and 3,000F if you want to climb the tower (which you should).

Back in the village, the waters just offshore here are part of a community marine reserve that is home to perhaps the largest African manatee (*Trichechus senegalensis*) population in Casamance. As such, a shaded **observation tower** has been built above the river so you can watch them float by from above, and it would be easy to spend the lion's share of a breezy afternoon up here watching the river drift by whether you spot the manatees or not; even better, it's free. Discussions are under way to turn the area between here and Mlomp into a community-run protected area as well, so it's possible that there could be further projects developed in the area during the lifespan of this edition.

As far as accommodation goes, Pointe Saint-Georges no longer has an official *campement villageois* but some residents of town have stepped into the breach, and it's now possible to stay in a few different places that tread a fine line between campement and homestay. Everybody in town will be able to point you to **Chez Ousmane** (m *77 575 8395*), which has standing tents and a few simple rooms right on the river. Guests can push off and paddle around the area in their canoes, or Ousmane can guide you anywhere in the area. **Chez Clara** (m *77 613 4231/731 5393*) is another excellent option, with a garden compound just off the river and simple huts, open-air ablutions and plenty of space for camping. The proprietors, Clara and Gigi, provide excellent meals and drinks, often sourced from their own gardens. Finally, you can always call up **village headman** Pierre Diémé (m *77 522 0568*) and he'll arrange a place for you.

Getting here is the tricky part: there are footpaths leading to Pointe Saint-Georges from Mlomp, and it's a relatively undemanding 9km walk, but it could get a bit longer when you include a few dead ends and wrong turns – don't hesitate to ask for directions! Just under 5km west of Mlomp at Kagnout, there's also a 13km 4x4 track that would probably be considerably easier to follow, and is, of course, passable in a 4x4 as well. By water, Djiromait is the closest jumping-off point to get here, and if you call up one of the campements they should be able to arrange a transfer for around 15,000F. If you get a taste for the isolation up here, it's an easy hop across the river to the wilder-still islands of the Petit Kassa.

ENAMPORE AND SÉLÉKI

Leaving the tarmac behind, the twin villages of Enampore and Séléki (not to be confused with Séléti on the Gambian border) sit along a silent (and bumpy) earthen road 12km from the junction with the main road at Brin. The two villages sit on either side of a bolong from one another, and are recognised as perhaps the best place in the region to check out traditional *cases à impluvium* – supposedly the oldest one in Casamance, predating the independence era, is here in Enampore and it's no problem to stop by and visit.

Wander a bit further through the villages and you'll find traditional apiaries, a sacred forest, animist shrines, a women's garden and school (funded by proceeds from the campement), and a hand-built wooden bridge over the bolong connecting the two villages. Continue on down the road for another 6km (a worthy hike or ride in itself) and stare out into the mangroves (or head out in a pirogue to explore) from the dead-end village at Bandial.

It's also quite simple to pop over to the staunchly traditional and truly back-of-beyond feeling **Eloubaline** from here and tour the village's eight *cases à impluvium* (a fair number considering there's no more than a few dozen houses here total), and an impressively geometric carpet of rice paddies south of town. Either of the campements will take you here, or Eloubaline resident Mr. Conakry (*www.eloubaline.over-blog.com*) shows people around as well. Eloubaline has a serious shortage of fresh water, so it's likely your pirogue over will be hauling some jerrycans along with you.

Enampore's historicity is further buttressed by its status as capital of the pre-colonial Bandial (Mof Awi) kingdom and, to celebrate that fact, the first *Festival du Royaume d'Enampore* was held in February 2015. It will hopefully become an annual event, and the tourism office in Ziguinchor will be able to let you know if it does. Expect pirogue races, traditional wrestling, plenty of feasting, dancing, art, and an earnest introduction to the traditions of the area.

There are usually a couple of *ndiaga ndiayes* running the 25km between here and Ziguinchor every day, or you could try your luck hitching a lift or hiring a *djakarta* at the turnoff in Brin.

WHERE TO STAY, EAT AND DRINK

Ecocampement Solidaire de Séléki
(10 rooms) m 77 731 6830; e jeanbassene29@ yahoo.fr or asociacion@campamentos-solidarios.org; www.campamentos-solidarios.org. About 1.5km further down the road, across the bolong from Enampore & set in another huge *case à impluvium*, this is also a community-run campsite, administered in partnership with a Spanish NGO. The location overlooking nearby rice paddies & bolongs might have an edge on its neighbour, but the en-suite rooms are similar in their simplicity. They organise excursions ranging anywhere from an afternoon of birdwatching to a 3-day pirogue safari down the river. The usual complement of meals & drinks are available, & prices are a bit higher than down the road, but still in the bottom half of this range. **$$**

Campement villageois d'Enampore
(10 rooms) \33 936 9160; m 77 441 4484/416 7324; e idrissamanga60@yahoo.fr; www. casamance-tourisme.sn. Way back in 1973, Enampore was the site of the first *campement villageois* in Casamance, & they certainly chose a good spot for it. The grand *case à impluvium* here has burned down & been rebuilt since that time, & more recently it's undergone a series of very welcome renovations. All the rooms are en suite with solar power & mozzie nets, & they arrange the usual Senegalese & Casamançais meals. There's a range of activities on offer, including guided village tours & pirogue excursions. **$**

ELINKINE

With a magnificent kapok tree at the dockside, rows of day-glo pirogues beneath it and a sandy, palm-fringed shoreline with views over to Carabane, Elinkine would do well for itself in a lineup of Senegal's prettier towns. Granted you're still in the bolongs here and not on the endless sands of the coast, but as far as a spot to string up your hammock and have a swim in the river goes, Elinkine is hard to beat, and the best beach in town is at the *campement villageois*.

The bustling fishing port and market stalls here are worth an afternoon's exploration, and the multi-ethnic population of the town means you'll get to try out your Wolof (or Mandinka, or Pulaar) here if your Diola is a bit rusty. Like Diogué, the fishing outpost at the mouth of the Casamance, Elinkine is also home to a fair few Ghanaian fisherman who've made their way here seeking fishy fortunes, and they're usually more than happy to chat with you in English – look for a few Twi *nyame adom's* mixed in with the *alhoumdoulilah's* on the sides of the pirogues.

Elinkine is also the easiest jumping-off point for Carabane, so it's quite likely you'll pass through here *en route* if you plan on getting over to the island. Even if you don't feel the need to see historical-but-crumbling Carabane town, this is also the starting point for trips to Elinkine innkeeper Mamadou Ndiaye's delightfully rustic *Campement de l'Île d'Efrane* (see pages 315–16) less than 2km across the water. There are occasional vehicles headed here from Ziguinchor (2,100F), but if for some reason you can't find one or you're coming in from Cap Skirring, aim for Oussouye first and change cars there.

WHERE TO STAY, EAT AND DRINK

La Casa Star (6 rooms) 33 992 6140; m 77 647 3272; e casa.star@hotmail.fr; www.casa-star-elinkine.com. The location about 500m from the pirogue launch towards the entrance to Elinkine isn't much to write home about, but the facilities at this new place are the most sophisticated in town, & it's home to what might very well be the only swimming pool between Ziguinchor & Cap Skirring. The en suite rooms are high-ceilinged & clean, & all come with writing desk, fan & mozzie nets. The resto-bar has a big stage for live music on the weekends, *plats du jour* for 1,000F or continental fare for 4,000F, & there's both Wi-Fi & a cyber café out front. They can arrange trekking, fishing, kayaks & mountain bikes, & the prices are excellent considering the facilities on offer. **$**

Campement Villageois d'Elinkine (9 rooms) 33 993 2289; m 77 229 0776; e djibril.attaya@gmail.com; www.campementvillageoiselinkine.e-monsite.com. In a wide, mango- & palm-studded compound about 400m north of the pirogue launch, this beachy community retreat snagged the finest stretch of sand in town you can swim just a few feet from your front door, with bobbing pirogues & the undulating waves of mangrove & bolong as a backdrop. The en-suite bungalows are scattered about the compound & come with nets, & maybe even fans if the power is on. They can arrange pirogue journeys & trips to Carabane, & the resto-bar is the type of place where both the hours & the beers tend to pass quickly. Wi-Fi is supposedly on its way as well. **$**

Campement Le Fromager (8 rooms) m 77 525 6401/465 6015/61 7640. Unsignposted, but smack dab in front of the pirogue launch & under a fantastic fromager (kapok) tree that gave the place its name, this easygoing campement isn't the prettiest one in town, but Mamadou & his wife Aysatou (who does batiks and would be happy to teach you) are a welcoming pair, & the en-suite rooms are totally lacking in frills but reasonable for the price. More interestingly, they also own a delightfully isolated new campement directly across the water on Île de Carabane (see pages 315–16), & will send you over in a pirogue for 2,000F per person return (minimum 3). **$**

CARABANE

The former trading post and administrative capital of Carabane is the perfect example of a town that has quite simply been overtaken by events and lost what was once its *raison d'être*. Reminiscent of the similarly somnambulant, mangrove-choked and lost-in-time Ibo Island in Mozambique, Carabane today is a quiet village of outsized and crumbling old colonial artefacts that date back to the decades in the late 19th century when it, almost unbelievably when looking at it today, served as administrative capital for all of the Casamance before Ziguinchor took on this rôle in 1901.

Though the Diola had lived here on and off for centuries and the Portuguese had previously visited the island, the first permanent European presence on Carabane began with the opening of a French *comptoir*, or trading post, here in 1836, and one of the island's most famous landmarks, the **grave of Captain Aristide Protet**, dates to exactly this year. Marked by a small whitewashed pyramid, the story goes that the former military man was buried here standing up and facing north, so as to better see his enemies in the islands across the river, who were notoriously resistant to the French presence in the area. The **French cemetery** nearby would expand in the years to come and can still be visited today.

As the century continued and the French cemented their presence on the island, Carabane continued to grow into a rather cosmopolitan trading centre populated by Wolofs, Serers, and *métis* residents in addition to the local Diolas. A number of **warehouses** sprang up here in the second half of the 19th century to facilitate exports of rice and cotton, and today make an excellent habitat for strangler figs. As is common, with trade came religion, and the Holy Ghost Fathers founded their Catholic mission here in 1880, setting to work on the mostly ruined **Breton church** that opened here a number of years later and is today perhaps the island's most compelling landmark. The **mission** they built would fare considerably better as the years passed, and today you can not only tour, but sleep at what is now the Hôtel Carabane.

After the turn of the century and the transfer of governance and administration to Ziguinchor, Carabane began what would become a long, slow and seemingly terminal decline. Trade would eventually all but bypass the island and the population began to drift away as well; today there are less than 1,000, mostly Diola residents who call Carabane home. As with other settlements in the Casamance, most people here make their livelihoods from fishing and farming, and this simple existence is made all the more compelling when surrounded by the vainglorious relics of empires past.

The most exciting thing to happen on the island for many years was the opening of the new pier in 2015, which, while vitally necessary, is almost comically large next to the diminutive village that Carabane has become. Still, it means the ferries to Dakar and Ziguinchor can again dock here (see page 315), which goes an immeasurably long way towards ameliorating the island's crippling isolation.

This isolation also means that tourists on Carabane are typically few and far between, but those who do make it out here almost universally regard it as a favourite destination in the Casamance, and it's not hard to see why – there just aren't many places where you can explore 19th-century ruins in your swimming shorts on the way back from an afternoon canoeing through the mangroves or lazing on under the palms of the riverside beach. All the hotels listed here are a short walk from the new pier, except for Campement de l'Île d'Efrane (Chez Mamadou), which is separated from Carabane village by bolongs and mangroves, and is much more easily accessed from Elinkine.

GETTING THERE AND AWAY There are a few ways of getting to Carabane, but the easiest approach is via Elinkine, from where there are several public pirogues daily (in the morning and afternoon) for 1,000F per person, or it'll cost you 10,000–15,000F for a private hire from here. There are also occasional public boats from the pirogue launch in Ziguinchor that take roughly four hours, but if you're pressed for time it's usually quicker to head for Elinkine by road and take a pirogue from there.

The COSAMA (\ *33 984 3190*) boats (*Aline Sitoé Diatta, Aguène* & *Diambogne*) also now call at Carabane *en route* between Dakar and Ziguinchor in both directions, though if you're supposed to be on either the *Aguène* or *Diambogne,* make sure they're going to call at Carabane, as we've had reports they aren't always doing so.

Tickets to Carabane from Dakar are the same price as to Ziguinchor, while one for the much shorter journey from Ziguinchor to Carabane is half price. Full-price non-resident rates for the *Aline Sitoé Diatta* are 30,500/28,500/18,500F for a bunk in a two/four/eight-person cabin and 15,500F for a seat, and seats are the only option on the *Aguène* and *Diambogne.* For Senegal residents, it's 26,500/24,500/12,500F for a bunk in a two/four/eight-person cabin, and 5,000F for a seat.

Finally, it's always possible to hire a private pirogue from various points around Basse Casamance, and these should cost around 20,000F from Cachouane, 35,000F from Niomoune and 40,000F from Cap Skirring (Katakalousse).

WHERE TO STAY, EAT AND DRINK All the following are within a few hundred metres of Carabane's new pier, except for Campement de l'Île d'Efrane (Chez Mamadou), which is way on the other side of the island and better accessed from Elinkine.

Hôtel Carabane (32 rooms) \ 33 991 2685; m 77 569 0284/648 9634; e hotelcarabane@ yahoo.fr; www.hotelcarabane.com. Housed in a whitewashed 1880 building just west of the pier, Carabane's most venerable hotel was once its Catholic mission, & the en-suite rooms here are still as no-nonsense & scrupulously tidy as you'd expect from a group of nuns, but the bar is (one would guess) considerably more active. The ceiling fans are a nice touch, & thanks to their new solar panels they even run all night! All the rooms cost the same, so ask for one upstairs with views over the riverside gardens – a divine place to sup on one of their seafood meals. It's also a good place to arrange pirogue trips & the only place in town with Wi-Fi. Rates approach the middle of this range. **$$**

Badji Kunda (9 rooms) m 77 537 3702/418 9841; e flora@badjikunda.com; www.badjikunda. com. This rootsy campement on the west end of town is covered in the artwork of the late founder Malang Badji & it's a great place to hang around, beat a drum, take a dip in the river & allow yourself to sink into the molasses-slow pace of Carabane life. They've got both en suites & rooms with shared ablutions, & all are simple, clean, cheap & steps from the river. The resto-bar does all the usuals, & don't be surprised if there's a jam session after dinner. **$**

Chez Héllèna (8 rooms) m 77 654 1772; www.chezhellena.wix.com/chezhellena. For more than 20 years, the proprietress here, Marie Hélène,

has graced guests with her irresistible smile & delectable home-cooked meals. The old adage about it taking more muscles to frown rings quite true in this cheerful riverside haunt, & it's more than likely you'll wind up smiling right along with her (especially after you've been fed). Rooms are decorated with a mishmash of mosaics & murals, & all come with nets & either en-suite or shared ablutions. You can't beat the prices, especially the full board rate – only 10,000F per person. **$**

Campement de l'Île d'Efrane (Chez Mamadou) [Map, page 285] (14 rooms) m 77 525 6401/465 6015/61 7640. If you've ever dreamt of having a deserted island all to yourself, this fleetingly small teardrop of sand at the edge of Île de Carabane might be just the place. Known as Efrane, & surrounded by river in front & mangroves behind, there's nothing here but pure, splendid isolation, and it's deceptively easy of access to boot. Less than 2km across the river from Elinkine, it's under the same ownership as the dockside Campement Le Fromager (see page 313), & they'll punt you over & back (when you're good & ready) for only 2,000F per person (assuming 3 passengers). Rooms consist of a cluster of reed huts equipped with mozzie nets & not much else, & ablutions are out in the fresh air. Unlike many deserted island residents, however, you're unlikely to be bored – nightly campfires, fishing, drumming, pirogues, & nearly 60km^2 of bolongs to explore right behind you are

12

315

only a few of the temptations that might lure you out of your hammock. Or not. **$**

🏠 **Le Barracuda** (12 rooms) m 77 310 2424/659 6001; e amath.barracuda@yahoo.fr; http://carabacuda.free.fr. The first place you'll see getting off the boat, this angler's hangout is a great place to put down your pack whether you plan on getting hooks in the water or not. The proprietor, Amath Mbaye, has been here since 1992 & is not only an expert fisherman, but a man about town;

& he can set you up with anything from excursions to see the animist *féticheurs* across the river in Itou to mucking in with the traditional farmers, carvers & cloth dyers here on Carabane. Rooms are all en suite, sleep 2–3, & come with nets, fans & views over the water. As you might imagine, the restaurant is a pescatarian's dream. Fully customisable fishing trips go for 50,000/80,000F half/full day, with a maximum of 3 passengers. **$**

AFFINIAM

Surrounded by an impressive expanse of rice paddies on the north bank of the Casamance in what was once the kingdom of Blouf, this kapok-studded village of Diola farmers is only 10km from the Trans-Gambia as the crow flies but, because of the wide bolong labyrinths so common in the Casamance, it's a circuitous (though admittedly very scenic) 25km trip on bouncy dirt roads to get here by car. Given its proximity to Ziguinchor on the south bank, a trip here by pirogue is a quick and easy way to get out on the water if you don't have too much time to dedicate to puttering around the region by boat.

Once you're here, you're in good hands at the *campement villageois*, and they'll roll out the red carpet for your tour around the village. Many people here work in crafts and trades, and it's easy to visit traditional blacksmiths, weavers, dyers, carvers and others at work here. If it's in season (roughly October to June), you can head out with the experts and spend the day tapping palms (and imbibing the produce) as well. There's a Chinese-built barrage on one of the channels nearby (you'll pass over it if you come in by road), and birders should know that Affiniam is also close to the *Île aux Oiseaux*, a sandbar that's above water at low tide and frequently visited by the Anhinga (*Anhinga anhinga*), African sacred ibis (*Threskiornis aethiopicus*), various types of cormorants, pelicans, kingfishers and more.

The real one-of-a-kind attraction here, though, is actually in the neighbouring village of Djilapao, down a winding set of footpaths some 10km away. The relief-covered **Jean Yéyié Badji's house** (✪ *12.609695, –16.370372; entry 500F*) is the arguably the region's most striking *case à etage*, and, along with the smaller building next door, is lovingly decorated with all manner of colourful scenes of daily life and mythology of the Casamance carved into the banco walls. Jean himself has since passed on, but his family tends the homestead with care and gives visitors a brief and well-informed tour around the property. Getting here alone, either by foot, bike or pirogue (just ask the campement), is eminently worth the detour, and they sell some cold drinks down here as well should the trip leave you parched.

Public pirogues cross to and from Ziguinchor every day except Thursday and Sunday. Check in the morning to see what time they're leaving; the trip is about 90 minutes each way and dirt cheap.

🏠 WHERE TO STAY, EAT AND DRINK

🏠 **Campement villageois Diaméor Diamé** (16 rooms) ✪ 12.654337, –16.356081; ☎ 33 936 9619; m 77 567 0044; www.casamance-tourisme.sn. First built in 1978 & rehabbed 2005,

the wide (15m across!) *case à impluvium* here sits under a magnificent fromager (kapok) tree along the road to the pirogue launch & takes fine advantage of its *banco* construction with a series of colourful reliefs carved into the sides. Rooms have mozzie nets, solar lights & shared bathrooms, & they do the usual meals on request – it's a great place to try *caldou*. There's a small craft boutique on site, & they can take you around the village to meet the local artisans. **$**

COUBALAN

In a rarely visited corner of Casamance at the edge of the Forêt des Kalounayes, Coubalan sits, much like villages throughout the region, tucked away between farm, forest and bolong, and splays unhurriedly along a quiet dirt road east of the Trans-Gambia Highway. It's a great launch pad for bike trips into the 166km² Forêt des Kalounayes just north of the village, or for a pirogue exploration of the upper reaches of the Casamance River where tourists rarely tread (or paddle). Another rewarding itinerary, especially on a bike, would be to simply follow the riverside roads and paths northeast of here (where there are a couple other compact campements) until you eventually wend your way back up to the Trans-Gambia.

The laterite road to get here starts at the RN4 in Tobor and arcs its way some 40km northeast through a dozen-odd villages along the Casamance and Soungrougrou Rivers until it reaches Ndieba, from where the RN4/Trans-Gambia Highway is 8km to the west, and there's a little car ferry that goes east across the Soungrougrou on the back route to Marsassoum and eventually Sédhiou. Coubalan itself is more or less equidistant between Ziguinchor and Bignona, and there's public transport that covers the 22km from either town and to neighbouring villages along the road, as well as public pirogues from the launch in Ziguinchor a few times weekly.

WHERE TO STAY, EAT AND DRINK

⌂ Campement villageois Ankadji (6 rooms) ⊕ 12.665555, −16.163028; ☏ 33 936 9473; m 77 578 2091/895 8811/736 4964; e badianepape@ hotmail.com; www.casamance-tourisme.sn. With common spaces & the restaurant in a gorgeous *case à impluvium* & rooms in standalone duplex bungalows nearby, this bolongside retreat at the east end of Coubalan is a beautiful example of what *campements villageois* can be. Here since 1979, it was fully overhauled in 2009 & rooms come with the usual solar lights & mosquito nets, as well as private terraces & clever local touches like calabash sink basins in the en-suite bathrooms. The standard meals are on offer, & if a swim in the bolong isn't enough excitement for you, they do bike & pirogue trips to the Forêt de Kalounayes & surrounding villages, along with fishing, hikes & visits to local artists & artisans. There are also small campements up the road in Ouonck & Ndieba (m 77 503 1694; e campementouoncketdieba@ hotmail.fr), & you can set up a circuit between the camps here. **$**

PETIT KASSA

With only two places to stay in the whole archipelago and no more than a small handful of villages overall, this clutch of islands on the north bank of the Casamance River between Diogué and Niomoune is about as remote as it's possible to get in the Casamance, and anyone who makes the effort to get out here will be amply rewarded with unspoilt calm, untouched landscapes, and an authenticity that defies imitation.

At the east end of the archipelago, the animist village of Niomoune sits on an island of its very own, crisscrossed with a lush quilt of rice paddies and surrounded by thick mangroves and pretzel-shaped bolongs on all sides. Continuing west, the oblong middle island is more than a dozen kilometres from end to end and home to several villages, all linked by a cluster of footpaths wending their way through the forests and farms: Bankassouk, Haere, Kande and Itou at the southern end, which is the most famous of the lot, known far and wide for its powerful fetish priests.

Finally, Diogué sits isolated at the very mouth of the Casamance and is home to a sizeable fishing & drying operation, and a number of Ghanaian fisherman who have rounded many capes to call this windswept spot home.

GETTING THERE AND AWAY There are public boats from Ziguinchor to Niomoune and Haere (also called Ahèr) on Sundays, Mondays and Thursdays, which return to Zig on Wednesdays, Saturdays and Sundays. They all depart from the pirogue launch (ancien bac/Embarcadère de Boudody) in Ziguinchor around noon (give or take a good while), but get there earlier to make sure you get a spot.

As always, private pirogue hire is an option from most any point along the river, and it's about 35,000F to get here from Carabane and roughly 25% less from Pointe Saint-Georges. With a hired boat, you could even theoretically continue into the Karone Islands (see page 323) and Kafountine to the north from here.

⌂ WHERE TO STAY, EAT AND DRINK

⌂ **Gîte Rural de Eringa** [Map, page 285] (5 rooms) Haere; ✣ 12.670554, −16.683637; m 77 545 1214/584 5461; e ylanneau@euz.be; http://propoze.free.fr. Lost deep in the seemingly infinite creeks & channels of the Petit Kassa, it really doesn't get much further-flung than this Belgian-Senegalese family-run campement on the shores of the Ounembene Bolong. A *New York Times* reporter managed to make it here for a 2015 feature on Casamance, but very few other visitors ever do, & it's a very convincing antidote to the mass tourism of Cap Skirring or Saly. Set in the bush outside the diminutive village of Haere, birds & little else punctuate the stillness of this extraordinary locale. Meals are taken communally, & there's plenty of opportunity to wander up & down the island & the river as you please. All the usual campement amenities are on offer – namely simple rooms with mozzie nets & a hammock everywhere you might need one. There's room for

campers, the owners can accommodate sailboats, & strangest of all, you can even – but shouldn't – get online. Rates at the bottom of this range. **$$**

⌂ **Campement Alouga** (4 rooms) Niomoune; ✣ 12.641505, −16.651212; m 77 576 0977/539 7128; e alouga1@yahoo.fr; www.alouga.com. Even though it's among the remotest spots in the Casamance, stepping off the boat here feels like coming home to a long-lost family at this bewitching campement stashed away on the tiny island of Niomoune. The simple whitewashed rooms come with hammocks out front, mosquito nets inside, & are painted in whimsical murals of local animals. All rooms use eco-loos & a delightful outdoor shower under a tree. They do eminently affordable pirogue, hiking & camping excursions deep into the Petit Kassa & beyond (including the Kalissaye reserve), & a day-long excursion for two starts at 13,000F. There are tents available for rent, & meals here are a treat. **$**

WHAT TO SEE AND DO More than perhaps anywhere else in Casamance, the islands of the Petit Kassa are simply a place to take a deep breath and revel in the profound isolation of your surroundings. The villages are all linked by walking paths, and you could easily spend a very pleasant day or two simply traipsing through the pinprick-small & overwhelmingly friendly villages along the way, from Itou up to Bankassouk. If you're feeling intrepid, it's also possible to hike between the two campements, but since they're separated by the Ounembene bolong, you'll have to find someone to punt you the 250m across to the next island, which shouldn't be too difficult. Both campements can also arrange rewarding cultural visits to local artisans, musicians, farmers and *féticheurs*.

When you're done wandering the rice paddies and footpaths, there are ample opportunities to get out on the water with pirogue and fishing trips, including excursions to the mouth of the river at Diogué. Also, though it's more typically accessed from Kafountine via Kassel, birders should know that the Réserve Spéciale des Oiseaux de Kalissaye (see pages 323–4) at the end of the Saloulou peninsula is actually closer to here than it is Kafountine, and both campements can set up pirogue trips to it.

KAFOUNTINE

With what seems like a higher percentage of dreadlocks than any other town in the country, Kafountine has a beachy rasta vibe that seems to at least partly spill over from The Gambia 15km to the north. As such, it's an easygoing and unaffected place, and it may well be the laissez-est of laissez faire towns in the Casamance, which is something of an accomplishment given the region's affinity for tranquillity and a good fête. Unfortunately, along with the irie vibes come a few hangers-on and false friends out for personal gain, known by the perfectly tailored and generally delightful Gambian term of *bumsters*. This is offered simply as a note of explanation; the *Kafountinois* are as warm and welcoming as anyone else in the Casamance, and with a postcard-perfect beach, active music and arts scene, and easy access to the mangrove swamps and ornithological reserves to the south, Kafountine packs a serious punch for backpackers and nature lovers alike.

It's also a living, breathing, working town, and its frenzied fishing port is the largest in the Casamance. Standing on its own, it's larger than many entire villages listed in this chapter, and it's nothing short of a sensory overload to wander through the rows upon rows of drying racks, smoking sheds and a small army of loaders dispatching their slippery cargo into the awaiting trucks with remarkable grace and agility. Your eyes will burn, your nose will pinch, and the absolute stillness as you walk out the other side at the south end of town will have never felt so fresh.

It's a reasonably active little town all year long (by Casamance standards, anyway), but it really comes alive every February during the Kafountine festival, when the whole village awakes to the beating of a thousand djembes and the stamping of just about every foot in town. (So there might be less than a thousand djembes, but the foot part is a guarantee.) Over several days in February, the whole town comes out to sing, drum, dance, wrestle and perform, and traditional troupes of all stripes flock here from all corners of the region.

TOURIST INFORMATION It's rather out of date, but **www.kafountine.info** has good information on culture, attractions and daily life in Kafountine and the surrounding villages.

GETTING THERE AND AWAY Kafountine is connected to the RN5 at Diouloulou by a surfaced road in reasonably good nick, and it's possible to get a *sept-place* all the way to Ziguinchor for 2500F. Otherwise, rattletrap *ndiaga ndiayes* ply the route to Diouloulou all day for 600F and you can connect to another vehicle headed north towards Seleti or south to Ziguinchor from there, though Diouloulou is rather languorous as far as crossroads go, so be ready for a wait.

Coming from The Gambia, *ndiaga ndiayes* trundle between Brikama and Kafountine on the back roads west of Séléti, crossing the border at Darsilami, where there is Gambian, but no Senegalese immigration. It's legal to cross this way, but something of an inconvenient route for travellers, as if you enter Senegal here it's advisable to make the trek up to Séléti for an entry stamp as soon as possible after you arrive in Kafountine: a nearly 70km round trip, though Kafountine hotels can often help with this.

As such, we'd recommend instead that travellers coming down from The Gambia pick up one of the *ndiaga ndiayes* in Brikama headed for Jiboroh, where there's a

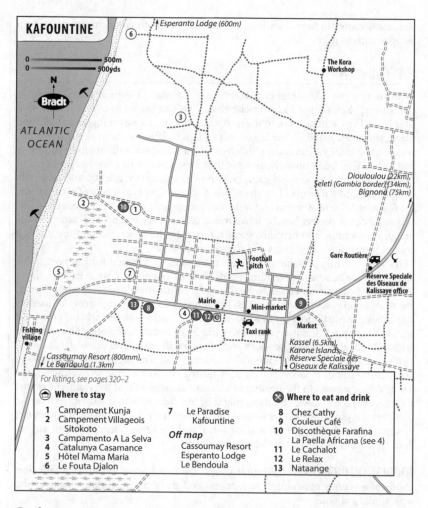

KAFOUNTINE

↑ *Esperanto Lodge (600m)*

0 ——————— 500m
0 ——————— 500yds

N

Bradt

ATLANTIC OCEAN

The Kora Workshop

*Diouloulou (22km),
Séleti (Gambia border) (34km),
Bignona (75km)*

Football pitch

Gare Routière

Réserve Speciale des Oiseaux de Kalissaye office

Mairie

Mini-market

Market

Taxi rank

Fishing village

*Cassoumay Resort (800mm),
Le Bendoula (1.3km)*

*Kassel (6.5km),
Karone Islands,
Réserve Speciale des
Oiseaux de Kalissaye*

For listings, see pages 320–2

🏠 **Where to stay**

1 Campement Kunja
2 Campement Villageois Sitokoto
3 Campamento A La Selva
4 Catalunya Casamance
5 Hôtel Mama Maria
6 Le Fouta Djalon
7 Le Paradise Kafountine

Off map

Cassoumay Resort
Esperanto Lodge
Le Bendoula

❌ **Where to eat and drink**

8 Chez Cathy
9 Couleur Café
10 Discothèque Farafina
La Paella Africana (see 4)
11 Le Cachalot
12 Le Relax
13 Nataange

Gambian immigration post. Senegalese immigration at Séléti is 3km down the road from here, and taxis run between the posts if you don't want to walk. From Séléti, it's not hard to get a lift to Diouloulou, and from there you can finally connect over to Kafountine.

If you're in a hurry to get back up to Dakar, there are direct buses that depart a couple of times weekly for about 8,000F – your hotel will know when the next departure is.

🏠 **WHERE TO STAY** *Map, above.*

🏠 **Esperanto Lodge** (8 rooms) m 77 635 0280/305 6756; e esperantolodge@gmail. com; www.esperantolodge.com. In an utterly tranquil corner of bush between the beach & a bolong some 2.5km north of central Kaf, this is worlds away from the rootsy Rasta vibes that predominate in town. Instead, guests are treated

to a marvellous collection of upmarket thatch bungalows, tastefully decorated in African art & sculpture, with full-length mirrors & wardrobes, mangrove ceilings, & smooth ochre *tadelakt* floors. Some have their own terraces overlooking the *bolong*, so birders could happily spend a day here without stepping off their front porch. The restaurant is known for its excellent seafood, & is worth the trip up here for a meal even if you stay elsewhere. Rates straddle the low end of this range & top of the one below, depending on the season. Recommended. **$$$**

🏠 **Campamento A La Selva** (6 rooms) m 77 714 5934; e alitibialaselva@gmail.com; www.sites.google.com/site/campamentoalaselva. In a rustic, tree-covered compound just north of town, rooms here are set in a big round building done up in thoroughly rastafied décor, & are basic but reasonably well cared for, with en-suite showers but shared toilet facilities. Meals are available on request, but there was a full resto-bar under construction when we checked in. At 10,000F per person, it's a bit pricier than most of its campement competitors. **$$**

🏠 **Campement Kunja** (15 rooms) m 77 609 3647/521 2930/724 8716; e info@campementkunja.com; www.campementkunja.com. Hidden away a few blocks north of the centre just as the town starts to give way to the forest, this place is barely 900m from the main road but the preponderance of fruit trees & vines make this agreeably rustic compound feel miles away. Rooms come in 3 categories but differ primarily in size; all are spotless & come with fans & nets, & all but the bottom category are en suite. Staff are warm & welcoming, & Senegalese meals are available on request at their resto-bar. Rates start at the bottom of this range. **$$**

🏠 **Cassoumay Resort** (4 rooms) m 77 241 8532/108 2846; e info@cassoumay.com; www.cassoumay.com. Directly on the delightfully peaceful stretch of beach about 1.5km south of town, you'd hardly even know this sleepy little resort was here, but it's actually some of the better-value accommodation in town, particularly in the off-season when rooms come at a deep discount. The rooms are very nicely refurbished & come with fans, nets, fridge & private terraces. The resto-bar does the usual meals, & they've also got a self-catering house that sleeps 4, should you come in a group. There's good birding & fishing on this stretch of shore (they can arrange both), & prices are in the bottom half of this range. **$$**

🏠 **Hôtel Mama Maria** (6 rooms) 📞 33 994 8541; m 77 517 0374; e hotelmamamaria@hotmail.com; www.hotelmamamaria.com. At the west end of town just north of the fishing village at the edge of the lagoon, this Spanish-owned retreat sits in a sandy garden dotted with palms & bougainvillea only 100m from the beach. The homey rooms are decorated in tapestries & batiks, & all come with en-suite ablutions, fans & mozzie nets. They open on to a fantastic veranda with *chaise longues* & hammocks facing the water. There's the usual range of drumming, dancing & pirogue trips, & an impressive library to choose from, though Romance languages are *de rigueur*. Meals run the gamut from Spain to Senegal, & prices are towards the middle of this range. **$$**

🏠 **Le Bendoula** (12 rooms) 📞 33 994 4598; m 77 269 5006/540 3114; e info@hotelbendoula.com; www.hotelbendoula.com. About 2km south of town & just past the Cassoumay Resort (but before you reach the defunct La Korone), this place feels a bit conventionally resort-like, but it's hard to argue with the location, & the tiled rooms are reasonably equipped with fans, nets & private terraces. Unfortunately we've had credible reports of theft from the rooms here. Prices in the bottom half of this range. **$$**

🏠 **Le Fouta Djalon** (8 rooms) m 77 368 3386; e lefoutadjalon@yahoo.fr; www.hotelsenegallefoutakafountine.e-monsite.com. The vibe here is on the sleepy side, but with big brick bungalows in a sandy beachfront compound, hammocks aplenty & campfires by night, it's hard to not get sucked in to the somnambulance. Rooms are simple but proper & all come with mosaic floors, nets & fans. If you read French, there's a sizeable library at your disposal, & if not, we were told that 'Wi-Fi is coming'. The usual land & water activities can be arranged, & the Franco-Senegalese kitchen has a reputation for quality. Rates towards the top of this range. **$$**

🏠 **Le Paradise Kafountine** (5 rooms) m 77 327 2123; e suka30@hotmail.com. In a centrally located compound overflowing with greenery, this hippyish haven has been a reliable backpacker hangout for more than a decade, & would certainly make a good stop if your primary goals in town are beating a drum & putting your feet up in a hammock. The bungalows are a bit musty but comfortable enough, & they're all set up with nets, fans, & murals on the walls. A room with shared bath goes for 6,500F per person, while an en-suite double is 15,000F. They do a good range of meals & can arrange excursions & drum lessons. **$$**

🏠 **Catalunya Casamance** (2 rooms) m 76 864 0055/77 163 5244; e catalunyacasamance@

yahoo.com; www.catalunyacasamance.org. With a couldn't-be-more-central location on the main drag through town, this Catalonian charitable organisation does a little bit of everything, but its main focus is running adult literacy courses for the community. As far as tourism goes, it's one of the best places in town to arrange activities, especially if you want to hire a bicycle or explore the islands south of Kassel. Rooms are set behind the centre's *case à impluvium* classrooms in neat little tiled bungalows (with kitchen) that sleep 3. All come with nets & fans. Prices are just about the best in town, but it's often full. **$**

🏠 **Campement Villageois Sitokoto**
(12 rooms) **m** 77 403 6218/949 7793; **e** sitokoto@hotmail.fr; www.casamance-tourisme.sn.
Kafountine's representative of the community-owned *Fédération des Campements Villageois*, this place is starting to look a bit long in the tooth next to its neighbours & would make a welcome candidate for some refurbishments, but serious penny-pinchers are well catered for, as their rooms with shared bath are definitely the cheapest in town. (The en-suite rates are more or less in line with the other campements.) The location is fabulous & if djembe's your jam, there's no shortage of rhythmically inclined folks around to give you a lesson. **$**

✗ **WHERE TO EAT AND DRINK** *Map, page 320.*
✗ **Couleur Café** 📞 33 994 8566; **m** 77 316 6111; **e** couleur.cafeym@yahoo.fr; ⏲ 08.00–22.00 daily. With a dining room appointed like a safari lodge that got lost on its way to East Africa, the interior here can feel a bit stuffy, but the gardens at the back & terrace out front are perfectly pleasant spots to while away some time over a beer (& free Wi-Fi), or with one of their *très raffinée* French dishes, which are easily among the most sophisticated in town. Mains start around 4,000F, & you've got plenty of choice, including *lapin aux champignons* (rabbit & mushrooms) & *barracuda à la provençale* (barracuda Provençal-style). They've got a few well-kept rooms at the back as well (**$$**).
✗ **La Paella Africana** **m** 77 163 5244. Connected to the Catalunya Casamance Centre, this is the place to be on Sun, when they serve up heaped pans of *paella* with a flair that rapidly (& happily) gives away their Iberian origins. They also do espresso coffee, & what is almost certainly the only *sangria* in town. The hours were in flux when we stopped by, but they're open more than just Sun & will probably have new hours by the time you read this.
✗ **Nataange** **m** 77 895 4455; ⏲ 07.00–22.00 daily. This tiny little café squeezed next to a shopful of African clothes & souvenirs is painted in white with Moroccan-style lanterns & a Rastafied clientele. They do a small selection of pastries, fresh juices & sandwiches, but don't expect *Dakarois* patisserie sophistication.
✗ **Le Cachalot & Musée Diola** **m** 77 448 4423; ⏲ 08.00–21.00 daily. Hidden away down a back road near Campement Kunja, this idiosyncratic little place is worth a stop for the food – which includes a couple of veggie options – but even more so to have a chat with Fred Sagna, the proprietor & curator of an oddball collection of Diola fetish shrines & artefacts (including a traditional catafalque & the *ekonting*, a stringed instrument widely considered to be forerunner to the modern banjo) set around the mud-pillared garden terrace. Meals tend towards traditional Senegalese fare & brochettes, but they also surprise with their excellent homemade jams.
✗ **Chez Cathy** 📞 33 994 4017; **m** 77 564 6103; ⏲ 08.30–late daily. With a winning smile, a flair for presentation & entirely unexpected free Wi-Fi, the charming proprietress here has more or less cornered the market on excellent & unpretentious local food in Kafountine. Shrimp & calamari are the specialities of the house, but they rustle up an equally satisfying chicken & chips, or a budget-beating *plat du jour* for 500F.
✗ **Le Relax** **m** 77 500 9185; ⏲ 10.00–14.00 & 16.30–22.00 daily. This new little place on the main drag has a funky, laid-back vibe (it's certainly in the right town), & serves up a rotating menu of affordable French cooking in its eclectic dining room & on the streetside terrace. Sat is the best deal, when there's a 3-course *menu* for only 4,000F.
☆ **Discothèque Farafina** **m** 77 570 3438; ⏲ midday–late. Long regarded as the fanciest of Kafountine's nightclubs, though that doesn't mean so much in this rootsiest of towns, this place is where Kafountine's kids come to drink & dance the night away. Worth a peek for the people-watching alone, & the building's retro exterior is one of the most notable façades in town.

WHAT TO SEE AND DO Kafountine's laid-back take on life is exactly what many people are looking for when they arrive here, but it's also likely enough to make a Type A person break out in hives unless you make a serious effort to schedule some activities into your day beyond adjusting your position in the hammock. Life for locals often revolves around the beach, & it's no different for tourists. Start with a swim, check out the fishing village at least once, and rent a bike or take a tour down to the Karone Islands or the Réserve Spéciale des Oiseaux de Kalissaye (see below).

It's also a fantastic place to learn an instrument, with djembe being the obvious choice, though it's also home to **The Kora Workshop** (m *77 489 5368;* e *info@ thekoraworkshop.co.uk; www.thekoraworkshop.com*) where, much as the name would indicate, you can learn not only how to play, but how to build your own kora. They've got an array of fully customisable tuition options with master players (details on their website), and if you've got a serious interest, these can be booked as a full-trip package, taking advantage of their comfortable guest rooms and home-cooked meals.

AROUND KAFOUNTINE Along a decent laterite road some 7km southeast of Kafountine, the largely Christian village of Kassel sits facing a seemingly impenetrable thicket of mangroves across the water and serves as the gateway to the **Karone Islands**, a sparsely populated and fiercely traditional smattering of islands and villages sandwiched between here and the islands of Petit Kassa further south. The villages hidden behind the wall of mangroves here are inhabited largely by animist Diolas and, much like in the rest of the delta, subsist primarily from fishing and rice cultivation, but these remote islands have also developed a not-unfounded reputation as centres for illegal marijuana – *yamba* as it's known locally – plantations. It's available rather openly here and you won't have any shortage of offers should you visit, but it would be very unwise to attempt to carry any out of the islands with you, especially if you plan on crossing The Gambia, where border checks are often thorough and you can expect a serious problem if found to be carrying drugs.

The main villages here are Hillol, Kouba, Boun, and Saloulou. There's no accommodation in any of them, so most visits are day trips, but you could certainly camp (always ask permission first), or even find a place in someone's house at a pinch. Hillol and Kouba are on the same island directly south of the pirogue launch at Kassel, and it's 200F or less if you catch the occasional public pirogue across, while chartering one for yourself is more like 2000F for the 1.5km trip. Once on the island, it's a straightforward 6km walk or *djakarta* ride through forests, fields and rice paddies to Hillol, and a further 2km to Kouba. Boun and Saloulou are north of the Saloulou peninsula at the west end of the archipelago & only accessible by boat, which will start at around 40,000F for a charter from Kassel.

Though it's possible to get here on your own, it's certainly simpler and very possibly more rewarding to go with the local guides at Catalunya Casamance/ Kafountine VTT, who offer day bicycling trips from Kafountine to Hillol and Kouba. An interesting itinerary would be to continue on from here down to Bankassouk and the Petit Kassa – you'd almost certainly have to charter your own pirogue, but you'd be so thoroughly off the beaten path that we'd love to hear about it – if you go this route, send us a note and let us know how it went!

Also in the neighbourhood, at the very southern tip of the Saloulou Peninsula (also called the Pointe de Sankoye) and bordered to the east by the Kalissaye bolong, you'll find the **Réserve Spéciale des Oiseaux de Kalissaye** (Kalissaye Avifaunal Reserve) (℅ *33 994 4546/832 2309*). Gazetted in 1978 and listed as an

Important Bird Area by Birdlife International in 2001, this 16ha ornithological reserve covers the very southern end of the peninsula and a handful of shifting sandy islets offshore, and though it's been poorly studied as compared with other sites in Senegal, at least one count reported between 20,000 and 30,000 breeding pairs of royal terns (*Thalasseus maximus*) here in 2004, which would be among the largest breeding colonies in West Africa. Other studies have failed to come close to matching these numbers, however, and observations in spring 2011 indicate numbers in the hundreds or low thousands are considerably more likely. There's been no permanent staff based in the reserve since the 1990s, so regular observations simply don't exist.

In addition to the royal terns, the same 2011 count found numbers of great white pelican (*Pelecanus onocrotalus*), African spoonbill (*Platalea alba*), greater flamingo (*Phoenicopterus roseu*), pink-backed pelican (*Pelecanus rufescens*), Caspian tern (*Hydroprogne caspia*), Sandwich tern (*Thalasseus sandvicensis*), little tern (*Sterna albifrons*), slender-billed gull (*Larus genei*), lesser black-backed gull (*Larus fuscus*), great egret (*Ardea alba*), and grey heron (*Ardea cinerea*) among others living or breeding here. Birdlife International estimates a breeding-season population that includes 500 pairs of western reef heron (*Egretta gularis*) and 6,000 pairs of great white pelican (*Pelecanus onocrotalus*). Back on land, both green sea turtle (*Chelonia mydas*), and loggerhead sea turtle (*Caretta caretta*) have been recorded breeding here, and as with many of the surrounding rivers and bolongs, African manatee (*Trichechus senegalensis*) is present as well.

Since there are no staff in the reserve, visits have to be arranged through the office in Kafountine (number listed on page 323) or any hotel in either Kafountine or Petit Kassa should be able to make this happen as well. Setting out from Kassel, expect to spend about two to three hours in each direction getting to and from Kalissaye and, since the reserve is quite small, in practice a visit will usually take in portions of the surroundings, such as Presqu'Île aux Oiseaux and possibly Lac de Kati and Île de Kati south of the peninsula.

The area around Kassel is also notable as a heronry, and is sometimes marked on maps as **Réserve Ornithologique de Kassel**, covering the mangroves to the east and south of Kassel village, where unknown, but presumably large, numbers of grey heron (*Ardea cinerea*) and western reef heron (*Egretta gularis*) descend to nest during the breeding season.

ABÉNÉ

Just up the shore from Kafountine (you can even walk it if you're feeling hardy) on the way to the Gambian border, the beachside retreat of Abéné in many ways feels like a smaller, more peaceful version of its southern neighbour, which really is quite the accomplishment considering that Kafountine is already the land of peace, love and rasta-coloured tank tops. Still, Abéné does seem to manage it somehow, and walking the long dirt road that forms the village's spine makes for a 2km promenade of endless greetings, more than likely a few stops for beer, maybe a couple of sales pitches from *bumsters* slipped down from The Gambia (see pages 334–5), and an entirely genuine, unaffected feel-good vibe that strikes at the core of what a beachside getaway in West Africa should be.

Life here moves slowly for most of the year (a trend in Casamance), and if you're looking for a place to slow down, collect your thoughts, and perhaps even write that novel you've always meant to, Abéné wouldn't be a bad choice. Things really perk up a couple of times a year, though, starting with the unofficial 'Bob Marley Day' which takes place every year on 11 May, when what seems like the whole village turns out to celebrate the anniversary of Robert Nesta's passing with a lot of music and probably a little *yamba* to boot.

From then on it's back into Abéné's easy everyday groove until the end of December, when the **Abéné Festivalo** takes over the village entirely with contingents of drummers, dances, musicians, artists and fans from all over the region and the world, and the music goes on late into the night. The festival runs from Christmas until after New Year's Eve every year, and some traditional spirits like the *koumpo* have been known to make an appearance as well. Whether or not you make it here for the festival, Abéné's musically inclined population means it's an excellent spot to do African drum and dance lessons as well. Souvenir shoppers or folks with an interest in the visual arts should swing by the unassuming **Marché Artisanal**, which is home to about a dozen workshops with a dusty but alluring selection of masks, paintings and more. There are usually a few more craft sellers along the main road too, some with a noteworthy and highly unusual selection of sculptures made from circuit boards, discarded electronics and more.

Beyond relaxing in a hammock and possibly drumming or dancing, swimming would have to be the second most popular activity in town; the **Aire Marine Protegée d'Abéné**, which covers 119km² offshore, ensures the windswept beach here remains a captivating and productive place for tourists and fisherman alike, and most of the campements can easily line up fishing excursions if you'd like to get out on the water.

Finally, if you're coming back from the beach and can't bear another round of greetings on the main road, taking a wander through the farms, fields, and homes hidden away on the sandy paths radiating off the main drag is a worthwhile way to get happily lost and perhaps even, if you're lucky, find the enormous **sacred fromager**, known as *Bantam Wora*, held dear by many residents. If you're not so lucky, ask nicely and someone might show you the way.

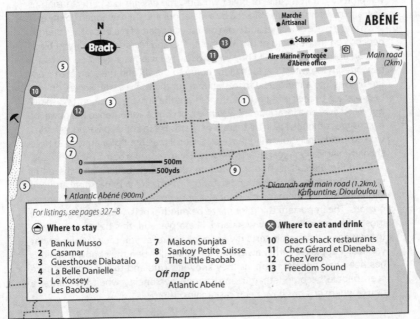

ABÉNÉ

For listings, see pages 327–8

🛏 **Where to stay**
1 Banku Musso
2 Casamar
3 Guesthouse Diabatalo
4 La Belle Danielle
5 Le Kossey
6 Les Baobabs
7 Maison Sunjata
8 Sankoy Petite Suisse
9 The Little Baobab

Off map
  Atlantic Abéné

✖ **Where to eat and drink**
10 Beach shack restaurants
11 Chez Gérard et Dieneba
12 Chez Vero
13 Freedom Sound

TOURIST INFORMATION For a rundown of different accommodation activities, and more general information about Abéné, the village has a website: http://abenevillage.wix.com/abene.

GETTING THERE AND AWAY Any transport headed for Kafountine can drop you off at Diannah, which is the junction village for Abéné. There are two turnoffs from the Kafountine–Diouloulou road from which you can reach Abéné; if you're using public transport, alight at the one in Diannah village (closer to Kafountine) as that's

---

GRIS-GRIS

Simon Fenton (www.thelittlebaobab.com), author of Squirting Milk at Chameleons *(Eye Books, 2015; www.eye-books.com)*

I live in Abéné, a village in the Casamance region of southern Senegal, where you do not need to scratch far beneath the surface to find traditional animist beliefs. This is a land of genies, spirits and spells. Almost everybody wears a *gris-gris* for spiritual protection.

West Africa was animistic before Islam and Christianity showed up at the party, and as in the rest of the continent, many of the traditional beliefs were absorbed and maintained within the new religions. It's not difficult to understand why the Abrahamic religions gained a foothold. Both Christianity and Islam offer Africans an afterlife, whereas traditional beliefs aren't so clear-cut, offering only the world of spirits and ancestors.

Although I've read that some Senegalese don't agree with *gris-gris* – they still believe they work but see them as blasphemous against God – I've yet to meet them. Everyone I know wears them and there's a *gris-gris* for every occasion – to find a lover, to become pregnant, for protection and even very strong ones that will protect you from knife or bullet wounds. The *gris-gris* is a perfect fusion of new and old. Koranic script blessed by a Marabout and then wrapped tightly and sewn into a piece of leather and worn on a specific part of the body. The strength depends on the strength of the Marabout. A Grand Marabout, a skinned black cat and a small fortune could buy you invisibility. I was recently asked to wear a new *gris-gris* to protect me for a flight home to the UK and I've seen men work themselves into a trance and then stab and cut themselves with knives, only to be protected by their *gris-gris*. In fact, once I was the only person unhurt when my bus rolled over on a local journey, which was of course attributed to the power of my *gris-gris*, although I didn't like to ask why those of the other passengers hadn't worked. Incidentally, following that crash, a local marabout pronounced I'd have children in Africa. One year later, to the very day, my son was born in Abéné village.

It's quite difficult to find information about such beliefs, and there are some things here I can never understand. *Gris-gris* are very personal and you shouldn't discuss them too much or else your enemy may prepare a counter-*gris-gris*. The important thing for me to be mindful of is, whatever my beliefs, most Africans believe they work and, like a placebo, this belief does make them work. Witchcraft is certainly not a joke here, as you can't laugh at what you fear. People do wither away and die or fall ill when they know a *gris-gris* has been cast against them, as they know it's true and that it works. I have seen people become lethargic and change personality when they enter a house where *gris-gris* have been cast against them.

where the *djakarta* guys hang out, and it's also slightly closer if you're walking the 2km into town.

If you're self-driving, note that all the roads in Abéné except the main drag can be very sandy and present a risk of getting stuck if you're not in a 4x4.

WHERE TO STAY Map, page 325.

Only a couple of places in town have Wi-Fi, and they're mentioned below.

Atlantic Abéné (6 rooms) m 77 578 7560; e atlanticabene@yahoo.fr; www.atlanticabene. com. Fisherfolk headed to Abéné would be well advised to make this isolated beachside place their first port of call. Just over 1km south of the main road, there's hardly any bustle to be removed from in Abéné, but this end-of-the-road spot does the trick nonetheless. With a 3-bedroom house & standard rooms in a *case à impluvium* for rent, it's a solid bet for self-catering groups, as well as couples or individuals who can take meals at their terrace resto-bar. Ablutions in the *case à impluvium* are shared, & the fresh whitewashed rooms come with the usual nets & fans, along with a writing desk. They've got 2 boats & all manner of fishing trips can be arranged, plus ornithological excursions & more. Rates at the lower end of this range. **$$**

Banku Musso (3 rooms) m 77 167 0024; e regulat@mac.com www.regula-trutmann.ch. Presided over by a Swiss artist-shaman, this new-agey organic retreat is so in-tune with its surroundings that the earthen *banco* walls would credibly seem to have risen from the ground of their own volition if not for the exquisite reliefs & traditional motifs that adorn them. The rooms are simple as can be & use shared ablutions, but are dotingly well kept & beautifully appointed. The owner gives painting & potting lessons, & her works can be seen throughout the house & tranquil gardens. It's certainly the most characterful accommodation for the price, which hovers at the very bottom of this range. **$$**

Guesthouse Diabatalo (12 rooms) m 77 618 8328; e info@guesthousediabatalo. com; www.guesthousediabatalo.com. With an organic garden, thick stands of bamboo, & no shortage of hammocks in their thickly forested compound, this Dutch-run place is a cool & shady retreat less than 500m from the beach. The rooms are nothing to shout about, but all are set up with nets, fans & bright textile accents. It's a good address if you want to tag along for a palm-wine

tapping, learn how to make batiks, & cook, drum or dance. Rooms with shared bath start at €12.50, while an en-suite dbl goes for €30. **$$**

Le Kossey (10 rooms) m 77 223 8052/226 6312; e abyissa@hotmail.fr. Long one of Abéné's more comfortable options, the beachside gardens here certainly don't suffer from a lack of charm. The en-suite duplex bungalows are scattered throughout the compound & are comfortably equipped with the usual nets & fans, along with small terraces overlooking the grove of coconut & eucalyptus trees where dozens of songbirds make their homes. The comfortable restaurant & bar does all the seafood usuals. Rates edging towards the centre of this range. **$$**

Les Baobabs (8 rooms) m 76 382 8024; e bienvenubalacoune@gmail.com; www. facebook.com/lesbabobas. In a wide, palm-studded compound with a windswept beachfront location 500m south of the main drag, it's a real surprise that this place is as sleepy as it is. The en-suite bungalows are simple & cheerful, with canopy beds, fans & nets. The beach bar does good seafood meals & has satellite TV, Wi-Fi, a billiard table, & once you're sick of all that, a stupendous ocean view. It's good value, with rates at the very bottom of this range. **$$**

Maison Sunjata (5 rooms) ℡ 33 994 8610; m 77 609 8070. Just south of the main road & across the (sandy) street from the beach, the high-ceilinged thatch-roof rooms here are clean & spacious, & come in either an en-suite or 2-rooms-sharing-1-bath configuration. The grounds are well-kept & unpretentious, & Oumar, the English-speaking owner, is a cheerful soul who is happy to help with any questions. There's a pleasant terrace restaurant as well, or you're just a couple hundred metres from Chez Vero or some of the beach-shack restaurants. Rates at the bottom of this range. **$$**

Sankoy Petite Suisse (12 rooms) m 77 831 1515; e sankoypetitsuisse@gmail.com; www. sankoy.info. In a comfortable compound just off the main road, this place suffers from a distinct lack of character but is otherwise very adequate at the price. The en-suite rooms feel rather sparse & impersonal, but are reliably clean, & meals can be taken either in the restaurant or on your terrace. They can also arrange local excursions. Prices at the bottom of this range (& dipping into the category below out of season). **$$**

🏠 **Casamar** (16 rooms) 📞 33 994 8605; m 77 565 8939. Right next door to Maison Sunjata, this is broadly similar but slightly more basic & dated-feeling than its neighbour, with Spartan rooms set in a few blocks around the sandy compound & nary a frill in sight. Ablutions are shared between 2 rooms each, & the resto-bar up front does the usuals upon request. Difficult to complain about at the price. **$**

🏠 **La Belle Danielle** (25 rooms) m 77 115 1281; e belledanielle69@yahoo.com. Next to Abéné's main junction as you come in from Diannah, this unassuming campement is about as basic as it gets (& so are the prices), but the manager, Mamadou Konta, is also the head of tourism in the area, so it's actually a great place to get info about excursions & activities in the area. The concrete rooms have beds with nets & little else, & Senegalese meals are available on request. They might have some bikes for rent, but these

didn't seem very operational when we stopped by. **$**

🏠 **The Little Baobab** (See ad, page 346) (2 rooms, more u/c) ⊕ 12.991560, −16.726961; m 77 341 4356/066 9497; e fentonhq@gmail. com; www.thelittlebaobab.com. It takes a bit of following your nose though Abéné's sandy, crisscrossing footpaths to get here (just ask anyone in town for Chez Simon), but rarely has there been a place so worth the hunt. Less hotel than happy homestead, your hosts here are British author Simon Fenton, his Diola wife Khady Mané & their 2 young children, who waste no time in making you feel a part of the family. They've got simple rooms with shared ablutions or an en-suite bungalow, as well as plenty of space between the fruit trees for campers. Simon is a consummate guide & storyteller, & can arrange anything from casual village tours to a border-to-border trek through the Casamance & beyond, along with language, dance & music lessons. Alternatively, you can while away the day in a hammock or on their shady 1st-floor terrace with a book from their fabulous English-language library. They whip up the usual Senegalese specialities, & meals can be taken communally with the family or in a quiet spot on your own. Warmly recommended. **$**

✖ WHERE TO EAT AND DRINK *Map, page 325.*

✖ **Chez Gérard et Dieneba** m 77 441 0256/274 7473; ⊕ lunch & dinner daily. Dishing up what are very likely Abéné's only hamburgers as well as a considerably more sophisticated range of French-inspired fare, this unassuming place on the west end of the main drag is a favourite stopover for local expats. Meat & fish dominate the menu, & mains start around 3.000F.

✖ **Chez Vero** m 77 617 1714/424 6388; ⊕ lunch & dinner daily. Right at the junction of Abéné's main drag & the coastal track, this low-key eatery is a well-loved standby for locals & visitors alike. There's a colourful bar, bougainvillea-draped terrace & a rotating selection of Senegalese &

continental favourites, & even some Lebanese thrown into the mix as well.

🍷 **Freedom Sound** m 77 505 0280/889 1845; ⊕ 18.00–late daily. There are plenty of little drinking holes scattered around Abéné, but with its big bright courtyard, outdoor stage & thoroughly Rastafied vibe, this is the place in town for live music, & a fab spot for a drink should you fancy getting out of your lounge chair & shaking a leg. Wed is reggae night (to be honest, most nights are), every Sat there's a live band, & Sun there's a jam session you're welcome to join, with koras, djembes, *akontines* & guitars.

NIAFOURANG AND KABADIO

The northernmost settlement on the Casamance coast, Niafourang sits just south of the Gambian border at Kartong, which is a quick 3.5km hop north across the narrow Allahein River. Dominated by a stunningly large fromager (kapok) tree in the village square, Niafourang is a delightfully scenic clump of houses wedged between twisting bolongs to the east and palm-punctuated rice paddies and the Atlantic Ocean to the west, and most of the few hundred Diola inhabitants here make their livelihoods either out in the paddies or on the waves with a paddle.

This idyll has been in serious jeopardy since 2004, however, when, under the Wade administration, a Chinese-Australian mining consortium was granted an exploration licence for zircon mining in a 410km² area of the Casamance shoreline, centred

THE *KONKOURAN*

Simon Fenton (www.thelittlebaobab.com), author of Squirting Milk at Chameleons *(Eye Books, 2015; www.eye-books.com)*

In central Abéné, doing some shopping on a day not especially different from the last, I nonchalantly regarded a procession of older local women dancing in formation to the beat of drums, but there was an unmistakably strange atmosphere in the air - an air of nervousness. As the low rumble of fear continued to spread through the neighborhood, I saw people running, and then I saw it – the *konkouran*. A flash of red as a hairy creature ran between two buildings. 'Fat-Fat!' (quick, quick!) cried my partner, Khady, as several adults and about 20 children ran into a house and barricaded ourselves indoors.

Often, this is a playful creature that chases kids around. Parents warn them that the *konkouran* will get them if they're naughty. But this was not a good *konkouran* – this one was hitting people. There was genuine terror in the air, and when I went to peer at it through the window, I was dragged back into the darkness.

For a while now, I've been trying to figure out what the *konkouran* is and why it terrorises people. I presumed it was ceremonial and wouldn't actually hurt someone. I made to go out and look, and it was at that point that a French friend had some sharp words with me: 'You have Khady and a baby – don't be stupid'.

'But I know karate,' I replied, like an idiot.

'Okay. Well, just so you know, a tourist was severely beaten up a couple of years back, and the *konkouran* have machetes. The police won't do anything, nobody will do anything. You are part of the community now so you have no excuse. You need to take these things seriously.'

That told me. We discussed further and I learnt that the *konkouran* come to a village to give a warning. For example, if kids pick mangos before they are ripe and that upsets the year's harvest, the *konkouran* will come and teach the village a lesson. If you keep out of its way it won't hurt you. If you go towards it or take a photo, anything could happen.

Local people believe it is a genuine spirit, not some guy in a Chewbacca suit. Although there are moves to ban them from hurting people in cities, it will be years before that trickles down to the villages. And, like a real life Boogeyman, parents warn their children, 'Be good or the *konkouran* will get you'.

By now the *konkouran* had moved down the street and I ventured outside. From a safe distance I saw it walking towards the procession of women who were still dancing. It seemed to be covered in red hair. One man taunted it and wouldn't move. Maybe, like me, he knows karate. If so, he forgot it and the *konkouran* struck him to the ground and beat him. I was too far away to see how serious it was, but he lay there for some time after the devil had gone, then got up, dusted himself down and wandered off.

on – but extending far beyond – the coastal dunes of Niafourang. Operations were scheduled to begin in 2015, but have so far been delayed in part thanks to concerted resistance from residents of Niafourang, Kabadio and surrounding villages. It remains to be seen what will happen to the project, but there's no better reason to visit now, before this bucolic backwater may be drilled, scraped, sifted, and carted away.

On the other side of the bolong about 2.5km to the east of Niafourang, its sister village Kabadio stretches some 800m along the road, in a patchwork of forest and farm fields that spread out in every direction until reaching the fringes of the bolong, where Kabadio's beautiful campement faces the sunset. Between the two villages, you'll pass the wooded *Cimetière des victimes du Joola*, a shady and contemplative space where several dozen victims of the 2002 disaster are interred.

GETTING THERE AND AWAY Coming from Gambia, pirogues cross back and forth from Kartong throughout the day, and you can look for a *djakarta* or walk the 3.5km south into Niafourang from here. It's legal to make the crossing but, since there's no Senegalese immigration on this side, you'll still have to get to Séléti to do passport formalities – ask your guesthouse for help with this.

From the Senegalese side, any vehicle headed between Diouloulou and Kafountine will drop you at the junction village of Bandjikaky, from where a reasonable laterite road leads just over 2km to Kabadio and a further 2.5km to Niafourang. There's no public transport along this route, so hire a *djakarta*, walk or call your hotel and they'll send someone (probably also on a *djakarta*) to fetch you.

WHERE TO STAY

Campement villageois Mansa Dambel (4 rooms) Kabadio; ✪ 13.054258, −16.720336; ☎ 33 995 8439; m 77 535 9755/709 3241; e campementdekabadio@yahoo.fr; www.campementkabadio.wordpress.com. With a delightfully remote perch at the eastern edge of a bolong some 3.5km northwest of Kabadio itself, it's actually only about 1.5km to get here from Niafourang but, regardless of direction, the only way here is by either forest tracks or following the eastern shore of the bolong. Built in 2012, it's the newest of the *campements villageois* & has two stilted wooden rooms at the edge of the bolong & 2 bungalow-style rooms further inland, all of which are en-suite, come with mosquito nets, & sleep 3. They can set you up with guided hikes in the surrounding forests & farms, pirogue trips in the bolongs, or visits to local artisans' village workshops. **$**

Chez Mikky (2 rooms) Niafourang; m 78 129 6419/77 495 6481; e africajack@hotmail.com; www.chezmikky.com. Sequestered down a forest track about 500m south of 'downtown' Niafourang, this Dutch-owned bolthole feels miles from anywhere & looks like a little Moroccan casbah that somehow got itself lost in the jungle. Surrounded by a farm of fruiting cashews, citrus & more, the rooms here are basic but breezy & immaculately clean, &

while the showers are en-suite, the 2 guest rooms share a bathroom. They do excellent Senegalese- or European-style meals on request, & are happy to go out of their way setting up activities & whatever else you'd like to do, including a visit to check out the school they're building. Campers are welcome & fees are nominal. No Wi-Fi. **$**

Tilibo Horizons (7 rooms) Niafourang; m 77 501 3879; e tilibo-horizons@hotmail.com; www.facebook.com/casamance.horizons.9. This long-serving campement on the bolong is a gentle return to Senegal if you're coming down from The Gambia, as the amenable owner, Ousmane, is perfectly happy to chat with you in English. He's also a leader of the anti-mine initiative, and can bring you up to speed on the latest developments. The campement itself has a fabulous location overlooking a bolong and is just a few steps (over an inordinately picturesque bridge) to the beach, some 200m across the mangroves. The bungalows are basic and a bit musty, but serviceable at the price, and the resto-bar does some nice and simple seafood dishes. Along with their associated tour agency, Casamance Horizons, they can line up hikes, fishing, kayaking, pirogue trips and excursions to meet local artists and artisans. It's also a good place to get rid of your leftover Gambian Dalasi. No Wi-Fi. **$**

CASAMANÇAIS ARCHITECTURE

Though this steamy, low-lying region might seem an unlikely architectural Mecca, Casamance has given birth to a building unlike any other in Africa, known as the *case à impluvium*. Shaped like a doughnut, *cases à impluvium* have an inward-sloping thatched roof not unlike a giant funnel, opening on to a central courtyard which can range from as small as a metre to more than a dozen metres wide. Here you'll usually find a small garden and a set of basins set up to make the most of the prodigious rainstorms that buffet the region and collect the rainwater funneled in off the roof. It's an elegant and quite fetching solution to the region's water needs, and the interiors tend to be cool and quite pleasant – especially the ones with a garden inside. The magnificent double *case à impluvium* at the Alliance Franco-Sénégalaise is undoubtedly the region's finest, while the oldest is in Enampore, and the arch-traditional village of Eloubaline is dominated by them. Many have been set up as campements, and you can spend a night in a *case à impluvium* in more than a half-dozen villages around Casamance.

The other of Casamance's two architectural treasures and another singularity in the region is the *case à étage*. Made exclusively from banco mud, wood and other local materials, these two-storey houses may not exactly be skyscrapers, but getting inside one to see the thick, rounded banco pillars, open courtyards, and wood beam ceilings will give you an appreciation for the craftsmanship that went into their construction and, in a land of one-storey dwellings, the inspiration required to build them in the first place. Though they're not as common as the *cases à impluvium*, there are some excellent examples to be seen in Affiniam and Mlomp, and you can get a good night's sleep on the first floor at either of the two *case à étage* hotels in Oussouye (see pages 308–9).

AROUND NIAFOURANG AND KABADIO Just across the border in Kartong, 300ha of lagoons and decommissioned sand mines between the Allahein River and the coast were recognised as an Important Bird Area in 2001, and the **Kartong Bird Observatory** (✪ *13.092137, –16.763418*; m *(+220) 733 2225/700 3147 (The Gambia)*; e *kartongbirdobservatory@hotmail.co.uk; www.kartongbirdobservatory. org*) has been here as an observation and ringing station since 2010. Their checklist at Kartong is a plump 357 species long, including northern carmine bee-eater (*Merops nubicus*), green-headed sunbird (*Cyanomitra verticalis*), and the black-legged kittiwake (*Rissa tridactyla*); while it's easy enough to make a day trip up here, given the traditional disdain with which birds treat national borders you can be certain to benefit from a fair bit of spillover from their checklist, even if you opt to stay on the Senegal side of the border. If you do cross over, the Observatory runs half- and full-day birding tours either on foot or on the river, and they've spotted 260 species from the terrace of their café-bar alone.

DIOULOULOU

Diouloulou is the type of place where watching the paint dry might be the most exciting thing going on in town on any given day – that is if anyone ever painted. Still, the town spills appealingly over the edge of a wide, lazy, eponymous bolong, and would certainly be a pleasant enough spot to while away a day or two with no set agenda, especially if you're here during the Diouloulou festival, held sometime over November and December every year.

Practically speaking, it's home to the closest accommodation to the Gambian border at Séléti, so it makes for a convenient staging point if you need to put up for a night on your way to or from The Gambia and don't feel like trucking over to Kafountine or Abéné. Most transport waits near the cluster of market stalls at the foot of the bridge, but vehicles to Kafountine are parked just out of sight (the *djakarta* guys will conveniently neglect to tell you this) a few metres up the road to Kaf.

🏠 WHERE TO STAY, EAT AND DRINK

🏠 **Kent Motel** (8 rooms) m 77 615 0895/960 2765; e info@kent-motel.com; www.kent-motel.com. Supposedly named in honour of the original owner's roots in the garden of England, today the management of this appealing riverside stopover has links to Sweden. Set about 250m from the central junction & facing a wide patch of mangroves (replanted by Oceanium, see page 92) fringing the expansive Diouloulou bolong, the hammocks & huts here have an enviable position with views over the river & bridge. Rooms are in simple & spotless duplex bungalows with fans, nets & en-suite ablutions, & the welcoming staff at the resto-bar will whip you up all the usuals upon request. Rates at the bottom of this range. **$$**

🏠 **Auberge Chez Myriam** (10 rooms) m 77 608 9521/633 9864. About 800m from the main junction & *gare routière* & just next to the Total fuel station & the military roadblock *en route* to the Gambian border at Seleti, this basic place has cheapness on its side & not a whole lot else, though it's surprisingly pleasant for the price, which, at 6,000F for a double, doesn't even crack our lowest price category. Some of the rooms are in bungalows while others are in a more standard block, but they're broadly similar in character (all come with fans & nets) & priority should be given to rooms on the far side of the compound from the potentially noisy restaurant & bar. **$**

BAÏLA

On the RN5 about two-thirds of the way between Diouloulou and Bignona, most people blow though Baïla without a second look, but this Diola village is a pleasant enough stopover if you want to break your journey and it's home to the **Campement villageois Lambita** (⊕ *12.898990, −16.352291;* \ *33 936 8076;* m *77 544 8035/618 7730; www.casamance-tourisme.sn;* **$**), which was founded here in 1977 and rehabbed in 2005. They've got new en-suite rooms and older ones using shared ablutions, but the nominal price difference between the two is eminently worth the upgrade. They can put on dance performances, take you out into the village to consult with the local *féticheurs* or paddle you out into the bolong for a day of fishing, and naturally they whip up big bowls of the usual Casamançais favourites. Don't just breeze by if you end up here in April, though, as this is when they put on their annual festival. It's a magical time to visit – drumming, dancing and supernatural visitors like the *koumpo* are the unquestioned rulers of the night.

BIGNONA

More junction town than tourist attraction, Bignona is where you'll come to draw money if you're staying in Abéné, Kafountine or any of the other villages up north, as it's home to the first ATM you'll encounter coming down from the Gambian border. It's an important road junction between the RN5 and RN4/Trans-Gambia Highway, and if you're coming from up the RN5 and headed for Sédhiou, Kolda or beyond, you'll more than likely change vehicles here. Additionally, as of 2015, all public transport between Ziguinchor and Kolda was travelling via Bignona

SECURITY IN THE CASAMANCE

As of mid-2015, FCO advice still advised against road travel in the Casamance west of Kolda, except the route between Cap Skirring and Ziguinchor. Our personal take was that this felt somewhat out of date and not especially reflective of the current situation, but it's absolutely advisable to seek information on the current situation (locally, if possible) when planning your visit and itinerary. During the course of our research in late 2014, we spent numerous weeks in all parts of the Casamance travelling by both public transport and private car, and aside from an increased (and for the most part professional) military presence as compared with the rest of the country, there was no sign of instability, nor of an increased risk to travellers. The RN4 and RN5 are still under a dusk-to-dawn curfew, however, and there's now a hotline (*33 994 1228*; m *77 173 7529*) you can call in case of danger on the roads (though what kind of assistance would be on offer is unclear).

Since the on-again-off-again rebellion kicked off here in 1982, any number of abortive peace accords and ceasefires have been signed and declared, but to little lasting effect. Most recently, hard-line leader Salif Sadio, who heads the largest MFDC faction, declared a unilateral ceasefire in April 2014 and, though there has yet to be an official peace treaty or a laying down of arms, more than a year since its declaration the ceasefire so far shows all signs of holding.

Still, the presence of a 33-year rebellion does mean that there's a fair few more guns floating around the region than in the rest of the country, and this has occasionally translated into opportunistic and non-political armed banditry on the roads. However, a combination of waning support for the rebels, increased investment in the region, and improved connectivity to Dakar has meant that today Basse Casamance is as peaceful as it's been in years – indeed, many Senegalese, Casamançais and Dakarois alike will tell you that you're at greater risk in the streets of Dakar than on the creeks of Casamance.

Additionally, landmines remain a small but serious problem; while the remaining mined areas have been demarcated and mapped, their removal has run aground on disagreements between the Senegalese armed forces and the MFDC and for the moment seems to be stalled. Still, to put the problem into perspective, 600,000m^2, representing half of the total mined area, has already been cleared, leaving only what is an estimated 0.6km^2 remaining. Despite the limited area, sporadic deaths and injuries do still occur, most recently in August 2014 when seven people were killed when the *calèche* carrying their wedding party triggered an explosion. More information (in French) is available through the Centre National d'Action Antimines au Sénégal (CNAMS) (*www.cnams.org*).

Ultimately the decision is up to you, but should the vagaries and vicissitudes of the political situation allow, Basse Casamance is an area truly unlike any other in the country, and not to be missed if you can help it.

and Carrefour Diaroumé, not on the RN6 south of the Casamance River. Note that this could very well change when the on-going reconstruction of the RN6 is complete.

Still, even if your reasons for putting up here are purely practical (like the roads closing after dark), there's good cheap accommodation on offer, and the frenetic

Many trips to Senegal, either by necessity or by choice, are combined with a visit to The Gambia, so while travellers planning to spend an extended amount of time here should check out Bradt's dedicated *The Gambia* guide by Philip Briggs, it's also worth knowing several of the primary routes that visitors to Senegal might use to transit between northern Senegal and Casamance.

To begin with, the only place you can transit The Gambia *without* purchasing a Gambian visa is on the Trans-Gambia Highway (RN4) that runs between Kaolack and Ziguinchor. Your passport will still be stamped at both border crossings, and there's a 1,000F fee payable to Gambian authorities on entry and exit at Farafenni and Soma, but no visa is required.

At any other border crossing, visitors must purchase a Gambian visa on arrival, even if they plan to continue directly through to Senegal. The single-entry visa is good for seven days and costs either 20,000F or 1,000 Dalasi, but note that it comes out significantly cheaper when you pay in Dalasi – €21 vs €31 when paying in CFA (as of June 2015). It should be available at all official Gambian border crossings.

Though it takes many steps, perhaps the most popular route between northern Senegal and Casamance besides the Trans-Gambia Highway is on the RN5 from the border at Karang (Senegal)/Amdallai (The Gambia). Note that if you get stuck here (the ferries to Banjul stop running in the evening, so there's no point in continuing south after sunset, and you may not even be allowed to do so), there's good accommodation for 400 dalasi (6,500F) per person per night at the NGO-run **Helping Lodge** (m *(+220) 994 5174/360 7148 (The Gambia)*; e *helping-lodge@helpingcharity. org.uk*; *www.helpingcharity.org.uk*) 2km south of Amdallai in Fass village. If you're stuck on the Senegal side, there's supposed to be a basic guesthouse in Karang, but your best bet would be to head 23km north to Toubacouta (see pages 188–91), where there's an excellent choice of accommodation.

Given the Amdallai / Karang crossing's relatively small size, it's a surprisingly hectic border; you should avoid the throng of crooked moneychangers here like the plague and convert your CFA to Dalasi inside a shop. From Amdallai, shared taxis run to Barra, where you can take either the somewhat dodgy government ferry or the also-dodgy private pirogues the nearly 5km across the mouth of the Gambia River. Once in Banjul, *ndiaga ndiayes* and shared taxis leave for Westfield Junction in Serrekunda (⊕ *13.446105, –16.674522*) and Brikama from the traffic circle at the junction of Rene Blain and Nelson Mandela Streets (⊕ *13.452761,*

city centre is home to a couple of forlorn-looking roundabout monuments and a whole lot of hustle and bustle. Both of the hotels are in the *Quartier châteaux d'eau* at the north end of town, just east of the RN5 heading towards Diouloulou, and about 1,200m north of the main junction with the RN4.

🏠 WHERE TO STAY, EAT AND DRINK

🏠 **Auberge Kayokulo** (7 rooms)
📞 33 990 4242; m 77 516 7167/236 5789;
e kayokulo@hotmail.com; www.facebook.com/ aubergekayokulo.guesthouse. With immaculate high-ceilinged rooms that all come with satellite TV & good free Wi-Fi, this family-style compound is an unexpectedly excellent option in town. It's all very simple, but lovingly done & it shows. Rooms come with nets & fans, AC is available for an extra 5,000F, & the chequerboard-tiled resto-bar does a good selection of Senegalese favourites upon request. The switched-on owner splits his time between Bignona & Ireland, so he's a great English-language resource on the area when he's around.

−16.575535), 1km from the port. If you're ultimately aiming for the Séléti border, get a vehicle going all the way to Brikama if you can.

Once in Serrekunda, you've got a couple of choices. To head for the sleepy river border at Kartong (The Gambia) / Niafourang (Senegal), you can pick up a vehicle at Dippa Kunda Station (✆ *13.434285, -16.691265*), which is 2km past Westfield on Sayerr Jobe Rd at Kololi Rd (Bakoteh Junction). Otherwise, simply change for a Brikama-bound vehicle at Westfield Junction.

From Brikama (✆ *13.275319, −16.648308*) there are occasional direct vehicles to Kafountine (see pages 319–24) via the border post at Darsilami (The Gambia), and regular *ndiaga ndiayes* to the larger border at Jiboroh (The Gambia) / Séléti (Senegal). If you somehow wound up here but are aiming for Kartong, it's also possible to get a vehicle to Gunjur and then to Kartong from here. Once you reach Séléti, you're back on the RN5 and it's easy to get onward transport to Diouloulou and beyond.

Note very well that the borders at Kartong and Darsilami are both **only** staffed by Gambian immigration, and you'll have to figure out a way to formalise your entry to Senegal (usually by a trip to Séléti) if using either of these crossings. Nearby hotels in Niafourang, Abéné and Kafountine can usually help with this.

Further east, the Trans-Gambia highway is a piece of cake by comparison. If you're not on a vehicle going all the way through, just go straight from the border at Keur Ayip (Senegal) / Farafenni (The Gambia) to the ferry, cross over, and find another vehicle heading to Soma (The Gambia) and onwards to Senoba (Senegal).

East of here, your options drop off considerably. We're not aware of any official border crossings between The Gambia and northern Senegal east of Farafenni, so if you wanted to head east through The Gambia, it's easiest to start by crossing to the south bank of the river at either Banjul or Farafenni and getting on a vehicle bound for Janjanbureh (Georgetown) or Basse Santa Su from here. Brikama station is a good place to do this, and vehicles all pass through Soma *en route*. (Of course, it's also possible to head east on the less-travelled north bank and cross over on one of the ferries at Janjanbureh, Basse Santa Su or Fatoto as well.) Following the south bank, you can get to Kolda via the Brikama Ba (The Gambia) – Pata (Senegal) crossing, and Vélingara via Basse Santa Su. Beyond Basse, completists and adventurers can aim for Fatoto and the rarely-used border crossing at Nyamanari (The Gambia)/Manda (Senegal) at the very eastern tip of the country.

Excellent value, with prices towards the bottom of this range. **$$**

🏠 **Auberge Kayanior** (6 rooms) ☎ 33 994 3014; m 77 650 3246; e kayanior@yahoo.fr; www.kayanior.over-blog.com. Right around the corner from the Kayokulo, this homey place is a very serviceable option, but a discernible step down from next door. The décor is pure, unapologetic kitsch, & your room may or may not come with a framed portrait of holographic fruit on the wall. It will, however, have a fan & mozzie net, be quite clean, & have what appears to be a purely theoretical Wi-Fi connection. The resto-bar has all

the standard meals & drinks, & a single room costs the same as the equivalent fan room next door, but couples will save a few thousand CFA on the double rate here. **$**

✗ **Bar-Restaurant Le Jardin** 🕐 10.00–late daily. With a 500F *plat du jour*, chicken & other meals starting around 2,000F, & a rough-&-ready dance floor that's known to attract punters until the wee hours, this place serves up a (very) unvarnished slice of Bignona life along with its heaped bowls of rice & frosty Gazelles. It's opposite the 2 hotels on the other side of the RN5.

CAMPEMENTS VILLAGEOIS

Scattered around nearly a dozen villages in the region, the *campements villageois* that have come to be synonymous with travel in Casamance today were the brainchild of Adama Goudiaby and Christian Saglio, who in the 1970s went about setting up this network of community-owned camps, all of which were built in a local style and run by local people, with profits going directly into the communities that hosted them. It was a fabulous idea and well ahead of its time, but like many things in Casamance, the camps suffered greatly in the 1980s and 90s when conflict dominated the region and tourists by and large stayed away.

The *campements* were given a new lease on life in the mid-2000s, however, when peace negotiations with the MFDC began and a tranche of funding was earmarked for the rehabilitation of the camps, most of which had been sorely neglected or even destroyed during the war. Today, the *Fédération des Campements Villageois* (FECAV) (m *77 556 4096;* e *fecav2012@gmail.com*) has nearly all of the original camps up and running again, and it's possible to explore much of the region by simply following the trail of *campements*.

Though quality can vary greatly between them, the camps are often set in *cases à impluvium* or *cases à étage* (see page 331), and these are some of the most characterful accommodation options in the region. Additionally, even though the rustic rooms are already the best deal this side of The Gambia, most will also allow camping for around 2,000F/tent. The FECAV website has thorough information on prices and offerings at each of the camps, and the Casamance Tourism (*www.casamance-tourism.sn*) office in Ziguinchor can make reservations or propose an itinerary between the campements. Most of them have also recently been signposted – keep an eye out for Casamance Tourism's multicoloured logo.

THIONK-ESSYL

Some 30-odd kilometres (on a brilliant new road) west of the turnoff from the RN5 at Tendième, Thionk-Essyl is the most important centre in the Blouf region – named after the historical Diola kingdom with its capital here – and is also among the largest urban centres in Basse Casamance, though it's still lush with vegetation & 'city' would be a wholly inappropriate term. Slung along a 2.5km main drag between the Forêt de Tendouck to the east and some of the many tributaries of the Diouloulou bolong to the west, it gets precious few visitors and remains well off of any tourist itineraries, but serves as a reasonably substantial trading centre for the region.

And while it may be true that traditional 'sights' are in short supply, Thionk-Essyl and the villages around it would still make a worthwhile stopover for anyone interested in seeing a workaday slice of Casamance life in a comparatively large Diola town, where traditions still run strong & the outside world seems far away indeed. The basic **Campement Abeukoum** (m *77 605 93 57;* e *campabeucoum@ hotmail.fr; www.les-amis-de-thionck-essyl.org*) is the only accommodation in town, and you can pick up road transport here from Ziguinchor, Bignona or potentially the turnoff at Tendième, with public pirogues from Zig a possibility as well.

13

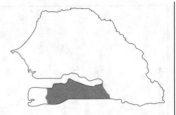

Haute Casamance

Long a black hole on most tourist maps, Haute Casamance is geographically larger than its downstream cousin, but there's little tourist industry to speak of, and traditional sights here are few and far between.

As you move inland from the sparkling beaches and never-ending creeks of the Casamance river delta, the landscape of steaming mangrove swamps and kilometre-wide waterways becomes ever so gradually less lush, slowly leaving the equatorial forests of Basse Casamance behind in favour of the more familiar (if your trip started in Senegal, at least) and more desiccated agricultural plains so common in the north. The river shrinks from its epic, labyrinthine vastness into a waterway of considerably more modest proportions, the trees take on a hardier look, and Diola influence fades, giving way to Fulbe (Peul) and Mandinka traditions.

Closest to the coast, Sédhiou still unwinds with a syrupy riverine charm similar to its downstream cousins and is by far the region's most compelling destination, while by the time you reach Kolda the river has very much ceased to dominate the landscape, and Kolda reveals itself as something of a garden-variety regional capital, of note primarily for its convenient geography and good facilities rather than any particular allure. At Vélingara the Casamance has long since meandered its way out of the picture, you've nearly rounded the bend on Gambia, and the landscape has noticeably declared its intention of joining the baking plains to the north. It's a form-follows-function market town through and through, but with a handful of good facilities and an easy crossing into The Gambia.

SÉDHIOU

The French colonial presence in Sédhiou dates to the establishment of a *comptoir*, or trading post, here in the 1830s, making it the earliest French presence on the Casamance (along with Île du Carabane). It went on to become an administrative centre of some importance, and was named the Casamance administrative capital in 1894. It enjoyed this status until 1909, after which the growing town of Ziguinchor upstaged it and the administrative seat was moved there. Even 100 years later, it seems that Sédhiou never really recovered from the blow, and today it remains a steamy, languorous backwater. It sits some kilometres off of the main road, and continues to be literally and metaphorically passed by, except by the most determined of visitors. The town itself may never regain its former glory, but the river here is magnificent and wide, the mood is most certainly mellow, and it's a perfect place to either get in a pirogue and get out on the water or just put your feet up and watch it slide by.

GETTING THERE AND AWAY Coming from Kolda, Sédhiou is accessed via the northern route (R21/22/23) to Carrefour Diaroumé (RN4/Trans-Gambia

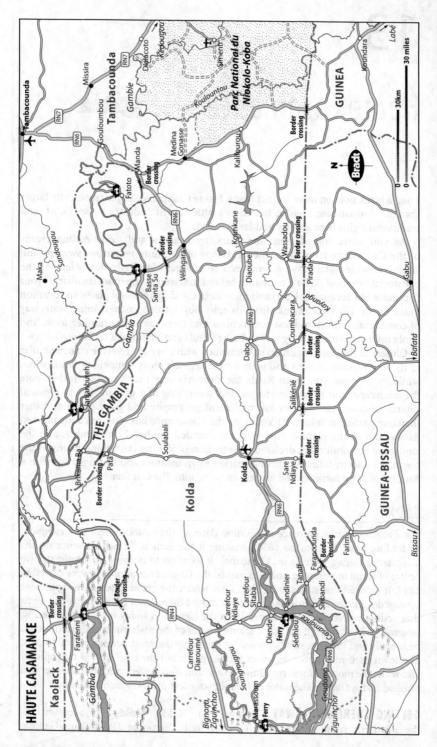

Highway). There are two turnoffs, both surfaced, and 12km apart, which rejoin some kilometres later at Diende on the way into Sédhiou. In the east is Carrefour Sitaba, and in the west is Carrefour Ndiaye. Ndiaye tends to get more traffic as it's on the route between Carrefour Diaroumé and Sédhiou, whereas Sitaba only sees vehicles coming from the east. There are direct *sept-places* from Kolda to Sédhiou for 2,300F, but these can take a long time to fill, so it may sometimes be more convenient to take one bound for Diaroumé and transfer at Carrefour Ndiaye, where you can wait for a lift or hire a *jakarta* to ferry you the last stretch to Sédhiou.

The approach from Ziguinchor, 150km to the west, is much the same. There are direct *sept-places* between Ziguinchor and Sédhiou for 3,500F, or barring that you can get a vehicle from Zig to Carrefour Diaroumé and change there for Sédhiou.

There's a ferry across the river to Sandinier, from where it's 15km to Tanaf on the southern RN6, and another 10km to the Guinea-Bissau border at Farancounda.

WHERE TO STAY, EAT AND DRINK   *Map, page 340.*

Bantabaa Too Lodge   Diende/Sefa village; \33 996 1170; m 77 407 3849; e diahobbe@ orange.sn; www.hotel-hobbe.com. Under the same ownership as the Hotel Hobbé in Kolda (see page 342), this secluded getaway 10km north of Sédhiou offers a similarly high standard of accommodation, with French-inspired cuisine & a welcoming swimming pool overlooking a gorgeous bend in the river. The colourful thatch bungalows have AC, four-poster beds & private terraces. As with the Hobbé, they also specialise in hunting, but river trips, fishing, bicycle treks & other excursions are also on offer. **$$**

Chez Nous & Chez Nous Annexe   \33 995 1741; m 77 252 0841; e cheznous2012@ yahoo.fr. A sleepy regional capital in Casamance might seem a pretty unlikely place to get your fix of *kimchi* or *bul-go-gi*, but the Korean proprietress here can do all that & more with enough notice. It's a low-key set-up that feels much like a family home, but the unpretentious en-suite rooms are kept scrupulously clean & come with AC, hot water, satellite TV & mosquito nets. The main house has a couple of fan rooms with shared ablutions as well & is right on the river; views from the terrace are lovely. Annexe rooms are equally nice, only further away from the river. They've got another hotel in the works (Nid du Paradis) just down the road, but it's some way from being finished. **$$**

La Palmeraie   \33 995 1102; m 77 507 9390/569 2799; e bertrandph@arc.sn; www. relaisfleuri.info. In a dense thicket of towering palms at the south end of town, this is easily the smartest accommodation in Sédhiou proper, & as with much of the nicer accommodation in this part of the country, hunters are very much the target (market).

Still, the facilities are excellent. Charming bungalows are scattered in a lush & neatly groomed compound, some of them with river views. All are done up in an understated African style with natural accessories; standard rooms have AC & hot water while VIP rooms come with a flatscreen lounge area. There's a pool, bar, restaurant & boat launch; aquatic & land-based excursions can all be arranged. **$$**

Auberge Faradala   (12 rooms) \33 995 8366; m 77 566 4846/70 454 8202; e diaiteo@ yahoo.fr. There's nary a frill in sight at this friendly place at the entrance to town, but the compound is full of flowering cordia trees & while they don't have Wi-Fi, the spartan rooms do come with their own terraces, so you can sit outside & read a book. Inside, rooms are pleasant, clean & equipped with fans, nets & a candle if the power goes out. The management is happy to help set up any activities in town, including fishing & pirogue trips to the islands. Meals are available with advance notice. **$**

✕ **Chez Tida/Restaurant Mme Gano**   m 77 658 7379; ◷ 08.00–01.00 daily. One of a (very) small number of bespoke restaurants in Sédhiou, the energetic ladies behind the counter here dish up fast-food favourites like burgers or chawarma & a Senegalese *plat du jour*, usually *thieboudienne* or *yassa*, & almost everything in between. 1,000F–2000F.

☆ **Bar-Dancing Therdo**   m 77 373 5587; ◷ 08.00–midnight daily (later at w/ends). It'd be easy to miss this nightclub tucked away on a side road, but it's *the* place in town for occasional live music & regular butt shaking. If it's a quiet night, the exuberant murals surrounding the dance floor should be enough to keep you entertained over a beer.

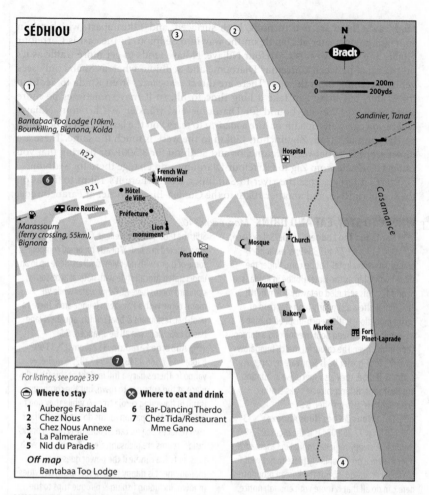

SÉDHIOU

Bantabaa Too Lodge (10km),
Bounkilling, Bignona, Kolda

R22

R21

Gare Routière

Marassoum
(ferry crossing, 55km),
Bignona

French War
Memorial

Hôtel
de Ville

Préfecture

Lion
monument

Post Office

Hospital

Mosque

Church

Mosque

Bakery

Market

Fort
Pinet-Laprade

Sandinier, Tanaf

Casamance

0 ——— 200m
0 ——— 200yds

N

Bradt

For listings, see page 339

Where to stay

1 Auberge Faradala
2 Chez Nous
3 Chez Nous Annexe
4 La Palmeraie
5 Nid du Paradis

Off map
   Bantabaa Too Lodge

Where to eat and drink

6 Bar-Dancing Therdo
7 Chez Tida/Restaurant
   Mme Gano

WHAT TO SEE AND DO The river here is over a kilometre wide and arguably constitutes Sédhiou's only real 'must-see'. The town butts right up on to the shore, and there are plenty of paths that lead right down to the water. Luckily, it's also an easy place to get out *on* the water as well. If you're feeling claustrophobic and need to get yourself to an even smaller town, there's a ferry to the village of Sandinier on the opposite bank, where you're sure to be the first tourist in a while. The forested and uninhabited **Île du Diable** (Devil's Island) sits about 1km upstream from town and any of the town's many *piroguiers* will be happy to punt you across for a visit; all the hotels in town can arrange this too. If you're a landlubber, you certainly won't go wrong with a riverside drink at La Palmeraie (see page 339). Finally, if you wind up here in April, don't miss the annual concerts, workshops and historical tours of **Rams'Fest** (*Rassemblement des Artistes Musiciens de Sédhiou*; ℂ 33 995 0225; m 77 690 1473; e ramsfest.sedhiou@gmail.com), first held here in 2014.

Completed in 1844, the **Fort Pinet-Laprade** (named after the two-time colonial governor of Senegal, Émile Pinet-Laprade) is between the main market and the river, and though it is in serious need of restoration, it's still a grand old building and the sight of the thick walls and arched porticoes overlooking both town and harbour can ever so briefly take you back to Sédhiou's fleeting days as the most important town in Casamance.

OTHER PRACTICALITIES

Money The nearest banks are in either Kolda or Ziguinchor, so bring enough cash to get you through to either.

Communications There was no public internet café in town at the time of writing, but all of the hotels except Auberge Faradala have Wi-Fi. They should give you the code if you go for a drink at La Palmeraie, even if you're a non-guest.

Hospital The hospital is at the north end of town facing the river (✆ *33 995 0116*).

KOLDA

Of interest primarily as a point to break the journey between Ziguinchor and Tambacounda, Kolda is today the most important trading centre in upper Casamance. It was once a centre of the late 19th-century Fulbe (Peul) kingdom of Fouladou, which under the leadership of Alpha Molo Balde and his son Moussa Molo Balde encompassed most of today's Kolda region, as well as parts of what are now Gambia and Guinea-Bissau until being destabilised and brought down by French colonial forces in the early 20th century. Today it's a pleasant enough town with little obvious historicity, and has good tourist facilities including banking, internet, postal services and pleasant accommodation, but bona fide attractions are in genuinely short supply.

The town centre is on the west bank of the Casamance, which is shockingly narrow here compared with its kilometre-wide expanses further downriver. The town itself doesn't take especially good advantage of its riverine location, though the new bridge is an excellent perch from which to soak up the household chores, laundry, and seasonal farming going on in the riverbed below. A couple of blocks inland from the river, the market hustles and bustles daily and can make for a diverting stroll if you've got some time in town.

GETTING THERE AND AWAY Surprisingly enough, Kolda is one of the handful of Senegalese cities with a regular **air service**, and Groupe Transair (✆ *33 865 2565/991 6774*; e *sales@groupetransair.sn; www.groupetransair.sn or www.facebook. com/groupetransair*) runs two flights weekly to Dakar (*Tuesdays and Saturdays, 80,000/140,000F single/return*); bookings can be made locally at Hôtel Hobbé.

By road, the RN6 to Ziguinchor is in such lamentable shape that all traffic goes north of the river via the R21/22/23 & RN4 (Trans-Gambia Highway), which are all in reasonably good shape; it's a 200km trip this way, as opposed to 185km on the southern route. Roadworks on the southern RN6 were under way in 2014, so this may very well have changed by now. Heading east, the RN6 to Vélingara (130km) was in considerably better shape to start with, but is also undergoing intensive upgrading as of late 2014. To the north, there's 65km of dirt leading to the sleepy Gambian border crossing at Pata. Southbound, there are several crossings to Guinea-Bissau nearby at Salikénié, Coumbacara and Sare Ndiaye, but we don't have any recent reports as to their condition.

All transport goes from the *gare routière* just south of town on the road to Sédhiou. *Sept-places* will take you to Sédhiou for 2,300F, onward to Ziguinchor for 4,500F, and in the other direction to Tambacounda for 5,500F. Lots of transport passes through Kolda full, so it doesn't hurt to get to the *gare* early. Le Kam (✆ *77*

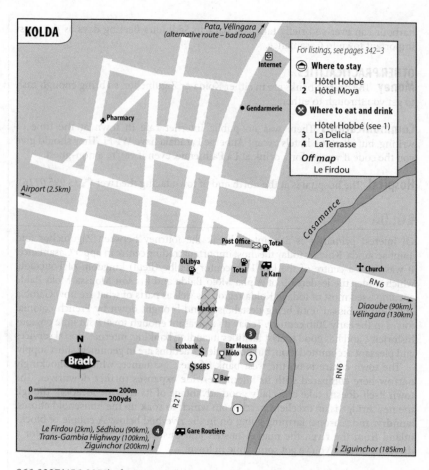

KOLDA

Pata, Vélingara
(alternative route – bad road)

For listings, see pages 342–3

Where to stay
1 Hôtel Hobbé
2 Hôtel Moya

Where to eat and drink
Hôtel Hobbé (see 1)
3 La Delicia
4 La Terrasse

Off map
Le Firdou

Internet

Gendarmerie

Pharmacy

Airport (2.5km)

Casamance

Post Office   Total

OiLibya

Total   Le Kam

✝ Church

RN6

Diaoube (90km),
Vélingara (130km)

Market

N

Bradt

Ecobank

Bar Moussa
Molo

0 — 200m
0 — 200yds

SGBS

Bar

RN6

R21

Le Firdou (2km), Sédhiou (90km),
Trans-Gambia Highway (100km),
Ziguinchor (200km)

Gare Routière

Ziguinchor (185km)

---

966 0227/456 2259) also runs a direct bus to Dakar every Monday, Thursday and
Sunday at 09.30. The departure point changes, so ask at the ticket office.

WHERE TO STAY, EAT AND DRINK *Map, above.*

Eating options in Kolda can be quite limited if you're not in the mood for
thieboudienne, *chawarma* or *fattayah*, but the poolside restaurant at the Hôtel
Hobbé is the exception to this rule, with an excellent French-inspired menu starting
around 4,000F.

Hôtel Hobbé 33 996 1170; m 77 567
0676; e hotelhobbekolda@gmail.com; www.
hotel-hobbe.com. Long known as Kolda's
swankiest address, the Hobbé continues to be the
most comfortable place to stay in Kolda & is worth
a visit for the excellent poolside restaurant & bar
even if you're sleeping elsewhere. The grounds
are sprawling & green despite being right next to
the town centre, & rooms are modern & equally
colourful. Standard rooms have large beds with

crisp blankets & sheets, & all the mod cons you'd
expect. VIP rooms are high-ceilinged & bright, with
flatscreen TV, mini-fridges & sleek, contemporary
décor. French hunters are their bread & butter;
don't be surprised to hear some boasting going on
at the bar after hours. **$$**

Le Firdou 33 996 1780/2; m 77 656
2475; e hotelfirdou@orange.sn; www.firdou-hotel.
com. In a leafy compound 2km south of town, this
place has a superbly tranquil riverside location &

342

takes good advantage of it with a swimming pool & stylish (for Kolda, anyway) bar & restaurant. Rooms are in widely spaced thatch bungalows with terracotta floors, TV, A/C, nets & hot water. The indifferent management explains a few frayed edges, but it's still decent enough value. **$$**

🏠 **Hôtel Moya** (62 rooms) ☎ 33 996 1175; m 77 535 3985; e moyakolda@orange.sn. Characterful it's not, but the Moya is a reliable budget option & as centrally located as can be. The en-suite tiled rooms are reasonably kept & come with nets & TV; ask for one on the 1st or 2nd floor to catch more of a breeze. Fan rooms here are the cheapest in town, but if you're going to spring for

A/C anyways, Firdou is a much nicer option & the prices are almost the same. Meals are available at request, but no alcohol is served. **$**

✖ **La Delicia** ⏲ lunch & dinner; m 77 532 1958/300 4994. Right around the corner from the Hotel Moya, this place does burgers, chawarma & other fast-food staples in addition to a Senegalese *plat du jour*, all fast & all cheap.

✖ **La Terrasse** m 77 727 8626/533 8178; ⏲ lunch & dinner. Directly opposite the *gare routière*, this is something of a rare breed: a *Koldois* sit-down restaurant. That being said, it does a typical array of fish & meat dishes for between 1,500F and 3,000F.

OTHER PRACTICALITIES

Money Ecobank and SGBS are both represented with branches and ATMs across from each other at the south end of the town centre.

Communications All of the hotels offer Wi-Fi, and there are also a couple of basic internet cafés scattered around town. The post office is near the base of the bridge as you enter town from the east.

DIAOUBE

Known for having the biggest *loumo* (weekly market) in Casamance and well beyond, the one-street town of Diaoube doubles (triples? quadruples?) in size every Wednesday, when traders from Gambia, Guinea, Guinea-Bissau, Mali, Mauritania and even further afield converge on the town with trunkloads of just about everything you could imagine: tapes and tarpaulins, grease and gris-gris, palm oil and pantyhose. The diversity of goods is matched only by those doing the selling; you could easily find yourself haggling in a dozen or more languages here on market day. Rest assured, though, that whatever your mother tongue may be, in Diaoube the language of commerce reigns supreme.

Because of the massive weekly migration from points near and far, it's possible to find transport heading in many directions after the market, with some buses even going as far as Conakry. It's also the best jumping-off point for the Guinea-Bissau border crossing at Pirada. There are no banks in town, but there are plenty of different currencies floating about, and it won't be hard to find someone willing to exchange some with you (though as always, be cautious). As far as accommodation here goes, there may be some basic guesthouses aimed at traders overnighting in town, but for something a bit more comfortable head to the **Hôtel Sehelia** (☎ 33 997 49 59), which is 9km east of town in **Kounkané** and has bungalows with AC for about 25,000F.

VÉLINGARA

Probably only of interest if you're headed to or from eastern Gambia via Basse Santa Su, Vélingara would do well at a forgettability contest, though it's got a few old colonial buildings hanging around and the steady, unhurried feel of a rural market town where village dwellers come to shop, but mostly to catch up with friends they haven't seen since their last visit. The market has all the usual clothing, tools and

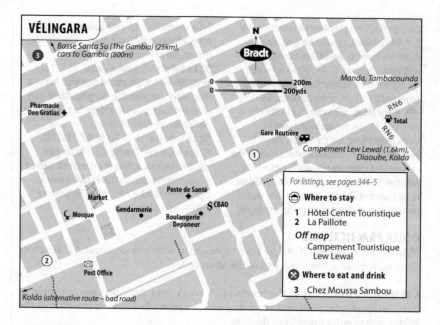

VÉLINGARA

Basse Santa Su (The Gambia) (25km),
cars to Gambia (800m)

Manda, Tambacounda

0 — 200m
0 — 200yds

Pharmacie
Deo Gratias ✚

RN6

Total

Gare Routière

RN6

Campement Lew Lewal (1.6km),
Diaoube, Kolda

For listings, see pages 344–5

🏠 **Where to stay**
1 Hôtel Centre Touristique
2 La Paillote
Off map
    Campement Touristique
    Lew Lewal

Poste de Santé ✚

Market

$ CBAO

Mosque   Gendarmerie

Boulangerie
Depaneur

✖ **Where to eat and drink**
3 Chez Moussa Sambou

Post Office

Kolda (alternative route – bad road)

various doo-dads you might expect, and a better-than-average selection of fruit and
veg for a town of its size. It's barely a dozen kilometres to the Gambian border, so
you're likely to hear some English spoken around here as well.

GETTING THERE AND AWAY At a 90-degree bend in the RN6, Vélingara sits 95km
from Tambacounda (40km of it on a carefully curated pothole collection cleverly
masquerading as a national route) heading northeast and 130km from Kolda to
the west. All traffic to or from Casamance that isn't going through Gambia passes
Vélingara, so there are usually a good number of cars headed in either direction. It's
3,000F to Kolda, 7,000F to Ziguinchor, 2,500F to Tambacounda, or 12,000F all the
way through to Dakar.

   If you're headed to Basse Santa Su, the road that was once marked as 'very bad…
avoid if possible' (on a map of Senegal and the Gambia, mind you!) has just been
surfaced and the trip is a breeze, though the border does close in the evening. Cars
leave from a separate *gare routière* just north of town and it'll cost you 1,400F or the
Dalasi equivalent.

🏠 **WHERE TO STAY, EAT AND DRINK** *Map, above.*

🏠 **La Paillote** (9 rooms) 📞 33 997 1326; m 77
510 2050. The closest thing you'll find to a business
hotel in Vélingara, this is a notch above the other 2
options in terms of facilities, but the staff can be a
bit surly depending on who you get. All the rooms
are en-suite with AC, nets & satellite TV, & the resto-
bar on site does meat, fish or chicken dishes on
request, whether or not you're staying there. **$$**

🏠 **Campement Touristique Lew Lewal**
📞 30 100 7506; m 77 725 5636; e dembamballo@
hotmail.com; www.campementlewlewal.blogspot.

com. Definitely the friendliest accommodation in
Vélingara, this quiet compound just outside town on
the RN6 towards Kolda has nice en-suite bungalows
with tiled floors, thatch roofs & mosquito nets. The
bar des amis (where there's Wi-Fi) does meals on
request, & the owner-manager, Demba, can arrange
excursions locally & further afield. Recommended. **$**

🏠 **Hôtel Centre Touristique** (13 rooms) 📞 33
997 1633; m 70 921 8089; e diallotige@hotmail.fr.
Spitting distance from the *gare routière*, the rooms
here come with the usual trimmings (TV, nets, en

suite), but are indifferent overall & rather musty. For penny-pinchers, the fan rooms are the cheapest in town, though not by much. Meals on request. $

♀ **Chez Moussa Sambou** It may look rough up front, but the plastic furniture every bar-goer in Senegal knows & loves is waiting patiently for you on the terrace at the back.

OTHER PRACTICALITIES

Money CBAO is the only game in town when it comes to banking, and they've got an ATM just opposite the hospital. If you want to change Gambian Dalasi, there are informal traders at the market, or barring that you could try at the Gambia-bound *gare routière*.

Communications There was no public internet café in Vélingara at the time of writing. The restaurant at La Paillote (see page 344) is the most reliable choice for Wi-Fi if you've got your own device, though all the hotels in town theoretically offer internet.

MANDA

Just inside Senegal at The Gambia's western extremity, Manda (sometimes called Manda Douane) is a small-time border crossing and junction town on the RN6, and you'll have to pass this way if you're going between Casamance and the rest of Senegal by road. It's also the junction for the newly tarmacked road to Guinea via the Tijani holy city of Medina Gounasse and Kalifourou, so it's a good place to pick up transport to Labè, or even Conakry, especially if you're here during the weekly market (*loumo*) on Tuesday. If you're aiming for Gambia, it's about 8km (5km of which is on earth tracks) to the village of Nyamanari across the border, so consider hiring a *jakarta* if you're not up for the hike.

FOLLOW BRADT

For the latest news, special offers and competitions, subscribe to the Bradt newsletter via the website www.bradtguides.com and follow Bradt on:

f www.facebook.com/BradtTravelGuides
🐦 @BradtGuides
📷 @bradtguides
📌 pinterest.com/bradtguides

THE LITTLE BAOBAB

TRADITIONAL HOSPITALITY IN ABENE, CASAMANCE

STAY - TREK - DRUM - DANCE - RELAX

READ THE BOOK: SQUIRTING MILK AT CHAMELEONS

77 341 4356

WWW.THELITTLEBAOBAB.COM

Appendix 1

LANGUAGE

FRENCH See also page 22.

French is the official language in Senegal and, as English is not widely spoken at all, you will need some basic French to get around. However, there's no need to be intimidated by the language barrier, as any efforts will be highly appreciated. Politeness is very important, although as a foreigner you'll be quickly forgiven any mistakes.

- Adults use *tu* (you) to children, but children use *vous* (you) to all adults
- Adults use *tu* to adults they know well, *vous* to other adults they do not know very well

English French

Greetings

Good morning	*Bonjour*	Goodbye	*Au revoir*
Good evening	*Bonsoir*	See you later	*À plus tard*
Good night	*Bonne nuit*		
How are you?	*Comment allez-vous (polite)/Ça va (informal)/*		
	Comment tu vas (informal)?		
I'm fine	*Je vais très bien/ça va bien*		

Basics

yes	*oui*	here	*ici*
no	*non*	stop	*arrêtez*
please	*s'il vous plaît*	Help!	*Au sécours!*
thank you	*merci*	Do you speak English?	*Parlez-vous anglais?*
thank you very much	*merci beaucoup*	I don't understand	*Je ne comprends pas*
you're welcome	*de rien/je t'en prie*	I don't speak French	*Je ne parle pas*
excuse me	*excusez-moi, pardon*		*Français*
I would like …	*je voudrais …*	a bit	*un peu*
there	*là*	Where is …?	*Où est …?*

Health

chemist	*la pharmacie*	malaria	*palu/paludisme*
doctor	*le médecin*	mosquito net	*moustiquaire*
hospital	*l'hôpital*		

Accommodation

toilet	*la toilette, le WC*	air conditioning	*climatisé*
How much is it?	*C'est combien?*	May I see the room?	*Puis-je voir la chambre?*
It is too much!	*C'est trop cher!*		

hotel	l'hôtel (all sorts of accommodation), l'auberge (inexpensive), le case de passage (cheapest)

Food

restaurant	le restaurant, le maquis (small, informal eatery)	pork	le porc
		chicken	le poulet
		fish	le poisson
market	le marché	grilled meat/fish	les grillades
bakery	la boulangerie	I don't eat meat/fish	je ne mange pas de viande/poisson
supermarket	le supermarché		
some food	de la nourriture/ quelque chose à manger?	bush meat	la viande de brousse
		only vegetables	juste des légumes
		eggs	les œufs
breakfast	le petit-déjeuner	fruit	les fruits
lunch	le déjeuner	apple	le pomme
supper	le diner	peanuts	les arachides
bread	le pain	drinking water	l'eau potable
butter	le beurre	soft drink	le jus
sandwich	un sandwich	fruit juice	le jus des fruits
chocolate bread	pain au chocolat	beer	la bière
vegetables	les légumes	wine	le vin
meat	la viande	coffee	le café
beef	le bœuf	tea	le thé

Getting around

car	la voiture	What time ?	A quel'heure ?
bus	le bus	Morning	le matin
bus/taxi station	la gare routière	Afternoon	l'après-midi
four-wheel-drive (4x4)	le quatre-quatre	Evening	le soir
bush taxi	le taxi-brousse	petrol/gas	l'essence
private taxi	le taxi	diesel	le gazole
aeroplane	l'avion	roundabout	le rond-point
boat	le bateau	street	la rue
canoe (dug-out or larger narrow fishing boat)	le pirogue	road	la route
		police	la police
boatsman	le piroguier	post office	la poste
Is it very far?	C'est très loin ?	forest	la forêt
		city, town	la ville

WOLOF by Tim Johnson; see also page 22.
Courtesies Greetings are the best way of showing respect in Wolof, and the more you learn of them, the easier time you will have.

Peace be upon on you	Asalaa Maalekum
Peace with you also	Maalekum Salaam
Spend the day in peace	Nu yendu ak jamm ak salam

How (where) is your family?	Ana waa kër gui
They are here	Nungiy fii

Good day/hello	Nanga yendoo? (literally: How's the day)

Good morning		*Naka suba si?* (literally: How's the morning)	
Good afternoon		*Naka ngoon si?* (literally: How's the afternoon)	
Good evening		*Nu fanaan ak jamm* (literally: Let us spend the night in peace)	
Sir		*Borom kër gui* or *Monsieur*	
Madam		*Soxna si*	
How are you		*Nanga def?*	
I'm fine, thank you		*Maangi fi rekk, jërëjëf*	
Please		*Jegel ma*	
Thank you		*Jërëjëf*	
Excuse me		*Jegel ma* or *Baal ma ak* (forgive me)	
Goodbye (morning)		*Ba ci kanam* (see you later) or *Ba benneen yoon* (until next time) or *Ba ngoon* (until the afternoon)	
Goodbye (afternoon)		*Nu yendu ak jamm* (literally: spend the day in peace)	
Goodbye (evening)		*Nu fanaan ak jamm* (literally: spend the night in peace)	
Goodbye (forever)		This isn't typically said but one could say: *Yalla nanu ko fekke ay at yu bari, Amiin* (May we be present for many years to come, Amen); *Mangiy dem ak jamm ak salam* (I'm going in peace); or *Dalal ak jamm* (Go in peace).	

NB: Shaking with the left hand is a gesture to indicate that you will not see someone for a long time.

Basic phrases

yes	*waaw*	It is nice (place or food)	*Neex na*
no	*déedéet*	It's hot	*Tang na*
That's right	*Dëgg la*	It's cold	*Cedd na*
maybe	*peuh-tet* or *xey na*	and	*ak*
It/he/she is good	*Baax na*		

Questions

How?	*Naka?*	When?	*Kañ?*
How much?	*Ñaata la?*	Where?	*Fan?*
What's your name?	*Noo tudd?*	Who?	*Kan* (plural: *Ñan*)?

Food and drink

breakfast	*ndekki*	milk	*meew*
lunch	*añ*	potatoes	*pomme de terre*
dinner	*reer*	onions	*soblé*
beans	*niebé*	chicken	*ginnar*
peas	*petit pois*	rice	*cheb*
beer	*biere*	salad	*salad*
butter	*beurre*	soup	*soup*
bread	*mburu*	sugar	*sucre*
coffee	*café*	tea	*ataya*
eggs	*nen*	tomatoes	*tomaté*
fish	*jën*	drinks	*liminate/boisson*
meat	*yapp*	water	*ndox*

Shopping

bank	*copofort* or *waxandé* or *bank*	battery	*buturie*
pharmacy	*pharmacie* or *dispenser*	film	*film*
		map	*carte*
		money	*xaalis*
shop	*butik*	soap	*savon*
market	*marcé*	toothpaste	*pates*

At the post office

post office	*bureau post*	postcard	*bataxa* or *lettre poste*
envelope	*envelope*		
letter	*bataxa* or *lettre*	stamp	*tembre*
paper	*caiet* or *fuille*		

Getting around

bus	*jegenjaye* or *car rapide* or *auto bu mag*	straight ahead	*tout droight*
		bridge	*pon*
		hill	*montaine*
bus station	*arrêt car*	lake	*gëj*
taxi	*taxi*	river	*gex* or *fleuve*
car	*auto*	road	*yonn* or *talibé*
petrol station	*estation*	street	*mbed*
plane	*ropran* or *avion*	town	*dekk*
far	*sori*	large city	*rew mu tax*
near	*soriul*	village	*dekk al* or *villas*
to the right	*à droite*	waterfall	*cascade*
to the left	*à gauche*		

Hotel

bed	*laal*	toilet/WC	*duce* or *toilette*
room	*nig*	hot water	*ndox bu tang*
key	*chay bi*	cold water	*ndox bu cedd*
shower	*sangu*		

Miscellaneous

dentist	*dentiste*	embassy	*embassade*
doctor	*doctor* or *kër doctor*	tourist office	*bureau touriste*

Time

minute	*waxtu*	tomorrow	*suba*
hour	*waxtu* or *heure*	this week	*semaine bi*
day	*bës* (plural: *fan*)	next week	*semaine be de nëw* or *semaine prochaine*
week	*ayubës* or *semaine*		
month	*weer*		
year	*at*	morning	*suba si*
next year	*dewen*	afternoon	*dëggbujekk*
now	*leggey leggey*	evening	*ngoon si*
soon	*leggey*	night	*guddi gui*
today	*tey*		
yesterday	*demb*		

Days of the week

Monday	*altine*	Friday	*ajuma*
Tuesday	*tallaata*	Saturday	*gaawu* or *samdi*
Wednesday	*allarba*	Sunday	*dibéer* or *dimaas*
Thursday	*alxamis*		

Numbers These are the Wolof numbers but when used for currency they must be multiplied by five to represent the number in CFA (eg: *juròom* means 25CFA; *téeméer* means 500CFA). Most often it is easier and better understood to use French numbers for currency.

1	*benn*	11	*fukk ak benn*
2	*ñaar*	50	*juròom fukk*
3	*ñett*	100	*téeméer*
4	*ñeent*	500	*juròom téeméer*
5	*juròom*	1,000	*junni*
6	*juròom benn*	5,000	*juròom junni*
7	*juròom ñaar*	10,000	*fukk junni*
8	*juròom ñett*	50,000	*juròom fukk junni*
9	*juròom ñeent*	100,000	*téeméer junni*
10	*fukk*		

DIOLA *By Khady Mané*
Diola is written phonetically.

Courtesies

Good day/hello	*Kassumaye*; reply: *kussumaye kep*
Good morning	*Buno moralay*; reply: *kassumaye kep*
Good afternoon/evening	*Buno ti na nalay*; reply: *kassumaye kep*

Sir	*Aney now*	Please	*abari*
Madam	*Asek cow*	Thank you	*Abaraka*
How are you?	*Katabo?*	Excuse me	*kobom folo*
I'm fine	*Kokobo*	Goodbye	*Woly ejow benachin*

Basic phrases

yes	*ey*	hot	*boly boly*
no	*hani*	cold	*giling gileng*
that's right	*more malagan*	and	*ni*
maybe	*molen molen can*		
good	*jayjak*		

Questions

How?	*Buma?*
How much?	*Butumbo?*
What's your name?	*Karesibu/Kassavibu?*
When?	*Noh nay?*
Where?	*Bobay ma?*
Who?	*Amba?*

Food and drink

beans	*kusakak*	potatoes	*potatay*
beer	*bonok* (palm wine)	rice	*emanay*
bread	*nboray*	tea	*kenkillyba*
eggs	*feyaf*	tomatoes	*kufinbarak*
fish	*ewoli*	drinks	*ran*
meat	*eluway*	water	*melam*
milk	*milem*		

Shopping

bank	*fiyafoff*	money	*ekoray*
market	*Marchay*	soap	*sefinay*
battery	*Bapillop*	toothpaste	*fo sorchi*

Getting around

bus/taxi	*ewoti*	straight ahead	*tilling*
bus station	*banku*	bridge	*kalum*
	kobinyassiwatas	hill/mountain	*fat iya*
petrol station	*ban kunomenem*	lake	*melam bammoo*
far	*lay lay*		*duray nya*
near	*laloff*	river	*bolong*
to the right	*canyon corid*	road	*burongap*
to the left	*canyon kumay*	town	*essukaye*

Hotel

bed	*bacha chap*	toilet/WC	*kammaye*
room	*kalim bisak*	hot water	*melam boly boly*
key	*echabaye*	cold water	*melam gileng gileng*
shower	*kanyowak*		

Medical services

dentist	*karup pem unyi nu*	doctor	*kudocer turak*

Time

day	*funak fimbar*	tomorrow	*kajom*
week	*locung*	this week	*lokung uyay*
month	*emit*	next week	*lokung uyah*
year	*finking*	morning	*bjomaray*
now	*In yay*	afternoon	*kaloff*
soon	*nyem nyemay*	evening	*fukaray*
today	*jat*	night	*bujon-jon*
yesterday	*fukeng*		

Days of the week

Monday	*tenengay*	Friday	*arijumaye*
Tuesday	*talataye*	Saturday	*sibit eh*
Wednesday	*arabaye*	Sunday	*dimanchaye*
Thursday	*aramisaye*		

Numbers

1	*akun*	50	*bu kan kugaba*
2	*gah ba*		*dunyen*
3	*fayji*	100	*chemi*
4	*ba chi*	500	*si chemi fu tok*
5	*fu tok*	1,000	*willy*
6	*fu tok daya kon*	5,000	*willy fu tok*
7	*fu tok di sigaba*	10,000	*si willy un yen*
8	*fu tok di si fayji*	50,000	*si willy bukan*
9	*fu tok di si ba chi*		*kukaba dunyen*
10	*un yen*		

PULAAR *By Alison Souders; in memory of her* baaba *and Pulaar teacher, Balla Baldé*
Courtesies

Good day/hello	*Jaraama*
Good morning	*Wallen jam* or *Jam walli*
How did you sleep?	Singular: *A fiini?* Plural: *On piini?/Pin don?*
Good afternoon	*Ñallen jam* or *jam ñalli*
How is your afternoon going?	Singular: *A ñaali?* Plural: *On naali? Naalu don?*
Good evening	*Kiiren jam* or *Jam hiiri*
How is your evening going?	Singular: *A hiiri?* Plural: *On kiiri? Kiir don?*
Goodnight	*Mballen jamm/Fiinen jamm*
What's up?	*Hono wei?/Hono hen?* Response: *Alaa noon* (Nothing really) or (less commonly) *Jamm tan* (literally: Peace only)
How are you?	*Hono mba(t)-daa?*
I'm fine, thank you	*Jam tan* or *Jam tan ngon mi*
Please	NB: Nobody uses a word for please in Pulaar dialects
Thank you	*Jaraama/Al-barka*
Excuse me	*Yaafo* or *Massa*
Goodbye (morning)	*Wallen jam* or *Jam walli*
Goodbye (afternoon)	*Ñallen jam* or *Jam ñalli*
Goodbye (evening)	*Kiiren jam* or *Jam hiiri*
Goodbye (forever)	*En/Haa lawol gongol*
See you later	*Haa yesso seeda/En burini han*
See you tomorrow	*Haa jango*

Basic phrases

yes	*ha or ey*	Really?! (surprised)	*Dee?!*
no	*aa ah* or *no no*	really	*tigi tigi*
That's right	*Ko goonga/Ko noon*	a lot	*buyi*
maybe	*na/di waawii wonde*	a little	*seeda*
good	*moyyi*	small	*tosoko*
bad	*moyyanni*	big	*mawni*
hot	*wuli*	tall	*juuti*
cold	*buubi* or *jahngaani*	short	*rabindi*
and	*e*	enough	*yoni*
but	*kono*	I am sick	*sellanni*

Questions

How?	*Hono?*	What's your name?	*Hono mbiete-daa?*
How much?	*Njelu?*		(one person)

When?	Tuma?	What?	Hodum?
Where?	Hoto?	Why?	Fii hodum?
Who?	Hombo?		

Food and drink

I'm hungry	Mi naalaama	milk	mayo or biradam
I want to eat ...	Mino faala naamde ...		(fresh milk)
I want to drink ...	Mino faala yarde ...	potatoes	pommes de terre
beans	nebbe	rice	maaro
beer	biere	salad	salat
alcohol	konyam	soup	sopa
butter	mbeurre	sugar	sucre
bread	mburu	tea	attaya/waarga or
coffee	cafe		worga
eggs	bochode	tomatoes	mentunaji/mantanaji
fish	liddi	drinks	boissons
meat	teyu	water	ndiyam

Shopping

Who sells .../(that)?	Hombo yayat .../	money	kalise
	(dum)?	soap	sabunday
bookshop	boutique defteere	toothpaste	pate
shop	boutique	stamp	timbre/tampon
market	lumo		

Getting around

Where is ...?	Hoto ... wonni?	next to	tacco
bus	bus	to the right	sengo ñamo
bus station	garage	to the left	sengo nano
petrol station	estation essence	straight ahead	haa feewat
far (distance)	woti	road	laawol
far (time)	booy	street (paved)	gudron
near (distance)	wotaani	town/village	saare
near (time)	boyaani		

Hotel

I would like a room	Mino faala suudu	toilet/WC	douce
bed	mballi	hot water	ndiyam nguldam
room	suudu	cold water	ndiyam buubdam/
key	cabbi (pronounced		wuubdam
	chabbi)		

Time

time	waktu	year/years	hiitande/duubi
What time is it?	Hono waktu jooni/	last year	rowani
	yooni?	next year	ñaagaro
minute	minitahji	now	jooni
hour	waktuji	soon	burini seeda
day/days	naande/balde	today	hannde
week/weeks	yonteere/jonte	yesterday	hanki
month/months	lewru/lebbi	day before yesterday	hetchanki

tomorrow	*janngo*	Monday	*al-tenen*
day after tomorrow	*fabbi janngo*	Tuesday	*al-Talaata*
this week	*nde yonteere*	Wednesday	*al-arba*
next week	*yonteere aronde*	Thursday	*al-kamisa*
morning	*bimbii*	Friday	*al-juma*
afternoon	*ñaloma*	Saturday	*aset*
evening	*kikiide*	Sunday	*alet*
night	*jema*		

Numbers These are the Pulaar numbers, but when used for currency they must be multiplied by five to represent the number in CFA (eg: *sapo* means 50CFA; *temederre* means 500CFA). Most often it is easier and better understood if you use French numbers for currency.

1	*goto*	10	*sappo*
2	*didi*	20	*nogass*
3	*tati*	30	*chappande-tati*
4	*naye*	40	*chappande-naye*
5	*joye*	50	*chappande joye*
6	*jey-go*	100	*temederre*
7	*jey-didi*	500	*temederre joye*
8	*jey-tati*	1,000	*wuulure*
9	*jey-naye*	5,000	*wuulure joye*

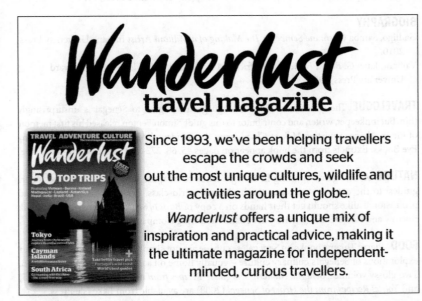

Wanderlust
travel magazine

Since 1993, we've been helping travellers escape the crowds and seek out the most unique cultures, wildlife and activities around the globe.

Wanderlust offers a unique mix of inspiration and practical advice, making it the ultimate magazine for independent-minded, curious travellers.

TRAVEL ADVENTURE CULTURE

Wanderlust

50 TOP TRIPS
Featuring Vietnam · Burma · Iceland
Madagascar · Iceland · Antarctica
Nepal · India · Brazil · USA

Tokyo
Journey from city to nature
explore its unified connected trains

Cayman Islands
A wild diving tourist lover

South Africa
Go roaming with the rhino
- the crowd-free way

Take better travel pics
Portugal's wild coast
World's best guides

Appendix 2

FURTHER INFORMATION

A number of the books below are out of print, but for the most part all are still relatively easily available through Amazon or other online booksellers.

LITERATURE The books below would make an excellent primer on Senegalese literature from the independence era to present-day, and indeed many regularly find their way on to syllabi for African Literature courses around the world.

Bâ, Mariama *So Long a Letter* Waveland Press, 2012.
Bugul, Ken *The Abandoned Baobab: The Autobiography of a Senegalese Woman* University of Virginia Press, 1991.
Diome, Fatou *The Belly of the Atlantic* Serpent's Tail, 2008.
Fall, Aminata Sow *The Beggars' Strike* Longman, 1986.
Kane, Cheikh Hamidou *Ambiguous Adventure* Heinemann, 1972.
N'Diaye, Marie *Three Strong Women: A Novel* Vintage, 2013.
Sembène, Ousmane *God's Bits of Wood* Longman, 2008.
Sembène, Ousmane *Xala* Chicago Review Press, 1997.
Senghor, Léopold Sédar *The Collected Poetry* University of Virginia Press, 1991.

BIOGRAPHY

Gadjigo, Samba *Ousmane Sembène: The Making of a Militant Artist* Indiana University Press, 2010.
Vaillant, Janet G. *Black, French, and African: A Life of Léopold Sédar Senghor* Harvard University Press, 1990.

TRAVELOGUE The selection of English-language travelogues to Senegal is unsurprisingly thin, but innkeeper, writer, and contributor to this guide Simon Fenton released his first memoir of life in Abéné, *Squirting Milk at Chameleons: An Accidental African*, in 2015, published by Eye Books. Extracts from the book appear on pages 45, 68, 272–3, 326 and 329 of this guide.

NATURE As the game-spotting in Senegal tends to be quite limited, there are no 'safari guides' to the country, but since the birding is world-class, ornithologists amateur and professional alike should get their hands on a copy of *Birds of Senegal & The Gambia*, by Nik Borrow and Ron Demey (Christopher Helm Publishing Company, 2012).

FOOD Pierre Thiam's books on Senegalese cuisine are not simply cookbooks, but full-colour explorations of Senegal's culinary culture – equally home on a coffee table as in the kitchen. Two glossy volumes, *Senegal: Modern Senegalese Recipes from the Source to the Bowl* (2015) and *Yolele! Recipes from the Heart of Senegal* (2008) are available from Lake Isle Press.

HISTORY AND CULTURE For an introduction to the history and culture of Senegal that goes beyond the confines of what we can cover in this guide, Eric Ross' *Culture and Customs of Senegal* (listed below) is the best place to start, while the other texts listed are for the most part better suited to those with an academic interest in Senegal or its history.

In addition to the below texts, the eight-volume *UNESCO General History of Africa* series is an excellent resource for scholars seeking a wider understanding of the regional and international forces that have shaped what is today Senegal.

Barry, Boubacar *Senegambia and the Atlantic Slave Trade* Cambridge University Press, 1997.
Barry, Boubacar *The Kingdom of Waalo: Senegal Before the Conquest* Diasporic Africa Press, 2012.
Brooks, George E *Western Africa and Cabo Verde, 1790s-1830s: Symbiosis of Slave and Legitimate Trades* AuthorHouse, 2010.
Green, Toby *The Rise of the Trans-Atlantic Slave Trade in Western Africa, 1300-1589* Cambridge University Press, 2012.
Jones, Hilary *The Métis of Senegal: Urban Life and Politics in French West Africa* Indiana University Press, 2013.
Klein, Martin *Slavery and Colonial Rule in French West Africa* Cambridge University Press, 1998.
Mark, Peter A *'Portuguese' Style and Luso-African Identity: Pre-Colonial Senegambia, Sixteenth–Nineteenth Centuries* Indiana University Press, 2002.
Mark, Peter and da Silva Horta, José *The Forgotten Diaspora: Jewish Communities in West Africa and the Making of the Atlantic World* Cambridge University Press, 2011.
Ross, Eric *Culture and Customs of Senegal* Greenwood, 2008.
Wilder, Gary *Freedom Time: Negritude, Decolonization, and the Future of the World* Duke University Press Books, 2015.

MUSIC AND ART Both *A Saint in the City* and *Senegal Behind Glass* are beautifully assembled large-format, full-colour books that prominently feature hundreds of Senegalese works of art, while the others are more text-based.

Bouttiaux-Ndiaye, Anne-Marie *Senegal Behind Glass, Images of Religious and Daily Life* Prestel, 1994.
Castaldi, Francesca *Choreographies of African Identities: Negritude, Dance, and the National Ballet of Senegal* University of Illinois Press, 2008.
Harney, Elizabeth *In Senghor's Shadow: Art, Politics, and the Avant-Garde in Senegal, 1960–1995* Duke University Press Books, 2004.
Roberts, Alan F and Roberts, Mary Nooter *A Saint in the City, Sufi Arts of Urban Senegal* UCLA Fowler Museum of Cultural History, 2003.
Tang, Patricia *Masters of the Sabar: Wolof Griot Percussionists of Senegal* Temple University Press, 2007.

RELIGION

Babou, Cheikh Anta *Fighting the Greater Jihad: Amadu Bamba and the Founding of the Muridiyya of Senegal, 1853-1913* Ohio University Press, 2007.
Diouf, Mamadou (ed.) *Tolerance, Democracy, and Sufis in Senegal* Columbia University Press, 2013.
Foster, Elizabeth *Faith in Empire: Religion, Politics, and Colonial Rule in French Senegal, 1880–1940* Stanford University Press, 2013.
Ross, Eric *Sufi City: Urban Design and Archetypes in Touba* University of Rochester Press, 2006.

LANGUAGE There are a few Wolof-language dictionaries and primers available on Amazon, but to get started, an eminently worthwhile resource is the **Live Lingua Project** (*www.livelingua.com/peace-corps-language-courses.php*), which offers a free archive of downloadable Peace Corps language lessons that includes courses in Wolof, Diola (Jola), Pulaar, Mandinka and others.

If you would like information about advertising in Bradt Travel Guides please contact us on +44 (0)1753 893444 or email info@bradtguides.com

Index

Page numbers in **bold** indicate major entries; those in *italics* indicate maps

Abéné 5, **324–8**, *325*
accommodation **56–8**
  budget accommodation 52, 58
  camping 58
  tourist taxes 57
  see also individual locations
Accrobaobab 147
Affiniam 316–17
Afia 278–9
African humpbacked dolphin 178
African manatee 6, 178, 310, 311
African oil palm 7
agriculture 3, 215
Aïnou Rahmati 251
air travel
  deep-vein thrombosis (DVT) 70
  domestic 52–3
  to Senegal 39–40
aircraft tours 157, 185
airlines 39–40, 80–1
airports 16, 40, 79–80
alcohol 61, 62
amusement parks 118–19
Ancienne Assemblée Territoriale 210
Andyel 275
animism 284, 306–7, 317, 326
architecture
  cases à etage 309, 316, 331, 336
  cases à impluvium 294, 309, 312, 331, 336
  Sudano-Sahelian 227, 231
art galleries, commercial
  Dakar 115, 117–18
  Saint-Louis 208–9
  Saly 157
art museums *see* museums
arts and entertainment 64
arts and music festivals 109, 152, 158, 207–8, 226, 243, 245, 287, 304, 325, 340
arts, visual **30–2**, 63–4
ATMs 51
auto-racing 146

Baïla 332
Bakel 232–4, *233*
Balanta 21
ballet 29
Bamba, Ahmadou 31, 61, 247, 248, 249, 250
Bambaras 21
Bandafassi 274–5
Bandia Reserve 4, 5, **146–7**
banks 52
baobabs 6–7, 147, 166–7
bargaining 46
Basilique Notre-Dame de la Délivrance 144–5
Bassari people 21, 22, 271, 272–3, 274, 276, 277, 282
Basse Casamance 284–336, *285*
Basse Casamance National Park 5, **310**
batik 32, 116, 294
Baye Fall 47
beauty treatments 121
Bédik people 21, 22, 267, 271, 274, 275, 282
begging 23, **46–7**, **196–7**
Bibliotheque Cheikhoul Khadim 250
Bignona 332–5
Bijagós Archipelago 302
bilharzia 71–2
bioluminescence 191
birdlife 4, 6
  Basse Casamance National Park 310
  Ferlo North and Ferlo South reserves 247
  Île aux Oiseaux 177, 191
  Îles de la Madeleine National Park 131
  Kartong Bird Observatory 331
  Lac de Guiers 222
  Niokolo-Koba National Park 260
  Parc Exotique de N'guerigne 150
  Parc National de la Langue de Barbarie 212
  Parc National des Oiseaux du Djoudj 4, 34, **217–19**
  Réserve Naturelle de Popenguine 146
  Réserve Ornithologique de Kassel 324
  Réserve Spéciale de Faune de Guembeul 4, 214
  Réserve Spéciale des Oiseaux de Kalissaye 5, 318–19, **323–4**
  Sine-Saloum Delta 5, 177–8
Blaise Diagne International Airport 16, 40
boat travel 56
  Dakar–Ziguinchor 288, 292
  river cruises 56, 198
  to Dakar 82
  to Senegal 43
book fair 110
books, recommended 356–8

bookshops, English-language 113
Bopp Thior 210
border crossings 40, **41–3**, 220
Bou el Mogdad 198, 225
Boucotte 301–4
Boun 323
Boundou Community Nature Reserve 263–4
bowling 112
bribery 47
budgeting 52
bureaucracy 47
buses 55–6
    Dakar 81, 83, 86–7
    to Senegal 40–1
business investment 66–7

Cachouane 305–6
Caillié, René 234
calèches 56
campements villageois 336
camping 58
    equipment 49
Cap Skirring 34, **294–301**, *295*
    getting there and away 296
    what to see and do 301
    where to eat and drink 300
    where to stay 296–9
Cap Vert Peninsula 78, *78*, 139
    see also Dakar
car hire 53, 88
Carabane 313–16
Casamance 3, 6, 7
    see also Basse Casamance; Haute Casamance
Casamance conflict **14–15**, 44, 333
Casamance Ecoparc 302
Cascade d'Affia 279
Cascade de Dindefelo 34, **279**
Cascade de Ingli 280
Cascade de Lombel 283
Cascade de Pélél 279
Cascade de Ségou 278
cases à etage 309, 316, 331, 336
cases à impluvium 294, 309, 312, 331, 336
casinos 108–9
Cathédrale du Souvenir Africain 122
Cathédrale Sainte Anne de Thiès 240
caves, Dande 282
central Senegal 235–51, *236*
ceremonial music 28
charettes 56
Château du Baron Roger 222
child beggars 23, **46–7**, **196–7**
chimpanzee trekking 5, 276, 278
cinemas
    Dakar 109
    Gorée 131
Circuit de Dakar Baobabs 146
climate 2, 4, 33
clothing 50
    made-to-measure 114, **116–17**
coffee 61
Collective of Women's Groups for the Protection
    of Nature (COPRONAT) 145

colonial era 10–12
communications 64–5
conjunctivitis 73
conservation 3, **4–7**
    see also national parks and preserves
contact lenses and glasses 51
Corniche des Almadies 125
Coubalan 317
credit cards 51
Croco Parc 166
crocodiles 6, 166, 260, 310
    crocodile farm 290, 294
cultural etiquette 66, 67
    dress code 48, 50
    gay and lesbian travellers 48–9
    greetings 66, 67, 347, 348–9, 351, 353
    photography 65–6
culture 14, **24–32**, 357
currency 2, 51
currency exchange 40, 51, 52, 121
cycling 54

Dagana 223
Dahra 235, **245–6**
dairy industry 245
Dakar 2, 33, **77–126**, *84–5*, *90–1*, *94–7*, *99*
    around Dakar 126–37
    arts and entertainment 109–10
    beaches 125–6
    for children 118–19
    galleries, workshops and museums 115–18
    getting around 83, 86–8
    getting there and away 79–82
    history 78–9
    maps and guides 88
    medical facilities 120–1
    nightlife and live music 107–9
    orientation 82–3
    practicalities 120–1
    safety and security 119
    shopping 112–15
    sport 111–12
    study centres 112
    tour operators 88
    what to see and do 121–6
    where to eat and drink 101–6
    where to stay 89, 92–100
Dakar Fashion Week 32, 110
Dakar Ralley 132
Dakar-Gorée swim 130
Dakar–Saint-Louis railway 196, 245
dama gazelle 4, 213, 247
dance **28–9**, 142
Dande 281–2
Darou Khoudoss Mosque 251
Darou Minam Mosque 251
deep-vein thrombosis (DVT) 70
dehydration 71, 73
dentists 121
Désert de Lompoul 34, **242–3**
desertification 251
Diakhanor 184
dialling codes 2, 65

Diama 215, 217
Diaoube 343
diarrhoea, travellers' 71
Diatta, Aline Sitoé 296
Diembéring 304–5
Dindefelo 279–80
Dindefelo Community Nature Reserve 3, 5,
    272–4
Diogué 318
Diola people 14–15, **18–20**, 22, 284, 307, 309,
    314, 323, 329
Diome, Fatou 26, 186
Dionewar 186
Diouloulou 331–2
Diourbel 235, **246–8**
disabilities, travellers with 49
Diuof, Abdou 14
Djallonkés 21
Djiffer 184
Djilapao 316
Djilor 178–80
Djinack 193
Djiromait 310
Donayé 227
dorcas gazelle 4, 213, 247
dress code 48, 50
drinking water 62
driving **53–4**
    car hire 53
    chauffeured cars 53, 74
    in Dakar 88
    fuel 53
    international licence 38
    night driving 54
    road hazards 44, 54, 74
    road systems 33, 53–4

Ebola 69
economy 2
Edioungou 308
education 22–4
Église Saint-François-Xavier de Fadiouth 166
electricity 2, 49
elephants 260
Elinkine 312–13
Eloubaline 312
email 65
embassies 38–9
Enampore 311–12
entry formalities 37
environmental issues 3, 151, 211
Ethiés 275
Ethiolo 277
Éthiwar 275
ethnic groups 17–21
European community 20
exchange rates 2, 51
eye problems 73

Fadiouth 34, 140, **165**
Falaises de Popenguine 145
Faoye 180
fashion 32, 110, 207–8

Fathala Reserve 4, 5, **192–3**
Ferlo North and Ferlo South reserves 4, **247**
Ferme de Djibelor 290, 294
ferries *see* boat travel
festivals
    Abéné 324–5
    Baïla 332
    Dakar 109–10
    Diembéring 304
    Enampore 312
    Gorée 130–1
    Koré initiation ceremony 272–3, 277
    Lompoul 243
    Louga 245
    Mbour 158
    Oussouye 307–8
    Podor 226
    Saint-Louis 207–8
    Saly 152
    Sédhiou 340
    Ziguinchor 287
film festivals 109–10
film industry 29–30
    see also cinemas
Fimela 178–80
first-aid kit 70
fish markets
    Dakar 115
    Kayar 136–7
    Mboro 241
    Mbour 161
fishing trips 6, 111, 150, 157, 208
fitness clubs and centres 111, 294
flora and fauna 6–7
    see also national parks and preserves
Fongolimbi 282–3
fonio grain 280–1
food and drink **58–62**
    alcohol 61, 62
    drinking water 62
    eating out 62
    hygiene 71
    juices 61, 62
    Liquer de Warang 61, 162–3
    mealtimes 59
    prices 52
    self-catering 62
    Senegal cuisine 58–60
    soft drinks 62
    street food 60
    tea and coffee 60–1, 68
food festivals 109
football 32
Forêt de Kanoufa 311
Fort Pinet-Laprade 340–1
Fort Senoudebou 265
Foundiougne 187–8
Fouta Djallon foothills 3, 267, 278
fuel 53
Fulani people 274, 275
Fulbe people 9, **17**, 22, 215, 230, 247, 271, 282
fungal infections 73

Galerie Nationale d'Art, Dakar 115
The Gambia 334–5
  travel to/from 42–3, 334–5
Gambia River 6, 279
gay and lesbian travellers 48–9
GDP 2
general information 2–74
geography 2, 3
getting around Senegal **52–6**
  by air 52–3
  cycling 54
  driving 53–4
  hitchhiking 54
  public transport 54–6
getting to Senegal **39–43**
  by air 39–40
  by boat 43
  overland 40–3
golf 111, 157, 301
good luck charms 57
Gorée 34, *124*, **126–31**
Gorée Institute 131
Goudiry 263–4
Gounoumane 183
Grand Côte 235, *236*
Grand Mosque, Dakar 122–3
Grand Mosque, Diourbel 248
Grand Mosque, Saint-Louis 210
Great Green Wall 251
Great Mosque, Touba 250
greetings 66, 67, 347, 348–9, 351, 353
griot praise-singers and storytellers 27, 28
gris-gris 326
Guet Ndar 211
Guinea, crossings to 42
Guinea-Bissau 302–3
  crossings to 42, 302

handicrafts 31, 64
harmattan winds 4
hassles 46–7
Haute Casamance 337–45, *338*
health **69–74**
  first-aid kit 70
  food hygiene 71
  insurance 69
  medical facilities 69
  medicines 49–70
  pharmacies 49, 63
  potential medical problems 71–4
  pre-travel preparations 69–70
  travel clinics 69, 70
  vaccinations 37, 69–70
  see also specific health problems
highlights 33
Hillol 323
hip-hop 27–8
history **7–16**, 357
hitchhiking 54
HIV/AIDS 72
hivernage 4
horse riding 111, 119, 142, 150, 208
hotels 58

see also individual locations
hyena spotting trips 185

Ibél 275
IFAN Historical Museum, Gorée 130
Île aux Coquillages 191
Île du Diable 340
Île d'Eguèye 306
Île d'Ehidje 306–7
Île de Gorée 34, *124*, **126–31**
Île de Guior 186–7
Île à Morfil 226–8
Île de Ngor 125
Île aux Oiseaux 177, 191
Île Sipo 191
Îles de la Madeleine National Park 5, **131–2**
immigrants 21
immunisations 37, 69–70
independence 12–13
insect-borne diseases 70, 71, 72–3, 74
insurance 69
internet cafés 65, 120
Islam 8, 22, 196
  Sufism 12, 22, **23**, 248–9, 250–1
  talibé system 23, 46–7, 196–7
itineraries 34–6
Itou 317
Iwol 275

Jant Bi dance school 142
jazz festival 207
Jean Yéyié Badji's house 316
jet skiing 157
jiggers 74
Joal-Fadiouth 164–5
John Paul II, Pope 130, 144
juices 61, 62

Kabadio 330
Kabrousse 295, *295*, 296, 299
Kafountine 319–24, *320*
  around Kafountine 323–4
  getting there and away 319–20
  what to see and do 323
  where to eat and drink 322
  where to stay 320–2
Kaolack 2, **169–74**, *171*
  getting there and away 170, 172
  history 170
  what to see and do 174
  where to stay, eat and drink 172–3
kapok (*fromager*) 7, 191, 325
Karone Islands 323
Kartong Bird Observatory 331
kayaking 111, 157, 181, 186, 190–1
Kayar 136–7
Kédougou 266, 267–83, *268*
  around Kédougou 271–83
  getting there and away 267, 269
  history 267
  what so see and do 271
  where to eat and drink 270
  where to stay 269–70

Keur Gou Mak 248
Keur Momar Sarr 223, 244
Keur Moussa Monastery 135–6
Kidira 264–5, *264*
kitesurfing 111
Koba Club cooperative 280–1
Kolda 337, **341–3**, *342*
konkouran 329
koras 135, 323
Koré initiation ceremony 272–3, 277
Kouba 323

La Somone 3, **147–50**
Lac de Guiers 222–3, 244
Lac Rose 34, 132–4
land area 2
landmines 44–6, 333
languages 2, 22
    language courses 112, 208
    resources 358
    useful words and phrases 347–55
Langue de Barbarie 211–13
Lebanese community 20
Lébou people 21
Léopold Sédar Senghor International Airport
    40, 79–80
life expectancy 2
Linguère 235, **245–6**
lions 5, 260
    lion walks 192, 193
Liquer de Warang 61, 162–3
literacy rate 22
literature **24–6**, 356
livestock 227
livestock market, Dahra 246
Lompoul 34, **242–3**
Lompoul-Sur-Mer 242
Louga 235, **243–5**
luggage 49–50
Ly, Oumar 31, 223–4, 225–6

Maal, Baaba 27, 223, 226
Magic Land amusement park 118–19
Maison des Esclaves, Gorée 129–30
Makhana 219
malaria 70, 71
Mali, crossings to 41–2
Mali Empire 8–9
Manda 345
Mandinka (Malinké) people 20, **22**, 191, 253
mangroves 7
Manjacks 21
Manufactures Sénégalaises des Arts Décoratifs
    240
Mar Lodj 182–3
marabouts 170, 326
marijuana plantations 323
marine life 178
marine protected areas 5
markets
    Dakar 113–15
    Diaoube 343
    Kaolack 174

Ourossogui 230
    see also fish markets
Massalikoul Djinane Mosque 123
Matam 230–1, *231*
Mauritania, crossings to 41, 220
mbalax music 26–7, 28
Mbodiène 140, **164**
Mboro 241–2
Mboro-Sur-Mer 241
Mbour 2, 139, **158–61**, *159*
medical care 69
    Dakar 120–1
medicines 49, 70
Medina Baye Great Mosque 174
megalithic sites 7–8, 175, 176–7
meningitis 72
métis 21, 127, 208
Missirah 191
Mlomp 309
mobile phone service 65
    SIM cards 120
money 51–2
    bargaining 46
    budgeting 52
    credit cards 51
    currency 2, 51
    foreign exchange 40, 51, 52, 121
    theft 43–4, 119
    travellers' cheques 51, 121
    wire transfers 52, 121
Monument de la Renaissance Africaine 123
Moors 21
Mosquée de la Divinité 123
mosquitoes 71, 73
moto-taxis 56
Mount Assirik 3, 258
mountain biking 301
muggers 119
Murid order 23, 248–9, 250–1
museums
    Galerie Nationale d'Art, Dakar 115
    IFAN Historical Museum, Gorée 130
    Maison des Esclaves, Gorée 129–30
    Musée du Centre de Recherche et de
        Documentation du Sénégal, Saint-Louis
        211
    Musée des Civilisations Noires, Dakar 116
    Musée de la Femme, Gorée 130
    Musée Jean Mermoz, Saint-Louis 210
    Musée Kadioute, Boucotte 302
    Musée Khelcom, Saly 157
    Musée Mbind Diogoye, Fadiouth 166
    Musée de la Mer, Gorée 130
    Musée Théodore Monod d'Art Africain,
        Dakar 115–16
    Musée de la Tradition Diola, Mlomp 309
    Thiès Museum 240
music **26–8**, 64, 357
    Keur Moussa Monastery 135
    see also arts and music festivals
musical instruments 28, 64, 135, 323

Nandoumary 279

national anthem 2
national flag 2
national parks and preserves 4–5
  Bandia Reserve 4, 5, **146–7**
  Boundou Community Nature Reserve 263–4
  Croco Parc 166
  Dindefelo Community Nature Reserve 3,
    272–4
  Fathala Reserve 4, 5, **192–3**
  Ferlo North and Ferlo South reserves 4, **247**
  Îles de la Madeleine National Park 5, **131–2**
  Kartong Bird Observatory 331
  Niokolo-Koba National Park 3, 5, 7, **258–63**,
    259
  Parc Exotique de N'guerigne 150
  Parc National de Basse Casamance 5, **310**
  Parc National de la Langue de Barbarie 4,
    211–13
  Parc National des Oiseaux du Djoudj 4, 34,
    217–19, *218*
  Réserve Naturelle d'Intérêt Communautaire
    de la Somone 5, **150**
  Réserve Naturelle Communautaire de
    Palmarin 185
  Réserve Naturelle de Popenguine 5, **145–6**
  Réserve Ornithologique de Kassel 324
  Réserve Spéciale de Faune de Guembeul 4,
    213–14
  Réserve Spéciale Botanique de Noflaye 136
  Réserve Spéciale des Oiseaux de Kalissaye 5,
    318–19, **323–4**
  Sine-Saloum National Park 5, **177**
nature reserves *see* national parks and preserves
Ndangane 180–1
Ndar Toute 211
Nder 222
ndiaga ndiaye 55, 86
Ndiouga Kebe mosque 174
Ndioum 226
N'Dour, Youssou 26, 28, 177
newspapers and magazines 64
Ngallou 183
Ngaparou 147–50
Ngawlé 226
Ngor 125
Nguethie 183
Niafourang 328–31
Nianing 139–40, **163–4**
nightclubs, Dakar 107–8
Niodior 186
Niokolo-Koba National Park 3, 5, 7, **258–63**, *259*
  back route through 263
  entry and fees 260–1
  flora and fauna 260
  getting there and away 261
  where to stay, eat and drink 261–2
Niomoune 317
Nioro du Rip 174–5
northern Senegal 215–34, *216*

optometrists 121
Ourossogui 228–30, *229*
Oussouye 307–9

overcharging 46

packing essentials 49–51
paintball 111
palm wine 61, 307
Palmarin 183–6
Parc Exotique de N'guerigne 150
Parc National de Basse Casamance 5, **310**
Parc National du Delta du Saloum 5, **177**
Parc National des Iles de la Madeleine 5, **131–2**
Parc National de la Langue de Barbarie 4, **211–13**
Parc National des Oiseaux du Djoudj 4, 34,
  217–19, *218*
Pavilon René Caillié 234
peanut production 246
Petit Kassa 317–19
Petite Côte *138*, 139–67
Phare du Cap Manuel 122
Phare des Mamalles 123, 125
pharmacies 49, 63
photography 65–6
  photographic art 31, 225–6
pickpockets 44, 119
pilgrimages
  Popenguine 145
  Tivaouane 241
Podor 34, **223–6**, *224*
Pointe de Sangomar 184
Pointe Saint-Georges 311
politics 13–16
Pont Faidherbe, Saint-Louis 209–10
Popenguine 3, 139, **142–6**
population 2, **17–21**
Porte du Troisième Millénaire 123
postal service 65
prehistory 7–8
prickly heat 73
Protet, Captain Aristide (grave of) 314
proverbs 18–19
public holidays 2, 62–3
public transport **54–6**
  boat travel 56
  buses 55–6
  calèches and *charettes* 56
  Dakar 83, 86–7
  moto-taxis 56
  ndiaga ndiaye 55, 86
  prices 52
  sept-places 44, 48, 54–5
  taxis 56
  trains 56
putsi flies 74

quad biking 157, 208

rabies 70, 72
radio 65
rainy season 4, 33
Ramadan 55
red tape 37–8, 47
red-fronted gazelle 247
religion 2, **22**, 357
Réserve de Bandia 4, 5, **146–7**

Réserve Naturelle Communautaire de Dindéfélo 3, 5, **272–4**
Réserve Naturelle Communautaire de la Somone 5, **150**
Réserve Naturelle Communautaire de Palmarin 185
Réserve Naturelle de Popenguine 5, **145–6**
Réserve Ornithologique de Kassel 324
Réserve Spéciale de Faune de Guembeul 4, **213–14**
Réserve Spéciale Botanique de Noflaye 136
Réserve Spéciale des Oiseaux de Kalissaye 5, 318–19, **323–4**
responsible tourism 67
Richard Toll 221–2, *222*
river cruises 56, 198
river dolphins 6
road travel
    overland to Senegal 40–3
    road accidents 44, 74
    road systems 33, 53–4
    to Dakar 81
    see also driving
rock hyraxes 282
Rosso-Senegal 220
Rufisque 134–5

sabar 28–9
safety 43–6
    Casamance conflict **14–15**, 44, 333
    Dakar 119
    landmines 44–6, 333
    road hazards 44, 54, 74
    theft 43–4
    wildlife hazards 74
    women travellers 47–8
sailing trips 43, 82, 157, 181
Saint-Louis 33, **194–211**, *195, 199, 200, 201*
    activities 208
    festivals 207–8
    getting there and away 197–8
    history 194–7
    nightlife 206–7
    orientation 198
    practicalities 207
    tour operators 198, 200
    tourist information 198
    what to see and do 208–11
    where to eat and drink 205–6
    where to stay 200, 202–5
Salemata 275–7
Sall, Macky 16, 48
Saloulou 323
salt ponds and lakes 132, 185
salt processing 132
Saly 139, **150–8**, *152*
    Saly-Niakhniakhal 151
    Saly-Portudal 151
sand dunes 242
Sangamar Peninsula 183
Saraya 283
schistosomiasis 71–2
scimitar-horned oryx 4, 213, 247
scuba-diving 111

sculpture 30–1
seashell islands 8, 165, 191
seasons 33
Secret Bay 150
Sédhiou 337–41, *340*
Ségou 278
Séléki 311–12
self-catering 62
Sembène, Ousmane 13, 24, 29–30, 177, 237
Senegal River 215
Senghor, Léopold Sédar 12, 13, 14, 24, 25, 29, 30, 237
    birthplace 178, 179–80
    boyhood home 164, 166
sept-places 44, 48, 54–5
Serer people 10, **17**, 22, 169, 182, 184, 191
Serigne Saliou Mbacké Mosque 161
Sëriñ Souhaïbou's Mosque 251
Seydina Limamou Laye Mausoleum and Sacred Well 125
Seydou Nourou Tall Mosque 123
shopping 63–4
Simal 178–80
Siné Ngayène 175, **176–7**
Sine-Saloum Delta 3, 7, 34, *168*, 169, **177–93**
Sine-Saloum National Park 5, **177**
skin infections 73
slavery **10–11**, 127, 129–30, 170, 195
snakes 74
Sobo Badè 140, 141
soft drinks 62
Sokone 188
Soninké (Sarakole) people **20**, 22, 215
sous-verre painting **31–2**, 240
spiders and scorpions 74
sport 32
steam crane, Saint-Louis 210
street food 60
study facilities 112, 208
Sudano-Sahelian architecture 227, 231
Sufism 12, 22, 23, 248–9, 250–1
sugar factory tour 222
Sun Park amusement park 119
sunscreen 49
sunstroke 73
surfing 150, 157
Sy, Oumou 32, 223

Tabaski sheep 227
talibé 23, 46–7, 196–7
Tall, Omar 226, 227, 232
Tambacounda 253–8, *255*
    getting there and away 253–4
    what to see and do 258
    where to eat and drink 256–7
    where to stay 255–6
Taxi Sisters 56, 87
taxis 56
    Dakar 80, 87
tea 60–1, 68
telephones 2, 65
television 65
temperatures 33

tetanus 72
textiles **32**, 64, 116–17, 118, 209
  batik 32, 116, 294
theatre
  Dakar 110
  theatre festival 287
Théâtre de l'Engouement 142
theft 43–4
Thiès 2, **235–40**, *238*
  getting there and away 237, 239
  history 237
  what to see and do 240
  where to eat and drink 239–40
  where to stay 239
Thiès Museum 240
Thionk-Essyl 336
thiouraye 77
tick bites 72–3
Tijani brotherhood 23, 170, 241
time zone 2
Tivaouane 241
toilets 51
tortoises 136, 213
Touba-Mbacké 2, 48, 235, **248–51**
  getting there and away 249
  what to see and do 250–1
  where to stay and eat 249
Toubab Dialaw 139, **140–2**
Toubacouta 188–91
Toucouleur people 215, 226–7, 230
tour operators 36–7
tourist information 36
  see also individual locations
tourist season 33
tourist taxes 57
train services 56
  Dakar–Thiès 82, 237
transport
  getting around Senegal 52–6
  getting there and away 39–43
travel clinics 69, 70
travellers' cheques 51, 121
travelling positively 67–8
tree climbing 147
turtles 6
  breeding grounds 178

UNESCO World Heritage Sites 4, 131, 169, 175, 176, 177, 197, 217, 258, 271, 277
universities 24

vaccinations 37, 69–70
Vallée de Nandoumary 279–80
Vélingara 343–5, *344*
Village des Tortues 136
visas 37–8
volunteering 67–8

Wade, Abdoulaye 14, 15–16
Wade, Karim 16
Wanar 175, **177**
Warang 139–40, **161–3**
waterfalls *see* Cascade
western giant eland (Derby eland) 192–3, 260
when to visit 33
Wi-Fi 65, 120
wildlife
  hazards 74
  poaching 258
  viewing *see* national parks and reserves; *and individual species*
windsurfing 157
witchcraft 326
Wolofs 8, 10, 17, 22
women travellers 47–8
wrestling 32, 112, 183, 184, 186, 308

Yang Yang 246
yellow fever 37, 69
Yoff 125
yoga classes 301

Ziguinchor 34, **286–94**, *289*
  festivals 287
  getting there and away 287–8, 292–3
  history 286–7
  tour operators 287
  tourist information 287
  what to see and do 293–4
  where to eat and drink 291–3
  where to stay 288, 290–1
ziplining 147
Zippyland amusement park 119

INDEX OF ADVERTISERS

Esprit d'Afrique (Camp du Désert and Gîte du Lac) 76
Hôtel Al Baraka 2nd colour section
Les Palétuviers 2nd colour section

Tama Lodge 167
The Little Baobab 345
The Senegal Experience x
Wanderlust 355

Oceanium
77 544 5398